John Charles McQuaid

Ruler of Catholic Ireland

So close yet so far: no eye contact between Dr Nöel Browne and
Archbishop John Charles McQuaid at the blessing in 1967 of
Dublin's Liberty Hall, sixteen years after the Mother
and Child controversy.

John Charles
McQuaid

Ruler of Catholic Ireland

John Cooney

THE O'BRIEN PRESS
DUBLIN

First published 1999 by The O'Brien Press Ltd.,
20 Victoria Road, Dublin 6, Ireland.
Tel. +353 1 4923333; Fax. +353 1 4922777
email: books@obrien.ie
website: www.obrien.ie

ISBN: 0-86278-594-4

British Library Cataloguing-in-publication Data
Cooney, John
John Charles McQuaid: Ruler of Catholic Ireland
1.McQuaid, John Charles 2.Catholic Church - History
3.Bishops - Ireland - Biography
I.Title
282'.092

1 2 3 4 5 6 7 8 9 10
99 00 01 02 03 04 05 06 07

The O'Brien Press receives
assistance from

The Arts Council
An Chomhairle Ealaíon

Layout and design: The O'Brien Press Ltd.
Colour separations: C&A Print Services Ltd.
Printing: MPG Books Ltd.

ACKNOWLEDGEMENTS

The publishers have made every reasonable effort to contact the copyright
holders of the material reproduced in this book. If any involuntary infringement
of copyright has occurred, the owners of such copyright should contact the
publishers immediately. The author and publisher wish to thank the following
for permission to reproduce photographs:
Blackrock College; De Valera Archives; Dublin Diocesan Archives; Paul McQuaid
Collection; The Irish Times; The Catholic Standard; John Moran; Irish Independent;
and Micheál Ó Nualláin for the cartoon by Kilroy.

The author would like thank Michael O'Brien, Íde ní Laoghaire and all the staff at
the O'Brien Press for their help and encouragement during the marathon effort
of retracing the footsteps of John Charles. In particular, special thanks are due to
Des Fisher, Marian Broderick, Susan Houlden, Lynn Pierce, Ivan O'Brien,
Rachel Pierce, Helen Carr, Susanna Coghlan and Valerie Cahill.

CONTENTS

the work of the Currency Commission • becomes de Valera's eyes and ears • organises advertising boycott against *The Irish Times* in protest against its coverage of the Spanish Civil War • uses a newspaper pseudonym to attack Dr W.R.F. Collis • monitors the Erasmus Smith Scholarship.

8 Co-maker of the Constitution, 1937–38

Persistent adviser in the drafting of the Constitution • disagrees with de Valera over naming Catholic Church the One True Church • diplomatic mission of Joe Walshe to the Vatican • enactment of the Constitution • staff strike at Blackrock College as a constitutional test case.

9 Dev's Man, 1939–40

Appeals in vain to Paris for extension as President • achievements as President of Blackrock College • becomes Director of the Castle • undertakes special education work for de Valera • on a visit to London when Britain declares war against Hitler's Germany • returns to Dublin and is reappointed chairman of the Catholic Headmasters' Association.

10 Father 'X', 1940

Death of Archbishop Byrne • de Valera and Archbishop Robinson promote McQuaid's candidature in Rome • McQuaid as Fr 'X' in telegrams • Robinson's despatches lost in transit • renewal of the lobby for Fr 'X' • Fr 'X's appointment • cold reaction of Dublin clergy • receives a good press • preparations for Consecration in Dublin's Pro-Cathedral on December 27, 1940.

PART III

Using Power – Ruler of Catholic Ireland: 1940–62

11 Pillar of the Emergency, 1940–45

Receives the homage of the senior clergy and City Fathers • first Pastoral Letter • negotiates with Government on Army chaplains • sets up the Catholic Social Service Conference • promotes 'domestic economy' studies for girls • persuades the Secretary of the Department of Education to overturn the Vocational Education Committee's opposition to nuns being paid for teaching homecrafts • promotes Church-State 'collaboration' • instances of charitable donations • attack on Irish censorship by Cardinal Arthur Hinsley • reorganises staff at Palace • impact of Catholic Social Service Conference • negotiates religious instruction programme in Technical and Vocational Schools • organises 'Day of the Pope' • launches the Catholic Welfare Bureau for emigrants • opens Youth Department of the Catholic Social Welfare Conference • resists American pressure against Irish neutrality • meets Archbishop Francis Spellman of New York • chairs Government Commission on Youth Unemployment • launches a Commission of Inquiry into 'pious abuses' • deplores Allied bombing of Rome • opens VD clinic in Dublin.

axis • fears that progressives have the ear of Pope John • end of First Session • 1963: Church-State negotiations on education, adoption, company law and a change in the age of consent for marriage • William Conway succeeds John D'Alton as Archbishop of Armagh and assumes leadership of Irish Church • McQuaid's *annus horribilis*.

CHRONOLOGY

1895   Born July 28 at Cootehill, Co. Cavan.

1905   Attends St Patrick's College, Cavan.

1910   Transfers to Blackrock College.

1911   Switches to Clongowes Wood College.

1913   Enters the Holy Ghost novitiate at Kimmage Manor.

1917   Graduates with B.A. First Class Honours in Classics, UCD.

1918   Awarded First Class M.A. Honours for thesis on Seneca.

1919   Takes a Higher Diploma in Education.

1924   Ordained priest at St. Mary's College, Rathmines.

1924   Studies at the Biblical Institute in Rome.

1925   Appointed Dean of Studies at Blackrock College.

1930   Takes over as President of Blackrock College.

1937   Assists de Valera in drafting the Constitution.

1940   Appointed Archbishop of Dublin by Pope Pius XII.

1950   In Rome for the dogma of Mary's Assumption into heaven.

1951   Embroiled in Mother and Child Scheme controversy with Dr Nöel Browne.

1961   Celebrated the 1500th anniversary of St Patrick.

1962   Attends Second Vatican Council.

1965   Celebrates Silver Jubilee but puts the brakes on the Council and becomes first bishop to open a diocesan press office.

1972   Obliged to stepdown by the Vatican. Closes his files on February 16 and hands power over to Fr Dermot Ryan.

1973   Dies on April 7 at Loughlinstown Hospital.

Dedication

For Liguori, Francis, Sarah and John who lived
with John Charles McQuaid for six years

For my father, Francis Cooney, and my late
Mother Mary, and family, who form the core of the
Irish diaspora in Scotland.

For the Glasgow Saturday Theology Journal Club,
especially the late Pat Bolan, Dr John Durkan,
Hugh Falls, Jim McMillan, Malcolm Sinclair
and Danny Baird.

INTRODUCTION

The McQuaid Shadow

Reflecting on the difficulties in writing a biography of any important public figure, the writer, Russell Braddon, observed shrewdly that real people in real life ignore the demands of narrative and plot in a way that no novelist would tolerate in any fictitious character.[1] This observation runs aground in regard to the life of Archbishop John Charles McQuaid, whose true life story at times reads like fiction: unlike many people who live shapeless lives, McQuaid had an unshakeable certitude that his path in life, though not without its share of emotional tumult and unexpected directions, was guided by Jesus Christ, whose representative in the succession from the Apostles he was as Archbishop of Dublin and Primate of Ireland. From early in life, John Charles McQuaid believed that he would be a man of divine destiny. More than any other twentieth century churchman, McQuaid could proclaim, 'Catholic Ireland, I am Catholic Ireland.'

Unlike most people, who throw away their letters, photographs and original documents that provide the straw for the biographer's bricks, McQuaid kept, with magpie-like diligence, the most extensive archives of any twentieth century figure in Irish public life. Paradoxically, the most secretive of modern Irish prelates kept the most expansive collection of personal records.

Some of the bizarre episodes in McQuaid's extraordinary life story, many of them recounted for the first time in *Ruler of Catholic Ireland*, would be dismissed instantly as mere fiction by the defenders of his memory were it not for the fact that either he himself documented their authenticity or they were vouched for by intimates or associates. It is, for example, a draft account of his childhood and youth compiled by the Catholic writer, Mary Purcell, that provides the sources for the death of his mother a week after his birth, the remarriage of his father when he was only a year old and his premature departure from St Patrick's College, Cavan, when he was fourteen years old. Indeed, it was in response to these findings by Purcell that McQuaid admitted to her that he was indeed unhappy at St Patrick's and, astonishingly, he alluded to the bestial side of life which he witnessed at the Catholic boarding school run by the local diocesan bishop.[2]

Further evidence of emotionally erratic school experiences comes from McQuaid's own pen. He wrote a memoir describing how his father moved him to Clongowes Wood College against his wishes, after he came under the influence of a devout but psychologically unbalanced Holy Ghost Brother, Gaspard O'Reilly, at Blackrock College, Dublin.[3] It was McQuaid's closest friend at Clongowes, Hugo Kerr, a future head of the Redemptorist Order in Ireland, who testified to John Charles's adolescent rebellion after discovering at the age of sixteen the facts of his mother's childbirth death and his father's remarriage. So acute was the alienation that reconciliation was brought about only on condition that Dr Eugene bowed to John Charles's determination to become a missionary priest of the Holy Ghost Congregation, an ambition kindled by Brother Gaspard.[4]

It is these dramatic disclosures that constitute the opening chapters of *Ruler of Catholic Ireland*. McQuaid's cold public image masked emotional scars from a tragic family background which were to shape his public life. These provide the framework for the relentless quest for respectability which was an integral part of McQuaid's adolescence and adult life, as well as contributing to his narrow devotionalism and excessive puritanism both as Dean of Studies and President of Blackrock College, and later as Archbishop of Dublin.

The most evocative description of McQuaid was written by his most outspoken political opponent, Dr Nöel Browne. A procession into Dublin's Pro-Cathedral, Browne noted in his autobiography, *Against the Tide*, was led by

> ...the demure child acolytes, the robed clerical students, the imposing shining gilt crucifix carried by its tall student bearer. Scented incense rose from the gently moving thurible. Embroidered vestments glowed, bejewelled, ornate and colourful, on the supporting clergy ... at its heart walked the Archbishop of Dublin. A broad white silk shawl covered his frail bent shoulders, falling down on each side to cover his hands, in which he clasped the glinting gold processional monstrance. His dark eyes, glittering in a mask-like face, were transfixed on the shimmering White Host. He had a long, straight, thin nose and a saturnine appearance, with an awesome fixity of expression, and the strong mouth of an obsessional.

As McQuaid passed by, Browne heard the British Ambassador, Sir Gilbert Laithwaite, whispering to him: 'What an impressive figure, Nöel, would he not make a notable addition to the distinguished company of the Spanish Inquisitors.'[5]

In a closed society in which the press was non-intrusive, McQuaid was an aloof and distant figure to his flock. Fortunately, for the bar of history, McQuaid left a massive archive. His monument, in the form of over seven hundred densely-packed boxes of papers, is a testimony to a superb administrator. As a professional churchman, not only did he keep files for business efficiency, he also did so, consciously, to provide an unquenchable reservoir of material for historians to assess his place in history.[6] Indeed, late in life, after declining an invitation from a distinguished journalist to conduct an interview which he would be allowed to vet before the details of his life and times were chronicled in a series of newspaper articles, he bragged that his archives would provide historians with numerous surprises.

What comes as no surprise, however, is that McQuaid's voluminous archives confirm that he stands as a giant of twentieth-century Ireland alongside the politician who helped to make him Archbishop of Dublin – Éamon de Valera. A major surprise, however, is how often de Valera, who was universally esteemed as a model Catholic statesman, found himself at loggerheads with a McQuaid often more Roman than Rome. Uncannily, the de Valera-McQuaid relationship has striking parallels with that of King Henry II and Archbishop Thomas à Becket, though in the end the stab in McQuaid's back came from the Vatican, not from the temporal power. On balance, the willingness of de Valera to stand up to the more extravagant of McQuaid's theocratic tendencies casts him in a much better light than he appeared in Tim Pat Coogan's pioneering book, *De Valera, Long Fellow, Long Shadow*.

Since McQuaid's death in 1973 no Irish churchman has exercised the enormous spiritual, let alone the almost unbounded temporal power which he exercised for over three decades. As the late John Whyte demonstrated in his classic book, *Church-State in Ireland*, the political auction to catholicise the independent State was begun by its two founding fathers, W.T. Cosgrave and Éamon de Valera, years before McQuaid's elevation to the archbishopric of Dublin in 1940. However, Whyte and other church historians have underestimated the extent of the tightness of the grip held over all aspects of Irish life by the Catholic Church in the McQuaid era. Unlike de Valera, the Fine Gael lawyer, John A. Costello, who headed two Inter-Party Governments, put few, if any obstacles in McQuaid's way when he sought to extend the censorious boundaries of his ecclesiastical jurisdiction into the nation's bedrooms and libraries.

The McQuaid files show how Costello wholeheartedly accepted an utterly subservient role in 1950–51 when the Hierarchy, led by McQuaid, opposed the Minister for Health, Dr Nöel Browne's, proposed free, non-means tested scheme for mother and child welfare. Not only was McQuaid briefed by Costello about cabinet discussions, he momentarily assumed the role of Cabinet secretary when he helped draft the Government's acceptance of the Bishops' condemnation of 'Socialised medicine' – written by McQuaid!

Even the hard-bitten Seán Lemass, who put Ireland on course to the European highway as Taoiseach in the 1960s, was wary of challenging McQuaid's moral monopoly. Furthermore, Lemass's successor, Jack Lynch, who talked a lot about a pluralist Ireland, shirked from removing the ban on contraception when McQuaid threatened a curse upon a nation that would legalise condoms. McQuaid's vast archives reveal him to have been an authoritarian prelate who used fear as an essential instrument for achieving discipline and conformity among his flock. At heart, he was a 'control freak'. At his palace in Drumcondra on Dublin's northside, McQuaid built up a highly effective homespun intelligence system that provided him with a constant supply of information about what was happening in Dublin and elsewhere. His agents ranged across all sectors of society and could inform him on the minutest details of Government policy, as well as the private peccadilloes of his clergy, nuns and laity. Across McQuaid's desk, both in his palace at Drumcondra and in his secluded residence in Killiney with its unsurpassed view overlooking Dublin bay, passed confidential reports from his 'collaborators' or 'helpers', as he was wont to refer to them, in Government Departments, Dublin Corporation, the medical, legal and teaching professions. Interested in military matters, he had close contacts with the Army and the Garda Síochána, the Irish police force.[6]

The professional middle class members of the secret organisation known as the Order of the Knights of St. Columbanus, of which he himself was a member, were particularly vigilant on his behalf. Another principal ally was the founder of the Legion of Mary, Frank Duff, who deferred to McQuaid on all aspects of his organisation's social and spiritual work, especially among delinquents and emigrants. McQuaid's surveillance of students at University College, Dublin was ensured by the appointment of a 'thought control' cleric, Monsignor John Horgan, who, in addition to his academic duties, operated as a kind of undercover agent sending reports to his Episcopal master about the activities of independent-minded chaplains and students. Frequently acting as McQuaid's hatchet-man in dealing with turbulent priests was the cultivated but pompous Father Cecil Barrett, who was known to his intimates as 'Balls Barrett'.

For those Irish people over forty years of age, the name John Charles McQuaid still conjures up vivid images of a Counter-Reformation prelate ruling the country with an iron will, secure in his knowledge of the divine will. For today's go-getting generation he is a figure from a bygone age, far removed from the music of U2, Sinéad O'Connor, the Corrs, Riverdance and Boyzone. For both age groups, however, McQuaid still casts a shadow when the Catholic Church in Ireland is struggling to redefine its identity after a long period of cultural dominance. For the majority, being Irish has ceased to be synonymous with being Roman Catholic. The story of John Charles McQuaid provides 'the hinge' which explains his time to us today at the turn of the millennium.

In his story lies the key to understanding the awesome power exercised by the Catholic Church in Ireland in the mid-twentieth century. McQuaid represents both the high point of Catholic power and an index by which to measure the subsequent dramatic decline of the Catholic Church's influence in society. His story offers a cogent explanation for the Irish Catholic Church's loss of status since his death just over a quarter a century ago. *Ruler of Catholic Ireland* is cast in the form of historical narrative structured in four parts covering his childhood and youth; his training for the priesthood and his years at Blackrock College; his reign as Archbishop from 1940 to the eve of the Second Vatican Council in 1962, and from the Council to his death in 1973. Reconstruction of his life is based on Church and State archival sources, his extensive published writings, newspaper reports, memoirs and interviews with his contemporaries. In addition to a detailed list of these primary sources, the bibliography cited at the end also sets out the secondary sources on which this study is based.

The one interruption from chronological sequence is the latter part of chapter eighteen which draws on an unpublished manuscript by Dr Nöel Browne in which he levels a charge against McQuaid of making sexual advances to a schoolboy. This charge was based on information supplied to Browne by a retired school inspector from the Department of Education at the funeral of Seán MacBride in January 1988.

Browne penned an essay based on this disclosure titled *A Virgin Ireland*. This exclusive manuscript, which was made available to me by Mrs Phyllis Browne, has been lodged with the Nöel Browne Papers at Trinity College, Dublin. As such, it is an important historical document, especially in the context of understanding the McQuaid-Browne adversarial relationship. However strenuously this manuscript may be disputed by supporters and admirers of the Archbishop, its existence cannot be overlooked in any historical assessment of the repressive climate of the period.

However shocking, Browne's 'outing' of McQuaid needs to be put into the public domain, because it raises fundamental questions about the Archbishop's attitude towards sexuality. Since McQuaid's death the stream of revelations about sexual and physical abuse by clergy in church institutions has shown that these evils were an integral part of the Catholic Church of the day. Just when the Irish public was recovering from the sensational disclosures that Bishop Éamonn Casey and Fr Michael Cleary had fathered children, it had to come to terms with the horrendous abuse perpetrated by a number of priests and brothers on children, most notably the late Father Brendan Smyth, the apparent cover-up of whose case contributed to the fall of an Irish Government headed by Albert Reynolds. Within the diocese of Dublin, prominent cases have involved three priests who had served under McQuaid, Fathers Paul Magennis, Ivan Payne and Patrick Hughes.[7]

Ironically, in 1995, the centenary of McQuaid's birth, the

constitutional ban on divorce which McQuaid had helped de Valera to draft in 1937 was repealed in a referendum. This came after a long 'moral civil war' in which the Catholic Bishops failed to prevent the liberalisation of the law governing contraception and the legalisation of homosexuality between consenting adults over the age of eighteen. Meanwhile, abortion has been ruled by the Supreme Court to be legal in certain circumstances. The Catholic Church in Ireland no longer exercises 'a moral monopoly.'[8]

Vocations to the priesthood and the religious life have plummeted. Clonliffe College, which was the jewel in McQuaid's pastoral crown, did not recruit even one student in October 1998, prompting one commentator to advise Archbishop Desmond Connell to sell the college. There has been a steady erosion in weekly Mass-going, and there are signs that many women feel alienated from the institution because of Rome's refusal to allow them ordination to the priesthood.

Three powerful television documentaries, *Dear Daughter*, *Sex in a Cold Climate* and *States of Fear*,[9] highlighting allegations of widespread sexual and physical abuse in religious-run orphanages and reform schools such as Artane and Goldenbridge, have added further to the poor image of the Catholic Church in Ireland. Today Artane Industrial School is the focus of a Garda investigation into allegations against seventy-five Christian Brothers, making it the biggest sex scandal ever in the Irish State. Two other institutions which McQuaid was involved in creating have also been subject to inquiries about abuse allegations. Madonna House, which was subject to a Government inquiry in 1995 into cases of child abuse, was opened by McQuaid in 1955, and assigned by him to the Sisters of Charity for the care of children whose mothers were ill. St Laurence's Remand Home in Finglas, which McQuaid persuaded Lemass to build to 'straighten the crooked souls' of boys, has also been the subject of Garda investigations into alleged abuse by the de la Salle Brothers. The storm of public indignation which followed the screening of *States of Fear* led to the announcement by the Irish Government of the establishment of a Commission on Childhood Abuse.[10]

The opening of McQuaid's archives has sparked off a major national debate about the respective roles of Church and State in his day. While it would be absurd to place all the blame on McQuaid, it is clear that the highly clericalist system over which he presided left his successors defenceless in the face of a more critical and educated laity. It is of crucial importance that this debate should be conducted on an informed basis.[11] *Ruler of Catholic Ireland* aims to situate that debate in its historical context. Primarily, it is the remarkable story of a boy of obscure origins who rose to the highest position of authority in the Irish Catholic Church, which enabled him to exercise personal power over a nation whose political, administrative and professional classes vied with one another for his favour.

PART I

MAKING OF A MILITANT –
EDUCATION TO PRIESTHOOD
1895–1925

1

Faith of his Fathers
1895–1910

'McQuaid was a native of Cootehill in Co. Cavan and
carried to Dublin with him the antagonisms of that
border area.'

León Ó Broin, in *All our Yesterdays*.

John Charles Joseph McQuaid was born in the Co. Cavan market town of
Cootehill on July 28, 1895. On the following day he was brought to the
church of St Michael the Archangel, where he was christened at the large
stone baptismal font. A hand-written entry in the Kilmore diocesan registry records that the witnesses were his uncle, Patrick McQuaid, a farmer,
and his grandmother, Mary McQuaid.[1] He was named John after his
grandfather, a leather salesman who had died in 1893.[2] The notifier of
birth both as father and as registrar was Dr Eugene McQuaid J.P. A week
after the joyous signing of his first son's birth certificate, Dr Eugene,
acting in his position as Coroner for East Cavan, signed the death certificate of his 22-year-old wife, Jennie.

The marriage, only 20 months earlier, of the highly eligible doctor
to the granddaughter of the town's popular postmistress, Jane Corry, had
been the talk of Cootehill. The local newspaper, the *Anglo-Celt*, reported
that Dr Eugene and his 'fascinating' bride, newly returned from their hon-
eymoon, were 'the cynosure of many eyes' at the Christmas 1893 charity
concert as they were 'highly esteemed and respected members of the
community.'[3] Their first child, Helena Maria Josephine, was born in
August 1894. Soon afterwards Jennie was pregnant again, and made her
last public appearance with her husband at a Percy French concert in
April 1895. Her death on August 5 stunned the people of the town and
surrounding countryside, who came in large numbers to her wake in the
modest two-storey McQuaid house in Market St. At the funeral Mass in
St Michael's Church the parish priest, Fr Thomas Brady, described Jennie's life as 'saintly', and as the coffin was carried to Middle Chapel
graveyard a few miles outside the town, all the shops and homes in Coote-
-hill closed their shutters and the townspeople filed behind the hearse.

Dr Eugene was consoled by his older brother, Dr Matthew McQuaid, the medical officer of Ballyjamesduff, as Jennie was laid in the grave.

Notably, only the sparsest details of the life of Jennie Corry, for whom a town of 1200 residents turned out to pay their last respects, were given in the newspaper coverage of her funeral.[4] On the Corry side, the chief mourners were her grandmother, Jane, a sister, Mabel, and an uncle, James Corry, who was the manager of the Ulster Bank in Tuam, Co. Galway. Widowed early in life, Jane was successful in business, firstly as a grocer and later as postmistress. Her outgoing personality made her friends in every social rank and she was a great benefactress to the church, having endowed St Michael's. Missing from the list of mourners was any mention of Jennie's mother and father.[5]

The world into which John McQuaid was born was one in which Queen Victoria's Empire dominated a globe that even included the whole of Ireland. The Conservative and Unionist party, led by Lord Salisbury, had just been returned to power on a wave of imperialist jingoism in England, and though these sentiments were not shared in Ireland, Scotland and Wales, the Government enjoyed a sufficiently commanding majority in the House of Commons to re-launch its policy of 'killing Home Rule by kindness'.

As the century drew to a close, the people of Ulster were anchored in ancient sectarian feuds. The year 1895 was one of competing centennial celebrations. For Protestants it was the 100th anniversary of the Orange Order, whose Lodges restricted membership to 'those born and brought up in the Reformed Religion'. Only a few weeks before John's birth, Cootehill's Orangemen were especially vigorous practising at their headquarters in Dawson Hall for their annual parade on 'the Twelfth', to commemorate the victory of the Dutch Protestant, King William of Orange, over the Catholic Englishman, King James II, at the Battle of the Boyne in 1690. The beating of their Lambeg drums was particularly loud that year: Ulster Protestants feared the growing power of the Catholic Church, which, since its emancipation from centuries of penal laws in 1829, was building churches, convents and schools at an unprecedented rate throughout the land.

For Catholics, 1895 was the centenary of St Patrick's College, Maynooth, a national seminary set up to train young men for the priesthood. In June, what writer Michael McCarthy described as 'a clerical army', consisting of a cardinal, three Archbishops, 25 bishops, two mitred abbots and some 3,000 priests and 600 students, assembled at Maynooth. Articulating the new triumphalist mood of the Catholic Church, the Cardinal Archbishop of Armagh, Michael Logue, declared: 'We shall never be satisfied until every tower and turret is built and every chair is established that will make the Irish Church what it should be, and what it will be, please God, in our own times.'[6]

If Cootehill, the second largest town on the north-east tip of Co. Cavan, belonged to the Orange Order on July 12, it was taken over on August 15 by the Ancient Order of Hibernians. Founded as a Catholic Friendly Society in 1884, the AOH effectively formed the socio-religious wing of the Irish Parliamentary Party, which had split in 1890 after Parnell's mistress, Kitty O'Shea, divorced her husband, a member of the Home Rule Party.[7] Apart from these two marching days, relations between Protestants and Catholics in Cootehill were marked by a spirit of neighbourliness, outwardly at any rate. Beneath the surface, the Protestant gentry and commercial elite feared an erosion of the social supremacy which they had enjoyed since Cromwellian times. On the authority of the Lord Protector, Oliver Cromwell, the estate of the local Gaelic and Catholic chieftain, an O'Reilly, was transferred to Thomas Coote, who married Frances Hill of Hillsborough, Co. Down. Muinchille – literally 'the sleeve of the O'Reillys' – became Cootehill, which later generations of the family, ennobled as the Earls of Bellamont, developed into a prosperous market town under Royal Charter.

A prominent member of the town's rising Catholic middle class, Dr Eugene McQuaid was the assistant to the Medical Officer for the Cootehill Union, Dr Thomas Hamilton Moorehead. Educated at Trinity College, Dublin, and listed in *Slater's Directory* as a member of the gentry, Moorehead's father had owned the property rented by Dr Eugene's father, 'Honest John' McQuaid. Working with a Protestant posed no religious scruples for Dr Eugene, who had trained at the Royal College of Surgeons in Dublin. Interested in astronomy, politics and horse-racing – he owned a horse, Scarlet Runner – Dr Eugene enjoyed socialising with the Protestant upper class.[8]

A widower at 35, Dr Eugene was forced to take stock. He turned to his mother and his sister, Annie, for help in rearing his two children. 'The tall and stately' Mary McQuaid was too old to take on this responsibility and Annie was planning to emigrate to America, so a local girl, Bridget Foy, was employed as a domestic to rear Helen and John.[9] The McQuaid and Corry families urged Dr Eugene to remarry.

Fourteen months after Jennie's death, a notice appeared in the columns of the Dublin and Cavan press. 'September 30, 1896, at St Joseph's Church, Terenure, Dublin ... Dr Eugene McQuaid, J.P., Cootehill, to Agnes, daughter of Thomas Mayne, Esq, Cremorne, Terenure, Co. Dublin.' A discreet trailer requested 'no cards'. While this diffidence might have been a social courtesy to the Corry family, there was a further complication. The wedding certificate carries the addendum: 'Dispensation received from Monsignor FitzPatrick, Vicar General.' Normally, this was indicative of a mixed marriage, but as Agnes was a Catholic, there may have been an impediment on Eugene's side which needed to be waived by the Church authorities.[10]

Agnes was a sophisticated and well-travelled woman. Her parents, Thomas and Susanna Mayne, owned Cremorne House, a stylish residence in Dublin's Terenure. Her father was an Alderman of Dublin Corporation and a confirmed Parnellite who had sat, in Westminster, as an Irish Party M.P. for Tipperary. Agnes lived in Chicago for a time, where she helped her sister, Annie, organise the 1893 Irish Pavilion at the World Fair. An accomplished musician, she played piano at the recitals given there by Miss Josephine Sullivan, the celebrated harpist and daughter of A.M. Sullivan, whose book *The Story of Ireland* was the bible of patriotism for that generation. Interested in literature, Agnes had become friendly in Chicago with the writer, Carmel Snow, and she loved to reminisce about the time she met the famous Bill Cody, 'Buffalo Bill'.[11]

A few years after her return to Dublin, Agnes was introduced to Eugene McQuaid at a doctors' party by a cousin who was on the staff of the Mater Hospital.[12] Adjusting to provincial life was not easy for her at first. She attended the Christmas Coal Concert for the poor, at which she played the piano and sang, as did Jennie's sister, Mabel, while Dr Eugene took part in the Percy French farce, *Borrowed Plumes*. According to local tradition, Agnes came with a sizable dowry which enabled Dr Eugene to buy the parochial house at Court View, after Fr Brady's death in March 1897. This purchase enabled Dr Eugene to take a considerable leap up the social ladder. Court View, which now forms part of the White Horse Hotel, was one of the finest buildings in the town, deriving its name from the court house directly across the street. The McQuaids' neighbour to the rear was owner of the Bellamont Estate, the Ampleforth College-educated, Captain Edward Smith, who had inherited a family fortune from coal mines in England. Their neighbour to the left was the Church of Ireland Rector, Mr Plummer, whose Tudor-style church stood guard at the foot of Main Street as the symbol of the Protestant Ascendancy.

Agnes hung Jennie's sketches in the drawing-room when they settled into their new home. Dr Eugene inherited a well-stocked library from Fr Brady, a Maynooth-educated priest who had written pious pamphlets about Faith and Fatherland under the *nom de plume* of *Missionary Priest*.[13] The doctor's medical and astronomical volumes and Agnes's literary and travel books were added to Fr Brady's religious tomes. John and his sister, Helen, grew up loving books, and the music and stories from Irish folklore which their stepmother, Agnes, taught them.

From time to time Dr Eugene took Helen and John to see their great-grandmother, Jane Corry. The children were too young to remember her before her dreadful death from cancer and delirium in November 1897 in the fever hospital attached to the workhouse.[14] However, the *Anglo-Celt* reported that wreaths were sent from 'Leeney and Charley'. Jane's Protestant origins were recalled at her funeral. 'Her holy faith, a divine gift bestowed when reason was mature' had inspired her in 'a life of unostentatious piety'.[15]

John's first memory was of being taken for walks, in 1898, with his sister in the nearby Bellamont forest by their nanny, Brigid Foy. He could recall the stream that ran down the hill past their home, and how 'We peopled that stream with our fancies. I distinctly remember the sough of the wind on a frosty December night in the pine trees. I thought it was Santa Claus making ready for Christmas.'[16]

The Christmas present for John and Helen that year was the arrival of the first child of Eugene and Agnes, a girl called Eugenia (or Deenie) after Dr Eugene's sister, Eugenia Connolly, who had died in 1893. When Eugenia's husband, John, died suddenly, Dr Eugene and Agnes adopted the Connolly children, Paul and Mary, and brought them up as McQuaids in a household which was growing rapidly with the births of Eugene Ward, known as Dean, in 1899, Marie in 1901, Thomas Mayne in 1902 and Matthew Joseph in 1907.[17]

In 1900 John began attending the National School in Station Rd, a bleak two-storey building which housed the boys in the basement and the girls on the ground floor. Evidence from contemporaries indicate that he was introspective – 'a tarribly quiet fella' – and bookish.[18] As he was precocious academically, his father arranged for him to be tutored in Latin and Greek by the local Presbyterian minister, the Rev. William Montford Henry. It was during his visits to the manse that John acquired a love of Cicero, Virgil and Homer.[19] From the age of nine, he wrote plays.

His early boyhood friend was Eric Dorman-Smith, later to become famous in the British Army during the Second World War as Brigadier Dorman O'Gowan, and immortalised by Ernest Hemingway as Chink. John was a regular visitor to Eric's home, Bellamont House, an elegant red baroque building overlooking the lakes and trees of the estate. John spent hours in the library there, reading the Arthurian legends, *Wars of the Eighteenth Century* and the *Illustrated London News* with its gory drawings of the Boer War battlefields of Spion Kop and Buller, in which Eric's father, Edward, had fought. Among the volumes were books by Lewis Carroll, Charles Dickens, Tennyson, Sir Walter Scott, Conan Doyle, Jules Verne, William Thackeray, Rudyard Kipling and Rider Haggard.[20] The military and chivalric codes seeped through Bellamont and made a huge impression on John.

Outdoors, John and Eric swam, fished for pike and boated on the lakes, went for long walks along the River Annalee and became first-class riflemen shooting woodcock, partridge and snipe in the Bellamont and Dartrey woodlands. 'The bark of a fox, the call of a cock pheasant, the great thrashing, splashing descent of a swan onto the water, the flutter of wild duck in the reeds, occasional woodcock,' Eric later recalled. 'We were stoutly shod and not minding the rain. Dogs and laughter, and the knowledge that on the hill behind stood a dignified redbrick house which could be cosy in its strength, and log-fires and lamplight and teas – such teas. Every believable kind of bread, far better bread than cake, barmbrack, soda cake, potato cakes, honey, home-made jam.' [21] Bellamont gave John McQuaid a taste for well-blended tea and scones.

If Eric imagined himself as a descendant of the Gaelic leader, Hugh O'Gowan, who came to Cootehill after losing to the English Elizabethan forces under the Great Hugh O'Neill, so John could claim (with justification) lineage from the Gaelic O'Reilly clan, and kinship with leaders of the Catholic Church in its darkest days of persecution and with the Wild Geese who fought for the King of Spain. These claims were vindicated in a parchment drawn up by his great granduncle Fr Matthew McQuaid, in 1852.

One hundred years before John's birth, his great-great-grandfather, Patrick McQuaid, from the Newbliss area of Monaghan, had married Lucy O'Reilly and inherited the family's farm at Lisduagh. An O'Reilly chart, dating back to the year 1700, revealed bonds of marriage between O'Reillys and MacMahons that linked John to three Archbishops of Armagh and Primates of All Ireland – Hugh, Bernard and Ross MacMahon. It also unveiled a complex web of family links which included a Bishop of Derry, Michael O'Reilly, and a Bishop of Raphoe, Philip O'Reilly. John could claim ancestors who kept the faith alive in Ulster.

The second family document, dated 1852, claimed that the McQuaids were rightfully entitled to a vast sum of money left by a member of the O'Reilly clan who had lived at Pamplona and served as a soldier in the pay of the King of Spain. By chance, after seeing a notice about the fortune published in *The Nation*, Fr Matthew claimed it for his mother, Lucy, as the only living grandchild of Charles O'Reilly from Lisduagh and Mary Ward from Co. Monaghan. But despite the McQuaid family's persistence, Fr Matthew failed to persuade the Spanish authorities to part with 'the O'Reilly gold'.[22]

Crouched in the east of a county renowned for its tumbled hills and awash with lakes, Cootehill lies on a plain 68 miles, north, north-west of Dublin. The produce of the surrounding countryside was sold on its streets and farmers gathered around the Green and Chapel Lane to buy and sell cattle. Bleeders – professional butchers – slaughtered pigs each week in the Market Hall, and there were seasonal hiring fairs at which farmers recruited young boys and girls for farm work and domestic service. The town's 80 shops, 19 of them draperies, did a brisk trade and the Ulster and Provincial banks competed for the business of the farming, professional, mercantile and trading classes. What had once been Jane Corry's post office provided an excellent mail service. The Bellamont Arms and the White Horse Hotel were thriving county inns, and provided commercial travellers with horse-drawn broughams to the railway which joined the Great Northern line at Ballybay just inside the Monaghan border. Cootehill looked beyond its own horizons to Belfast and Glasgow rather than to Dublin.[23] As for the rest of the world, Cootehill was immortalised by Percy French in his song, *Come Back Paddy Reilly to Ballyjamesduff*, with its advice to 'turn to the left at the Bridge of Finea, And stop when half-way to Cootehill.'

John loved to accompany his father, Dr Eugene, on his medical rounds. As was the case with boys at that time, John was often beaten harshly by his father,[24] though such ill-treatment, rather than causing alienation, made him even more attached. John came to know every byroad and boreen as he travelled the district with his father.[25] At first hand he saw the horrors of poverty and the stigma attached to the Poor Law system, with its black tickets to allow a sick person attend the doctor at the dispensary, and red tickets – called scarlet runners – entitling the sick person to a visit at home.[26]

As medical advisor to the local council, Dr Eugene drew up reports on housing and sanitation and together with Dr Moorehead campaigned to improve the conditions of the local workhouse. Their campaign brought them into conflict with the Board of Guardians, whose chairman, John Primrose, was a prominent worthy in the Orange Order. A deputation from the *British Medical Journal* subsequently visited the area to investigate conditions in the workhouse, and reported that it housed lunatics as well as destitutes, that the milk was sour and sometimes mixed with paraffin oil.[27]

Dr Eugene was also a Justice of the Peace under the British Crown and built up a reputation as a severe man, not unknown to demand that offenders promise to give up drink, which he considered a root cause of their social degradation. Yet despite his social status, he found it a struggle to rear and educate his own family. Deenie recalled her mother complaining one evening about the rather shabby curtains in the drawing-room. 'Agnes,' Dr Eugene shouted, 'Do you want to put us all in the workhouse?' Terrified, the younger children ran into the garden and cried. 'We were not well off,' the teacher's son, Jim Fitzsimons, recalled, 'but I got two new suits for every one John McQuaid did.'[28]

Another of Dr Eugene's duties was to attend the nuns in the Convent of Mercy, which his cousin, Sister Joseph, had co-founded in 1880. John often accompanied him to the huge four-storey building which towered over Cootehill and the surrounding countryside. The convent had 40 large rooms including two bathrooms and six toilets with wash handbasins, as well as an elegant staircase. Every room had an ornamental fireplace and was well-furnished. Sister Joseph was a model figure of the ideal nun for the impressionable young John McQuaid.[29]

Each Sunday Dr Eugene and Agnes escorted the family to Mass and Benediction in St Michael's, where they paid one penny for a place in the better part of the chapel, in contrast to the halfpenny area where the poorer Catholics congregated. Dr Eugene's relations with the new parish priest, Fr Patrick O'Connell, an advanced nationalist, were strained, how-ever.[30] O'Connell supported the Gaelic League, begun by a West of Ireland Protestant, Dr Douglas Hyde, when it opened up a branch in Cootehill. Although from 1900 the rival wings of nationalism had come together to form a reunited party under the leadership of MPs John Redmond and John Dillon with the extra-parliamentary support of the United Irish League, O'Connell supported the writers, Arthur Griffith and William Rooney, who founded Sinn Féin, a separatist party based on the nationalist philosophy, 'ourselves alone'.

A Vicar General of the diocese, O'Connell was believed locally to have been miffed at Dr Eugene's purchase of Fr Brady's house. He built a splendid parochial house on a hill overlooking an entry road to Cootehill, signalling that Catholicism in Cootehill was challenging the Protestant social dominance.[31] At catechism class O'Connell did not spare the cane. He was quick to chastise young people caught 'company-keeping', His anger was also directed at the proselytism of the Plymouth Brethren, known as the Dippers for their practice of baptising converts, especially women, in the Diamore River, where one December an 80-year-old man nearly drowned.[32]

From 1902 the *Anglo-Celt* published articles in Irish and gave prominence to Gaelic League news. Dr Eugene arranged for John to learn Irish. An upstairs loft in a terraced house was the makeshift venue for his Irish tuition from a travelling language teacher. Although McQuaid never learned Irish as well as he was to master the Classics and French, he spoke the Ulster Irish dialect competently.[33] Unlike many of his school friends, John was not interested in the Gaelic football club, Cootehill Celtic.

When John finished national school in 1905, his report was outstanding. 'The most intelligent boy I ever taught,' schoolmaster Fitzsimons wrote. 'His ability to assimilate knowledge was a revelation. With such intellectual attainments this boy will have a brilliant scholastic career and will rise to great heights in whatever profession he adopts.'[34]

St Patrick's College, Cavan

Dr Eugene decided to send John to St Patrick's College in Cavan, originally the diocesan seminary for the training of boys for the priesthood, but now a diocesan school for the sons of the post-Emancipation Catholic middle class, with a catchment area covering Cavan, and parts of Leitrim, Fermanagh, Meath and Sligo. Two personal reasons influenced this choice: Dr Eugene's granduncle, Fr Matthew, had been the first President of St Augustine's College, the forerunner of St Patrick's; and Dr Eugene's brother, Dr Matthew McQuaid, had worked there before taking up his post in Ballyjamesduff. In September, a few weeks after his tenth birthday, John left Cootehill on the 16-mile journey by pony-and-trap to St Patrick's, an imposing but bleak Gothic-imitation building, situated beside the Bishop of Kilmore's residence on the Cullies estate on the outskirts of Cavan town. His leaving home was accompanied by tears. 'We were so lonely for him. We were a happy, united, very affectionate family, but we loved him most of all,' his oldest half-sister, Deenie, recalled.[35]

St Patrick's was as cut off from the commercial life of Cavan as Bellamont was from the daily routine of Cootehill. A distinctively ecclesiastical atmosphere filled its corridors and rooms. A portrait of Cardinal Paul Cullen, who had laid the first stone of the college in 1871, dominated the dining-room. Looking down on the boys, too, was Bishop Nicholas Conaty, an ultramontane ally of Cullen's at the First Vatican Council which proclaimed the doctrine of Papal infallibility in 1870. There was also a portrait of great-grand-uncle Fr Matthew McQuaid, a notable figure in the diocese of Kilmore not only as president of the first diocesan seminary and contributor to *The Nation* journal founded by the Protestant Young Irelander, Thomas Davis, but also as the theologian to Bishop James Browne at the Synod of Drogheda in 1854. Colleges like St Patrick's were regarded as a key feature of diocesan revival, and John took pride in how Fr Matthew's brother, Fr Eugene McQuaid, also a Kilmore priest, died administering the sacraments to the poor in the Famine of 1847.[36]

By today's standards, life in St Patrick's was spartan, even inhumane. Except on Sunday, when the boys could sleep until 7am, the bell for rising was at six. However, a contemporary, James Galligan, recalled that, because John was so young, he was allowed to sleep until seven in his first year.[37] In winter students went to bed at 9.30pm, by candlelight. The prefect in charge of the lights – called 'Blow' – went around the corridors to make sure that all candles were out.[38] Often homesick and ill, John looked forward to the visits from Dr Eugene, Agnes and the other McQuaid children. 'Whenever our parents piled as many of us as could fit into the trap and took us to visit him in Cavan, we cried all the way home,' Deenie recalled.[39]

During John's five years at St Patrick's major changes in Rome began to alter the character of Irish Catholicism. In 1905, Pope Pius X, who had succeeded Pope Leo XIII, introduced frequent and early Communion for children. Two years later he condemned Modernism as 'the meeting place of all heresies', and in 1908 he promulgated the *Ne Temere* decree requiring the Protestant partner in a mixed marriage to give a written promise to raise the children as Catholics.[40] Ireland, too, was changing under the influence of Asquith's Liberal Government, which introduced social welfare reforms and with the support of John Redmond's revamped Irish Parliamentary Party committed itself to legislating for Home Rule in Ireland.

In 1910 John returned to Cootehill before completing his final year at St Patrick's. He was extremely unwell. Two reasons were offered for his hasty departure from the college. The first was that he was so poor at mathematics that his parents were anxious to improve his grades elsewhere, but while it was true that he was weak at the subject and it was taught badly at St Patrick's, this hardly accounted for such a deterioration in his health. The second reason given was that he was expelled for smoking; this smacks, literally, of 'a smokescreen'.[41]

A boy who only missed school two days in five years when he was at National School in Cootehill from 1900 to 1905 became so physically ill that he could not finish the college course in 1910. Something untoward had happened to John McQuaid during his period at St Patrick's. He had suffered a serious breakdown in his physical health and emotional outlook. Miss Elizabeth Dempsey of Cootehill recalled that Agnes went to Cavan and brought John home. 'He was in a terrible condition when he came home but after a while he was returned to health and enjoyed the summer in Cootehill.'[42]

'I was not happy there,' McQuaid confided to the writer Mary Purcell shortly before his death. 'If I were to record the barbarities practised in most boys' boarding schools at that time, I might fly this country.'[43] His comments suggest that he witnessed – and perhaps experienced – physical or sexual abuse. The regime at St Patrick's was harsh, as in other boarding schools, and the prevalence in Britain and Ireland between 1880 and 1914 of what is now known as child sex abuse has been documented by the Christian Brother and historian, Brother Barry Coldrey.[44]

Though John had spent five years at St Patrick's,[45] Dr Eugene and Agnes decided that he needed further secondary schooling. They were attracted by an advertisement publicising Blackrock College, not only for its educational excellence but also for its location overlooking Dublin Bay where, the prospectus boasted, 'the students can bathe with perfect safety'. The brochure also explained, in terms which might have persuaded his parents that John would be safe from whatever 'barbarities' he had experienced in St Patrick's, that 'each student has his private room and can enjoy every educational and social advantage at a safe distance from the dangers of city life'. However, as Dr Eugene and Agnes were to discover, Blackrock College was to produce another emotional upheaval for their teenage son, when he fell under the influence of an elderly Holy Ghost Brother known for his devotional extremism.

2

Chosen by God
1910–1913

'A priest? I thought so.'
Brother Gaspard to John McQuaid.

On a wet autumn evening in October 1910, John McQuaid raced around the corner of the billiards room in Blackrock College and collided with an old man. 'I have been anxious to meet you,' the stranger said to the startled teenager. 'God expects great things from you. Correspond with your present grace; that is all that is in your power – and be devout to Our Lady.' This unexpected encounter had a profound effect. 'I was astonished,' the 15-year-old later wrote. 'I had no remembrance of having ever met the man before and could not rid myself of the impression made on me. I distinctly remember the joy I felt that evening at Benediction, as I recalled his words.'[1]

This was John's introduction to the saintly but eccentric Brother Gaspard O'Reilly. Born John O'Reilly in Ballymughe, near Ardagh in Co. Cavan, he had joined the Holy Ghost Congregation in 1869, and on professing his vows as a Brother two years later took the religious name of Gaspard. Assigned to the bakery at Blackrock College, he proved to be so good that he was still there 45 years later.[2]

John's second meeting with Gaspard, outside the bakehouse, was an anticlimax. When John told Gaspard that he had been thinking over what he had said and had reached the conclusion that he wanted to enter the religious life, the Brother replied off-handedly, 'Oh, don't bother about that,' and passed on. The rebuff did not, however, discourage John.

Gaspard was not the only member of the Holy Ghost Congregation who thought that John had the makings of a priest. His spiritual director, Fr John Kearney, had observed his piety in the junior Sodality of the Holy Angels. After hearing John's confession on the eve of Passion Sunday in 1911, Fr Kearney broached the question of his becoming a priest. When John confided that Brother Gaspard had already said that he had a vocation, Fr Kearney tried diplomatically to convey to him that though undoubtedly a holy man, Brother Gaspard was not to be taken too seriously.

Kearney shared the general view that Gaspard was prone to hallucinations. One of the college founders, Fr Jean Martin Ebenrecht, often told of how during a visitation of the Superior General from the Holy Ghost mother house in Paris, Gaspard had disrupted Solemn Benediction by going into a trance in front of a boy and trying to consecrate him to the religious life. He said that God had inspired him to do so. Along with his natural brother, Andy O'Reilly, and other disciples, Gaspard was known for his nocturnal habit of assembling in the college chapel to say the Stations of the Cross and re-enact the Passion of Christ.[3]

Gaspard's anointing of students and bodily mortifications were frowned upon by the college staff and the priests would sometimes humiliate him verbally, but his behaviour was tolerated because of his bread-making skills. John was undeterred by his spiritual director's reservations about Gaspard, and approached the old man to tell him that he had decided to become a Holy Ghost priest. Gaspard responded: 'A priest? I thought so.'[4]

Shortly afterwards, the bond between John and Gaspard became even closer following an accident which they came to regard as a sign from God. On Easter Monday 1911, John tripped and fell from a fast-moving tram outside the college gates. He was rushed to the college infirmary with a badly gashed leg and his shoulder seriously injured: one side would remain slightly higher than the other for the rest of his life. Gaspard visited him daily while he was in hospital. They grew convinced that God had saved John from death or serious injury because greatness was expected of him. During one of their many discussions about the interior life, Gaspard told John: 'You will have great power in the confessional because of your purity.' This remark flattered John and stuck in his mind.[5]

After his return to college routine, John visited Gaspard every Sunday in the bake-house for about half an hour. He believed that the Brother possessed supernatural powers which enabled him to perform miracles through the intercession of the fourteenth-century Italian ascetic and mystic, St Catherine of Siena, whose fasting and self-mortification resulted in her receiving the stigmata, or wounds of Christ.

Gaspard stressed the favours God accorded those who accepted His words and the punishment He inflicted on those who rejected His grace. 'He did not hesitate to speak to me of the highest spirituality,' John later wrote. 'I distinctly remember his talking one evening of self-annihilation.' Gaspard was steeped in the teachings and sayings of Francis Libermann, a convert Jew from Alsace who had just been declared Venerable by Pope Pius X. Libermann had co-founded the Congregation of the Holy Ghost and Immaculate Heart of Mary in Paris, a foundation which expanded to Ireland in the 1880s with the opening of schools by 'the French Fathers' at Blackrock, Co. Dublin, and Rockwell in Co. Tipperary.[6]

As well as preserving a distinctively French ethos, Blackrock

College was dedicated to Jesus's mother, Mary. A replica of the statue of Our Lady of Victories in Paris held pride of place in the extensive grounds, which included a number of impressive buildings such as Castle-dawson House, formerly part of the Pembroke estate, and the college chapel, a gem of Romanesque architecture of the Gothic type. Blackrock's primary object, its founder Fr Jules Leman wrote, was to train its boys to be strong Catholics who would discharge their duties to the world and to God. Great emphasis was put on good manners and politeness. Blackrock inculcated in John a deep sense of the connection between chivalric conduct and honour to Mary.[7]

In awe of Gaspard, and happy, John came eighth in Ireland in the Classics in his Junior Grade examinations and won an Exhibition scholarship in Latin in which he took first place with a mark of 98 per cent. He scored 96 per cent for Greek and 80 per cent for French. His poorest subject was maths. Though not on the examination curriculum, church music was given a high priority in Blackrock, whose Holy Ghost hymnal was commended by Pope Pius X in a letter to the college president in 1911. John grew to love the Gregorian Chant.

As the summer holidays came round in June 1911, the college celebrated its golden jubilee with a Mass at which the Archbishop of Dublin, Dr William Walsh, presided. The Bishop of Clonfert, Dr Thomas Gilmartin, preached on the importance of Catholic education, a subject of conflict between the Hierarchy and the 'secularising' Dublin Castle authorities. Afterwards many prominent former pupils, including a young mathematics teacher, Éamon de Valera, mixed with the boarders over lunch. This was probably John's first glimpse of the man who would not only shape Ireland's destiny but determine the course of his own career. This occasion also marked John's reluctant leave-taking of Blackrock College, and of Brother Gaspard to whom he had grown extremely attached.

Clongowes Wood College

In September 1911, John began the third phase of his secondary schooling, at the élite, Jesuit-run Clongowes Wood College in Sallins, Co. Kildare, where he was accompanied by his half-brother, Dean. The oldest Catholic college in Ireland, Clongowes prided itself also on being the best. John, however, was extremely perplexed by the move, which had been decided by his parents after a retreat given in Cootehill by a member of the Clongowes staff, Fr Charles O'Connell S.J. It would seem that Dr Eugene and Agnes confided their anxieties about Brother Gaspard's influence on their son to Fr O'Connell, and they hoped that a switch to Clongowes would broaden his outlook.[8] Another factor behind the change was financial: Dr Eugene was in arrears at Blackrock and was listed on the college's bad debts file.[9] On foot of a favourable reference from Fr O'Connell, he was able to do a more economic 'package deal' for John and Dean. John, however, was unsure about the motives behind the change of college and felt unsettled and extremely anxious. He already wanted to become a Holy Ghost priest. He missed Brother Gaspard badly.[10]

Downhearted, John was less than fully enthusiastic about his studies at his new school. Teaching him French was a Jesuit scholastic, Joseph Walshe, who later became a diplomat and he had a close relationship with him as Archbishop. The Prefect of Studies was Fr James Daly S.J., who was immortalised by Clongowes' most famous past pupil, James Joyce, in his *Portrait of the Artist as a Young Man*, as Fr Dolan, the priest who thrashed the writer for allegedly smashing his own glasses. John's Classics master and spiritual director was Fr John Sullivan S.J., whose cause for sainthood is being processed in Rome.[11]

John's two closest friends at Clongowes were the tall and rugged Hugo Kerr from Belfast and the tall but frail Daniel O'Connell, who had been born in Rugby, England, but had moved to Ireland at the age of 12 after his Irish father and English mother died.[12] Dan had a passion for astronomy which he shared with John, who had learned it from his father. Hugo, the son of a Belfast solicitor who was adviser to the Redemptorists at Clonard Monastery, excelled in the debating society at which John spoke with less sparkle.

John was more retiring than his friends, according to the Jesuit educationalist, Fergal McGrath S.J., but he was already showing 'great qualities'. He used every spare moment – in class, in the corridors and in the college grounds – reading French literature.[13] Even when he played in goal for the Gollymockies, he could be seen with a book in his hand when his team was on the attack.

Academically he did reasonably well, winning the gold medal for English in 1913 and taking first place in religious knowledge in 1912 and 1913. John, however, felt that he failed miserably in the middle and senior grade examinations. 'Not only did I not retain the Latin medal and prizes and exhibition, but I did not even win a good honours mark,' he wrote.[14] Hugo's memoirs confirm that John did not achieve his full academic potential at Clongowes. According to Hugo, it was the custom for those who had obtained an exhibition at the public intermediate examinations to sit at a special Exhibitioners' Table in the refectory. As Hugo and John had won exhibitions in the junior examinations – and had collected the munificent sum of £10 each – they were privileged to have a seat at this prestigious table . To their common misfortune, both Hugo and John failed in maths in middle grade and therefore lost the overall examination. In disgrace, 'we forfeited our position at the Exhibitioners' Table and had to retire to the adjoining table which we christened 'starvation corner', Hugo wrote.[15]

It was also Hugo Kerr, who recorded an estrangement which John experienced in his relations with Dr Eugene and Agnes McQuaid. In the summer of 1912, the year which saw the sinking of the *Titanic*, John's inner emotional world capsized. He found out that Agnes was not his real mother. 'My father married a second time. That is bad news for me,' the sixteen-year-old Cavan youth blurted out to Hugo as they sat one day in the refectory. So distraught was John that he vowed that he would not return to his home in Cootehill for the approaching summer holidays. Not only did John accept Hugo's immediate offer to stay the summer with him in Belfast, he also spent the Christmas holidays there, an indication of the depth of his alienation from Dr Eugene and Agnes.[16]

There are two oral versions as to the circumstance in which John made his discovery. The first is that Agnes told John that his real mother had died a week after giving birth to him, and that his father had remarried soon afterwards.[17] The second and more likely account is that John was told about his real mother by the son of a doctor who was a fellow student at Clongowes.[18]

The revelation had a devastating effect on the introverted teenager, and may account for a moodiness that marked his character in adult life. Remarkably, his adolescent hurt, far from plunging him into an antireligious lifestyle, reinforced his belief that pain and suffering were central to life as God willed it. Later, John had in his possession a photograph of Jennie Corry, a pretty woman with a thin face and curly hair, wearing a high-collared blouse and smiling shyly.

John spent his birthday on July 28, 1912, with Hugo's family at their home in the fashionable, and Protestant, Upper Malone Road, where they were the only Catholics to drive to Mass in St Brigid's Church. The weeks he spent there brought him into close proximity with Ulster Unionism at a time when Protestant Ulster was mobilising against the nationalist and Catholic demand for Home Rule. Strenuous opposition to a third such Bill tabled at Westminster by the Liberal Prime Minister, Herbert Asquith, was being mobilised by Conservative leader, the dour Andrew Bonar Law in conjunction with a Dublin-born lawyer, Edward Carson.

Belfast that summer was the centre of ugly sectarian confrontation. When an overzealous member of the Ancient Order of Hibernians, returning from a Home Rule demonstration, tried to seize a Union Jack from a Protestant child participating in a Sunday School procession, the brawl that followed resulted in 35 prosecutions. In retaliation, 3,000 Catholics were hounded out of the Harland and Wolff shipyard. In this crisis atmosphere the Bishop of Down and Connor, John Tohill, summoned a meeting of the clergy and senior laity of his diocese, including Hugo's father, who was the first Catholic councillor in Belfast's City Hall. In late July Bonar Law visited Belfast to assure Unionists that the British public would support their attempts to overturn Home Rule, no matter what lengths they went to. That summer, too, Carson collected signatures for a Covenant to be launched in the autumn to defeat 'the present conspiracy to set up a

Home Rule Parliament in Ireland'.[19]

John and Hugo's return to college that autumn shielded them from these turbulent events. In their final year, Hugo became prefect of the Sodality of Our Lady Immaculate and John assistant prefect. Other members of the sodality were the future diplomat, Count Gerald O'Kelly, and future Attorney General, Conor Maguire. Each Tuesday evening Hugo and John prepared the oratory for the sodality meeting, which was addressed by Fr Sullivan. John revered Fr Sullivan, though Hugo offered the more critical view that, while he was undoubtedly a holy man, his style of oratory had little appeal.[20] A more charismatic Jesuit priest, the ascetic Fr Willie Doyle, addressed the sodality and helped reinforce John's belief that he was called by God to be a missionary priest. Fr Doyle was the inventor of the 'black baby card' which invited Irish students to subscribe half a crown to baptise and name an African child. This method of saving black children from the slavery of the devil captured John's imagination.[21]

As office bearers in the sodality, one of the perks for John and Hugo was the special tea that was laid on for them by a Brother 'Plum'. Looking on the boys as potential recruits to the Society of Jesus, 'he seasoned his conversation with broad hints about novitiate life, to which we invariably made objections,' Hugo recalled. 'He had only one answer to these, to retire to a pantry or some inner sanctum and emerge with a plate of even more scrumptious cakes. Needless to say the objections continued non-stop, thus ensuring an abundant supply of cakes.'[22]

John, Hugo and Dan announced their intention of becoming priests during a novena to St Francis Xavier in March 1913. When the Jesuit Provincial arrived at Clongowes to interview prospective recruits in early June, he succeeded with only one of the three, Dan. He later became a distinguished Jesuit astronomer, firstly as Director of Riverview Observatory, New South Wales, in Australia, and afterwards as the Director of the Vatican Observatory and confidant of Pope Pius XII. Hugo, who felt that the Jesuits were too like the Christian Brothers, opted for the Redemptorists, where he rose to the rank of head of the Irish Province.

John insisted on joining the Holy Ghost Fathers, in line with his pledge to Brother Gaspard 'to plant the faith of Christ in the African bush'.[23] Faced with his stubborn determination, Agnes persuaded Dr Eugene to accept John's wishes. According to Hugo, John's relationship with Agnes improved immediately as a result. Father and son were reconciled too, and in the summer Dr Eugene took John on his first trip to the continent. It became a tour of pilgrimage centres including Lourdes and Lisieux. They also visited the cathedrals of Notre Dame in Paris, Chartres, Nancy, Metz and Strasbourg. One of the places they visited remained long in John's memory – a shrine to Our Lady at Les Trois-Épis, a village in the Vosges overlooking the plain of Alsace.[24] That summer, John's eighteenth birthday marked his adieu to ordinary secular life.

3

Sanctity and Terror
1913–24

'My yoke is sweet.'

Fr John Kearney C.S.Sp.

Intent on becoming a saint, John McQuaid began his year-long novitiate as a Holy Ghost probationary in September 1913 at Kimmage Manor, a towering mock-Elizabethan building on a wooded estate close to the mountains in suburban South Dublin. This House of Studies, with an adjoining farm, stood in majestic isolation from the capital's populace in accordance with the prevailing orthodoxy that priests were a caste superior to ordinary mortals. His training in the hard doctrines of humility and self-denial encouraged constant penance to control bodily and worldly desires. 'The saints became saints only in doing violence to themselves, and in sacrificing without reserve all that was most dear to them,' he recorded in a black-bound notebook. 'Therefore I resolve to sacrifice everything to follow the voice of the Lord.'[1]

His time was governed by the rules of the Congregation. The chores of religious life were fixed in a preordained schedule set in motion by the ringing of the bell: rising in the early morning, followed by prayers before the Blessed Sacrament, meditation and Mass. There was spiritual reading, recital of the Divine Office and the Rosary, Benediction and the Stations of the Cross; then study, examination of conscience, gardening, meals and sleep. Even the walks in the grounds alongside the River Poddle took place in obligatory silence.[2]

A novice's individuality was subordinated to the directives of his religious superiors as the interpreters of God's will for him, and the rules were reinforced by regular retreats. The system was a form of indoctrination designed to control emotions and will power. The striving for personal perfection was compared to that of a young man dreaming of becoming a perfect footballer. 'We join a club which is there to make the end easy for the individual,' John wrote in his spiritual-exercise notebook. 'We go through certain exercises day after day, giving up or taking on certain things.'

John's novice master was Fr Dan 'Spuds' Walsh, from Skibbereen, Co. Cork, who instilled in him the rigorous teachings of the Venerable Francis Libermann, already known to him as Brother Gaspard's spiritual guide. Libermann's writings revolved around the constant struggle between the individual's imperfect human nature and the supernatural life of God's grace for the possession of the soul. In the battle between Adam and Jesus Christ, the spirit needed to annihilate the flesh through self-denial – *renoncement* – in God's presence.[3]

This teaching was rooted in the French school of spirituality, whose towering figures from the sixteenth to the eighteenth century were Cardinal Berulle, Jean Jacques Olier, St Vincent de Paul, St John Eudes, John Baptist de la Salle and St Louis Grignion de Montfort. McQuaid's mental companions were the giants of the Catholic Church's age of spiritual grandeur.[4] Central to French religious thought was a Jansenist concentration on mortal sin, especially sexual weakness. Bodily austerity was regarded as the hallmark of holiness, and the École Française extolled severe corporal mortification in order to achieve it. 'Let us suffer, weep, fast and pray,' de Montfort counselled. 'You must destroy the man of sin who has reigned heretofore in you,' preached de la Salle. For protection against the lust of the flesh, John prayed regularly to John Berchmans and Aloysius of Gonzaga, two saints renowned for their purity, and, with his special interest in medical matters, he developed a devotion to the patron saint of hospitals, St Camillus de Lellis. Influenced by French spirituality's cult of Jesus and Mary, McQuaid collected devotional aids such as the blue scapular of the Immaculate Conception, a badge of the Immaculate Heart of Mary on green cloth, and prayer cards conferring a Plenary Indulgence which would absolve all sins at the hour of death.[5]

Beyond Kimmage's walls, 100,000 Dubliners were gripped in a struggle against starvation during an eight-month lock-out of workers led by the Liverpool-born head of the Irish Transport and General Workers' Union, Jim Larkin. Although Archbishop William Walsh of Dublin subscribed to the strikers' children's fund, Larkin's decision to ship the children of the strikers to Britain for a holiday fell foul of Catholic clergy and pious laity who saw their evacuation as a danger to their faith and morals, and they 'rescued' them from their parents and guardians as they gathered at ports and railway stations for the journey. The lock-out highlighted the lack of social conscience which existed in Irish Catholicism, and inspired a number of priests to take up 'the social issue'.[7]

Dublin had not long returned to an uneasy peace after its first taste of class warfare when the old European order collapsed. On August 3, 1914, Britain declared war on Germany on behalf of Belgium. Some 150,000 Irishmen volunteered for service in the British Army, among them John's boyhood friend, Eric Dorman-Smith, while nationalist leader John Redmond agreed on a postponement of Home Rule for Ireland until after the war. A heartbroken Pope Pius X died pleading vainly for peace, and was succeeded on September 3 by a professional diplomat, Cardinal Giacomo della Chiesa, as Benedict XV. His priorities were peace in the world and an end to the anti-Modernist witch-hunting in the Church promised by his hard-line predecessor.

A few weeks later, John McQuaid, now aged 19, presented himself before the tabernacle in Kimmage to be professed as a member of the Congregation of the Holy Ghost and the Immaculate Heart of Mary. He solemnly vowed to observe poverty, chastity and obedience for three years, as well as to obey the Congregation's rules and constitution. Proud of his membership of the Holy Ghost Congregation, he believed it was superior to other religious institutions on account of its dual recognition of the Holy Ghost and the Virgin Mary.

'WE then are the brothers of J.X. – a privilege unique in the Church, because of the special title and Consecration,' he wrote. 'WE, then, are called to a closer imitation of Jesus Christ. To attain this we have withdrawn our minds and senses to study the Divine Model.' [7]

University student

In October 1914, John McQuaid, now wearing the soutane, collar, coat and soft hat of the Holy Ghost Congregation, began his studies for a Bachelor of Arts degree at University College, Dublin. Although it claimed to be the spiritual descendant of the short-lived Catholic University founded by Cardinal Paul Cullen of Dublin in uneasy partnership with the English scholar John Henry Newman, UCD owed its formal origins to the English liberal system which had conferred a non-Conformist statute on it as a constituent college of the National University of Ireland, along with sister colleges in Cork and Galway. In practice, it had developed a broadly Catholic ethos as the rival to Trinity College, a bastion of Protestantism founded in 1592 by Queen Elizabeth I of England. An indication of growing Catholic influence at NUI was the election of Archbishop Walsh as University Chancellor.

Usually, John cycled to and from college with a fellow Holy Ghost student, Dan Murphy, a Kerryman from Knocknagoshel who was older than him and as able intellectually. They became rivals rather than friends. Murphy once said that he could write two books about John McQuaid, to illustrate the two sides of his personality.[8]

Clerical decorum kept John and Dan Murphy from taking part in student social life. In his book *The Man and the Mask*, John Feeney claimed that 'the young McQuaid was disconcerted with the lives of many youths from the countryside, which he considered wanton and corrupt.'[9] Numbering just over 1,000 students in McQuaid's day, the hub of college extra-curricular life was the Literary and Historical Society which provided a platform for many of the country's leading figures to make their debut as debaters – among them John A. Costello, Conor Maguire, Arthur Cox and George O'Brien, a future Taoiseach, Chief Justice, President of the Incorporated Law Society and Senator respectively.[10] Neither John nor Dan took part in these events: when lectures finished, they cycled back to the cloister to study and pray. When examinations came round in summer 1915, McQuaid took first-class honours in his five subjects and won the Delany Prize for obtaining the highest aggregate of marks among former Jesuit pupils.

He was selected for part-time secretarial work by the Holy Ghost Provincial, Fr John T. Murphy, under whom he learned the importance of keeping accurate records of the Congregation's work and personnel. Fr Murphy was an accomplished fund-raiser – he had shown his financial flair in the United States where he raised the money to purchase and develop Kimmage Manor – and was not slow to demonstrate that investments, land management and balanced books were also vital to the life of a religious institute. Murphy had broken the tradition of scholastics studying in France by opening Kimmage and sending them to NUI. Although Murphy had secured a degree of decentralisation from the Congregation's mother house, the Irish Province was still largely controlled by Paris. On the outbreak of the First World War, the French superiors moved personnel and assets to the Congregation's house in Freiburg, Switzerland, while many clergy – Irish as well as French – volunteered as army chaplains. As a missionary Congregation, the outcome of the war against Germany was clearly going to have enormous implications for its missions in Africa.[11]

The Superior General of the Holy Ghost Fathers, Archbishop Alexander Le Roy, himself a veteran of the mission field, looked increasingly to Ireland for recruits to take up the mantle of the Celtic missionaries of earlier centuries. In Ireland there was a phenomenal growth of interest in the work of foreign missionaries that was as revolutionary in its impact on public attitudes as was fermenting within the nationalist movement. This interest centred on the Maynooth Mission to China, and in the work of the Holy Ghost Bishop of Southern Nigeria, Joseph Shanahan, who inspired the founding of the Missionary Sisters of Our Lady of the Holy Rosary and of the St Patrick's Missionary Society.[12]

Like the majority of the Irish people, the Holy Ghost Fathers were surprised by the armed rising for national independence from Britain which took place in Dublin in Easter Week 1916. The Order's Provincial condemned the Rising as the work of 'foolish and uptight men', and one Holy Ghost priest, Fr Jules Botrel, denounced it as 'a stab in the back.'

However, with three former 'Rock' men involved in the Rising – Éamon de Valera, Fionán Lynch and Willie Corrigan – there was considerable sympathy for the rebels among the Holy Ghost priests.[13] The brutal execution of the 1916 leaders swung public opinion in favour of the rebels, especially when publications such as the pro-Sinn Féin *Catholic Bulletin* published obituaries highlighting the piety they had shown before their deaths. Archbishop Walsh's favourable attitude to Sinn Féin was a significant help in that movement's victory in a by-election in Longford the following year.

John McQuaid graduated in the summer of 1917 with a first-class honours B.A. degree in Classics. In October he renewed his vows for a further five years and began work on a dissertation on 'A Roman of the Early Empire: Lucius Annaeus Seneca.' His thesis won him a first-class M.A. honours in 1918.[14]

McQuaid characterised Seneca, the philosopher-statesman of first-century Rome, as a pre-Christian moralist living in an age of immorality, sinfulness and confusion. 'It is a great sign of strong virtue to abstain from pleasure when the crowd is wallowing in filth, to be sane and temperate when it is vomiting and drunk,' he wrote. 'But it is a much greater sign not to withdraw from the crowd nor mingle with it in all things. We can be merry without debauch. 'In a licentious age, Seneca commended chastity and upheld by his own example the natural sanctity of marriage. In days of brutal selfishness and callous cruelty, Seneca reverenced the slave and the outcast.

McQuaid compared the horrors Seneca experienced during Nero's reign with the growing troubles he saw in Ireland. Referring to 'the stealthy fear that crept around Seneca', McQuaid argued that this was a feature of the Roman writer's life which 'it seems those only can fully appreciate who have themselves undergone a period of unnerving terrorism.'

McQuaid saw himself as living through 'Senecan' times. In addition to the horrendous carnage of the world war, the ungodly Bolshevik revolution in Russia and the slide towards guerrilla warfare in Ireland, there was an outbreak of Spanish 'flu in 1918 in which the deadliest virus thus far in the twentieth century killed an estimated 20 million people worldwide, including Fr Dan Walsh.[15]

As McQuaid was putting the finishing touches to his thesis, national politics focused on the East Cavan by-election, where the frantic efforts of the Bishop of Kilmore, Patrick Finegan, to unite the constituency behind the Parliamentary Party were frustrated by the parish priest of Cootehill, Fr O'Connell, who presided at the convention which chose the Dublin journalist, Arthur Griffith, as the Sinn Féin candidate. Griffith was returned with a majority of 1,200.

With the end of the world war, that saw the defeat of Germany and the collapse of Austro-Hungarian Empire, the Vatican hoped to participate in a diplomatic settlement on the reordering of European society. Like other Holy Ghost members, McQuaid believed that a secret Treaty between Italy, England, Russia and France prevented Pope Benedict, despite all his peace efforts, from being represented at the peace negotiations at Versailles.[16] McQuaid, who noted that the Turks acknowledged the greatness of Benedict in a magnificent statue of him in Constantinople, believed that the Pope was excluded by a plot hatched by the Freemasons.

From autumn 1918 to 1920, turbulent years which saw the electoral triumph of Sinn Féin and the outbreak of the War of Independence against Britain, McQuaid taught as a prefect in Blackrock College while pursuing a Higher Diploma in Education at UCD under the country's leading educationalist, Fr Timothy Corcoran S.J.[17] Corcoran was strongly nationalist and pro-Sinn Féin. A product of Clongowes, in 1909 he was appointed Professor of the Theory and Practice of Education at UCD, where one of his earliest students had been Éamon de Valera, with whom he remained close. He had co-authored with Seán T. O'Kelly *The Case for Ireland* which O'Kelly, as the envoy of the Provisional Government, took to Paris as part of the campaign to lobby America's President Woodrow Wilson for recognition of Ireland's right to self-determination.[18]

In McQuaid, Corcoran found his most able, receptive and diligent disciple to share his vision of an Ireland that would reincarnate the old Catholic-Gaelic values. Their aim was to undo the work of the 'so-called' Protestant Reformation, which destroyed the monastic schools and shattered Catholic unity with Rome. An élitist – he believed in selecting a privileged minority to dominate the professions – Corcoran denigrated self-development in education as 'soft pedagogy' and set a high store on memorisation and repetition of facts. He expected that, in an independent Ireland, the Irish language and classical education would be revived. Corcoran's villains became McQuaid's villains: Jean Jacques Rousseau for his advocacy of emotional freedom; the progressive American educationalist John Dewey for attempting 'to carry into popular education the antisocial and selfish tenets of Rousseau'; Pestalozzi, Froebel and particularly Maria Montessori for promoting a naturalistic or child-centred approach to education.

McQuaid also learned from Corcoran the importance of engaging in polemical journalism. Corcoran had begun editing *Studies*, a review of letters, philosophy and science, in March 1912, but by early 1914 the journal's losses were so heavy that it faced bankruptcy. To meet the crisis, the Jesuit Provincial undertook to finance the publication on condition that the editor appointed by him was supported by the Jesuit Superior, and a new editor and manager, Fr P.J. Connolly S.J., took over in July 1914.[19] Corcoran's own literary output spanned a range of publications, including the *Irish Monthly* and the *Catholic Bulletin*, which under its editor, 'Sceilig' – J.J. O'Kelly – was noted for what historian Patrick Maume has called 'hate--filled diatribes' against Protestants and Freemasons'.[20] At this time too

McQuaid came in contact with Fr Finbar Ryan O.P., the Cork-born and Clongowes-educated editor of the Dominican magazine, *The Rosary*.

When the Holy Ghost Fathers founded the *Missionary Annals*, the new magazine provided an outlet for McQuaid's writing. His first published article was a profile of 'the apostle to Mauritius', Fr Jacques Désiré Laval, a Norman doctor who converted 60,000 Mauritians to the Catholic faith and whose tomb became a place of pilgrimage after his death in 1864, with miraculous cures being attributed to his intercession. It was a topical article as Laval's beatification process had been introduced in 1918 by John T. Murphy, now Bishop of Mauritius.[21] McQuaid manned a stall selling copies of the Missionary Annals at the Donnybrook fête held to raise funds for the missions in Sierra Leone, Zanzibar and Nigeria.[22] He joined the *Annals'* editorial team and also helped to produce the *Holy Ghost Manual*, a study of Catholic writers like Monsignor Robert Hugh Benson, the convert son of an Archbishop of Canterbury, whose historical novels, ghost stories, mystical writings and fascination for gargoyles in chapels and for carvings and embroideries in old country houses attracted him.

By autumn 1920 the 'unnerving terrorism' of the War of Independence was at its most intense. Rockwell and Blackrock colleges were raided for arms and 'collaborators'. The bishops, meeting at Maynooth College, roundly condemned a grim catalogue of British atrocities and declared that the only parallel to the misdeeds of their 'Black and Tan' troops were the outrages of the Bolshevik Red Army.

The growing nationalist mood at Kimmage was highlighted in the community's response to the death of 17-year-old Kevin Barry, executed for killing two British soldiers collecting bread in North King St, Dublin. 'Another tragic death unites us all in prayer today,' the *Missionary Annals* reported. 'Many Masses were offered in our communities this morning for the gallant Kevin Barry, who was up to a few weeks ago a pupil in one of our colleges, and whose name is now inscribed on the list of those who died for Ireland. God send us many more like Kevin Barry. He is a splendid type of Catholic Irishman. He is a worthy model in every sphere of life – in church, in army or in State: unselfish, brave and true.'[23]

Only hours after Bishop Joseph Shanahan celebrated his first Pontifical Mass in Blackrock College on November 20, 1920, news arrived from Croke Park of the indiscriminate killing of 14 sports fans by British troops, a retaliatory action for the killing of 14 of their officers by Michael Collins's squad, the 'Apostles'. In December, just days after the Government of Ireland Act was passed by the Westminster parliament, there was a Christmas Eve raid on the Holy Ghost college of St Mary's, Rathmines.

When Dublin's Archbishop Walsh died in the spring of 1921, Catholic Ireland mourned the passing of a leader whose 35-year reign stretched from the Land War to the campaign for Home Rule. His untimely death left the country on the verge of the partitionist settle-ment he had worked so hard to avoid. Three weeks later, a letter from Pope Benedict referred to Ireland as 'unflinching, even unto the shedding of blood, in her devotion to the ancient Faith and in her reverence for the Holy See.'

The Irish bishops welcomed the Pope's rebuke of Britain. In Rome the credit for Benedict's April letter was attributed to the Cork-born Archbishop of Melbourne, Daniel Mannix, whose striking personality had impressed the Pope when they met. A confidant of Éamon de Valera, now a leading rebel against Britain, Mannix's role had not gone unnoticed in the *Missionary Annals*, which described him as 'our suffering country's most brilliant son and stoutest champion'. Mannix and his colleague, Archbishop Foley of Ballart, responded to this praise by taking out life subscriptions to the magazine.[24]

Against this unsettled background, John McQuaid pursued his courses in theology and philosophy under the direction of Holy Ghost Fathers who had studied in Rome at the height of Pius X's uncompromis-ing campaign against Modernism. Two in particular, Fr Denis Fahey, from Tipperary, and Fr James Murphy, from Mullagh, Co. Clare, had been imbued with the anti-Rationalist spirit that swept Rome during his Papacy. Both men were strongly influenced by the movement known as 'integralism' which regarded Revelation as a body of truths delivered by God to the Apostles and to their successors, the bishops, authoritatively to be laid before the obedient intellects of the faithful. Essentially, Catholic integralists saw the whole system of doctrine as given by God to his Church, like a package deal for all time.[25] Fahey summed up integral-ism when he wrote that in Rome he vowed to St Peter to 'teach the truth about the Master in the way that the first Pope and the Roman Pontiffs wanted it to be done.'[26] While science and intellectual thought might change, integralists regarded faith as immutable. They denounced liberal-minded Catholics as agnostics and vehemently opposed the emphasis placed by Immanuel Kant and Georg Wilhelm Friedrich Hegel on the value of exploring human experience.

Fahey and Murphy had been taught by the chief exponent of inte-gralism, the Professor of Dogmatic Theology at the Gregorian University, Fr Louis Billot S.J. Created a cardinal in 1911, Billot, a Frenchman, loathed the French Revolution and all forms of liberalism, and admired Charles Maurras, a non-believer whose anti-Semitic *Action Française* move-ment and newspapers championed the Catholic Church's right to a spe-cial place in French life. Above all, Billot was a follower of the thirteenth-century scholar, St Thomas Aquinas.[27] Like Billot, Fahey also regarded Aquinas as the apostle of modern times, one whose integration of intellectual and spiritual life in his *Summa theologica* provided Irish youth with an antidote to the anti-religious naturalism arising from

Martin Luther's revolt against the authority of Rome in the sixteenth century.[28]

John McQuaid accepted completely these neo-scholastic teachings on the unchanging nature of the Catholic Church. He was taught that the Roman Missal would endure for all time, as decreed by the Papal Bull of 1570, *Quo Primum Tempore*, while Bossuet's classic text, *Histoire des Variations des Églises Protestantes*, confirmed his belief that Protestantism was a recipe for doctrinal chaos.

The nineteenth century was, in McQuaid's words, a time of 'the dirtiest intrigue', in which the Freemason, Count Camillo Cavour, united Italy and dispossessed Pope Pius IX of his estates, known as the temporal power. McQuaid believed Italy was 'inspired by a hatred of the Papacy that stopped short only at assassination: they were afraid to murder the Vicar of Christ, so the cowards robbed him instead.' [29]

Steeped in the Papal tradition that 'error has no rights', McQuaid accepted Rome's opposition to democracy and its advocacy of political and press censorship. Like Fahey, he became an expert on the Papal Encyclicals. He studied Pope Pius VI's condemnation of the French *Declaration of the Rights of Man and Citizen* of 1789, and the writings of Pius IX, who in his 1864 *Syllabus of Errors* condemned the proposition that 'the Roman Pontiff can and should reconcile himself to and agree with progress, liberalism and modern civilisation'. He also read *The Pilgrimages of Switzerland* by the ultramontane writer, Louis Veuillot, with its memorable quotation regretting that the reformer, Huss, was not burned earlier in life and that Luther had not been burnt at all.

With nationalism on the ascendant in Ireland McQuaid reflected on its relationship with Catholicism. In 1913 the celebrations to honour the centenary of the birth of Thomas Davis, the Protestant Young Irelander and editor of *The Nation*, recalled the role Protestants had played in the struggle for a united Ireland. This invitation to Protestants and Catholics to work towards a common national identity ran contrary to the exclusively Catholic outlook McQuaid was nurturing at Kimmage. Referring in his notebook to Davis's much-quoted verse:

> **What matters that at different shrines**
> **We pray unto one God?...**
> **If you're to Ireland true,**
> **We heed not race, nor creed, nor clan,**
> **We've hearts and hands for you.**

McQuaid answered Davis's question: 'Yes for a logical Protestant.' But the answer must be 'No' for Catholics, for whom religion was not merely an individual affair. 'We must heed what is the creed,' he wrote, rhetorically posing the question: 'If a neutral nationality be set up, if Protestants are drawn in and not converted, is not the supernatural end missed?'[30]

This equating of the supernatural purpose and Catholicism preju-
diced McQuaid against Protestant leaders of Irish nationalism, particularly the head of the United Irishmen, Theobald Wolfe Tone, whose
attachment to French Revolutionary ideas and politics 'did immense
harm to the Irish character'.[31] McQuaid's anti-Protestant outlook was
reinforced by a third Holy Ghost teacher, Fr John Kearney, who had
taught him at Blackrock. A staunch advocate of the dogma that 'Outside
the Church there is no salvation', Kearney was fond of saying that when St
Paul said 'I chastise my body,' he meant 'I beat myself black and blue.'

McQuaid's rigidity was further confirmed by his teacher in Canon
Law, scripture and catechetics, Fr Bernard Fennelly, who was also his
confessor, a position which gave him enormous, and life-long, influence.
From Fennelly, McQuaid inherited the habit of according great respect
for the minute details regulating Church life as defined in the Code of
Canon Law, promulgated by Pope Benedict XV in 1918.[32]

A tragic State

Aquinas and Billot were worlds away from the negotiations in London
between an Irish delegation led by Michael Collins and Arthur Griffith
and British Prime Minister Lloyd George which produced a Treaty establishing the Irish Free State on December 6, 1921. The sovereignty of the
new State extended over only 26 of Ireland's 32 counties. Six of the nine
Ulster counties remained under British rule and would henceforth to be
governed from the Stormont parliament by the Protestant Unionist leaders, James Craig and Basil Brooke. McQuaid's Cavan was one of three
Ulster counties which found itself under the jurisdiction of the Irish
State.

After heated debate in which Collins argued for the Treaty as a
stepping stone to greater autonomy at a later date, the Dáil ratified it by
64 votes to 57. The Irish Free State became an independent dominion
within the British empire, the first but not the last nation to achieve this
status. At 26 years of age, John McQuaid was now a citizen of the Irish
Free State, though it was still required to profess ultimate allegiance to
the British Crown, and when the President of the Executive Government,
Éamon de Valera, and a minority of Sinn Féin refused to accept the
Treaty's ratification, the country moved inexorably towards Civil War.

The Catholic bishops came out in support of the Treaty, describing
it as a settlement which brought civil strife to an end and restored lawful
governance in the two jurisdictions on the island. The Treaty, the bishops
also argued, had re-established a framework in which theological principles might again be unambiguously applied. The bishops' theological
authority was the Professor of Ethics and Politics at UCD, Michael
Cronin, whose two volumes on *The Science of Ethics* taught that rebellion

was a grave violation of the divine law and a grave sin'.[33]

The establishment of the Irish Free State coincided with a new pontificate in Rome following the death of Benedict XV. McQuaid, who thought Benedict had been a man of greatness, believed that because he showed himself above all else to be 'the Pope of Charity' his name would never die in human memory. However, Benedict is probably the least remembered Pope of the twentieth century. When he died unexpectedly, he had given so much money to aid the victims of war that, while his humanitarianism offset the hostility of the major powers, who were angered by his pacifism, the Vatican did not have enough money to cover the expenses of the conclave convened to elect his successor.[34]

On February 2, 1922, the Archbishop of Milan, Achille Ratti, a scholar and librarian, and formerly Papal Nuncio to Poland, was elected Pope. His first act was to appear on the balcony of St Peter's as a gesture of goodwill to the Italian people, something which no new Pope had done since Pius IX in 1846. Taking as his motto *Pax Christi in regno Christi*, he reaffirmed his belief in the centrality of the Latin language and the scholastic method of St Thomas Aquinas in the training of the clergy. These had been fundamental elements of John McQuaid's education as he graduated through the several stages on the way to the priesthood. On March 10 in Dublin's Pro-Cathedral he knelt before the new Archbishop of Dublin, Edward Byrne, to receive the tonsure. The circle shaved on the crown of his head was a sign that he was now a cleric.

On May 7 the bishops condemned the IRA's defiance of civil authority as 'an immoral usurpation and confiscation of the people's rights', and warned that they would face excommunication. Asked in later years about his attitude to the excommunication of republicans led by de Valera – known as the Irregulars – McQuaid said that there was 'a great deal of confusion and that these men were given the sacraments when they were dying'.[35]

As his 27th birthday came round, McQuaid confided in his private notebook on July 26, 1922: 'Lord Jesus, save me from a bitter tongue. Often and often I sin by sarcasm and irony, by abruptness of speech and manner, by chilly politeness towards those who even without reason irritate me, by remarks, ill-timed, misplaced and impertinent, because lacking in respect due to others, who are my superiors or my confreres.' A remorseful McQuaid struggled to overcome this character defect. He was sorry that he 'wounded fraternal charity and made life hard for those around me.'[36]

McQuaid's aloofness, especially in the company of women, was noted by Eileen Finlay, who was being courted by his half-brother, Dean. An intelligent young woman and a niece of Fr Thomas Finlay S.J., John, on holiday in Cootehill, appeared to her as a strait-laced, austere man who kept his distance from her. 'He had a very cutting manner,' she recalled.

'His eyes were sneaky.'[37] Nor was his sister, Helen, friendly. Eileen's impression was that Dr Eugene's second family did not sit well with Helen and John. Dean, who was a doctor in the Free State Army, had a very different temperament from his half-brother. He took Eileen to a dance in Clones in the neighbouring county of Monaghan, and assured her they would be safe as he had been given an escort by the head of the anti-Treaty forces, Frank Aiken.

On February 23, 1923, McQuaid received the news that Dean had been wounded by the Irregulars in an ambush at Furnace schoolhouse on a remote mountainside near Newport in Co. Mayo. He had been on patrol as a Red Cross medical with the First Western Division of the Free State Army. Accompanied by his cousin, Mary Connolly, an anxious McQuaid set out on the long journey to Mayo. The *Freeman's Journal* had reported that during a six-hour battle a Free State soldier had fallen mortally wounded and 'a young doctor who accompanied him rushed to render assistance and in doing so he was fired on and wounded, though happily not seriously.'[38]

On arrival at Claremorris hospital, John and Mary found that Dean's wound was much more serious than had been reported. Dean died on Monday, February 26, at the age of 23. Under army escort, John and Mary travelled with Dean's hearse to Cootehill, where he was given a huge funeral.

Anxious to know the exact circumstances of his half-brother's death, John wrote to the officer in command, Captain Joe Togher, who had been wounded in the ambush. 'The doc was a universal favourite,' Togher wrote from Galway. 'It was impossible not to love him, he was such a gentlemanly chap, so cheerful and unassuming, and with all that refinement that came from a perfect home life, and liberal education. From Mac's ways, I could tell what pals you and he must have been.'

Dean had had a painful, lingering death. Pale and cold as ice, he had lain on the schoolhouse floor wrapped in children's coats. 'We then got the fire going with pieces of wood and turf, and covered him with our own greatcoats,' Togher went on. 'I lay down beside him and rubbed his hands while the Sergeant Major rubbed his feet, but it was impossible to keep him warm. He lost a fearful amount of blood and his clothes were saturated. I could hear him breathing through the hole in his lung, and I was in positive agony not knowing what to do for him. We bound him up and plugged the wound with dressing. He was in great pain.'

In despair Togher sent one of the children out waving a white apron to the house where the Irregulars were positioned to ask for blankets, clean sheets and some water and milk, but the Irregulars refused to give the provisions. Instead they sent Togher an ultimatum to surrender. Togher refused. The siege of the schoolhouse continued. 'Dean tried to clear his throat. He asked me to lift him up. I lay down and shoved his shoulders up to enable him to spit out. He did so. It was a clot of blood. ''That's a piece of my lung Joe,' Dean said.' At about 7.30pm reinforcements arrived with a doctor and stretchers. Dean was moved to Westport, and later to Claremorris.

The Free State troops wanted revenge for the loss of their comrade. 'We had eight prisoners. They were only arrested on suspicion, but officers and men went so mad when they heard about Mac that they wanted to shoot the lot. I explained we weren't sure about them, and I think that's all that saved them. I never saw men so mad.'

This account of Dean's death gave McQuaid a bitter insight into the cruelty of the Civil War. He took consolation from the fact that Dean had been in a state of supernatural grace when he met his death; he had said an Act of Contrition, which Togher considered unnecessary, knowing that he had been to confession the previous Saturday. The teacher had also got the children to say the Rosary for 'the poor doctor'. [39]

Concern for the spiritual welfare of combatants appears to have been John McQuaid's main response to a Civil War in which his sympathies lay with the Free State Forces rather than the republicans who resorted to armed insurgency. In later life McQuaid persuaded army chaplain Fr John Piggott to write a personal account of what was perhaps the most tragic episode of the Civil War: the government-sanctioned execution of four republican prisoners – Liam Mellows, Rory O'Connor, Dick Barrett and Joe McKelvey – in reprisal for the assassination of a Dáil deputy, Seán Hales. Piggott was able to confirm that Mellows was not refused the sacraments before his death. And he disclosed that Archbishop Byrne had pleaded with the President of the new Executive Council, W.T. Cosgrave, a devout Dublin Catholic, to stop the executions, Afterwards Byrne protested that 'the policy of reprisals seems to be not only unwise but entirely unjustifiable from the moral point of view'.[40]

Dean's death was followed by the death of Brother Gaspard, John's spiritual mentor. Their loss spurred on his determination to complete his preparations for the priesthood. The culmination of 11 years of study[41] came on June 29, 1924, when he was ordained a priest at St Mary's College in Rathmines by the Vicar Apostolic of Bagamoyo in East Africa, Bishop Bartholomew Wilson C.S.Sp., a Corkman who had received the Distinguished Service Medal and the Military Cross as a British Army chaplain.[42] The tall, heavily built Wilson called on the slender, ascetic McQuaid, his hair already slightly receding, to recite the anti-Modernist oath. McQuaid vowed to accept 'those principal dogmatic truths which are directly opposed to the errors of this time' and to uphold until his last breath the Faith of the Fathers communicated through the Episcopal succession from the Apostles.[43]

Shortly before John's ordination, the Irish Holy Ghost Province had been praised by the Vatican for the high quality of its teaching of

Aquinas. 'The philosophy of St Thomas Aquinas has always been inculcated by the Catholic Church as that which most conforms to the truth of
our dogmas,' Cardinal Pietro Gasparri wrote to the Holy Ghost Provincial,
Fr Joseph Byrne C.S.Sp.[44] To help consolidate the Irish Province's academic standing in Rome, Fr Byrne selected McQuaid, his best Thomistic
scholar, to study sacred scripture there. McQuaid had already begun to
learn Hebrew under Professor of Scripture and Oriental Languages at
UCD, Dr Patrick Boylan, who had studied in Berlin under Adolf von Har-
nack and was building an international reputation as a linguist and biblical
scholar. Throughout July and early August McQuaid helped Boylan complete his second volume of *The Psalms* and was warmly thanked for his
assistance by Boylan in a generous tribute in the preface.[45] The book was
completed before McQuaid left Ireland for Paris, which he found greatly
altered since his visit with his father in 1913. The traditional spectre of
'the clerical threat' remained at the centre of French politics, however,
with the *Cartel des Gauches* – an alliance of the Left led by the Radical,
Édouard Herriot – whipping up anti-Catholic feeling rather than tackling
the country's post-war economic difficulties. To counter these attacks a
National Catholic Federation was set up under General Castelnau, who
believed that *le Pays légal* – as distinct from *le Pays réel* – was once more
under the control of Freemasons and Jews, a view that also held sway with
the Holy Ghost Fathers at their headquarters in Chevilly.

It was at Chevilly on September 17 that Fr John McQuaid was consecrated to the Apostolate, the formal confirmation of his priestly vows by
the Mother House. After a short stay McQuaid travelled by train to Rome,
where he believed, mistakenly, that his destiny was to become a biblical
scholar.

4

Biblical Scholar
1924–25

'You might sometimes, too, have met him in early
morning prayer and Mass at the tomb of the Eucharistic
Pontiff, Pius X.'

Fr Michael O'Carroll C.S.Sp. on McQuaid's Roman days.

Fr John McQuaid C.S.Sp. watched Pope Pius XI advance steadily towards him along the corridor of the Lateran Palace. Portly and imperial in a white soutane, with black cape and rounded hat, Pius approached the stall to browse through the literature and artefacts relating to the missionary activities of the Holy Ghost Fathers which were on display under McQuaid's supervision. On the Pope's arrival at the stall, McQuaid, robed in a black cloak, fell to his knees and bowed his head. The Pope, his gold-rimmed spectacles glistening in the sunlight, held out his hand for the young priest to kiss his ring and imparted his blessing. In this face to face encounter, at the Missionary Exhibition during the Holy Year in 1925, McQuaid was enthused by the granite-like character of a Sovereign Pontiff, whose every action bore the hallmarks of self-confidence and authority. It was not only the highlight of McQuaid's period in Rome, but also the highpoint of his career to date. He had met 'the Pope of the Missions', Christ's representative on Earth.[1]

His Roman experience, from late summer 1924 to late autumn 1925, entrenched John McQuaid's Papalist outlook. During the Holy Year jubilee of 1925, Rome was the focus of the Catholic world as never before. More than 1,500,000 pilgrims came to the Eternal City as pilgrims, while 750,000 visitors attended the Missionary Exhibition which displayed how extensively the Church had followed its mandate to bring Catholic values to bear on societies world-wide. With the prestige of the Papacy reaching new heights, Pope Pius staged a number of impressive canonisation ceremonies in St Peter's Square, including those of a number of saints to whom McQuaid was devoted, like St Thérèse of Lisieux,[2] St John Baptist Vianney, more popularly known as the Curé d'Ars, St John Baptist de la Salle and St John Eudes. Beatified was Bernadette Soubirous of Lourdes, while St Francis de Sales was proclaimed a Doctor of the Church. For someone of McQuaid's devotional temperament such colourful ceremonies provided endless fascination, as he studied the decorum of clerical protocol, the nobility of the Papal Court and the trappings of the diplomatic world and, above all, listened to the beauty of the plain chant of the Sistine Chapel Choir with his Holy Ghost colleague Fr Michael Kennedy, a tenor who regularly sang in the choir.[3]

Rome was an aesthetic as well as an intellectual experience for McQuaid, who spent hours visiting the city's magnificent churches. He would sometimes take pilgrims on a special tour of the basilicas of St Peter's, St Paul's Without the Walls, Santa Maria Maggiore, and St John Lateran, and spent hours looking at Rome's art treasures and archaeology, particularly admiring 'the golden simplicity' of the artists Giotto and Fra Angelico.[4] He visited the graves of the early Christians in the catacombs. On his regular visits to St Peter's he prayed at the tomb of Pius X 'for whom he never concealed his admiration'.[5]

The combative spirit of Pius X was shared by Pius XI, whose religious agenda was also deeply political. 'The larger project of the Pontiff was always to revive and revitalise an intransigent and ultramontane version of Catholic Christianity,' writes the historian, James McMillan. 'As the Pope of Catholic Action, he hoped that the laity might become apostles of Christ alongside the clergy – though always subject to the authority of the Hierarchy. What Pius wanted was not a reconciliation between the Church and the modern world but a holy crusade against it in the name of Christ the King.'[6]

The compromise between the Vatican and Mussolini's Fascist state was well underway during McQuaid's stay in Rome. *L'Osservatore Romano* had welcomed Mussolini's seizure of power in 1922, and the Vatican Secretary of State, Cardinal Pietro Gasparri, was already embarked on the secret negotiations with Mussolini which would lead to the signing of the Lateran Treaty in 1929, an agreement between the Pope and the *Duce* which, in McQuaid's view, 'repaired to some extent' the loss of temporal power by Pius IX in 1870.[7]

Although Mussolini 'displayed a hostility that bordered on the obscene' towards Christianity and Catholicism,[8] he was also a pragmatist. To placate the Vatican, he curtailed the freedom of Protestant missions in Italy and stopped the building of a mosque in Rome. Launching a campaign to present himself as a model Christian, Mussolini had his marriage regularised and his children baptised by the Catholic Church. The former advocate of free love and the author of a novel, *The Cardinal's Daughter*, in which he portrayed priests as 'black microbes as fatal to mankind as tuberculosis germs', now advocated large families, the apostolic number of twelve being promoted as the ideal. Childless couples were subjected to penal taxation. Adultery and passing on syphilis to a sexual partner were made punishable in law. Short skirts and skimpy bathing costumes were banned, as were negro dances. Women were urged not to participate in sport. For his part,

Pius XI regarded Mussolini as an improvement on the Socialist or Communist alternatives. His *modus vivendi* with the dictator was also to carry the heavy price of disowning the moderate *Partito Populare* under the dynamic Sicilian priest, Luigi Sturzo, and the dissolution of Catholic trade unions. Historians like Professor A.J.C. Jemolo have argued that by associating with such a fundamentally anti-Christian and anti-clerical movement, the Papacy became less capable in later years of taking a firm stand against Fascism and German Nazism.[9] Clearly, Mussolini's pro-Church phase provided the devout young Cavan priest with a model of how the State could co-operate with the Vatican in enforcing its Catholic teachings.

McQuaid had taken up residence in the Via Sancta Chiara at the Holy Ghost Fathers' Pontifical Seminary, Gallico de Urbe, better known as the French seminary. Here he came into daily contact with the academic wing of Papal militancy. Entrusted by Pope Pius IX in 1853 to counteract Gallican tendencies towards greater independence from Rome, the seminary's priorities were widened at the request of Pius X to engage in the battle against Modernism. Its superior, Fr Henri le Floch C.S.Sp., an ardent royalist and supporter of the anti-Semitic *Action Française* movement, was also a close friend of Cardinal Billot, who often visited the college. His combination of theological rigidity and political conservatism rubbed off on the seminarians, who were from all parts of France, among them Marcel Lefebvre, the future Holy Ghost Superior General and rebel-traditionalist Archbishop of the 1970s.

The same blend of anti-Modernist attitudes also dominated the Pontifical Biblical Institute in the former Papazurri Palace, where McQuaid attended scripture lectures. Its founder-rector, Fr Leopold Fonck, a German Jesuit, had established the Institute in 1909 on the personal request of Pius X to counteract Modernist thinking. Fonck had assembled a vast library and museum, stocked with publications which promoted the worldview of Pius X. Thanks to Frs Murphy and Fahey, McQuaid came to Rome already well versed in this firebrand-style of Catholicism. In studying for his Licentiate in Biblical Studies at the Pontifical Institute, McQuaid had joined the ranks of the Vatican's intellectual élite. Through Fonck he mingled with the leaders of a highly organised conservative faction in Rome that stressed fidelity to tradition and opposition to the new method of biblical criticism pioneered by the Dominican founder of the École Biblique in Jerusalem, Fr Marie-Joseph Garrigou-Lagrange. Fonck's scholarship did not stray beyond the directives issued by Pius X.[10] Fonck's students, including McQuaid, saw themselves as 'integral Catholics' who inherited from Christ the certitude that Catholicism embodied an objective order of divine facts and teachings that were true for all time and place. Integralism, too, contemptuously treated Protestantism as the product of anarchic individualism. In such a climate of ideological hostility to modern thinking, McQuaid belonged to a school that accepted an unchanging Church. In accordance with a decree of the Biblical Commission in 1906, he was taught that the first five books of the Bible were written personally by Moses, an instruction regarded as nonsense by subsequent generations of scholars. One of his lecturers was a highly intelligent young Austrian Jesuit, Fr Augustin Bea, who in later years was to move far beyond the confines of Fonck's narrow system and become one of the leading champions of the *aggiornamento* of the Second Vatican Council.

A pilgrimage to Aquino

As part of his studies, McQuaid combed through the works of the leading authorities on St Thomas Aquinas.[11] Fatigued by the heat of Rome on a late April day in 1925, he was sitting limply behind a pile of books in his study at the French seminary when there was a knock at his door. It was a messenger informing him that the Superior, Fr le Floch, wanted to see him. A vacancy had arisen on the following day's international pilgrimage to the birthplace of St Thomas Aquinas at Aquino – did McQuaid wish to go? McQuaid accepted at once. At 3.30 next morning he rose for prayer, said Mass and had breakfast before crossing Rome to board the bustling train for the three-hour journey to Aquino. Under the pseudonym of *Peregrinatus Hibernicus* he wrote a vivid account of the pilgrimage for the *Missionary Annals*. Like a budding travel writer, he captured the flavour of Mussolini's Italy. With the train departing on time, he described its slow ascent in the Alban mountains, its picking up speed on the slope towards Naples, rattling and puffing across miles of pasture and tillage on its way up the snow-clad Apennines, glistening in the spring sunshine, passing through Old Praeneste and Angani, crossing the Lirio and the river valley before reaching its destination. With their banners unfurled, the pilgrims walked the remaining three kilometres to Aquino.

'*Fascisti* soldiers passing along our ranks invited us to form in fives,' McQuaid wrote. 'That done, a band somewhere in front struck up a march; the whole column moved forward, bareheaded and somewhat silent, into the town of St Thomas Aquinas. A narrow street, bordered by houses, old and new, that sometimes lean forward, sometimes recede, side streets that are stone stairways, a large square, off which, to the right, in a tiny square stands the old Cathedral and the house of St Thomas's family, the whole village perched on the brow of a precipice; that is Aquino.' The Solemn High Mass in honour of St Thomas was sung in the cathedral by the Procurator-General of the Dominicans, Fr Catharani. The deacon was Fr Thomas Garde, the Prior of the Irish Dominican Church of San Clemente, a Corkman who had studied in Jerusalem and now taught at the Angelicum. The text of a telegram from Pope Pius XI was read to the congregation before the local bishop, Monsignor Bonnani, raised for the veneration of the pilgrims a crucifix with a silver figure that had belonged to the Counts of Aquino.

After some sightseeing and dining with 'excellent relish' at an *osteria*, McQuaid and three companions walked six kilometres in the hot sun to the fortress town of the Aquinas family at Rocca-Secca in the mountains. They were determined to reach the summit. 'Tell me,' McQuaid said earnestly to a young French seminarist, 'do you think St Thomas is watching us now?'

'We talked pure Thomism all the way, and while his young enthusiasm kindled and flashed, I could watch the flush of his eager face, at my side, as the thoughts of his Angelic Teacher sped through his mind. We passed several shrines at the cross-roads, always of the Cross, always the recognition of a world redeemed by the Precious Blood of God Himself. Oh how good it was to breathe in such air the perfume of Christ and the love of Mary in the home of our Saint and Teacher, Thomas.'

After climbing up the cliff-face, McQuaid met 'a Dominican head which could only have come from Ireland'.[12] He greeted the stranger in Irish with the words, *Dia's Muire dhuit*. Back came the name of St Patrick. 'We had just time for a handshake and a promise to meet again. Is it the first time God and his Mother and St Patrick were named in our tongue in the home of St Thomas?' McQuaid wondered. Making straight for the ruined tower, McQuaid recalled that this had been the saint's prison, where 'his fiendish enemies had tempted his chastity and where, in the hour of his triumph, God's angels had girded him in sign of the gift of perpetual virginity.' Kneeling down at this sacred spot, McQuaid and his friends said a prayer. Kissing the stones, they imagined that Thomas had touched them or that his white Dominican habit had brushed against them.

Marvelling at the intense devotion of the local people to God and his Blessed Mother, McQuaid's thoughts returned to Cootehill, 'to the old home-country, especially to my own North-land, while I caught the traces of the characteristics of our Catholic people in this other Catholic people of the Italian mountains. Wherein lies the common cause of this resemblance? In God and his Blessed Mother. Ah we, who have lived among Protestants, know it.'

The trip to Aquino further stimulated McQuaid's interest in the Angelic Master, but his preference in terms of travel was for the north of Italy rather than the south. Later that year he visited Siena, the capital of the Chianti region: His purpose was to make a pilgrimage to the birthplace of St Catherine to pray for the soul of Brother Gaspard. It also produced another piece of writing, in which McQuaid again combined a good eye for his surroundings with a densely mystical and romantic style. 'There it stands yet, the old building beyond the Cathedral Square, unchanged, like other features in medieval Siena,' he wrote. 'In her home, too, still you see her lantern and her staff.'[13]

Just as he was showing promise as a biblical scholar and writer, McQuaid's life took an unexpected direction as the result of a manpower crisis in the Irish Province of the Holy Ghost Fathers. Alarmed at falling enrolments to their Blackrock and Rockwell colleges, the Superior General in Paris, Monsignor Louis Le Hunsec, had appointed Dr Edward Crehan as an official visitor – an investigator – with the task of drawing up a confidential report on the state of affairs in Ireland.[14] Crehan discovered that, although the Irish Province contained a broad spectrum of political opinion, it had become too identified with the defeated republican side through its association with Éamon de Valera. As a result it was losing support from those who backed the Cosgrave Government, which was consolidating its hold on power. It was also feared that the Holy Ghost Fathers had lost the confidence of the bishops.

In the light of Crehan's report, Le Hunsec authorised an administrative shake-up at the highest levels of the Irish Province. The Provincial, Fr Joseph Byrne, a loyal friend of de Valera, was transferred to Paris, while Fr Dick Hartnett, an apolitical figure, was promoted to the post of Provincial. Crehan himself became President of Rockwell, with Fr Dan Murphy, McQuaid's UCD rival, as Dean of Studies.

Fr Edward Leen, a friend of W.T. Cosgrave and Eoin MacNeill, was made President of Blackrock College in place of Fr Michael Downey, another close friend of de Valera's. The final place on the new team was assigned to Fr John Charles McQuaid, who became Dean of Studies at Blackrock College. In what effectively was a purge of the pro-de Valera leadership, the new men were given the task of getting back on side with the Cumann na nGaedheal Government and the Hierarchy.

McQuaid was not destined to become a biblical scholar or a foreign missionary after all. Whatever his sense of shock on receiving word of his transfer to Blackrock without having completed his higher studies, he put into practice the teaching of Brother Gaspard by submitting to the will of God as directed by his superiors. The closing of his Roman period, however, coincided with the ending of his links with Cootehill. McQuaid had no sooner arrived in Ireland in late autumn 1925 when he had to rush to Cootehill where his father's health was deteriorating rapidly. As he was walking him home in silence from morning Mass to Court View, a frail and unsteady Dr Eugene suddenly said: 'People are hungry and thirsty for doctrine.' It was a remark that John never forgot.[15] When Dr Eugene died on December 13, there was an 'extremely large' funeral at which Bishop Finegan presided, according to the *Anglo-Celt*, which described him as a most successful medical practitioner whose medical abilities were sought over a wide area.[16] It was John who arranged for his father to be buried in the family plot in Middle Chapel alongside his mother, Jennie Corry. It was his way of making their marriage permanent in the grave as in heaven. Agnes resolved shortly afterwards to sell Court View and to return to Dublin, where her stepson was about to become a national figure in his mission to satisfy the nation's 'hunger and thirst for doctrine'.

PART II

BUILDING A POWERBASE
1925–40

5

Man of Mystery
1925–32

'There was about the man at this time a distinctive aura.'
Fr Michael O'Carroll C.S.Sp.

In his first speech as Dean of Studies at Blackrock College on December 21, 1925, Fr John McQuaid C.S.Sp. flattered the average performers rather than the academic high-fliers when announcing the Christmas examination results. Enthused more by Gregorian Chant than rugby, he listed his priorities as their mental training, character formation and life-long commitment to 'the supernatural work of social charity'. Not a speech likely to woo adolescents, McQuaid's words, spoken in a low but commanding voice, nevertheless cast a spell.

The Holy Ghost priest Fr Michael O'Carroll, who listened to that speech as a student in the Intermediate Certificate class, remembers vividly that an 'air of wonder' hung over McQuaid. His teaching of art appreciation and literary criticism was informed by 'a sense of style that was inherent in him, by a characteristic precision and by subtlety of manner down to the intonation and gestures,' says O'Carroll, recalling the finely chiselled lettering on the blackboard. 'We felt that behind it all was something deeply spiritual, perhaps mysterious.'[1]

'A slight narrow-featured man whose generally ascetic air and bearing were somehow emphasised by the fact that he carried one shoulder higher than the other,' is how McQuaid is remembered by the writer and poet, Anthony Cronin. 'He had a piercing eye, a mouth that betrayed a certain humorous expectancy and an undoubted presence.'[2]

His mannerisms were imitated by the boys, who nicknamed him 'Mixer McQuaid' after the pipe tobacco known as 'Mick McQuaid'. The story is often told of the boy who mimicked his manner of walking with one shoulder drooping slightly, but who was surprised to have his own shoulder tapped by McQuaid, whispering in his ear, 'The other shoulder'. Brian O'Nolan, who would win literary fame under the *noms-de-plume* of Flann O'Brien and Myles na gCopaleen, imitated McQuaid's writing, and provided his versions to other boys as official excuses for undone homework.

Although McQuaid tended to keep his distance, his image as a teacher is not that of an aloof or timid man. Indeed, the stereotype of McQuaid as 'a shy, retiring man' has been challenged as totally inaccurate by Brian O'Nolan's brother, Ciarán Ó Nualláin, who found him to be a strong personality, 'He was a friendly, sociable, learned man with a good sense of humour.' [3]

McQuaid was enthusiastic about the college's debating society, but his choice of subjects could be heavy. One of the debates grappled with the question: 'Can fallen man, in his present historical circumstances, all strictly supernatural assistance apart, perform some of the acts which in the natural order are to be deemed in every sense, morally good?' 'No' was his answer. This was the doctrinal core of his pedagogy. Convinced that a pupil's will was defective as a result of the original sin of Adam and Eve in the Garden of Eden, he argued that a balance needed to be struck between moral order and personal freedom. To achieve this, the Catholic system was 'fatherly, both in the firmness with which it apportions penalties and in the delicacy with which it judges individual frailty'.[4]

As Dean of Studies, McQuaid administered corporal punishment sparingly. 'I was flogged by McQuaid,' recalls Robert Geldof, father of singer Bob Geldof. 'I had to kneel down and lift up the shirt after being reprimanded for impudence for defending another student who was victimised by a priest unfitted for the Blackrock classroom after a traumatic spell in Africa.' According to Geldof, who described McQuaid as a 'likeable man with a tough face and a quiet manner,' he tried to understand why students had been reported for punishment by asking them to explain themselves.[5]

Yet as Fr O'Carroll has noted, McQuaid was moody. He could be abrupt and prickly. Asked by a colleague, Fr Francis Howell, to translate from French into English a biography of the Holy Ghost Superior General, Monsignor le Roy, he replied sharply, 'You have not the faintest idea of what my work here means, especially at this season of the year. I return it with regret that you did not first ask me whether it was possible. I should not then have been obliged to do what may seem very ungracious. I may later find time.'[6] He often conveyed a hint of deep sadness in his own life. 'You are young and grief of soul is not your lot, as yet,' he told the boys during a talk on guardian angels. 'One day you will know it and in that day God's angel will be with you.'[7]

His other duties as Dean meant that McQuaid was responsible for planning the curriculum, for grading and grouping the boys in classes and for the day-to-day supervision of order and discipline. He organised the school timetable and allocated classes and duties to the staff. Interested in medical advances, he consulted doctors and psychologists on applying psychology to the personality development of his boys.[8] He helped Joseph Egan to get over shyness by telling him, 'You are much too timid, Joseph.

Go into the corner and shout at me!'⁹ A shrewd judge of a boy's aptitude, he pioneered career guidance in the college. He failed, however, to impress a young lady who came to discuss her younger brother's poor school reports and assess his prospects for a job in the banks. This was Edel Quinn, the future Envoy of the Legion of Mary and now a candidate for sainthood. 'The Dean is fairly young and has a most doleful way of speaking. Like the younger priest in the Abbey play, he would really send you into the depths!' she wrote. Edel was annoyed by McQuaid's remark to Ralph, 'Are not sisters terrible bosses!'¹⁰

McQuaid kept his promise to encourage the average student. When he discovered that a class of sixth-year boys lacked even the rudiments of Latin late in term, he announced in his low steely voice: 'Gentlemen, we shall begin with *mensa*.' By the end of that term, his systematic exposition of grammar and syntax enabled 17 of the 18 boys to pass the examination.¹¹

In the English literature class, McQuaid taught that the purpose of writing was 'to interest, to amuse, to elevate'. A master of précis, he presented thumbnail assessments of the great writers: William Shakespeare had unprecedented mastery of language, Sir Walter Scott provided a great portrait-gallery of characters of every rank and style, Charles Dickens left a legacy of good beyond all accidental faults, William Makepeace Thackery was a good prose writer whose novels lacked firm plots, William Goldsmith was a naive but shrewd humorist, John Keats embodied the ideal of what was popularly considered to be 'poetry', William Wordsworth was egotistical, Samuel Coleridge was intensely imaginative, Lord Byron was deliberately outrageous and lacking in deep vision, Percy Bysshe Shelley was the supreme lyrical poet, Robert Browning was direct and precise but capable of writing carelessly, Arthur Tennyson possessed craftsmanship of very high power, and Robert Burns was Scotland's drunken and dissipated national poet who made permanent a dying dialect.¹²

For McQuaid the greatest living prose writer was Hilaire Belloc, the English Catholic convert whose famous bestseller, *Europe and the Faith*, captured the imagination of a generation of Irish as well as English Catholics.¹³ With Belloc came that other literary convert, Gilbert Keith Chesterton, who taunted his secular opponents with the conviction that St Thomas Aquinas knew all that there was to be known. A third prose model was the French neo-Thomist scholar, Jacques Maritain, who, sickened by the materialism of university life in Paris, made a suicide pact with his wife, only to revoke it after hearing a lecture by the Catholic philosopher, Henri Bergson. Through the publishers Wilfrid Sheed and Maisie Ward, McQuaid came to know personally this trio of unyielding Catholic apologists.

According to Anthony Cronin, McQuaid himself was 'something of a prose stylist in a rag-bag Edwardian, mandarin way'.¹⁴ Others have described his frequently pedantic and purple prose as 'the language of the corset-maker'.[15] Certainly, his use of language is archaic, and often laden, in today's soundbite age; but well-crafted gems of irony or observation keep surfacing and make his prose memorable and trenchant in places.[16] There was no place for Protestant writers like Jonathan Swift, William Butler Yeats or Sean O'Casey in McQuaid's classroom, and most certainly not for the Clongowes renegade, James Joyce, the Blackrock rebel, Liam O'Flaherty, and the UCD poet, Austin Clarke.

The new order

McQuaid quickly discovered that he had a natural flair for 'networking'. While the President, Fr Leen, was preoccupied with educational theory and highbrow spirituality, McQuaid – while not lacking in either of those demanding specialisms – excelled in the social graces and was a generous host. The old Blackrock and Clongowes school-tie connections meant that in a short time there was no one of importance in politics, the civil service, the judiciary, industry and commerce, the army and Garda Síochána that he did not know – or who did not know of him. Blackrock College was McQuaid's gateway to the Free State's political, social and ecclesiastical elite.

Encouraged by Leen, he became friendly with the head of Government, W.T. Cosgrave, a proud bearer of Knight of the Grand Cross of the Order of Pius IX. Before long, Cosgrave agreed to speak at Blackrock's Prize Day, and not long afterwards his wife, Louisa, presented the prizes at the revived college Sports Day. However, to the dismay of *The Irish Times* and its mainly Protestant readers, Cosgrave used Blackrock College as a platform on which to insist on compulsory Irish.[17]

Government ministers like Patrick McGilligan, Fionán Lynch, Michael Corrigan and John Marcus O'Sullivan became a regular sight at Blackrock functions. This generation of politicians was receptive to the claims of the Catholic Church in society. Already underway was a process of State abdication of its authority. In the immediate post-independence period Cosgrave had considered giving the Vatican the power of veto over legislation contrary to faith and morals in return for Papal recognition of the new State. Another quixotic plan to convert the General Post Office in O'Connell Street into a cathedral also failed to materialise. But the new State did not baulk at enforcing Catholic teaching forbidding divorce. Attempts in 1923 by the Attorney General, Hugh Kennedy, to preserve for Protestants a parliamentary procedure granting marriage dissolutions with right to remarry were scuppered by the Hierarchy. Ignored was the eloquent warning by the Senator and poet, William Butler Yeats, that the task of reconciling the Protestant minority's constitutional freedom with the will of the majority would be the state's most delicate problem. Yeats carried no weight with the Cosgrave Government, which used censorship to cultivate a closed society, reinforced by Church control of the education system.[18]

The catholicisation of the Free State proceeded steadily. In 1923 a law on film censorship was approved. In 1924 and 1927 laws curtailing the consumption of strong alcoholic drink were introduced at the prompting of the bishops. By 1926 the census showed that the Protestant population had begun to decline, and over the next decades would fall from 11 per cent of the population to its present low of around 5 per cent.

The ethos in which McQuaid operated was inherited from the unchallenged dominance of the Catholic Church in the Free State. Since 1919 the bishops had drawn up a uniform syllabus and examination in religious instruction which was totally under Church control. In addition to the catechism, pupils in their first three years of secondary schooling were taught the creed and the commandments, as well as learning about virtue, vice, grace and the sacraments; they also studied the Gospels, church history and liturgy. In the final two years students followed courses in apologetics and Catholic social science, which covered elementary economics and the teachings of Popes Leo XIII and Pius XI. A course in Plain Chant was obligatory.[19]

McQuaid boasted that there was not a single State school in Ireland: the country's 280 Catholic secondary schools were built, equipped and managed by the Religious Orders or the diocesan clergy. Because they received government subsidies, they were subject to State inspection and followed the State examination system; however, the Minister for Education, John Marcus O'Sullivan, who was regarded as a Catholic intellectual, believed that it was the State's duty to finance the Church-owned schools, while recognising the Catholic Church's right to educate its members without further State involvement.[20]

In Fr Leen, Blackrock College could claim an educationalist who was second only to Professor Timothy Corcoran S.J. but who was also a Catholic writer with a considerable international appeal. From Abbeyfeale, Co. Limerick, he had been educated in France by Pierre Genoud, later Archbishop of Guadaloupe, and in Rome by Fr Billot. Before his appointment to Blackrock his horizons had been broadened through two years spent in Southern Nigeria, where he had been secretary to Bishop Shanahan and diocesan director of education. His blueprint for Irish education hinged on making the system Christian and Catholic; it also aimed 'to liberate the teachers from the Anglo-Saxon mould'.[21]

Leen's objective of catholicising the British educational legacy corresponded with the outlook of his chief assistant, John McQuaid, who wanted to promote the integralist ethos in the school curriculum. They did not believe that secular instruction and religious education could be kept apart. On the contrary, they inculcated into their students the belief that religion must influence their civic, commercial and private lives.

Direction to do so was coming from Rome itself, where at the end of 1925 Pius XI published the Encyclical *Quas Primas*, fixing the last Sunday in October annually as the feast of Christ the King. On that day Catholics were to affirm their commitment to 'the Kingship of Christ on Earth' and to study the Papal teaching that the Catholic Church provided the principles on which could be built a just order for the nations of the world. In Ireland this meant, first of all the healing of divisions arising from the Civil War. Under the leadership of the Professor of Church History at Milltown, Fr Edward Cahill S.J., around 40 priests and lay Catholics, including Éamon de Valera, founded the League of Christ the King, *An Ríoghacht*.[22]

Deeply involved in this movement, McQuaid arranged for its first feast-day meeting to be held in Blackrock College on October 31, 1926. It was addressed by Fr Cahill and Fr Denis Fahey. The League aimed to educate Catholics in their Church's social principles and to work 'towards the gradual building up of a Christian State on the lines of the Catholic national tradition but suited to modern circumstances'.

As part of its blueprint for the development of a Free State based on Catholic social order, its ambitious programme involved the devising of economic plans to develop forestry, fishing, manufacturing industry, banking and the control of credit and the currency. Particular attention was given to the training of young persons as lay defenders of the Faith against the Communist challenge. The promotion of Catholic education rather than State education was a central plank in its policy. It called for an exacting system of censorship to control the evil of the cinema and imported newspapers from Britain. An advocate of State control of public morality, it frowned on 'an excessive craze after dissipation and excitement' at cinemas, ballrooms and race-meetings. It also aimed to control the new medium of radio, which had begun in Ireland as 2RN at the start of 1926.[23]

Prior to the launching of *An Ríoghacht*, McQuaid had returned to the continent to keep abreast of theological developments. In Rome, he passed the examination for his Doctor of Divinity degree at the Gregorian University, a consolation for not having completed his course in biblical studies. There he applied for membership of the Society of Thomist scholars (*Unio Thomistica*) and was admitted as John C. McQuaid D.D.[24]

He spent some time in France, where he cultivated old and new friends. One of these was Count Biver,[25] with whom he shared a devotion to a holy priest who was being compared with the Curé d'Ars for humility and saintliness. This was Père Jean Édouard Lamy, a mystic whose visions of Jesus, Mary and Satan had attracted a cult following. Lamy's appeal resided in his teaching that in the daily struggle against Lucifer, the Blessed Virgin Mary had mastered the Evil One.

The Blessed Virgin was Lamy's life. He claimed that Mary appeared to him before his First Communion, which he made at the age of eleven, and that in 1883 she cured him of eczema. In September 1909 the Virgin appeared to him with Lucifer, and on this occasion she foretold the onset of the First World War and condemned Modernism. After showing him a spot in the woods at Clairvaux, Mary asked him to build a shrine to her, Notre Dame des Bois.

On his return to Ireland, McQuaid often spoke to his friends, colleagues and students about the miraculous powers of Père Lamy, who had taken hold of his adult spiritual life as completely as Brother Gaspard had directed his religious outlook in adolescence.

With his fluent French and Italian, McQuaid was courted at diplomatic receptions and dinners of the resident ambassadors. He was a regular guest at functions in Iveagh House, headquarters of the Department of External Affairs, especially after Patrick McGilligan became minister in October 1927. Worried that this lifestyle might run contrary to his vow of poverty, he sought advice from his confessor, Fr Fennelly, who reassured him that he was in fact 'unworkably severe concerning reparation to be made for violations of poverty'.[26]

Triumphalism was becoming the dominant characteristic of Catholicism in the Free State, which was also submitting its social mores to the control of the clergy and a devout laity – described by the writers Liam O'Flaherty and Peadar O'Donnell respectively but not respectfully as 'the soutaned bullies of the Lord' and 'the yahoo laity'. At the Synod of Maynooth in 1927 the bishops complained of 'the dance hall, the bad book, the indecent paper, the motion picture, the immodest fashion in female dress, all of which tend to destroy the virtues characteristic of our race.' The State responded to the Church's cue by introducing the Censorship of Publications Act 1929 against 'evil literature'.

The first big event in the life of the new State was the celebration in 1929 of the centenary of Catholic Emancipation. Oblivious to the feelings of the Protestant minority, this event produced a remarkable demonstration of national thanksgiving to God for a century of Catholic religious freedom. A highlight of the celebrations was a garden party for 4,000 guests in the grounds at Blackrock College, hosted by the Hierarchy but organised by McQuaid and his colleagues. It was hailed as the largest and most fashionable garden party ever held in Dublin. 'Beautiful weather favoured the event,' the *Irish Independent* reported. 'The crowds of fashionably dressed ladies moving in a setting of sylvan grandeur made a most impressive spectacle.'[27] There was a new confidence running through Blackrock, evident in the relaunch of the *College Annual* and the revival of the college theatre, and the introduction of a junior conference of the St Vincent de Paul Society inaugurated by former Blackrock luminaries Sir Joseph Glynn and Frank Duff.[28] McQuaid, for his part, had established his

name in social and educational circles, and in 1929 he was appointed special delegate on the Department of Education's Commission of Inquiry
into the Teaching of English. He represented Ireland at the first International Congress of Independent Secondary Education in Brussels.

In January 1930 Archbishop Paschal Robinson,[29] the first Apostolic
Nuncio to Ireland since Archbishop Rinnuccini in the seventeenth century, was welcomed by Archbishop Byrne and Government ministers
when he arrived at Dun Laoghaire. He was met with scenes of fervent
devotion in the south Dublin seaside town, and at Blackrock McQuaid
lined the road with his students, who waved as the Nuncio passed in his
car. This was the first street demonstration by the college since Queen
Victoria had been welcomed to Ireland 30 years earlier.[30]

By 1930, too, the political pendulum was swinging towards de
Valera, who had broken with Sinn Féin and had founded a new political
party, Fianna Fáil, to advance his objectives of a united Catholic and
Gaelic Ireland. The college, which had fostered a close relationship with
Cosgrave's party, now had to revise its attitude towards de Valera. The
bridgehead to de Valera was McQuaid. He had befriended Éamon and
Sinéad de Valera when they visited the College almost daily for ten days
in December 1928 during a serious illness of their son Vivion. McQuaid's
attentiveness to Vivion, then and later, was greatly appreciated.[31]
Although Vivion had begun his studies at University College Dublin, he
lived in Blackrock College, where the climate was conductive to his recov-
ery from asthma attacks.

A shared pastime of McQuaid and Vivion was target practice using
.22 rifles which they fired to great abandonment in their joint mission of
decimating the rat population which bred around the Willow Park mansion and the out-offices. For years afterwards, colleagues marvelled about
the day McQuaid spotted a cat ambling across the quadrangle some 60
yards away with a rat in its jaws. Taking careful aim, McQuaid fired and
shot the rat from the cat's mouth. To show it was not a freak hit, McQuaid
picked out another distant object and put two bullets through it in quick
succession. 'She is firing a little to the left!' he commented.

With student numbers beginning to rise, McQuaid had assumed
more administrative responsibilities. Increasingly, he undertook 'parlour
work', meeting parents and relatives of students with special problems, to
relieve Leen from routine duties. He built up a reputation for being
accessible, and 'clientelist' in the efforts which he made to place boys in
good jobs, especially in the harsh days after the economic collapse of 1929.

McQuaid found himself him in a highly sensitive position when he
detected in Leen, a man prone to sharp outbursts, the early signs of a
mental and physical breakdown. The strains on Leen were showing from
his heavy workload as retreat and conference preacher, as the co-founder
with Bishop Shanahan of the Killeshandra Foundation,[32] as the chairman

of the Catholic Headmasters' Association and as a member of a Government Commission into Proselytism. His worries were significantly added to by his plans for a new college wing which would include a kitchen, pantries and a boiler-room. Psychologically he nursed a continuing hurt from the bishops' disapproval of an article he had written in the *Irish Ecclesiastical Record* on the Mass in 1924. In late 1930 Leen felt no longer able to continue as President and he petitioned Paris to be relieved of his office. The Superior General, Bishop Le Hunsec, appointed Leen Professor of Psychology and Ethics in the Senior Scholasticate, a post which gave him time – after recovering from his temporary collapse – to write books that made him one of the bestselling spiritual writers of his period.[33]

There was little doubt as to who would succeed Leen. In Paris on December 24, 1930, the Holy Ghost Superior General signed McQuaid's appointment as President of Blackrock College, an appointment that was confirmed on January 6, 1931, by the Irish Provincial, Fr Hartnett. He was 35 years old.[34]

President of Blackrock College

A change of style from the Leen years immediately marked McQuaid's presidency of Blackrock College. For the college sports in 1931 each invitation card had to be presented for control at the college entrance and the names of the guests were supplied to the press. The distinguished visitors included the Governor General, James McNeill, the Garda Commissioner, General Eoin O'Duffy, the French Minister and Mme Alphand, the Belgian Consul-General and Mme Goor, as well as 'Mr É. de Valera, T.D., Miss M. de Valera and Mr V. de Valera'.[35]

In his address welcoming O'Duffy as guest of honour, McQuaid boasted that 'in the great revival of athletics inaugurated by him in Ireland, it will please him to see Blackrock in the vanguard.' It was not an idle boast: over the next few years Blackrock won numerous trophies in college tournaments. Bright rugby prospects combined with good examination results and increasing school numbers quickly enhanced his position as a dynamic and successful president. While holding the reins tightly over both the college staff and the Holy Ghost community stationed in Blackrock, McQuaid delegated much of the day-to-day management to his subordinates, Frs Daniel Liston, James Finucane and Walter Finn, organising his own schedule to give himself ample time to pursue his many other interests.

In his first presidential address to the Blackrock Union, McQuaid commended Catholic Action as 'the apple of Pope Pius XI's eye'.[36] This was a reference to the publication by Pope Pius XI of his Encyclical, *Quadragesimo Anno*, only five months into his presidency. This Encyclical proposed that class struggle should be displaced by the creation of corporations or guilds representing each class and caste in society, a system modelled on medieval Christendom. It attacked the centralised State, as found in Bolshevik Russia, and advocated 'subsidiarity' so as to favour decision-making at local level. Priests were urged to promote social study among working men, employers and youth in accordance with Catholic doctrine. *Quadragesimo Anno* gave an enormous stimulus to the vocationalist (or corporatist) movement in Ireland and elsewhere, and came just at a time when an ascendant Fianna Fáil party was borrowing heavily from the Papacy's language of social democracy. With de Valera's establishment of the *Irish Press* as 'the Truth in the News', McQuaid's Blackrock speeches – as well as those as chairman of the Catholic Head-masters' Association – were reported prominently in that newspaper. In his address to the Blackrock College Union he declared that his daily prayer, when mounting the altar-steps to say Mass, was that the boys under his care would take their place in 'the Catholic life of our young State, [as] integral Catholics of Blackrock training'. Not for his boys were indulgence in the sins of social laziness, nor membership of the self-constituted intelligentsia of pagan movements, literary and artistic. Nor too would they become the tool of unquiet agitators.

> **It is our present endeavour so to enlighten and discipline our boys that each, with God's help, may be an intelligent and willing cooperator with the Hierarchy and the parish clergy in social charity. And by social charity I mean no small thing, nor any mere freelance effort. Rather I mean that work of years that lies ahead of us, work of head and heart and will for the social betterment of this Catholic people.[37]**

McQuaid went to France over the Christmas period, perhaps to visit the grave of Père Lamy who had died on December 1: Éamon de Valera, in whom McQuaid had nurtured a devotion to the French priest, had asked him to bring back a relic. McQuaid noted that anti-clericalism had abated somewhat in France. There was a remarkable vitality in spiritual writing and social thinking, which was also spreading to Belgium and Switzerland, and on a visit to the Loreto House in Paris he met a group of Sisters who were preparing to work as missionaries in East Africa and Mauritius.

McQuaid was spiritually recharged when he returned to Ireland in early January 1932 – and in an apocalyptic frame of mind. In an address to the Society of St Vincent de Paul, he told the officers that they were doing apostolic work in preparing boys to work under the parish clergy for 'the coming struggle for the faith in Ireland'.[38] The form that struggle would take was about to be revealed by McQuaid at a special sermon back in his native Cavan.

6

War against Satan
1932–34

'Lucifer is tall, with quite a good-looking face,
bony, bearded.'

Père Lamy.

Fr John McQuaid C.S.Sp. returned to Cavan on Passion Sunday, March 13, 1932, to preach on the subject of: 'Our Divine Lord Jesus Christ or Satan? – the real struggle in the modern world.' Addressing his 'own countryfolk in the interests of Catholic Truth', he warned them that this struggle involved Satan – the banished Archangel Lucifer – and his companions in a perennial battle against Christ's Church and the good angels. The struggle, he argued, was being fought in all parts of the globe – including Cavan – in the guise of a conspiracy led by Jews, Freemasons, Protestants and Communists.[1] McQuaid's sermon was praised by the Bishop of Kilmore, Dr Finegan, who had invited his county kinsman to preach in the Town Hall in aid of new buildings for the Loreto College at Drumkeen. The local newspaper, the *Anglo-Celt*, published his every dire word on Satan.[2]

Warning that Satan's enmity had not abated over the centuries, McQuaid declared that Jews were always to be found leading the attacks against the Church. 'From the first persecutions till the present moment, you will find Jews engaged in practically every movement against Our Divine Lord and his Church,' he said. 'A Jew as a Jew is utterly opposed to Jesus Christ and all the Church means. But further, Satan has other allies; all those who by deliberate revolt against God and his Church set themselves under the government and direction of the Evil One. I want you to remember the truth very clearly: by Satan we mean not only Lucifer and the fallen Angels, but also those men, Jews or others, who by deliberate revolt against Our Divine Lord have chosen Satan for their head.'

McQuaid proceeded to give his Cavan audience the truth as taught by 'the Billot-Kimmage school of history'. Until the thirteenth century, society, based on the family and the guild system, had acknowledged the Vicar of Christ as the supreme judge of doctrine and conduct on Earth. Tragically, a fatal blow to order in society was inflicted by a hireling of

Philip the Fair of France, Nogaret, when he struck Pope Boniface in the face. The rest of history was a story of rapid decay, with the revival of interest in Greek and Latin literature hastening paganism in thought and life. Within 200 years, Europe was ripe for Luther.

It was the fearful distinction of that fallen priest not only to separate men from the One True Church but also to 'rend' society. Luther's legacy – a widespread indifference to God – accelerated the decay of all belief in the supernatural life of grace, and paved the way for the Naturalistic Society, one based on the teaching that men could become good and true without the aid of God. 'This is the prime doctrine of Freemasonry, a sect that arose from the ruins of Luther's division,' he declared.

Even if it might shock his listeners, McQuaid insisted that they had better know the facts: the French Revolution of 1789, an orgy of blood and lust, was a Masonic achievement. Yet when the murdering was over and the guillotine lay silent, something more terrible remained. This was the infamous *Declaration of the Rights of Man*, which blasphemously proclaimed that man is God.

> The *Declaration of the Rights of Man* is the political creed that explains the modern world. As a result of its teaching, States have almost everywhere been separated from the Church. Modern constitutions are based on this Masonic declaration. Modern law, in all its texture, is inspired by it and especially, modern Parliaments are only instruments for putting its theories into effect, while the modern Press and Cinema are the direct outcome of this virulent document, which after the manner of Satan, sets man in the place of God. Thus, the *Declaration of the Rights of Man* has inspired the whole modern attack on Our Divine Lord Jesus Christ and his Church.

Turning his attack on the scientific approach to the Bible, McQuaid maintained that for more than 70 years scholars, from Ernest Renan to the Abbé Loisy, had used their perverted genius to prove that Christ was a fraud and that the sacred scriptures were false. Modern scholars denied the evidence being found in the sands of Egypt and the monuments of the Near East which were vindicating the Christian faith.

Like the Jews of old, modern Jews were also busy denying the divinity of Christ. The German Jew, Émile Ludwig, had written a blasphemous *Life of Christ* which was given massive publicity by the Jewish-controlled world press. So too, Jewish writers like Eisler and Klausner praised Christ as a man of the Jewish race, but in doing so denied his divinity.

Topically relating his talks to the cinemas of Cavan, McQuaid also denounced Hollywood's false portrayal of the person of Jesus Christ.

'How many of you who saw *Ben Hur*, *The King of Kings* and *The Ten Commandments* realised that these films were based on this very desire to show Christ as only a Great Man and a member of the Jewish race?'he asked. 'I hold here copies of the telegrams by which the powerful Masonic and Jewish group, the Benai Berith, compelled the Jewish film producers even to alter the sacred history of the Gospel!'

Referring to a photograph in a society paper of a Western Girls Rowing Team, McQuaid regretted that the young girls were dressed in men's scanty athletic attire. 'Poor children, if they but knew it! They are carrying out Satan's programme,' he lamented. 'Has Pius XI spoken in vain: "In gymnastic exercises and deportment, special care must be had of Christian modesty in young women and girls, which is so gravely impaired by any kind of exhibition in public."'

Cavan's Catholics were put on their guard against one of the unfailing forms of attack upon their Church: propaganda against the bishops and their teaching.

> We in Ireland are not unacquainted with this form of ambush, for such it is. It is in truth a favourite device of Satan to weaken reverence for the authority of those who command in the name of Christ: the next step, rejection of authority, is rather quick to follow. Hence we may be prepared to hear more and more the plea that Bishops and priests must keep out of politics.

It was, in fact, the great crime of modern society that very few States officially acknowledged Christ and his Church. This apostasy had resulted in the harsh tyranny of the Satanic masters of world finance, the Jews. A recent editorial in the Parisian daily newspaper, *L'Ami du Peuple*, had proved that the financial distress caused by the Wall Street Crash in 1929 was the deliberate work of a few Jewish financiers, among them Paul Warburg.

To combat this, the Church needed to engage in politics as a matter of moral conduct, he continued:

> Till the crack of dawn, while the Church is the Church, Pope and Bishops and, in due submission to the Bishops, priests also, must interfere in politics, as by Divine right to guide the Faithful, not of course in mere politics where no moral issues are threatened, but whenever political or social or economic programmes are at variance with Divine Law.

Lay Catholics should also become engaged in the combat, as Pope Leo XIII had advocated: 'publications to publications, schools to schools, association to association, congresses to congresses, action to action'. To educate the laity for this task, McQuaid saw study clubs as a vehicle for moulding the outlook of the emerging middle-class intelligentsia and working-class leadership. He was an enthusiastic supporter of the Pro Fide Society in University College, Dublin, which promised 'to do vast work among the picked students of our land,' and he encouraged adult education through *An Ríoghacht*. He also took a keen interest in the Catholic Young Men's Society's courses in social science, the Study Circle of St Thomas Aquinas in Cork and the rural revival movement, Muintir na Tíre. The Catholic Boy Scouts and Girl Guides were a major force for Catholic revival, but McQuaid regretted that these organisations were centred in urban areas and not active in the countryside, where he feared that Communists and Protestant proselytisers, the enemies of the Church, were burrowing away.

In identifying Satan as a living spirit engaged in non-stop warfare with Christ's Church, McQuaid was merely giving expression to mainstream Catholic thinking. Later that year the Scottish bishops issued a joint Pastoral Letter, given prominent coverage in the *Irish Independent*, in which they warned their flocks against the Satanic anti-God campaign being conducted by Communists. But the extremism of his anti-semitic and anti-Protestant views marked him out as being on the far right of Irish Catholicism, led by Frs Cahill and Fahey.[3] Since his return from Rome McQuaid had come under the strong influence of Fr Fahey, who was teaching theology and philosophy to the senior Holy Ghost scholasticates at the Castle in Blackrock College.

One measure of the closeness of their relationship was the preface written by McQuaid to Fahey's *The Kingship of Christ*, published in 1931. McQuaid commended it as the first work in the English language to present a synthesis of dogmatic truths and historical facts. It was 'a storehouse of defensive arguments' for Catholic students, clerical and lay. More especially, 'he explained the interrelation between Church and State which is called the Indirect Power'. Abstract though that term might sound, McQuaid went on, in real life the Indirect Power meant the acceptance or rejection by all states of Jesus Christ and His Church. The true progress or certain decay of these states followed as a consequence.[4]

McQuaid, Fahey and Cahill looked to Éamon de Valera as the political leader who would create the Catholic social order – now being called 'vocationalism' in the Free State. They were encouraged in this expectation by Fianna Fáil's deputy leader, Seán T. O'Kelly, who claimed during the general election campaign that 'our policy was that of Pope Pius XI'. The perception of an alliance between Catholicism and Fianna Fáil was reinforced when Seán MacEntee boasted that the party had won 'the Catholic vote'.[5]

As the Dáil prepared to meet on March 9, 1932 to elect Éamon de Valera as President of the Executive Council after Fianna Fáil's victory at the polls, rumours circulated that Cosgrave would stage a coup d'état to stop the party from assuming power. Fully aware of the tense political situation, McQuaid said a Mass for peace in the college chapel. What McQuaid did not know was that, on the night before the Dáil vote, Vivion de Valera recovered a gun belonging to the late republican, Cathal Brugha, from its hiding place on the altar where the Blackrock president was to pray. Acting as his father's bodyguard, Vivion had the gun in his pocket while they entered the precincts of the Dáil, but it was not needed: Cosgrave conceded defeat and the authority of government was passed to Fianna Fáil.[6]

One of the first to congratulate the new head of Government was the President of Blackrock College. 'I have great pleasure in wishing you, on my part and from all the Community,' he wrote, 'sincere good wishes for the blessings of God and Our Lady, in every detail of your enormous work.'[7] Fearing that de Valera might never see a letter sent through civil service channels, McQuaid had Rory de Valera bring his note directly to de Valera's home. McQuaid also secured an audience for the Blackrock College Union at Government Buildings, where they reassured de Valera that he would have the support of former 'Rock men at a time when he was uncertain of the loyalty of the civil service.

The Eucharistic Congress

During its first three months in office, de Valera's Government oversaw the erection of a high-powered radio station in Athlone capable of transmitting Pius XI's broadcast from his study in the Papal apartments live to the international Eucharistic Congress being held in Dublin in June. McQuaid had been preparing for the Congress since his appointment as president: Blackrock had been chosen as the venue for the reception to be hosted by the Hierarchy. He arranged for the construction of a new road linking the Willow Park and Clareville gates to ease the flow of traffic through the grounds, and through his bursar, Fr James Burke, liaised regularly with the Congress organisers under Frank O'Reilly of the Catholic Truth Society.

Éamon and Vivion de Valera were McQuaid's personal guests at lunch in the college on Palm Sunday, when McQuaid produced a Blackrock solution to a Fianna Fáil problem. During the election campaign de Valera had promised to abolish the post of Governor General, but he had hesitated in doing so because the Papal Legate would wish to meet the Governor General, James McNeill, when they attended the Congress, and now there might be an embarrassing McNeill-de Valera encounter at the garden party. McQuaid promised to work out a plan to ensure that two political leaders would enjoy the occasion without coming into contact with one another.[8]

At 3pm on Tuesday, June 21, the first day of the Eucharistic Congress, 23,000 people filled the grounds. 'In the brilliant sunshine the wonderful gathering of ecclesiastics with their various robes of scarlet, purple, brown, grey, white and black and the immense and dignified multitude of laity representing everything that was best and most Catholic in Ireland, made an unforgettable picture,' the official Congress chronicler wrote.[9]

McQuaid was at his charming best, personally welcoming guests, from the most distinguished prelate to the lowliest seminarian. A young Jesuit novice, Roland Burke Savage, was to recall that when his turn in the queue came he was received by McQuaid with the same exquisite courtesy with which he had received cardinals, archbishops and ministers of state.[10]

The Papal Legate, Cardinal Lorenzo Lauri, drove into the college at 4pm and was received by Cardinal MacRory, the bishops, and McQuaid. Keeping his promise to spare de Valera any diplomatic embarrassment, McQuaid had assigned his own room at the top right-hand side of the main stairway of the imposing building to the Legate, and brought him there to meet Governor General McNeill and various clerical and lay dignitaries. After these introductions, McQuaid led the Legate across the landing to the reception room, where he met de Valera and his ministers, then escorted the Legate back to his office where other guests awaited him.

Cardinal Lauri's entourage included two of the Curia's rising diplomats who would influence McQuaid's own career. The Under Secretary of the Sacred Congregation for Extraordinary Ecclesiastical Affairs, Monsignor Domenico Tardini, was a brilliant but blunt-speaking Roman, and Francis Spellman, of the Secretariat of State, was an energetic and worldly American, who was writing and translating Lauri's speeches. McQuaid was reverential in his attentiveness to the Pontifical Master of Ceremonies, Monsignor Calderari, as well as the Cardinal's Private Chamberlains of the Sword and Cape, Commendatore Croci and Commendatore Vignoli.

McQuaid had familiarised himself with the biographies of his guests, who included the giants of contemporary English Catholicism: 'the quiet Cardinal', Francis Bourne of Westminster, whose mother was Ellen Byrne of a Dublin merchant family; the flamboyant Archbishop Richard Downey of Liverpool, a worldly Dubliner who personified the hopes of Irish emigrants and boasted that he ruled the North of England; and the Bishop of Southwark, Peter Amigo, an open admirer of Mussolini who would secure the canonisation in 1935 of Thomas More and John Fisher as martyrs of the Reformation under King Henry VIII.

The garden party acquainted McQuaid with the most powerful dignitaries of the American Church, among them the Archbishop of Philadelphia, Cardinal Dennis Dougherty, known as 'His Immense' on account of

his enormous girth, and the scholarly Cardinal Patrick Hayes of New York
and Irish-born Archbishop John Glennon of St Louis. Archbishop Michael
J. Curley of Baltimore brought with him a reputation as an outspoken
opponent of President Franklin D. Roosevelt's New Deal, while Archbishop Samuel Stritch of Milwaukee responded to the Depression with a
call for a rebirth of Christian doctrine. Perhaps most splendid of all was
Cardinal William O'Connell, the Archbishop of Boston, a social snob possessing an art collection to match that of a Renaissance prince.

Among the many prelates representing the Irish diaspora with
whom McQuaid would keep in touch over the coming years were the
Archbishops of Sydney, Cardiff, Birmingham, Edinburgh and St Andrews.
He also entertained European prelates who would become world famous
for their stand against Hitler's Germany, notably Cardinal August Hlond,
the Primate of Poland, and Cardinal Josef Ernst van Roey, the Archbishop
of Brussels-Malines. McQuaid had a special welcome for the Cardinal
Archbishop of Paris, Jean Verdier, whose welfare drive among the working
class had helped to ease tensions between the Third Republic and the
Catholic Church. While he was in Dublin, Verdier, accompanied by Minister for Finance Seán T. O'Kelly, took the opportunity to visit the tomb
of the reformed alcoholic, Matt Talbot, and to distribute Congress medals
and badges among the poor of Dublin's slums. As G.K. Chesterton wrote
in his book, *Christendom in Dublin*, the poor were 'better pleased than if he
distributed sixpences'.

The garden party was followed by a reception in Dublin Castle,
where de Valera formally welcomed Cardinal Lauri in a speech composed
in Latin but delivered in Irish and English. The Latin text with its
numerous references to Popes bore McQuaid's imprint, as did de Valera's
enunciation of a concept of Irish nationalism rooted in St Patrick's bringing of the faith from Rome to Ireland. Congress week reached a popular
climax with a Mass in the Phoenix Park attended by one million people
and crowned by the tenor John McCormack's memorable rendition of
Panis Angelicus. It was a moment which symbolised the bonding of Catholicism and Irish nationalism in the new State.

As the celebrations drew to a close, McQuaid oversaw a second
garden party at Blackrock hosted by the Irish National Teachers Organisation for 3,500 teachers from all parts of the globe. Attended once more
by de Valera, 'This was the largest function ever held under the auspices
of the INTO,' wrote the union's general secretary, T.J. O'Connell, paying
tribute to McQuaid's formidable managerial skills. On Sunday McQuaid
entertained visitors including the Papal Legate's ebullient speech-writer,
Francis Spellman, to lunch at Blackrock.

It had been a remarkable week for McQuaid. He had met the most
powerful leaders of the Catholic Church. De Valera and his ministers were
full of praise for his skilful avoidance of a showdown between them and

Governor McNeill. Under McQuaid's guidance, the Blackrock garden party was judged to be the greatest day in the history of the college. Yet in the crucial period prior to the Congress he had been ill and absent from the college, staying with his sister, Dr Helen, in London. The real organiser was his deputy, Fr Burke, but as president McQuaid was given and took the glory.[11]

'Uncharitable Protestantism'

Fr John McQuaid's reputation as a robust public figure of note was confirmed on November 13, 1932, when he became embroiled in a Letters Page controversy in *The Irish Times* with Canon T.A. Harvey of the Church of Ireland.[12] This exchange was sparked off by a sermon which McQuaid gave to the Society of St Vincent de Paul in the Church of the Assumption in Booterstown during which he attributed the decay of charity to Protestantism.[13] McQuaid was quoted as saying that Protestantism had rent the body of Christ – the Roman Catholic Church. He argued that Protestant spirit had made every man fight for his own selfish existence, and therefore grasp all the wealth within his reach. Protestant capitalism had had no use for the charity of Christ.

An angry and insulted Harvey, whose parish was in Booterstown, took McQuaid to task for making his sweeping claims against Protestant capitalism in a Catholic church which had been erected in 1811 at the expense of Richard, seventh Viscount Fitzwilliam, who lived and died a Protestant. Harvey also drew attention to how his parishioners raised funds each year to provide coal for both the Protestant and Roman Catholic poor in the run-up to Christmas. Some of his parishioners had even threatened to withdraw their contributions if the distribution was confined to Protestants. Of the millions of pounds subscribed annually by Protestants, 75 per cent of this went to Roman Catholics. And he pointed out that, in contrast to McQuaid's line of argument, a very high Roman Catholic dignitary had acknowledged the help which the St Vincent de Paul Society received from Protestants.

Unfazed by this critique, McQuaid sent a copy of the text of his sermon to Harvey so that he could 'attempt to grasp its meaning'. It was, he repeated, a grim fact that Protestantism had rent the body of Christ, and Protestants who talked about reuniting Christendom would not be confronted with the task in the first place had Protestantism not been guilty of its disruption. Capitalism, as the unlawful concentration of vast wealth in the hands of relatively few men, was a logical derivative from the basic tenet of Protestantism, the alleged right of uncontrolled private judgement.

Uncontrolled private judgement has for issue inordinate individualism,' McQuaid continued. 'Inordinate individualism begets unrestrained competition. Unrestrained competition has for child the right of the strongest. The right of the strongest engenders in politics, State absolutism, and, in economics, post-Reformation capitalism. Thus, Protestant capitalism is, indeed, alien in spirit from the charity of Christ. As for Catholics, we, too, admit a capitalism, but strive for the diffusion of personal ownership.

Disposing of Harvey's list of Protestant benefactions to Roman Catholics, McQuaid argued that the Canon should have distinguished between true charity and mere benefaction. True charity was a supernatural, infused virtue, existing in the soul of one who possessed sanctifying grace.

In second letters Harvey and McQuaid still differed on their substantial points but expressed cordial wishes to each other. Harvey thanked McQuaid for his text which he had read with 'the deepest pleasure and profit', though he saw individualism as preceding and giving rise to Protestantism, and could not accept McQuaid's distinction between the spirit of Protestantism and the spirit of Protestants. Harvey was willing to accept that McQuaid's remarks contained an economic theory rather than a general insinuation against Protestants. McQuaid, however, insisted that he had set out doctrinal teaching, not economics, and he felt he had demonstrated that Protestantism was inimical to charity without minimising the charity of Protestants.

Seducing de Valera

De Valera, capitalising on the popularity arising from the Eucharistic Congress, called a snap election in January 1933 and won an overall majority. McQuaid again sent his congratulations and invited de Valera to dinner at the college on February 12. 'He remained with us in the Library until 6pm,' *The College Annual* recorded. The de Valera-McQuaid axis was now so solid that McQuaid's clerical colleagues came to hold him in awe and informed students in hushed tones that he discussed the theory of relativity with de Valera.[14]

It was probably McQuaid's friendship with de Valera that caused Fr Joseph Byrne C.S.Sp. to select the Blackrock President as the preacher at his Episcopal Consecration as Vicar Apostolic of Kilimanjaro in today's Tanzania. Archbishop Harty of Cashel was the celebrant at the ceremony in Rockwell College on March 13. Bishop Le Hunsec came from Paris. De Valera represented the Government. It was McQuaid's biggest audience to date. In a learned sermon on the office of Bishop, McQuaid declared that through Byrne, 'the voice of Pius and of Peter, nay of Jesus Christ Himself, will now be heard by the pagan tribes of Kilma that are grouped around the wondrous, snow-clad mountain, lovely image of the tranquil grandeur of the eternal God, and of the steadfast permanence of the one True Church.'[15]

McQuaid's Latin skills and organisation abilities were in demand by the heads of Church and State. In May, de Valera visited Rome where he met Mussolini and Pope Pius XI, taking with him Latin scripts drafted by McQuaid and returning with the Grand Cross of the Order of Pius to match that of W.T. Cosgrave. In June Archbishop Byrne selected Black-rock College as the venue for a reception for the British Medical Associa-tion. At the height of the economic war between Britain and Ireland, de Valera and his whole cabinet came out in force. It was on this occasion too that a photograph was taken of de Valera and McQuaid escorting Arch-bishop Byrne to the centre area.[16]

Immediately after the reception McQuaid set off for the Hague, where he delivered a paper to the International Congress of Secondary Schools that was described by the *Irish Independent* as 'brilliant and com-prehensive'. His survey of education in Ireland concluded that the secon-dary schools had the power 'to train, in the fullest Catholic manner, a nation of fully Catholic men and women'.[17]

McQuaid contended that, while the curriculum in the Free State was imbued with a strong national emphasis, it was liberal enough to afford wide avenues of approach to the traditional Catholic and European culture. In Classics, the Free State matched the leading classical coun-tries – Italy, France, Belgium and French Canada. As regards modern lan-guages, 44.4 per cent of secondary pupils pursued French and 1.3 per cent German. Interestingly, the instinctive ease with which children learned to render the Gregorian Chant was attributed by McQuaid to the close affinity between it and Irish native music. McQuaid was convinced that Irish would become the vernacular of everyday life and of all educational courses within a few years. 'Much remains yet to be done in utilising the vast resources of Irish music as a means of restoring the vernacular. In our enchanting cradle-songs, pure love-songs and vibrant martial airs, lies buried a treasure too little explored.'[18]

McQuaid also nurtured the romantic notion of the lay-teachers as 'worthy heirs of the Catholic schoolmasters and schoolmistresses who once risked everything for Faith and Scholarship'. He believed that sec-ondary education was becoming more accessible to ordinary people, due chiefly to 'the magnificent work of the Irish Christian Brothers and the Sisters of Mercy'. In his eyes, the involvement of the religious Orders in education marked a return to the Catholic traditions of late medieval Europe. Church and State had everything to gain from 'so liberal and Catholic a policy' as that which would place the best Catholic education, free of charge, within the reach of every Catholic pupil who wished to receive it.

With such a strong Catholic hold over secondary schooling, few

Catholics opted for neutral or mixed-religion schools. Only an insignificant minority – 'a few weak persons for various unworthy motives' – had entered the Protestant University of Trinity College. In 1927 the traditional Catholic attitude towards education was reiterated by the bishops at a National Synod in Maynooth. For McQuaid, this attitude 'was splendidly voiced' by Bishop John Dignan of Clonfert, in a pamphlet denouncing Trinity College as a Protestant university.[19]

After this spate of public appearances, McQuaid maintained a low profile for the remainder of the year and the early months of 1934, when he spent much of his time arranging the Blackrock pilgrimage to Rome as the climax of a special Roman Holy Year commemorating the nineteenth centenary of the death of Christ. He helped to raise funds for the De Burgho-style chalice which the boys presented at their audience with Pope Pius XI, and he wrote the text pledging the loyalty of the Blackrock pilgrims to 'the integral teaching of the Sovereign Pontiff concerning both education and human conduct'. It was co-signed by McQuaid, Willie Corrigan and Éamon de Valera.[20]

McQuaid's position as headmaster, educationalist and figure of the establishment was now well entrenched, so much so that he was confident enough to flex his muscles in public controversy.

7

Catholic Campaigner
1934–36

'The Lord will continue to use you as an instrument of
good in various departments of life.'

Fr Bernard Fennelly C.S.Sp. to McQuaid, October 8, 1935.

On Wednesday February 7, 1934, *The Irish Times* carried the eye-catching
headline 'Women in athletics: Protest from Blackrock College' over a
letter from the Very Rev. John C. McQuaid C.S.Sp. He wrote to complain
about the National Athletic and Cycling Association's decision to allow
women compete in track and field events at the same athletics meetings
as men, a decision he found 'un-Catholic and un-Irish'. The President of
Blackrock College bolstered his protest with a threat: 'I hereby assure you
that no boy from my college will take part in any athletic meeting controlled by your organisation at which women will compete, no matter what
attire they may adopt.'[1]

McQuaid had earlier sent copies to other clerical school managers
seeking their support for his action and, as intended, the letter sparked off
further public criticism of the association. The first to give him public
endorsement was the head of Rockwell College, Fr Edward Crehan
C.S.Sp., who also threatened to prohibit his students from taking part in
sports organised by the NACA[2] while the director of the Camogie Association, Sean O'Duffy, criticised the organisation for basing its decision on 'the
cross-channel or continental idea' and advocated a modified form of athletics for Irish girls.[3] The *East Galway Democrat* joined the attack: 'On the
grounds of delicacy and modesty there is grave objection to women taking
part in athletics with men, and women should not be blind to this,' its editorial thundered. 'The strong protest of the Reverend President of Blackrock College is one that must not go unheeded by those concerned.'[4]

The NACA secretary, James J. McGilton, responded to McQuaid's
missive by trying to play for time. 'I appreciate the motive which
prompted you to forward your protest on the question of athletics for
women. I cannot give you any definite reply until the question has been
considered by the Council of my association,' he wrote to McQuaid

privately,[5] but the growing controversy forced him to appease McQuaid publicly by pointing out that women had been competing in reserved events at men's meetings without any previous objections. The sports chief's observation was supported by a well-known runner, Eileen Bolger, who pointed out that the civil service and Gardaí held a women's event at their sports days.

By the weekend, however, nearly every Catholic college in Ireland had announced its willingness to join McQuaid's boycott; indeed, the 'fierce opposition' of the Irish clergy and school authorities to mixed athletics made headlines in Britain. The *Sunday Chronicle* quoted an anonymous source as saying that the decision would spell the National Athletic Association's death-knell. 'We will certainly have nothing to do with any athletic body which intends to follow the lead of continental bodies on this question,' an unnamed athlete said. 'To have women compete with men is all wrong.' [6]

McQuaid, meanwhile, was encouraged by like-minded priests to hold his ground. Fr Peter, a Dominican priest in St Mary's College, Belfast, felt that 'if there were a few more leaders of the Catholic people to follow your example, we would surely put an end to unChristian impositions on a Catholic people'.[7] Fr J.P. Noonan of St Mary's, Marino, Dublin, congratulated him for giving the lead to kill 'the pagan proposal'.[8] From St Mary's, Dundalk, Fr John F. Roe S.M. thanked McQuaid for his 'splendid protest' and added: 'Please God your timely action will prevent the carrying out of the monstrous suggestion'.[9]

In mid-October the Athletic Association's standing committee considered McQuaid's objections and referred his letter to its General Council which was scheduled to meet on March 10.[10] On February 23, however, McQuaid published a second letter to McGilton, which described mixed athletics as 'a social abuse outraging our rightful Irish tradition'. This claim, he said, did not require proof, only reflection. Mixed athletics was un-Catholic, because it was a moral abuse, formally reprobated by the Sovereign Pontiff, Pius XI. It was a truth clearly proved by the Encyclical letter of Pius XI, *Divini Illius Magistri*, in which he invoked 'God's plan for the different sexes against the deceptive system of modern coeducation which is the enemy of Christian upbringing'.

Arguing that this principle was 'highly relevant' to the athletics controversy, McQuaid referred readers to the official source of Papal documents, the *Acta Apostolicae Sedis*, Vol. xxii, no. 2, pages 72–75, and gave the Latin text, which was faithfully reproduced by the newspapers. He provided his own translation of Pius's admonition that 'the Christian modesty of girls must be, in a special way, safeguarded, for it is supremely unbecoming that they should flaunt themselves and display themselves before the eyes of all.' [11]

Clearly taken aback by the strength of the support which McQuaid had mobilised, the General Council of the NACA met in a crisis atmosphere on March 10 at its headquarters in Dublin. When a Mr McManus of the Dublin board warned that it would be unfair to drive women out of sports, he was shouted down with the remark that 'We cannot flout public opinion.' The proprietor of the *Western People*, Fred de Vere, proposed that the association's decision should be suspended for a year, during which time the county boards could resolve the matter in the light of the Pope's Encyclical and the attitude of the clergy. This was agreed unanimously in an atmosphere of nudges and winks that ensured that the matter would be laid to rest.[12]

When McGilton informed McQuaid of the outcome, McQuaid congratulated him on 'this correct and courageous decision', but he warned that 'you will, however, understand that my protest in so far as it concerns the Annual Congress stands unchanged until the Annual Congress will have rescinded the decision.'[13]

McQuaid had won. The association did not dare to challenge the teaching of the Pope and the clergy as so vehemently articulated by him. The mood on the victorious side was summed up by the President of St Jarlath's College, Fr Joseph Walsh, the future Archbishop of Tuam: 'You must have the satisfaction of feeling that you have led the way to victory in a really important fight. I certainly have no doubt about the victory of our cause. I thank you for your magnificent lead and I hope you will be long spared to lead the way whenever similar perils threaten our country.'[14]

Keeping education under clerical control

Another peril which McQuaid was already confronting was a plan put forward by the Irish National Teachers' Organisation (INTO) to establish an Educational Advisory Council which would give lay teachers a consultative voice in school policy and management for the first time since the foundation of the Free State.

The INTO had long urged the Minister for Education to set up a council representing educational groups to advise in regard to legislation, administration and policy, but although other departments had appointed similar bodies, two successive Ministers for Education – O'Sullivan and his Fianna Fáil successors, Thomas Derrig – had refused to do so.

In a circular dated October 3, 1933, the INTO General Secretary, T.J. O'Connell, proposed convening a meeting of the educational bodies to continue their discussions. 'It is felt that though such a body would not be officially appointed by the Minister, no Minister could afford for long to ignore its views,' O'Connell wrote. Invitations to a preliminary meeting, fixed for mid-November, were sent to the main bodies including the Catholic Headmasters' Association of which McQuaid was chairman.[15] It was proposed that the meeting would establish a Joint Council to develop its programme in detail.[16] Confident of a positive response, O'Connell briefed the press a few days before the meeting and gave the impression that the proposal, which was designed as much to weaken the clerical hold over education as to make the department more accountable, would win the support of 13 educational interest groups.[17]

On November 11 some 40 delegates assembled at the Teachers' Club in Parnell Square, Dublin. The INTO, the Technical Schools and the Protestant Associations were strongly represented. The National University did not send a representative and Trinity College did not wish to attend either, because in its view the organisation seemed hostile to the Government. Opening the conference, chairman Cormac Breathnach T.D. denied this and said the proposed council was not meant to be in any way hostile. Then he called on McQuaid to speak.[18]

McQuaid pointed out the apparent discrepancy between the chairman's benign remarks and the tenor of the official correspondence, an observation which 'greatly disconcerted those present', he recorded.[19] The meeting was flung into still greater confusion when he announced that as chairman of the Catholic Headmasters' Association he could not support the project and listed four reasons as to why it was not needed: successive Ministers for Education had opposed the idea; there was already good access to the Minister and the Department of Education; the Joint Council's constitution was unwieldy and the divergent interests of its members could draw the Catholic Headmasters' Association into controversies outside its scope; and the problems of secondary education could be more equitably treated under the existing machinery rather than by the majority vote of the proposed advisory council.[20]

McQuaid's statement drew a great deal of dissatisfied comment from the floor, where all delegates except the Christian Brothers and the de la Salle Training College expressed unqualified approval for setting up a council. An attempt to establish one there and then, without any clear statement of its aims or constitution, was opposed by McQuaid and his colleague, Canon James Staunton. The meeting ended in confusion, after adopting a resolution that 'delegates be invited again to attend a Convention to consider terms of reference for a further meeting'.[21]

McQuaid's filibustering tactics were approved by the Archbishop of Dublin, Edward Byrne, to whom he had sent a confidential background note on the INTO-led initiative. Byrne, a traditionalist prelate, agreed that it represented a serious challenge to the Catholic Church's influence in education. 'He hopes that your efforts to frustrate the movement will be successful,' the Archbishop's secretary, Fr Tom O'Donnell, wrote to McQuaid on November 15.[22]

Encouraged by the Archbishop's support, McQuaid arranged an interview with the Minister for Education, Thomas Derrig, who expressed his satisfaction with the Catholic Headmasters' Association's statement and condemned the INTO's 'big stick' methods. McQuaid then secured a united stance by the Catholic Headmasters, the Christian Brothers and the de la Salle Brothers.[23]

At the poorly attended Convention on March 24, 1934, INTO's Chairman O'Connell, who was also a Labour Party T.D. and party leader, proposed as a compromise alternative to the controversial advisory council the formation of a looser federation, to be called 'an Education Dáil'. O'Connell ran into difficulties straight away with McQuaid, who asked for clarification of what was being planned. On McQuaid's formal proposal, seconded by the de la Salle College, Waterford, the convention agreed that 'the INTO should itself explain the aim, constitution and actual function of the Body they wished to see formed, and should supply the delegates with a draft answer on these points.'[24]

In a confidential memorandum to Archbishop Byrne, McQuaid pointed out that neither the INTO nor the ASTI 'consider it in any way opposed to Catholic principles to constitute a Federation of any and every religious body.' He noted that 'The INTO and the ASTI are ... by their constitutions undenominational, and on that account perhaps seem to see no difficulty in entering an undenominational council.'[25] He reminded the Archbishop that Catholic educational groups did not have a joint body of their own to express their views on the federation now being proposed. As a result, 'There would seem to be a certain danger of the commanding position being seized by these lay organisations, at least in the eye of the public, with consequent division and misrepresentation. Hitherto the CHA has succeeded in keeping the proceedings as private as possible.'[26] And while the INTO's Cormac Breathnach had admitted that the Catholic Headmasters' Association had the power to make or break the proposed federation, McQuaid was worried that the two teachers' bodies were strongly organised and knew how to sell their message in the press.

When the educational bodies reconvened on May 26, 1934, McQuaid and Canon Staunton raised so many objections to every speech and proposal that the meeting broke up in disarray – though not until after a resolution was adopted classifying the INTO document as confidential in order 'to prevent useless or hurtful discussions in the public Press'. When McQuaid protested against plans to offer the Hierarchy only one nominee to the proposed education body, the INTO's General Secretary took his words as a personal attack and professed to the meeting his complete respect for the bishops.[27]

To prevent INTO becoming the dominant force in education, McQuaid suggested to Cardinal MacRory that the Catholic Truth Society should organise an annual Education Day with the official approval of the bishops. Apart from providing a platform for Catholic educational associations, such a body would draw Catholic education more closely under the wing of the Hierarchy. In the public mind, it would be seen as part of

'Catholic Truth' and regarded as a serviceable part of 'Catholic Action'. [28] MacRory advised McQuaid to discuss his idea with Archbishop Byrne and Archbishop Harty of Cashel.[29] After consultations with them, McQuaid sent a revised document to the bishops for consideration at their meeting in June at Maynooth, where they adopted his Education Day proposal.[30]

McQuaid informed ASTI and INTO secretaries T.J. Burke and T.J. O'Connell of the Hierarchy's plans when he met them in the autumn. The teachers' leaders promptly abandoned their federation scheme. Burke, a teacher at Blackrock College, was most deferential to McQuaid, while O'Connell, again professing his complete respect for the bishops, dismissed his dearly held federation plan as 'a thing of the past'.[31]

When, at their October meeting, the bishops discussed how the educational advisory body had been successfully blocked, the President of Blackrock College was the toast of Maynooth. Archbishop Byrne praised McQuaid for having handled 'a very delicate situation with great tact and skill'.[32] Cardinal MacRory trusted that the bishops would not hear any more about the federation.[33] A servant of the Hierarchy in all things, McQuaid asked MacRory for 'a blessing on my work [as he] kissed the Sacred Purple'. [34]

McQuaid had been active on another front in the meantime, foiling an attempt by an inter-denominational debating body, Cumann na hÉireann, to establish a branch in Blackrock College. The Catholic Headmasters' Association subsequently ratified his refusal to sanction debates between Catholic and Protestant schools, seeing it as a further blow to the menace of nondenominational schooling.[35]

In June 1935 St Kieran's College, Kilkenny, was the venue for the launch of the Catholic Education Day during a spectacular session of the Congress of the Catholic Truth Society of Ireland, whose climax was an Open Air Pontifical Mass attended by Cardinal MacRory and most of the Hierarchy. Along with Canon Staunton, Archdeacon Kelleher, and Professors Timothy Corcoran and Michael Tierney, McQuaid was a keynote speaker. His address on Catholic education: its function and scope was highly acclaimed and further marked him out as the dominant figure in the Irish secondary school system. 'Catholic education, of whatever particular age, ancient or modern, in old Cathedral or monastic schools, in this or that more modern system, in this or that country aims at one essential thing – Catholic living,' he said, arguing that the Catholic Church alone held the balance between Lutheran pessimism and Rousseauist optimism.[36]

War against impiety

A bonus extracted by McQuaid from T.J. Burke in the education council negotiations was a promise to form a Regnum Christi guild for men and women secondary teachers. Preaching at the launching of the guilds in

Blackrock College chapel on October 28, 1934, McQuaid felt that it was no accident that they were being formed at a critical stage in the young life of the Free State, to combat 'the desolate horror of modern impiety'. Heads of states held their authority from Christ and exercised it in his name, he said. 'Therefore, they owe Him public recognition of divine worship, they may not be neutral. No man can be neutral in face of Jesus Christ. Family, School, Law-court and Parliament have each the bounden duty publicly to accept Jesus Christ the King.'[37]

Much of the early activity of the Catholic guilds, especially the doctors' Guild of St Luke, centred around the headquarters of the Knights of St Columbanus at Ely Place in Dublin. McQuaid had solid medical contacts and became an adviser to some of the major Catholic practitioners of the day, Dr A.B. Clery, Dr M.S. Walsh, Dr H. Quinlan, Dr H.W. Daly, Dr T.A. Moynihan, Dr J. McPolin, Dr J.J. McCann, and especially Dr J. Stafford Johnson, who was to become McQuaid's closest lay friend.[38] Together with a group of high-ranking doctors, McQuaid pored over lists of hospital personnel, identifying those who were Catholics and those who were Protestants. He was convinced that Protestants held a disproportionate number of the better posts and that the balance needed to be swung in favour of Catholics.

McQuaid was also alarmed at the inroads being made by Protestant preachers among Catholics, especially the Irish Mission directed by the Presbyterian Church in Dublin's city centre. A report prepared for the Presbyterian General Assembly in Belfast by the Rev. W.G. Wimperis claimed that never before had its missionaries been more kindly received in the homes of the Roman Catholic people of the Free State. They had sold some 16,000 Bibles to Roman Catholic homes during their Spirit of Enquiry campaign. 'The desire of the people for conversation with our agents on religious subjects is a marked contrast to the spirit of the past,' Wimperis reported. 'The Perils of the Times are very great in this land. The influence of the Church is unquestionably on the wane. The priest is not now the power he once was. The menace of Communism is with us in Southern Ireland. If proof be needed, it is found in the Pastoral Encyclicals of the Roman Catholic Bishops. The only way to save the Irish people is by giving them the Word of God. The Eucharistic Congress in many cases, instead of engendering loyalty to the Church, awoke a spirit of perplexity in the minds of the people.'[39]

McQuaid urged middle-class women who belonged to the Sodality of Mary to open club rooms in Dublin, where nurses could spend their leisure time and attend conferences in dress-making, cookery, child-welfare and homecrafts. 'A narrow creature, uninterested except in frivolities,' by instinct a nurse would spend her free time going to the cinema, McQuaid said, or walking around the city centre, gazing into shops and tea-rooms. Such a girl should be provided with the chance of a deeper, more

Christian use of her leisure in sodality-run clubs. 'In these pleasant surroundings, a young girl, whether she be lonely at her first experience of
life in a city or happy in the possession of a position and of friends, will
find some reflex of her own home atmosphere. By instinct, one may say,
she will tend to trust the ladies in charge of such a Club ... If, in addition, a
girl finds these ladies to be sympathetic, tactfully cultured, willing to chat
about all that interests her, she will ... confide in them and make them her
friends.

> The Club can be a nucleus of literary and artistic training.
> A small library, a few good pictures will suffice for an
> introduction to something better than the novels of a circu-
> lation library or cheap oleographs. Of her nature a girl
> chooses lovely things; it is her taste that requires educa-
> tion. The costume that a Directoress of the Club may wear
> is itself a lesson in better taste. In the Club room, lectures,
> or better, Conferences can be given. There are many
> members of the Sodality who have seen the best and most
> interesting that life can give. It is not too much to ask them
> to share a portion of their experience with the less
> fortunate.

McQuaid also counselled the Sodality of Mary to consider establishing Catholic-run restaurants for the poor. The efforts of many well-meaning
non-Catholics to remedy the poverty of the city's Catholics were, at best,
suspect, especially when run by 'non-sectarian' Committees.

> You are well aware that havoc has been wrought by Prot-
> estant benefaction. You would do well to remember that
> members of the present minority of non-Catholics are not
> the less bitter and crafty foes of Catholic life. It is entirely
> certain that very well-planned and very determined efforts
> are being made now to hold every vantage point already
> gained, social, cultural, commercial and especially profes-
> sional. Social clubs, work-rooms, tea and dinner rooms,
> not to mention Hospital visitation and almoner work, are
> among the chief instruments used for the retention of
> power and spread of influence.

McQuaid urged the Sodality of Mary to run a modest restaurant and
to visit the Catholic sick, assuring them that Christ would be found in
every hospital bed at which they paused.[40]

Meanwhile, through *An Ríoghacht*, McQuaid took an active interest
in its submissions to a Commission of Inquiry into the currency and banking situation which was set up in November 1934 by Finance Minister
Sean MacEntee as part of Fianna Fáil's objective of making the Free State

economically self-sufficient. *An Ríoghacht* made three submissions to the commission in 1935, advocating that the existing banking system be replaced by a credit-issuing department which would have the level of independence enjoyed by the judiciary, and they called for a programme of rural reconstruction.[41] The group's main spokespersons included the economist Mrs B. Berthon Waters and Mr Cox Gordon. McQuaid was deeply involved with Waters in researching material for their proposals, and took to reading copies of a new journal, *Prosperity*, edited by the veteran republican Bulmer Hobson and published by the League against Poverty. The League was regarded as socially subversive and was under surveillance by the Special Branch. De Valera and the political establishment dismissed the work of the minority Commission as coming from the lunatic fringe.[42]

De Valera's eyes and ears

By 1934, McQuaid's friendship with de Valera was so close as to allow him privately to make numerous attempts to influence the head of Government's attitude to matters of public policy. 'I am grateful for the kindness that allows me to make such suggestions,' McQuaid wrote in November 1934 after drawing de Valera's attention to 'discontent' concerning the Criminal Amendment Bill's proposal that contraceptives could be imported freely once they were not for sale. Worried about the provision that the Post Office could not in that event open a package, he proposed that the phrase 'for sale' should be deleted. He wanted the Post Office to have an automatic right of search so that no contraceptives could be sent to private individuals for personal use from Britain or elsewhere.[43]

So wide was the range of subjects which McQuaid raised with de Valera that he appeared at times to be acting more as a backbench Dáil deputy than a school headmaster. He intervened in relation to the election of a home assistance officer in Clonmel, Co. Tipperary, the appointment of a doctor in Sixmilebridge, Co. Clare, the possibility of securing a commercial contract for Roads and Roofs Asphalt Ltd, queries about the McHale Road housing scheme in Castlebar, Co. Mayo, and the thwarting of police deportations from Ireland of a M. Bouquet and a German, Alfred Langenbach.[42] McQuaid also proposed a project to gather personal reminiscences and contemporary narratives of the struggle for national independence, which were to be stored in the National Library of Ireland.[44]

Catholic medical interests were frequently raised by McQuaid with de Valera. In late 1934 he sent de Valera confidential documents – 'for your own eyes' – on pending negotiations between Archbishop Byrne and Minister Seán T. O'Kelly following 'a very secret breakthrough' in attempts to get St Vincent's and the Mater hospitals to form 'a proper' – that is, Catholic – medical teaching school with Holles Street, in conjunction with UCD's Medical School.[45]

In a series of letters, McQuaid tried to persuade de Valera that plans by Protestant medical interests, especially Dublin's Harcourt St Children's Hospital, to a establish a joint children's hospital was a danger to Catholic children.[45] Returning to this topic on another occasion – while on holiday with his sister in London – McQuaid warned that plans to amalgamate a number of hospitals, including St Ultan's, would 'for generations to come, hand over the Catholic children to an almost exclusively non-Catholic control'.[47]

When on December 1, 1934, McQuaid heard from Sir Joseph Glynn that O'Kelly had refused 'point blank' to attend the Inauguration of the new Maternity Hospital, he complained to de Valera that 'someone has bungled the matter'. Although Byrne knew nothing about the Minister's refusal, McQuaid feared that O'Kelly's absence would be widely commented on. 'The less ground of offence that can be given, the better for other interests that will be coming up, continually, in the near future, in the sphere of the Hierarchy,' he confided to de Valera. 'If I can do anything, you can count on me.'[48]

As well as keeping de Valera up to date on the politics of secondary schooling by giving him copies of his correspondence and addresses,[49] McQuaid, on one occasion, informed de Valera that he had obtained a copy of the Diploma in Social Studies which was being offered by Trinity College and which was ahead of anything the National University was providing for aspiring Catholic civil servants.[50]

McQuaid's friendship with the director of the Catholic Truth Society, Frank O'Reilly, involved him in schemes to promote Catholic interests in the State's fledgling radio station at Athlone. He alerted de Valera to 'some very interesting developments' which he would like to explain to him before the President proceeded 'to appoint a new Director of Broadcasts or to revise the Athlone programme and methods'.[51] On another occasion he acted as an intermediary with Archbishop John Harty of Cashel to stop a potentially fiery broadcast by Bishop Daniel Mageean of Down and Connor on the grievances of Northern nationalists, and he was successful. 'In view of the perfectly Catholic attitude adopted by President de Valera, Dr Mageean is quite willing to drop his broadcast,' Harty informed him.[52]

The affairs of the Vatican and the League of Nations also came up for discussion between the two men. In early autumn 1935, McQuaid translated for de Valera an extract of an address on peace and the horrors of war by Pope Pius XI,[53] which would suggest that he had an input into the Christian philosophy which marked de Valera's speeches as President of the League of Nations. When de Valera made his famous address to the League in Geneva in September 1934 on the proposed admission of Russia, McQuaid and the Blackrock boys listened to the broadcast on radio, though they were disappointed by the poor reception.[54] On another occasion McQuaid received a note from Fr Fahey asking him to bring to de Valera's attention a news report carrying the headline , 'League to be asked to ban Masons'.[55]

At a more relaxed social level, McQuaid and de Valera shared an interest in astronomy, with the priest advising the politician on how to focus a telescope according to the directions sent by the firm, Messers Negretti and Zambra.[56] When the de Valera family suffered the tragic death in 1936 of the youngest son, Brian, in a horse-riding accident, McQuaid remained with the younger ones at Bellevue, while the parents and older children were at the hospital. In later life Emer de Valera always recalled how McQuaid had distracted them from the horror of Brian's accident by telling them stories and playing word games with them.[57] Sinéad de Valera never forgot McQuaid's kindness at that time, but she did not feel socially able to accept the President of Blackrock's invitation to Pentecost Sunday dinner and the sports on June 9. 'As you know, Sinéad can hardly be prevailed on to go anywhere,' de Valera informed McQuaid when accepting the invitation himself.[58]

The difficult side of McQuaid's nature was revealed in two incidents relating to members of the Fourth Estate. Aggrieved at the coverage given in the *Irish Press* to a match involving the Blackrock College rugby team, he threatened to complain to de Valera if the editor did not sack the reporter in question.[59] McQuaid did not get his own way. Also, in midsummer of 1936, McQuaid refused the photographer Charlie Fennell permission to take pictures of Blackrock College for a series of articles on famous past pupils which were being written by the journalist Sean Piondar for the *Sunday Graphic*. 'Mr Fennell, the *Press* photographer, tells me that you have threatened to take all kinds of drastic action against me such as seeing Mr de Valera and writing to my employers,' a puzzled Piondar wrote to McQuaid. 'This sounds so silly that I can hardly believe it. Surely you do not claim the right to censor anything ever written by journalists about your college or about the President of the Executive Council? I must say you are the first College President in the Free State to refuse cooperation with me in the series.'[60]

The Spanish Civil War

No information has so far emerged as to whether McQuaid tried to persuade de Valera to end Ireland's non-intervention policy during the Spanish Civil War. However, on August 27, 1936, Hugh Allen of the Catholic Truth Society wrote to McQuaid suggesting that 'the conduct' of *The Irish Times* in regard to the War between General Francisco Franco's Nationalist forces and the Republican militias provided an opportunity for the Catholic Headmasters' Association to put that newspaper out of bounds for members of the Association, as far as school advertisements were concerned.[61] Specifically, Allen asked McQuaid to damage *The Irish Times* financially by organising an advertising boycott among the headmasters and sisters of the secondary schools.

Allen was referring to the reports by Lionel Fleming, who had been given £50 by the editor, Robert M. Smyllie, to combine a holiday in Spain with 'coming down on the republican side.'[62] Unlike the pro-Franco reports in the *Irish Independent*, which characterised the fighting as 'a battle between Christianity and Communism in which there can only be one victor',[63] Fleming's coverage had infuriated Catholic Ireland, not just Allen and McQuaid. Though de Valera's government was a signatory to the Non-Intervention Act, pro-Franco support was being mobilised by the Irish Christian Front under the leadership of Patrick Belton T.D. Allen's suggestion came as pro-Franco sentiment in Ireland was reaching its peak. It was a feeling shared by McQuaid, who regarded the bloody events in Barcelona and the execution of priests as opening 'flood-tides of obscenity' and as 'signs that Communism was on the upsurge.'[64]

Allen was careful to stress that his suggestion of an advertising boycott against *The Irish Times* was made to McQuaid in his capacity as chairman of the Catholic Headmasters' Association, and he asked him to bring this proposal forward for discussion at the Association's next meeting. 'If all agree not to advertise in this anti-Catholic organ, the necessity of advertising in it will disappear,' Allen said. 'Perhaps too the Association could give a lead to the nuns.' Allen added a postscript to say that this was a personal letter, and that the Catholic Truth Society was not responsible, even remotely, for the boycott idea.[65]

McQuaid responded promptly and duly won his association's approval for a commercial offensive against *The Irish Times*. 'I knew you would do the needful,' Allen remarked. 'The explanation of the attitude of *The Irish Times* everybody knows,' he added. 'But none of our newspapers so far have had the courage to give the reason except the Irish representative of the *Catholic Times*. Bertie Smyllie is a Mason – and his actions are taken in sympathy with his Masonic brethren in Barcelona.'[66]

As a result of the McQuaid-Allen conspiracy, virtually all Catholic educational advertising was withdrawn by the religious-run schools. The boycott hit the newspaper's finances so badly that Smyllie was obliged to recall Fleming.[67]

Generally, McQuaid had friendly relations with Smyllie, who had succeeded the anti-Catholic John Healy, who was a Freemason. Indeed, shortly before the outbreak of hostilities in Spain, an *Irish Times* staff member, Kevin Collins, who was organising Blackrock College Union events, had persuaded McQuaid to renew advertising for the *College Annual* in the paper. 'You, or may I say we, have made a protest against a certain bigoted statement, the author of which has now been removed by death from control of the paper,' Collins wrote to McQuaid. 'The present editorial policy is a liberal one and has no anti-Catholic bias. Indeed, as I have said, the *Irish Press* is more anti-Catholic than we are in many ways.'[68]

Catholic slums

The *Irish Press* headline on October 13, 1936, 'Rotarians accept doctor's slum tour challenge,' caught McQuaid's attention. It was a report of a crusading address to the Dublin Rotary Club lunch by the noted paediatrician and former rugby international, Dr W.R.F. Collis, in which he invited the members to take a humanitarian interest in the plight of those one in four Dubliners who were living in tenement slums.[69]

McQuaid read Collis's vivid description of how 93,000 persons were living in one-roomed tenements which were a breeding ground for illness and disease. Collis highlighted the case of a young girl convalescing after two months of treatment for rheumatic heart disease, and whom Collis was sending home from the National Children's Hospital. When he advised plenty of rest for the girl, her mother asked how she could get any rest in a bed which was crawling with bugs that would eat her alive. 'Seven others sleep in the same attic room on the sixth floor,' the mother explained. 'The roof is leaking. The only water supply is in the yard. The only lavatory is down six flights across the yard. And you say she is to rest there in bed!'

The tale moved the Rotarians to promise to accompany Collis on a fact-finding tour of the slums, with the aim of persuading Dublin Corporation to switch its policy of building outside the city to rebuilding houses in the inner city.

McQuaid agreed with much of what Collis said about conditions in the slums, but he took exception to his remarks that the country needed to develop a new outlook on health policy. Collis pointed to the example of Germany, where, though he did not agree with Hitler's methods of government, he was struck by the happiness and health of the young and the standard of social services. He also emphasised the link between poverty and disease, and insisted that 'Mental health is a hopeless ideal without physical health,' Collis said. 'And the health of one class without the health of the community is utterly un-Christian.'

McQuaid found the report so offensive, particularly when it came from a Cambridge-educated Protestant, that he scoured the newspapers over the following days in expectation of seeing either a correction or an apology. When none appeared, he decided to challenge Collis in print, and on October 17 a five-paragraph letter appeared in the *Irish Independent* under the heading 'Children's mental and moral education.' It was signed by *Observer*.

'Catholic Dublin must have been at least mildly roused by the excursions of Dr W.R. Collis into the mental and moral education of the city children,' McQuaid began, though Collis had mentioned neither Catholicism nor moral education. McQuaid's anti-Protestantism and his belief that the Rotary Club was linked to Freemasonry revealed themselves in his dismissive remark that 'if this medical gentleman' was referring to the small percentage of his co-religionists, he was welcome to the platform of the Rotary Club. It was quite another matter, however, if he intended to lecture Catholics on the mental and moral health of the Catholic children who formed the overwhelming majority of his patients.

> **The Canon law declares that every Catholic child must receive a fully Catholic education. Dr Collis can very safely leave the mental and moral education of Catholics to those whom it properly belongs, the Church and the parents. But Dr Collis should realise that education means all the processes of upbringing, medical treatment included. A Catholic child then, by the fact that it is a Catholic, has the right to a fully medical treatment.[70]**

McQuaid asked whether Dr Collis could guarantee that Catholic children were given this treatment in the non-denominational hospitals.

> **Are there, for example Crucifixes in the wards? Are the hospitals, to put the case briefly, in all their organisation, just a substitute for the Catholic home, even the Catholic home of the slums? We have the right to demand that where our Catholic children are treated the very atmosphere shall be Catholic.**

McQuaid's resorting to anonymity is most telling. His own script is detectable in corrections he made to a typewritten version of the letter on non-headed notepaper. Even if this letter was originally drafted by someone else, McQuaid, at the very least, collaborated in its construction. He may have thought it imprudent to sign his own name on account of the fact that Collis graduated in medicine in England a year ahead of Helen McQuaid, and would most certainly have been known to her. And, of course, there may also have been other undercover letters from McQuaid's pen.

McQuaid, the anti-Protestant lobbyist, was everywhere in the 1930s. Perhaps an abiding insight into his style is offered in a description of his attendance at meetings of a committee which agitated for years for Tipperary town's Christian Brothers School to be given a share in the Erasmus Smith School scholarships. The committee met periodically in Dublin. 'Precisely five minutes after each meeting began McQuaid glided into a seat. He never spoke and never addressed anyone afterwards, because the very second that the proceedings concluded he was out the door like an Olympic sprinter.'[71]

8

Co-maker of the Constitution
1937–38

'It is a Constitution which embodies the Catholic
principles of the Irish nation – a Constitution which found
its inspiration in the Papal Encyclicals.'
Vatican Radio, Christmas 1938.

From early 1937 Éamon de Valera was bombarded with letters almost daily – sometimes twice a day – from Fr John McQuaid C.S.Sp. They were crammed with suggestions, viewpoints, documents and learned references on nearly every aspect of what was to become *Bunreacht na hÉireann* – the Constitution of Ireland. McQuaid was the persistent adviser, 'one of the great architects of the Constitution, albeit in the shadows'.[1] However, McQuaid's efforts to enshrine the absolute claims of the Catholic Church as the Church of Christ were frustrated by de Valera.

The constitutional process, which involved at least six drafts, began as far back as May 1934 when de Valera set up a committee of four civil servants to review the Free State Constitution of 1922. On April 30 and May 2, 1935, he instructed the legal adviser to the Department of External Affairs, John Hearne, to draw up the heads of a new constitution. During the summer of 1936 Fr Edward Cahill S.J. heard about the project and wrote to de Valera offering advice. De Valera accepted this offer from an old friend whose views he shared on the national question, though not on Church-State relations.

However, the Jesuit Provincial, worried about Cahill's extreme views, neutralised him by setting up a committee of eminent Jesuits which drew up a Joint Document that was sent on October 21 by Cahill to de Valera. This consisted of a draft preamble and articles on education, family rights, marriage. De Valera also discussed the constitutional project with Fr Denis Fahey during their vigorous walks in the grounds of Blackrock College. Although it is highly likely that McQuaid joined Fahey and de Valera for informal talks on the outlines of the constitution at de

Valera's home, of the three priests, it was to the youngest and most practical that de Valera turned for detailed drafting advice after passing the Jesuit document onto McQuaid.[2]

From January 1937, McQuaid was soon immersed in Papal teachings on economic and social policy, and on Church-State relations. Not even de Valera's private secretary, Maurice Moynihan, knew of McQuaid's hefty labours in the Blackrock constitutional vineyard.[3] He was indefatigable in checking sources for de Valera. 'His Reverence has spent the day in our elaborate research of the origins and the uses of the present and future of the verb, *to be*,' an exhausted Vivion de Valera reported to his father. 'His conclusions are no doubt accurate. I have been treated to discourses on the Hebrew, Latin, Greek and Old English uses, which reminded me of similar agonies in the past with such theories as quadratic equations and Binomial Theorem.'[4]

McQuaid's tone was generally courteous and deferential. From de Valera's underlining of passages it is clear that he treated his contributions with great attention. The Holy Ghost priest gave de Valera two key books, both in French: *Manuel Sociale* by the Belgian Jesuit, Vermeersch, and the *Code of Social Principles*, published at Malines by the International Union of Social Studies. He also supplied de Valera with two copies of the 1918 *Codex Iuris Canonici*, noting that the smaller one had a better index and would be very handy on a desk, while the larger one could fit in his library at his office in Government Buildings. McQuaid gave the Fianna Fáil leader a long lecture on Rousseau's *Theory of Civil Authority* when the two men were discussing the death penalty; on another occasion he told de Valera that he had been 'rummaging in the heads of the last few Popes'.[5]

The thoroughness which McQuaid brought to the process was evident in his first letter, dated February 16, 1937, enclosing 'a most interesting and useful criticism of the French Constitution of 1814 by Pius VII'. Along with this Papal gem from the time of the Bourbons, McQuaid sent three paragraphs on private property, saying 'I hope they are according to the idea you had in mind.' At least they were accurate, McQuaid assured him, 'for I spent the day in an analysis of *Quadragesimo Anno* and *Rerum Novarum*'.[6]

Next day, McQuaid presented a draft on free competition which he considered to be a logical and compact improvement on an existing text. He hoped that the correction would not prove inconvenient, an indication of his confidence that de Valera would be incorporating the addendum. McQuaid had recast one section, 'Share in the land', making it 'more accurately represent the famous passages in *Quadragesimo Anno* and also *Rerum Novarum*'.[7]

On March 8 McQuaid was wrestling with the State's obligations towards widows, orphans and the elderly. 'It devolves on the family to support – where it can – its own aged members, in a spirit of charity,' he stated, explaining his philosophy that it was unfair to expect, as so many did, that the State would somehow take care of everything.[8]

On strikes, which McQuaid described as 'the most potent form of social agitation', he advised de Valera that 'a great deal of the venom of Communism could be neutralised, if, where strikes do occur, a mode of settlement, fair to both sides could be found.' To achieve this, he proposed the insertion of a small paragraph which was 'both correct in social doctrine and capable of averting immense evils'. He would be delighted to call at de Valera's house, he added. 'When next we meet, perhaps we could discuss the paragraph, unless you see fit to incorporate it at once.'

The strikes issue had become a major social problem for de Valera, who had faced a tram strike the previous year and in 1937 was confronted with a widespread strike in the building industry, a situation characterised by McQuaid as 'a state of social unrest with intervals of quiet'. McQuaid advocated a remedy for this 'state of social unrest' similar to that put forward by the Bishop of Cork, Daniel Cohalan, in a Pastoral Letter that February.[9]

When de Valera sent McQuaid draft proofs of the Constitution on March 9, he did more work on the text, paying particular attention to ensuring that the inverted commas were in the right places! Next day McQuaid informed de Valera that he had been through the text very carefully and appended a few points for consideration.[10] He added his thanks for the present of Dorothy Macardle's recently published *The Irish Republic*, which presented de Valera as the central figure in 'the birth of a nation'.

On March 16 confidential copies of the draft text were distributed to the Executive Council and to select individuals, including McQuaid. On finding that the section on religion was left blank, McQuaid did not question its omission, though both he and the Jesuits had made a lengthy submission on this point. He was more than pleased with the progress that had been made and looked forward to its implementation. 'It is such a joy to see it in print: now it remains to see it enacted. It reads very well. I think I note the few changes made,' he wrote.[11]

From this remark, it can be deduced that McQuaid felt that the bulk of his suggestions were being incorporated by de Valera. According to the historian of Blackrock College, Fr Séan Farragher, de Valera 'had long and frequent discussions with McQuaid who actually provided the most satisfactory draft of the Preamble to the Constitution',[12] a passage which had undergone many revisions and taken up a lot of time. Farragher's observation is borne out by the draft text of the Preamble in the McQuaid Papers, where a typescript with some changes in McQuaid's hand-writing is close to the final version. The reference to the Trinity, a specifically Christian belief, was already in its final form, but McQuaid's description of Éire as 'the Motherland of the Irish Race' was dropped by de Valera.[13] The final text of the Preamble read:

> In the name of the Most Holy Trinity, from Whom is all authority and to Whom, as our final end, all actions both of men and States must be referred.
>
> We the people of Éire,
>
> Humbly acknowledging all our obligations to our Divine Lord, Jesus Christ, Who sustained our fathers through centuries of trial,
>
> Gratefully remembering their heroic and unremitting struggle to regain the rightful independence of our Nation,
>
> And seeking to promote the common good, with due observance of Prudence, Justice and Charity, so that the dignity and freedom of the individual may be assured, true social order attained, the unity of our country restored, and concord established with other nations,
>
> Do hereby adopt, enact, and give to ourselves this Constitution.

As an Ulsterman, McQuaid proved to be an invaluable interlocutor when it came to the wording of the national question. McQuaid's pen put brackets around the draft heading, 'Fundamental Declaration,' and inserted in his own hand 'The Nation.' This became the heading for Articles 1 to 3 of the Constitution. Article 2 defined the national territory as consisting of the whole of Ireland, its islands and territorial seas. While McQuaid's penmanship is to be found in all three articles, he appears to have played a pivotal role in drafting Article 3, which was to enrage Ulster Unionists for many years afterwards. McQuaid's handwritten wording read:

> Pending the reintegration of the national territory, the jurisdiction of the State established by this Constitution shall extend to that part of the national territory recently termed the Irish Free State.[14]

This provided the nucleus for the final text:

> Pending the reintegration of the national territory, and without prejudice to the right of the Parliament and Government established by this Constitution to exercise jurisdiction over the whole of that territory, the laws enacted by that Parliament shall have the like area and extent of application as the laws of Saorstát Éireann and the like extra-territorial effect.'

Despite his busy schedule of liturgical events in the run-up to Easter, McQuaid continued to work on the Constitution. On Holy Thursday, March 25, he apologised for being 'somewhat late' with a submission. 'I enclose the more useful excerpts connected with Religion. There are a few more valuable ones but they can follow.'[15] In a second letter later that day McQuaid sent 'with great pleasure the remaining dossier, point by point for the Family, Education and Private Property. By tonight I hope to have Church and State all typed ... these are auspicious days for the work.'[16]

Although he was engaged in the Good Friday services, McQuaid completed his task and despatched 'the last of my dossier: with the sincere hope that it will prove of some avail'. His appetite for work was undiminished. 'What of the Secret Societies clause?' he enquired, adding, 'I hope you are not too tired after these nights of labour: and that it all goes well. Would a Note on Law and the Common Good be of some use?'[17]

He wrote to de Valera again on Holy Saturday. 'This letter is unusual from me,' he stated. 'It is only one of good wishes for a peaceful Easter. I hope you will soon draw breath – whatever breath, my friend, the jurists will have left you.'[18]

McQuaid kept working over the Easter weekend and on the following Tuesday sent a further batch of materials which he thought was 'safe and sure'. He added a postscript, asking de Valera if he would have the sheet of suggestions on Article 41 – the Family – by the evening. 'I can work on them too,' he volunteered.

In an early draft of what was to become Article 41, McQuaid anchored the concept of family in the traditional model of 'a valid marriage' – a husband, wife and four or five children, the average size in late 1930s Ireland. He proposed that: 'The State guarantees the constitution and protection of the family as the basis of moral education and social discipline and harmony, and the sure foundation of ordered society.'[19]

To preserve the sanctity of marriage and family life, McQuaid proposed giving constitutional status to the legal ban on contraception as set out in the 1935 Criminal Law Amendment Act. Specifically, he proposed to incorporate in the Constitution a clause stating that 'contraception and the advocacy of contraception and the possession, use, sale and distribution of contraceptives shall be punishable by law'.[20] De Valera rejected McQuaid's proposal, however, on the grounds that the legal provisions against contraception already provided the necessary protection to the family.[21]

De Valera was more ready to accept the substance of McQuaid's argument against divorce. McQuaid had proposed that 'no law shall be enacted authorising the dissolution of a valid consummated marriage of baptised persons'. De Valera trimmed this to read: 'No law shall be enacted providing for the grant of a dissolution of marriage.'

In a briefing note, McQuaid wrote that it was:

> ...hardly possible to describe how great are the evils that flow from divorce. Matrimonial contracts are by it made variable; mutual kindness is weakened; deplorable inducements to unfaithfulness are supplied; harm is done to the education and training of children; occasion is afforded to the breaking up of homes; the seeds are sown of dissension among families; the dignity of womanhood is lessened and brought low, and women run the risk of being deserted after having ministered to the pleasures of men...

> So soon as the road to divorce began to be made smooth by law, at once quarrels, jealousies, and judicial separation largely increased, and such shamelessness followed, that men who had been in favour of these divorces repented of what they had done, and feared if they did not carefully seek a remedy by repealing the law, the State itself might come to ruin.[22]

McQuaid proposed that the State should encourage early marriage and foster large families by providing tax allowances for children, promoting saving schemes and providing housing at reasonable prices. In this, McQuaid appears to have shared Fr Cahill's thinking on the need to enshrine a denominational health policy in the Constitution. 'Maternity is under the special protection of the State. Provision may be made by law for the supervision and inspection of lying-in hospitals and maternity nursing homes,' he had proposed.[23]

McQuaid is generally recognised as being the primary craftsman of Article 42 on education, in which the State acknowledges that 'the primary and natural educator of the child is the family, and guarantees to respect the inalienable right and duty of parents to provide, according to their means, for the religious and moral, intellectual, physical and social education of their children.'[24]

Dev's Roman diplomacy

De Valera kept McQuaid in the dark about his reservations concerning the churchman's attitude towards Protestants and Jews. In the Joint Submission from the Jesuits the text on religion was based on the Polish Constitution of 1921, which gave specific acknowledgement to the Catholic faith; McQuaid had been working on this, developing the idea of having the Constitution recognise Catholicism as the One True Church.[25] Realising, however, that such a declaration would be divisive, and contradict Arthur Griffith's assurance to the Protestant minority that they would be given fair play in the new State, de Valera decided to engage in some unilateral ecclesiastical diplomacy.

On April 3 he visited the Papal Nuncio, Archbishop Paschal Robinson, and told him that such a clause would not work. From April 3 to April 27 he had ten contacts with the Nuncio, two meetings with Archbishop Byrne, one with Cardinal MacRory, as well as meetings with Protestant leaders including the Anglican Primates, C.F. D'Arcy of Armagh and John Gregg of Dublin, and the Jewish leader, Dr Isaac Herzog. He had a particularly difficult meeting at the Nunciature with MacRory, who pressed his own formula on the President: 'The State, reflecting the religious convictions of 93 per cent of its citizens, acknowledges the Catholic religion to be the religion established by Our Lord Jesus Christ; while guaranteeing at the same time to all its citizens the fullest liberty to practice their religion in public and in private, with due regard however for public order and morality.'[26]

McQuaid was working along similar lines. On April 10, as a second revision of the draft was being circulated, McQuaid sent de Valera additional material along with 'a very useful little work ... an excellent treatise on civics ... The author is a friend of mine, who worked with me in Rome. He was already a Barrister and Doctor of Civil Law and had been through the war, before doing his doctorate in Theology and Canon Law studies.'[27]

But McQuaid's moment of truth came four days later at de Valera's home, when he was given the text of Article 44 for the first time.

Article 44.1.3 recognised the 'special position' of the Holy Roman Catholic and Apostolic Church, but also recognised the Church of Ireland, the Presbyterian Church in Ireland, the Methodist Church in Ireland, the Religious Society of Friends in Ireland, as well as the Jewish Congregations and 'the other religious denominations existing in Ireland at the date of the the coming into operation of the Constitution.' This fell short of recognising Rome as the One True Church.[28]

The Holy Ghost priest lost his temper and had harsh words to say about the wording proposed. Next morning McQuaid, moving quickly to heal the rift, wrote to de Valera asking pardon for sending another note. 'I fear my many notes and papers must have only bothered you these last ten days. It occurred to me as I said Mass this morning that last night I may have so shown my disappointment as to seem wanting in courtesy. If I did in the least way I am very sorry for it.'[29]

De Valera telephoned to put the disagreement behind them, but found McQuaid reticent. 'It was kind of you to phone and I am grateful,' McQuaid stated in a second letter that day. 'At the time, I was surrounded by people and could not say any more than I did, in a bald way. I do not judge myself so indulgently as you have done. I was clearly at fault and I am sorry for it. Should I be able to serve, now or in the future, even to a small degree, I should like to think that you will not hesitate to ask me and to believe that I bow willingly to those who are placed above and who

give their decisions.' In the meantime he would work on the property sections, he said, and if anything occurred to him he would send it on.[30]

McQuaid had deferred to de Valera out of respect for his position as
head of Government, but this did not mean that he had been converted to
the politician's point of view. McQuaid was to nurse privately his belief
that de Valera had anchored the Constitution on the false principle of the
separation of church and state. It was only years later that he made his real
belief known to de Valera in circumstances much more acrimonious than
those of 1937.

Conscious of McQuaid and MacRory's criticism, de Valera decided
on April 15 to send the Secretary of the Department of External Affairs,
Joe Walshe, to Rome on a secret mission – to obtain, confidentially, the
approval and blessing of Pope Pius XI on three points. First, the religious
part dealing with the special position of the Catholic Church. Second, the
official name of the Catholic Church that would be used in the Constitution. Third, the state's recognition of 'the other Christian churches'.

A ten-page memorandum instructed Walshe to apologise that the
Constitution did not go further in embodying 'the full Catholic ideal' in
Church-State relations, but to explain that any attempt to do so 'would
cause an immediate outcry from the Protestant section of the population
and result in a bitter religious controversy'. With recollections of their
past supremacy, 'the Protestants find it very difficult to accept a second
or subordinate place,' the memorandum stated. 'A religious controversy in
present circumstances would be deplorable and could result in the Government being accused of inviting renewal of the bitter attacks on our
fellow Catholic countrymen in Belfast.'

Walshe was to stress that the Catholic Church would be associated
with the state on all public occasions, and that ministers, who were all
likely to be Catholics, would profess their religion openly. 'Religious functions in the Catholic Church will be attended by them on all occasions in
which it is right that there should be a manifestation of religious belief.'
On the other hand, Walshe was to let the Pope know that the recognition
given to the Protestant churches, 'even though they are put in a subordinate place, will bring about considerable appeasement, will lead to better
feelings between the different religious bodies and may even be a step
towards the desired political reunion of our country.' All this would help
to unite all Christians 'against any inroads of Atheism which in the present world conditions would seem to be the enemy most to be feared.' [31]

In Rome, Walshe met the Assistant Secretary of State, Monsignor
Giuseppe Pizzardo, who foresaw no difficulties in getting the Pope's
approval for the Constitution. He was overly optimistic, however. The
Secretary of State, Cardinal Eugenio Pacelli, subsequently informed
Walshe that the Pope had refused to approve the draft because it did not
recognise the Catholic Church as the one 'founded by Our Lord'. Pacelli

even implied that the wording was 'heretical'. He told Walshe that 'Ireland was the Catholic country of the world and he thought we should have made a very special effort to give the world a completely Catholic Constitution.' He also said that the annulling of marriages in civil courts was heretical, as this was the exclusive domain of the Catholic Church. However, the Papal pill was sweetened by the fact that the Vatican did not intend issuing a public condemnation of the Constitution. In classic Vaticanese, Pius XI said: 'I do not approve. Neither do I not disapprove; we shall remain silent.' [32]

The question of the status of religions in the new State did not stop there, however. Even after the Constitution was circulated to the members of Dáil Éireann and published on May 1, McQuaid wrote to de Valera urging that the title 'Church of Ireland' should not be allowed to remain in the final draft.' Coming back to this theme more than a week later, McQuaid queried the use of the expression 'other Christians' in Article 44. 'I have been thinking very much about it,' he wrote to de Valera. 'Of course, they claim the title but as very many in all these churches deny the divinity of Christ unlike their ancestors they have truly ceased to be Christians. Very often they are only ethical.'[33]

On the question of the special position of the Catholic Church in Ireland, when De Valera piloted the Constitution through the Dáil, he said: 'There are 93 per cent of the people in this part of Ireland who belong to the Catholic Church, who believe in its teachings, and whose whole philosophy of life is the philosophy that comes from its teachings ... If we are going to have a democratic State, if we are going to be ruled by the representatives of the people, it is clear their whole philosophy of life is going to affect that, and that has to be borne in mind and the recognition of it is important.'[34]

By now de Valera was under criticism from lobby groups, not least women, for some of the draft text's assertions as to the place of mothers in the home, largely drafted by McQuaid. Aware of the criticism, McQuaid told de Valera that the feminists' thoughts were 'very confused'. 'Both *Casti Connubii* and *Quadragesimo Anno* answer them,' McQuaid said, and he referred to Pius XI's statement that 'mothers will above all devote their work to the home and things connected with it'.[35]

The Pope's thoughts shaped the context of Article 41:5. 'The State recognises that by her life within the home, woman gives to the State a support without which the common good cannot be achieved. The State shall, therefore, endeavour to ensure that mothers shall not be obliged to engage in labour to the neglect of their duties within the home.'

McQuaid appears to have convinced de Valera that men and women did not have equal rights to work of the same kind. He insisted that:

Men and women have equal right to appropriate work.
The law of nature lays diverse functions on men and

women. The completeness of life requires this diversity of
function and of work. This is diversity not an inequality of
work. In the desire to cut out unfair discrimination against
women, diversity of work is being constantly confused
with inequality of work. [36]

This thinking was reflected in Article 40.1: 'All citizens shall, as
human persons, be held equal before the law ... This shall not be held to
mean that the State shall not, in its enactments, have due regard to differences of capacity, physical and moral, and of social function.' As Tim Pat
Coogan has commented: 'The diversity argument was one which was to
hold sway, not only in the Constitution, but in Irish life generally for many
years after de Valera had retired from politics.'

McQuaid did further research to rebut the criticisms being aired
about the inequality of men and women's roles as laid out in the Constitution, and on May 10 sent de Valera 'the enclosed ammunition' which he
had checked with his Holy Ghost colleague, Fr Edward Leen. 'It is impeccable,' Leen had told McQuaid, who added chirpily, 'As he is an expert, I
think we are safe on this very knotty question.' McQuaid's material was
used by de Valera in a major speech which he delivered in Ennis rebutting
critics. McQuaid also read the text and assured de Valera that 'the Ennis
speech reads very well indeed; 'Anytime you want me, I am available.'[37]

Christian democracy

On June 14, 1937, the Constitution was approved in the Dáil by 62 votes
to 48. The public voted on it in a Referendum on July 1, held the same day
as the general election. The Constitution was passed by 685,105 votes to
526,945, while de Valera was returned as head of Government, the first
'Taoiseach' under the new Constitution. McQuaid kept an annotated
copy of the Constitution alongside the autographed copy of the final
document presented to him by de Valera. McQuaid's Catholic and nationalist fingerprints were everywhere in the new *Bunreacht*, third only to
those of de Valera and his chief draughtsman, John Hearne.[38] His influence is found in the Preamble, the definition of the nation and the status
of private property. He was a key figure in determining the constitutional
prohibition of divorce, its outline of education and social policy, and even
on its use of the death penalty. Most controversial of all, perhaps, was his
input into establishing that the role of mothers was in the home. But the
final product, although thoroughly Roman Catholic in its ethos, was made
more 'broad church' by de Valera in its formal recognition of Protestants
and Jews. In doing so, de Valera frustrated the efforts to fashion the Constitution in the image of the Catholic State advocated by McQuaid and
his fellow travellers of right wing extremism, Frs Fahey and Cahill.

That summer and into the autumn, McQuaid helped de Valera to translate the Constitution into Latin for presentation to Pius XI. He found time off to host a reception at Blackrock for delegates to the Second International Catholic Conference for Peace, which brought together leading churchmen and laity from Ireland, Britain and the continent. A press photograph captures the most influential triumvirate in the land – McQuaid, de Valera and the Papal Nuncio – as they walked together in the college grounds.[39] In late October McQuaid visited his sister, Helen, in Putney for 'a quiet rest here, close to the noise of London town, strange as it may seem … for sake of quietness'. But his rest was interrupted by de Valera wishing to check part of the Latin text. In letters sent via the College bursar, Fr Finn, the text was duly amended and improved.[40]

The Constitution was enacted on December 29, 1937. De Valera made a special broadcast on Radio Éireann to launch the new document. He emphasised its Christian character and its conformity to the Christian philosophy which the Irish people had held for more than 1,000 years. Its chief significance was that it was in complete accord with national conviction and tradition. 'It bears upon its face, from the first words of its Preamble to the Dedication at its close, the character of the public law of a great Christian democracy.'[41]

Writing to de Valera that same day, McQuaid remarked that it seemed strange to be calling him Taoiseach instead of President. At the Mass which he had offered for de Valera on that eventful day, McQuaid quoted the scripture: 'Many have desired to see what we see and have not seen.'[42] In his New Year message for 1938 Cardinal MacRory praised the Constitution.'The Cardinal's words have been a great joy to us – Happy New Year,' McQuaid greeted de Valera on January 3.[43] Agreement on the first President to hold office under the new Constitution was not reached until Easter Week 1938, when the Gaelic League founder, Dr Douglas Hyde, was nominated for the post. His installation, however, was deferred until June 25, following a snap general election which returned Fianna Fáil to Government. Separate religious ceremonies were held in Dublin prior to Hyde's installation at St Patrick's Hall in Dublin Castle. A solemn Mass in the Pro-Cathedral was presided over by Archbishop Byrne and attended by Government ministers and T.D.s, churchmen and diplomats, the judiciary, army and civil service. However, the President, who was Protestant, was at a service in St Patrick's Cathedral where he was greeted by Archbishop Gregg and seated in the former Lord Lieutenant's Pew, now named the President's Pew. Separate services were also conducted by Presbyterian, Methodist and Jewish communities.[44]

After Hyde took the oath and received his seal of office at Dublin Castle, de Valera, echoing McQuaid's scriptural quotation, 'Many have desired to see what we see and have not seen,' saluted him on behalf of the nation and the dead generations who longed to see this day, when an elected President inherited the authority of the Gaelic chiefs and closed the breach which had existed since the undoing of the Irish nation in 1601 at Kinsale. Predicting that the unity of the country would be put right, de Valera praised Hyde as the man whose 'foresight saved from death our own sweet language', without which 'we could but be a half nation'.[45]

The Blackrock College strike

Ironically enough, the priest at the centre of drafting a constitution for a Catholic nation found himself embroiled not long after its enactment in what he believed was a constitutional test case against Communist infiltration of the Irish State. This legal battle arose in the Dublin district court after McQuaid had dismissed in September two Blackrock College waiters and a hall porter who had joined the Domestic and Household Workers' Union of Ireland; their work was taken over by three Holy Ghost Brothers. The union instituted legal proceedings against McQuaid and placed a picket on the college proclaiming that the men were barely being paid a living wage – 14 shillings for a 75-hour week. When McQuaid called the Gardaí to clear the way into the college, 20 men, including union officials, were arrested and brought to trial in the Dublin District Court. The law found in favour of the school authorities.[46]

McQuaid sent a memorandum to the Episcopal secretary, Dr Jeremiah Kinane, for the Hierarchy to consider at its meeting at Maynooth in October.[47] He insisted that the union organiser, James Bower, had given 'great bent of bitterness against Religious as being too wealthy and very bad employers. He used the normal Communistic language.'

Describing Bower's action as lamentable, and pointing out that it was spreading discontent among domestic servants in Dublin, McQuaid informed the bishops that he had twice met the Attorney General about the case and that he was also convinced of the union's Communist tendency. McQuaid noted that the solicitor advising the servants, C.B.W. Boyle, had previously worked for Mr James Larkin. 'The significance of these events would seem to be more than local,' he warned. 'The Secretary of the Union has assured my bursar that the movement is not merely against us but is meant to extend to all the Irish Colleges, and has boasted that this is the first strike brought off.'[48]

After the collapse of the strike, one of the former servants, Patrick Daly, begged to be reinstated in the post. 'I would like you to know that I feel very sorry for my part in the strike. I know I was wrong and I see now that I acted unjustly towards the college where I was always treated generously. I would be very grateful if you would take me back, although I know I do not deserve it. I apologise to you, Very Rev. Father, for having picketed the college gates and I give you my word that under no circumstances will I do the like again. You were, Father, very kind to Mrs Daly and got her looked after and I know I ought not to have forgotten that. All

I can do now is to ask your pardon and assure you that if you see your way to take me back I will with God's help serve you faithfully.'[49]

In marked contrast to this apologetic note, an anonymous correspondent ridiculed the notion that the strikers were Communists and suggested that 'the Bastille of Blackrock' was producing rebellion. 'Blackrock breeds Bolshies' by its treatment of servants, the writer told McQuaid, pointing out that the servants had prayed to the Blessed Sacrament before going on strike.

> **Humbly examine your conscience and ask yourself whither you are driving these boys. Ask yourself if how the action is dictated by pride and patrician instinct. God forgive me if I wrong you as much as Dublin is saying you have wronged those boys. For the story is spreading despite the suppression.**[50]

As 1938 ended, McQuaid was able to bask in the reflected glory of a tribute by Vatican Radio to the Catholic nature of the Constitution, but it had not been the best of years for his public image, and within the Holy Ghost Congregation the perception was growing that McQuaid had become too much of an independent force. The appointment of McQuaid's old rival, Dan Murphy, as the head of the Irish Province signalled the opening of a new chapter in the history of the Holy Ghost Fathers. The McQuaid era in Blackrock, too, was coming to a close.

9

Dev's Man
1939–40

'Gifted but flawed.'
Fr Michael O'Carroll C.S.Sp. of McQuaid.

In June 1939, some weeks before his forty-fourth birthday, Fr John McQuaid C.S.Sp. learned from Fr Dan Murphy that his term as President of Blackrock College was to expire at the end of the summer term. He had been a record nine-and-a-half years in office. Although he had known for more than a year that a change was almost certain, confirmation of the move struck a raw nerve. It was his first career setback since he had been recalled 15 years previously from the Biblical Institute in Rome. The news signalled a loss of professional prestige and the diminution of his national standing as an educationalist.

McQuaid, a member of a Religious Congregation which equated obedience to a superior with obedience to God, tried to have the decision reversed, and wrote to the Superior General in Paris pleading for an extension.

'If I am changed, I cease to be Headmaster and Chairman of the Headmasters' Association,' McQuaid told Bishop Louis Le Hunsec. 'Frankly, no one in Ireland has my knowledge of the situation or my power with the bishops, priests, sisters and especially lay teachers at the present time.'[1] It was a revealing self-assessment, and McQuaid was not deluding himself about his unique position in national education; indeed, his friends were already lobbying to ensure that he would maintain it.

The Papal Nuncio, Archbishop Paschal Robinson, wrote to Le Hunsec on July 1, urging him to grant McQuaid at least two further years as President of Blackrock College. Robinson made this special request following a visit to the Nunciature by the head of the Irish Government, Éamon de Valera. The Taoiseach was concerned that McQuaid's departure from Blackrock College and the Headmasters' Association would harm negotiations on a revised secondary school curriculum which were approaching a critical stage.

Robinson informed Le Hunsec of the highest regard in which McQuaid was held and praised his singular achievement of having devised the regulations governing the role of lay teachers in secondary schools controlled by Religious Orders and secular clergy.

'In connection with these and other important matters,' Robinson continued, his candour conspicuous for a Papal diplomat, 'Dr McQuaid has often acted as intermediary between the Government and the Irish bishops with whom he is *persona gratissima*. If Dr McQuaid now retires from the Presidency of Blackrock College, he will cease *ipso facto* to remain Chairman of the Headmasters' Association, and will thus be obliged to give up the direction of the work in question which will consequently suffer considerable detriment and delay.'

He informed Le Hunsec that de Valera had discussed the possibility of McQuaid's term being extended with Fr Murphy, who 'kindly' promised to bring the matter to the Mother House in Paris. Casting diplomatic niceties aside, Robinson put the full weight of the Holy See behind McQuaid: 'I need hardly say that I do not wish to intervene in any way in the internal affairs of your Congregation, but, in view of the grave reasons put forward by Mr de Valera, I have no hesitation in endorsing his opinion with reference to the great importance of Dr McQuaid's continuance in office, for the present, as President of Blackrock College.'[2]

On foot of this extraordinary appeal, Le Hunsec convened a special meeting of his principal advisers, who responded to the dilemma with an ingenious Gallic solution to an Irish problem. On July 5 Le Hunsec informed Robinson that he could not extend McQuaid's term as College President: to do so would be inconsistent with the Congregation's rules. However, he would continue to be a member of the community at Blackrock. 'We are only too pleased to think that he will continue to act as an intermediary, if necessary, between the Government and the Irish bishops. His prudent and enlightened advice will always be at the disposal of those who work on the revision of the Secondary School Programme.'[3]

As soon as he received news of the decision, McQuaid turned to de Valera. 'I rang up this morning to find you had gone, for I was anxious to let you know, first of all, that I have ceased to be Superior,' he wrote. He rationalised this turn of events as God's plan. 'I can believe now, if ever I was tempted to think the contrary, that I am not necessary here'.

McQuaid knew that he was to be kept at Blackrock but did not yet know in what capacity. 'I have only one desire now,' he wrote ingratiatingly, 'to thank you for your extraordinary goodness to me and to thank Mrs de Valera who has been so motherly in her kindness. You know that to the last, I am willing to serve in any measure I possibly can.'[4]

In his formal reply to Le Hunsec next day, McQuaid 'very willingly' accepted the decision and offered himself for whatever work might be chosen for him. 'I only hope that God will be indulgent to the many faults and negligences of my Superiorship,' he wrote disarmingly.[5]

But there was a further surprise in store for him. His successor was not to be his friend and protégé, Fr Vincent Dinan, who for nine years, successively as Dean of the Day School and Director of the Juniorate with additional responsibilities for running the Sodalities and training the rugby team had been groomed in McQuaid's ways. Instead, Dinan was to be transferred to Rockwell College as President, bringing about a separation that was to be painful for the two men who had grown so close. The McQuaid succession fell on Fr John English, OBE, who had lived in Trinidad since 1919 and had just completed a term as the President of St Mary's College, Port of Spain. In the words of the chronicler of Blackrock College, Fr Seán Farragher, English was seen as 'a rank outsider'. In due course, English was to show just how out of touch he was with McQuaid's Blackrock and de Valera's Ireland.

In his last address to the College Union as President, McQuaid took special pride in looking back on the restoration of the Castle. The scholastics had departed it in 1938 for the new seminary at Kimmage Manor, leaving McQuaid free to combine his fund-raising and artistic skills to renovate the building, which he did magnificently. He trusted that the final-year boys who now occupied the Castle would enjoy 'so large a measure of controlled freedom' that they would learn 'to appreciate more fully the Christian dignity of self-restraint and personal devotedness to duty'. He had established a praesidium (or branch) of the Legion of Mary there to 'develop in our boys a chivalrous love of Our Blessed Lady, a spirit of loyalty, even of affection, towards the drudgery of daily life, and especially a readiness to place oneself with obedience and intelligence, at the service of the parish clergy.'[6] He was especially pleased that the College Union had established a Boys' Club in Dun Laoghaire. 'In such a venture, may we not be allowed to see,' he said, 'the proper fruit of a Catholic education.'[7]

McQuaid was offered the directorship of the Castle, the post overseeing the final year boys which he had created only the year before. To facilitate him, Fr Thomas Maguire, who had been appointed director by McQuaid moved to the Preparatory School in Willow Park. McQuaid's new duties included a return that autumn to the classroom as a teacher of Latin and English, but he was given full scope to pursue his educational work for de Valera, in addition to his apostolic work with the bourgeois leaders of Catholic Action. Since May he had assumed the chairmanship of the education and youth sub-committee of the Catholic Truth Society and was collaborating with its director, Frank O'Reilly, on schemes to maximise Catholic influence on radio.[8] He was also involved in a history project with Fr Corcoran.[9]

Although he had lost his President's 'stripes', McQuaid's hallowed place in the history of Blackrock College was recognised when the Past Pupils' Union commemorated his achievements in a plaque that was erected at the entrance hall to the college chapel, alongside the panels he had set up in 1937 bearing the names of the Presidents of the Union. It set out his educational ideals.

During his tenure he had purchased the freehold for Blackrock College, Willow Park and Clareville from the Pembroke estate, making the Holy Ghost Fathers the first native owners of the land since the Norman invasion. He had transformed Blackrock into a magnificent building, commissioning windows in the college chapel by Evie Hone, Michael Healy and Hubert McGoldrick. St Patrick's Hall was bedecked with replicas of della Robbia figures imported from Italy. In the Hall of Fame he installed a set of Arundel prints from the Medici Masters, and he renamed the centrepiece of the hall as Our Lady's Hall, furnishing it with a marble Madonna bust by Pachini which he had brought from Italy. Two plaques to Our Lady were stationed in the Jubilee Hall.

With the professional assistance of Mrs Berthon Waters, a heraldic artist as well as a social campaigner, he had redesigned the college crest with its motto *Fides et Robur* (Faith and Fortitude). He made wearing the school's blazer and flannels compulsory during sports' days in the summer and, most ostentatiously of all, had bought Blackrock's first car, a Daimler, purchased in London.

McQuaid became a legend in the lives of several generations of 'Rock boys. He encouraged them to read widely and to appreciate the arts, and in his sociable moods often gripped them with the story of how one of the original buildings had been haunted when the first group of Holy Ghost fathers arrived there, and had to perform an exorcism to rid the place of evil spirits before they could move in.

The writer, Anthony Cronin, recalls how staff would tell pupils that McQuaid had learned French overnight from a book, and he recalled the system of bells which McQuaid had fitted into his presidential office: a touch of an illuminated panel on the ante-room door told the visitor to wait or enter, or that the president was absent.[10] Such ploys all added to 'the air of wonder' which surrounded the president.

McQuaid had also made Blackrock College synonymous with national celebrations, such as the Eucharistic Congress, and he made it a centre for Catholic apostolic work when, in association with the Legion of Mary, he pioneered an experiment in 'convert-work', the first initiative of its kind since the Reformation. With Archbishop Byrne's approval, McQuaid developed a programme which provided 'the interested inquirer' with instruction in Catholic doctrine and a practical introduction to liturgy. Meetings were held in the college on Sundays, giving those who attended an insight into the atmosphere of a Catholic religious community. Many Protestants who undertook instruction did become Catholics. McQuaid's most famous convert was the artist Evie Hone, who was impressed by his 'power of clear expression, sensitive understanding of the temperament and vocation of the artist in society, and a firm faith.' Not so impressed was the writer Lennox Robinson, who found the talks enormously interesting but came away 'a Blacker Protestant'. The experiment was, however, so successful overall that it was put into operation by the Legion in Australia, America and Trinidad.[11] McQuaid still ranks as Blackrock's greatest President since its foundation by Père Leman.

Dev's Plenipotentiary

Relieved of the presidency, McQuaid plunged himself into his work on the new national curriculum. From July 30 to August 5 he attended the International Congress of Catholic Secondary Education in Fribourg, Switzerland, as the delegate of the Catholic Headmasters' Association. He saw the build-up towards war as he travelled across the continent. Just as he had witnessed the final days of the old European order before the outbreak of the First World War, twenty-six years later he could see the eclipse of Versailles Europe.

While McQuaid was in England, visiting his sister Helen, Britain and France declared war on Germany on September 3, after it invaded and occupied Poland with Russian connivance. He witnessed the tears of mothers as their children were evacuated by train from London. In his haste to return to Ireland, McQuaid left laundry, two keys and a mackintosh in Welwyn, Hertfordshire. Before his departure McQuaid asked his host, Joscelyne Finberg, to send him on a copy of Cardinal Arthur Hinsley's Pastoral Letter on the reaction of English Catholics to the war.[12] 'We cannot stand idly by and allow our neighbour to be enslaved or ruthlessly done to death,' wrote Hinsley, who also sent a message to Prime Minister Neville Chamberlain pledging him the absolute loyalty of the English Catholic community, including its strong Irish immigrant element.[13]

'Emergency Ireland' to which McQuaid returned in early September had already declared itself neutral. The Dáil had amended the Constitution to give the Government emergency powers. De Valera, in his biggest cabinet reshuffle since coming to power in 1932, promoted Seán Lemass from Industry and Commerce to the new post of Minister for Supplies, demoted Seán MacEntee from Finance to Industry and Commerce, and transferred Seán T. O'Kelly from Local Government and Public Health to Finance. The principal levers of Justice and responsibility for Coordination of Defensive Measures, particularly the enforcement of censorship, were given to the dependably tough Gerald Boland and Frank Aiken respectively. The hardline republican P.J. Ruttledge took over Local Government and Health from O'Kelly, while Derrig was moved from Education to Lands, and Oscar Traynor took charge of Defence. The only newcomer was P.J. Little as Minister for Post and Telegraphs.[14] Initially, for three weeks, responsibility for Education was given to O'Kelly. But O'Kelly's timetable was monopolised by the mandarins of Finance.[15] Accordingly, before the end of September de Valera

took charge of Education in addition to his duties as Taoiseach and Minister for External Affairs. 'The McQuaid factor' was behind this move. In
effect, McQuaid had become an unofficial Government plenipotentiary,
entrusted with work which de Valera wanted done but could not oversee
personally. First, however, McQuaid had to plot a scenario in which he
would hold his grade in the upper ranks of headmasterly politics.

For the first time in nine years, McQuaid did not take the chair when
the Catholic Headmasters' Association assembled for its autumn plenary
meeting at the Gresham Hotel, Dublin, on October 19, 1939. Indeed, he
was not even admitted to the opening session, and was asked to wait outside as the chair was taken by Fr William Meagher of St Vincent's College,
Castleknock. But in accordance with a plan worked out in advance at a
standing committee meeting McQuaid had chaired, Fr Meagher formally
proposed that the outgoing chairman, Dr McQuaid, should be co-opted as a
member of the association. When this proposal was accepted, Meagher
immediately tabled a follow-up motion that McQuaid should be elected
chairman for the coming year. This move was accepted unanimously by the
29 members present.[16] His peers knew that he was Dev's Man, and were as
eager as McQuaid to exploit their conduit to the heart of Government.

It was a masterly stroke. McQuaid was invited back into the room
and, feigning surprise at his unprecedented re-selection, he thanked the
association for the extraordinary kindness it had shown him. Immediately
re-possessing the chair, with his customary crisp despatch McQuaid
steered the meeting through a busy agenda that included consideration of
the draft of a Uniform Contract of Employment and a Conjoint Appeal
Agreement that he had negotiated with the Association of Secondary
Teachers of Ireland. The details were approved and McQuaid was
instructed to recommend both documents to the Hierarchy and to the
heads of the Religious Orders.[17]

It was not until towards the end of the meeting that McQuaid
played his 'de Valera card' when he tabled the Taoiseach's request that
'the association should examine the working of the Revised Programme,
especially the prescribed texts, with the aim of making recommendations
the following April on suitable material in Irish and English.' It was
nodded through enthusiastically. McQuaid was instructed to thank de
Valera, wish him well as Minister for Education and assure him that the
association 'would endeavour to meet his desire in the present instance'.[18]

This McQuaid did so next day, and dutifully expressed the Association's hope that de Valera would 'promote strongly the best interests of
secondary education and its conjoined departments'.[19] De Valera replied
on October 26, and widened the time available for the special study to 'a
year or two'.[20] As McQuaid would conclude the special mission well
within that time-span, it was clear to those close to the Chief that he had
other plans for his man in Blackrock.

10

Fr 'X'

1940

'This most secret of missions.'
Joe Walshe to Éamon de Valera.

While Fr John McQuaid C.S.Sp. was advancing de Valera's educational agenda – and also seriously considering the prospect of becoming a missionary priest in Africa – the Archbishop of Dublin, Edward Byrne, died on February 9, 1940. No sooner had his body been laid to rest in the crypt of the Pro-Cathedral than the play for the succession to the See of Dublin and Primacy of Ireland began in earnest. The elderly Bishop Francis Wall, who took temporary charge of the diocese as Vicar Capitular, instructed the clergy to invoke the guidance of the Holy Spirit in special prayers at Mass until 'a worthy successor to his Grace has been given to bless us by the supreme authority of the Apostolic See'.

On account of Byrne's long illness from Parkinson's disease – he was known as 'the silent Archbishop' – opinion strongly favoured the appointment of a prelate who would shake up the Dublin diocese and play a greater role in the nation's affairs. This prescription, together with Wall's emphasis on the Church's need to respond to Dublin's poor, matched the ideas being shared privately by the Nuncio and the Taoiseach.

This was not to be de Valera's first intrusion into the shadowy politics of Episcopal appointments. Having formally protested to the Vatican about the anti-Government speeches of the Bishops of Killaloe and Achonry in 1933, de Valera subsequently launched a 'charm-offensive' to convince Pope Pius XI that he was a solid son of the Church. His proactive policy had helped secure the promotion of Maynooth Professor Michael Browne, known as 'Cross Michael', to Galway in 1937, and the Derry priest, Neil Farren, to Raphoe in early 1939. An attempt to influence the outcome of the selection procedure for the Primacy of Ireland, however, was a more hazardous operation, compounded by the exceptionally high level of self-interested wheeling and dealing which was taking place among the Dublin clergy.

Discreetly, de Valera contacted Fr English at Blackrock College and requested a dossier on McQuaid's career. English sent some details to de Valera on March 4, and apologised for not having completed the file in time for the Taoiseach's meeting with the Nuncio. 'Hoping that God will bless your efforts in what we believe to be an excellent cause in the interest of both Church and State,' English wrote, indicating that he knew the significance of de Valera's activities.[1]

At the crucial meeting with the Nuncio, de Valera was assured of Robinson's support for McQuaid. The Papal representative was unhappy with the laxity that had crept into the Dublin diocese as a result of Byrne's prolonged illness, when the diocese had been run by his senior secretary, Fr Tom O'Donnell, and a group of powerful clergy, which included another of the Archbishop's secretaries, Fr Patrick Dunne. This group would regularly settle diocesan business while playing billiards, and came to be known as 'the billiards room cabinet'.[2]

Robinson, independently of de Valera's support for McQuaid, had concluded that McQuaid was the man to succeed Byrne. Robinson had been impressed by McQuaid's management of the Blackrock garden party and had met him regularly at Church-State functions. Prior to Byrne's death Robinson had visited him to discuss, among other routine matters, the future stewardship of the diocese. After the meeting Byrne told O'Donnell: 'I am happy to know that that my choice of successor has the support of the Nuncio. And you will be happy too.'[3]

But the task of securing McQuaid's appointment was tricky. Both Taoiseach and Nuncio knew that procedures had to be observed, at least outwardly. According to Canon Law, the Cathedral Chapter was required to present the Nuncio with a list of three priests – known as the *terna* – who were deemed suitable for the post of Archbishop. As a result, three leading candidates emerged. Thought to have been listed as *dignus*, or 'worthy', was the parish priest of the Pro-Cathedral, Fr Edward Gallen, who shared McQuaid's enthusiasm for the Regnum Christi organisation. A strong candidate and most likely *dignior* – the second or 'worthier' preference – was one of Byrne's secretaries, Dr Patrick Dunne, a mild-mannered and thoughtful Dubliner who had done his postgraduate studies in Rome after his ordination at Clonliffe College. The position of *dignissimus* was almost certainly held by McQuaid's professor of Hebrew, Monsignor Patrick Boylan, the diocese's most outstanding intellectual and the only one with a truly international reputation as a scholar. Also canvassed for the post was the president of Maynooth College, Monsignor John D'Alton, a Classics scholar and former classmate of de Valera at Blackrock College.[4]

The discreet championing of McQuaid by Nuncio and Taoiseach meant that these nominees had to be circumvented, especially the Dublin priests' much-respected favourite, Boylan. In his report to Rome,

Robinson appears to have argued that the wishes of the clergy should be put aside in the interests of an exceptional candidate who would restore order to a diocese which had descended into clerical factionalism, and recommended McQuaid who, as a member of a Religious Order, would not be beholden to any group.

While the canonical process was taking its course, de Valera was pursuing the diplomatic route. A memorandum to Government outlined the role of the next Archbishop of Dublin in a way that was tailor-made for McQuaid. 'The Archbishop should be a man of wide interests and have a considerable knowledge of public affairs, particularly in regard to social and political matters. It is obvious also that he must be in general sympathy with the Government. In order that the Archbishop's influence may be as great as possible, it is not necessary to point out that he should be a man of culture and dignity as well as being a good administrator.'

Two other factors pointed in McQuaid's favour. First, the Government felt it was a matter of the greatest importance that Church and State would cooperate in social and other matters for the common good. Secondly, such co-operation could best be secured by frequent meetings between the head of Government and the Archbishop of Dublin. Against this, however, was the uncertainty surrounding how the new Pope, Pius XII, the former Eugenio Pacelli, who had succeeded Pius XI in February, 1939, would handle Episcopal appointments.[5]

De Valera instructed the Secretary of the Department of External Affairs, Joe Walshe, to inform the Vatican authorities of their views. Walshe in turn instructed the head of the Irish Legation to the Holy See, his former Clongowes pupil, William J. Babbington Macaulay, to press the case for McQuaid, who was to be code-named 'X' in secret correspondence between Dublin and Rome.[6] Macaulay, who had already encountered difficulties in promoting Paschal Robinson's case for a Red Hat as a member of the College of Cardinals, advised that they move cautiously. State interference in appointments had become a very sensitive issue at the Vatican, he pointed out, since friction had arisen between General Franco and the Vatican over the nomination of bishops in Spain. 'The late Pontiff [Pius XI] was entirely opposed to State interference ... and the present one [Pius XII] is even more so,' he warned.[7]

On March 8 Macaulay submitted a précis of the Government memorandum to Curia officials.[8] 'The need for a person of no ordinary attainments and character is realised as they recognised the defects of the last incumbent, owing to ill health,' Macaulay reported to Walshe. He hesitated to mention names, but Roman gossip indicated that the Belfast priest, Arthur Ryan, was highly thought of. Significantly, Macaulay added: 'I was told the Nuncio was already interesting himself in finding the best man. I think that what he suggests will carry great weight, perhaps decisively so.'

Walshe was not satisfied with this state of affairs, however, and instructed Macaulay to expedite matters. On May 29 Macaulay telegrammed encouraging news to Dublin following an audience he had had with Pope Pius XII the previous day. Pius expressed 'great concern at our situation and promised attention to filling Dublin vacancy in terms of my request,' Macaulay reported, but aware that Pius had not made a specific pledge to endorse Dublin's wishes – only to look at the case for 'X' – he again cautioned against pressing 'X's' case too strongly as this might offend the Pope.

The following month, de Valera was encouraged to hear that the Legation had engaged the interest of the Substitute Secretary of State, Monsignor Giovanni Battista Montini, the future Pope Paul VI, in the appointment. This was an important contact, as Montini was responsible for liaising with diplomats accredited to the Holy See. Nor was Montini unfamiliar with Ireland and Robinson: he had spent four days on holiday in Dublin in 1934, when he stayed at the Nunciature. A rising star of the Curia and one of the two key advisers to the Pope, Montini had taken over from Monsignor Domenico Tardini as director of the Secretariat of State in December 1937, when Tardini had been promoted as head of Extraordinary Ecclesiastical Affairs, the section which dealt with Governments. Macaulay reported that he had had a good meeting with Montini, who accepted the Government's view that the Dublin See should not be kept vacant for much longer.

In June de Valera returned the Education portfolio to Derrig after ten months. As well as piloting legislation through the Oireachtas setting up the Institute for Advanced Studies, de Valera, with McQuaid, reintroduced specified texts in language courses and literature which had been abolished in 1924. That same month, McQuaid consolidated his reputation in the eyes of the bishops as a superb negotiator when the Hierarchy approved his proposals covering the new contractual terms for the employment of lay teachers in secondary schools, and the financial position of lay secondary teachers who joined the Defence Forces.[9]

By late July, however, there was near-panic in Dublin's Government Buildings at the Holy See's continued silence on the Dublin succession. After further inquiries were made by the Irish Legation, a coded telegram was sent to the Department of External Affairs in Dublin. Deciphered, it read: 'Regarding the Dublin vacancy, delay is due to Robinson's despatches having been lost in transit. Matter is now being dealt with by cable.'

The loss of Robinson's mail recommending McQuaid's selection was deeply frustrating. Almost six months after Byrne's death, de Valera and Robinson had to re-start the campaign all over.

In the intervening months the map of Europe had changed drastically. Hitler's forces had conquered Denmark, Norway, the Netherlands,

Belgium, Luxembourg, and most spectacularly of all, France. Mussolini's Italy had extended its power-base in the Mediterranean basin, while Stalin's Soviet Union had absorbed Finland, Lithuania, Latvia and Estonia. With the fall of France on June 21, British forces and a sizable number of French troops had been evacuated to England. Britain now stood alone against the Axis powers, and political and diplomatic circles in Dublin gave her little chance of winning, not least Joe Walshe. The London Blitz added enormously to McQuaid's concerns. He was anxious for Helen's safety and for his younger half-brother, Tom, who had joined the British Army in India as a medical officer.

McQuaid had been busy all through the summer. In July he gave the first annual retreat in the Castle for the Past Pupils' Union. However, he was feeling increasingly on edge as the mood within the college became distinctly anti-English – against the new president, that is, whose austere cut-backs made him unpopular. English was compared most unfavourably with his predecessor. It was by now an open secret in Blackrock circles that he was being considered for the archbishopric. His Holy Ghost colleagues were privately speculating that he was being backed by de Valera and Robinson. According to Fr Michael O'Carroll, McQuaid's pending appointment was 'all the talk of the town for a time', but as time passed, McQuaid's colleagues began to think that 'it was off and he was not going to be chosen.'[10] McQuaid was aware of the gossip and the weeks of waiting tested his nerves. Towards the end of September a Holy Ghost colleague, Fr James Keawell, seeing that McQuaid looked utterly morose and dejected, asked him if anything was wrong. 'I could wish I had never been born,' was the frosty reply. Fr Keawell later suggested that his enigmatic response showed that McQuaid knew of his impending promotion and was brooding on it.[11]

McQuaid held strong opinions about the weaknesses of the Hierarchy which he often privately expressed to de Valera and others – and he had definite ideas about how these inadequacies should be addressed. His name had even been mentioned in connection with the succession to his native Kilmore diocese in 1937 after the death of Bishop Patrick Finegan, but there is no indication to show that he would have relished a return to what would have been an ecclesiastical backwater.[12] McQuaid believed that dioceses which looked to Dublin had not found leadership on account of Byrne's long-running infirmity, and as a result the intelligence and especially the goodwill of both clergy and lay-people were 'unharnessed' as regards the development of 'a Catholic sociology'. He realised that the Communist threat was minimal, but he detected a restlessness among the people arising from what he called the inevitable existence of unemployment. To remedy this he thought the Government should embark on social programmes which tapped into the strong Catholic life that existed, especially among the working class.[13]

Parallel with Government action, McQuaid wanted parishes throughout the dioceses to set up committees of educated laity to work towards developing Catholic structures in economic and social life. Secondary school pupils, who would form the élite in the professions, must be 'gripped' through existing church organisations; those with only primary school education needed to be catered for in their religious formation by after-school enterprises. He saw the Legion of Mary as a crucial force in creating a socially minded Catholicism, and thought that priests and seminarians should be encouraged to pursue higher studies and education in Catholic sociology abroad.[14]

Characteristically, McQuaid had thought too about how this Catholic action programme might be delivered. He dismissed the idea of sending a letter to the Hierarchy: he feared that would prove to be ineffective, even hurtful, and would be misinterpreted both in Ireland and among Irish people abroad. He decided that a special report should be sent to the Holy See, and that its contents could be taken up with each bishop on his five yearly visit to Rome.[15]

In Rome, meanwhile, Colman Donovan, the second-in-command at the legation, had taken over from Macaulay, who had taken leave and was in mourning for his wife, the wealthy Genevieve Brady. His departure turned out to be fortuitous for McQuaid's candidature. Though younger and less experienced than Macaulay, Donovan, a product of St Mungo's Academy in Glasgow, was prepared to take the kind of risks that his boss shied away from.[16] Donovan arranged a meeting with Montini on September 25 at which he pressed McQuaid's case. He was told, however, that such interference was *inauditum* – not heard.[17] This was the kind of rebuff which Macaulay had warned against, but Donovan was undeterred and continued to pursue the matter until, finally, Montini suggested that he should seek an audience with the Pope. He consulted Iveagh House and was urged to follow it up. Donovan also related that Vatican sources were saying that Bishop Browne was to be transferred from Galway to Dublin, which was not at all what de Valera and Robinson wanted.

Five days later Donovan reported excitedly to Dublin that Montini had spoken to Pope Pius, who had still heard nothing from the Curial officials. 'This means that the appointment has not yet been made. The Holy Father is asking to have the matter expedited and will have the name communicated to me,' Donovan wrote. But Donovan was running ahead of the Vatican. On October 3 he wired that at an audience that morning the Pope had promised to give attention to the appointment when Cardinal Rossi, head of the Consistorial Congregation which would select the name for ratification by the Pope, returned to Rome towards the end of the month.

On November 5 Donovan reported that Rossi had been received by Pius, and he alerted Iveagh House that 'We shall be informed after nomination and only a few hours before publication' of the outcome. The breakthrough came two days later. Donovan wired Dublin: 'An official in the Secretariat of State told me privately today that he had heard "X" had been appointed, but all I could get from Tardini was that he hoped to have information for me within a few days. He made, however, reference to "X", which I took as a deliberate hint.'

On receiving Donovan's decoded message next day, a senior diplomat, Freddie Boland, wrote in the margin: 'Personal letter to Secy. X noted to be Fr McQuaid C.S.Sp. (Blackrock Coll).' It was the first mention of McQuaid's name in the official Vatican-Ireland correspondence.

In a second coded telegram sent that day, Donovan reported: 'Vatican has just informed me officially of the appointment of "X".'

The telegram from Rome formally nominating Fr John Charles McQuaid as Archbishop of Dublin and Primate of Ireland was received by Robinson on Saturday evening.

Archbishop-elect

On Monday morning of November 11 McQuaid was in his study at the Castle when he received a phone call at ten minutes to nine from the Nuncio. Robinson needed to confirm McQuaid's acceptance of the post before officially informing the Government and the Dublin clergy. Robinson made it clear to McQuaid that he could not decline the post.

On obtaining McQuaid's consent, Robinson phoned Walshe at the Department of External Affairs to convey the formal news. A telegram was sent to Donovan : 'News officially confirmed by Nuncio. You should take very early opportunity of informing Holy Father through Secretary of State of pleasure of Government at appointment.' The quick-witted Donovan wired back: 'I had already used exactly your words when informed of appointment and had already asked for interview with Secretary of State for purpose indicated.'

McQuaid immediately wrote to his step-mother, Agnes: 'I want you to be the first to know that His Holiness the Pope has appointed me Archbishop of Dublin. It is due to you, and you alone, that this great honour has been conferred on me.' This was an acknowledgement of the strength of character shown by Agnes when she helped persuade Eugene to relax his opposition to Brother Gaspard O'Reilly and allow McQuaid's entry into the Holy Ghost Fathers. The letter was sent by special messenger.[18]

At twenty minutes to ten McQuaid broke the news to his Blackrock College colleagues. At an impromptu meeting with staff and pupils in the Jubilee Hall, he asked them for their prayers and urged them to be strong in their Catholicism. Turning for confirmation to Bishop John Neville C.S.Sp., retired from East Africa, he revealed that on four occasions his requests to be sent to the missions in Kenya had been turned down. His appointment as Archbishop of Dublin, however, was one which he was not allowed to turn down! 'I have been asked to accept and not refuse. So I have accepted.' [19]

Later that morning McQuaid drove to the Phoenix Park to pay his respects to the Nuncio. Next he called on Bishop Wall at Archbishop's House in Drumcondra. By then, Wall had made the official announcement to the Dublin clergy: 'The Holy See has once more gladdened our hearts by appointing as our Archbishop the Most Rev John McQuaid, M.A., D.D., C.S.Sp., Blackrock College, County Dublin. In your name, I offer him a hearty welcome amongst us as our spiritual ruler and guide, and wish him many happy years in his exalted office. His Grace may rest assured that he can always rely on the unfailing obedience and loyalty of his priests and people'.[20]

Behind the scenes, however, frantic efforts were being made to secure McQuaid's acceptance by the Dublin clergy. While McQuaid had been the confidant of Byrne and Robinson and was well known to the Hierarchy through his educational and hospital work, he was not one of the rank and file of the Dublin diocesan clergy. He was an outsider, a member of an élite Religious Order. Most damningly of all, he was from Cavan.

The news from Rome of his appointment was received coldly, if not resentfully, by the Dublin clergy, according to John A. Costello, the future Taoiseach.[21] Only 'the iron discipline of the Church' prevented 'the widespread indignation' from becoming vocal, the British Delegation in Dublin reported to London.[22] Even in the late 1990s, a Dublin parish priest recalled how older clergy would speak of their shock on the day they heard about McQuaid's appointment. These elderly priests 'could remember exactly where they were and what they were doing when they were told the news.'[23]

According to British diplomatic intelligence, McQuaid's promotion was an even 'more sensational appointment' than that of Michael Browne to Galway. The note pointed out that McQuaid had no experience of pastoral work and that his position as a Regular priest (belonging to a Religious Order) was greatly disliked by the secular clergy, and concluded that one of McQuaid's 'most important qualifications seems to have been his friendship with Mr de Valera, for whom he drafted the clauses in the Constitution dealing with religion'.[24]

Deeply disappointed though he was at being overlooked for the top ecclesiastical post in the State, Monsignor Boylan made a joke out of his loss. Referring to his physical ailment of a nervous twitch in his neck and the dark-horse nature of McQuaid's victory, he would often remark that he was 'beaten by a neck'. Influential, too, among the middle-ground clergy was Fr Patrick Condon, who urged colleagues at least to give McQuaid a chance to prove himself.[25]

Despite the negative reaction of the Dublin clergy, McQuaid's appointment was greeted with a surge of support from people in all strands of Irish public life, especially from those who knew his mettle. Resolutions were passed by educational boards throughout the country – even the Irish Auctioneers and Estate Agents Association sent a message of congratulations. The euphoria was best summed up in a statement issued by Sir Joseph Glynn at the annual meeting of the National Maternity Hospital, which declared that McQuaid's 'scholarship, saintly life, love of the poor and experience in training the rising generation, render him the ideal of the people.'[26]

As messages of congratulations poured in from all parts of Ireland and abroad, Fr R.J. Glennon, one of the Drumcondra secretariat, assumed the role of the Archbishop-elect's 'chief of staff'. Among the messages was a telegram from Clongowes Wood, McQuaid's Jesuit alma mater. Within the hour, the reply read: 'Deeply moved ... Grateful for prayers.'[27]

McQuaid, too, knew the importance of making a good first impression with the press. That Monday afternoon, as the rain fell steadily, the Archbishop-elect received journalists and photographers at Blackrock College. Despite his innate shyness, he needed little tutoring in PR skills, as reported by 'Spectator' in the *Irish Independent*.

> Tall and wiry of frame, he sat in his chair, one arm thrown over the back, his head slightly tilted – the typical gesture of a scholar. From underneath the high clerical collar gleams the only colour – as yet – in the black of his clothes: the light blue stock of the Holy Ghost Fathers. In his tanned face glows a slightly ruddy complexion as of a man much out in the open. Nose and chin are pointed, his head broadens towards the brow and crown, over which the dark hair is thinning. His eyes are the grandest feature of his face, fine and searching, lined with innumerable crows-feet.

'Spectator' warmed to McQuaid's strong and engaging personality as he submitted to the cross-fire of questioning with great friendliness and patience.

> Yet, again and again, he would beg, with a disarming smile, his questioners to desist. For points of policy, it was much too early yet, and at personal questions, his retiring disposition still flinched ... It was fascinating to watch how, at a very leading question, his face would ... light up with that winning smile which is so typically, so essentially his own. The crows-feet deepen, the corners of his mobile, sensitive mouth uncurl into a smile because it is so genuine and which the multitude will take to its heart.

McQuaid deflected questions about his family background. 'This is my tribulation,' he said laconically when asked about his mother, Jennie Corry. More openly, he concurred that his strong social interests were inherited from his doctor father. His fondest recollections centred on his European 'wanderings' – to Paris, Rome, the Hague, Luxembourg and Fribourg. What struck the *Irish Independent* writer most was McQuaid's intimate contacts with the country and with the world: he bridged rural Ireland and cosmopolitan scholarship. He summed McQuaid up as 'a man who knows what he wants, and sets to it winningly'.[28]

That evening McQuaid was at his most charming as he received visitors. De Valera called and stayed for a long chat. McQuaid's inner circle of friends were there, among them Sir Joseph Glynn, Chief State Solicitor M.A. Corrigan, Mr Justice C. Maguire, Dr P.D. O'Rourke, the President of the Blackrock Union, Dr J.A. Harbison, Dublin City Manager P.J. Hernon, and a Miss Jennings. The celebratory mood was only slightly diminished by the sombre tones of Seán Lemass on the wireless, warning of a scarcity of coal, tea, butter and petrol on account of the serious deterioration in Ireland's situation since July.

McQuaid enjoyed a favourable press next morning. The *Irish Press* presented him as well-known educationalist and a brilliant scholar, whose chief interests outside his work as a churchman were music, archaeology and art. The de Valera organ noted that he was the second youngest prelate in Ireland (Browne of Galway was younger) and the youngest Archbishop in Ireland or Great Britain.[29]

The editorial in the *Irish Independent* highlighted his intellectual qualities and thought that 'At a time when our educational system has not yet quite emerged from a period of delicate transition, it is singularly appropriate that the new Archbishop of Dublin should be a man who has had such an exceptional career as a scholar and an educationist.'[30]

Even *The Irish Times*, the bastion of Protestant opinion, was positive in its coverage, confidently predicting that the Dublin diocese would enjoy wise and firm guidance in the years to come. 'Its new Archbishop is not only a scholar of eminence, but a keen student of educational and other social problems, and a man of practical mind. He is young – very young for so exalted an office – and in the full vigour of life. Concerning the wisdom of his appointment, there is only one verdict, among priests and people alike; and the Protestants of this Archdiocese will share the satisfaction of their Catholic fellow-citizens.'[31]

Later that morning McQuaid received the formal congratulations of the Blackrock College staff and senior pupils at a reception in the Aula Maxima. It was on this occasion, according to Fr Michael O'Carroll, that McQuaid 'acknowledged publicly something which the community had only known vaguely – that his first steps to the priesthood had been directed by the saintly Brother Gaspard O'Reilly.'[32]

In the afternoon McQuaid travelled to Áras an Uachtaráin, where he met for 20 minutes with President Douglas Hyde, now aged 80 and virtually invalided. His next call was to Government Buildings in Merrion Street, where he was greeted by the Secretary to the Government, Maurice Moynihan, who escorted him to the cabinet room where de Valera was waiting. After a brief conversation, de Valera introduced the Archbishop-elect to the members of the Government.

Now wearing a red biretta with his Holy Ghost soutane, McQuaid had another round of engagements over the following days. The US Ambassador to Ireland, David Gray, called on him at Blackrock College, as did W.T. Cosgrave, George Noble Count Plunkett, Count O'Byrne and the chairman of the Currency Commission, Joseph Brennan. A delegation from the College of Physicians led by its president, Dr Howley, and numbering influential members of the Knights of St Columbanus, called to present him with 'the Borgia ring', a precious amethyst dating from the fifteenth century and believed to have been worn by some of the medieval Popes.[33]

McQuaid also met the legendary trade union leader, Jim Larkin, who received the Archbishop-elect at his Liberty Hall headquarters and harangued him about the many social ills that existed in the city of which he was soon to become the spiritual head. Visiting Liberty Hall was a daring gesture and one that was well received by Dubliners. The encounter was the start of a relationship with Larkin which was to be of mutual benefit in resolving many labour disputes over the next six years.[34]

McQuaid chose December 27, the feast of St John the Evangelist, as the day of his Episcopal Consecration. When preparing his coat of arms, he selected as his motto a quotation from St John's Gospel: *Testimonium perhibere veritati* – 'To give Testimony to the Truth'.

McQuaid moved into Kimmage Manor to undertake a spiritual retreat before the ceremony, but he was frequently interrupted by well-wishers. On November 15 Joe Walshe sent him a cutting from the *Daily Telegraph*, which referred to de Valera's 'preponderating voice' in the appointment and speculated that McQuaid would succeed Cardinal Mac-Rory in Armagh. 'I need hardly say,' the column's punch-line declared, 'how important it would be if Mr de Valera had such a friend and confidant north of the border at Armagh.' McQuaid took this speculation in his stride. 'Isn't it interesting?' he wrote back impishly. 'What a strange tribe these journalists.'[35]

Among those who sent him their blessings was Dr Thomas Arnold Harvey, his adversary in the letters' column of *The Irish Times* who was now Church of Ireland Bishop of Cashel and Waterford. 'I have been deeply touched by your most kind letter,' McQuaid replied. 'You have referred to old times with great gentleness. Pardon me again if I was in the least hurtful: you know my feelings. I have prayed for you every day since. I do hope that God will realise your beautiful prayers: strength for the burden that has been put on me so unexpectedly. May I assure you that at any time you can call. You will be a very welcome visitor.'[36]

It was impossible to have the Archbishop's Consecration in Rome as was usually the case; instead it was planned to hold it in Dublin, the first ceremony of its kind in the city for almost 170 years. Because of difficulties in war-time communications Rome dispensed with the traditional lead-sealed Bull to confirm the appointment, but the continuing non-arrival of the Papal Letters threatened to postpone the Consecration date.

As the day of his elevation approached, McQuaid was the guest of honour at a dinner in Blackrock College attended by the priests of the Holy Ghost province, including Dan Murphy, Edmund Leen and Vincent Dinan. Similar dinners were held in Kimmage, St Mary's and Rockwell, the other Holy Ghost establishment in Ireland. Prior to his consecration, McQuaid publicly donned the archiepiscopal robes – which had been presented to him by the Dublin clergy in a gesture of obeisance – when he joined de Valera and members of the Blackrock Union at the College opera. He also sat for an official photograph taken at Blackrock College by J.J. Mooney. With McQuaid's permission, specially framed prints were offered for sale at prices ranging from 13 shillings to a princely 114 shillings.[37]

There was a grim reminder amid the celebrations of the fragility of Ireland's neutrality when two bombs fell on Sandycove on December 20. 'No deaths, thank God,' the *College Journal* reported, 'but two or three injured, and windows shattered; roofs pierced with flying blocks of concrete. A crater 30 feet wide and 15 feet deep made in the tramline.[38]

The weekend before his Consecration, McQuaid visited Cootehill with his close friend, Fr Vincent Dinan. They drove to the McQuaid family farm at Maudabawn and then to Middle Chapel cemetery, where McQuaid stood in silent prayer at the grave of his parents, Eugene and Jennie. He also called on his schoolteacher, Mr Fitzsimons, and his nanny, Bridget Foy.[39]

Consecration

John Charles McQuaid's Consecration in Dublin's Pro-Cathedral brought a badly needed dash of colour and pageantry to the city after a bleak Christmas during which petrol pumps ran dry all over Ireland. There were coal shortages, tea was rationed and the weather was bitterly cold. By chance, McQuaid's big day coincided with a sale in Clery's stores in O'Connell Street, which added to the sociable buzz in the city centre as shoppers searched for bargains and a first glimpse of their new spiritual leader. And for the first time ever, the nation was able to follow the Consecration of a Primate of Ireland on the radio, the pomp and ritual of the ceremony lifting the spirit of a nation.

The congregation in the Pro-Cathedral was in place by 9.45am. President Hyde, owing to ill health, was represented by his secretary, Michael McDunphy. De Valera, in sombre black, sat in a special place on the Gospel side of the nave, with Tánaiste Seán T. O'Kelly on his left. Behind sat members of the cabinet. 'The fact that this is a Catholic nation was brought home when one watched every single minister reverently bending his knee before taking his seat,' the *Irish Independent* noted.[40] The Lord Mayor, Mrs Kathleen Clarke, the widow of the executed Easter Rising leader and veteran Fenian, Tom Clarke, sat in a prie-dieu, keeping herself warm in a mink coat, accompanied by her chaplain, Fr Vergilius, a bearded Capuchin.

Even though Ireland was a neutral State, the divisions wrought by the war were mirrored in the seating arrangements for the resident diplomatic corps: the representatives of Canada, France, Poland, Belgium and the Netherlands sat on one side, while those of Germany, Italy and the still-neutral United States on the other. The British Representative, Sir John Maffey, who failed to turn up, issued a statement explaining that the poor weather conditions prevented him from returning to Dublin from Meath, where he had spent Christmas. Another victim of the weather was Dr Richard Downey, the dynamic but flamboyant Dublin-born Archbishop of Liverpool, whose flight was forced to land in the Isle of Man. The Archbishop of Westminster, Cardinal Hinsley, aged 70, was represented by his auxiliary bishop, David Mathew, a grand-nephew of Fr Theobald Mathew, the famous Cork temperance campaigner. Among the ranks of the clergy was McQuaid's old Clongowes classmate, Hugo Kerr, now a senior member of the Redemptorist Order.

The McQuaid family sat as proud witnesses among the guests. Over from England was McQuaid's sister Helen, who was accompanied by his step-mother Agnes, his half-sister, Marie, his uncle Matt and Matt's wife Frances, as well as his cousin, Dr Mary F. Connolly. Conspicuous in his officer's uniform was McQuaid's half-brother, Lieutenant Matt McQuaid, of the Army Transport Corps.

The Nuncio, in his silk *cappa magna* with its long flowing train, moved to his place in the sanctuary. Behind him trooped the purple-vested members of the Hierarchy, their pectoral crosses sparkling under the lights. To the loud strains of '*Ecce Sacerdos Magnus*' the consecrating prelate, Cardinal MacRory, resplendent in cerise vestments, moved to the centre of the altar, followed by his two assistants, Bishops Wall and Collier.

Behind them the Archbishop-elect moved briskly to a special chapel inside the altar-rails where his pontifical vestments – sandals, amice, alb, girdle, pectoral cross, stole, dalmatic, gloves, chasuble, embroidered mitre, the pastoral staff, maniple and gremial – were laid out for him. White silk shoes were put on his feet. With the Borgia ring sparkling from his right hand and a brand-new purple biretta on his head, McQuaid positioned himself in front of MacRory. When the Cardinal asked for the apostolic mandate, Bishop Wall replied that the sacred Bull was not at hand and Canon Walsh of Glasthule read out the special dispensation. McQuaid knelt before the Cardinal to take the oath of fidelity and obedience to Blessed Peter, to the Holy Apostolic and Roman Church, and to the Pope. He swore that he would visit Rome, 'the threshold of the apostles', every five years and would report regularly to the Roman Congregations as required by the Council of Trent. McQuaid was subjected to the *examen*, which consisted of 17 questions on faith and morals, dwelling on the virtues expected of a bishop – chastity, temperance, humility, patience, justice, constancy of faith, purity of love and sincerity of peace. To each question, he answered, '*Volo*' – I will. With each answer, he rose slightly further up the altar-steps and uncovered part of his head.

McQuaid, now in archiepiscopal robes with pectoral cross and stole, began Mass at the side altar as MacRory began Mass at the high altar, both with their backs to the congregation, as was the practice then. After the Gradual, MacRory resumed his seat on the faldstool while McQuaid moved to the high altar and prostrated himself at its steps. The Litany of the Saints was sung. MacRory placed the Book of the Gospels on McQuaid's head and shoulders to symbolise the burden of office. Then the Cardinal and the assistant bishops placed their hands on the head of the elect, invoking the Holy Ghost upon him. The Cardinal rubbed his finger in the dish of chrism and with it made the sign of the cross on the kneeling McQuaid's head and on his hands. When Fr McQuaid stood up he did so as Archbishop McQuaid of Dublin and Primate of Ireland. John Charles McQuaid was now Rome's principal representative in Éire.

Cardinal MacRory and Archbishop McQuaid, standing side by side on the high altar, co-celebrated the remainder of the Mass and shared the host and chalice at the Communion. Before the last Gospel, MacRory, Wall and Collier blessed McQuaid's mitre, 'the helmet of salvation', and placed it on his head. He donned the gloves which symbolised the skin of the Lamb of God and was led to the throne where MacRory handed him a crozier, the symbol of Episcopal power in his role as shepherd of the flock. To the loud cheers of 'Long live the Pope!' the prelates began their slow exodus from the Pro-Cathedral.

When Archbishop John Charles McQuaid moved from the sanctuary, the choir began a lusty rendering of '*Ecce Sacerdos Magnus*' – Behold the Great Priest. He walked down the nave of the church, imparting his first Episcopal blessing to the congregation. 'Bishops, priests, representatives of Emperors and Kings went on their knees and received the blessing – a sublime scene,' the *Irish Catholic* reported.

'As the congregation filed out,' the *Standard* noted, 'one could sense the excitement in the air as the crowds outside waited for their first glimpse of their new Archbishop, the 47th successor to the line of Danes, Irishmen, Normans, and English, who had filled the See of Dublin, this latest embodiment of a tradition of hundreds of years of loyalty to the Holy Roman Catholic Church and its Sovereign Pontiff. The throng opened their hearts in a full-throated cheer as the new Archbishop emerged from the church.'

Saluted by the Catholic Boy Scouts and flanked by two senior priests, McQuaid walked briskly from the Pro-Cathedral to the door of the nearby parochial house, constantly raising his hand in blessing to the crowd. A few minutes afterwards McQuaid came out again, evidently to everyone's surprise, and posed for photographs on the steps. The crowds lingering outside the parochial house gave him a rousing cheer as he left in his car to take up residence in Archbishop's House, Drumcondra.

In a gesture of solidarity with the poor, McQuaid had dispensed with the custom of providing a meal and refreshments for the Pro-Cathedral guests, but the suddenness of his departure also meant that he did not meet them socially. McQuaid, however, had arranged for a private reception in Archbishop's House at Drumcondra, where he entertained Episcopal colleages, especially his suffragan (subordinate provincial) bishops, Patrick Collier of Ossory and James Staunton of Ferns.[41] After his first day's work at Drumcondra, that evening the new Archbishop paid an unannounced visit to Blackrock College and joined his former colleagues for supper. An uneasy Fr English was overheard making small-talk to McQuaid: 'I thought the Nuncio looked very pleased today.' This remark prompted one of the priests to chirp *sotto voce*: 'And I thought Dev looked a bit sheepish.'[42]

There were awkward silences. The atmosphere had changed. Everyone sensed that, under Archbishop McQuaid, life would somehow be different.

John Charles's step-mother, Agnes McQuaid, a lover of music and books, was a member of the RDS in Dublin.

The mother he never knew – Jennie Corry, who was 'highly cultivated but meek and retiring'.

An early photograph of his father, Dr Eugene McQuaid, a well-known dispensary doctor in counties Cavan and Monaghan, but not known as particularly pious.

Court View, not where John McQuaid was born, as claimed,
but where he grew up after its purchase by Dr Eugene in 1897.

A maid at Court View.

John Charles McQuaid
at Blackrock College
in 1911, already noted
for 'a delicate and
reserved demeanour'.

Ordination day at St
Mary's College
Rathmines, June 29,
1924: Frs McQuaid
and Meenan with
Bishop Bartholomew
Wilson C.S.Sp.

Kneeling for the personal blessing of Pope Pius XI.

The President of Blackrock College had 'a distinctive aura' that marked him out as a man of mystery.

Members of the Holy Angels' Sodality of Blackrock College with Fr Vincent Dinan C.S.Sp.

Discussing arrangements with the Papal Nuncio, Archbishop Paschal Robinson, for the visit of the Papal Legate to Blackrock College during the Eucharistic Congress in 1932.

Escorting the Archbishop of Dublin, Edward Byrne, and the head of Government, Éamon de Valera, at the BMA Garden Party in 1933 at Blackrock College.

McQuaid prostrates himself on the altar steps during his Consecration ceremony in 1940 as Archbishop of Dublin and Primate of Ireland.

The first blessing outside the Pro-Cathedral after the first Episcopal Consecration in Dublin in 170 years.

The new Archbishop, described as pale by onlookers, poses for photographs on the steps of Dublin's Pro-Cathedral after the two-hour Consecration ceremony.

From left: His older sister, Dr Helen McQuaid, with his younger half-sister, Marie McQuaid and his cousin, Dr Mary Connolly.

Pillars of the Emergency: McQuaid with de Valera in June 1941.

PART III

USING POWER – RULER OF
CATHOLIC IRELAND
1940–62

11

Pillar of the Emergency
1940–45

God bless those lips empower'd with mystic words.
And touch them unto wisdom fearless, kind.
Poem to McQuaid, Irish Catholic, *January 2, 1941.*

On January 13, 1941, the day James Joyce died in exile in Zurich, the writer's native city officially welcomed its new spiritual leader, John Charles McQuaid. The senior Catholic clergy and the City Fathers, at separate appointments, assembled in the library at Drumcondra, where they were received by the Lord Archbishop seated on his throne. Dean Patrick Walsh read an address on behalf of the clergy, pledging their obedience to him as 'a Priest noted for faith, piety and humility, as a Preceptor skilled in sacred and profane sciences, as a Master distinguished for fashioning and forming the morals of youth, as a Governor of long experience in ruling the minds of men and in inspiring them to higher things.'[1]

In the afternoon the Lord Mayor, aldermen and burgesses of Dublin Corporation filed into the library. After kneeling to kiss the Archbishop's ring, Alderman Cormac Breathnach T.D. read out a handsomely framed address in Irish. He was followed in Latin by the city manager, P.J. Hernon, who pointed out how well qualified McQuaid was to lead the people, especially youth, and assured him of the effective cooperation of all citizens in regard to their moral and material advancement.[2]

Replying in Latin, Irish and English, McQuaid accepted the Corporation's promise to build harmonious relations between the Catholic Church and the civic authorities. 'It is one of our deepest sources of consolation that in the perils of our day, an increasing sense of danger has called forth, in every department of our social life, a more earnest desire for the rational and disciplined unity that is the mark of the Christian State,' he declared in his first policy statement as Archbishop. Pledging to work with the City Fathers to bring about a reign of peace and sinlessness, of piety and discipline among the clergy and the people, he applauded the Christian spirit of their civic rule and urged them to make Dublin's housing needs their first priority.

> More especially, I should like to commend your earnestness
> in providing houses for the poor, despite the claims upon
> you of many other schemes of necessary and public utility.
> Such an achievement deserves great praise from a Bishop
> inasmuch as it tends to promote the good of that natural and
> essential unity of society: the Christian family.[3]

Although this plea received wide publicity, McQuaid was still fret-
ting over the non-arrival of the Papal Bulls confirming his appointment.
The Nuncio, Archbishop Robinson, assured him that the Holy See had
issued a dispensation, giving him formal possession and jurisdiction of the
Archdiocese.[4] 'This prompt official action of His Holiness will be most
helpful and gratifying to Your Grace,' wrote Bishop Collier from Kilkenny.
'Through it many difficulties will vanish, and the government of the Archdiocese will proceed with authority and power. You will find your position
made easy in every way, with loyal and undivided allegiance. All young
bishops are afraid of the future, and we are inclined to anticipate troubles
that never come as heavily as we feared. And while Dublin must always
have its special heavy responsibilities, I think you will be happily surprised later on to find ruling so comparatively easy'.[5]

Guided by Robinson, McQuaid reached a 'happy' understanding
with Bishop Wall, who consented to be auxiliary once more, and accepted
the suggestion of becoming an assistant at the Pontifical Throne. This
arrangement allowed him stay on as parish priest in the prestigious parish
of Haddington Rd.[6]

With Wall's loyalty assured, McQuaid quickly asserted his authority
over the 373 secular priests and 423 members of Religious Orders under
his sway. 'I came away for a week's rest on Tuesday night, having made 46
changes of parish priests, curates and chaplains – a very vigorous beginning!' he wrote to de Valera from Rockwell on January 25. 'It may seem as
if I took to the woods after having done the damage.'[7] The groundwork
was laid for McQuaid's introduction of a strict disciplinary code governing
the lifestyle of his priests. No longer would priests buy cars, leave the diocese, renovate or expand their parochial houses, or publish articles in
newspapers or periodicals without his approval.[8]

A key section of the clergy, led by the triumvirate of Fathers
Condon, Carton and Boylan, rallied to the new man and became his
trusted advisers. Boylan was also one of McQuaid's Council, which
included his two other Vicars General, Monsignor Walsh of Glasthule and
Monsignor Cronin of Rathgar.[9]

Instilling Obedience

In his first Pastoral Letter, issued on February 22, 1941, McQuaid wrote
that prayer, especially the nightly Rosary, was the distinguishing mark of a

Catholic home. Parents, he said, must regard their children as souls to be prepared for carrying the Cross of Christ. 'It will be impossible to train youth to the maturity of Christian virtue,' he said, 'unless from infancy the habit of obedience has become, so to speak, an instinct.'[10]

Parents and schools also needed to be more vigilant in making the young virtuous and in preventing them from lapsing from the faith. He urged girls' schools to inculcate in their pupils a Christian reverence for the divine vocation of motherhood to which most of them would be called. Rebuking those of social position and higher education for giving scandal to the poor, he warned that 'the law of God which commands modesty in dress, temperance in drink, chastity of conduct and avoidance of all that is dangerous to Faith, has the same binding force in all stations of life, whether lowly or exalted.'

McQuaid called on the Government, public authorities, educationalists, charity and social workers 'to make it their first concern to appreciate the vast riches of the treasury of our Faith, with its divinely given remedies for all our social life.' Catholics, he said, were to accept in a spirit of obedience the censorship and food-rationing measures which 'the Supreme Civil Authority' found it necessary to ordain.

McQuaid's concerns rose above mere civics. 'No activity of life may be withdrawn from the guidance of the Faith and the control of Charity,' he wrote.

> **For a Catholic people the only Civics which may be lawfully taught or practised is that which, because it is deliberately based on the teachings of our Faith, is treated as an exercise in social life of supernatural virtues.**

The widespread yearning for social peace was proof of the need for social reform, he said, but whatever shape reform of the social structures might ultimately take, the only lasting basis for reconstruction could be the True Faith.

> **Hence any merely human approach to a solution, in the present or the future, for our social problems, especially in what concerns the entire life of the poor, the sick and the children may indeed bring a certain momentary relief: it must, however, fail in regard to that which alone is permanent and divine, the supernatural aspect of our people's life.**

Wartime measures

In an Emergency Ireland, fearful of invasion at any moment from either Churchillian Britain or Nazi Germany, McQuaid studied Episcopal plans for the evacuation of Catholic boys and girls from Dublin to Catholic homes in the countryside. He considered the use of convents as hospitals and anticipated a refugee problem.[11]

Of immediate concern to him was the regularisation of the status and role of Army Chaplains. Assisted by Bishop Thomas Keogh of Kildare, in whose diocese the Curragh Army Camp was situated, McQuaid drew up a document for circulation and signature by all the bishops. This entailed a Form of Delegation of Faculties from each bishop, conferring on the Head Chaplain the spiritual authority to hear the confessions of soldiers and to absolve their sins, as well as other spiritual functions. In turn, the Head Chaplain was given the power to sub-delegate these faculties to other Army Chaplains. The document also provided for the wearing of Army uniforms by the chaplains. Each bishop was to arrange for a further supply of chaplains.[12]

'You have made the matter very simple for the Bishops so that there should not be too much delay in replying,' the Episcopal secretary, Bishop Jeremiah Kinane, informed McQuaid ahead of the March meeting of the Bishops at Maynooth.[13] Typical of the positive response was that of Bishop James Roche of Cloyne, who felt it 'quite in order' that the chaplains should wear a uniform.[14] Reflecting the national anxiety that Eire would be sucked into the War, Bishop William MacNeely of Raphoe, writing to McQuaid from Letterkenny in County Donegal, close to British bases across the Border in Derry, hoped that 'the people's worst fears' would not be realised. 'Your Grace and the Bishop of Kildare are managing Army affairs in a manner worthy of the crisis.'[15]

McQuaid's friendship with de Valera and Joe Walshe, the Secretary of the Department of External Affairs gave the Archbishop unprecedented access to the workings of Government.[16] He consulted the Department of Finance regularly on currency rules and the current rate of sterling with the lira. He himself was courted for advice and briefed on confidential developments. Opposition politicians were eager to find favour with him – the Labour Party leader, William Norton, was just one who let McQuaid know how much he upheld Catholic values. He sent McQuaid a copy of correspondence he had had with a Mrs M.J. Cullen, who had complained about candle-shrines in Catholic Churches. 'I can scarcely imagine that there is a single Catholic in this country who, notwithstanding his poverty, would not willingly sacrifice all he possesses in order that lighted Shrines might bear testimony to the unquenchable faith of our people,' Norton had replied to her. 'But that is a form of faith which some people, still enjoying residence in this country, do not appear to be able to fully comprehend. I fear that your letter indicates that you are in the latter category.'

'These times call forth all kinds of queer complaints,' McQuaid noted dryly.[17]

Catholic Social Service Conference

Since his first day as Archbishop, McQuaid had more serious complaints occupying his mind. He had wanted to tackle the problems of Irish emigrants by establishing a Catholic social-welfare organisation, but after consulting friends and experts his focus shifted to the city's poor, whose conditions were rapidly worsening as a result of food scarcities and rising prices, a situation aggravated by the severe winter. McQuaid decided to amalgamate the existing diocesan charities into a single body in order to establish a structure to deal with the problem. He hoped this would maximise the effectiveness of the social, educational and medical services at the Catholic Church's disposal.[18]

Early in the new year, McQuaid invited some 40 Catholic organisations to a meeting in the Mansion House. McQuaid himself did not attend, but his ideas were presented to the gathering by the secretary of the St John Bosco Society, Owen Cowley, whom he had briefed in detail. This somewhat chaotic meeting, which General Seán MacEoin had to call to order, was not open to the press.[19] Despite the disorder in the hall and the rivalries among the organisations present, the meeting led to the formation of a provisional body to draw up proposals to alleviate poverty in the city. Its members included a number of prominent Catholic activists, including Frank Duff of the Legion of Mary, Fr John Hayes of Muintir na Tíre, Fr Edward Coyne S.J. of Milltown Park, Fr John Ryan S.J. of UCD, Frank O'Reilly of the Catholic Truth Society, John T. Lennon of the St Vincent de Paul Society, A.J. O'Connell of the CYMSA, Brian MacCaffrey of *An Ríoghacht* and Patrick Reynolds of *Regnum Christi*.

The roll-call, however, was dominated by the Knights of St Columbanus, among them the Deputy Supreme Knight, Dr J. Stafford Johnson, the Provincial Chaplain, Fr Daniel Delany, the Supreme Advocate, W.G. Fallon, the Supreme Warden, Michael Kelly, former Grand Master Dr M.S. Walsh, and Grand Knight Kevin J. Kenny. Others such as the Treasurer of the INTO, M.P. Linehan, Labour Party T.D. William Davin, Fine Gael T.D. Seán MacEoin, and the Dean of UCD, Fr M. O'Halloran were members of the Knights. Key businessmen such as the chairman of the Dublin Ports & Docks Board, Percy McGrath, the Secretary of the Motor Traders' Association, Frank J. Lemass and T.J. Gallagher of the Electrical Traders' Association were card-carrying Knights, as were the Director of the Dublin Branch of the Irish Red Cross Society, David M. O'Kelly, the past president of *An Ríoghacht*, Brendan J. Senior. Significantly, too, Michael L. Burke of Dublin Corporation's Housing Department and W.A. Geraghty of the ESB belonged to the Knights.

Their dominance was consolidated by the election of the Secretary of the St John Bosco Society, Owen Cowley, who was secretly the Supreme Chancellor of the Knights, as chairman of the new body.

Cowley's right-hand man and secretary was Eugene Kavanagh, who doubled as the Supreme Secretary of the Knights. The Knights formed the conference's backroom as well as its backbone.[20]

In mid-March the planning group met for two days at the headquarters of the Knights in Ely Place, and set about exploring solutions to the crisis developing in Dublin and elsewhere – there was general agreement that if the war went on, the existing shortage of food and fuel would become critical. It was proposed that unemployed men should be channelled into new food and fuel production schemes while retaining their unemployment benefit as part payment of their wages. It was also proposed that the State should act as guarantor of bank loans to farmers and producers for the purchase of machinery, manure and seed.

A voluntary evacuation scheme to suitable rural parishes was proposed in which it was envisaged that country parishes would adopt unemployed Dublin families and provide them with a house and employment. The conference also adopted a controversial plan to have single unemployed men who had lived in Dublin for less than five years return to the countryside to work on the food and fuel schemes. Most ambitiously of all, the conference proposed setting up five large communal food and fuel distributing centres in Dublin, which would cater for about 500 families in each district.

While he prepared the conference report, Cowley was in constant touch with McQuaid, who refined and edited the proposals. The finished document was put to the provisional committee on April 15, 1941, and two days later the Catholic Social Service Conference (CSSC) was formally inaugurated under McQuaid's patronage. Its four main aims were defined as: supplementing and supporting the State during the Emergency; providing means of employment and supplying the needs of those who were in distress; channelling public effort and goodwill into a single agency; and mobilising all available resources for the common good.[21]

The presidents of 30 diocesan organisations made up the CSSC's membership, and there were nine sub-committees to oversee the different areas of its operation. Pooling what McQuaid called 'the counsel and energy' of the city's Catholic bodies, under his direction the new superentity was to supervise the activities of its constituent organisations and other voluntary agencies. On the suggestion of the War Relief Agency in Liverpool, McQuaid also gave the CSSC permission to recruit qualified specialists to give professional advice; many came from Dublin Corporation and Government departments. Executive committees were set up to deal with the five key areas of food, fuel, clothing, housing and unemployment, and provision was also made for publicity, fund-raising and 'unobtrusive surveillance' of poverty blackspots.

Despite the successful launch of the Conference, McQuaid was preoccupied with how to maintain control over the organisation and its finances. He sought the advice of Monsignor Cronin, who warned him against allowing the proposed central secretariat to develop into a lay or mixed lay-clerical body, a futile and dangerous experiment that had previously been suggested by the Catholic Young Men's Society. Cronin also advised that the Conference should be diocesan rather than national in scope so that McQuaid could take charge of it more effectively, and he proposed that the large sums of money being handled by the Conference should be managed by three treasurers, one of them a priest, and that the signature of all three should appear on every cheque.[22]

McQuaid's organisational skills were tested when Belfast was devastated by German air-raids in mid-April and evacuees brought south to Dublin came under his pastoral care.[23] When they arrived at Amiens St station, many were brought by the Irish Red Cross Society and the St John Ambulance Brigade to emergency accommodation in Mespil Rd, while McQuaid helped to organise an Episcopal appeal urging Catholics to contribute financially towards the care of the evacuees, and to 'ask the Almighty to save our own country from the horrors of war'[24]

In May the Secretary at External Affairs, Joe Walshe, asked McQuaid's opinion of the public's 'devotional strength' in favour of preserving peace. McQuaid assured him that since the country's neutrality had been threatened, attendance at daily Mass and visits to the Blessed Sacrament had multiplied greatly. The previous Sunday, a day of special atonement to keep Ireland safe from the scourge of war, the piety across the social classes was comparable to the devotional fervour at the Eucharistic Congress in 1932. 'The desire of our people to be preserved from the present conflict is shown to be extraordinary intense, by reason of the uninterrupted recourse to God that is evident in all our Churches, in city and suburbs and country.' [25]

On May 30 the horror of warfare hit Dublin when German bombers, mistaking the city for Belfast, dropped landmines on the North Strand, killing 34 persons and injuring 90, and leaving 2,500 persons homeless. In clerical frock-suit and top hat, McQuaid visited the scene of the disaster to console victims, the television cameras for international newsreel concentrated on the diffident young prelate rather than the boisterous but diminutive Minister for Health, Séan T O'Kelly. A few days later he sent the President of the Red Cross Society, Mr Justice Conor Maguire, a £500 (£12,500 in present-day terms) cheque for the victims.[26] The bomb devastation dramatically increased the demand for meals at CSSC centres.

Teaching the VEC a lesson

In June when McQuaid accompanied the Minister for Education, Thomas Derrig, at the opening of St Mary's College, Cathal Brugha St, he welcomed the teaching of domestic economy in the school curriculum as 'a great thing for the national well-being that would shake the foundations of society.' He looked forward to the day when schools would advertise 'the multitude of girls whom they shall have trained, first, to help their mothers at home, and later, to build for themselves a happy home.' Congratulating Derrig and Dublin City Vocational Educational Committee (VEC) for putting an emphasis on homecrafts as an essential element of women's education, McQuaid noted approvingly that St Mary's was attached to a hostel run by the Sisters of Charity of St Vincent de Paul, and that the college had been named after 'the Supreme Home-maker and Protectress of Catholic homes'.[27]

Behind the scenes, McQuaid was putting pressure on Derrig to remove the Dublin VEC's ban on nuns teaching domestic economy. The ban had been brought to his attention in April by the Superior General of the Sisters of Charity, Mother M. Bernard Carew, after the education committee refused to sanction the appointment of a Sister to teach domestic economy in a school for girls in Crumlin.[28] On hearing of this McQuaid immediately called for all the correspondence in the case.

On May 8 the chief executive officer of the vocational committee, L.E. O'Carroll, wrote to Sister Josephine Dodd, Mother Superior of the convent in Crumlin, informing her that because the school was now within the City boundary, it was entitled to six hours of domestic economy tuition weekly, though the requisite material and equipment had to be provided by the convent. When the vocational committee's head of domestic economy, Miss O'Sullivan, came to inspect the school, she was impressed by the equipment available but surprised to learn that a nun would be in charge of the classes. On foot of Miss O'Sullivan's report, O'Carroll wrote to Sister Josephine on June 20 repeating the offer of a domestic science instructress from the committee's own staff, but insisting that the VEC was 'not prepared to assume control or remunerate an instructress on any other lines'.[29]

After private consultations with McQuaid's office, Sister J. Patricia, another of the Crumlin nuns, called on O'Carroll on July 1 and asked him why the committee refused to sanction the appointment of a nun. In her report to Fr Patrick Dunne, Sister Patricia wrote that O'Carroll said that the committee wished to keep these classes entirely under the control of their own executive. 'If a nun were appointed, Mr O'Carroll seems to think that they would lose the control which is their right,' she continued. 'I fail to see that they would. Mr O'Carroll does not think it quite fair to the ratepayers that their money should go to pay a nun. Not a very reasonable statement!'[30]

McQuaid immediately sent Derrig a copy of O'Carroll's letter of June 20 in which the chief executive had set out the principle that he would not appoint nuns in an area controlled by the VEC. 'The implications of this principle, in regard to the status of Religious, both men and women, in the whole area of Catholic schools, are so grave,' McQuaid told Derrig, 'that I shall be grateful if I could be furnished with a statement of the reasons by which it is attempted on the part of the Vocational Education Committee for the City of Dublin to justify the existence of this principle or the introduction of the principle.'[31]

McQuaid's letter hit the Department of Education with precise force. Derrig responded next day, saying that he was inquiring into the matter and would communicate again as soon as possible. The Secretary of the Department, Joseph O'Neill, travelled to the Archbishop's residence to discuss the matter at a meeting on July 24. He left the Archbishop in no doubt as to where he stood on the matter.

O'Neill attributed the committee's 'liberal' attitude to a Mr Ingram, an otherwise excellent Catholic who believed that the committee should keep control of technical and vocational schools. 'There is evidence in Cormac Breathnach [another committee member] of anti-clerical feeling and L.E. O'Carroll is evasive,' McQuaid recorded in a note of his conversation with O'Neill.

'The Sec. means to keep at it till the answer is given,' McQuaid continued. 'He admitted that there was no answer to my letter except the revelation of a policy which is untenable and wrong. He admitted with pleasure that my bringing the case to the level of 'principle' as distinct from 'particular case' makes the Committee incapable of defending itself.'[32]

O'Neill's assessment proved accurate. Following representations from Derrig, O'Carroll sent a VEC sub-committee, including Cormac Breathnach T.D., to Crumlin for discussions with Sister Josephine. They recommended 'That financial assistance towards the classes be made by the Committee to cover general expenses including maintenance of equipment, provision of fuel, lighting materials, & by payment of a sum equivalent to the cost of the teaching instruction to be given by a fully qualified Sister of the Community ... It was further agreed that if the need should arise for the services of an additional teacher, a lay teacher would be appointed by the Committee.'

The recommendation was adopted and approved by the VEC at a special meeting on September 11. Writing from the Technical Institute at Bolton Street to a Department of Education official, O'Carroll said that the recommendation would be put into operation as soon as he received Derrig's approval. 'I trust that this solution will be acceptable to the Minister and to His Grace the Archbishop of Dublin.'[33]

Derrig wrote to McQuaid saying that his representations had produced the outcome outlined by O'Carroll, whose letter he attached. 'I assume from the terms of the letter that the arrangement is satisfactory to the Sisters of Charity,' Derrig wrote. He himself was quite satisfied with the outcome. 'I should like to take this opportunity to thank Your Grace most heartily for the deep interest you have shown in Vocational

Education and for the extremely helpful arrangements you have been so good as to make for the provision of religious instruction in the schools,' Derrig concluded. 'I feel that as a result of these provisions there is bound to be most valuable progress not only in religious knowledge but in the growth of a sense of civic duty and responsibility at a very critical period in the lives of the pupils.'[34]

Thanking Derrig[35] for his kind remarks, McQuaid assured the minister that 'For Crumlin, there need never be any difficulty and may I say that I wrote straight to you instead of to Mr O'Carroll, because I knew that any implications that had already been created could thus be gently smoothed away.'[36]

'Divine charity'

Instances of 'praiseworthy collaboration' between Church and State multiplied under McQuaid's vigorous direction. He was a master at harnessing State resources to social and educational initiatives which were run by clergy or lay Catholic organisations. He was particularly adept at persuading the State authorities to finance Church involvement in the voluntary sector, while retaining ecclesiastical control of projects. State funds flowed into 'divine charity'.[37]

McQuaid used his power to direct nuns and laity into specific State-aided projects, such as the opening by the Loreto Order of secondary and kindergarten schools in the fashionable Dublin suburb of Foxrock.[38] He persuaded the Legion of Mary to start a club for deaf-mute girls, and appointed two chaplains to attend to their spiritual needs in St Mary's, Cabra.[39] At his prompting the Sisters of Charity took over the St Patrick's Guild, founded in 1910 by Miss M.J. Cruice, and ran St Patrick's Infant Hospital, Temple Hill, Blackrock.[40] A home for delinquent girls in St Anne's, Kilmacud, run by the Sisters of Our Lady of Charity of Refuge, was inspired by McQuaid.[41] At his instigation the Little Sisters of the Poor, based in the working-class Kilmainham district, purchased Roebuck Castle in Clonskeagh for £16,100 in September 1943 and converted it into a home for the aged poor.[42] A home for the care of 'adult female mental defectives' under the Sisters of Charity was opened in Clonsilla with his encouragement.[43] Particularly novel were schools for girls on probation which were opened at McQuaid's direction by the Sisters of Charity in Gardiner Street and Harold's Cross.

The extent of this Church-State collaboration was acknowledged in the Dáil by the Minister for Justice, Gerald Boland, when he said that it was only with McQuaid's assistance that the Government was able to initiate a scheme for juvenile delinquents in which voluntary workers assisted probation officers at two youth training centres.[44] As many as 46 Legion of Mary members were engaged in probation work. Boland's comments were echoed by Derrig, who thought McQuaid's work was 'of immeasurable benefit to the State as well to the Church.'[45]

The Parliamentary Secretary for Health, Dr Conor Ward, discreetly called on McQuaid to tell him of a request from the Master of the Rotunda Hospital for increased pre-natal work by the St John's Ambulance Brigade. Both hospital and brigade were Protestant bodies, and 'Dr W. wished the Catholic Society to get both credit and probable money-grant for such services, as Cath. approach to problem is very much more necessary and desirable,' McQuaid noted after their meeting. Next day Ward was furnished with a memorandum from McQuaid on the pre-natal and post-natal care undertaken by his Conference.[46] Under P.J. Hernon, Dublin Corporation's planning department provided McQuaid with advance information on the availability of land in the city, as in the case of the developing Cabra area where McQuaid chose sites for a church and a school 'according to the plans of the Corporation maps'.[47] Combined with the information received from the Department of Education about future school developments, McQuaid acquired the best sites to build churches and schools in the new towns around the city. One of his earliest land transactions was the negotiation of a 99-year lease in Dublin's North Strand at a rent of £12 6d,[48] while early developments included the £70,000 (£1.75 million) Church of Corpus Christi in Griffith Avenue, the Church of the Most Precious Blood in West Cabra, a new Irish granite extension to the Church of St Agnes in Crumlin, and the Church of St Bernadette at Clogher Road, Crumlin. A new national school at Drimnagh was declared to be one of the most advanced in Europe.[49]

While the danger of being dragged into the war receded following Hitler's decision in June 1941 to turn his armies east to the Soviet Union, the Social Service Conference grew at a phenomenal pace throughout Dublin. Some 23 food centres, in which nuns cooperated with women and girls as paid helpers, operated in convents and other buildings which the Corporation made available free of charge. Farmers, creameries, grocers and butchers all helped to provide food. A free booklet on diet and health was distributed.[50]

McQuaid became legendary for his personal charitable donations. He gave £100 (£2,500) to the Duke of Gloucester's Red Cross and St John's Fund through the British representative, Sir John Maffey. The overseas committee chairman, Lord Huntingfield, on the Duke's direction, expressed appreciation of the Archbishop's 'liberality' which was to be used 'to provide for the manifold needs of His Majesty, King George VI's Forces serving abroad and the civilian population which has suffered untold hardship and distress as a result of aerial warfare.'[51]

McQuaid combined generosity towards Empire royalism with assistance to Irish republicanism, subscribing £50 (£1,250) to the Green Cross Fund, a charity formed by republicans to alleviate distress among the dependents of prisoners and internees in the North of Ireland. As the biggest donor in the Free State, McQuaid's name at the head of the list of subscribers was publicised by the Fund organisers. However, when Gerald Boland, the Minister for Justice refused to allow the Green Cross to broadcast an appeal on Radio Éireann, McQuaid made no public fuss over the ban.[52]

McQuaid regularly gave money to the poet Patrick Kavanagh, whom he had met in 1940 when he visited Blackrock College. Kavanagh told McQuaid that he would never have accepted money from him had he not believed that it was a prelude to a job. He would have gone long ago to England, he said, but was glad to have stayed in Ireland, and he felt there must have been a special grace attached to McQuaid's money to make him stay.[53]

Other beneficiaries were Donal O'Donovan and his brother, who were educated at Blackrock College from 1942 to 1946 but 'were never made to feel any different from the others,' except that Donal was told to complete his Leaving Certificate course in one year and was denied the privileges associated with residence in the Castle.[54]

As the winter of 1942 approached McQuaid turned his attention to raising funds for the CSSC, whose operations were rapidly spreading across the city. In September 1941 he organised a special church collection 'to see to it that no good child would go unclothed, no sick, especially no aged, person would be left untended, especially as every person who mutely called for aid was none other than Christ Himself.'[55] The appeal raised £15,000, (£375,000) with an additional £5,000 (£125,000) coming from raffles and personal donations.

Confronted with such a super-agency, it would appear that both de Valera's Government and Dublin Corporation abandoned plans to become more directly interventionist in the social sphere and confined themselves to the role of supplementing the Archbishop's efforts. No other Catholic diocese had developed such a structure. Not surprisingly, McQuaid's innovation was praised by the Hierarchy at its autumn meeting.[56]

Cardinal Hinsley hits out

Unlike some other Irish bishops who fell foul of the Government censors during the Emergency, McQuaid was staunch in his support of the 'Supreme Civil Authority'. He made no specific condemnation of Nazism or Bolshevism. He even stayed silent about censorship by the Irish State of Vatican Radio broadcasts on the persecution of the Catholic Church in Poland and Germany, even though a Polish visitor, Count Balinski, found him to be 'well acquainted with the facts of religious persecution carried out by the Germans and the Russians'.[57]

McQuaid's silence contrasted with the outspokenness of the Arch-bishop of Westminster, Cardinal Arthur Hinsley, whose statements were regularly censored in the Irish State. Hinsley regarded himself as defending religion against Nazism, Communism and Fascism. The secretary of the Department of Justice, Tommy Coyne, however, thought his pronounce-ments were 'pure jingo' and described him as 'the most tactless member of the Sacred College, constantly identifying English interests throughout the world with the success of the British cause.'[58] The Minister for Defence, Frank Aiken, supported the ban on Hinsley and defended it in the Senate.

The Cardinal turned to McQuaid for an explanation. 'I am put down as a propagandist and as one paid by the British Government to say things,' Hinsley wrote. 'Personally I do not care a straw for what those who place politics before their religion say against me. I shall continue to defend religion, and to despise such a calumny.'

Hinsley asked McQuaid if there was a campaign against him. 'Am I blacklisted in Éire because I have spent money – my own and that of charitable persons zealous for the salvation of souls and the good name of Catholic Ireland – in an endeavour to prevent the scandal of Irish girls and Irishmen who have left their unwanted babies to be maintained by us?' he asked. 'Mr de Valera and Cardinal MacRory and the Bishops of Ireland know the facts: the problem is of many years standing. If you want further information ask the Legion of Mary over here, or the head of our Crusade of Rescue.'

And he wondered if he had been 'blackened and calumniated because I have all my life spoken and acted on behalf of a free united Ire-land? For this attitude I have been represented by the ultra-English as out-Irishing the Irish. If I love England as the country in which I was born and educated, I have had a great love for Ireland as the one-time home of my mother and as a Catholic land which has suffered for the Faith ...' Hinsley vowed to defend religion against totalitarianism, by whatever manner it was designated, and trusted McQuaid would pardon his frank letter.

Hinsley raised questions as to whether Papal Encyclicals and let-ters of German bishops were also censored in the Irish State:

> There are some other pertinent questions: does Éire censor or ban *Mit Brennender Sorge*? Or the words of Pius XII about the awful persecution and martyrdom of Poland? Or the broadcasts of the Vatican Radio regarding the pagan and anti-Christian character of Nazism? Is it unlawful to denounce totalitarianism in Ireland?

> Are the strong utterances of the German and Bavarian Hierarchy – by Cardinal Faulhaber and Bishop Von Preysing – banned in Éire? Is the book, *The Persecution of the Catholic Church in the Third Reich* forbidden by the

Censor in Éire? Is Éire under the sway of Berlin and
Moscow?

The Nazi inspired attack on the Archbishop of Westminster shall not quench the devotion I entertain for the Archbishop of Dublin and for my fellow Catholics in the land of
my mother.[59]

Hinsley's questions raise issues which need further exploration by
historians of Emergency Ireland.

The Palace

In October 1941, ten months after his Consecration, McQuaid completed
the renovation of Archbishop's House, which had been run down badly
since Archbishop Walsh's time and was damp and musty. So splendid was
the renovation that Bishop Collier described it as his 'new' house.[60] Dubliners later simply called it 'the Palace'. The renovation was accompanied
by a staff reshuffle which saw Fr O'Donnell, who had been closely identified with Byrne, being transferred from the secretariat to parish duties.
Fathers Patrick Dunne and Dick Glennon remained in key positions at
Drumcondra, while a recently ordained priest, Fr Chris Mangan, was
appointed secretary, which meant living at Archbishop's House.

Although the financial situation inherited by McQuaid has not yet
been published, it would appear to have been in healthy balance, enough
to enable him to be one of Dublin's élite owners of a de luxe Dodge.[61] In
addition to his refurbishment of Archbishop's House, he set about
improving conditions in the diocesan seminary of Holy Cross in the
adjoining Clonliffe grounds, and invited the Sisters of St Vincent de Paul
to look after the kitchens and infirmary for the 99 students there. The
Red House, formerly Clonliffe House, was designated by McQuaid as the
Sisters' convent, but it needed extensive repair and the cost of renovation
came to almost £4,000. (£100,000). He also built a new sacristy in the
Clonliffe College chapel at a cost of £3,600 (£90,000).[62]

Whenever possible, McQuaid spent time either at Rockwell as the
guest of Fr Dinan or at a bungalow in Delgany, Co. Wicklow, which he had
inherited from his predecessor. He liked to put a distance between his
working and leisure environments, as he had done in his Blackrock College
days.[63] In turn, he brought the atmosphere of a busy headmaster's room to
'the Palace'. His hours at home were advertised as being from 11am to 2pm
on all week days except Saturdays, and he responded swiftly to requests for
appointments from clergy and others. His Vicars General, like assistant
headmasters, could be contacted five days a week at Westland Row.[64]

'After supper at night, six nights a week, he would go out visiting
hospitals,' his secretary, Fr Mangan, recalled in an interview.

When he came back in he would sit down at his desk and start writing letters. His study was his sitting-room, and he would send you down to the post at 11.00pm with a bundle of letters which you had to copy. He wouldn't use a dictaphone although we tried to get him to use one. He would write letters by hand, both business and personal ones, and he wrote at terrible speed.

With some he would give you the gist of the letter and tell you to do it and sign it yourself. Sometimes he would have a number of queries to answer. When answered, he would sit down and keep you chatting for an hour. You would go out and within about half an hour he would have about half a dozen letters in to you.[65]

McQuaid needed to work efficiently to deal with the enormous amount of paperwork that passed between Drumcondra and the Vatican. 'Papers pour in from the Curia,' wrote the former Rector of the Irish College in Rome, Monsignor Michael Curran, who advised him on protocol and procedure.[66] McQuaid kept archival copies of Papal briefs, rescripts (legal judgments), *moduli* (forms), to be filled and returned to the Roman congregations on subjects ranging from parochial loans to the granting of relics, benefices or favours to Religious Orders. When the chaplain of St Joseph's Blind Asylum in Drumcondra wanted to bless candles, ashes and palms at Holy Week functions, McQuaid had to apply to Rome for permission on his behalf. With such an administrative workload, he could fall behind, as when he was reminded by the Nuncio to provide the annual returns of diocesan matrimonial cases.[67]

On December 7 Japan attacked the United State's airbase at Pearl Harbor, bringing Roosevelt's America into the war.[68] Finding it increasingly difficult to secure fuel supplies, the Government empowered the Minister for Supplies, Seán Lemass, to regulate school and college hours under the Emergency Powers Act. Immediately after the cabinet meeting on December 19, Derrig informed McQuaid that from January 1, 1942, schools would not open before 10am and would close at 5.30pm. 'I understand at once its necessity and its reasonableness,'McQuaid replied. 'With gratitude for informing me.'[69]

The escalation of the war persuaded McQuaid to recall his students from the Irish College in Rome. He sought the assistance of the British Representative, Sir John Maffey, and Bishop David Mathew in London,[70] and when it proved impossible or inopportune for the British to assist him he relied on the Department of External Affairs and the Irish Shipping Company to have his six students brought over in small Irish cargo boats, the last arriving in early February, 1942.[71]

Wartime restrictions on trade meant that living conditions grew steadily worse in the poorer parts of Dublin, and demands on the CSSC stretched the organisation to the limit. Through the winter, it served over seven million meals at its food centres, and though the destitute were never refused nourishing food, to avoid the stigma of pauperisation a penny was charged for the main course. Hot food was also supplied in containers and distributed to families in their homes. When the Dublin City Fathers met McQuaid for tea at the presbytery in the Pro-Cathedral in April 1942, the Mayor, Alderman Peadar Doyle T.D., paid tribute to McQuaid's 'unfailing generosity and paternal vigilance' towards the poor.[72]

The operation of his CSSC had spread through layer after layer of city life. Creameries donated milk, butchers gave bones and oxtails, and the farmers of Dublin, Wicklow and Kildare gave sacks of potatoes. Eighty-four clothing guilds produced baby clothes, First Communion and Confirmation outfits. The CSSC distributed 500 blankets and warm garments to the elderly and bedclothes to pregnant women. Women in wealthy parishes and former convent schoolgirls were encouraged to help clothe the poor.

Five dilapidated buildings were purchased by the housing committee and within two years were transformed into 40 three-roomed flats, mainly for newly married couples, while a building society run by the Conference converted houses into flats which were let at a low rent. Pre-natal and post-natal clinics addressed Dublin's chronic infant mortality rate. The junior doctors of St Vincent's Hospital offered their services free.

With coal stocks scarce, the Conference's fuel committee, whose membership included officials of the Turf Board and the Department of Agriculture, purchased 8,000 tonnes of turf and transported it to the city, where Dublin Distilleries provided free storage space in their depots and the army stockpiled it in the Phoenix Park. The fuel was distributed to the poor in parishes close to the depots, and the St Vincent de Paul supplied 1,000 tons to primary schools and orphanages.

Only 2.5% of the CSSC's £20,000 (£500,000) budget was spent on administration.[73] The Conference, according to Professor Patrick Corish, 'transformed the quality of welfare work that still had too much degradation of the Poor Law System attached to it.'[74]

Reporting to Maynooth

The Hierarchy meeting at Maynooth on June 23, 1942, was a personal triumph for McQuaid and confirmed his credentials as its dominant member only 18 months after his Consecration as Archbishop.

His reputation as an educationalist was sealed when the bishops approved his report on religious instruction in the vocational sector, where he had won major advances for Catholic educational interests. McQuaid informed his Episcopal colleagues that he had established a new system of instruction by priest-teachers in all the technical and vocational schools of the Dublin diocese. And though the admission of priests in fact altered the non-sectarian complexion of the 1931 Vocational Act, he had brought this about without recourse to parliamentary legislation. It was an enormous step forward in his drive to Catholicise the whole education system.[75]

When it adopted McQuaid's scheme, the Hierarchy also rescinded its resolution of June 1931 which forbade payment for priests who gave religious instruction in vocational schools. As a result, McQuaid's initiative also gained the Church a massive long-term injection of cash from the Department of Education.

McQuaid also told the meeting that he was preparing a booklet on Catholic citizenship, and in his note on how Catholic civics should be taught, he recommended that every pupil should have a copy of the Constitution. This, however, was considered to be a dangerous idea by Bishop Collier, who feared that it would injure the programme by provoking controversy and opposition. 'The country is still much divided on the Constitution,' he wrote. 'It is looked on as a Party Instrument.'[76]

Not one to neglect practical details, McQuaid also informed the bishops that because of the ongoing fuel shortages there was no prospect of the dioceses' religious instruction inspectors receiving permission to use their motor cars; he had learned this from an authoritative source.[77] Nor on his recommendation did the bishops raise any objection to amending the rule which prevented a woman teacher from marrying the owner, part-owner or occupier of a public house.[78]

Next day, the Hierarchy gathered in the Pro-Cathedral, Dublin, to celebrate Pope Pius XII's Episcopal Jubilee, the 'Day of the Pope.' The celebration was a further personal triumph for McQuaid, who had taken on the task of organising a fitting commemoration for the Pope's anniversary.

Three months earlier, Bishop Jeremiah Kinane had informed him privately that the Nuncio was most disappointed that there was to be no central celebration in Dublin to mark the event.[79] The bishops had planned to organise spiritual ceremonies in each diocese, but this had not met Rome's expectations, and Cardinal Marchetti-Selvaggiani, head of the Curial body coordinating events, had made this clear to the Nuncio.[80]

McQuaid resolved to rescue matters, and on April 14 the bishops' standing committee meeting gave him the authority to arrange a Jubilee service in the Pro-Cathedral in association with the Nuncio. Already he had made March 12, the anniversary of the Coronation of Pope Pius XII,[81] and March 17, the feast day of St Patrick, diary events on which de Valera and his ministers, the diplomatic corps, the judiciary, the Dáil and the Seanad congregated in the Pro-Cathedral for a sung *Te Deum* and Solemn Benediction, over which McQuaid and the Nuncio presided. In the event, the Pope's Jubilee on June 24 was attended by the bishops, Government and the diplomatic corps, and enhanced by the grandeur of the Palestrina Choir under conductor Vincent O'Brien. 'The Foreign Representatives say they never saw the ceremonies so well carried out. Nor did they hear such beautiful church music before,' Joe Walshe told him.[82] McQuaid's reputation as a professional churchman was beginning to reach international levels.

Emigrant welfare

In June 1942, McQuaid also launched the Catholic Welfare Bureau, whose aim was to give advice to emigrants, especially women and girls, in England and elsewhere. Although emigration had risen dramatically during the Emergency no organisation had paid much attention to the spiritual or material well-being of the Irish flowing overseas. According to Columban priest Fr Timothy Connolly, this new initiative was to establish for McQuaid a reputation as the man who did more for the Irish in Britain than any other politician or churchman.[83]

McQuaid had laid the foundations for the project in 1941 when, with the help of the Secretary of the Department of External Affairs, Joe Walshe, and Britain's Sir John Maffey, he arranged for Irish priests to obtain work visas in England.[84] The success of the CSSC in the meantime meant that it could provide finance for the new bureau.

Initially, McQuaid assigned responsibility for running the bureau to the Legion of Mary. And though he secured the cooperation of the Irish and English hierarchies and Irish State authorities, he warned the Legionaries: 'You will have no State aid, no municipal grant. Your work must be altogether voluntary.' [85]

The Legion was entrusted with a dual spiritual-material mandate: to arrange for 'proper introductions' for emigrants in their adopted country, especially with a view to ensuring their continuing religious practice, and to provide for their social welfare in what were new and often difficult surroundings.[86] Legion of Mary members also gathered regularly at railway stations and shipping quays to try to persuade emigrants to stay at home.

As the Catholic Welfare Bureau's work grew more demanding, McQuaid encouraged the Knights of St Columbanus to become involved. They liaised with the Catenians and the Knights of St Columba in England and Scotland in regard to particular cases, and provided accommodation for returning emigrants at the Sisters of Mercy's hostel in Baggot Street.[87]

McQuaid personally took up some hardship cases in the Archdiocese of Birmingham. A social worker for the Birmingham diocese, Helen Murtagh, subsequently visited Dublin and, enthused by what she saw of the bureau there, she arranged with the British Home Office for the drawing up of a list of instructions on the repatriation of unmarried Irish mothers and their babies from all the major cities in Britain. As a result of that initiative, 'We ought not to have any more of the inhuman treatment to which some of them were subjected,' Archbishop Thomas Williams of Birmingham informed McQuaid.

Williams also told McQuaid that a lot more work was needed to ensure that the many Irish girls who went to England to do war work were properly billeted in decent homes. While some firms supplied the addresses of newly arrived Irish girls to the local parish priests, others did not, and it was to this latter group that Mrs Murtagh was looking for cooperation. 'My object all through is to try to get better relations between Irish and English Catholics,' Williams wrote.[88]

Williams had sent a Fr William O'Malley to act as chaplain to a large crowd of 'muscular Irishmen' who were working for a contractor in the Birmingham diocese. 'I took him off parish work,' Williams explained, 'and asked him to tackle a job which no one but a brave Irish priest could have tackled. The camp was a disgrace and a danger to the locality when he went there about Easter; it is now a model camp and it's all down to Fr O'Malley.'[89]

McQuaid developed a friendship with the Auxiliary Bishop of Birmingham, Bernard Griffin, the future Cardinal Archbishop of Westminster, which proved especially important in forging a closer relationship between the Irish and English Hierarchies. 'Your programme for Youth is marvellous and I know you will not object if we borrow some of the ideas,' Griffin told him, proposing joint meetings of the English, Scottish and Irish hierarchies after the war.[90] Meanwhile, he kept McQuaid informed of conditions in Birmingham, where thousands of Irishmen were working. He hoped to acquire the land to build a big concrete hut to house Irish women workers under the chaplaincy of Fr O'Malley. Mrs Murtagh had told him that McQuaid had trained workers: would he be able to send a lady to take the post of club leader?[91]

Youth mission

As part of his social action programme, McQuaid took a third major initiative with the establishment of a youth department within the CSSC to run youth training centres for 'difficult' boys who were in trouble with the law. With the support of the Department of Education, the Vocational Educational Committee, the Legion of Mary, the St Vincent de Paul Society and the St John Bosco Society, two centres were established. The building at Mount St was opened in September 1942 by the Minister for Education, Tom Derrig, in the presence of Taoiseach Éamon de Valera, the Leader of the Opposition, W.T. Cosgrave, Lord Mayor Doyle and members of Dublin Corporation. Blessing the centre, McQuaid praised the VEC for its 'immediate and generous collaboration' in providing for the religious and moral training of the boys. He described the Church-

State training programme as 'the beginning of an enterprise that must have far-reaching effects upon this city'.[92]

McQuaid also thanked the City Fathers for their cooperation in the vocational schools. 'The testimony given during the year by the principals concerning the advantages derived by their boys and girls from this essential training is already a reward to the civil authorities and a benefit to the city. To have set in the very first place of honour our bounden duty to God is an unfailing guarantee of the blessing of God upon our city.'

The following year, in June 1943, the Government appointed McQuaid as chairman of a national Commission on Youth Unemployment. Launching the initiative, the Minister for Supplies, Seán Lemass, remarked that other members were ready to serve because the new body was under the Archbishop's stewardship and they knew its report would command attention and action. McQuaid, too, had high expectations that the commission's proposals would benefit 'the welfare, natural and supernatural, of the youth of Éire'.[93] He now had access to the corridors of power, while the commission's secretary, Fr Timothy Counihan S.J., had an office in Government premises.

American pressure

Although he made no public statements on the matter, McQuaid appears to have shared the views of de Valera and Cardinal MacRory that President Roosevelt's decision to accept Britain's invitation to station American troops in Northern Ireland in January 1942 condoned the Partition of Ireland. Through Joe Walshe, McQuaid knew of the Government's distrust of America's ambassador to Ireland, David Gray,[94] while the elderly Cardinal had kept McQuaid informed of his correspondence with Gray on the moral iniquity of Partition.[95] Bishop Mathew, Auxiliary Bishop of Westminster, told McQuaid that anti-Irish feeling in Britain was stronger than at any other period in his lifetime because of the Free State's refusal to allow the British navy use Irish ports.[96]

In late January and early February 1943 McQuaid met the US Secretary of the Navy, Francis Matthews, who had been visiting American troops in Lough Foyle, Co. Derry. Matthews was the Supreme Knight of the Knights of St Columbus in America, and a devout man who was anxious to improve the services for Catholics serving in the American forces. Whatever his political views, McQuaid saw in Matthews a Catholic who could promote Catholic interests and he arranged with Bishop Collier to bring him to Sunday lunch, which was also attended by Bishops Staunton and Keogh.[97] In a letter to the Archbishop of Detroit, Edward Mooney, McQuaid wrote that he felt Matthews' visit had done something to strengthen the traditional friendship of Ireland and the United States.[98]

Irish-US relations were strained, however, as a result of the irish

State's neutral stance in the war. In March, the Archbishop of New York, Francis Spellman – a friend of McQuaid's from the Eucharistic Congress of 1932 – visited Dublin as a private envoy of President Roosevelt. Spellman was charged with the highly delicate mission of encouraging de Valera to join the Allies against the Axis powers, and looked to his fellow Archbishop for support in persuading the Taoiseach to abandon Ireland's neutrality. American military intelligence compiled a file on McQuaid for Spellman: he was described as having tremendous influence over Éamon de Valera and as being 'difficult'.[99]

McQuaid was invited by Ambassador Gray to a dinner in Spellman's honour attended by de Valera, Tánaiste Seán T. O'Kelly, Sir John Maffey, the Canadian High Representative, John Kearney, and the Secretary at the Papal Nunciature, Monsignor Domenico Enrici. In hawkish mood, Spellman said that Roosevelt would prosecute the war to a final and definite victory, but while McQuaid did not support his view, like de Valera he had no option but to raise his glass when Spellman proposed a toast 'To the President of the United States and the cause he serves.'[100]

Role of Religious

'Few acts of my administration since I became Archbishop have given me deeper satisfaction than this,' McQuaid wrote to Bishop Collier in August 1943 after approving the admission of the Sacred Heart of Mary nuns into the diocese. Collier had recommended them as 'a most excellent Sisterhood' that might be of help to the diocese 'in the big educational problems unfolding themselves through new parishes and schools'.[101] McQuaid informed Collier that the nuns' arrival was very apposite, coming just as he had consecrated his diocese to the Immaculate Heart of Mary, 'a fact which augurs very happily to the new foundation'.[102]

Despite their undoubted good works, the Sisters of the Sacred Heart of Mary and other Religious Orders had their darker underside.

Disturbed by allegations of fraudulent practices and financial corruption by the priests of Religious Orders, McQuaid launched a commission of inquiry into 'pious abuses' which reported to the Diocesan Council on July 13, 1943. New rules were introduced to govern the fund-raising activities of four Religious Orders. The Capuchins were instructed to abolish their penny-a-week collection and replace it with a monthly one, permission for which had to be renewed each year with McQuaid. The Franciscans, who had built up a considerable debt at their Merchant's Quay Church, were given permission to continue a special collection till the end of 1944. The Oblate Fathers (O.M.I.) were ordered to close a bureau in Dame St forthwith, though they were allowed to continue their system of collection till the end of 1943, after which they had to seek permission each year to continue. More significantly, when the commission asked for direction in regard to the Holy Ghost Student Missionary Burse, on McQuaid's suggestion it was unanimously agreed that the burse 'must cease to exist'.[103] McQuaid had settled a score with the Holy Ghost Provincial, Fr Dan Murphy, for Murphy's part in his removal from the presidency of Blackrock College in 1939.

Ireland's dominant Catholic teaching Order, the Christian Brothers, commemorated the centenary of the death of its founder, Edmund Ignatius Rice, in 1944. McQuaid acclaimed Rice, 'the Educator of Catholic Youth', as heir to the hedge schoolmasters linking Ireland to its ancient tradition of European culture. The Christian Brothers had 106 communities in Ireland and 159 in the United States, Canada, Australia and New Zealand. At a fundraiser in the Mansion House McQuaid donated £1,000 (£12,000 today) for a House of Formation to train prospective Brothers, while the Knights of St Columbanus raised £7,000 ((£175,000 today).[104]

The centenary celebrations took place as two senior Gardaí at Dublin's Fitzgibbon St station were prevented from pursuing allegations of abuse by two Christian Brothers of boys at Artane Industrial School. The Superior, the Rev Brother T.M. Lennane, and the school chaplain, Fr William Kenny, succeeded in hushing up a potential scandal with the assistance of McQuaid and Justice Minister Gerald Boland. In a climate of opinion hostile to prosecution of clergy, the two Gardaí were told not to proceed with the case.[105]

Worse even than the austere regime which applied in industrial schools such as Artane for boys and Goldenbridge for girls, were the conditions for 'fallen women' engaged in laundry and menial work in the four Magdalene penitentiaries in the archdiocese, at Donnybrook, Drumcondra, Dun Laoghaire and Lower Gloucester St. A particularly harrowing story was that of 14-year-old Martha, who was sent to Drumcondra in 1942 to repent for 'telling a shameful lie' – she had been indecently assaulted by a relative, but her aunts did not believe her.

Prostitutes were also sent to Drumcondra instead of prison. Martha was put to work in the laundry. It was hard labour – at 15 she had varicose veins from standing over sinks – and there was no recreation: just work, prayer, and atonement for her sins. If she committed a misdemeanour, she would have to kneel in front of a nun and kiss the floor. The nuns rejoiced in shaving girls' heads down to the scalp as a way of crushing their pride.[106]

Protection of Rome

In Europe the tide of war was turning, but now the security of Rome was threatened by the Allies' advance. In July 1943 American aircraft bombed 40 kilometres of railway line and two airports around Rome, killing over 100 civilians and injuring about 1,000. The Church of San Lorenzo was also badly damaged. A distraught Pius XII visited the scene of the devastation, distributed 60,000 lire at random and said the *De Profundis* for the dead. The Pope's grief moved McQuaid to send a telegram to Cardinal Maglione: 'The Archbishop of Dublin, prostrate at the feet of his Holiness, in his own name and in the name of the Clergy and Faithful of the city and diocese of Dublin, desires to express profound sympathy with the sufferings of the Holy Father and sorrow at the destruction of Sacred Monuments of our Faith in the See of the Vicar of Christ and the centre of the Catholic world, and begs to offer assurance of devoted loyalty and constant prayers.'[107] There was no condemnation by McQuaid of the loss of human life.

When McQuaid offered 8,000 Mass stipends to the Vatican, he was requested to deposit £2,000 (£50,000) to the credit of the Opere di Religione at its bank account in the Foreign Branch section of Barclay's Bank. McQuaid transmitted this sum to London through the Hibernian Bank in College Green.[108]

After a second bombing of Rome in August, McQuaid instructed the US embassy in Dublin to stop sending him its propaganda material, *The Letter from America*. 'We were amazed that Rome should have been bombed again,' he told Freddie Boland, Assistant Secretary in the Department of External Affairs. 'We cannot help feeling that the apparent indifference of the Governments concerned to the unanimous and clearly expressed sentiment of Catholics throughout the world is of particularly evil augury for the future.'[109]

That autumn, through the good offices of Joe Walshe, McQuaid received confidential diplomatic accounts of the measures being taken to protect the Irish in German-occupied Rome, and he was allowed to pass this privileged information on to the other bishops.[110] Deploring the fact that the Eternal City was being treated as a military objective, McQuaid called on Dubliners to pray daily for the 'Pope's safety and the preservation of Rome, the centre of the Catholic world.'[111]

There was more bombing following the Allied invasion of Italy in January 1944. On March 12, Pius XII pleaded from the balcony of St Peter's for a stop to the bombing. His words inspired de Valera to launch an appeal to the belligerents to prevent 'a major calamity for the human race' by sparing Rome, 'which for almost 2,000 years has been the seat of the sovereign authority of the Catholic Church and contains the great central temple of the Catholic religion and the great central seminaries and libraries of the Christian Faith.'[112]

In April Walshe canvassed a second Irish initiative, 'acting exclusively in our capacity as a Catholic State,' calling on Rome to be administered by a neutral commission, possibly involving Franco's Spain, after the German withdrawal in face of the American-led Allies. In the event, on June 5 the Allied troops entered Rome and the city escaped destruction. It was a miraculous hand-over that could never be explained, wrote the

Irish representative to the Holy See, Tom Kiernan. A week later Pius XII asked Kiernan to inform de Valera that he attributed the safety of Rome to his timely and persistent pressure.

VD clinic

Through the influence of his sister, Helen, who was specialising in the treatment of venereal diseases as Assistant Medical Officer at the Elizabeth Garrett Anderson Hospital in London,[113] McQuaid took an interest in the spread of such diseases as a result of what he considered was the breakdown of traditional morality during the war. When a sharp increase in the incidence of VD was reported in May 1944 by the Dublin City Medical Officer, McQuaid drew the attention of the management committee of Jervis Street Hospital to this 'grave menace'.

To the surprise of church and medical personnel, he requested the establishment of a first-class modern unit in Dublin for the treatment and cure of the disease. After the Jervis Street committee endorsed the proposal, McQuaid sent a cheque for £3,000 (£75,000) with the advice that a doctor should be selected for post-graduate training in the Stokes Institute of the University of Philadelphia.[114]

Despite initial opposition from the Sisters of Mercy, McQuaid arranged with them and the medical staff of the Mater Hospital and St Michael's Hospital, Dun Laoghaire, for similar clinics to be established in these hospitals. Dr Conor Ward, the Parliamentary Secretary for Health, sanctioned the proposals.[115]

'I know of some of the difficulties which you have had to overcome already,' the President of the Irish Medical Association, Dr John Stanley, wrote to McQuaid. 'It is about time, however, that our Catholic hospitals took their part in this fight. This is not the first occasion that you have placed the public and the medical profession under a deep debt of gratitude for Your Grace's great and wise helm in the struggle against disease. I need only mention tuberculosis and antenatal care.'[116] 'Not every Catholic doctor has expressed himself in your kind manner,' McQuaid told Stanley, 'but I have confidence that, under your guidance, many of your colleagues will ultimately appreciate the import of my direction and suggestions.'[117]

Such progressive medical work, combined with the expanding Catholic Social Service Conference and other thriving agencies of 'divine charity', cast McQuaid as the creator of 'a State within a State'. The criticism was dismissed by McQuaid, who thought it failed to grasp that 'we are but entering into our proper sphere: the care of our own poor, in the spirit of the Faith.'[118] By now, however, McQuaid's emerging power-base was coming into conflict with de Valera's commitment to a Catholic but not aggressively sectarian Ireland in which Protestants, Jews and the liberal intelligentsia could feel at home.

12

Hammering Dissent
1940–44

The chief means of expressing public opinion or criticisms
in Éire are being progressively tuned to a Gregorian mode.
Professor W.B. Stanford, The Bell, *1944.*

'Since his appointment Dr McQuaid has shown himself to be not merely austere but also narrow and intolerant,' a diplomat at the office of the United Kingdom's Representative to Éire wrote in a confidential report in 1944. 'There is little doubt that he will follow a rigidly Ultramontane line.'[1]

Three years into his reign there were numerous instances of McQuaid's narrowness, intolerance and rigidity to support the diplomat's assessment. McQuaid's insistence on 'Catholic civics' in his first Pastoral Letter resulted in the collapse of the inter-denominational Civics Institute. His Catholic Social Services Conference helped to close down Judge William Wylie's non-denominational Guild of Goodwill, which ran two non-profit-making companies, Goodwill Restaurants and Goodwill Fuel Producers.[2] He dismissed the Masonic Order as a sect based on the religion of naturalism and dissuaded Catholics from joining the Rotary Club, which he branded as an off-shoot of naturalism. He insisted that the Catholic Boy Scouts keep their distance from the Baden Powell Scouts.

He encouraged Religious-run schools to take milk from a Catholic, effectively damaging the business of a Protestant-owned creamery. Efforts by the Consul General for Poland, W.N. Dobrzynski, to involve McQuaid in his country's affairs resulted in his being sent two copies of *The Life of Père Lamy.*[3]

To curtail the influence of Protestant youth charities, McQuaid wrote in June 1941 to the Superior General of the Irish Sisters of Charity, Mother Mary Bernard Carew, offering her £500 (£12,500) to provide holidays for Catholic boys in north Co. Dublin seaside resorts. 'Already, I have had to block Trinity College Holiday Camp,' he confided. 'But I cannot succeed unless I have an alternative to offer. The matter is very urgent.'[4] Within a fortnight Mother Carew received a cheque from

McQuaid to help run a holiday home in Baldoyle exclusively for poor Catholic boys.

At the request of Bishop Kinane of Waterford in 1942, McQuaid stopped a priest of his diocese, Fr Jack Hanlon, an artist who had been taught by the Cubist painter Mainie Jellett, from opening an exhibition of paintings in a Protestant school in Waterford.[5]

McQuaid's primary concern was to apply Roman regulations, and apply them strictly, a preoccupation that led to charges that he operated like a colonial governor of the Roman Catholic Church.

Nuns' habits

In mid-1941 the Mother Superior of the Missionary Sisters of Our Lady of the Holy Rosary arranged an interview with McQuaid at which she asked permission for her Sisters to attend medical courses in lay attire. When McQuaid rejected her arguments about the absurdity of young religious women learning surgery skills in the full habit of the congregation, she cited a prescription from the Sacred Congregation of Propaganda Fide, dated February 11, 1936, allowing them to wear lay attire. But McQuaid interpreted the Roman document as stipulating that as far as possible Sisters should acquire the necessary diplomas before their solemn profession of vows. He refused her request.[6]

Pluckily the Mother Superior submitted a written request: 'It is imperative to have Sisters trained not only for nursing but also as fully qualified medical practitioners in view of the urgent and increasing demands of our missions in Africa, Southern Nigeria and the Transvaal,' she wrote. Coupled with this request was an application for the Archbishop's permission to rent or even buy a house close to the university, where the Sisters could lead their religious life while following the five-year medical course. It was intended that the Sisters would wear the religious habit at home and wear 'becoming lay dress' at university.

As 'a strictly personal kindness,' McQuaid granted permission for the Sisters to attend medical courses and to look for a hostel, but he insisted that they wear their full habits at all times. When five sisters started medical studies in the autumn and took up temporary residence at Muckross Park, the Superior promptly received a letter from McQuaid's secretary, Fr Mangan. 'His Grace bids me to say that it not open to you to obtain even a temporary residence without first obtaining the sanction of the ecclesiastical authority as to its general suitability,' he wrote. 'When therefore you have submitted to His Grace the proposed site of your temporary residence and the site has been approved, His Grace will furnish you with the formal document outlining the canonical position as to all aspects of your residence in his diocese.'

Mother Superior apologised. In due course, she was told that the

Archbishop had no objection to a property in Lower Leeson St. Meanwhile, the nuns acquired the use of a neighbouring garden for the summer, an initiative which further incurred McQuaid's displeasure. 'I may be allowed,' he wrote, 'to express my surprise that a Congregation would negotiate the use of a garden in an adjacent house, without even a word of consultation with the Ordinary. It is a procedure that is most unusual with Sisters in this diocese and I trust that if your Congregation comes to reside here temporarily it will not be repeated.'

Muintir not welcome

On November 4, 1941, the founder of Muintir na Tíre – the People of the Countryside – Fr John Hayes, notified McQuaid of a weekend seminar he had organised on rural development at Lucan Spa Hotel in Co. Dublin at which both Éamon de Valera and W.T. Cosgrave were scheduled to speak. He invited McQuaid to attend one of the sessions or at least to send a letter supporting Muintir na Tíre. Next day McQuaid drafted a reply stating that he would be absent on another engagement. He refused to send a message of support. Instead Hayes was told that 'the Archbishop has not yet had the occasion to examine the nature and claims of Muintir, more especially in regard to the place that such an Association might hold in his diocese.'[7]

This was an astonishing comment from McQuaid, who in his Cavan address in 1932 had cited Muintir as one of the new movements doing battle against Satan. In the intervening decade Muintir's work to regenerate rural society was recognised by de Valera, who rated it 'the most valuable movement in the country'. Muintir na Tíre put into practice Papal social teaching through the formation of guilds at parish level representing farmers, farm labourers, the unemployed and the professions. By 1941 the guilds employed 1,000 men in food and turf production to meet war-time scarcities. Its 'Rural Weekend' seminars and annual 'Rural Weeks' discussed practical social issues. Its appeal stretched beyond the diocese of Cashel to which Hayes, a Tipperary man, belonged. As the Dublin diocese contained a large rural population, particularly in south Dublin and Wicklow, Hayes had high hopes of securing McQuaid's official approval.

Trouble, however, was brewing. On November 6, McQuaid read in the *Irish Press* that Fr Edward Coyne S.J. and 'other well-known speakers' would address a public meeting in Ballsbridge that evening 'for the formation of a Sandymount-Ballsbridge group of Muintir na Tíre'. McQuaid had not been informed of the meeting or Muintir's intention to organise a branch in Dublin city.

Writing to the parish priest of Sandymount, Fr MacMahon, McQuaid stated: 'I am not convinced that the Association has yet proved that it deserves a place in the Dublin diocese, in the country and the City.

Therefore I have not sanctioned the formation of any group in the diocese. I should be grateful if you could give me any help in understanding
the Ballsbridge-Sandymount movement.'[8]

The Dublin diocese was closed to Muintir since McQuaid's
appointment as Archbishop in 1940, Hayes's biographer, Stephen Rynne,
wrote.[9] A request by Hayes for an interview in May 1942 failed to win
McQuaid over, even though the Tipperary priest assured the Archbishop
of his 'loyalty and obedience to you in all matters'.[10] Tom Fitzpatrick, Fr
Hayes's driver, recalls that Hayes was so furious after a meeting with
McQuaid at Drumcondra that he fumed in silence almost the whole way
to Bansha, his parish in Tipperary.[11] Hayes was later to remark that 'this
country is becoming so Catholic, it forgets to be Christian.'

A number of reasons suggest themselves to explain McQuaid's
opposition. A fundamental one is that he perceived Muintir as a rival to
his Catholic Social Service Conference, which was firmly under his control. As the correspondence shows, McQuaid was hostile to Muintir's
seminar in Lucan even before he discovered the attempt to organise a
branch in Ballsbridge-Sandymount, a move which he regarded as an
affront to his prerogative to decide an organisation's status in the diocese.
Moreover, apart from not being keen on the mixing of men and women in
the same organisation, McQuaid disapproved of Muintir's admission of
Protestants to its membership. McQuaid's attitude was considerably nar-
rower than that of the elderly Archbishop Harty of Cashel, who advised
Hayes to use the title Christian rather than Catholic.

'Dressings-down'

McQuaid could be difficult on matters of protocol, a fact which officials of
all rank discovered sooner or later. McQuaid was piqued, for example,
when civil servants from the Department of Education called on him to
secure his agreement to increases in the cost of building three primary
schools in Crumlin – the original agreement had been negotiated by the
Minister and the Secretary of the Department, with the late Archbishop
Byrne. McQuaid left Derrig in no doubt that he wanted to deal with him.
'I shall very much value the opportunity of discussing problems personally
with you and Mr O'Neill, as in former days,' he told Derrig pointedly.[12]
Derrig responded immediately by making an appointment to see the
Archbishop.

Prominent lay Catholic leaders also found themselves stung by
McQuaid's aura of superiority and his sharp tongue. Frank and Jack Nagle
of the St Vincent de Paul Society received 'curt, hurting messages of dis-
approbation' from their Archbishop, who warned them against mistaking
their 'spiritual caprice for the manifest will of God'.[13] When the founder of
the Legion of Mary, Frank Duff, presented him with a chalice

incorporating a design of the Legion's standard, McQuaid gave him 'a dressing-down' about his supposedly exaggerated opinion of the Legion's work.

Duff was particularly demoralised by McQuaid's censorship of his account of Bentley Place, the notorious red-light area behind Dublin's Pro-Cathedral, which was cleaned up by the Legion of Mary in the 1920s. The Dublin Diocesan Censor, Dr Kelly, phoned the editor of *Maria Legionis*, León Ó Broin, to tell him that because of its references to prostitutes he had forwarded Duff's article to McQuaid, who had ordered 'the series be discontinued as being unsuitable for general reading'. When Ó Broin demurred, Kelly said the Archbishop's decision was final. An appeal by Duff to McQuaid for truthful history rather than 'invented storyettes' was not entertained.[14]

The Bell

When in September 1941, the Auxiliary Bishop of Westminster, Dr David Mathew, asked for advice on whether to write for the independent literary review, *The Bell*, McQuaid told him that it would be a very grave mistake to do so. 'An article on Catholicity in England would be very useful to that organ in restoring an appearance of dignity,' he wrote. 'Such an article, however, by a Bishop would surprise us, unless it appeared in a review of weight, e.g. the *Dublin Review*. I should feel worried by the possible juxtaposition of some short story or article of scant decency.'[15]

McQuaid was puzzled as to how the editor, Seán Ó Faoláin, could have spoken to Mathew of his general approval of *The Bell*. 'I have met him at my house on one occasion and showed the ordinary courtesy, more especially as I felt that he and his associates were nursing the grievances of being outlawed,' he commented. McQuaid was far less sympathetic towards Ó Faoláin and his colleagues than the writer imagined: 'My belief is that the group is infected with the liberalism that considers it may give rein to 'realistic expression', that is, to the unworthy aspects of life in books. They suffer much from the disregard of the Irish Catholic public.' Attacking them, McQuaid told Mathew, 'would give publicity, but for the most part, no one notices and that hurts much. Therefore, they look towards London for an appreciative public, and go to live there or get books published there. They would look to New York or any other centre, where paganism thrives, if it were convenient.'[16]

The private life of Ó Faoláin's fellow writer and Cork man, Michael O'Donovan, better known by his *nom de plume*, Frank O'Connor, was a matter of concern to McQuaid who had been told by Frank Duff that O'Connor was trying to secure an ecclesiastical annulment of his first marriage from the Archdiocese of Westminster.[17]

In late September 1942, McQuaid sent an intermediary to

O'Connor's house where his common-law wife, Evelyn, who had previously been married to the English Catholic actor Robert Speaight, allowed him entry and innocently sent him upstairs to the writer's study. McQuaid's representative offered O'Connor work on condition that he split up with Evelyn. No mention was made of the well-being of children. Ironically, O'Connor, who was finding it difficult to obtain work on Irish radio, was about to throw the messenger out when Evelyn proposed that if a job were offered to her, she would consider a separation. Two days later she took up a position in Radio Éireann.[18]

O'Connor remained *persona non grata* with McQuaid. In 1940 the Censorship Board had banned O'Connor's novel *Dutch Interior*, which he dedicated to Evelyn, and his 1941 play, *The Statue's Daughter*, was banned for its portrayal of a national hero fathering an illegitimate daughter and its evident approval of Catholics marrying Protestants.

Heenan rebuked

McQuaid's wrath was not confined to left-leaning writers. In December 1941 he wrote to the Apostolic Delegate to Britain, Archbishop William Godfrey, complaining of 'a scandalously offensive calumny' against Catholic thought and life in the Dublin diocese which appeared in an article in the *Catholic Herald* written by a priest, Fr John Heenan, the future Cardinal Archbishop of Westminster.[19]

The article, 'Where Ireland makes an unfavourable impression,' was the fourth in a series which Heenan had written following a visit to Ireland which was sponsored by the British Foreign Office as part of a campaign run by their press attaché in Dublin, the poet and writer John Betjeman, to counteract the isolationism imposed by neutrality and the censorship laws. Through the Secretary of the Department of External Affairs, Joe Walshe, Heenan was introduced to the Irish political and religious élite, including de Valera and McQuaid. Heenan, who was himself of Irish stock, was sympathetic towards Ireland and took a liking to McQuaid, whose 'sanctity and humanity' were 'applauded by both Catholics and Protestants'. He quoted McQuaid as saying: 'Hatred is unchristian. We must all work together, Irish, English or German, we are all the children of God. The Church will go on. *Non prevalebunt* – the gates of hell will not prevail, if only we preserve charity.'

Heenan struck a more critical note when he reported what he had heard and seen about Dublin's poverty, of religious formalism and anticlericalism, and of the 'dancing problem'.

His first and most unfavourable impression was the 'appalling poverty' of Ireland's capital city. 'Allowing for the impoverished state of Éire and for its dependence upon foreign currency, it is hard to believe that a Catholic Government could not in twenty years have done more to put into operation the principles of *Rerum Novarum*,' he wrote. 'Ireland is a Catholic country and it is disturbing that in Catholic Ireland degrading poverty should be tolerated. Many times late at night I saw small boys selling newspapers, and in certain sections of Dublin it was hard to go many paces without being accosted by beggars. Allowing for the easygoing ways of Irish administration one must not expect the neat and tidy parcelling up of beggars that takes place in other countries. But my impression was that the poor are too numerous and too miserably poor.'

Heenan commented on the lack of religious instruction and 'short' Masses, and posed the question as to whether the people's Catholic faith was a formality. 'In every congregation a notable percentage will go to work abroad where, without religious instruction, they will not be in a position to defend and sustain their Faith.' He also noted that in Ireland there was far less loyalty to the clergy than in the much-criticised England. And he detected the beginnings of a cleavage between young people and the clergy over teenage drinking and late-night dancing. 'It is remarkable that not only the priests but also Protestant ministers were at one in naming dances as one of the great curses of modern Ireland,' Heenan wrote. 'I therefore lost no opportunity in seeking the views of the young people themselves. I found, as I had suspected, that they were sullen and resentful of the attitude of the clergy. The days of the docile laity gladly accepting the dictates of the soggart aroon are surely numbered in Ireland.'

In his complaint to Godfrey about the impression the article had created, McQuaid wrote that he had had the four members of his Council read Heenan's report individually, and each one of them had condemned it.[20]

Diplomatically, Godfrey thanked McQuaid for his 'helpful' letter which would enable him to know the view of the Dublin Council if ever the matter came within the range of his competence. 'But I am, of course, entirely aloof from any expression of opinion regarding Ireland which might appear in the Catholic Press of Britain,' he wrote. Cleverly he added that if the Nuncio to Ireland, Archbishop Paschal Robinson, thought that he could be of help in any way, he was ready to do whatever was possible, though 'my position as Delegate of the Holy Father is a delicate one here in London, where are gathered so many of the Allied Governments.'[21]

Godfrey's reference to Robinson was an unexpected twist. McQuaid wrote back to explain that he had merely wished to inform Godfrey of his council's reaction to the article, and that 'I cannot see my way to suggest to His Excellency the Nuncio Apostolic that any method of helping us in the situations would be indicated to Your Excellency.' He repeated, however, that articles such as Heenan's had 'deeply angered both clergy and people in this country.'[22]

Fahey under a cloud

Even a close former colleague such as Fr Denis Fahey C.S.Sp. could find himself under fire from McQuaid, who would not sanction any usurping of his role to proclaim orthodoxy in Dublin. 'Dr Fahey will certainly not err in doctrine, but he is capable of making statements and suggestions that are not capable of proof by any evidence available to the Censors,' McQuaid wrote to Cardinal MacRory in 1942. MacRory had sought advice on whether to give his imprimatur to Fahey's new book. McQuaid told him that he did not have the least objection to the book being printed in Dundalk, but he had not allowed Fahey to print it in Dublin and Bishop Staunton had done likewise in Ferns.[23]

'I have been obliged to watch carefully his remarks upon the Jews,' McQuaid added damningly. 'Fahey will frequently err in good judgement, and this error will take the shape of excerpts from newspapers as proof of serious statements, unwise generalisations and, where Jews are concerned, remarks capable of rousing the ignorant or malevolent. In his own Congregation, Fr Fahey is not regarded as a man of balanced judgement. He is a wretched Professor, obscure and laborious.'

McQuaid feared that Fahey would incur legal action sooner or later, and would lose in court. But he willingly admitted that Fahey was 'a most exemplary priest, of deep sanctity, and a man who will very generously sacrifice his time and health to help anyone: not a small sign of genuine holiness.'

Trinity rebuffs

When the new Provost of Trinity College, Dr Henry Alton, asked to pay a courtesy call on McQuaid, he was told that the Archbishop was prepared to receive him out of Christian politeness, but 'in view of the existing law of the Catholic Church concerning attendance at Trinity College by Catholics, the AB may not return the courtesy call at Trinity College.'[24]

The same year, 1942, the Auxiliary Bishop of Westminster, Dr David Mathew, informed McQuaid that Trinity wished to confer an honorary LL.D. on him in recognition of his work as a historian, and asked McQuaid if he should accept the honour. While insisting that the decision was the Englishman's own affair, McQuaid pointed out that as a member of the English Hierarchy, 'Your action in accepting the degree will tend to make still more difficult the execution of the existing law of the Maynooth Synod by which Catholics may not enter Trinity College. I have enforced that law and I will enforce it. I am well aware that a certain proportion of Catholics disregard the law, for many reasons, among which I must reckon a sojourn in English Catholic schools. It seems to me that acceptance of a degree by an English Catholic Bishop can only help to strengthen the mentality that I profoundly deplore.'[25]

After Mathew declined the honorary degree, McQuaid trusted that 'Your Lordship's method of explaining the situation to Trinity College will not only succeed in making the authorities of that University understand the law of the Church in Ireland but also prevent them from regarding my opinion as but another example of what so many on their side call intransigent bigotry.'[26]

'His Grace is not pleased'

In late 1942, just a year after Heenan's report criticising Catholic formation in Ireland, McQuaid complained to the Jesuit Provincial, Fr John MacMahon, that an article in *Studies* cast serious doubts on the quality of catechism teaching in the Dublin diocese. It suggested that rote learning did not impart real assent to Catholic teaching, and as a result Irish emigrants were failing to maintain their religious beliefs. As far as McQuaid was concerned, evidence supplied by the English Hierarchy gave 'no countenance' to the review's claims, and his Council wanted *Studies* to publish 'a reparatory note' – a euphemism for a grovelling apology.[27]

Fr MacMahon duly apologised and begged permission to show His Grace the 'reparatory note' before it went to the printers. The author, Fr Sean Ó Catháin S.J., also regretted the difficulties his article had caused for his Provincial and offered no resistance to the climb-down, although he felt strongly that McQuaid had distorted his meaning. 'Nowhere in the review did I speak of 'gross failure' on the part of Irish emigrants, and nowhere did I connect that entire loss of faith with them. Such an interpretation seems to me, let me say it frankly, hasty and ill-considered to say the very least.'

When an apology was drafted for the winter issue, McQuaid described it as perfect. But shortly afterwards the Superior of the Jesuit Community at Leeson St, Fr Aubrey Gwynn S.J., threw intriguing light on McQuaid's attitude when he informed MacMahon that at a recent conference of priests engaged in religious instruction, McQuaid voiced the opinion that the ordinary catechism was most unsatisfactory and was one of the causes of the failure of Irish Catholic emigrants to keep their faith in England. 'We can only learn our lesson,' Gwynn wrote, 'that what His Grace may wish to say in a conference to the priests of his diocese may not safely be said, or even hinted, in a review in *Studies*. But that is, I suppose, an ancient lesson!'

Anti-Tuberculosis League

A few months later on February 15, 1943, McQuaid intervened to oppose the launching of an Irish Anti-Tuberculosis Society by Dr Dorothy Price and Dr John Duffy at a public meeting in the Hibernian Hotel. This inter-denominational campaign aimed to reduce the high incidence of tuberculosis by enlisting the support of veterinary and medical experts as well as public figures. No sooner had the chairman, Dr R.J. Rowlette, opened the meeting than a priest stood up and waved a piece of paper which he claimed was from the Archbishop, mandating him to act as His Grace's official representative. This was Monsignor Daniel Moloney, one of McQuaid's trusted advisers, who obtained permission from a flustered Rowlette to read out the message.

'May I explain to you that I am very much interested in the effort to reduce the incidence of illness and death due to tuberculosis,' McQuaid's message began. 'I should like to state my view that a nation-wide campaign of medical character can succeed only under Government patronage. It is my definite opinion that such a campaign can be carried through in Éire only by the Red Cross Society. That Society enjoys Government patronage, is in fact nation-wide, and has a large membership of trained workers. Further, at the end of this war emergency, the Red Cross Society will find ample opportunity for devoting its trained energies to an anti-tuberculosis campaign with undistracted attention.'[28]

This intervention threw the meeting into disarray. From the floor the chairman of the central council of the Red Cross, Chief Justice Conor Maguire, assured those present that the Archbishop's suggestion had not been made at his organisation's instance – though he made it clear that the Red Cross would be prepared to take charge of the campaign. In a counter-move, Dr Theo Dillon proposed a motion that the Irish Anti-Tuberculosis Society be founded. Seconding the motion, the Independent Senator for Trinity College, Owen Sheehy Skeffington, argued that the Red Cross was not the proper body to fight TB as it had no expertise in dealing with the disease. Rowlette, however, ruled that he could not put the motion to the meeting on account of the Archbishop's clearly expressed wishes.

A compromise emerged, establishing a provisional executive committee for one year which would work in cooperation with the Red Cross Society. This situation, wrote Andrée Sheehy Skeffington, 'created a deep feeling of unease among the original committee, whose members were indignant that the campaign should be taken over by a single body, trained in little more than first aid, and under virtual Catholic control.'[29] Summing up the demise of the Anti-Tuberculosis League, Dr Mitchell of the Adelaide Hospital concluded: 'It had taken so much cooperation to bring the scheme that far, and only one letter to bring it to a halt.'[30]

'For a doctor's son and a man of the cloth, McQuaid appears to have had a rather odd attitude to public health issues,' the social critic, Nöel Coghlan, has commented in regard to McQuaid's role in this episode. 'Could it possibly be that Mammon rated higher than the Lord's teachings?'[31] Coghlan appears to have read the situation correctly. At the next

meeting of the Red Cross Society, its future course was made safe when
Bishop Browne of Galway intervened effectively to accept the anti-
tuberculosis work. 'This work will be a God-send for the Red Cross,' Archbishop Walsh of Tuam wrote to McQuaid. 'When the Emergency is over
the Red Cross would have no occupation and this fine organisation, which
is almost entirely in Catholic hands (towards which the Knights of St
Columbanus helped), would fade away.'[32]

'The Artistics'

Despite their earlier differences about Catholic publications, in 1943
McQuaid allowed Frank Duff and León Ó Broin to set up a discussion
group known as *Common Ground* with writers who formed the small
nucleus of the Irish intelligentsia of the time. Keen to improve the position of the writer in Emergency Ireland, Seán Ó Faoláin became involved
in discussions on the censorship laws and felt that Duff and Ó Broin
should be held accountable for what was being done to writers by fanatical
'Holy Joes' in the name of the Catholic Church. *Common Ground* failed to
live up to its name: Duff took umbrage at remarks made by Mervyn Wall,
Ó Faoláin lost interest in talking to Duff, and the group soon fell asunder.
Years later, in correspondence with journalist Brendán Ó Cathaoir, Ó
Faoláin described Duff as 'a very sentimental chap completely subservi-
ent to J.C. McQuaid at the latter's most painfully ingenuous.'[33]

Frank O'Connor, who edited the poetry section of *The Bell*, did not
take part in the *Common Ground* dialogue, but suggested to Ó Faoláin that
Bishop Browne of Galway was an intelligent man who might be invited to
address the writers. Ó Faoláin, who had been to see McQuaid, told
O'Connor that he had found the Archbishop sympathetic to writers,
which prompted O'Connor to say that perhaps 'His Grace might honour
us, at least once, by dining with us'.[34]

Such an encounter between McQuaid and the literary figures of his
day did not take place. What Ó Faoláin and O'Connor did not know was
that Duff was sending reports on the writers directly to McQuaid, who
patronisingly called them 'the Artistics'.[35]

McQuaid and Radio Éireann

In June 1943 McQuaid became chairman of the Hierarchy's sub-
committee on religious broadcasting. Its specific mandate was to explore
with Radio Éireann the possibility of introducing practical religious programming on the network.[36]

The original idea had been to broadcast the Rosary but McQuaid
had succeeded in broadening the scope of this proposal. As for the Rosary
itself, in a letter to Bishop Staunton, now secretary to the Hierarchy,

McQuaid thought that it would be a mistake to transmit the Rosary by itself, as 'its repetition repels Prots.'[37]

Following his meetings with the chiefs of Radio Éireann, in October McQuaid reported to the Hierarchy that there was 'real sympathy' among the authorities for the idea of a religious programme. With this, he began laying the foundations of a system of religious broadcasting on Radio Éireann where all such material was handled by his censor, Fr Cathal McCarthy, of Clonliffe College.

On his knees

Three years into his reign, McQuaid had become so powerful that even fellow members of the Hierarchy lived in fear of him. In late 1943 the newly consecrated Bishop of Waterford and Lismore, Daniel Cohalan, delivered an address on temperance at the request of the Pioneer Total Abstinence Association. During a long diatribe against drunkenness, he compared the spectacle of young girls socialising in hotels in Dublin's fashionable O'Connell St, 'powdered and painted, smoking cigarettes, and in and out of bars,' with life in the nearby slums behind the Pro-Cathedral, where neglected, ill-clad, pinched-looking children lived in derelict houses with broken windows.

'Is this a Christian land?' Cohalan demanded. 'With these little beings, just around the corner, looking from their life and habitation as if they were little animals of a lower class: and then you see the luxury, the make-believe, the adoration of appearances and the amount of unnecessary expenditure in O'Connell St.'[38]

Not surprisingly, Cohalan's remarks made headline news in the daily press, the Catholic weeklies and his own local newspaper, the *Waterford Star*. Privately, he himself suffered the equivalent of a hangover when he saw his comments on Dublin low-life given such prominence. His premonition of a sharp response from McQuaid was realised with the arrival of a letter from Drumcondra.

'The matter has been a source of anxiety to me for a week,' Cohalan confessed to McQuaid. 'When I saw your envelope and felt that the letter was from Your Grace, I knelt down at once and said three Hail Marys before opening it.'[39]

Cohalan opened the letter to read that McQuaid had raised the temperance address at a meeting of his council. 'I wish, in union with all the members of my Council,' McQuaid wrote, 'to express my profound grief that Your Lordship should have chosen, publicly, in your own Cathedral, to select my See as the special and single type of grossly unchristian contrast between rich and poor. In particular, I wish to express my deep resentment at the language which describes the children of my own parish as little animals of lower class.'[40]

Regretting the displeasure or annoyance which his address had caused, Cohalan explained to McQuaid that he had lost his way recently between Gardiner St and O'Connell St and had walked into a slum-clearance area. 'When trying to emphasise the unreasonableness of spending money on drink, the experience must have quite inadvertently crossed my mind and so have been the occasion of words I regret so much. I was extremely worried when I saw the words quoted in the press and detached from context.'[41]

Cohalan begged to be excused from any pain which he had caused McQuaid through lack of care. He hoped that the incident would not make any difference in their relations. McQuaid accepted the apology and promised to raise the letter at the next meeting of his council in order to remove the unfortunate impression which had been created. And he reassured the Waterford bishop that the incident would not change their relations.[42]

Trinity ban

On February 7,1944, McQuaid issued his Lenten Regulations in which he stipulated that no Catholic might enter the Protestant university of Trinity College without his permission. 'Any Catholic who disobeys this law is guilty of mortal sin and while he persists in disobedience is unworthy to receive the Sacraments,' he decreed. Permission for Dublin Catholics to attend Trinity College would be granted 'only for grave and valid reasons,' and would involve the acceptance of 'definite measures adequately to safeguard the Faith and practice of Catholic students'.

Founded by Queen Elizabeth I in 1592, as the stronghold of the Protestant Ascendancy in Ireland, Trinity College had been condemned by the Hierarchy at the Synod of Thurles in 1850 and by Maynooth Councils in 1875, 1900 and 1927. These denunciations aimed at discouraging Catholics from attending its courses and at preventing priests from advising Catholic parents to send their children to Trinity. Although the decrees were strongly worded, they fell short of a formal prohibition. Through this loophole, by 1944, Catholics in fact constituted about one-third of Trinity students. McQuaid opposed this trend, and became the first member of the Hierarchy to check Trinity's integration into the educational mainstream of independent Ireland. His counter-offensive was ridiculed by the *Church of Ireland Gazette*, which noted that mortal sin was strong language and commented that as 'no provision is made to bring actions for alleged slander before the heavenly courts, those who are attacked in such pronouncements can only receive them with their annual smile.'[43]

One of the few commentators to spot the significance of McQuaid's move was Seán Ó Faoláin. 'An important and interesting incident occurred in February,' he noted in *The Bell*.[44] 'The Lenten Regulations of His Grace, the Most Reverend Dr McQuaid, Archbishop of Dublin, announced the closing of Trinity College to all Catholics resident within the Dublin diocese – if not, ultimately, to all Irish Catholics.' McQuaid's 'first tightening of the screw' against Trinity went further than the traditional position. While the regulations applied only to the Dublin diocese and were not equal to an absolute interdiction, Ó Faoláin pointed out: 'their intention is obvious, and in their wider influence and repercussions they are poles apart from the spirit of conciliation which marked earlier efforts to establish a unified National University in Ireland.'

Ó Faoláin argued that McQuaid could not touch religion without also touching politics and affecting society. 'We cannot, to give a homely example, tell our children not to mix with our neighbours' children on religious grounds, and at the same time expect our neighbours to believe that we have no personal objection to them. Irish Protestants would have to be angels, not human beings, not to feel a sub-implication that there is something sinister about their creed, and their society. And all of this ... in its enlarged form is of vital importance to us in connection with Partition and the whole political future of Ireland.'

Referring to McQuaid's belief in the paramount importance of 'a Catholic society, of a Catholic order,' Ó Faoláin warned that history taught that such great ideals caused untold human misery without achieving their desired result. Cardinal Henry Manning's interdict in 1864 against Catholics attending the universities of Oxford and Cambridge had failed, he reminded readers.

To ensure that his clergy enforced the anti-Trinity decree and an accompanying prohibition on attendance by Catholic children at non-Catholic schools, McQuaid sent copies of the ecclesiastical legislation to all parish priests in the Dublin diocese. Not only were they to communicate its contents to their curates, they were requested to acknowledge receipt of the document personally. It read:

> Having duly considered the matter, having consulted the Council of the Diocese and having obtained its unanimous consent, WE, JOHN CHARLES, ARCHBISHOP OF DUBLIN, hereby declare that:
>
> 1. If any priest, secular or religious, subject to our jurisdiction, shall have, by material assistance or counsel or approval, aided in sending a Catholic to be educated in a non-Catholic School or College or University in this Diocese, he shall, by the fact, incur suspensio *a divinis*, reserved to the Ordinary.
>
> 2. If any priest, belonging to a Religious Order or Congregation, which in this matter is exempt from censure

inflicted by Us, shall have, by material assistance or counsel or approval, aided in sending a Catholic to be educated
in a non-Catholic School or College or University in this
Diocese, he will be deprived of any diocesan faculties
which he may hold from Us and his name will be forwarded to the Holy See.

Given at Dublin, the Seventh Day of February, in the
Year Nineteen Hundred and Forty-four.[45]

McQuaid's edict caused great anxiety to many Roman Catholic parents who nurtured Trinitarian ambitious for their sons or daughters. In his
autobiography *The Time of My Life*, broadcaster Gay Byrne, recounts how
his devout Catholic mother believed that allowing her eldest son, Al, to
attend Trinity would improve his prospects of a senior management job in
Guinness's, then a Protestant organisation. 'Ma suffered agonies every
Lent when the Archbishop's Pastoral Letter was read from the pulpit of
every church in Dublin,' he wrote. 'Everyone in our neighbourhood knew
Al Byrne was going to Trinity College, and as the renewal of the ban on
the attendance at this sinful repository of all that was harmful was
renewed, she was convinced that all eyes in the church were turned in our
direction. I was aware of it myself, young though I was, and sat there, part
of a solidly Byrne phalanx, tight and rebellious, holding out against the
neighbourhood and John Charles McQuaid.'[46]

Youth Unemployment Commission

In February 1944, McQuaid, in his capacity as chairman of the Commission on Youth Unemployment, was also in the thick of theological battle
with the country's most pragmatic politician, the Minister for Supplies,
Seán Lemass over how to handle submissions from Protestants. The dispute arose when McQuaid informed Lemass that he would not receive
from non-Catholic teaching and welfare associations answers to a questionnaire concerning the religious and spiritual welfare of their members.
Instead of these answers being sent to him as chairman, McQuaid proposed that Protestant responses should be sent to Lemass, who could
'duly provide for the freedom of conscience of non-Catholics' in whatever
decisions were later taken by the Government. 'It will thus be made clear
to the non-Catholic Teaching and Welfare Bodies that I shall not, being
Archbishop of Dublin, take cognisance of what properly pertains to the
consciences of non-Catholics, either during the sessions of the Commission on Youth Employment or in the Report which it is expected the
Commission will ultimately issue.'[47]

Lemass offered the counter-proposal that the commission should
exclude questions about people's spiritual and religious welfare from its

remit,[48] but this suggestion infuriated McQuaid who went over Lemass's head and complained to de Valera that it would be 'a grave error' to draft a report on youth unemployment without explicitly basing the recommendations on Catholic social principles. And 'a chairman, who is Catholic Archbishop of Dublin, cannot sign a declaration of incompetence to deal with spiritual and religious matters that pertain to Catholics,' he insisted.[49]

After discussing the issue with Lemass, de Valera wrote defiantly to McQuaid. 'The Commission is essentially a lay body, set up by the civil authority, and the fact that the chairman of the Commission is at the same time the Catholic Archbishop of Dublin seems to me not to alter its fundamental character in this respect.' It would not, therefore, be open to the State, as he was sure McQuaid realised, to take any action that could reasonably be regarded as 'involving religious discrimination or to cooperate in any such action on the part of a body established by its authority.'[50]

Next day McQuaid replied that de Valera's alternative so gravely affected his spiritual office that he felt obliged to consult his Administrative Council, as the Canon Law prescribed in questions of major moment.[51] After consulting his advisers, he threw down the gauntlet to de Valera in a six-page letter. He could not accept the Taoiseach's contention that his being the Archbishop of Dublin did not alter the character of the commission. 'No intention of the Government to constitute a lay or neutral Commission can alter the fundamentally spiritual character of the office of Archbishop, and the Archbishop, if he acts as chairman of the Commission, must always act in the person and capacity of authoritative Teacher of Faith and Morals in this diocese.'[52]

And echoing his row at Bellevue during the drafting of the Constitution in 1937, McQuaid taunted de Valera: 'Even under the Constitution of Éire, which admits the false principles of the separation of the Church and State, it is allowed in article 44.1.2 that 'the State recognises the special position of the Holy, Catholic, Apostolic and Roman Church.' Consequently, as Archbishop of Dublin, he was obliged to dissent from the procedure proposed by de Valera.

'Much as I regret it, I must accept your decision as final,' de Valera replied calmly two days later. 'We have, therefore, reached the impasse which I had sought to avoid ... The Commission was set up to consider a certain problem which is an integral one and affects the community as a whole.'[53]

In a move worthy of Machiavelli, McQuaid arranged for the Taxing Master of the Courts, Henry B. (Bertie) O'Hanlon, one of his close friends through the Knights of St Columbanus, to call on de Valera and tell him that the Archbishop had written a letter resigning as chairman of the Commission. O'Hanlon delivered his message at Government Buildings shortly before midnight on Monday February 28, but he did not manage to faze de Valera. The Taoiseach explained to him that the Government could not be a party to any procedure which would involve discrimination. The terms of his letter still stood.[54]

His bluff called, McQuaid wrote defiantly on March 4: 'I am left with no other option but to notify the Government formally that, while I am permitted to be Chairman of the Youth Unemployment Commission, I intend to act in all matters pertaining to the spiritual and religious welfare clauses of the Terms of Reference, in the person and capacity of the Archbishop of Dublin.'[55] He did not resign.

No adoption

In March 1944, the Secretary of the Department of Justice, Stephen Roche, wrote to McQuaid to sound out the Hierarchy's attitude to the introduction of an adoption law in the Irish State.

'It has been represented to me,' Roche wrote to McQuaid, 'that many people would be willing to adopt destitute children if they could acquire parental rights over the children and if they could be secured against the fear that the parents of the children might demand their return at any time. It is also urged that the procedure would give illegitimate children a better status: they would be registered as adopted children under the new name.'[56]

Specifically Roche wanted to know what McQuaid's reaction would be to the insertion in a Bill of a provision 'prohibiting the making of an adoption order in any case where it is not proved to the court that the religion of the adopter and the religion of the child are the same.'

McQuaid told Roche that if his draftsmen could put forward such a provision it would be a matter of great interest to him. Legal adoption was not contrary to the Catholic faith, he said, but 'If my advice be sought, I should urge that no step be taken in respect of Catholic children – and you know what a proportion that category entails – without referring the matter to the Catholic Hierarchy.'

A week later Roche briefed the Minister for Justice, Gerald Boland, on McQuaid's response. 'If the Archbishop of Dublin is not in favour of the proposal, it is unlikely that the Catholic Hierarchy as a body would agree to it,' Roche advised. 'I suggest therefore that we should drop, for the present at any rate, any idea of introducing legislation which would enable the courts to make orders transferring to adopters parental rights and duties in regard to adopted children.'

After reading Roche's memorandum, Boland appended his ministerial signature: 'I agree that it is unlikely that the Hierarchy would be more favourable than the Archbishop, so we had better drop the matter.'[57]

McQuaid also monitored the behaviour of students and by the academic year 1943–44 had imposed a tight grip on chaplaincy services at

University College, Dublin, which found students suitable 'Catholic accommodation' and kept an eye on their attendance at Mass, retreats and the university's annual pilgrimage to Lough Derg. The provision of a residential hostel was a priority for the chaplains, Frs Herbert McKernan and Fergus O'Higgins, who visited all 3,039 Catholic students in UCD – there were only 41 non-Catholics, 15 of them German. An Austrian student, absent from Sunday Mass for eight months, promised to overcome his indifference and laxity, while another student returned to the sacraments after an absence of two years. The Auditor of the Literary and Historical Debating Society, on 'the matter being brought to his notice by the chaplains, agreed to see that no suggestive subjects be allowed in *ex tempore* debates.'[58]

Efforts by the Legion of Mary and the St Vincent de Paul Society to recruit students were reported by the chaplains to be 'flagging', but 'the most useful and most successful work' undertaken by the Legion was that of the Magnificat Society, which met fortnightly during term to provide lectures by prominent guest speakers on 'the great Catholic principles and doctrines'. Celebrity speakers in 1943–44 included Professor Sherwood Taylor of Oxford on 'From Science to Catholicism,' the Minister for Post and Telegraphs, P.J. Little, on 'Catholic Rural Life,' actor Gabriel Fallon on 'Drama,' Frank Pakenham on 'Social Security' and James Meenan on 'The Corporate State.'

Not even soccer was free from McQuaid's interference. In his determination to make Irish society respect the sanctity of Holy Week, he wrote to the parish priest of Ringsend, Fr J. Neary, deploring the practice of holding soccer matches on Good Friday. At the Archbishop's behest, Neary forwarded a copy of the letter to Shelbourne Football Club, which subsequently informed the Leinster League that no matches would be played at Shelbourne Park on Good Friday. The Football Association of Ireland extended Shelbourne's ban to all Good Friday matches.[59]

As part of a process of reclaiming for Catholicism symbolic areas of Irish public life associated since the Reformation with the Protestant Ascendancy, McQuaid, in June 1944, solemnly re-dedicated the former Chapel Royal in Dublin Castle as the Military Church of the Most Holy Trinity. It was history in the making, according to the *Irish Press*, which marvelled at how the atmosphere of a bygone world still clung to the Gothic arches and stained-glass windows. 'The head of Government and his ministers with most of the principal chiefs of the military High Command knelt in line with the rank and file of the Army, while the Archbishop presided at High Mass. Young soldiers, holding six-foot candlesticks, swinging the incense thurible, kneeling with Mass book at the Archbishop's throne, uniformed chaplains in the choir, colour party and guards with fixed bayonets gave a military background to the church ritual.' After McQuaid exchanged the kiss of peace with his priests, de

Valera left his pew and knelt at the altar rails to kiss the *Instrumentum Pacis*, offered only to high dignitaries and heads of Government. Everyone attending the Mass was granted 200 days indulgence.[60]

But Protestants were not only losing their symbols of past power; they were effecting little influence on current decision-making. A clear instance of this came in July when the Red Cross and the Department of External Affairs were considering a residential scheme for housing 500 French refugee children, and turned to McQuaid for guidance.[61] He advised Mr Justice Maguire of the Red Cross that no accommodation scheme would succeed which did not segregate boys and girls, and that he would be inviting grave difficulties if the refugees' education did not take into consideration French class distinctions.[62] Because of their French training, McQuaid recommended the Sisters of St Joseph of Cluny in Chapelizod and put them in contact with Freddie Boland to work out a solution to 'this very grave problem of Catholic children'.[63]

In a defence of McQuaid from the charge of being a 'sectarian bigot', the late Fr Roland Burke Savage S.J. argued that he was never anti-Protestant, as such, but conceded that he was 'most definitely and vigorously anti-non-sectarian in his outlook.' There was nothing underhand or sinister, Burke Savage contended, in McQuaid's conviction that given the historical situation, Dublin charities in which priests participated were better under completely Catholic control.[64] In short, the Jesuit pleaded that McQuaid should be judged by the circumstances prevailing in the 1940s – and should not be judged by ecumenical criteria arising from the 1960s, sound advice in itself.

Burke Savage's plea to the bar of history was a piece of admirable but unconvincing apologetics for the 1960s when he wrote his famous article, but his distinction between anti-Protestantism and his vigorously non-sectarian outlook appears extremely thin some sixty years on from the 1940s which can now be studied from the historical files as a decade when Protestantism was under severe threat for survival from McQuaidian Catholicism. Burke Savage's argument that McQuaid was not anti-Protestant is hard to sustain under detailed scrutiny. It would become even harder to sustain as evidenced by his dealings with the Mercier Society, a discussion group for Catholics and Protestants, which provided a classic study of his deviousness and duplicity.

13

Defending the One True Church

1942–44

The unity of Christians can be achieved only through a
return to the One True Church of Christ of those who are
separated from it.

Pope Pius XI, Mortalium Annos, 1928.

In late September 1942 Archbishop John Charles McQuaid discussed
with the Professor of Dogma at Clonliffe, Fr Michael O'Connell, his
anxieties about the Mercier Society which ten months earlier he had
allowed Frank Duff to set up under the auspices of the Legion of Mary.
The Mercier Society encouraged debate on religious matters among educated middle-class Catholics and Protestants, and was named after the
Belgian Primate, Cardinal Désiré Joseph Mercier, who had conducted the
Anglican-Roman Catholic Conversations from 1921 to 1926 in Malines
with Lord Halifax of the Church of England. The inter-church dialogue
had failed to win the blessing of Pius XI.

The Mercier Society, whose leading lights were Frank Duff and
León Ó Broin, adopted the motto 'Towards better understanding' and a
joint committee composed of eight Protestants and ten Catholics was set
up to arrange speakers at its meetings in the National University buildings,
St Stephen's Green. Each month an invited speaker, alternately a Catholic
and a Protestant, gave an address which was followed by refreshments and
informal discussion. The meetings were by invitation and were not open to
the press. Members of the society included former Government minister
Desmond FitzGerald, the diplomats Joe Walshe, Freddie Boland and John
Betjeman, and churchmen George Otto Simms, P.C. Hanson, Rodney
Coote as well as the writer Thomas MacGreevy. Its chaplains were two
Holy Ghost priests, Fr Edward Leen, McQuaid's former boss at Blackrock
College, and his former Blackrock pupil, Fr Michael O'Carroll.

McQuaid's uneasiness stemmed from the tendency in the Mercier
Society's proceedings to provide a platform for what he regarded as

Protestant polemicism: his original expectation had been that the society would offer an opportunity of converting Protestants to Catholicism. McQuaid feared that the Mercier Society allowed single-minded Protestants to engage in controversial debate with well-intentioned and intelligent but theologically unqualified Catholic laity, and his suspicions appeared to be confirmed when the Church of Ireland Rector at Harold's Cross, the Rev. W.G. Proctor, attacked the primacy of Rome, Papal infallibility and the uniqueness of the Catholic Church in the course of a paper on 'Protestantism and the Scriptures.'

To confirm his fears, McQuaid sent O'Connell to meetings of the Mercier Society, effectively as his spy. He also delegated O'Connell to convey his anxieties to the society's chaplain, Fr Leen, whom he did not appear to trust. O'Connell let Leen know of McQuaid's misgivings on September 29, 1942; up until then, McQuaid had tolerated the society in the hope that 'great good' would result from its meetings, but since Proctor's lecture he was uneasy with its direction. The fact that Protestants were on the committee caused the Archbishop further anxiety.

O'Connell told Leen that the Archbishop considered that the controversial character of its discussions brought the group into conflict with Canon 1325, paragraph 3 of the Code of Canon Law, which warned the faithful against disputations and conferences with non-Catholics without the special permission of the Holy See or, in urgent cases, the local bishop. McQuaid was prepared to allow the next meeting to take place as scheduled in October, because the lecturer, Christopher Hollis, was an English Catholic. However, the Archbishop was opposed to a Protestant speaking in November. Overall, O'Connell made it clear that McQuaid felt that the Mercier Society's procedures needed to be amended.

According to O'Connell, Leen indicated his complete agreement with McQuaid and promised to assist in every way. He told O'Connell that he was personally pained by the relaxed attitude of the Catholic members to Proctor's contentious remarks about the Papacy and the Catholic Church. He accepted that controversial discussions should not be allowed to continue. Leen warned O'Connell that an attempt to alter the character of the meetings might enable the Protestant participants to claim that open discussion was being forbidden owing to 'Proctor's Protestant victory'.

Leen felt strongly that the Mercier Society's lectures should be given exclusively by Catholics for the sole benefit and enlightenment of non-Catholics, but such a radical policy amendment would need to be submitted to the group's committee, where the Protestants were most likely to reject it and refuse to participate further. 'Such a decision,' O'Connell concluded, quoting Leen, 'would be no concern of the Catholic members.'[1]

Before the Mercier Society's committee met on October 2, McQuaid personally explained to Duff why the society was in conflict with Canon Law, and he asked the Legion of Mary founder to provide him with a memorandum on the the Mercier's origins and aims.

McQuaid's reservations dominated the meeting, at which all the members – except Frs Leen, O'Carroll and O'Connell – were unanimous that if Protestant speakers were excluded it would mean the end of the society. Duff asked the members to give him their comments if they wished to ask McQuaid's permission to continue with the society as it was.[2]

A new difficulty arose when it emerged that, contrary to McQuaid's instruction that there should be no more Protestant speakers, the Church of England Dean of St Paul's, Dr Matthews, was confirmed as the speaker for November. However, McQuaid was assured by O'Connell that Leen did not think the Dean would be controversial as his topic was 'The reactions of the war on religion in England.'[3]

In mid-October, the society's Catholic committee met and approved Duff's memorandum, except for a foreword that was to be written by Joe Walshe on the decline of Protestantism in Ireland. The document traced the history of retreats for Protestants at Blackrock College, which had resulted in over 100 converts, and stated that the Mercier Society had been formed to reach those Protestants of goodwill whose circumstances did not permit them to attend the Blackrock retreats. It was given the name of Mercier Society purely to attract prestige; it did not aspire to a re-run of the Malines Conversations, which had been condemned by Pius XI.[4]

Leen, who received an advance copy of Duff's report, accepted that there was a risk in inviting Protestants to lecture which was not fully appreciated by the Catholic members. Indeed he criticised the fact that they felt that the response of 'the ordinary sensible man in the street' was adequate to deal with difficult theological matters. Nor could Leen detect any sign of a favourable attitude towards Catholicism among the Protestant participants. Unwittingly, Leen was supplying McQuaid with ammunition for his assault on the society, and putting his own head on the block by vouching for the non-polemical nature of the Church of England contribution.[5]

Trouble was brewing. O'Connell reported to McQuaid that a disservice to the Catholic cause occurred after Christopher Hollis' lecture on English Protantism. 'A former student of the Irish College in Paris, who is now reading Economics at Dublin University, Sheehy by name, made an unwarranted attack on the Irish educational system and seemed to laud Materialism,' O'Connell wrote in confidence to McQuaid. Sheehy had not been rebuked by Duff. Worst still, three Protestant speakers had 'deliberately introduced controversial matters.' Notice too was given of the likelihood of Quakers and Christian Scientists being elected to the society's joint committee.[6]

Although McQuaid was assured that a Catholic majority would be retained on the joint committee, he assigned another Clonliffe priest, Fr Michael Dempsey, to gather information for him on the Legion of Mary's spiritual directors and to make proposals regarding the spiritual formation of Clonliffe seminarians and the Legion's members. In his report delivered in early November, Dempsey recommended improvements in Clonliffe's depleted Library and was critical of the Legion's reliance on its handbook rather than on a systematic course of spiritual formation. While Legionaries had sound instincts of piety, devotion and zeal, they were lacking in theological knowledge. Ominously for the future of the Mercier Society, Dempsey provided McQuaid with the Latin commentaries on Canon 1325 of the two key authorities, Vermeersh and Wernz-Vidal.[7]

When Duff presented his memorandum to the Archbishop a few days later, McQuaid's response was immediate. He informed Duff that, regrettably, he could not sanction the development of the Mercier Society on his own authority as the matter was beyond his competence. If Duff wished to have the society continue as it was, he would have to petition the Holy See. To avoid undue inconvenience or scandal, however, McQuaid indicated that he would sanction an occasional meeting pending the decision of the Holy See, but on the explicit condition that the precautions outlined by him would be observed.[8]

Duff told McQuaid that it was the Mercier Society's 'earnest desire' to carry on its work and 'we would beg Your Grace to make the petition' to Rome; or, if McQuaid felt the Legion should make the petition, he would be happy to obey his wish on the matter. Duff also wanted Rome's approval for two other spheres of activity in which the Legion of Mary was involved – dialogue with Jews and with Communists.[9]

By return of post, McQuaid advised Duff that the Legion of Mary should draft and present the petition, which he would be happy to sign, seal and forward to Rome. 'I would suggest that the petition should be brief, full and clear, and that in view of the difficulties of communication, it should be made ready without delay.'[10]

When Duff sought McQuaid's personal views, the Archbishop raised no objection to the papers due to be given by two Catholics, Fr Arthur Ryan and Mr Seán Moynihan, but without his explicit permission no other paper was to be read after that, pending a reply from the Holy See. 'I wish no increase in Protestant membership of the Committee to be allowed,' he directed. 'The mixed Committee must restrict itself to the merest business routine.' [11]

'Society of the Jews'

When he read Duff's memorandum on the Mercier Society, McQuaid was surprised to see reference to 'a Club or Society for making contact with Jews and another for discussions with Atheistic Communists.' In regard to these two activities he directed Duff 'to undertake no further step without any explicit reference to me and subsequent approval.'[12]

The first club referred to was the Pillar of Fire Society, which was set up in 1942 by Duff and Ó Broin to promote dialogue with the small Jewish community in Ireland against the background of reports of massacres of Jews throughout Europe. Its aim was to bring together influential Catholics and Jews in a convivial atmosphere. Ó Broin had given the society's inaugural lecture. The second lecture was due to be delivered on Sunday November 22 1942 by Dr Leonard Abrahamson.

As regards what he called 'the Jewish Society', McQuaid ruled that there should be no further development pending the decision of the Holy See. He would allow Dr Abrahamson to read his paper but after that papers were to be given by Catholics only, at intervals of two months up until Easter. 'The strictest control must be exercised concerning the Catholics who attend,' McQuaid wrote to Duff. 'I do not wish any mixed committee to be formed, or if formed to meet. I shall appoint one of my own Priests to attend.'[13]

Duff explained to McQuaid that he had discussed a proposal to form a 'Joy of Israel' society at the Legion of Mary praesidium meeting the previous April, when McQuaid had given it his approval and ratified Fr Arthur Ryan as the first speaker. (When Ryan turned out to be unavailable, Ó Broin had launched the project instead.) Duff quoted from the Legion minutes of April 30, 1942: 'Brother Burgess reported that the Archbishop had sanctioned the formation of a society to work for the Jews and to bring them into closer contact with Christianity.' On hearing this, McQuaid said he 'was not aware that the matter would be entered in the minutes' and he dictated that: 'For the future, no permission may be regarded as valid, unless I give it in writing. I shall take care to limit the explicit terms of any permission. This in my view is the only satisfactory course to adopt in matters of such grave importance.'[14]

In regard to encounters with young atheists, Duff explained that this matter was in a different category. The meetings were run by the Legion's 'Mirror of Justice' group, which specialised in labour studies and conducted conferences in Tallaght. McQuaid, however, directed that the Legion should avoid all encounters with Communists. 'If, by chance, encounters arose, the issue must be faced on the spot or, should the Director think more prudent, at a later moment. In general, it must be recognised that any person undertaking to work for the Church, as a priest or as a layman, has the strictest obligation to make himself competent in the specific work he undertakes,' he told Duff.[15]

Dean criticises Pope

The Mercier Society fell into even deeper trouble with McQuaid after the Dean of St Paul's delivered an outspoken address to the society in November. Unknown to the organisers, Dr Matthews decided to change his topic

to 'The Christian ethic and the planned society,' one in which he suggested the dominant ethic would be control over the immigration of Jews,
birth prevention and the discouragement of the sexual mating of the
physically unfit. According to the Dean, these were pressing problems for
the man-in-the-street in England; but neutral Ireland had more time to
think out these problems in the light of the philosophical tradition represented by the eighteenth-century Anglican Bishop of Cloyne, George
Berkeley.

Bad as the lecture's content was in McQuaid's estimation, worse
still came at the end of question time, when Dean Matthews criticised
Pope Pius XII for a lack of outspokenness against Nazism. While admiring
many of the Pope's pronouncements, Matthews said he felt that it was
comparatively easy to lay down general principles, but he would have
more respect for the Pope – and the Pope would have more influence on
nations – if he had condemned evil when he saw it triumphant.[16]

An angry McQuaid demanded an assurance from Duff that there
would be no repeat of this kind of performance, and he criticised Catholic
members who had failed to respond to the Dean's remarks. 'No person,
priest or layman should speak at a meeting unless his words have been
prepared,' he ordered. 'It ought to be arranged in the Catholic Committee
who will speak to the paper and what his contribution will be. No priest
has my permission to speak without the previous knowledge and consent
of the very Rev. Chaplain, Dr Leen, and Rev. Dr O'Connell, even though
that priest holds the faculties of the diocese. Entrance of Catholics to the
meeting must be still more strictly curtailed.'[17]

Ó Broin supplied McQuaid with a copy of an apology offered by the
Rev. W.G. Proctor for the Dean of St Paul's 'seemingly slighting' reference to the Pope's Encyclicals. 'The letter is all the more valuable in that
it is the spontaneous act of a gentleman,' McQuaid acknowledged. 'Mr
Proctor's letter is a generous effort at an apology. Unfortunately, the Dean
of St Paul's was neither required to apologise, nor in fact apologised.'

Unmollified, McQuaid brooded on this slight to the Pope. 'I protest
against the insult which accused the Sovereign Pontiff of failing in his
duty of condemning wrong where he saw it,' he told Ó Broin. 'I authorise
you and I direct you to read this letter at the next meeting of the Mercier
Society Committee of Catholics.'[18]

Duff colludes with McQuaid

On November 18, 1942, Duff presented McQuaid with a draft of the
Legion of Mary's petition to Rome, which had been prepared by Fr Leen
and a Dominican priest, Fr Heuston, in consultation with Fr Fennelly of
Kimmage. Duff was unhappy with two points: Leen and Heuston had
insisted in specifically naming McQuaid twice, and they had omitted as

unimportant a passage which had read: 'There is no intention of combining with non-Catholics from a common platform of any description, whether of social action or religious defence, or anything else.'[19]

Duff felt that just such a statement was desirable, to make it plain to the Holy See that 'we are not a movement of the Sword of the Spirit type, about which it is rumoured that the Holy See has misgivings.' The Sword of the Spirit was a movement in England in which educated Catholics such as Christopher Dawson, Barbara Ward and A.C.F. Beales discussed social and moral issues with Anglicans and other Protestants. It was supported by Cardinal Hinsley, who believed that it was important that English Catholics should counteract charges of being supporters of the Catholic traditionalist values identified with Mussolini and more recently with Marshal Pétain in Vichy France. Hinsley, a Mercier-style ecumenist, had said the Our Father in public with the Anglican Bishop of Chichester, George Bell, after the House of Commons had been bombed by the Germans.[20]

Duff pointed to a religious service at Westminster Abbey in which the Catholic chaplain to the American Forces was to take part, and said that this could not fail to arouse uneasiness in Rome in regard to joint church services with Anglicans. 'It seems to me that a Petition should make evident the fact that our minds and our actions are at opposite poles to all that sort of thing,' he suggested to McQuaid.[21]

By return the same day, McQuaid 'hastened to assure' Duff that he approved the double use of his name and agreed with his concern to insert a phrase conveying the uniqueness of the Mercier Society. 'You are, in my opinion, accurate in fearing the Sword of the Spirit confusion,' he confided. 'There is a danger that the Legion might well be regarded as following an example of risky precedent. The only precedent that could justly be invoked is the Catholic Evidence Guild – and even that group worked under completely different circumstances.'[22]

When Duff received McQuaid's note he arranged for a private meeting with him that evening and, with McQuaid's assistance in Latin, he altered the Leen-Heuston text. Next morning and without consulting others in the Mercier Society, Duff sent the petition in its final form to McQuaid, amused that this was the first time that he had signed himself Franciscus Duff.

'A reading does not disclose to me any comma out of place,' Duff wrote. 'We will now commit the Petition and Your Grace's *Votum* to the care of Her under whose banner we work. I was glad to have that talk last night.'[23] The alterations he had suggested now intact, McQuaid arranged for the petition to be put in the next Nuncio's Bag to Rome. 'Our Lady will have to obviate the delays,' he told Duff.

The Duff-McQuaid relationship

As President of the Legion of Mary, Duff had regular contacts with McQuaid, characterised by docility and self-interest on his part and by a mixture of high-handedness and collaboration on the Archbishop's. A civil servant by profession who had worked briefly as private secretary to Michael Collins, Duff, a Dubliner, had taken early retirement to engage in full-time religious work. He was anxious to use his extensive contacts within the Irish civil service and public life to promote his Church work. From correspondence between McQuaid and Duff, it emerges that McQuaid exercised detailed control over all Legion of Mary activities. The Archbishop found in the Legion president both a source of intelligence and a conduit for channelling public funds into charitable projects, ostensibly run by the Legion but effectively controlled from the Archbishop's palace. Duff found that he had access to an Archbishop who was open to suggestions about new projects and who knew how to finance them. Duff acted as both a spy and a facilitator for McQuaid.

At the same time as Duff was working with McQuaid on the petition to Rome, he was also in November 1942 reporting to the Archbishop on a proposal to have the Corporation provide three playgrounds in Dublin's inner city which were to be run by superintendents chosen by the Legion. The scheme received a positive response from a Mr Sherwin of Dublin Corporation, though it presented the Legion with a problem in that it would become the employer of the playground superintendents. Duff suggested that if McQuaid would devise a means of relieving the Legion from 'the role of employer of paid labour', the Legion would be ready to undertake this new work with the prospect of good success. Meanwhile, he confirmed that 46 Legionaries were engaged in probation work and that Mr Justice McCarthy would be glad to see McQuaid on the work in general.[24]

Legionaries were preparing, at McQuaid's direction, to start visiting juvenile offenders in Dublin's Mountjoy Prison, and they had been invited to give day-retreats to 'the probation children' in the Sisters of Mercy's convent at Goldenbridge: 'The idea has been proposed to Reverend Mother Cyprian, and she had welcomed it, subject to the concurrence of Your Grace.'[25]

One spin-off from the Mercier Society's contact with Protestants was that Duff had learned that the Baptist church on the corner of St Stephen's Green and Harcourt St was for sale. McQuaid encouraged him to explore the possibility of purchasing it. 'It is really a fine building,' Duff reported, recommending that it would be worth having as a hall in addition to the Leinster Club which he had also inspected. Duff thought that the republican revolutionary and founder of the Irish Hospitals' Trust Sweepstakes, Joe McGrath, might be a suitable benefactor.

'It has occurred to me that suppose Joe McGrath could be interested,' Duff suggested, 'he might get together a group who would buy the Church and give it to us. Then we would have both places. Joe McGrath is not easy to interest or influence. This is inevitable, for I suppose everyone in Ireland has already written to him for money. But supposing it got to his ears (say via Alfred Jones) that Your Grace were interested in the project, no one knows what might happen!'[26]

As part of his espionage for McQuaid, Duff reported to Fr Mangan that the Legionaries had come across 'an aberration' in the existence of 'The Thinkers' Circle', a 'rationalist gathering' which met every month in Hynes's restaurant in South Great George's St. A Legionary named Tuke had infiltrated the group and reported to Duff that it was attended by 35 persons, six of whom were women.

'In the main the type of those attending was very good,' Duff told Mangan. 'Beckett, the architect and Quaker, was there. Rationalistic views were definitely in the ascendant. Possibly about six people could be described as pro-God. Stanley, the milkman of Parnell Street was present and showed himself to be bitterly anti-religion. I do not know if you are acquainted with this man. He was a Catholic and was formerly in the IRA ... the Honorary Secretary of the Circle is Marjorie S. Brook, 24 Lower Beechwood Avenue, Ranelagh, Dublin. She is a young girl of about 25 years.

'If there is no objection, we will continue to follow up this circle. Mr Tuke, whom we would propose to send there, forms an admirable representative. He has an excellent Catholic grounding, is self-possessed and is able to intervene effectively in the discussions. He has a very pleasing personality and a capacity for making contacts and following them up. I might mention that he brought out five Protestants to the last of the Labour Days held in Tallaght on Sunday last. The Protestants professed themselves delighted with the experience and anxious to repeat it.'[27]

What McQuaid told Rome

Unknown to Duff, McQuaid wrote to the head of the Holy Office, formerly known as the Inquisition, Cardinal Marchetti-Selvaggiani seeking his permission to send to Rome his own report and commentary on the Legion of Mary along with the Legion's petition. His report gave an account of the genesis and development of the Mercier Society, the Society of Jews and the Overseas Club, and was followed by the Archbishop's recommendations on each of the three organisations. It concluded with a commentary on the Legion of Mary which was quite critical of Duff. [28]

McQuaid's version of the origins of the Mercier Society was that in late 1941 Duff had asked leave to continue the one-day retreats for non-Catholics by holding meetings of an informal, private character, and to hold uncontroversial discussions on religious subjects, with entrance controlled by ticket and without any report being allowed to be printed or circulated. Its purpose was to establish a better understanding of Catholicism 'by the exposition of the tenets of the Faith.'

After consultation with his Vicars General, McQuaid had agreed 'to permit the experiment, which was after all directed at educated Protestants of goodwill who could not attend the one-day retreats. From small numbers, it soon attracted 70 Protestants, and the practice was established of alternate Catholic and Protestant speakers. A joint committee was considered necessary by the Legion 'to allow an appearance of equity' and to maintain cordial relations.

McQuaid recognised that the Catholics were well-educated, some of them holding most influential positions, and he stressed that he had 'taken measures to control very strictly Catholics who speak or even attend the meetings.' But he was scathing in his criticism of the Protestants, both clergymen and layfolk. 'The non-Catholics have on no occasion given proof of power to sustain a well-measured case,' he told the Cardinal. 'On the contrary, even they themselves admit that their speakers have been distinctly poor, in contrast with the Catholics. The ignorance even of their clergymen is so deep as almost to be beyond belief.' (This assertion amounted to a professional smear of Protestant theologians such as the two Hanson brothers, both future bishops, and George Otto Simms, the future Archbishop of Dublin and Armagh. Had the Protestants known his assessment of their theological worth they would have made their calibre known to him in no uncertain terms.)

'What is very remarkable for Irish Protestants,' McQuaid went on, 'the atmosphere has continued to be from the very beginning one of great courtesy and cordiality. This is a singular achievement on the part of the Legion of Mary, in view of the Calvinist bitterness that so frequently marks the attitude of Irish non-Catholics. Only on two occasions was a bitter note introduced by a Protestant, one of whom was the English Dean of St Paul's, but it was immediately resented by Protestants. It can truly be said that the non-Catholics appreciate and desire to hear spiritual subjects, rather than religious-social subjects exposed by Catholics.' (McQuaid's assertion here is contradicted by the documentary evidence, which shows that Protestants were in fact eager to expand the society's social and moral agenda.)

When the society seemed to have become controversial, McQuaid consulted his Vicars General and appointed four priests, 'all of them experts in their subjects and graduates of the Roman Universities ... to attend the meetings of the committee and the Society, watch over the interests of the Faith, answer objectives, set forth Catholic doctrine and report to me all the proceedings. These priests have acquitted themselves with most praiseworthy zeal, in securing that the safeguards suggested by me be faithfully observed.'

McQuaid claimed that the four priests were unanimous in stating that the Mercier Society had done and was capable of continuing to do great good to a certain class of educated Protestants: already a group of five young Protestant clergymen had asked a Dominican priest to give them priestly conferences on the doctrines of the faith. These priests, he wrote, agreed with his six conditions that would enable the Mercier Society to obtain 'a good that is otherwise impossible to maintain.' These safeguards were:

1. Selected priests, experts in the relevant branches of ecclesiastical science, be present at all meetings to guide the procedure, choice of subjects and of speakers.

2. One of these priests to be responsible to the Archbishop and report faithfully on every meeting.

3. Laymen in the Society who are chosen to speak, be of proved competence; and no layman or visiting priest is allowed to speak without previous preparation and the consent of the priest in charge.

4. Such laymen receive from the expert priests special instructions to fit them for their work.

5. All controversy, as at present, be strictly excluded and only exposition or defence of the Faith be allowed.

6. Entrance of Catholics to the meetings, as at present, be strictly controlled.

On the background to the Society of Jews, McQuaid explained that Duff had asked his leave to present a lecture by a distinguished Irish priest on the Jewish question, which was a notable success. (This differs from the Duff-Ó Broin account which claimed that Fr Arthur Ryan was unable to give the address.) 'Duff then asked leave to make contact with Jews, who had shown such an immediate interest, somewhat on the private lines of the Mercier Society,' McQuaid recorded. 'I agreed to permit a beginning.'

Noting that this initiative aroused a quite astonishing interest among the more educated Jews of Dublin, he next heard that a prominent Jew (Dr Abrahamson) was to give a conference. 'I at once interposed but gave due permission, in order not to damage gravely the good impression created. None the less, I have ordered that no further development take place and have directed that, pending the decision of the Holy See, only Conferences by Catholics, one every two months, may be given, with due safeguards arranged by me with the Vicars General.'

McQuaid told Rome that he feared that the society would achieve far less with Jews than with Irish Protestants, because of their general character, attitude to the faith and foreign nationality.

'I should distinctly suspect that many would use the Society merely to secure their position in Ireland, for social and commercial reasons, more especially because a certain fear concerning that position is often manifested by Jews, and because Irish Catholics frequently feel justified in resenting the number of Jews who have come to this country and the wealth they have amassed. It cannot, however, be said that there exists a hatred of Jews amounting to desire to expel or persecute them.

'A certain good can be done to Jews of goodwill and of better education. The number of educated Jews in Ireland is, on their own admission, remarkably small.

'Accordingly, I would venture to believe that the same regulations as suggested for the Mercier Society should be applied to this Society, with the added condition that Conferences by Catholics only, not on alternate occasions by Jews, be allowed. Jews who wish to state their opinion can do so after the Catholic has spoken.'

Turning to the Overseas Club, McQuaid reported that this was established by the Legion before his appointment to provide a club for foreigners, chiefly Africans and Asiatics. It had a reputation for showing Catholic hospitality to these strangers but had practically ceased to exist in war conditions. As it was more a social club than a society for the exposition of the faith, there were less dangers to be apprehended from it. However, McQuaid proposed that it should be subject to the same regulations as the Mercier Society.

In his commentary on the Legion, McQuaid acknowledged that the members were noted for their excellent lives and their charitable zeal. 'They undertake works for which no other workers practically can be found. They are docile towards authority. As lay-folk they achieve a good that is impossible for priest or religious to obtain. It seems to me that in the actual conditions of our society and in the reconstruction of society after the war, the Legion of Mary can be an instrument of good, than which it is difficult to conceive a more effective.'

Yet, McQuaid pointed out, the Legion was recruited largely from the less well educated and its members suffered from a lack of systematic spiritual and intellectual religious formation; neither were the qualities of its aspirants tested by subjecting them to a period of probation. McQuaid's remedy for these defects was the provision of a systematic course of instruction by priest-directors which would be obligatory for all Legion members during and after the probation period, and suited to the type of education and work of the Legionaries.

McQuaid informed Rome that he had set up a commission of priests to examine this matter and had suggested that the basis of the course should be the catechism of the Council of Trent and the social Encyclicals of the Popes. 'Until these deficiencies are supplied, it seems to me', McQuaid continued, 'that the Legion of Mary, not only in Ireland, but the very many countries where it now operates, will fail to do the good that it could in very striking measure achieve.'

'Having made inquiries from well-informed priests and laymen, having consulted my Council and received its full approval of this *Relatio*, I beg to suggest that the activities of the Legion of Mary described above are worthy of praise and that with the safeguards that Your Eminence may prescribe, they may be permitted to continue by way of experiment.'

Clearly, McQuaid's emphasis on a reorganised Legion developed by way of an educational training programme controlled by him was at variance with Frank Duff's vision of the group he had founded and his wider aspirations for intellectual dialogue with Protestants, Jews and Muslims from Africa and Asia. Rome would have to choose between them.

Ó Broin pleads for Jews

In early December 1942 Ó Broin reported to McQuaid on Abrahamson's lecture to the Pillar of Fire Society, an encounter which had been by ticket invitation bearing the instruction, 'No press references.' Ó Broin described the meeting as having a better atmosphere than the Mercier Society: 'There is nothing hoity-toity about the Jews. They are uniformly humble, respectful and yet quite frank. They are afraid of persecution. They want justice and sympathy.'

Ó Broin believed that the Jews needed the society as a safety valve, as a means of expressing their feelings on matters of current interest and of making contact with representative Irish Catholics. 'There is room for a great work of charity in just meeting them socially and giving them these opportunities. We can, moreover, use the Society for doing what we could never do in any other way, namely for teaching Christian doctrine to the Jews.'[29]

McQuaid did not share Ó Broin's expectations. He saw the society's chief value as offering an occasion of exposing Catholic doctrine to the Jews. And he added: 'The chief value of the Society, in Jewish eyes, is a chance of staving off persecution or expulsion, by making friendly contact with the dominant element in our State, the Catholics. Their purpose, however it be masked by an appearance of suavity and accommodation, is and will remain material.'[30]

Bluntly admitting that he had little confidence in the Jewish dialogue, McQuaid took the view that results would be visible only when the Jews sat at conferences on Catholic doctrine given by recognised and competent Catholics. McQuaid took this narrow view at a time when European Jews were looking for help against Hitler. That same month, the Chief Rabbi of Palestine, Isaac Herzog, sent de Valera a telegram informing him of the Holocaust: REVERED FRIEND PLEASE LEAVE NO STONE UNTURNED TO SAVE TORMENTED REMNANT OF ISRAEL DOOMED ALAS TO UTTER ANNIHILATION IN NAZI EUROPE.

On January 4, 1943, Ó Broin wrote to McQuaid thanking him for giving Duff permission to hold a meeting of the joint committee of Jews and Catholics as a necessary preliminary for a further meeting between them – it was intended to propose Duff as the next speaker and that would be agreed to. On the basis of an understanding with the Jews, one of their creed would give the fourth talk in February. Ó Broin thought that overturning this agreement would kill the society and make further work among the Jews impossible. 'What we would like,' he wrote, 'is permission to continue the arrangement of a monthly talk, turn-and-turn about.'[31]

In a reply drafted in his own hand but sent on January 5 in the name of his secretary, Fr Mangan, McQuaid pointed out that, as he was not the author of any understanding with the Jews, he was not bound by any arrangement. While recognising Ó Broin's good intentions, he directed him to obey his Archbishop. 'The Archbishop fails to see how with equal goodwill to accept his decision, you cannot safeguard the Society of the Pillar of Fire from extinction, until the Holy See has given its judgement on the advisability and procedure of the enterprise.'

The sting was in the last sentence: 'The Archbishop, in virtue of his office, has the right and duty to expound Christian doctrine and all others in his diocese, priests or layfolk, expound Christian doctrine lawfully only when they are duly subordinate to his authority.'[32]

On January 7 Ó Broin asked Mangan to explain to the Archbishop that he had written on his own responsibility, not on behalf of the Legion. There was no question of the Legion or himself being unwilling to do as McQuaid had directed. Ó Broin disclosed that when he wrote to the Archbishop he had not known that McQuaid had communicated to Rome his original direction of confining the society to Catholic speakers only. He realised now that he might have been quite wrong in assuming that delay would kill the society; nor was there a formal understanding with the Jews about rotation of speakers. No joint meetings had taken place. 'I am sorry that there should have been such casualness about any of my phrases as to suggest the contrary. I can only repeat that I was speaking to my Archbishop in the way I thought he expected me to. Of what assistance would any letter of mine be to His Grace if I were not therein to express my point of view? I did not anticipate that my letter would be treated as if it were a carefully drawn-up official document.'

Ó Broin was dumbfounded at McQuaid's attitude. The *raison d'être* of the Pillar of Fire was to teach Christian doctrine: 'The sooner we get down to that, the sooner we shall have converts.' But Ó Broin warned: 'We cannot begin to teach the Jew Christian Doctrine within the Society, if the Jews are not to have a corresponding right to express themselves.' Ó Broin 'ventured in all seriousness to suggest for His Grace's consideration that the further meeting should not be held.'[33]

It was not until February 15 that McQuaid replied, again in Mangan's name, and he merely thanked Ó Broin for the explanation he had offered. 'May I say, from myself,' Mangan wrote in accordance with McQuaid's outline, 'that you scarcely grasp the attitude of H.G. even in the current letter and if it would be of any use in your opinion to have a chat about the matter, I should be glad to see you.'

The final indignity for Ó Broin was that McQuaid left the advisability of holding a meeting to him and his committee, as he 'had not yet begun to consider the abandonment of the work at a later stage.'[34]

Waiting for Rome

Throughout 1943, as Duff harboured illusions of his petition succeeding in Rome, McQuaid made it clear privately that he expected a negative reply. In March he rejected a request from Leen on behalf of the Mercier Society to allow clergy to take part in efforts with Protestants to draw up a plan for the social order which would be equally acceptable to Catholics.[35] McQuaid had told Leen in November: 'The more I see of the Mercier Society, the less I can accept it as an instrument of conversion. It seems to me to be little better than a debating club, where, under cover of affability, each side scores its points.'

Intriguingly, McQuaid also told Leen that neither could he see the Legion accepting the essential need for trained speakers. 'Their attitude is still concerned with calling into play the emotional harmony of a social meeting.' He was willing, however, 'to tolerate the existence of the Society, until Rome gives a clear ruling'.[36]

Further evidence McQuaid had effectively written off the Mercier Society was his remark to the President of Maynooth College, Dr Edward Kissane, who was due to address the Society: 'I just tolerate it, for I am not convinced of either its legitimacy or its usefulness. And I have not found full cooperation in my very explicit instructions to secure only expert Catholic exponents, for the Legion people think it is a mistake to use priest-experts.'[37]

Holy Office decree

A request from Leen on January 21, 1944, to hold meetings of the Mercier Society in March and April, which would be addressed by the Professor of Philosophy at UCD, Rev. Professor John D. Horgan, and the Holy Ghost priest, Fr Bernard Kelly, was refused by McQuaid. Unknown to the Mercier group, McQuaid had already received the Vatican reply. 'I regret,' McQuaid wrote to Leen, 'that in view of the answer received from the Holy Office, I cannot see my way to renewing the permission of the Mercier Society as requested for March and April, until such time as the necessary adjustment has been made in the procedure of the Society.'[38]

McQuaid duly supplied Duff with the relevant paragraphs of the document. There was no mention of the Mercier Society by name in the decree signed by the Head of the Holy Office, Cardinal Marchetti-Selvaggiani. It was dated November 13, 1943.

> The matter is to be committed to the prudence of the Most Reverend the Archbishop of Dublin, who, by way of experiment only and for a period of five years, is empowered to grant leave to the Association of the Legion of Mary to proceed in its enterprise of propagating the light of Catholic Truth among non-Catholics, in such wise however that:
>
> 1. The Authorities of the Association of the Legion of Mary sedulously take care that lay Catholics who, together with priests, meet non-Catholics, especially in Conferences, be altogether trustworthy in respect of Faith and Catholic teaching; and
>
> 2. Further, that the said Authorities, in every subject matter and conduct of affairs, comport themselves with docile attention and fidelity to the commands of the Ordinary (ie McQuaid).
>
> Protestants, however, who assist at these meetings, while they seek for declarations of doctrine, must not, on any occasion, dare to defend the teachings and opinions of their own sect.

McQuaid coldly informed Duff that it was the usual practice of the Church to address the Archbishop personally. 'I should be grateful if, having considered the reply of the Holy See, you would kindly submit to me the measures you deem advisable, in order that I may judge their conformity with the Decree of the Holy Office.'[39]

Rigging a scheme

When the Mercier Society met to discuss the decree on February 5, 1944, no one was quite sure what to do next. Fr Leen said he felt that the general tenor of Rome's response was positive and suggested that, as long as Protestants did not attempt to win Catholics over to their views, the Mercier Society could carry on. Fr O'Carroll judged it to be unfavourable to the society as it stood, by limiting the activity of Protestants to listening to Catholic papers and asking questions about Catholic doctrine.

Duff disagreed with O'Carroll and argued that the decree did not forbid Protestants to expound their teachings and opinions – it demanded that they should not be allowed to defend them. Joe Walshe felt that if O'Carroll's interpretation were correct, Rome would be demanding something that could not be reasonably expected from the type of Protestant who attended the Mercier Society. Desmond Fitzgerald took issue with O'Carroll, too; he suggested that Protestants could be kept to neutral subjects. The Dominican, Fr Heuston, thought that it was up to the committee to hammer out a procedure that would effectively cut out all Protestant defence during the discussions, but Jack Nagle questioned whether such methods could be relied on – past experience had shown that the unforeseen happened at meetings. Leen proposed that the only effective way to prevent Protestants from defending their teachings was to ask them not to do so, but this view was rejected by the committee as unfeasible and as meaning the end of the society.

León Ó Broin said that the committee was wasting its time trying to rig a scheme which would be most difficult and unpleasant to carry out. Insisting that they had gone far enough in doing the unpleasant, he proposed that Duff and his colleagues put down on paper what they considered to be moderate and reasonable, and if McQuaid thought that was insufficient, then they should drop the whole business.

Ó Broin's suggestion was ruled out by the rest of the committee and he left shortly afterwards. Instead the meeting mandated Heuston to draft a full statement on the position of the Mercier Society for discussion at their next meeting before sending it for McQuaid's approval.[40]

'The Committee of the Mercier Society have received notification of the Decree of the Holy Office with great pleasure,' Duff wrote to McQuaid on February 20, 1944. 'They wish me to convey their thanks to Your Grace for what you have done to secure so favourable an outcome to my petition.'[41]

Promising McQuaid docile attention and fidelity to the instructions of the Holy See, Duff professed that their only desire was to work under the direction of their ecclesiastical superiors for the propagation of the light of Catholic Truth among those non-Catholics for whom the Mercier Society was first instituted.

'After much deliberation in the Committee,' he continued, 'it has not seemed feasible to us to publish the provisions of the Decree directly, even as from ourselves. The Committee have drawn up a draft scheme of regulation for the Society, which in our opinion, will provide for the continuance of the Society and at the same time secure that the requirements of the Holy See be fulfilled. And we respectfully submit this to Your Grace's consideration and judgement.'[42]

McQuaid was quick to draw Duff's attention to 'some misconceptions' in his letter and directed him to read out the following statement at their next meeting:

> The Decree of the Holy Office was not an answer to your petition. Your petition is not even mentioned. It is an answer to me as Ordinary of this Diocese.

The Decree may not be regarded as being favourable in the sense that it sanctions the existence or work of the Mercier Society, least of all that it gives any sanction to the existence or work of a similar Society organised in any other Diocese by the Legion of Mary.

The Decree allows me as Ordinary, if I consider it advisable, to tolerate for a period of five years in this particular Diocese, the existence and work of the Mercier Society, on certain conditions of which I am the competent judge.

One condition is very explicitly laid down by the Holy See – that on no occasion, while they seek for explanations of Catholic doctrine, 'may Protestants dare to defend the doctrines or views of their own sects.' Accordingly, it now remains for me to decide whether your memorandum, in theory and especially in practice, gives me the guarantees I require to tolerate the existence and functioning of the Mercier Society.

There can be no question whatever of your publishing, in whole or in part, the terms of a Decree addressed to me as Archbishop. Only inexperience in handling Roman documents can explain to me how you could speak of publishing the Decree and, what is more serious, of publishing it as from yourselves. I am very willing to accept your profession of docility to the measures I may submit.[43]

Mercier Society suspended

On April 6, 1944, McQuaid informed Duff that the revised regulations did not meet the conditions laid down by the Holy Office. 'It is the unanimous opinion of my Council that the Regulations could not in practice succeed in averting the defence of non-Catholics of their doctrines and opinions. Accordingly, I regret to say that I cannot sanction the Draft Regulations by you in the name of the Mercier Society.'[44]

McQuaid arrived at his decision despite the fact that the document presented by Duff had stipulated that 'in every subject-matter and in all conduct of affairs they must comport themselves with docile attention and fidelity to the commands of the Archbishop.' It also stated that 'the name Mercier Society does not imply imitation of the Malines Conversations'.[45]

Duff relayed McQuaid's decision to his collaborators in the Mercier Society. 'We all accept Your Grace's decision with docility,' he told the Archbishop. 'We have failed to devise more practical steps or further regulations capable of averting in practise the defence by Non-Catholics of their doctrines and opinions. Accordingly, the meetings of the Mercier Society remain suspended.'[46]

Two days later, McQuaid thanked Duff and the others for 'the immediate and admirable docility' they showed in accepting his decision.[47]

14

The Hidden Ruler
1944–48

'He is particularly able – a very quiet, unassuming little
man, but possessed of a big brain and a strong character.'

Francis Matthews, US Secretary of the Navy.

A bizarre exchange between Archbishop John Charles McQuaid and
Éamon de Valera on reasons why a new cathedral should not be built in
Merrion Square casts intriguing light on a question which has remained a
puzzle for Dubliners for more than half a century. What becomes clear
from two documents classified as 'secret' in the McQuaid Papers is that
their disagreement on the matter marked a dramatic deterioration in relations between the two men. These documents challenge the conventional view that it was McQuaid's decision not to proceed with the
building. On the contrary, it is clear from the correspondence that, far
from abandoning it, McQuaid felt it to be his duty to start work on the
project, which he feared would not otherwise be completed in his
lifetime.

It was McQuaid's predecessor, Archbishop Edward Byrne, who
announced in 1930 that Dublin needed a new cathedral because the Pro-
Cathedral, which had been built prior to Catholic Emancipation in 1829,
was 'inadequate as a Cathedral for Catholic Dublin, and is still not worthy
of the Catholicism of the Irish nation'.[1] With the secret assistance of the
then Head of Government, W.T. Cosgrave, in May 1930 Byrne bought
Merrion Square from the Pembroke Estate for £10,000 specifically for a
cathedral site, with a clause requiring payment of a further large sum if
the archdiocese failed to erect the cathedral within a specified period.

Under the terms of the contract, Merrion Square did not come into
the archdiocese's possession until May 1938, but by then, Byrne, a sick
man, was incapable of launching the project. On his appointment in 1940,
McQuaid found that Dublin Corporation and the diocesan authorities
were in head-on conflict over the Merrion Square site. Indeed, the last act
of Bishop Wall as Vicar-Capitular on Christmas Day, two days before
McQuaid's Episcopal Consecration, was to deliver a firm protest to the

Corporation against 'the grave discourtesy shown to the Ecclesiastical Authority in all that related to the site for a Cathedral, chosen by the Town Planners'.[2]

The Corporation wanted the cathedral to be built on a location close to its own offices near the River Liffey. Like Byrne, McQuaid wanted to build a national cathedral at Merrion Square, close to the seat of Government and parliament. McQuaid's ambition to site a Notre Dame-style cathedral there was further kindled in September 1942, when he attended the opening of St Phelim's Cathedral in Cavan by Bishop Lyons, who proudly proclaimed that it was 'a great day of victory not merely for the diocese of Kilmore but for the whole of Ireland and for the Church.' Lyons's achievement in the relatively poor diocese of Kilmore was a spur to McQuaid to provide Dublin and Ireland with a worthy cathedral.

McQuaid became increasingly irritated by the Corporation's stand. Nor was his displeasure lessened as a result of stories in *The Irish Times* that the Merrion Square site had been abandoned. He was further annoyed to read reports of how Jim Larkin had asked in the Dáil if Merrion Square would be thrown open to the citizens. It was therefore a shock for McQuaid when he discovered that among those querying the development of Merrion Square was Éamon de Valera.

The Government had decided to issue a declaration discouraging land speculation in the vicinity of Government Buildings and Merrion Square. On November 12, 1944, McQuaid wrote to de Valera to say that he was puzzled by their decision. Before it issued any such declaration, he wanted de Valera to bring to his Government's attention the fact that Merrion Square had been chosen as a cathedral site, and finding a suitable alternative would mean serious delay and additional expenditure. Indeed, finding an alternative would probably mean relinquishing the project for their lifetime, a prospect that was regarded by his advisers 'as gravely to be deplored'.

Referring to Cosgrave's involvement in the purchase of the site, McQuaid pointed out that the Head of Government was proposing to change an arrangement made with his predecessor. 'What ... must one expect from the Head of the next Government?' McQuaid wondered. 'I think you will agree that we have in this situation the heads of a possible misunderstanding which even the passage of years would not remove.'

McQuaid told de Valera that if the Government felt obliged to call for the use of Merrion Square, he would not consider it proper to oppose them on a merely physical issue such as the ownership of a strip of land. 'Government and Archbishop have to live in concord concerning issues of a spiritual and, therefore, incomparably greater value,' McQuaid wrote.[3]

Late the following night, de Valera phoned McQuaid. The Taoiseach's general remarks about 'a later stage' and 'a preliminary announcement' in regard to Government plans further puzzled the Archbishop, who took a note of the conversation. 'Tentative things had been done and firm action must be taken. Was it certain that I understood?' McQuaid recorded. In reply, McQuaid said that he was not sure if he did understand, for the situation was very nebulous. 'Yes,' de Valera answered, 'pretty nebulous and must be so now.'

McQuaid said his understanding was that the Government wanted to control property prices in view of the nature of future building in the area. De Valera said: 'That is accurate.' Merrion Square would almost certainly be included in the development of the area, and once it was it would be necessary to get an alternative site for the cathedral.

McQuaid's explanation that the diocese proposed building the cathedral on the east side of Merrion Square, de Valera replied that it would be necessary to have consistent design in the square. He went on to speak of how New York Cathedral was dwarfed by the buildings surrounding it. McQuaid pointed out to de Valera that variety of design was often a considerable aid to beauty and in the cities of Europe some cathedrals embodied as many as four styles. De Valera, however, held to the view that if McQuaid did not get an alternative site for the cathedral, it would be necessary to leave the matter alone or consider arbitration.

Reading over his notes again next day, McQuaid described them as an unsatisfactory but accurate record of a conversation that had been 'elusive and shadowy' on de Valera's part. He was still completely ignorant of the Government's actual plans.[4]

However, an interview which McQuaid's secretary, Fr Christopher Mangan, gave shortly before his death in 1989 casts further light on the 'bizarre' events of 1944. Mangan revealed that the Archbishop and the Taoiseach disagreed over the cathedral early on. 'They fell out over that and Mrs de Valera had to intervene to bring them together again,' Mangan disclosed. 'It seemed quite a serious falling-out. It was an extraordinary thing.'[5]

The cathedral was never built. McQuaid would not have given up easily on a project which he linked to the faith and generosity of centuries of Dublin Catholics, unless he feared that de Valera's opposition undermined his capacity to overcome planning procedures and to raise the necessary finance. The heavy demands of church and school building also bore down on him as the years passed. By the 1960s McQuaid had set his face resolutely against building a splendid cathedral in Ireland's capital city.

De Valera's challenge to McQuaid over the cathedral issue and their dispute over the running of the Youth Unemployment Commission were rare exceptions to the general attitude of deference accorded him. Four years into his reign, even the Jesuits, noted for their intellectual independence, were cowed by the Archbishop. An Apostolic visitor from Rome, Fr Dugré, reported that it had been said in the course of enquiries that the Irish Provincial, Fr John MacMahon, did not cooperate with

McQuaid in the work of his diocese. 'If it is true that the Archbishop is under this impression, I consider that this is most unfortunate; it is most necessary for us to cooperate to the best of our endeavour with those in positions of authority,' he wrote in a clear rebuke to MacMahon. The Jesuit headquarters in Rome had taken a strategic decision not to cross swords with McQuaid.[6] Little wonder then that de Valera was elusive and shadowy over the cathedral project.

Vocationalist Ireland

McQuaid's ambition to control the political contours as well as the religious boundaries of post-war Ireland emerges in previously unpublished correspondence in late 1944 and early 1945 with the veteran Bishop of Clonfert, Dr John Dignan. The Bishop was nursing his wounds after a verbal mauling by the Minister for Local Government and Public Health, Sean MacEntee, over his proposals for a social insurance policy based on Catholic social principles. Dignan had been appointed by the Fianna Fáil Government in 1936 as chairman of the Committee of Management of the National Health Insurance Society, whose remit was to consider policy responses to new social challenges. Dignan was highly respected within Fianna Fáil as an opponent of the 1921 Treaty and supporter of the 1937 Constitution, which he described as a second spring heralding the moulding of the nation as a truly Christian people.[7]

A paper which Dignan delivered to the society on October 11, 1944, made headlines in the newspapers on account of its scathing criticism of the dispensary medical system and its proposal for a restructured health service to be administered by an enlarged National Health Insurance Society rather than the Department of Health.[8] Although Dignan's plan captured the press and public imagination it angered MacEntee. If the scheme purported to be a factually detailed and costed proposal, MacEntee's private secretary replied dismissively in the newspapers, the Minister could categorically state that no such evidence had been submitted to him.

From his residence in Loughrea, Co. Galway, Dignan sent McQuaid a copy of his paper, accompanied by an apology for any apparent lack of courtesy in not doing so earlier. 'I had not the remotest idea it would receive such a favourable reception from the press and the public generally,' Dignan confessed. 'Did I think of or expect this publicity, you would have been the first to receive a copy.' Without referring to MacEntee's response, Dignan told McQuaid that he was fully aware of the paper's many defects, and he knew that when its implications were examined many vested interests would be up in arms. 'It will do some good, however, and if it does, I am more than rewarded for my trouble in writing it.'[9]

It was a more chastened Dignan who sought McQuaid's advice in early 1945, after MacEntee had dismissed his paper 'under almost every heading' in a Dáil debate. The Bishop wrote privately to the Minister asking for his detailed objections, but this request was fobbed off by MacEntee on the grounds of pressure of work. Exasperated, Dignan publicly demanded a reply from MacEntee as to whether a social security scheme based on the Christian principles of social justice and charity was impractical. To his Lordship's dismay, the sharp-tongued MacEntee lashed into him next day at a Fianna Fáil function in Dublin, accusing him of arrogating to himself functions belonging to the Minister and the Government. A week later, MacEntee's response was supported in the Senate by the Minister for Finance, Seán T. O'Kelly.

Describing O'Kelly's response as an 'apologetic explanation', McQuaid assured Dignan that he deeply regretted the 'great anxiety and greater pain' that the controversy with MacEntee must have caused him. A few days later Dignan thanked McQuaid for his letter's 'friendly and kindly tone,' but he admitted: 'I now fear that I should not have replied to Mr MacEntee at all and I should have continued to bear with his outburst in silence. People are often forced through good motives – in this case, truth and justice – to do things that were better left undone.'[10]

Dignan also appreciated McQuaid's advice not to give a public lecture at that juncture in Dublin, because the atmosphere was confused and 'a Bishop's dignity' might not easily fit with such surroundings. 'The Labour people are not to be trusted in their desire to hear a Bishop,' McQuaid told him. 'Political opportunism is always to be suspected, in view of the divisions in their ranks. This judgement may seem severe, but the recent disputes and some utterances of the two Larkins (Jim and Jim Junior) indicate the attitude of some members. The vast bulk of labouring men in Dublin is genuinely Catholic: so, too, some of the prominent leaders. To have explained sound social policy must always be of benefit to these decent people. But at the moment I find the situation rather disturbed by Mr MacEntee and Mr Lemass. I believe it would be well to allow a certain time to elapse.'[11]

McQuaid's reference to Lemass concerned the Minister for Industry and Commerce's outright rejection of the Vocational Organisation Report which had been issued by a commission chaired by Bishop Michael Browne of Galway. In response to Lemass' dismissal of the report as 'slovenly', Browne defended its call for structures involving vocational interest groups to be set up in place of the centralised bureaucracy in Dublin. The lines for a future Church-State battle were drawn by Browne when he told Lemass that it was his duty to defend the principles of the report, 'because they have been taught to us by Pope Pius XI'.[12] But McQuaid knew that the time for a trial of strength with the de Valera Government had not yet arrived, and that neither Dignan nor Browne had chosen the right issue.

Behind the scenes, McQuaid was building up diocesan support for Browne's report. Principally, he allowed a number of Catholic organisations to form the Catholic Societies Vocational Organisation Conference in May 1945 as a pressure group in favour of the report's implementation. However, the national archives reveal that the real economic battle taking place was inside Government, where a Memorandum on Full Employment tabled by Lemass was scuttled by de Valera, now aged 63. Influenced by the free-trade thinking of the economist J.M. Keynes and the social-welfare theories of Sir William Beveridge, Lemass wanted to move beyond what the British Representative to Éire, Sir John Maffey, called 'de Valera's Gaelic sanctuary'.[13]

From his regular contacts with Lemass, McQuaid knew how dictatorial he could be in applying regulations concerning fuel supplies. As late as spring 1945, Lemass refused to relax war-time restrictions on the use of candles in churches. Besides, McQuaid knew that he needed the good will of the Minister and his secretary, John Leydon, for licences to send food and clothing to the victims of liberated Western Europe and to the refugees from the Soviet Union and Eastern Europe. The Iron Curtain signalled the arrival of the Cold War era.

While watching the tide of events closely, McQuaid was pursuing a subtle strategy of twinning post-war celebrations to the Catholic Church's institutional interests. Through the Irish Red Cross Society, the Irish State sent Rome £100,000 (£2.1m approximately today) towards alleviating distress in Italy, a gift described by Pius XII as 'a truly bounteous contribution'.[14] In contrast to de Valera, who visited the German Minister, Eduard Hempel, to offer his condolences on the death of Hitler, McQuaid, on being tipped off by Walshe, prevented an unidentified group from having Mass celebrated in Fairview Church for 'the repose of the soul of Herr Hitler and the welfare of the German nation'.[15]

Just as de Valera was facing universal opprobrium for his ill-judged gesture of respect to Hitler, he was rescued by a ferocious attack on the Irish State's wartime neutrality by the British Prime Minister, Winston Churchill, during his 'Victory in Europe' broadcast on May 13.[16] In his reply on Radio Éireann, de Valera asked if Churchill could 'not find in his heart the generosity to acknowledge that there is a small nation which stood alone, not for one year or two, but for several hundred years, against aggression.'[17]

McQuaid listened to the Taoiseach's speech in Greystones, Co. Wicklow, and wrote to him next day. 'The broadcast was unusually good and its dignified restraint was, if I may say so, its chief feature. I hope that much good will come of it,' and he offered his assistance in arranging a Mass of Thanksgiving for keeping Ireland safe from the war. However, he advised that the manner of approach to Cardinal MacRory and the other bishops would need a little care. If de Valera was free on Saturday night, he could call 'at the usual hour for a little time.'[18] Clearly, the row over the cathedral site had not prevented the two men from pursuing their mutual interests.

De Valera's popularity soared after he stood up to Churchill. This surge of national pride coincided with the holding of nine days of prayers and benediction in churches throughout Ireland for the canonisation of the seventeenth-century Archbishop of Armagh, Blessed Oliver Plunkett. As in 1920 when Plunkett was declared Blessed, the Hierarchy celebrated the Silver Jubilee of his beatification linking Irish Nationalism with Catholicism. McQuaid had little difficulty with de Valera's notion of Éire as 'a sanctuary', though he preferred it anchored to the Catholic faith rather than the Gaelic language, which he now realised was not being spoken by the bulk of the people. And an unexpected concession in controlling the intellectual outlook of post-war Ireland was about to fall McQuaid's way.

Censorship: 'an unhoped for triumph'

On May 18, 1945, Senator William Magennis informed McQuaid of the outcome of 'an exceedingly friendly conference' which he had had the previous day with the Minister for Justice, Gerald Boland, in a private room at Leinster House on amending the censorship of publications legislation. Magennis, the *béte noir* of writers, was described by Frank O'Connor as 'a windbag with a nasty streak of malice'. In McQuaid's reckoning, however, for 35 years as Professor of Metaphysics and as an expert on education, Magennis 'at all times and on many questions fearlessly maintained the Catholic teaching of Faith and Morals'. As a result of the Archbishop's adulatory recommendation, he had been rewarded by Rome in January 1944 when he was created a Knight of St Sylvester.[19]

Boland had made a number of major concessions to Magennis, whom he knew was acting on behalf of the Archbishop of Dublin. He undertook to write to McQuaid asking His Grace to recommend a member to the Censorship Board to bring it up to its statutory number of five. He agreed to hold off his legislation until the autumn, provided Magennis gave him a memorandum which would serve his purpose and the country's interests. He also dropped his idea of replacing the board, as set up in the 1929 Act, with a single censor, similar to the legislation governing films. 'I countered his claim of superiority for the one–mind Censor as being the inferior and unsuitable type of judgement to bring to bear on so difficult a problem as estimating the probable influences of a novel on readers' minds,' Magennis gleefully told McQuaid.[20]

Magennis also claimed that he had won Boland over to the idea of establishing an Appeal Board. 'I explained that we consider the lack of a proper appeal from our findings a denial of natural justice which impaired the Act of 1929.' He had also explained to Boland that his and the Archbishop's scheme envisaged a board of three members to examine and report on books, plus a board of five to be available to consider an appeal against any book which had been banned. The setting-up of such an appeal board would free the Minister from making a judgement on a book, and the writer or publisher would have to pay a fee for the appeal. 'In view of these considerations, he swung round at once to this plan as eminently feasible if only we could provide the three and the five.'

McQuaid hastened to congratulate Magennis on an unexpected triumph, and he informed him that the Secretary of the Department of Justice, Stephen Roche, had asked him to nominate a successor to Fr Camac on the Censorship Board. 'I am very grateful and you know, I feel, that you can count on my aid in furthering your scheme.'[21]

Before the end of May, Boland's private secretary wrote to the Censorship Board secretary enquiring if Magennis had presented his memorandum, as the Minister wished to raise it in cabinet in explanation of his proposal to postpone his Bill. 'I had thought there was no urgency in the matter,' Magennis wrote to McQuaid, explaining that he was drafting his proposition for the next cabinet meeting. 'I consider it, however, essential to submit the plan for Your Grace's consideration and criticism before lodging it with the Minister.'

While believing that Boland had allowed it to be known – or guessed – that he was scrapping his original Bill and its one civil servant censor, Magennis feared that there was still a danger that he would retain a proposal for a seven-man Appeal Board with retrospective powers to review all previous bannings as far back as 1932!

Magennis explained that his scheme was as he had outlined to McQuaid in conversation, but he had put it in the form of a draft Act of Parliament to make it easier for the cabinet to grasp the idea; he also thought the legislation he proposed would reduce the Minister of Justice's contacts with censorship to an absolute minimum. In view of the urgency of the situation, Magennis suggested that the Archbishop's secretary might phone him to let him know if he could deliver the draft to the Palace next day.[22] 'Send in Manuscript,' was McQuaid's immediate response.

'I have carefully read the Draft of your Act,' he wrote to Magennis next day, praising its definitions of 'unwholesome literature' and what constituted 'indecent and obscene' reading material. 'One can always go on looking for a perfect censorship, while the tide of evil stuff keeps flowing in over the country, even into the recesses of the most backward districts.'[23]

By the end of the year, the Dáil and Senate amended the 1929 Act broadly along the lines proposed by Magennis-McQuaid, though both the Publications Board and the Appeal Board were composed of five members each. Boland had handed over ministerial responsibility to 'vocationalist' bodies effectively under McQuaid's hidden rule.[24]

'A Catholic country'

No surer proof of God's Providence was needed for McQuaid than the decision of President Douglas Hyde, a Protestant, not to seek a second term as president. On June 18, Seán T. O'Kelly was inaugurated as the second President of the Irish State with far grander pomp and ceremony than Hyde had been accorded in 1938. With meticulous care, McQuaid arranged that the music and liturgy at the Solemn Votive Mass in the Pro-Cathedral was worthy of a Catholic head of State.

McQuaid and the pious O'Kelly were soon engrossed in the task of providing a Catholic chapel for a Catholic president. McQuaid sent Fr James McArdle to Áras an Uachtaráin to examine the chapel used in Fitzallen's time under the British Crown. Knowing McQuaid's taste in ecclesiastical art, McArdle found the room too small, badly lit and approached by dismal stairways through a derelict part of the building. However, the Board of Works, anticipating McQuaid's requirements, favoured the building of a proper chapel in another part of the house. The board took the view that 'such a new chapel should be worthy of the President of a Catholic country'.[25]

Post-war Ireland was becoming steadily less attractive to the country's shrinking Protestant population. As was to be confirmed in the 1946 census, there was a 13 per cent decline in the number of Protestants living in the Irish State since 1936. In view of this trend Walshe confided to McQuaid that they could feel quite certain of being able to bring down particular Protestant organisations one by one. The Society for the Prevention of Cruelty to Children should be easier than the St John's Ambulance Brigade. 'From all sides I hear that the P's are very much on the run except in the higher economic spheres like the Bank of Ireland. So the time is ripe for action,'[26] Walshe observed to McQuaid.

McQuaid was not short of initiatives to put a Catholic stamp on every aspect of Irish life. He had formed a committee of Maynooth professors to translate the New Testament into Irish under the chairmanship of Monsignor Boylan.[27] Through the Supreme Knight of St Columbanus, Stafford Johnson, he floated his pet project of establishing a Catholic Institute of Writers and Journalists.[28] He established an Irish Catholic Stage Guild to organise special retreats and conferences for actors under the direction of Fr Cormac O'Daly O.F.M., whom he appointed its first chaplain.[29] Under McQuaid's patronage Our Lady's Choral Society was founded, with Vincent O'Brien as conductor, out of the Amalgamated Catholic choirs of the Diocese of Dublin: its first performance was Handel's *Messiah*, played in the Pro-Cathedral on December 16, 1945, with McQuaid acting as host to President O'Kelly, the Taoiseach and the Lord Mayor of Dublin.[30]

Meanwhile, the Catholic Social Service Conference continued to expand and was operating its own ambulance service to deliver pregnant Catholic women to and from the Catholic hospitals. The Catholic Welfare Bureau, whose referral services were being used by other bishops, reported that it had assisted 37,000 emigrants since its opening in 1942.[31] McQuaid supported the establishment of the Dun Laoghaire Guild of St Luke, and Sts Cosmas and Damian in St Michael's Hospital, and urged the publication of a journal for Catholic doctors in Ireland comparable to *The Catholic Medical Guardian* in England.[32]

In collaboration with the Mother General of the Irish Sisters of Charity, Mother Bernard Carew, he oversaw the provision of 145 beds at an extended Temple Hill children's hospital, without availing of Sweepstake Funds. 'I think it very important that both the Department [of Health] and the Corporation should understand that this extension is a private venture undertaken at the express request of the Archbishop of Dublin with a view to coping with very grave moral problems, and that the extension will neither ask for nor accept any subvention from Sweepstake Funds, either for erection or for maintenance, on the express wish of the Archbishop of Dublin,' he directed Mother Carew. 'A statement by you to that effect at the outset would mark the venture as a deliberately voluntary hospital, and therefore will be a demand on the very many Catholics who still believe in the Providence of God and in voluntary offerings to works of charity.'[33]

McQuaid enjoyed his celebrity status. Two nuns who visited him from Dumfries were so overawed by his wonderful kindness that, on their return to Scotland, they coaxed the Bishop of Galloway, William Mellon, to write to the Archbishop requesting a signed photograph. 'With some difficulty the nuns procured in Dublin a copy of Your Grace's photograph which they intend to hang on the wall of their Community room,' Mellon explained. 'They would like to have your autograph on it. I am taking the liberty of posting the copy to you and it should reach you by post following this. Please be good enough to sign and return.' McQuaid was happy to oblige.[34]

In a drive to expand youth clubs under his control, McQuaid told the first Leader Training Course, attended by 200 youths from all over the diocese, that they were 'only apprentices in the supernatural apostolate of youth' who needed to follow men and women 'rich in the counsel that was the fruit of grace and age and prayer'.[35] He thought the segregation of teenage boys and girls promoted moral discipline and was a marked advance in educational practice. It was at his behest that Dublin Vocational Educational Committee decided to build separate schools for Catholic boys and girls.

> The sanity of that policy is truly based on sound reason, on valid experience, and therefore, on the age-long favour of the Church. I feel sure that the years will amply justify the

wisdom of respecting the differentiation that is grounded in the diverse but complementary natures of the boy and the girl. It is a matter of pride to me that Dublin has taken an educational decision of which the intelligence and the courage must yet provoke admiring imitation.[36]

McQuaid did not countenance any show of independence on the part of young people. When Bishop Keogh of Kildare sent him a copy of a resolution passed at a Fianna Fáil Árd Fheis urging the setting up of a youth organisation that 'should cater for every class and type and should not worry what the parents thought', McQuaid noted that this was the second occasion on which such a move had been made. 'The resolution as put by a single speaker would not receive the support of the Party,' he told Keogh. 'Neither would it be worth our powder and shot. I think we must watch the movement vigilantly at the moment. So far I can find no sign of life, nor any plan. And they who may be working on the scheme know full well what forces they must reckon with, particularly if a wrong principle be set down at the start. It is not the remark or the resolution that worries me: it is the silence.'[37]

'Catholic' humanitarian aid

At first glance, McQuaid's anxieties about incipient youth rebellion in Ireland appear to be out of proportion to the far greater global concerns about the partition of Germany and the expansion of Soviet-led Communism. But his anxieties were, in part, fuelled by his conspiratorial cast of mind and partly by the potential appeal of the Communist ideal to Irish youth. Especially with the creation of the atomic bomb, McQuaid feared a renewal of warfare between Christianity and Communism. Once again, he looked to Pius XII for leadership against the forces of darkness.[38]

In close collaboration with Joe Walshe and Freddie Boland at the Department of External Affairs, McQuaid continued to build contacts with Vatican officials and leading European bishops. After hearing from the Apostolic Nuncio in The Hague, Monsignor Giobbe, McQuaid arranged with Boland, who was in charge of Ireland's aid programme which was run through the Irish Red Cross, to send £600,000 (£12.6m) worth of food and textiles to Holland. Writing to the Archbishop of Utrecht, Johannes de Jong, who had become a national hero for his resistance to Hitler, McQuaid told him that he was 'not a stranger to Holland and to its magnificent Catholic life,' and he expressed his confidence that 'Your Excellency's flock will emerge from the trial purified and stronger.'[39]

Boland, in regular consultation with McQuaid, also made arrangements to send aid to the Catholic countries of France, Belgium and Italy, and through the International Red Cross they were also able to get the food into the most stricken areas of Hungary, Poland, Austria, Germany and Yugoslavia.

As Primate of Ireland, McQuaid found himself inundated with appeals for assistance from all over Europe. Père Jacquinot, the head of the Paris-based International Committee of Catholic Charities, was introduced to McQuaid by the Nuncio, Archbishop Robinson, with whom the French priest stayed during his visit to Ireland. Jacquinot requested the appointment of a Fr Travers as Ireland's representative on the committee. 'This was done after consultation with the Cardinal, External Affairs and myself,' McQuaid informed the secretary of the Hierarchy, Bishop Staunton. 'And, as far I could see after much negotiation, this was all we ever can do, in view of the fact that the Government, using the Red Cross, has taken over all food and clothing which is being sent to the aid of Europe.'[40]

On occasion, McQuaid vented his anger at Red Cross officials for not following his wishes. 'I feel quite certain that the Irish Red Cross did not intentionally do anything which they believed would be disrespectful to Your Grace,' Walshe wrote soothingly when some unspecified action not to McQuaid's liking had been taken. 'Some of them just don't know but I have no doubt of their good intentions and of their gratitude to you for all you have done for them.'[41]

Lord of Killiney

In 1945 John Charles McQuaid became a Lord Archbishop in lifestyle as well as in ecclesiastical title. Shortly after celebrating his fiftieth birthday, McQuaid moved into a palatial residence in south Co. Dublin. Ashurst, a magnificent 100-year-old Victorian-Gothic mansion, was situated on 12 acres of farm and woodland off Military Road in the exclusive Ballybrack-Killiney district. With a spectacular view of Killiney Bay and the Wicklow Mountains, the mansion contained entrance and hallway reception rooms, 13 bedrooms and a well-cultivated garden. A gatehouse guarded the entrance, while the house was screened from public view and was reached via a long tree-lined drive. His chaplain-secretaries stayed with him, while his driver lived in the gatehouse. An order of nuns ran the household.

In memory of his French spiritual mentor, the late Père Lamy, McQuaid changed Ashurst's name to Notre Dame des Bois – Our Lady of the Woodlands – and he erected a statue of Our Lady in the grounds. Shortly after McQuaid took up residence, this part of Killiney became known as the Holy Land, even though many of his new neighbours were Protestant Freemasons. Built in 1845, Ashurst's first occupant was a wealthy Protestant landowner, Sir Compton Domville, Member of Parliament and leader of the House of Commons. The estate passed in 1874 to Elinor Jones Dobbs, whose husband William was a member of the

Westminster Parliament. Their daughter, Mildred, lived in the house until 1945. The circumstances under which Mildred Dobbs sold the property remain mysterious. According to the records in the Register of Deeds, Dublin, she sold Ashurst to the Master of the High Court, Henry B. O'Hanlon, on January 13, 1945. No price is given on the record. However, more than ten months later, on November 30, O'Hanlon endorsed this sale in the names of the Most Rev. John Charles McQuaid, the Right Rev. Monsignor Patrick Boylan and the Rev. Michael Patrick O'Connell. It would seem that he acted as an unofficial agent for the diocese.[42]

A mansion of such proportions might seem contrary to McQuaid's priestly vow of poverty but it fitted his perception of his special status as Primate of a Catholic nation. Its acquisition was a signal to the dwindling propertied Protestant class that Catholics were taking possession of the best land as well as the most senior posts in the professions. In Ashurst McQuaid was able to indulge in his hobbies of shrub planting and astronomy. He built his own shooting range and a installed a lift in the 60-foot-high belfry tower, where he fitted a telescope to watch the stars. From here he loved to shoot magpies with his .22 rifle. He kept cattle and Rhode Island hens, enjoyed his own cream, home-made butter and honey. He bred wolfhounds. He had become a country squire.

This acquisition came at a time when the diocese had built up debts for church expansion. Parochial improvements to the Holy Family Church in Aughrim St cost £6,000 (£130,000 in today's money). The site for a church in Rialto and the purchase of two houses for priests totalled another £6,000. In September 1945 McQuaid sent £2,000 (£43,333) to Rome, accruing from 8,000 Mass stipends.[43]

Before long, tongues were wagging about McQuaid's new-found affluence. The gossip affected the morale of leading members of the Knights of St Columbanus. Out of a sense of duty, the Supreme Knight, Dr Stafford Johnson, drew McQuaid's attention to 'the widespread criticism of the furnishing of some materials by firms called non-Catholic' to the new residence. Stung by the criticism, McQuaid refused to be called to account. 'There are some aspects of the criticism which intimately concern my own conscience and to these I shall not refer,' he wrote to Stafford Johnson in late October. I am willing to leave to God's justice and mercy both the accusations and the defence.'

However, in a move designed to win over the Knights, McQuaid allowed Stafford Johnson to bring some 'facts or truths' to their attention:

> I was obliged to find another residence, because I was obliged, under the new Canon Law, with the growth of the archdiocese to 646,000 Catholics, to set up a Chancellery at Drumcondra, with a resident Chancellor, with an Assistant and with all that a Chancellery demands in the matters of Diocesan Courts.

I am financially incapable of furnishing a new house. Therefore, I furnished my new house with all the effects of Drumcondra (furniture, carpets, curtains) which I could reasonably use in the new and MUCH SMALLER house at Killiney. All the rest (furniture, carpets, curtains) was donated to me, and donated so secretly that my benefactors will never be revealed; nor can their identity even be guessed. That donation was made because of my poverty.

Not a shilling of the alms, attributed to my personal use, on which ALONE I live, was used by me to furnish a new house for the Archbishops of Dublin and Primates of Ireland.[44]

The Red Hat succession

Just as McQuaid was supervising his move to Killiney, Cardinal MacRory died on October 13, aged 84. For his first official visit to the Six Counties to attend MacRory's funeral, McQuaid was supplied by Walshe with a *laisser passer* for the Northern security authorities once he crossed the Border. 'I don't believe you will be asked for any papers, and we have asked them not to do so, but it is better to be armed with it in case of need,' Walshe counselled.[45] In a panegyric, Bishop Lyons of Kilmore praised MacRory as the embodiment of the nationalist ideals of the Irish people at home and abroad, but the late cardinal's relaxed ways with money caused a major panic for the bishop and McQuaid, who found themselves searching frantically for a cheque which the President of the Red Cross Society, Mr Justice Conor Maguire, had sent him a few days before his death for refugees being accommodated in Glencree, Co. Wicklow.[46]

MacRory's death made McQuaid the senior as well as the dominant Irish prelate at a time when Pius XII was preparing to create additions to the College of Cardinals for the first time since 1935. For McQuaid, aged 50, in full health and at the height of his intellectual powers, the timing could not have been more propitious. An indication of his high standing in the Vatican was the conferral on him on November 13 of the Grand Cross of a Knight of Magistral Grace by the Grand Master of the Sovereign Military Order of St John of Jerusalem, of Rhodes and Malta, Prince Luigi Bangoni-Machiavelli. The most ancient religious Order of Chivalry in Christendom, it was traditionally a nobiliary body, which through appointments of Knights of Magistral Grace extended its membership to well-deserving Catholics of a respectable position, especially in those countries where nobility no longer exists as an institution.[47]

McQuaid's previous difficulties with de Valera may have weakened the Taoiseach's support for his candidature for the Red Hat. On December 18, Walshe instructed Ireland's representative at the Vatican, T.J.

Kiernan, that if the question of Ireland's next cardinal was raised by the Pope, he was to say that he had not yet ascertained de Valera's attitude. However, in the unlikely event of Rome offering Ireland two Red Hats – for McQuaid and Archbishop Mannix of Melbourne – they should be taken![48]

Another potentially damaging influence was the tall, thin and bespectacled number two at the Nunciature, Monsignor Domenico Enrici. Secretary since 1938 to the ailing Archbishop Robinson, Enrici had recently been appointed Auditor of the Nunciature, a promotion which gave him more responsibility and influence.[49]

Just as Walshe had detected a reservation in de Valera's attitude, so the wily head of the Department of External Affairs knew that Enrici had assembled a catalogue of complaints against McQuaid. 'If Enrici does the damage and damns John so that he won't be thought of in connection with a hat, we may not get a Cardinal at all for the present,' Walshe warned Kiernan. It would seem that 'the damage' was more than mere pique on the part of a junior official over McQuaid's frequent personal abruptness and exaggerated sense of his own prerogatives as Archbishop of Dublin, especially in matters of liturgical ceremonial. Had Enrici, with his access to the highest sources in Rome, spread stories about McQuaid's new lavish home and hinted at other handicaps?

As Christmas approached speculation mounted in Rome that Pius XII was finalising his first appointments to the College of Cardinals. During the War the membership of the College had dwindled to 38 members from the ceiling of 70 fixed in 1588 by Pope Sixtus V. McQuaid seemed a sure bet for promotion. It was not to be so. Just before Christmas Pius XII announced the creation of 32 cardinals, including Griffin of Westminster, Frings of Cologne, de Jong of Utrecht and four Americans – Archbishops Francis Spellman of New York, Samuel Stritch of Chicago, Edward Mooney of Detroit and the elderly John J. Glennon of St Louis.[50] McQuaid was not on the list. Ireland had been by-passed.

However disappointed he was, McQuaid put on a brave public face when Glennon, a native of Westmeath, was fêted on his way through Ireland to Rome for the consistory on February 18, 1946. But Glennon was to be a Prince of the Church for only a short time: he took ill in Ireland on his way home and died in Dublin. On March 10 his remains were received by McQuaid at All Hallows College. Next day McQuaid presided at the Solemn Requiem Mass said by Monsignor John P. Cody, who later as Cardinal Archbishop of Chicago was the model for the womanising prelate in a novel by Fr Andrew Greeley, and was named in Gordon Thomas's *Pontiff* as a suspect killer of Pope John Paul I in 1978.

Glennon's funeral was a national event. De Valera chartered a special plane for Cardinals Griffin of Westminster, McGuigan of Toronto and Gilroy of Sydney, Australia, to fly to Dublin for Glennon's funeral. On

March 12 McQuaid and de Valera met the three cardinals, who stayed with President O'Kelly at the Áras. McQuaid attended the funeral in Mullingar and hosted a lunch for McGuigan and Gilroy, who regaled him with the latest gossip from Rome. It was little consolation for the loss of Dublin's Red Hat.

Cardinal Spellman's conspiracy

On June 12, 1946, Joe Walshe presented his credentials to Pope Pius XII as Ireland's new Ambassador to the Holy See. During his 20-minute audience he expressed the hope that Ireland would soon be given a cardinal. 'The Holy Father eagerly answered at once that there was no doubt whatever about that point and that I could tell Mr de Valera that we should most certainly have a Cardinal at the next consistory,' Walshe informed Dublin. But, intriguingly, he added that Pius had said something so secret that this would have to be reserved for a verbal report.[51] Walshe intended to travel to Dublin to see de Valera but pressure of work kept him in Rome for the summer, and finally on August 28 he sent the Taoiseach the secret communication from Pope Pius in a handwritten note marked 'confidential'. The news concerned Archbishop John Charles McQuaid. Pius's exact words to Walshe were: 'I was going to make Dublin a Cardinal but the Americans were opposed to it. I yielded, because after all, they are the same as yourselves.'[52]

This was a stunning twist to the passing over of McQuaid at the previous consistory. Staggered by the news, Walshe had let Pius talk on without interruption. In his own thoughts, Walshe wondered if McQuaid's omission was brought about by Cardinal Spellman influenced by Ambassador Gray, or whether it was the work of the senior American in the Vatican Secretariat of State, Monsignor O'Connell, acting on information from Spellman. In the world of post-war politics, Spellman was a close adviser of Pius XII.

Walshe informed de Valera that Pius had decided that the next Irish cardinal would be the former Bishop of Meath, John D'Alton, who in April had been promoted to Armagh in succession to MacRory. 'John McQuaid will not be the next Cardinal, at any rate, as the H.F. told me positively it would be D'Alton,' he wrote. 'So unless you instruct me to the contrary I shall go on the general lines indicated.'

Walshe resolved that de Valera and himself should keep their counsel about the matter. De Valera was inclined to the view that it might simply have meant that the Americans had pressed for an extra cardinal for themselves and had used the twin arguments that their candidate was of Irish origin and that, with Armagh vacant, Ireland could wait.[53]

Walshe's suspicions about Spellman's role in an anti-McQuaid conspiracy were probably well founded. Spellman had cause to feel aggrieved at McQuaid over his unwillingness to side with America in 1943, and depriving the Dublin Archbishop of a Red Hat would have been sweet revenge for making him lose face in President Roosevelt's eyes. It remains a matter of conjecture as to whether de Valera ever told McQuaid how close he was to becoming a cardinal in 1945–46.

By August 1946 rumours from Rome were also reaching McQuaid. 'It is true that you are the cynosure of all eyes, and not all sympathetic,' his old friend Finbar Ryan O.P., now Archbishop of Trinidad, wrote to him on August 5. 'But for your comfort, let me tell you that there are many, very many, who see in you God's Chosen "man in the gap". Stand fast.'[54]

Still worried about stories of his princely lifestyle, McQuaid bared his soul in a letter to Ryan on August 9. 'I have destroyed it as you desired,' Ryan replied a week later. 'I heard some of the things you mention but the most diplomatic enquiry elicited no evidence, rather did it seem to me that, as you say, it was merely parrot-talk – and on the lips of such as count least before God. What you can clasp to your heart is the assurance that God's poor trust you.'[55]

In Rome, McQuaid was adding to his reputation as a meddler by taking up the cause of a holy French nun, Soeur Olive, who was in dispute with her religious superior in Paris. Against the advice of the Dominican head of San Clemente, Fr Tom Garde, that 'internal dissensions' between Olive and Mother Gabriel Mary would harm Olive's case, McQuaid had enlisted the support of Walshe to get 'a really fair hearing' for her from 'the more saintly men' among the cardinals and principal monsignori.[56] McQuaid's ally in the Olive case was his friend and follower of Père Lamy, Count Biver, who had drawn up a *relatio* or submission to Rome on her behalf.

The only consolation McQuaid could take from this period of unproductive Roman diplomacy was the appointment in August 1946 of Fr Dunne as his auxiliary bishop. 'An excellent choice,' was Ryan's verdict.

McQuaid plays the Roman card

Analysing the fall-out from McQuaid's failure to secure the Red Hat, Walshe decided that he should make it a priority to re-build Vatican-Irish relations from the bottom up, and he won de Valera's support for this policy. As a first step, the diplomat urged the appointment of able young Irish priests to the Secretariat of State, and advised de Valera that McQuaid was the prelate to implement this. 'In the end he is the one member of the Hierarchy we can really rely on for the big view notwithstanding his minor peculiarities, which please God will disappear rapidly,' Walshe wrote to de Valera.[57]

This was a godsend to McQuaid. 'Among the many evils that I deplore in this war, not the least is the fact that I have been unable for five years to send my best men to Rome. And I had some magnificent boys!' In due course, he selected one of his brightest priests, Fr John Gordon, for service in the Vatican diplomatic service, where he joined a Tipperary priest, Fr Tom Ryan.

Advised by Walshe to take a higher profile in Rome, McQuaid attracted positive attention in the Vatican by becoming the only Irish bishop to send a letter of support for the Archbishop of Zagreb and Primate of Yugoslavia, Aloys Stepinac, as the first 'prelate martyr' to Communist advances in East Europe.[58] When Tito established Communist rule in Yugoslavia in 1945, Stepinac – who had served during the war on the council of the fascist Croatian dictator, Pavelic – led the opposition to the new regime. After a political show-trial that captured world media attention, in October 1946 Stepinac was sentenced to 16 years forced labour at the dreaded Lepoglava prison. Pius XII rallied the Catholic world on behalf of his Slav protégé. (In 1999 Stepinac, controversially, was beatified by Pope John Paul II.)

On October 26, the Feast of Christ the King, McQuaid held a day of prayer throughout his diocese for the deliverance of Stepinac and all Catholics in Eastern Europe from atheistic Communism.[59] His protest letter was published in *L'Osservatore Romano*.[60] Walshe's advice was making McQuaid's name better known in Roman circles.

As the Dáil took up Stepinac's cause, McQuaid was kept informed of developments in Rome, particularly in regard to how Monsignor Tardini had prepared a memorandum on the Slav prelate's case for de Valera. De Valera used it to maximum advantage to mobilise the Dáil Opposition parties, the bishops and the public behind his national protest that was hailed as 'a superb lead to the world'.[61]

As part of Walshe's diplomatic offensive, McQuaid intensified his fundraising activities for Roman charities. In July he transferred through the Nunciature £14,164 (£300,000 in today's money) to the Holy Father's Fund for the Suffering Children which he had collected in the diocese, plus a £1,000 (£21,000) offering from himself.[62] In November he sent £213 (£4,873) to the Holy See as offerings for European relief, and by separate cheque £4,500 (£94,500) as St Peter's Pence from Dublin.[63] 'Cardinal Pizzardo knows of your great charity and believes you will help him,' Walshe assured McQuaid after Pius had assigned the Curial Cardinal to organise aid for Italy.[64] McQuaid's star in the Vatican was on the rise.

Teachers' Strike

Notwithstanding their cooperation in foreign affairs, McQuaid's relations with the de Valera Government were strained domestically as a result of his support for 1,200 national-school teachers who went on strike for higher wages in March. 'Your Organisation must have no doubt that the clerical managers of the city and the religious superiors have full sympathy with the ideal of a salary in keeping with the dignity and responsibility of your profession as teachers,' McQuaid wrote to the teachers' leaders publicly.[65]

McQuaid's letter gave the teachers an enormous morale boost, according to a member of the Drogheda Branch of the INTO, Padraig Faulkner. 'It removed any lingering doubts in the minds of Dublin teachers or of the Dublin Catholic Managers as to the justification of the action taken by the INTO.'[66]

However, McQuaid's public support angered the Government, which turned down a move to appoint him as mediator in the dispute. Derrig, the Minister for Education, stressed that the Government could not invite His Grace to mediate in an issue which it had already decided. McQuaid tried to appear unruffled by this snub. 'I am sensible of the pains you have taken to make clear to me the considerations on which the Government declares that it has based its decision not to invite the mediation of the Archbishop of Dublin,' he informed Derrig.[67]

When the Government refused to budge from its position, McQuaid provided the teachers with a face-saver which allowed them to return to school in late October. The Archbishop wrote to the General Secretary of the INTO, T.J. O'Connell, inviting the teachers to return to work as soon as possible for the welfare of the children. This was to be done without prejudice to 'the natural rights of the Government and the teachers, or to the just and equitable claims of the teachers'.[68]

'In deference to the wish expressed by the Archbishop of Dublin, as the Spiritual Authority responsible for the education of the children of the diocese, the Central Executive Committee, the better to consult the welfare of the children, unanimously decided to accept the invitation of His Grace.'[69] With that, the teachers went back to their jobs.

Larkin's Rosary beads

In a city gripped by Arctic weather and short of fuel, transport, light and food, McQuaid presided at the funeral Mass in January 1947 of the great Labour leader, Jim Larkin, universally mourned by the Dublin working class. While the poor poured out their grief at Larkin's death, McQuaid thanked God that the man long feared as the anti-Christ had died with Rosary beads wrapped around his hands. Larkin's pious death was McQuaid's most treasured conversion.

At the funeral, McQuaid told the writer Gabriel Fallon that Larkin had received the sacraments from the Capuchin priest, Fr Aloysius, who had notified him of the Labour leader's reconciliation to the Catholic Church. The Archbishop visited him at the Meath Hospital and gave him the Rosary beads on the evening before his death. McQuaid found Larkin propped up in bed with a tiny prayer-book held in his left hand, at arm's length, as he prepared to receive Holy Communion for the dying, the Viaticum. When Larkin talked about current trade- union rows, McQuaid calmed him and told him to put his faith in the Mother of God. 'I never did anything else before,' Larkin told an astonished Archbishop.

Revealing the gift of the Rosary beads years later, Fallon disclosed that McQuaid felt that it was 'not an unfitting gesture in the light of what the clerical attitude had been in the early days of Larkin's attempt to lift Dublin's working men off their knees.'[70] It was a magnanimous insight by McQuaid, who had developed close contacts with trade unionists, including Larkin. He confided to Joe Walshe that 'one of the most interesting social events recently was the public expression of gratitude to me issued by the Trade Unions for my share in settling the Dock Strike. Few things cost me such secret toil, but I was able to make most valuable contacts and helped, I think I can say, in very great measure, to end a strike which was already promising to be a national paralysis. It is a new feature to have the Trade Unions thank the Archbishop of Dublin.'[71]

At the same time, McQuaid was anxious to counteract the Communist-Socialist menace, and as an antidote to the vision of a militant working-class, secured Rome's permission to open the case for the beatification of 'the humble Dublin worker', Matt Talbot, a reformed alcoholic who had died in 1925. Visits to his grave in Glasnevin were encouraged. Aspects of his life which were emphasised in the promotion of his cause were prayer, self-denial, love of Christ and cultivation of character.[72]

If the Church could spread its influence among the working class, the centenary of the death of Daniel O'Connell, 'the Liberator', provided a further opportunity to highlight the established bond between Catholicism and nationalism. With the collaboration of the Knights of St Columbanus, McQuaid spearheaded a fundraising campaign for the restoration of O'Connell's home at Derrynane in Co. Kerry. Launching the O'Connell Centenary Commemoration in the Mansion House, McQuaid appealed to 'our faithful people here in Ireland and all their places of exile' to save the home which because once it cradled the home of the Emancipator had now become a Holy Shrine of God.[73]

Inside Killiney

McQuaid's lifestyle in Killiney was closer to the grandeur of O'Connell's Derrynane than Talbot's tenement hovel in Rutland St. Visiting churchmen such as Cardinal Griffin and members of the diplomatic corps such as Sir John Maffey, with whom he had a warm relationship, were regular guests. Unfortunately, their table talk is not recorded![74]

As a noted francophile, McQuaid was presented by the former

Resistance leader and founder of the pro-Christian Democrat MRP party (Mouvement Républicain Populaire), Georges Bidault, with a book on *The France that the Trials of the War has not Notably Changed.* The French Ambassador to Ireland, Stanislas Ostorog, delighted in ordering books from Paris for McQuaid's library. Ostorog, who was a regular visitor to Notre Dame des Bois, was enchanted by the piety of Irish people and loved to tell the Archbishop how the wife of a visiting colleague told him that she believed that the whole of Ireland was in state of grace. McQuaid also loved to hobnob with Ostorog's assistant, Vicomte de la Tour du Pin, who was from a well-known Catholic family.

Ostorog lavished even greater praise on the Archbishop after attending his first Holy Week services in the Pro-Cathedral – so magnificent was the conduct of the Passion ceremonies that it brought to Ostorog's mind the splendour of the Sistine Chapel itself. 'I never heard such beautiful church hymns. To hear them one understands the heights which the human genius can rise to when it is inspired by the Christian faith.'[75]

McQuaid may also have invited the English novelist, Graham Greene, to dinner at Killiney. 'I am most grateful to you for the kindness in seeing Mr Graham-Green *(sic)* and for all the help which you have given to him.' Cardinal Griffin acknowledged, after asking McQuaid the favour of meeting him.[76]

Freeman of Kilkenny

Disastrous winter floods in Kilkenny paved the way for what Bishop Collier described as a 'personal triumph' for McQuaid. The Archbishop had sent Collier a 'magnificent cheque' to help the flood victims: 'It was of course totally unexpected and we are therefore the more touched by the bigness of mind and heart that prompted you to remember and help in such a princely way sufferers at such a distance as we are.'[77]

As a result of McQuaid's generosity, Kilkenny City Corporation nominated him as a Freeman of the City, its highest civic honour. In early August 1947, Bishop Collier briefed McQuaid on the conferring ceremony. The speakers would touch on his achievements under four headings of 'Great Churchman, Metropolitan and Primate; Great Social Worker: interest in Poor and Young; Educationalist and his Sympathy and help to Kilkenny in the recent disaster.' The Bishop described the Mayor, James Pattison, as 'a very decent fellow and a good Catholic, being one of the National Labour Party who seceded on the question of Communism from the old Labour Party. 'The members of the Corporation are all Catholics. The speakers may wander a bit,' Collier warned, 'but they will mean well, and speak from the heart rather than from the head'.[78]

In his acceptance address in the City Hall, McQuaid supposed that it was his office rather than his person which had called forth such 'gracious tributes of courteous appreciation' from the Corporation members, who had conserved the culture of city life, while escaping the levelling serfdom of urban civilisation. After the ceremony McQuaid and Collier made a short inspection of the city by car – the Bishop was sure that the people would like that!' [79] The attendance of Your Grace and the provincial bishops gave it that touch of liturgical magnificence which is such a help to our good and simple people,' Collier wrote to McQuaid afterwards. 'It will be a tonic to their faith and piety for many a year to come.'

The populist reverence for 'liturgical magnificence' had become so widespread that even a Jewish member of the Dáil, Robert Briscoe, was moved to take action when he came upon an instance of the Religious appearing in a less than ideal display. After visiting Grangegorman Mental Hospital as a member of the board, he wrote to McQuaid looking for guidance on 'a delicate matter' which he did not intend to refer to in his report. He had been shocked to see five nuns – inmates of the institution – dressed in their robes, and it worried him that visitors would see their condition, a situation which did not accord with the dignity and status of nuns or of the Church itself.

'I am not competent to discuss the illness or the treatment of any of these Nuns and particularly as I am a non-Catholic the matter may be regarded by you as none of my business,' Briscoe wrote. 'I would, however, feel much more happy if Your Grace could see your way to have a member of your staff visit and examine the question and on the basis of his report Your Grace could then indicate to me whatever view is held. In my report to the Board, copy of which I here enclose, I make no reference whatever to this matter for obvious reasons.'[80]

Ad Limina Apostolorum

Archbishop McQuaid was seen off at Dublin Airport with the full honours of Church and State for his first *Ad Limina*, the official visit to Rome which all bishops are required to make every five years. Because of the war, his *Ad Limina* had been postponed until now, but as he was escorted by Aer Lingus staff onto the plane for London on September 4, 1947, he knew his reputation was high as Ireland's outstanding supporter of Papal charitable work, and that he was assured of a warm reception from Pope Pius XII and his senior officials, including Monsignor Montini. He also wished to crush the rumours which continued to circulate about his personality and lifestyle, or more precisely, as his friend the Archbishop of Trinidad, Finbar Ryan, put it, 'to counter any hostile propaganda in high places'.[81] McQuaid knew from Ryan that making a good impression could clinch the Red Hat which had eluded him the previous year. Significantly, the Primate of Ireland had arranged his appointments for September, a month ahead of the visit of Archbishop D'Alton and the other bishops.

With his usual thoroughness, McQuaid had compiled an exhaustive corpus of data highlighting the thriving state of the Archdiocese of Dublin during his seven years' reign, even though his well-intentioned but more relaxed mentor, Bishop Collier, had counselled him not to be anxious nor to bother too much about his Roman preparations. 'You will find the *Ad Limina* visit much less formal and troublesome than a first visit might lead one to fear, Collier wrote to him. 'It will in fact be easy and pleasant.'[82]

De Valera had instructed a senior diplomat at Iveagh House, Con Cremin, to make that visit as pleasant as possible by putting the State's resources and personnel at McQuaid's disposal on his way to Rome. McQuaid travelled on a diplomatic passport and was met on his arrival in London by the High Commissioner, John Dulanty. In Paris, McQuaid was entertained to dinner by Freddie Boland, who was in the French capital on State business. In Rome he stayed at the Irish College, where the rector, Monsignor Denis McDaid, had laid in a supply of whiskey for the guests, courtesy of Ambassador Walshe.

In October, when the 15 other Irish bishops visited Rome, Walshe told them that D'Alton would be the next Irish cardinal. 'The relief expressed was quite spontaneous, for reasons which I need not elaborate,' Walshe reported to de Valera. 'There was clearly fear of another appointment,' a clear but unexpressed reference to John Charles.

Walshe also told de Valera that McQuaid had 'let us down' by not coming with the rest of the bishops, because 'he put his own fears of petty difficulties arising with the other bishops here before the general interest.' But Walshe was even more critical of D'Alton, whose 'timidity' was aggravated by ill-health all the time he was in Rome. 'He seemed to have lost grip and power of decision during these past few years and I am afraid he is not going to set the world on fire unless he changes considerably,' Walshe wrote.[83] While he may have been passed over once more, McQuaid knew that with D'Alton so feeble, he could not be so easily ruled out for the Red Hat.

Seán MacBride T.D.

On October 29, 1947, the day on which he was elected to the Dáil for Dublin South-Central, the former IRA Chief of Staff, Seán MacBride, offered his unconditional loyalty to Archbishop McQuaid. Fifteen months earlier, MacBride had launched a new political party, Clann na Poblachta, which combined republicanism with a broadly-based economic and social agenda. MacBride claimed his party championed political principles which had been abandoned by Fianna Fáil, and certainly de Valera's party looked set to lose ground to its youthful republican rival.

MacBride made his respect for the Archbishop clear in a letter which he delivered to the Palace on the evening of his by-election victory:

> I hasten, as my first act, to pay my humble respects to Your Grace and to place myself at Your Grace's disposal. Both as a Catholic and as a public representative I shall always welcome any advice which Your Grace may be good enough to give me and shall be at Your Grace's disposal should there be any matters upon which Your Grace feels that I could be of any assistance. It is my sincere hope that Your Grace will not hesitate to avail of my services should the occasion arise.[84]

McQuaid assured MacBride that he would not fail to take advantage of his generous suggestion if the good of the faith were in question. 'When that occasion arises, I will not hesitate to avail of your services, now so frankly offered.'[85] In a second letter MacBride reminded McQuaid not to hesitate 'to call upon him at any time to impart such advice either formally or informally, as may from time to time occur to His Grace.'[86]

To meet the MacBride challenge, de Valera that same day announced a general election in early 1948. As the country settled down for a long campaign, McQuaid was able to follow events in the knowledge that he would not have to endure the fuel shortages which added to the winter harshness for most of the citizenry. The Archbishop of Baltimore, W.G. Toolen, advised him that a consignment of 50 bags of coal had been sent from the Port of Baltimore on the SS *American Forwarder* for his collection at the docks in Dublin. 'Doubtless you will be notified when the ship arrives and can make arrangements in the meantime to have the coal released by Custom Officials and delivered at the Episcopal Residence.'[87]

Papal medals

By early 1948 McQuaid had won Rome's approval for three Papal honours to be conferred on the Minister for Industry and Commerce, Seán Lemass, the Secretary of his Department, John Leydon, and Freddie Boland of the Department of External Affairs for their aid work on behalf of refugees in Europe. Industry and Commerce had sanctioned the export of supplies for charitable purposes and Boland had secured Government agreement that monies from the European Relief Vote would be allocated to cover the cost of transporting aid being sent by McQuaid to seminaries in Italy in response to an appeal by Cardinal Pizzardo.[88]

'I can say, though, of course, not publicly, that if it were not for Mr Boland, I could never have succeeded in having so much assistance voted and, what is more delicate, passed through private Catholic channels, as distinct from international and non-denominational channels,' McQuaid confided to the Nuncio, Archbishop Robinson, when processing the commendations.[89] But because of the election, McQuaid advised that the awards should not be presented until later; he did not want to be seen as giving an electoral advantage to Lemass.

Although he had been appointed Archbishop with de Valera's support in 1940, McQuaid shared the deep sense of relief felt generally throughout the country at the Fianna Fáil leader's defeat in the February 1948 general election.[90] Five political parties – Fine Gael, Labour, National Labour, Clann na Talmhan and Clann na Poblachta – combined to form an Inter-Party Government which ended 16 years of Fianna Fáil rule. The Dublin barrister, John A. Costello, emerged as the compromise choice as Taoiseach after MacBride vetoed the appointment of Richard Mulcahy. Labour leader William Norton became Tánaiste, but MacBride's ascendancy in cabinet was reflected in his appointment to the Ministry of External Relations.

The tone of the first cabinet meeting on February was like Gregorian music to McQuaid's ears: it sent a telegram to the Vatican expressing its intention 'to repose at the feet of Your Holiness the assurance of our filial loyalty and of our devotion to Your August Person as well as our firm resolve to be guided in all our work by the teaching of Christ and to strive for the attainment of a social order in Ireland based on Christian principles.' It may well have been written by McQuaid, especially the wording 'repose at the feet' of the Pope, a phrase which was opposed by the Government secretary, Maurice Moynihan.

This act of homage signalled the aspiration of Costello and MacBride to have Ireland engage in the battle to recover parts of Communist-dominated Central Europe for Christianity. The application of Christian principles to international politics was to bring the Costello Government to the forefront of the Vatican's campaign to preserve Italy from Communism. It was also to bring McQuaid onto the international stage as a doughty anti-Communist Cold War warrior.

15

Cold War Churchman
1948–49

'Pastor of the Church Militant.'
Michael Tierney on McQuaid.

On Sunday evening, April 11, 1948, Irish people tuned into their wireless sets to listen to a special broadcast by the Archbishop of Dublin and Primate of Ireland, John Charles McQuaid, on the crisis facing democracy in Italy. His stark message was that a Communist victory in the following Sunday's general election in Italy would result in the demise of the Papacy and the collapse of Christian civilisation. In such a situation, Ireland would not be immune from 'the pestilence of evil ideas' embodied in atheistic Communism and would be exposed to the danger of falling under the dictatorship of Joseph Stalin. 'The issue now being fought in Italy is as vital for peaceful Ireland as it is for every land where the name of Christ, Our Lord, is still revered,' he warned.[1]

As he spoke to the nation, McQuaid had already raised £19,933 (almost £400,000 in today's money) from Irish Catholics in support of their fellow Catholics in Italy. His appeal was inspired by the Easter message of Pope Pius XII, who had prophesised the arrival of 'momentous world decisions which would perhaps be final and irrevocable' between Christianity and atheistic Communism. His purpose was to rouse 'tranquil Ireland' to the realisation that 'the great hour has struck for Christian conscience'.

'Atheistic Communism has not yet attempted violence in this land,' McQuaid said. 'It has not openly pronounced its brutal sentence on all the principles of our Catholic Faith and culture. Its agents have been content to disguise their aims, under the mask of a Socialism, which seems to look only for fair conditions of a decent livelihood, and under the mask of a patriotism which appears to foster only the unity of our partitioned country.'

Defiantly, McQuaid asserted that the Irish people would not accept 'enslavement at the hand of hidden masters who, because they think they have no God, have, in fact, no country, no principle, no faith.

Our people have certainly understood that the issue in Italy is none other than the triumph of the One True Faith over the blasphemy and tyranny of atheistic Communism.'

Writing from Kilkenny, Bishop Collier described the broadcast as very impressive and he assured McQuaid that it read perfectly in the newspaper. 'Except for a small part near the beginning, it came over the air very well,' he wrote. 'The people were very touched, and the clergy spoke highly of the performance. It was called for and has done much good. Must impress the Holy Father.'[2]

McQuaid's broadcast certainly impressed the American Minister to Ireland, George Garrett, who described it as being 'by far the strongest evidence of a more aggressive attitude on the part of the Irish people towards the Communist menace.' The people of Ireland, through their Hierarchy, were going 'into battle for Europe and in such a bold fashion that any Irish Government must be forced to adopt the same line,' Garrett informed the State Department in Washington.[3]

Although no recording of the broadcast exists, McQuaid, the 'Cold Warrior' churchman, had nailed his colours to the mast in the manner of a Christian crusader. It was unprecedented for an Irish Catholic prelate to intervene in Italian politics and appeal for funds for fellow Catholics. McQuaid took this exceptional step on the grounds that he was acting for religious, not political motives. Remarkably, too, his broadcast was approved by the Inter-Party Government, which shared his outlook on the threat Communism posed to Christianity.[4] In 1948, neither Church nor State was neutral in the Catholic cause against Communism.

McQuaid's broadcast was the culmination of nearly three weeks of hectic fund-raising that had begun on March 24 when the Minister for External Affairs, Seán MacBride, called on the Archbishop to deliver a report from the Ambassador to the Holy See. Joe Walshe's report disclosed that an appeal had been made to Catholics in America to assist their fellow Catholics in Italy. A dramatic interview with the Pope had convinced him that Ireland was now of supreme importance as a Catholic bulwark in Europe. Shocked to find the Pontiff 'hunched up, almost physically overcome by the weight of his present office', Walshe suggested that it would be the greatest moment in Irish history if the Pope made Ireland the home of the Holy See 'for the period of the persecution.' Deeply moved, Pius replied that while Ireland was the only place he could go to, his duty was to stay in Rome, where he was ready to be martyred.[5]

Convinced that Pius XII was 'the stuff of great warrior Popes', Walshe told Dublin that the Pontiff meant to fight Communism, but he failed to persuade MacBride to send money secretly to the anti-Communist campaign in Italy where, under the direction of the Pope and Monsignor Montini, the Vatican had helped build 18,000 'civil committees' as part of Catholic Action. Outwardly independent of the Vatican, the committees took their instructions from the Pope. The chain of command stretched from the Vatican via the Turin-based leader, Dr Luigi Gedda, to all 300 Italian dioceses and from there into every parish. Gedda was Pius's man. Like McQuaid, he was an 'integralist', on the Catholic Right.

Fundraising for the faith

Within 24 hours of contacting Dr Stafford Johnson and other senior Knights of St Columbanus, McQuaid received a cheque for £5,000 (£100,000) which was to be placed at the Pope's disposal for the defence of the faith in Italy. 'Such a gesture of faith and courage is magnificent,' McQuaid told Johnson.[6] Next day McQuaid handed a cheque for £7,500 (£150,000) to the Nuncio, Archbishop Robinson, for immediate transfer to the Holy See. On top of the £5,000 (£100,000) raised by the Knights, McQuaid personally donated £2,500 (£50,000). 'In the name of these lay folk and in my own name,' McQuaid asked Montini to offer to the Holy Father 'this small sum for the use of His Holiness in combating the present attack upon the Faith in Italy.'[7]

Offerings poured into the Palace from Dublin and every county in Ireland, but also from England and abroad. The President of Ireland, Sean T. O'Kelly, sent a 'handsome cheque'. Éamon de Valera gave a 'generous contribution to the cause of the Faith in Italy'. MacBride apologised for only being able to give 'a small sum'.[8] Among the many contributions of 'outstanding liberality' were those from the Bishops of the Province of Dublin, as well as from priests and sisters. A fund for Italy opened by the Licensed Vintners' Association raised £2,800 (£56,000).[9] The Ancient Order of Hibernians sent £250 (£5,000). Other striking instances of 'great-hearted goodness' mentioned by McQuaid were those of the many individuals who gave £100 or even £200 'out of their poverty and out of their abundance'.[10] The total raised was described by Robinson as the splendid sum of £42,327 (£846,540).

On April 18, polling day in Italy, McQuaid awaited the result of the election on his radio at Notre Dame des Bois with Stafford Johnson. When the news of a Christian Democratic victory came through, the Irish Primate and the head of the Knights celebrated a triumph which they ranked with the Crusaders' defeat of the Mohammedans at the Battle of Lepanto. McQuaid wondered if history would record the part which the Knights had played in achieving a success which had 'flung back the forces of evil, one might say, with decisive force'.[11]

Five days later, Gedda sent a telegram to McQuaid extolling his part 'in the glorious fight'.[12] There was a month-long silence from the Vatican itself, which appears to have perturbed McQuaid as to whether his efforts had been really appreciated. 'What Gedda told me about the gratitude of the Italian people to Your Grace would do your heart good,'

Walshe reassured McQuaid on May 19. 'If, on the Vatican side, there has been a certain slowness in acknowledging the wonderful work you have done for Catholicism in this country, as well as in the whole of Western Europe, you must take it as part of the dreadfully inefficient machinery of the Vatican.'[13]

Writing from Rome three days later, after having had an interview with Montini, Walshe informed McQuaid that the Pope's gratitude was very real and that Gedda would express his gratitude in his report. 'In reality you were the only Bishop or Archbishop in the whole world who gave such help,' Walshe wrote flatteringly.[14] It was only after Walshe had spoken to the Pope that *L'Osservatore Romano* belatedly named McQuaid as the source of the funds from Ireland.

In confidence, Walshe explained the Vatican's 'bewildering' attitude to money. Irish aid would have been considerably lower if Walshe had not intervened to ensure that it was exchanged at the best rate, which was available through the Banca di Roma rather than the Opere di Religione (the Vatican Bank). But for Walshe's persistence, millions fewer lira would have been credited to Ireland. 'If these precautions had not been taken by yourself and me, we should now be feeling extremely bad indeed about the whole affair which would be in the state of unimaginable confusion in which the Vatican officials seem to delight.'

Walshe advised McQuaid that in future, when he was sending money to individual projects rather than to the Pope or the Curia, he should not use the Vatican Bank but should switch to the Banca di Roma, which he described as a thoroughly Catholic institution.

McQuaid followed Walshe's advice, and the following month reported the smooth transaction of a further cheque for Gedda. By return, Walshe sent McQuaid the Civil Committee's distinguished helper's medal on behalf of Gedda, who planned to set up an international organisation as the Communist attack had, in his view, only just begun.[15]

Although McQuaid believed Communism did not exist in Ireland, Walshe helped confirm his determination to continue the battle against any Socialist infiltration. The Hierarchy condemned the Socialist Youth Movement as a Communist front whose aim was to destroy the Christian faith.[16] On McQuaid's direction the Students' Representative Council at UCD agreed unanimously to disaffiliate from the Communist-sponsored International Union of Students.[17] McQuaid received a confidential 'Report on Communism in Dublin' compiled by a committee of Knights of St Columbanus 'whose duty it is to watch the activities of Communist bodies and organisations with Communistic tendencies'.[18] 'Big Brother' was not inactive in McQuaid's Dublin.

McQuaid-MacBride rivalry

One of the finest tributes to McQuaid's role in the Italian campaign came from the Minister for External Relations, Seán MacBride. Although MacBride felt 'intense pleasure' at receiving a letter conveying the gratitude of Pius XII, he disclaimed any special mention as his part was a small one in cooperation with McQuaid. 'The real work was done by Your Grace, without whose tireless help and intervention I would have been powerless,' he told McQuaid. 'I feel that Ireland's contribution, for which Your Grace was in the main responsible, was of very material help to the Italian Catholics in their hour of stress and to the cause of world peace.'[19]

Yet according to the British Ambassador to Ireland, Sir John Maffey, McQuaid did not trust MacBride on account of his antecedents as the son of the troubled marriage of Major John MacBride, shot by the British in 1916 for his part in the Easter Rebellion, and Maude Gonne, the Republican agitator and heartbreaker of the poet W.B. Yeats, as well as his membership of the IRA, of which he had been Chief of Staff.[20] MacBride, although he was a married man, was also known to be fond of women, especially when in Paris.

With his French accent and access to the Christian Democratic parties forming the Council of Europe and other post-war institutions, MacBride competed with McQuaid on the international stage as Ireland's European expert. McQuaid was mindful, however, of MacBride's personal pledge to act in the Catholic interest, an interest which he suspected that the leader of Clann na Poblachta equated with his ambition of ousting de Valera as the lay leader of Catholic nationalism.

Outwardly the two men gave the appearance of being cordial collaborators. When the Nuncio, Archbishop Paschal Robinson, died in August 1948, MacBride told McQuaid he was relieved that the Archbishop had taken charge of the arrangements in the Pro-Cathedral to fulfil the Nuncio's written instruction to have a simple funeral.[21] McQuaid applauded a speech MacBride made in Galway calling for a new approach in education that would allow the Catholic Church freedom in moral and spiritual spheres. The statement interested McQuaid, who believed that Catholics had to live under a grave disability imposed on them by 'the less than pagan Charter of the National University'. Until the charter was changed, 'the Church could not possibly have the liberty that you have courageously and rightly advocated,' McQuaid told MacBride.[22]

However, as chairman of the Commission on Unemployment, McQuaid was uneasy about a Government Memorandum on emigration prepared by MacBride, which proposed to prohibit certain females under 21 years of age from travelling abroad. McQuaid was sceptical of MacBride's claim that, from his informal conversations with members of the Hierarchy, 'some restriction on the emigration of girls would secure [their] warm approval'. But when he consulted the commission, McQuaid found them in favour of the MacBride proposal.[23]

A more serious difference of outlook between McQuaid and MacBride, over Ireland's attitude to the defence of the West against Communism, was highlighted by Maffey. The diplomat quoted McQuaid as saying to him in August 1948 that it was ridiculous for MacBride to argue that Éire could not play her part in the defence of the Western Union as long as Partition existed. 'Naturally the Archbishop's views are coloured by his detestation of Communism,' Maffey reported to London.[24]

Maffey's testimony is corroborated by the American Ambassador, George Garrett, who informed the State Department in Washington that McQuaid was in favour of Ireland accepting an invitation to join the North Atlantic Treaty Organisation (NATO).[25] Garrett concluded that it would be exceedingly difficult for MacBride to discount McQuaid's view, though he thought MacBride was prepared for some degree of difference between the Church and the Government on this issue.

Garrett appears to have misread the uneasy nature of the relationship between the prelate and the politician when he observed that 'MacBride, a highly religious man, not only holds the Archbishop in great esteem but a personal bond of friendship has developed between them.'[26] MacBride, in fact, reciprocated McQuaid's negative feelings. The late Desmond Williams witnessed him speaking to McQuaid on the phone with great deference, then becoming dismissive to the point of contempt after he put the receiver down.[27]

Another telling point in assessing the McQuaid-MacBride relationship is that the Secretary of the Department of External Affairs, Freddie Boland, reached the stage where he could no longer work with MacBride and sought a move as Ireland's Ambassador to London. With Marshall Aid now flowing into Europe, McQuaid, however, continued to work closely on aid issues with Boland, whom he regarded as the best-informed man in Ireland on this 'tangled question'.

Experience of aid agencies had taught McQuaid that the Americans 'talked least and did most' in the impartial distribution of aid all over Europe. Rather than relying on Secours Catholique or the Swiss-based Caritas, he found that the best way to channel aid to Catholics in Europe was through the American Catholic War Relief.

McQuaid's role in sending Irish relief aid to Europe brought him to the attention of leading Catholic churchmen such as Cardinals Suhard of Paris and Frings of Cologne. Frings warmly thanked McQuaid for 'the big amount of meat that has recently come from Ireland', and requested more aid on account of the economic conditions prevailing in Germany.[28]

McQuaid's work was also highly appreciated in Austria. Thanking McQuaid for a consignment of 30 tons of meat delivered through the National Catholic Welfare Conference (NCWC), Bishop Joseph Fliesser of Linz informed him each can of meat was distributed with a tag saying that this was 'a contribution of the Irish Catholics'.[29]

McQuaid and Boland liaised effectively with the chairman of the NCWC, the Archbishop of Cincinnati, John McNicholas, who calculated the Irish contribution to food aid in Europe at £6 million (£120 million). When McNicholas sent his representatives to Dublin, McQuaid ensured that they met the Taoiseach, John A. Costello, as well as MacBride.[30]

What McQuaid told London

McQuaid held Costello and Patrick McGilligan, Minister for Finance, in high regard but considered that the Labour Party leader, William Norton, was weak on the Communist threat. In McQuaid's view, Norton's sole criterion was 'votes from anywhere and how to get them'. A call by Norton for the release of republican 'so-called political prisoners' in Parkhurst Prison was scathingly dismissed by McQuaid as 'an unholy racket.'

The Partition of Ireland was seen by McQuaid as a godsend to extremists and Communists. Describing the anti-Partition campaign as 'a complete racket', he told Maffey that there were many people in the North and South who hotly denounced the Border, but who would be horrified if their efforts led to the ending of Partition. He had nothing to say in defence of Orangemen, but recognised they could not be forced into a united Ireland.

McQuaid was opposed to any weakening of the South's connection with the Commonwealth, which had become a hot political issue in the hands of the Inter-Party Government, and he argued that if a poll were taken a majority would be in favour of maintaining the relationship with King George VI. When Maffey said he was apprehensive of the future of the External Relations Act, which established Éire's status within the Commonwealth, McQuaid said he could not imagine that the Costello Government would commit the folly of repealing it. 'We would meet again and see who was right,' Maffey concluded.[31]

Within a month Maffey was proven right. In Ottawa on September 7 Costello announced that the Government intended to break from the Commonwealth and establish the Free State as a Republic. In retaliation, the Labour Government led by Clement Attlee passed the Ireland Act, which gave Ulster Unionists a guarantee that their status in the United Kingdom would be retained.[32]

Rugby priest

At this sensitive juncture in relations between the two islands, and between Ulster Unionists and Irish nationalists, McQuaid narrowly missed becoming a figure of ridicule in Britain and Northern Ireland.

In January 1949, McQuaid wrote to Archbishop Joseph Masterson expressing his displeasure that a Birmingham diocesan priest had been chosen to play for Ireland in a rugby international against France at Lansdowne Road which was in the Dublin diocese. Pointing out that this 'honour' was contrary to decrees issued by national and diocesan Synods forbidding clergy to participate in public sports, McQuaid alerted Masterson to the 'very adverse effect of such a violation on the Irish people', and requested his assistance in avoiding a scandal.[33] McQuaid felt he was acting on behalf of the whole Irish Hierarchy, which had agreed the previous October to draw attention to the fact that priests who played in public games in contravention of the Maynooth Statutes were causing scandal to the faithful.[34]

Taken aback by the tone of the request, Masterson admitted that he had granted Fr Tom Gavin, who was studying at St Edmund's House in Cambridge, permission to play in the trial and indeed had wished him luck. And when Gavin, who had already played in Ireland for London Irish and in France for Cambridge, asked if the ecclesiastical authorities in Ireland would be against his taking part, Masterson had lightheartedly shrugged off the suggestion, as he had heard that Irish priests were prominent in Gaelic games.

While sorry to have caused any offence in Dublin, Masterson indicated to McQuaid that, personally, he was pleased that the publicity in England about Gavin's selection had boosted the prestige of St Edmund's and had offset several 'unsavoury cases' involving priests which had been headlined in the English press. From his own enquiries Masterson had found that his priests were extremely pleased at Gavin's selection.

Privately, Masterson had also consulted Cardinal Bernard Griffin of Westminster and other senior churchmen, who shared his view that withdrawing Gavin from the team would cause more adverse comment in England than could possibly be caused in Ireland by his playing. 'May I therefore beg of you to regard him as outside the Synodal laws since he is a student coming from another country,' Masterson pleaded. 'I suggest that this explanation, which already has been well publicised, would take away any likelihood of scandal. Certainly, any ban which prevented him from playing next Saturday would cause such an uproar here that I should not like to be responsible for it. I hope therefore that you will be able to see your way to avoid any stricture being placed on Fr Gavin.'[35]

Masterson's common-sense reply did not satisfy McQuaid, who regarded his arguments as very poor and weak. 'The "offset" is not indeed supernatural,' he complained to his auxiliary, Bishop Dunne, whom he directed to consult with the Vicar Generals, Monsignor Boylan and Monsignor Dargan, on the matter. The three appear to have persuaded McQuaid to accept Masterson's plea as Gavin became a distinguished player on a Triple Crown team. McQuaid had been saved from 'uproar' in the British press, a controversy that would have been extremely difficult for the Irish newspapers to ignore.[36]

Mindszenty, 'the martyr'

By late 1948 the focus of the Cold War turned to Hungary, following the arrest of the Hungarian Primate, Cardinal Josef Mindszenty, who was listed for a state show-trial. In response to an appeal by Pope Pius XII, McQuaid sent a telegram to Monsignor Montini praying for the triumph of religious liberty and human rights of which Mindszenty had been the unflinching defender.[37]

From Rockwell College, where he was visiting his friend Fr Vincent Dinan, who had been very ill with a burst appendix, McQuaid sent his protest to the Budapest authorities via the Irish Department of External Affairs in early January 1949. 'It may not do any good but it will assist in swelling the chorus of disapproval before the trial,' he told Boland.[38]

McQuaid's prognosis proved to be accurate. When Mindszenty was sentenced to life-imprisonment on February 8, McQuaid sent a telegram to Rome declaring his 'execration of the cruel sentence'. Dublin Catholics were instructed to recite the Litany of Loreto at the end of Mass for Mindszenty's release, as Catholic organisations in the diocese, including the Catholic Social Service Conference, issued resolution after resolution in support of Mindszenty, who had by now become the best-known Hungarian in Ireland. Following McQuaid's lead, the Hungarian Primate's plight became a major preoccupation of the Irish bishops, the Government and the Dáil.

Only three days after Mindszenty's incarceration, McQuaid received in his morning's post a Communist circular without any covering note. 'It is the first Communist circular sent to me,' he informed Boland at the Department of External Affairs. 'The handwriting is unknown to me, but it is distinctive.'[39] However, neither Church nor State were able to unearth the identity of the sender.

'Your Grace can have no idea of the gratitude and praise one hears on every hand for the attitude, so largely promoted by you, taken by Ireland in regard to Cardinal Mindszenty,' Walshe wrote from Rome. 'The Holy Father himself mentioned it to me in the warmest terms.'[40] He told McQuaid that Vatican officials and resident diplomats acknowledged that the lead was given by the Irish Hierarchy and Government. 'So far as national protests and prompt action are concerned we have again been easily first. Naturally, this enormously increases our prestige in Rome and disposes the Holy See most favourably in our regard.'

It was against this background of swelling public support for Mindszenty that McQuaid's reputation as a Cold Warrior churchman of international stature was applauded by Ireland's tightly knit Catholic academia when the highest honour in its gift – an Honorary Doctorate in Literature – was conferred on him by the Chancellor of the National University of Ireland, Éamon de Valera. The Taoiseach, John A. Costello, and the Tánaiste, William Norton, were in attendance at the ceremony held in the Department of External Affairs.

In the citation speech, the Pro-Vice Chancellor and President of UCD, Michael Tierney, hailed McQuaid as 'Pastor of the Church Militant' who had given proof of his watchfulness and valour during the Italian election campaign, as a man 'most noteworthy for sanctity and scholarship, wisdom and high-mindedness'.[41]

Congratulating McQuaid on 'the highly deserved honour,' Walshe saw it as giving McQuaid 'an additional point of vantage' from which he could carry out his ambition of making UCD a truly Catholic university. 'The Lord knows it is about time we had a Catholic University where laymen can learn Catholic philosophy and apologetics.' Walshe wrote from Rome. 'In this we are so terribly behind the continental Catholic with a university training.'[42]

McQuaid's attention was distracted from Rome and Budapest as he prepared the guest list and music for the ceremony that would mark the Inauguration on the world stage of the newly constituted Republic of Ireland. On Easter Monday 1949, the first day in the official life of the new Republic, McQuaid presided at Solemn High Mass in the Pro-Cathedral attended by President O'Kelly and the members of the Costello Government. However, the public enthusiasm for the new Republic seemed pale in comparison with its concern for Mindszenty.

As Mindszenty languished in a Budapest prison amid rumours of his imminent death, McQuaid convinced the Labour Party and trade unions to ally with Catholic lay organisations to make the traditional May Day celebrations a Mindszenty protest day. On May Day, 140,000 Dubliners passed a resolution in support of Mindszenty, 'the martyr for the Faith'. Describing the scene in a letter to Monsignor Montini, McQuaid wrote:

> Not only the Sodalities and Confraternities, but the political parties, in particular, the Labour Party, aligned themselves firmly on the side of loyalty to the Faith and to our Holy Father. And what I had never seen before: the Papal flag flew, alone, on the headquarters of the Irish Transport and General Workers' Union, where the Citizen Army had flown its Plough and Five Stars in former times. This manifestation is but a continuation of the spirit that was roused at the time of the Italian elections. And what is genuinely consoling, the result is a practical devotion to Mass and the Sacraments such as even the Eucharistic Congress of 1932 has not exceeded.[43]

That month, too, the Pioneer Total Abstinence Association applied for permission to hold a Golden Jubilee Mass on O'Connell Bridge, as had happened at the 1932 Eucharistic Congress. The application was turned down by McQuaid, who was not 'a pioneer bishop', but he gave his approval for the 80,000 Pioneers who took part in the celebrations to arrange for a Mass in Croke Park. He himself declined to attend on the grounds that he would 'be so occupied with more pressing matters.'[44]

Unmasking Communists

Those more pressing matters included the setting up by the Hierarchy of an intelligence-gathering bureau to keep a close watch on any attempts to build a Communist movement in Ireland. This was done by the Catholic Information Bureau, which operated from the headquarters of the Catholic Truth Society at Veritas House in Lower Abbey St under the general direction of Bishop Willam MacNeely of Raphoe and Bishop James Staunton of Ferns.

Lists of Communists were compiled, and in its second annual report for 1949 the bureau credited itself with passing on authoritative information to unsuspecting trade union leaders about the activities of union members who were Communist. Priests throughout Ireland were also tipped off as to the identity of Communist agents in their parishes.

During 1949 Communist agents were sent over from London to explain the party's line on the trial of Cardinal Mindszenty and on Marshall Aid, only to discover that Catholic agents had infiltrated Communist cells and leaked information of their activities to the Catholic Information Bureau. Unofficially, the bureau handed on its information to the Government about the few real Communist recruits. 'Among their most active propagandists have been a few British ex-internees who had belonged to the left wing of the IRA and who have been involved in the terrorist activities of that body in England,' the report noted. 'They are now settled in Dublin.'[45] The bureau enjoyed another triumph when it uncovered the Communist past of the newly appointed Irish branch secretary of the National Union of Railwaymen, William Shearer, a Glaswegian.

The almost hysterical anti-Communist climate was reinforced by McQuaid's condemnation of Communism as a blasphemous doctrine and a perverse way of life. It denied God; it hated the Church; it attempted by every weapon of lying, treachery and persecution to wipe out the One True Faith of Jesus Christ. 'Communism for its own ends,' his Lenten Regulations decreed, 'fosters social restlessness, and thus prepares for the violence of tyranny. Before it seizes power, Communism shows itself as gentle and cultured, interested in patriotism, the language, art and drama, athletics and debating societies. Very many are deceived by these tactics, in particular, by fraudulent campaigns in favour of Peace ... The cruel experience of other countries shows that no sacrifice is too great to unmask and defeat Communism. Communism is wrong in itself, and no one may without sin collaborate with it in any undertaking whatsoever.'[46]

If the Irish Hierarchy was united in his hatred of atheistic Communism, it was less certain as to how Catholic workers should best be represented in trade unionism, an issue on which McQuaid did not see eye to eye with Archbishop D'Alton. In his 1948 Lenten letter, D'Alton received widespread news coverage for his suggestion that Irish trade unions should affiliate with the Christian International, a suggestion which resulted in a proposal being formally tabled for ratification. Dismayed by what he regarded as a naive intervention, McQuaid wrote to D'Alton complaining that his own investigations indicated that the move would be rejected in a manner that 'would gravely damage the interests of the Faith' in Dublin. Effectively blaming D'Alton for creating 'this quite sudden situation', McQuaid also direly predicted that the resulting disunion among good Catholic trade unionists in the Dublin diocese 'would help still further the machinations of our Communists'.[47]

Stoutly, D'Alton responded that although his proposal might have been premature, it should be the ideal in a predominantly Catholic country for Catholic trade unionists to affiliate with the Christian International. As the issue raised by McQuaid affected trade unionists throughout the country, he hoped that McQuaid would bring the matter up at the next meeting of the bishops.[48] In the event, the disagreement between the two bishops proved to be academic. Neither of the two Trade Union Congresses joined any of the Internationals when they found that the affiliation fees were excessively dear.[49]

McQuaid's pastoral strategy was to encourage trade unions to appoint a spiritual director, who would encourage workers to undertake the study of Catholic social principles and attend special residential retreats. Union leaders were also encouraged to have their headquarters dedicated to Our Lady. At the blessing of the Dublin headquarters of the Irish Bakers', Confectioners' and Allied Workers' Union, a priest assigned by McQuaid to the workers' apostolate, Fr Cecil P. Crean, explained that it was through the protection of Mary that trade unions could best safeguard the legitimate interests of workers.[50]

So great was the fear of being tainted by Communism that even officials in the Department of External Affairs, such as Brian Durnin, applied to the Archbishop for permission to read Marxist literature whenever their duties as diplomats demanded it.[51] Tomás Roseingrave, a leading figure in Maria Duce, the fundamentalist movement led by Fr Denis Fahey, was given permission to read Communist publications for a year,[52] while his colleague, John Ryan, was allowed read the *Irish Workers' Voice*, the *Irish Democrat* and *Young Ireland for Democracy* so that he could refute Communist arguments.[53]

Special attention was given to checking any signs of Communist infiltration in the university campus. In his confidential review of student activities for the Hierarchy, the chaplain at UCD, Fr Herbert McKernan, reported in June 1949 that two students were members of a Communist cell. 'One, a son of indifferent Catholic parents, comes from a non-Catholic school and denies he is a Catholic,' McKernan wrote. 'The other, a woman student, is a Protestant. Since these students have no following, and there is no evidence of Communist infiltration in the College, I think it would be unwise to press for any penal action.'[54]

A 23-year-old member of Maria Duce, John McCarthy, who was a student at UCD, asked permission from McQuaid 'to join Communist-sponsored societies and organisations with the sole purpose of acting as an observer or spy.' His aim, he explained, was to contact the inner ring which controlled Communist activities in the university. In reply, Fr Mangan told McCarthy that he was told by His Grace to state that 'the matter is one which properly concerns your confessor or spiritual director'.[55]

In mid-1949 this anti-Communist mood was further consolidated in Ireland, as elsewhere among Catholics, when reports appeared of religious persecution in Czechoslovakia. McQuaid led the Hierarchy and lay organisation in sending telegrams expressing deep sympathy with Archbishop Josef Beran of Prague and his flock.

Nuncio crisis

An indication of McQuaid's growing stature in the Vatican as Ireland's premier Cold War churchman was that in mid-July 1949 Monsignor Montini conveyed to him confidentially his anxiety about the long interval that had elapsed between the death of the Papal Nuncio, Robinson, and the appointment of his successor.[56] Within a week of Robinson's death in August, Montini had put in motion the diplomatic machinery to secure the Irish Government's agreement to the appointment of an elderly and mediocre Italian, Archbishop Ettore Felici, but both Government and Hierarchy favoured the appointment of a Nuncio of Irish birth or extraction. After making enquiries, McQuaid replied that he was deeply aggrieved that the Holy Father should have been placed in such a position, and he at once intervened with the Government to stress 'the necessity of accepting even the wish much less the direction of His Holiness'.

McQuaid explained to Montini that 'in the briefest possible period, a situation, which ought never to have been permitted in respect of the Holy Father, will be rectified by the Government of Ireland. May I be permitted to request Your Excellency to make known to His Holiness on my behalf the expression of my profound regret and the assurance of my filial desire to serve the Holy Father in this and in all other matters to the best of my powers.'[57]

In a second letter that day, sent by a different channel, McQuaid explained to Montini the background to the delay. After the country's change of status to the Republic of Ireland had become operative internationally, the first opportunity on which he could 'discreetly and effectively intervene' to end the delay was in early June. 'I was then able to intervene strongly in favour of the acceptance of Monsignor Felici, and the intervention was received with distinct favour, and even acquiescence.'

Since then, MacBride had been proposing to call on McQuaid every weekend but had not done so until August 3. MacBride's attitude was described by McQuaid as completely correct towards the Holy See and he accepted 'without difficulty' McQuaid's proposal that if possible, even that evening, he should secure Government ratification of the appointment. The delay, McQuaid concluded, was 'without excuse'.[58] The cabinet approved the appointment on August 4, a decision acknowledged by the Vatican on August 27.

McQuaid's account makes no mention of any complicity with MacBride and Walshe in stalling the process, as recounted by Professor Dermot Keogh in his pioneering work, *Ireland and the Vatican*. Keogh has argued that MacBride, at the outset, informally apprised McQuaid of Government wishes, and he quoted a Department of External Affairs note recording that McQuaid had expressed 'strong views against the appointment of an Italian prelate and suggested that the Irish Government should make its views known in unequivocal terms to the Holy See as soon as possible.'[59]

According to Keogh, too, after the October 1948 meeting of the Hierarchy, the Archbishop of Armagh, D'Alton, met MacBride before sending a telegram to Rome expressing the support of the Irish bishops for a non-Italian Nuncio, and in early December Iveagh House officials prepared a diplomatic note giving their reasons for rejecting of Felici. Boland suggested to MacBride that he should consult McQuaid about the acceptability of the draft.[60]

Keogh's version of events primarily presents MacBride's viewpoint and does not take account of the power-play which was taking place between the Minister of External Affairs and the Archbishop of Dublin. Even accepting that McQuaid's initial preference was for a Nuncio of Irish origin, the Archbishop's own account shows that he was not prepared to challenge Rome's selection. The suspicion must be that MacBride was economical with the Nunciature file and that he was engaged in an anti-McQuaid intrigue with a pliable D'Alton. A key player in MacBride's political games was the Ambassador to the Holy See, Joe Walshe.

Red Hat intrigues

Having resolved the Nuncio crisis, McQuaid's standing with Rome was the highest it had ever been, when in early September 1949 Walshe met Montini in his office at the Secretariat of State. In his report to Dublin, Walshe wrote that Montini said he was prepared to be 'a bit indiscreet' about McQuaid: he told Walshe that McQuaid had been 'a tower of strength' to him and 'a true son of the Church in the little crisis'.[61]

Walshe agreed that John McQuaid was 'unsurpassable as a churchman and was doing splendid work for the welfare of the people in the diocese, but argued that Armagh was the key to the Catholic and national unity of Ireland, and that if a Red Hat went to Dublin rather than Armagh, it would be regarded as a triumph for England.'

Walshe said that having been the intermediary between the Nunciature and McQuaid on several occasions involving ceremonial rows, he was able to assure Montini that if the Archbishop of Dublin 'became Cardinal, the Nuncio would have endless difficulties, in every sphere of his activities, owing to this deplorable weakness in John's character, already so well known to the Holy See.'

This reference to McQuaid's unspecified 'weakness' appears to have arisen in the conversation between Montini and Walshe in connection with McQuaid's known sensitivity to matters of precedence when both he and the Nuncio attended religious or civic functions. It appears that this had been reported to Rome by Domenico Enrici, a former official at the Dublin Nunciature. This would explain Walshe's remark that 'John was making constant difficulties on matters of precedence whenever the Nuncio had to be present at a ceremony in the Pro-Cathedral.'

Walshe claimed that from the beginning he had frequently tried to resolve difficulties and had tried to keep the Holy See 'fully alive to the traits in John's character which gave so much pain to his friends'. Walshe said he had always tried to re-establish the balance in McQuaid's favour.

Thanking Walshe for his frankness, Montini assured the Ambassador that his remarks would remain 'absolutely secret except in regard to the Holy Father himself'. Walshe declared he was not speaking out of want of charity but that 'his sole motive is the common interest of the Church and Ireland ... so completely one in this case.'

Walshe was sure that Montini and Pius XII were 'now at least sufficiently alive to the value, from the Catholic point of view, of a united Ireland not to allow the major interest to be submerged in the minor consideration of rewarding an individual prelate.'

This was an astonishing performance by Walshe, even by his own duplicitous standards, as recounted by Conor Cruise O'Brien in his memoirs.[62] At worst it was a betrayal of a long-standing friend and protégé; at best it was a diplomatic hatchet-job carried out under orders. The most likely explanation is that Walshe took this line with the specific instruction of his minister, Seán MacBride. Two pieces of evidence in the McQuaid Papers point the finger of suspicion at MacBride. The first is a letter sent to McQuaid informing him that MacBride regularly told his colleague, Dr Nöel Browne, that the Archbishop of Dublin was 'moving heaven and earth in Rome to get the Red Hat' and that MacBride was 'seeing to it that he [McQuaid] did not succeed'.[63] The second letter, written in 1957 by Walshe to McQuaid, amounts to a savage character assassination of MacBride for his duplicities when in public office. Whatever the full story behind the Red Hat intrigues, the fact is that McQuaid was unaware of Walshe's disclosures against him to Montini. As far as McQuaid was concerned, his anti-Communist stand, his contribution to Catholic international aid programmes and his moulding of the Dublin diocese into a model See meant that he was now recognised in Rome as 'the Pope's man'. As 1950 beckoned, a Roman Holy Year, McQuaid would have been forgiven for thinking that Pope Pius XII would make amends for the omission of 1946.

16

'The Arch-Druid of Drumcondra'

1950–51

'He is a true Roman.'

Monsignor Montini.

As the curtain rose on the second half of the twentieth century, McQuaid's Dublin was on its knees to observe a Roman Catholic Holy Year. To avoid overcrowding in churches McQuaid banned the saying of midnight Masses and imposed a curfew until dawn on New Year's Day for the celebration of Mass. So resurgent was the mood of popular piety in Dublin that a Jewish member of the Dáil, Robert Briscoe, remarked that the more Catholic the people became, the more he liked it. The Lord Mayor of Dublin, Alderman Cormac Breathnach T.D., offering the Corporation's 'filial homage and devotion to His Holiness', claimed that Dublin was the most Catholic city in the world after Rome.[1]

A substantial Holy Year achievement, which still endures, was made by McQuaid on August 15, the feast day of the Immaculate Conception, when at six o'clock that evening the first broadcast by Radio Éireann of the bell of Dublin's Pro-Cathedral beckoned Irish Catholics to recite the Angelus prayer to Mary. Technicians had designed special equipment controlled by a master clock in the General Post Office, O'Connell St, to ring the bell at set times.

The idea had originated within Radio Éireann but McQuaid seized this suggestion as an important means of evangelisation. He blessed what he loftily called 'the mechanism' linking the national radio station and the church dome, and explained that it was intended that all who heard the bell each day at noon and six o'clock would recite the Angelus prayer 'in union with Our Blessed Lady, as a prayer of thanksgiving for the Grace of the Incarnation'.[2]

The Angelus Bell was a significant medium for McQuaid's shaping of the religious outlook of mid-century Ireland. As a channel for promoting the daily observance of Catholic devotion on national radio, the

Angelus was as important to McQuaid's catechetical mission as the *Irish Press* was editorially to de Valera's Fianna Fáil. The presence at the Inauguration ceremony of the Minister for Posts and Telegraphs, Bill Everett, the head of the department, León Ó Broin, and the Director of Radio Éireann, C.E. Kelly, signalled clearly that the Angelus initiative had the full blessing of the State and the national broadcasting station. Although by the 1990s the Angelus had become a source of controversy as an allegedly sectarian feature of Irish broadcasting, it was hugely popular on its inception in 1950. Indeed, the story was told of how a Labour politician and former IRA man, Seán Dunne, was in full-flowing speech at a Dublin rally when the Angelus rang, and he stopped and bowed his head in prayer.

In an era of economic stagnation, high unemployment and mass emigration, religion was one of the more dynamic sectors in Irish society. Under McQuaid's brisk management, the diocese kept pace with the expansion of the capital, whose 639,500 Catholics were served by 443 priests spread throughout its 90 parishes. McQuaid's pastoral strategy aimed at fostering more recruits to the priesthood and he sanctioned a major expansion of Clonliffe College, with a new wing to accommodate 40 students and six professors, an auditorium and diocesan archives. Of the £70,220 (about £1.4 million) cost of the Clonliffe extension, McQuaid had just £300 (£6,000) in hand. 'All the rest I must find among the Faithful of my Diocese,' he told the Delegate-Apostolic for South Africa, Archbishop Lucas. 'At the same time, I am faced with the building of 11 churches in the city and suburbs not to mention a cathedral which is waiting some 21 years for someone to start.'[3]

Launching a fundraising drive for Clonliffe, McQuaid explained in a Pastoral Letter that the anticipated debt – which he put at £80,000 (£1.6 million) – would be 'immediately extinguished' if 80,000 households gave £1 (£20) each or if 160,000 households contributed ten shillings (£5) apiece.[4] The Clonliffe development showed the confidence which McQuaid had in the generosity of Dublin Catholics as it followed on the heels of a national appeal by the Hierarchy to renovate St Patrick's College, Maynooth, which up to October 1, 1949, had raised £642,567 (£12.9 million).[5] With McQuaid ordaining a record 67 students to the priesthood at Maynooth, 1950 was the high-water mark of an era when every family aspired to produce a priest or a nun.

A striking indicator of the strength of mid-century Catholicism came when McQuaid opened a retreat house for 20 men at St Doulough's Park, Balbriggan, run by the Marist Brothers – and urged them to treble its capacity. And the expansionist *zeitgeist* was further revealed at the opening of the Bon Secours Hospital, Glasnevin, run by the Bon Secours Sisters, when McQuaid proudly announced that it was built at his request as a completely voluntary institution with no money from the Hospitals' Sweepstakes or from the State. McQuaid's diocese did things his way!

As a result of his admiration for the seventeenth-century French educationalist, John Baptist de la Salle, McQuaid lifted the veto on the participation of the de la Salle teaching order in the Dublin diocese; indeed, he assigned the Order responsibility for running schools in the new housing estate at Ballyfermot, and in June 1950 he laid the foundation stone for a new £76,000 (£1.5 million) de la Salle monastery accommodating 36 Brothers close to the estate.[6]

McQuaid liked to point out to foreign prelates that all the headquarters of the Missionary Orders, and quite a number of missionary enterprises which had no claim on the diocese as such, were annually collecting 'a vast sum of money', quite apart from the Pontifical Works for the Propagation of the Faith and the Holy Childhood. 'I believe it can very fairly be stated that this City and Diocese are contributing more money to the missions all over the world than any other territory in relation to size and population,' he told South Africa's Archbishop Lucas.[7]

McQuaid v Redemptorists

Many Religious Orders became exasperated at what they regarded as McQuaid's excessive meddling in their affairs – his dealings with the famous preaching order, the Redemptorists, was a case in point. The Redemptorists declared their interest in opening a Retreat House in the diocese after McQuaid had dropped hints about the need to expand religious facilities in the city. The Provincial, Fr Jack Treacy C.S.S.R., found that negotiating with McQuaid was not straightforward and he was amazed at how the closed inner circle around the Archbishop operated. Although he had initiated the move, McQuaid kept a distance and delegated his auxiliary, Bishop Dunne, to act as his intermediary. The first meeting between Dunne and Treacy was interrupted by the arrival on a social visit of the President, Seán T. O'Kelly, with his chaplain and aides.

After McQuaid gave his written permission for the Retreat House to go ahead, Treacy requested an interview at which he explained that their house at Marianella in Rathgar was too small and that they would like to purchase a property to accommodate both their students and the planned Retreat House. McQuaid suggested Edenmore, a property in Raheny which he considered fit for the Provincial's double purpose. 'It is because I have seen the plans for future development that I have suggested to you Edenmore as safe from the uncomfortable aggression of building prospectors,' he wrote to Treacy on April 1.[8]

A few months later when it emerged that other religious communities were interested in Edenmore, McQuaid assured Treacy that he should have no scruple about bidding for the house. 'The Sisters in question will not purchase it, for it is I who will not consent to their purchase,' he told him.[9] However, the Redemptorists suspected that McQuaid was not as well informed as he thought he was: Treacy's property adviser, Mr J.J. Walsh, had information that Dublin Corporation intended to run a road through the property at some time in the future and did not recommend its purchase. The Redemptorists decided to look at other premises, including Drimnagh Castle and Kilmacud House, but none proved suitable. To avoid losing face, Treacy explained to McQuaid that the relocation of students from Limerick to Dublin would not take place for many years and that there was no immediate need for a place like Edenmore. McQuaid then sanctioned the building of the retreat house at Marianella, but linked the making permanent of its status in the diocese to the purchase in the future of a house for students.

Shortly afterwards the Redemptorists were attracted by a property which had come on the market at Oakland, stretching from Highfield Rd to Orwell Park in Rathgar (the site today of St Luke's Hospital). The property shared a boundary wall with Marianella and offered ample scope for expansion, but unfortunately for the Redemptorists they came up against 'an archepiscopal brick wall' when they sought McQuaid's approval for the purchase.

Even the friendly Bishop Dunne sounded a note of warning. 'Since the grounds of Oakland are extensive, I should tell you there will be objections to their purchase by any religious community,' Dunne told them. The plan was duly turned down by McQuaid's council.

Next, the Redemptorists tabled the compromise proposal of acquiring Oakfield and giving up Marianella. 'The hope is slender,' Dunne informed them. 'It is that the southside of the city is the difficulty. Go to the northside and you will easily get all you want!' Despite this advice, Treacy took the proposal to McQuaid, advancing the ecological argument that since the Corporation wished to preserve the site as 'a breathing lung for the city' and the Redemptorists would not undertake any large-scale development there, planning permission would be easily obtained.

'It is still the opinion of the Archbishop and the Council that it would be inadvisable to exchange, if such exchange could be effected, Marianella for the Oakland property,' McQuaid's secretary replied. This was 'the final brush-off', the Redemptorist archivist, Fr Brendan McConvery, suggests. 'The signature is the signature of the secretary, the tone is the tone of the Archbishop.'[10]

The Holy Places

Religion so dominated the world outlook of Dublin Catholics that McQuaid could afford to adopt a menacing tone when he warned Irish Jewish leaders, Edwin Solomons and Chief Rabbi Jakobovits, that a 'sentiment of apprehension' was more widespread than he had at first calculated about continued Christian access to the Holy Places in Jerusalem and

Palestine following the establishment of the State of Israel in 1948. The two Jewish leaders had expressed their worries to McQuaid about anti-semitic strains in Irish society which they feared might result in violence.

McQuaid told the Jewish leaders that if they could secure 'adequately firm and authentic guarantees' from the Israeli Government, they would do much to allay Irish Catholics' fears. 'An official declaration from the Control Government will receive wide publicity in Ireland,' McQuaid assured them,

> But, what is equally important, it will be carefully noted wherever Irishmen are found, that is, throughout the universe and especially in the United States of America. Such a declaration would greatly assist, too, in preventing unfortunate repercussions, such as you stated you fear may arise in Dublin.

> It would indeed be a grievous pity, if after having safely traversed a period of worldwide and unexampled crisis, innocent people of your Community should now suffer hurt, because of the attitudes and activities of religious members of Israel; whose merely political or commercial aims would never be countenanced by the peaceful members of your Community in Dublin.[11]

McQuaid had taken up the matter with the Irish Government and he could not see *de jure* recognition being accorded to Israel without definite guarantees being given concerning the Holy Places. Informing Monsignor Gino Paro at the Nunciature in Dublin of his contacts with the Irish Jewish leaders, McQuaid quoted Chief Rabbi Jakobovits as saying to him: 'We Jews, to put the matter on its lowest basis, have too many hostages in the Christian countries to wish to have trouble in the Holy Places.' In speaking so candidly, McQuaid felt that Jakobovits put his finger on what most worried Jews: the fear of reprisals. On the basis of these contacts, McQuaid sharply disagreed with the view of the American 'Goodwill Ambassador', Professor O'Brien of New York, that Cardinal Spellman would effect more influence on the Jews through private negotiations with President Harry Truman than public opinion could. 'Every manifestation makes for some good where Jews are concerned,' McQuaid told Paro, promising to keep the Holy See updated on his future contacts with Irish Jewish leaders.[12]

A particular cause of anxiety to the Jewish leaders was the campaign being run against the Israeli Government by the extreme right-wing Maria Duce, which was based in Dublin. The executive of Maria Duce sent copies of a resolution to McQuaid and the Taoiseach, John A. Costello, condemning the 'calculated and persistent persecution in Palestine of the Catholic Church, Christ's Mystical Body, by the so-called Israeli

Government, which represents the Jewish Nation.' And Maria Duce claimed that the Israeli Government had come to power by means of deceit, terror and huge financial resources. The Maria Duce leadership scrupulously sent copies of this and other resolutions to McQuaid.[13]

Maria Duce

Of all the lay organisations under his control, Maria Duce caused McQuaid the most soul-searching. On the one hand he was sympathetic to the movement's core beliefs, but on the other he was uneasy with their exhibitionism and lack of theological education. Established in 1945 by McQuaid's former Holy Ghost confrère, Fr Denis Fahey, 'to incorporate Christ's Kingly Rights in all aspects of Irish life', Maria Duce embodied the goals McQuaid had himself articulated in his 1932 Cavan speech.[14] However, by 1948 McQuaid, as Archbishop, was reluctant to give his official approval to the organisation, and when it pressed for recognition McQuaid's secretary, Fr Chris Mangan, told them that 'the Archbishop would prefer you at the moment not to insist on obtaining from him a statement of approval or toleration.'[15] Mangan received a copy of the Maria Duce constitution and a list of its executive committee.[16]

In 1949 T.J. Agar, President of Maria Duce, sent the Archbishop a draft copy of a proposed leaflet on associate membership of Maria Duce which they hoped would carry his imprimatur.[17] On McQuaid's instruction, Mangan sent the draft to the diocesan censor, Dr John Kelly, for his opinion on the possibility of letting the card circulate without the note, *Permissu Superiorum*. Maria Duce, however, expecting the green light from Drumcondra, went ahead and published membership forms printed with McQuaid's approval – *permissu Ordinarii Diocesis Dublinensis*.

Agar enclosed a copy of the membership card issued to 82 persons who accepted individual membership. 'Please accept our apologies if we stepped out of line in not submitting them before printing but at the time the necessity for so doing did not occur to us,' Agar explained to Mangan when their breach of the rules was pointed out to them.[18] All told, Maria Duce escaped with only a mild censure. McQuaid's attitude towards the organisation was remarkably tolerant compared with his hostility towards Muintir na Tíre and the Mercier Society.

Behind the scenes, McQuaid inspected Maria Duce's programme, 'The Plan for Catholic Social Order,' and suggested amendments which the group agreed to incorporate.[19] A leaflet which Maria Duce also presented privately to McQuaid was circulated throughout the country 'to expose the grave defect in Article 44 of the Constitution [recognising the special position of the Catholic Church] and to bring before the Irish people their obligation to establish the Social Reign of Christ the King.' Maria Duce's objective of strengthening the constitutional relationship between Church and State was in accord with McQuaid's view that in 1937 de Valera had admitted the false principles of their being separate. Maria Duce also sent a memorandum to local Government authorities as part of a campaign to secure the promise of a referendum to amend Article 44.[20]

McQuaid's public ambivalence towards Maria Duce was detectable in his noncommittal response to an enquiry from Eithne Curley, who asked 'if the organisation known as Maria Duce has your approbation'.[21] The answer was noncommittal: 'Approval of an organisation by His Grace is an official declaration which is very unusual. His Grace has not ever approved Maria Duce in that sense. It is for you to make up your own mind as to the advisability of your joining an organisation by examining the aims and methods of that organisation and by taking advice of your clergy, if in doubt.'[22]

A trickier situation arose when Maria Duce became entangled in a row in the *Standard* with theatre critic Gabriel Fallon after he dismissed the movement as conducting 'a totalitarian academy' whose curriculum included anti-semitism as well as opposition to the theatre![23] Efforts by both sides to enlist McQuaid's authority were skilfully bypassed by the Archbishop, though he summoned the leaders of Maria Duce for a talk. 'Saw Mr Agar, Roseingrave, Duggan, J.P. Ryan,' McQuaid's note of the meeting read. 'Expressed view that they were doing good, but not nearly as much as they could, if they were trained. Urged them to consider taking Catholic Social Guild Certificate and Diploma. Asked them to postpone answer.

'They could help their special line of interest in the Diploma. In present Apostolate: systematic training, continuous study necessary, under direction. They asked for a Chaplain. I agreed to consider it, but expressed sympathy for the priest who would be their chaplain. They were docile, receptive, but adamant on THE plan of their six points.'[24] The reaction of Maria Duce to this pep-talk was summed up by Roseingrave in the exclamation: 'But his Grace told us that he will not condemn us.'[25]

No joy Sundays

A major worry for McQuaid and the bishops in 1950 was the pressure being put on Dáil deputies by the Vintners' Association to support repeal of the Sunday Closing Act by allowing public houses to open for at least a few hours on the Sabbath. In 1948, a strong protest by the bishops had killed a Private Members' Bill which had proposed as much, but to their dismay a renewed attempt was now being made to introduce liberalising legislation in the Dáil. The clamorous lobbying of the Vintners' Association was met with a lengthy statement from the bishops in June setting out the divine and ecclesiastical law. 'It was the will of God to sanctify one day in each week and the Catholic Church had decreed that this day

should be Sunday, or the Lord's Day,' the bishops declared in their statement, which also pointed out that article 1248 of the code of Canon Law
forbade Sunday trading. The opening of public houses, which was calculated to lead to drunkenness and other sins and temporal evils, would be
particularly repugnant to the sanctity of the Lord's Day.

Accordingly, where there has been no existing and longstanding
custom, to open public houses on Sundays even for a few hours would be a
serious violation of this ecclesiastical law. So long as this ecclesiastical law
remains it would be sinful to agitate for their opening. Furthermore, those
to whom God has given authority to rule the State should in their legislation on this matter have for their object, not to satisfy the clamour of an
interested group, but to promote the true welfare of the whole community.

The bishops also warned publicans who broke the law and sold
drink on Sundays that they could be committing mortal sin. 'We warn
these that their conduct is reprehensible not only from the standpoint of
the civil authorities but also in the eyes of Almighty God especially because
of the scandal they give in leading the young into intemperate lives.'[26]

The hauteur of the Hierarchy was revealed in their comment that,
now that the divine and ecclesiastical law had been made clear, the agitation for the opening of public houses on Sundays could end and that publicans should remove existing abuses in connection with the sale of
Sunday drink. Many of these abuses were due to breaches of a law which
allowed *bona fide* travellers to order drinks in hotels en route. Inevitably,
many locals became travellers on a Sunday, encouraging the bishops to
urge the civil rulers to restrict the application of that law. Another source
of abuse which McQuaid and his colleagues wanted tightened up was the
granting of exemptions by local authorities.

Greyhound racing on the Sabbath was frowned upon by McQuaid
every bit as much as Sunday drinking. With his approval, the Knights of St
Columbanus lobbied a Department of Agriculture advisory committee on
the greyhound industry with a view to prohibiting racing and coursing on
Sundays and Church holidays.[27]

The Hierarchy was generally reluctant to encourage any signs of
'modernisation' of a traditionally hidebound society. Even their decision
to cooperate with the Genealogical Office and allow photocopying of old
parochial records, mainly to meet a demand from Irish Americans and
Irish Australians interested in tracing their roots, was restricted by the
habit of secrecy which still clung to McQuaid and his colleagues, who
made their agreement conditional on the requirement that photocopies
would be preserved in the diocesan archives under the control of the
Diocesan Curia.[28] Another concern of McQuaid at mid-century was that
there should be no burial of non-Catholics in those parts of cemeteries
reserved for Catholics.[29]

Religion might have been thriving, but Irish society was becoming more moribund, not just in terms of depopulation but also in intellectual life. By this time, the censorship system had banned writers of the stature of James Joyce, Sean O'Casey, Sigmund Freud, Maxim Gorky, Thomas Mann, Alberto Moravia, Graham Greene, H.G. Wells, George Bernard Shaw, Seán Ó Faoláin, Frank O'Connor, Liam O'Flaherty, Kate O'Brien, Oliver St John Gogarty, Bertrand Russell, George Orwell, Noel Coward, Christopher Isherwood, Aldous Huxley, Compton MacKenzie, Sinclair Lewis, W. Somerset Maughan, Ernest Hemingway, Taylor Caldwell, Upton Sinclair, Truman Capote, Henry Morton Robinson, Robert Penn Warren, Sherwood Anderson, William Faulkner, F. Scott Fitzgerald, Margaret Mead, Martha Gellhorn, John Dos Passos, Joyce Carey, Marcel Proust, Anatole France, Jean Paul Sartre, André Gide and Simone de Beauvoir. This system, supported wholeheartedly by McQuaid, was described by Paul Blanshard as offering 'honourable dishonour' to the banned writers.[30]

Anti-porn drive

With the approval of Archbishop McQuaid, the Knights of St Columbanus took on the 'wholesale clean-up of evil literature' as their principal work for 1950. The Supreme Knight, Stephen McKenzie, obtained the Archbishop's support for an action plan to set up 'committees of readers' in all branches of the organisation. These 'readers' were to visit libraries and bookshops to inspect and read free of charge any of the books available to the public. In cases where librarians or shopkeepers refused to grant the 'readers' these facilities, they were to be reported to the Knights' headquarters at Ely Place. Readers were urged to send pornographic books or periodicals to the secretary of the Censorship of Publications Board, with a covering note outlining offensive passages.[31]

Of particular concern was the importation of 'crime comics', particularly *The Eagle* with its star feature, Dan Dare versus the Mekon in outer space. Similar agitation was underway in Britain and Canada, where it was feared that such comics would turn young boys into raging criminals. It was therefore with a sense of considerable achievement that Ireland's most vigilant censorship campaigner, Fr R.S. Devane S.J., informed McQuaid that '*The Eagle* is now banned.'[32] Devane also directed his venom against the importation of British newspapers, rhetorically asking a Dublin Mass-meeting sanctioned by McQuaid: 'Can we call ourselves a free people and a sovereign state when we are so dependent for our reading matter on papers whose ideals are not our own?'[33]

McKenzie sought McQuaid's direction when the Knights began a cinema surveillance system. Under discussion were ways of classifying films as 'A' and 'U' as in Britian, and of excluding children from cinemas after 7.15pm. Bowing to the mood of the country, the film censor banned as blasphemous the Italian film, *The Miracle*, which had been denounced in New York as sacrilegious by Cardinal Spellman.[34]

At McQuaid's suggestion a group of Dublin Knights formed a Theatre Censorship Committee to watch plays being performed in the city and draw up critiques as to their suitability. The Knights were moving into an area which was already being kept under review by the Catholic Cinema and Theatre Patrons' Association, an arm of Maria Duce, whose constitution allowed the Archbishop of Dublin to appoint a nominee to the association's governing body.[35] The association kept McQuaid informed of its progress, including the Holy Year campaign to keep the harmonica player and raconteur Larry Adler from appearing in the Theatre Royal. They pointed out to the manager that Adler had been listed by the US Un-American Activities Committee as a member of a Communist-front organisation, and warned him that 'As a caterer of entertainment for audiences which are preponderantly Catholic, it is felt that you will appreciate your responsibility in this matter and act accordingly.' Without explanation, Adler did not appear for his well-advertised show.[36]

When a UCD student, Michael Gorman, visited Séan O'Casey at Totnes in Devon during 1950, he asked him why he wouldn't come back to Ireland, where he was assured of a warm reception from a younger generation who regarded him as one of their great models. O'Casey told Gorman, 'I shall never come back to Ireland as long as the arch-druid of Drumcondra is alive.'[37]

In the name of McQuaid

Despite McQuaid's best efforts to make UCD a Catholic enclave, some students were in sympathy with wider cultural trends. But when Michael Gorman, director of the Dramatic Society, planned to stage a production of Jean Paul Sartre's *Huis Clos* in the Aula Maxima, he was summoned to President Michael Tierney's office where he was asked if he wanted to turn UCD into a second Gate Theatre. 'What would the Archbishop say if I allowed you to go ahead with this production?' Tierney quizzed Gorman. Permission, which had not been sought for the production, was refused. Tierney's reaction to the Sartre play highlighted the shadowy atmosphere in which decisions were made to avoid offending the Archbishop. According to Gorman, this was McQuaid's most effective way of exercising power. 'If things went wrong the well-intending minion could be disowned very readily by pointing out that Dr McQuaid knew nothing about the matter.'[38]

A classic instance of this phenomenon concerned the Quaker-founded Meath Hospital and the Knights of St Columbanus. At the hospital's annual meeting in 1949 a group of Catholic doctors swelled the membership ranks and took control by securing a majority vote. The takeover

caused a public uproar when some of Ireland's leading non-Catholic physicians were discharged or resigned. Besieged Protestant board members
turned to McQuaid to redress their grievance.

McQuaid granted an interview to Professor Jessop and Dr Cyril
Murphy. Over tea, Jessop told McQuaid that he had lost his job and that
the Protestants were being 'persecuted'. McQuaid was adamant that he
had nothing to do with the affair and only knew what he had read in newspapers. Promising to do what he could, he invited them to come back two
days later.[39]

Stephen McKenzie assured McQuaid that the Knights had not
organised the coup, but he was forced to admit that it had been arranged
by a small section of members without any authority from the main body.
McQuaid sent for one of the culprits, Senator Michael Colgan, who was
left in no doubt that he should undo the damage. When Jessop and
Murphy came for their second visit, McQuaid could assure them that they
would see results very soon. As a result of McQuaid's remonstrance, three
members of the takeover committee – vice chairman Senator Michael
Colgan, Joseph Bowden and Charles H. Macauley – resigned in February
1950. A Private Members' Bill was rushed through the Dáil to regularise
the position in favour of Protestants.

While writers such as Jack White and Kurt Bowen have judged this
reversion to the status quo as evidence that McQuaid had not sanctioned
a policy of discrimination against Protestants, it would be more correct to
see this as an instance where McQuaid acted to undo a specific injustice
which his general policy had inspired.[40] He remained opposed to Catholics attending Protestant institutions, a stance underlined once again in
1951 when he was asked for advice by Bishop Daniel Cohalan of Cork
about sending a Catholic boy to the Stewart Institution in Co. Dublin.
'The place is very Protestant. I would not advise a child to be sent there,'
he replied.[41] At this time also McQuaid was supportive of the Knights'
campaign to infiltrate the Irish Trade Protection Association so as to
introduce 'a true Catholic flavour into the atmosphere of businesses'.[42]

It suited McQuaid to do his bullying in private. In 1950 he was outraged when the Irish National Teachers' Organisation sent a questionnaire to national school principals without seeking the permission of the
bishops and parish priests who were the school managers. McQuaid summoned the INTO's general secretary, D.K. Kelleher, and conveyed to him
'the surprise and grave resentment of the standing committee of the bishops' at the INTO's audacity. Kelleher was duly cowed: McQuaid reported
to the Hierarchy's June meeting that the INTO general secretary had
agreed that the answers to the questionnaire, which would have painted a
negative picture of conditions in many national schools under church
management, would not be published.[43]

Tilson mixed-marriage case

McQuaid's dexterity in pulling the strings of State from behind the scenes extended to the judiciary. A letter from the Irish Ambassador to the Holy See, Joe Walshe, links McQuaid to a landmark legal ruling in July 1950 by the President of the High Court, Mr Justice Gavan Duffy. Known as the Tilson Case, this *cause célèbre* gave Roman Canon Law on mixed marriages legal force in Ireland.

A Protestant, Ernest Neville Tilson, aged 34, had married a 16-year-old pregnant Catholic girl, Mary Josephine Barnes, in St Mary's Church, Haddington Rd, in December 1941. Before Bishop Wall, both parties had signed the *Ne Temere* promises that their children would be brought up as Catholics. After husband and wife fell out, Tilson removed three of their four children to a Protestant institution for children in need, known as Mrs Smyly's Home. When she discovered where the children had been placed, Barnes sought a High Court order requiring Tilson to return her sons to her.

Mr Justice Gavan Duffy ruled that without just cause Tilson had attempted to break up the home and had relegated the boys as mock-orphans to the care of a charity, where he would have them brought up as Protestants in defiance of his holy undertaking, cognizable by the High Court. He ordered the return of the children to Barnes, whom he described as a good mother who would fulfil the antenuptial agreement and would continue to bring up her children as good Catholics.

'I can echo your Grace's expression of relief at the Gavan Duffy decision – and I am above all delighted that it was brought about by your patient and consistent work,' Ambassador Walshe wrote to McQuaid. He informed the Archbishop that the Vatican had paid special attention to the case – whenever he met Monsignor Tardini, the Vatican official mentioned it, though he was puzzled as to why the *Ne Temere* promise was not instantly applicable in such a Catholic country as Ireland. His bafflement made Walshe feel 'like a Protestant'. 'Thanks be to the Lord that is all over and that it has been done in the best possible way,' he wrote in August.[44]

To Walshe's great relief, Mr Justice Gavan Duffy, with McQuaid's covert guidance, had given Canon Law the force of Irish law by basing his judgement on Article 44 of the Constitution, which referred to the special position of the Catholic Church. 'In my opinion,' he stated, 'an order of the Court designed to secure the fulfilment of an agreement peremptorily required before a "mixed marriage" by the Church whose special position in Ireland is officially recognised as the guardian of the Catholic spouse, cannot be withheld on any ground of public policy by the very State which pays that homage to the Church.'[45]

Protestant opinion was alarmed by the judgment, which made the ecclesiastically required written promise in mixed marriages enforceable in Irish law, even when the non-Catholic partner wished to revoke that promise. The judgement sensationally overturned constitutional precedent inherited from English law which would have upheld Tilson's case on the grounds that a husband was entitled to make decisions on behalf of his children as the sole head of the family.

Gavan Duffy's decision was upheld by a four-to-one majority in the Supreme Court, under Mr Justice James Murnaghan, McQuaid's contemporary at Clongowes Wood College. Pointing out that the Supreme Court did not hold that Articles 41 and 44 conferred any privileged status before the law on members of the Roman Catholic Church, Murnaghan based his judgement entirely on Article 43, relating to the rights of parents. He ruled that Tilson had no justification on the ground of religious upbringing or any other ground for taking the children from the family home.[46]

American adoptions

Because of the absence of legislation permitting adoption in Ireland, there were growing numbers of unwanted Irish babies with no legal status or rights whatsoever. Many of these babies were being bought by American couples from orphanages controlled by nuns and were illegally taken to their new homes overseas. This traffic in adopted babies appears to have begun in 1947 when de Valera was Taoiseach and Minister for External Affairs. By 1951 over 300 children a year were being sold abroad. Nearly all were Catholics 'born out of wedlock', many of respectable parentage but with no prospect in a society whose Constitution instituted the family as the basic unit of society. Described by the Catholic Social Welfare Bureau as 'fallen women' and 'grave sinners', the single women involved looked for help to two Dublin diocesan agencies, St Patrick's Guild in Abbey St and St Patrick's Home on the Navan Rd.

When the file on foreign adoptions landed on McQuaid's desk in March 1950 as the result of a casual enquiry from America, he ordered an immediate ban pending an investigation to satisfy himself that the children's Catholic faith would be safeguarded in all circumstances. Before McQuaid imposed this unilateral ban, Irish diplomats had taken no supervisory measures, despite the expressed concerns of the Minister for Health, Dr Nöel Browne.

McQuaid, however, waived his own ban soon afterwards following vigorous representations from two nuns, Sister Frances Elizabeth, of the Daughters of Charity of St Vincent de Paul, and Sister Monica of the Sisters of Charity, who pleaded on behalf of potential adopting parents, one of whom was a friend of Cardinal Spellman. McQuaid granted these exceptions but insisted that Pan American Airways should 'close down on publicity' when Irish children were being taken to the United States.

A few months later, after discussions with Monsignor John O'Grady of the Washington-based Catholic Charities, McQuaid introduced guidelines governing foreign adoptions. Prospective adopting parents were to fulfil six conditions laid down by him:

1. Obtain a written recommendation from their diocesan director of Catholic Charities.

2. Supply their baptismal and marriage certificates for inspection.

3. Supply a reference from their parish priest.

4. Submit a statement of their finances so as to ensure a good home and good prospects in life for the adopted child.

5. Submit medical certificates stating age, physical and mental health, and that they were not deliberately shirking natural parenthood.

6. Swear an affidavit that they were Catholics, guarantee to rear the adopted child as a Catholic, undertake to educate the adopted child, during the whole course of its schooling, in Catholic schools; and that if the child went to university, it would be to a Catholic University, and that they undertook to keep the adopted child permanently and would not to hand it over to any other party or parties.[47]

Once McQuaid had published his guidelines, Government departments accepted and enforced them. He went completely unchallenged by the State in his activity.[48]

Boys' holiday camps

One of McQuaid's special-interest projects was the building of a boys' holiday home in Balbriggan on the north Co. Dublin coast. He worked closely with Dermot O'Flynn of the Knights of St Columbanus in securing a suitable site and gave a gift of £1,000 (£20,000) towards the cost.[49]

McQuaid also encouraged the Catholic Social Service Conference to support boys' summer homes. Addressing the conference, he declared: 'Parents can feel assured when they know that their children are being enrolled in the clubs and holiday camps which the Conference controls. In your groups the teaching of the Faith is honoured, especially in regard to right moral conduct.'

Parents, he added, had a serious duty 'to examine the credentials of any organisation that now seeks to enrol their children under the cover of affording opportunities for debates, sport, hiking, cycling and dramatic performances.'[50]

Year of pilgrimages

Not only was 1950 a Holy Year, it was also the occasion of Pope Pius's solemn declaration of the dogma that the Virgin Mary was assumed body and soul into heaven. Amid rumours that Pius would crown the year's proceedings by giving Ireland a cardinal, it was also a year of numerous pilgrimages from the Emerald Isle to the Holy See. President O'Kelly placed his 'personal homage and that of my people at the feet of His Holiness', while Taoiseach John A. Costello, who assured Pius that Communism was virtually non-existent in Ireland, told him of his admiration for McQuaid.

'You can have no conception of the esteem you enjoy here,' Walshe assured McQuaid. 'Montini could not say enough about your great work in the diocese.' Costello, the Ambassador said, had told him 'so much about your extraordinary kindness to him, and to his family, and your readiness to see him at all times, that I felt back in the old atmosphere once again.'[51]

Montini had discussed with Walshe 'the wonderful favour' proposed by Pope Pius XII of constructing a chapel to the eighth-century Celtic missionary, St Columbanus, in the crypt of the Basilica of St Peter's. Although other bishops baulked at the financial undertaking which would be involved, McQuaid responded positively, and Montini was overjoyed when Walshe told him that McQuaid would see the chapel through. 'He is a true Roman,' Montini said of the Archbishop.[52] McQuaid arranged for a cheque of £3,000 (£60,000) to be given to the Pope that autumn by the Supreme Knight of Columbanus, Stephen McKenzie.[53]

The commemoration of the fourteenth centenary of Columbanus's birth brought McQuaid that July to the small town of Luxeuil in the French Alps, which was ablaze with tricolours at 50-yard intervals. The event was attended by 20,000 pilgrims and brought together the heads of Church and State of France and Ireland, including Cardinal Maurice Feltin of Paris and the Foreign Minister, Robert Schuman.[54] The star attraction was the Papal Nuncio to France, Archbishop Angelo Roncalli, the future Pope John XXIII. He was guest of honour at a convivial and animated luncheon which was captured in a unique photograph: the table plentifully supplied with excellent wines, while cigarette in hand beside McQuaid stood Seán MacBride, both of them waiting to be introduced by Costello to the Nuncio, whose ring was being kissed by de Valera.[55] MacBride later told the story of how when McQuaid threatened to be awkward about not having the correct Crozier, Roncalli smoothed matters by handing him his own.

McQuaid along with Costello, MacBride and de Valera, were guests of honour at a dinner offered by Monsignor Dubourg. Speaking in French, McQuaid prescribed 'the strong and saving influence of the genuinely Catholic school' as the antidote to the 'new barbarism' in the form of the Communist threat from the East. 'Coming from the country of St

Columbanus, I have learned the value of Catholic schools, to which in Ireland we owe the practice of the faith and the prodigious fertility of priestly and apostolic vocations,' McQuaid said, underlining the close fraternal bonds between 'my little country of the Faith and the land of ancient Catholic civilisation'. Ireland would remain ever grateful to France, he said.[56]

McQuaid's status as the premier Francophile in the Irish Hierarchy was confirmed when he was made an Honorary Canon of Besançon Cathedral. 'Luxeuil was a great triumph for Ireland and the presence of your Grace and the Prime Minister was a most fortunate circumstance for us,' Joe Walshe wrote from Rome.[57] 'Ireland,' Bishop Collier of Ossory thought, 'was well and worthily represented.'[58]

In September, McQuaid was in Lourdes with the Dublin diocesan pilgrimage as he had been the year before. This was a adventurous initiative from Dublin in view of the decision of Archbishop D'Alton of Armagh and Archbishop Kinane of Cashel not to join a national pilgrimage because of the disturbed state of Europe, especially France.[59] It was certainly not a question of money that held back D'Alton and Kinane, who had learned that the Hierarchy's Lourdes pilgrimage fund, which had been frozen during the war, stood at £32,000 (£640,000).

In late September, McQuaid travelled to London for the centenary celebrations of the restoration of the Hierarchy in England and Wales at the ruined cathedral of St George's, Southwark. He stayed with the Auxiliary Bishop of Westminster, Monsignor George Craven, and was the guest of the Minister for Civil Aviation, Frank Pakenham, at a luncheon attended by Cardinal Konrad von Preysing, the Under Secretary of State for Foreign Affairs, Lord Henderson and the Vice-chairman of the House of Lords, Lord Holden. Before returning to Dublin, McQuaid called on Cardinal Bernard Griffin, whose idea of enlarging the scope of the proposed Irish Centre in London to include all denominations had not won the Archbishop's favour.[60]

The following month McQuaid spoke at the Institut Catholique in Paris, where he handed over the supplies of meat donated by the Irish Government to the 'necessitous' French seminaries. 'Here in France one scarcely realises the sympathy that exists among our people for the land of France,' he said. 'In a very sombre period of history your seminaries imparted to thousands of Irish students the traditional clerical formation. Ireland in that sense owes to you the incomparable gift of the Priesthood, with all that that Priesthood means for the preservation of the Faith.'

McQuaid, who had celebrated Mass that morning in Notre Dame Cathedral, was the guest of honour at a luncheon in the Quai d'Orsay hosted by the Minister for Public Health and Deputy Minister for Foreign Affairs, Monsieur Schneiter. He also found time to pay a call on the Nuncio, Monsignor Roncalli, who accompanied him to the Comédie

Française for a gala performance by Our Lady's Choral Society of Dublin.[61]

At their meeting in Luxeuil, McQuaid had been impressed by Roncalli, with whom he found a mutual bond in their regard for St Francis de Sales. Not schooled in French intellectual history, Roncalli's view of France was coloured by his readings of de Sales, whom he regarded as his 'great teacher'. In the France of the 1950s, however, the Nuncio had a difficult time keeping Pius XII happy with Rome's 'eldest daughter'. There were tensions between Paris and Rome over the decline in religious practice and the control of schools in France. Roncalli was also being put under increasing pressure from Pius to halt the growth of the progressive wing of French Catholicism, centring on theologians like the Jesuit Henri de Lubac and Dominican Yves Congar.

On August 12, Roncalli, contrary to his own personal views, had the duty of informing Cardinal Feltin of the Encyclical letter, *Humani Generis*, which condemned *la nouvelle théologie* of the French Dominicans and Jesuits. As soon as he had done Pius's business, Roncalli retreated to his home in Bergamo for a break. So traumatised was he by these events that he stopped writing up his diary for several weeks.[62] He met McQuaid on one of his first working days back in Paris. No record of their conversation has yet emerged.

Dogma in Rome

In his Pastoral Letter on the Assumption of Mary, McQuaid showed no awareness of the doubts circulating in liberal Catholic and non-Catholic circles about the new dogma. On the contrary, he declared that the doctrine was in no sense new. 'Only the solemn proclamation will be new,' he said. 'Our belief will not now be changed; nor will any addition be made to that belief. Rather, a new reason for merit will be given to our faith, once the doctrine will have been explicitly, and with infallible authority, proposed by the Sovereign Pontiff.'[63]

On October 16, McQuaid climbed on board the *Hibernia* at Dun Laoghaire pier as head of the Second National Pilgrimage to Rome. In Rome he conducted the pilgrims on a tour of the four patriarchal basilicas, celebrated Mass in the catacombs at an altar over the tomb of the martyred Pope, St Melchiades, called on Montini at the Secretariat of State and attended a reception given by Prince Casa di Roda of the Knights of Malta, where he met Cardinals Pietro Fumasoni-Blondi and Canali. He also accompanied a group of Irish trade unionists to a special audience with Pius XII at Castel Gandolfo. In Rome he distributed money, given to him by the Knights of St Columbanus, to poor children.[64]

What the *Irish Press* described as the most moving moment in the history of the Catholic Church, took place at 8.38am Irish time on November 1, the feast of All Saints. McQuaid was among the 1,000 prelates who gathered around the Papal throne on the steps of St Peter's Square. Irish pilgrims carrying banners in English, Irish and Latin were among the estimated 700,000 crowd which stretched from the square to the banks of the Tiber half a mile away. The Irish Government was represented by Tánaiste William Norton and Ambassador Walshe. MacBride arrived late from fog-bound Zurich.[65]

Before leaving for Rome, McQuaid had left precise instructions as to how Catholic Dublin would honour Mary. Thousands of Dubliners, men, women and children, flocked to the early morning Masses so as to get back home in time to listen to the ceremonies being broadcast from Rome. As the Pope gave his Apostolic Blessing in St Peter's Square, families throughout Dublin knelt with Rosary beads in hand to receive the extended plenary indulgence wiping out the time they would spend in purgatory for their past sins. Homes and offices were bedecked with statues of Mary, lighted candles, Papal and national flags, and many businesses closed for the day or part of it in honour of the Virgin Mother. At midday, 1,500 dungaree-clad CIÉ workers marched with flags to the Oblate Church of Mary Immaculate for High Mass.

The splendour and sanctity of the ceremonies enhanced Irish trade unionism's links with the Christian religion, the President of the Congress of Irish Unions, John Conroy, claimed. 'In the circumstances, no one will question the cost of the delegations sent by Congress to Rome, nor will there be a single demur about it,' he said. The Trade Union Congress, numbering 181,040 members, went into debt on account of its Holy Year expenditures.[66]

Catholic Ireland's allegiance to Rome provided photographic opportunities for politicans. All Government ministers put Rome on their Holy Year itinerary, except for the Minister for Health, Dr Nöel Browne. Behind the scenes of celebration, the stage was being set for a major trial of strength between Browne and Archbishop John Charles McQuaid, one that was to reverberate through Irish society for the next 50 years.

Mother and Child
1950–51

'My most powerful and uncompromising opponent was
Dr John Charles McQuaid.'

Dr Nöel Browne, Against the Tide.

In a letter to the Papal Nuncio, Archbishop Ettore Felici, marked 'Secret'
and written on April 16 1951, four days after Dr Nöel Browne's resignation as Minister for Health, Archbishop John Charles McQuaid boasted
that the Hierarchy's condemnation of the Mother and Child Scheme, and
the condemnation of it by the Inter-Party Government led by Taoiseach
John A. Costello, was the most important event in Irish history since
Daniel O'Connell had achieved Catholic Emancipation in 1829.

The accuracy of this claim had been assured to him by a highly
placed Catholic judge, who had predicted that such a clash was bound to
come between Church and State. McQuaid believed that history would
vindicate him as the prelate who successfully defended the right of the
Catholic Church to manage its own voluntary hospitals and practise
Catholic medical ethics against the encroaching and potentially totalitarian powers of the State.

'That the clash should have come in this particular form and under
this Government, with Mr Costello at its head, is a very happy success for
the Church,' McQuaid wrote. 'The decision of the Government has
thrown back Socialism and Communism for a very long time. No Government, for years to come, unless it is frankly Communist, can afford to disregard the moral teaching of the Bishops.'

This was a candid assessment of the Catholic Church's moral power
30 years after Irish independence from Britain. The ideological reality of
the 1950s was that Browne, a democratically elected politician with a
social vision, was a pawn in McQuaid's Cold War struggle against Communism and its milder but no less insidious form of 'socialised medicine',
which had spread to Britain and Northern Ireland in the guise of the Welfare State.

In his report to the Nuncio, which McQuaid knew would be read avidly in the Vatican by Monsignor Giovanni Montini – and even by His Holiness, Pope Pius XII – he highlighted the influence he had exercised over Costello as the decisive factor in that Government's abandoning of Browne's scheme. McQuaid knew that the public declarations by Costello and his ministers, including Seán MacBride, that they were Catholics first and Irishmen second, would be welcome news in a Vatican embattled by Communism in Eastern and Central Europe and dispirited by war in Korea.

If McQuaid, deservedly by his own light, was to win the Vatican's esteem for his handling of the welfare controversy, he was to lose the propaganda war in Ireland against his younger and more charismatic opponent. McQuaid's personal perspective on the significance of the issues at stake in 1951 was swept into oblivion by Nöel Browne's mastery of publicity. Until his death in May 1997 at the age of 81, Browne believed that he was the victim of a conspiracy by the bishops and doctors led by McQuaid to subvert the implementation of his free, State-sponsored scheme for the welfare of mothers and children. Although the details of the controversy have faded from the public mind, the popular memory remains of McQuaid as a clerical villain and Browne as a medical Robin Hood.

McQuaid's account, published here for the first time, shows that Browne was a more conventional Catholic then, compared with his subsequent anti-clerical tirades. Notwithstanding his failings and political inexperience, he remains entitled to his status as modern Ireland's first socialist martyr.

The McQuaid version of events also disproves the thesis of those academics who have tended to play down the brutal use of *force majeure* exercised by McQuaid and the bishops against Browne. McQuaid confirms beyond doubt that, with Costello's collusion, the elected Government capitulated to the bishops behind closed doors, and shamelessly abandoned the principle of elective democracy when presented with a theocratic diktat. The McQuaid papers also confirm his central role throughout the crisis. With the cuteness of a Cavan man and the prejudices of the son of a doctor, McQuaid chose the moment to strike at Browne when he knew that the Minister for Health was totally isolated in Cabinet and was anathema to the medical profession.

McQuaid's account explains his motivation and action, but it does not absolve him from the verdict of history, that the bishops' intervention against Browne's welfare scheme was their biggest miscalculation in Church-State relations. It was an intervention which enabled the Church to bully the State on issues of public morality throughout the 1950s and even, to a diminishing degree, into the 1980s, but at the price of sowing the seeds of the Church's dramatic decline in the 1990s.[1]

Round one

The battle-lines between Church and State were drawn up several years before Browne came into office. Towards the end of 1945 the Department of Local Government and Health produced a radical blueprint for the reform of the health services which identified two key areas: tackling infectious diseases and providing better welfare care for mothers and children. This shift towards communal medicine reflected a trend highlighted by the Beveridge Report in Britain which had pinpointed the five enemies of public health as disease, ignorance, loss of income, squalor and idleness.[2]

Piloting the 1945 Public Health Bill through the Dáil was the combative parliamentary secretary, Dr Conor Ward. The Bill proposed to give the Minister the power to declare by administrative order that a particular disease was infectious. For the first time it would enable county and county boroughs to take under custody persons infected with venereal disease and tuberculosis. It also aimed at ensuring proper inspection of children with skin infections, vermin and malnutrition. Doctors treating infectious children were to notify the district medical officer; parents of infectious or verminous children were to keep them away from school, church and public places such as cinemas and parish halls. Dismissively, in the Dáil, Fine Gael's front-bench spokesman, Richard Mulcahy, attacked a provision which he said would prevent a child attending Mass 'because it has nits in its hair'.

Ignoring Opposition complaints that the Bill was bureaucratic and centralist, Ward captured the attention of the press gallery when he hinted that 'by far the most important' sections of the Bill were those dealing with the mother and child welfare scheme. Ward's nod was the midwife to next day's *Irish Press* headline heralding 'Free Care for Mothers and Children.'

The headline did not escape the attention of the Palace in Drumcondra. Ahead of the Bill's committee stage, McQuaid informed de Valera of 'serious considerations' which had been noted by the bishops' standing committee. 'It is feared,' McQuaid wrote, 'that the unusual and absolute power of medical inspection of children and adults, by compulsory regulation, and, if needs be, by force, is a provision so intimately concerned with the rights of parents and the human person, that only clear-cut guarantees and safeguards on the part of the Government, can be regarded as an adequate protection of those rights.'[3]

On de Valera's desk, too, was a tirade from the Conference of Superiors of Convent Secondary Schools against compulsory medical inspection. Echoing McQuaid's complaint, this powerful nuns' lobby opposed the inspection of adolescent schoolgirls by doctors as altogether undesirable.[4]

Aware of McQuaid's control of most Dublin hospitals and his personal contacts in the medical profession, de Valera promptly arranged to meet McQuaid to defuse potential problems. This respectful response flattered McQuaid's egotistic belief that protocol required him to deal with heads of Government, not ordinary ministers. De Valera arranged for Ward to call on McQuaid a week later.

When he met Ward, McQuaid acknowledged that the Bill had excellent features, but took issue with the powers of interference accruing to the State. Ward assured McQuaid that at committee stage he would introduce amendments exempting from inspection the better-type secondary school children who held a certificate from the family doctor. McQuaid subsequently approved draft amendments sent to him by Ward.[5]

Despite these amendments, Fine Gael compared the proposed powers of intervention to Russian totalitarianism and the Nazi concentration camps. Before the Bill reached the final stage, Ward, however, fell from power as a result of a scandal regarding irregularities in his tax returns.

Ward's downfall was used by de Valera to restructure Government portfolios in January 1947, when he made the former Agriculture Minister, Dr James Ryan, Ireland's first head of the combined Department of Health and Social Welfare. Within five months of taking office, Ryan introduced the Health Bill 1947. Basically the same as Dr Ward's Bill, Ryan identified a comprehensive service for mothers and children up to 16 years of age as the most important of his reforms. When he announced that the mother and child services would be free of all charge to the patients, there was no opposition from any Dáil deputy.

After the Bill became law in August 1947, its provision for a local authority which would compel schoolchildren to undertake medical examinations was challenged in the courts by James Dillon T.D. as being unconstitutional. A further set-back came in October when the bishops registered their objections privately with de Valera. Specifically, they disapproved of Part 3 of the Act, which empowered a public authority to provide for the health of all children, to treat their ailments, educate them in regard to health, educate women in regard to motherhood and provide all women with gynaecological care. To claim such unqualified powers was 'entirely and directly contrary to Catholic teachings, the rights of the family, the rights of the Church in education, the rights of the medical profession and of voluntary institutions', the bishops wrote privately.[6]

De Valera did not reply to the bishops' letter until February 16, 1948, two days before he left office. Citing Dillon's constitutional challenge as the reason for the delay, he included Ryan's revised memorandum in his reply. Ryan had made alterations after consulting McQuaid. 'Their Lordships,' de Valera wrote, 'may be assured that the Government, both in their legislative proposals and in administration, have constantly in mind, not only the State's function as guardian of the common good, but also the respect which is due to the fundamental personal and family rights.'[7]

De Valera's delaying tactics had avoided a potential Church-State showdown. The major question now was whether the incoming health minister would have the political skills to defuse the time-bomb left for him by McQuaid and the bishops.

Defying holy orders

Dr Nöel Browne, a 32-year-old socially minded doctor and member of Clann na Poblachta, a radical republican version of the old Fianna Fáil, became Minister for Health on his first day in the Dáil on the recommendation of his party leader, Seán MacBride. In his memoirs, *Against the Tide*, Browne has written movingly of how his parents and two sisters died from tuberculosis, and of how he himself had suffered from the disease. Eager to eradicate tuberculosis, Browne was also enthusiastic about the mother and child welfare project, though, amazingly, he did not know for some time about de Valera's valedictory correspondence with the bishops.

Although Browne was later to attribute his education in the Protestant medical school of Trinity College, Dublin, as a drawback in his dealings with McQuaid, he claimed that as a committed Catholic his scheme was not contrary to Catholic teaching. For his part, McQuaid felt that he was personally kind and sympathetic towards the youthful and soft-spoken Browne, who looked more like a student than a Government minister.

Browne's commitment to the Mother and Child Scheme became clear at a Cabinet meeting on June 25, 1948. Although no formal decision on the substance of the scheme was taken by the Government, Browne took the absence of dissent against it being free and non-means-tested as a green light to go ahead. The one formal decision taken was to repeal the clauses providing for women's education as regards motherhood, which Dillon, who was now Minister for Agriculture, had objected to. That alteration caused Browne no difficulty.

So confident was Browne of Cabinet support that in August he informed the Irish Medical Association (IMA) that the Government would not agree to a means test. He sent the IMA details of the scheme which provided women with free family practitioner care, specialist, consultant and hospital treatment, visits from public health nurses, and dental and eye treatment during and after their pregnancy. For children up to 16 years the Minister planned to provide free medical care (including inoculations and injections) for all illnesses, specialist, consultant and hospital treatment, home visits by public health nurses, dental and eye treatment, and their choice of doctor (including family doctor).

Employing what are now known as media spin-doctors, Browne used advertisements and radio to build up strong public support for his scheme under the slogan: NO DOCTORS' BILLS. He insisted that the health plan was necessary in a country with the highest infant and maternal mortality rates in Europe. The 1946 Census of Population had shown that the infant mortality rate in lower income groups in Dublin was 133 per 1,000 compared with 29 per 1,000 in higher income groups.[8]

By early 1950 the tide was running in Browne's favour. Intriguingly, in the McQuaid papers there is a letter from Browne's private secretary, Richard (Dick) Whyte, to McQuaid's secretary, Fr Michael O'Connell. Overlooked in any of Browne's accounts, it reveals that the Archbishop and the Minister were in touch about the details of the scheme, apparently amicably so at this stage. 'It is understood,' Whyte wrote, 'that in course of conversation recently with His Grace, Dr Browne promised to forward the enclosed particulars of the suggested Mother and Child Health Service Scheme for Dublin County Boroughs.'[9]

In McQuaid's possession, too, was a copy of the Explanatory Memorandum for the Health Bill 1950 with an instruction handwritten on the margin: 'Corrected and returned to Dáil office 18.1.50.' McQuaid also had a draft copy of the 1950 Health Bill, dated February 1950 and marked 'confidential'. The Archbishop evidently had a mole in or close to the Department of Health.

Armed with this advance intelligence, McQuaid instructed one of his key officials, Monsignor Dick Glennon, to obtain the opinion of a medical friend, Dr Patrick Dargan, on the Health Bill. After careful study, Dargan told McQuaid that Browne's Bill dealt satisfactorily with the features of Ryan's 1947 Act which the Hierarchy had found objectionable.[10]

The tide, however, was about to turn against Browne. The IMA was growing more agitated about the thrust of his plans, and the Minister for Defence, Dr Tom O'Higgins, a powerful figure in the doctors' lobby, was becoming a formidable opponent both inside and outside Cabinet. O'Higgins sided with the doctors in maintaining that the scheme represented a dangerous advance towards complete State control of medicine and would be harmful to the whole community. As early as June 1948 the Minister for Justice, Seán MacEoin, a member of the Knights of St Columbanus, had assured the Supreme Council that 'every step possible would be taken to eliminate the threatening conflict between Church and State'. Nöel Browne's plans were understood in these terms by McQuaid, who was himself a Knight, and his confidants in the organisation, Dr Stafford Johnson and Dr Stephen McKenzie.[11]

McQuaid rejected Dargan's advice on the Health Bill. Tension began to build between Browne's department in the Custom House and the Archbishops's Palace in Drumcondra. A personal request by McQuaid to exempt religious nursing sisters from night duty at St James's Hospital was refused by Browne; in response, the Archbishop withdrew their services from the hospital. Browne refused to allow the Sisters of Charity to use their vacated building in St Stephen's Green as a private hospital. More seriously, he bungled an attempt to transfer control from McQuaid of his prized Sick Children's Hospital in Crumlin to Department of Health nominees on the Dublin Health Authority. The Minister was by now being typecast as a 'Communist' in clerical circles for advocating equal job opportunities for nurses with religious sisters. Browne also believed that McQuaid was annoyed because he was the only minister not to travel to Rome for the Holy Year ceremonies in 1950.[12] As relations between them grew colder, McQuaid was not amused to discover the details of Browne's 'revolutionary plan' in the *Sunday Independent* in September 1950. The predictable response from the Palace was about to land on Government Buildings.

Drumcondra calling

On October 10, 1950, Browne received a phone-call from a priest secretary 'peremptorily' ordering him to a meeting next day at the Palace in Drumcondra to discuss the scheme with McQuaid. When colleagues told him that it was protocol for a minister to go to an Episcopal palace rather than for a prelate to come to the minister, Browne kept the appointment.

'Dr McQuaid brought me into a small ante-room, and courteously invited me to sit down,' Browne recalled. 'Contrary to what I expected, he had a particularly warm smile. In opening conversation Dr McQuaid chose, of all subjects, to discuss child prostitution, informing me: 'The little child prostitutes charge sixpence a time.''[13]

Steering Browne through to a bigger room, McQuaid introduced him to the plump, bespectacled Bishop of Ferns, James Staunton, and the tall and talkative Bishop of Galway, Michael Browne. As a courtesy, McQuaid read out to Browne the text of a letter agreed by the Hierarchy before its transmission to the Taoiseach. It threw down the gauntlet to the Government:

> The powers taken by the State in the proposed Mother and Child Health Service are in direct opposition to the rights of the family and of the individual and are liable to very great abuse. Their character is such that no assurance that they would be used in moderation could justify their enactment. If adopted in law they would constitute a ready-made instrument for future totalitarian aggression.

> 'The right to provide for the health of children belongs to parents, not to the State. The State has the right to intervene only in a subsidiary capacity, to supplement, not to supplant. It may help indigent or neglected parents; it may not deprive 90 per cent of their rights for 10 per cent necessitous or neglected parents. It is not sound social policy to impose a State medical service on the whole community

on the pretext of relieving the necessitous 10 per cent from the so-called indignity of the means test.

The right to provide for the physical education of children belongs to the family and not to the State. Experience has shown that physical or health education is closely inter-woven with important moral questions on which the Catholic Church has definite teaching.

Education in regard to motherhood includes instruction in regard to sex relations, chastity and marriage. The State has no competence to give instruction in such matters. We regard with the greatest apprehension the proposal to give to local medical officers the right to tell Catholic girls and women how they should behave in regard to this sphere of conduct at once so delicate and sacred.

Gynaecological care may be, and in some other countries is, interpreted to include provision for birth limitation and abortion. We have no guarantee that State officials will respect Catholic principles in regard to these matters. Doctors trained in instruction in which they have no confi-dence may be appointed as medical officers under the pro-posed service, and may give gynaecological care not in accordance with Catholic principles.[14]

According to Browne, the three prelates signalled that the inter-view was over when McQuaid finished reading the letter. Instead of leav-ing, Browne pointed out that there was no question of compulsion in his scheme, and he challenged the accuracy of various Episcopal claims. 'Dr McQuaid asked why it was necessary to go to so much trouble and expense simply to provide a free health service for the 10 per cent neces-sitous poor,' Browne later wrote. 'This comment was not only wrong, since the percentage involved was 30 not 10, but surely represented a strange attitude from a powerful prelate of a Christian Church towards the life and death of the necessitous poor and their children.'[15]

Browne left the palace convinced that he had satisfied the bishops with his undertaking to meet their objections on the education provi-sions. He recalled the meeting as most friendly, ending with a cup of tea and the Archbishop graciously seeing him to the door and enquiring about his wife and family. This was not McQuaid's account, however.

On October 12, when Costello called on McQuaid at Drumcondra, he was told by the Archbishop that during an 'incredible' interview Browne brushed aside all suggestions about the invalidity of the means test and stood by his plans for a scheme which would be free for all. Browne would concede nothing but the question of education, on which he said: 'You have a point there.' Browne terminated the interview and walked out.

Believing McQuaid, Costello claimed that he told Browne on October 13 that he wanted time 'to adjust the matter' between his minister and the bishops; and that McQuaid understood that he would not send a formal reply to the October 10 letter.[16] Browne, however, claimed that the Taoiseach informed him that the bishops were satisfied with the interview. Browne also briefed his department and prepared a departmental memorandum that would answer the bishops if needed.[17]

McQuaid watches

Browne's dispute with the IMA escalated into open warfare in autumn 1950. At a stormy meeting on October 24, Browne bluntly told the doctors that their proposal for a means test was not acceptable. This put him in total conflict with the medical association, which did not want the scheme to be free for those who could afford to pay for treatment. The IMA decided to ballot its members on the issue. A minute of this meeting found its way onto McQuaid's desk.[18]

On November 7 McQuaid received further documents detailing the dispute between Browne and the IMA from Dr Brendan Roantree of Adelaide House, Dun Laoghaire. In an accompanying analysis of the internal divisions within the IMA, Roantree bemoaned State influence over the medical profession. 'Our only hope then is the Church – if the Church can come to our rescue and incidentally to the rescue of the Irish people.'[19] McQuaid met the Taoiseach on the same day, and afterwards Costello gave Browne a copy of the bishops' October 10 letter, which the Archbishop had earlier read out to him.[19]

The outcome of the IMA ballot was announced on November 23. To the question 'Do you agree to work a Mother and Child Scheme which includes free treatment for those who could pay for themselves?' 78 per cent of respondents voted Yes and 22 per cent No. The turn-out was only 54 per cent, which enabled Browne to claim that opposition to the scheme came only from an intransigent rump of doctors.

Next day, November 24, McQuaid and Costello took stock of the vote. McQuaid also sought the views of Norton, MacEoin and the Attorney General, Cecil Lavery.

'The possibility of the Mother and Child proposals being accepted by the Cabinet and implemented, as they exist in the Draft, is not even to be considered,' McQuaid confided to Bishop Browne of Galway on December 9.

> **Negotiations are being conducted since the result of the Doctors' Referendum was made known, between the Doctors and the Taoiseach and with the Tánaiste. These**

are confidential talks. Time and silence are proving very helpful. I prefer not to write what I know, but my information is most reassuring from the very commencement of my own negotiations.[20]

McQuaid had learned that the Government–IMA discussions had reached such an acute crisis that Costello, Norton and O'Higgins had taken over completely from Browne and begun to negotiate directly with the doctors. It was agreed that the doctors would put forward a scheme within the framework of the Act, and they proposed that the State would give mothers an allowance of £5 to pay for the medical services they needed.

Meanwhile, instead of keeping quiet as promised, Browne made speeches which McQuaid deplored as 'provocative, inaccurate and gravely embarrassing.' An impasse had been reached as matters drifted into the New Year.

On January 16, 1951, McQuaid, having met Costello the previous evening, outlined 'the actual position' to the Hierarchy's standing committee:

The Bill is not Government policy. Not a single Minister wants it, except Dr Browne. The Taoiseach has affirmed twice in public that he will not stand for State medicine. To me he has given the assurance that whatever the Church declares to be right in respect of the Mother and Child Health Service will be unequivocally accepted by him, even if the Minister had to resign or the Government fall. In fact, the Minister is the greatest single embarrassment that the Government endures.

After giving an account of the October meeting at which Browne agreed to amend the clauses on 'education to motherhood' but was adamant that the scheme should be provided free, McQuaid told the bishops that Costello had assured him that Browne was also prepared to safeguard the clause on professional secrecy as to records, a major IMA concern. Browne, however, was still asserting his absolute determination to bring in a scheme which would be free to patients. But Costello had assured McQuaid that a Minister for Health, under the Act, was under no obligation to implement the section on Mother-and-Child services. Costello, however, feared Browne might resign and bring down the Government.

McQuaid outlined for the bishops the political options facing them: 'The Taoiseach proposes to have Dr Browne answer the Hierarchy's letters, to send to us that answer, to await our decision as to whether Dr B's answer is in accord with the Bishop's desires, and thus to put the Hierarchy's answer squarely to Dr Browne.'

Urging the bishops to allow as much time as possible to elapse before making a move, McQuaid explained:

I do not consider it advisable to give Dr Browne and the Clann the chance of going to the country on the basis that the bishops destroyed the Mother and Child Scheme for poor women and children.

But I am convinced that, even at that risk, we may yet be obliged to break the certain introduction within our country of Socialist State medicine. I have already broken Dr Browne's scheme to socialise the Cancer Services: and my success so far, I say so far, gives excellent ground for hoping that we can break the free-for-all Mother and Child Scheme.

Browne at close quarters

Unexpectedly, on March 8 McQuaid received his first formal communication directly from Browne since their Drumcondra meeting five months earlier. The Minister's letter, dated March 6 and signed by Browne, shocked and enraged McQuaid. Addressed *A Thiarna Árdeasbaig* – My Lord Archbishop – it curtly announced: 'I have the honour to send Your Grace the enclosed copy of MOTHER AND CHILD, a booklet explaining the principles of the Mother and Child service, which I am about to introduce.'[21]

This letter came three days after Browne abruptly had broken off negotiations with the IMA. *The Irish Times* reported that Browne had not consulted ministerial colleagues before going ahead with the scheme, and that a Cabinet caucus of Costello, Norton, Mulcahy, McGilligan, Dillon and MacBride had met informally at Leinster House to express their dissatisfaction at this breach of solidarity. The *Irish Independent* reported that Browne would resign, and that the Government Information Bureau, when releasing details of his scheme, said it was doing so at the request of the Department of Health. Reading these reports, McQuaid sensed that Browne was causing – and was in – serious trouble. It was time for a belt of the crozier.[22]

In a four-point letter to the Taoiseach, McQuaid expressed his surprise 'to read in the daily press of the sudden determination of the Minister for Health to implement the Mother and Child Health Service in the manner in which he conceives the Service.' Referring to the booklet he had just received from the Minister, he enclosed a copy of the response which he was sending to Browne. McQuaid had offered Browne's political death warrant to the Head of Government. Aware of the significance of his move, McQuaid noted on his own carefully kept copy that his letter was sent by hand at 3.30pm to Government Buildings.[23]

By the same courier delivery, the original letter was despatched to Browne at the Custom House. Despite the polite language, Browne could not fail to understood the ecclesiastical ultimatum:

> I welcome any legitimate improvement of medical services for those whose basic family wage or income does not readily assure the necessary facilities. And, if proof be needed of my attitude, I may be permitted to point to many actions of my Episcopate, in particular to the work of the Catholic Social Service Conference founded by me, more especially its Maternity Welfare services ...

> Now as Archbishop of Dublin, I regret that I must reiterate each and every objection made by me on that occasion (October) and unresolved, either then or later, by the Minister for Health. Inasmuch as I was authorised to deal with the Taoiseach, on behalf of the Hierarchy, I have felt it my duty to send to the Taoiseach today for his information a copy of this letter. I shall report to the Hierarchy at its General Meeting the receipt today of your letter, with enclosed pamphlet.[24]

To McQuaid's amazement, Browne did not reply. In sharp contrast, Costello answered next day: 'It is hardly necessary for me to say that Your Grace's views will receive respectful and earnest consideration.'[25]

Costello cautioned Browne that his action might well seem to be a defiance of the Hierarchy:

> I have no doubt that all my colleagues, and in particular yourself, would not be party to any proposals affecting moral questions which would or might come into conflict with the definite teaching of the Catholic Church. Having regard to the views expressed in the letters received from the Hierarchy I feel that you should take steps at once to consult their Lordships so as to remove any grounds for objection on their part to the Mother and Child Health Service, and to find a mutually satisfactory solution for the difficulties which have arisen.

> I can assure you that immediate steps will be taken to dispose of any financial matters which may be outstanding in regard to the proposed Service on the understanding that the objections raised by the Hierarchy have been resolved.[26]

On March 17, St Patrick's Day, McQuaid was briefed by Costello for half an hour on the latest developments: Browne was saying that, on the basis of consultations which he had had with theologians and Bishop Dignan of Clonfert, there was nothing in the scheme contrary to Catholic

teaching. Browne had been excessively difficult, unreliable and contentious. He had demanded money 'to fight the doctors. He threatened he
could "break the doctors tomorrow in their meeting".'

On March 19, Browne wrote to Costello informing him that he had
sent the explanatory booklet to all the bishops, and that he had received
acknowledgements, including one from the Bishop of Galway. 'In none of
these acknowledgements is there any suggestion of an objection to the
scheme except in the letter from His Grace of Dublin,' he wrote. Browne
still believed that the opposition was from one bishop – McQuaid.

On March 20, Costello updated McQuaid on Browne's moves.
'From morning to night he [Browne] was incapable of being trusted to
remain consistent,' McQuaid wrote. The IMA had unanimously rejected
Browne. The doctors were furious. Browne had told a Clann meeting that
only political bishops were in opposition, 'especially the chief political
Bishop, the Archbishop of Dublin.'

Browne, McQuaid added, in a revealing insight into the political
divisions, 'had wanted a declaration from his party of support for the
Scheme. This was avoided in public press. Mr MacBride had been
deterred by Taoiseach from issuing a public statement of Clann support,
by saying that Fine Gael would issue a public disavowal of the Scheme.'

Costello phoned McQuaid on March 21 to let him know that
Browne had issued a statement to the Government Information Bureau
declaring his scheme to be Government policy and that no persons however influential would be allowed to oppose it: he was going to implement
it at once. Costello told McQuaid that he had countermanded the statement and forbidden the bureau to issue it to the press. He had warned
Browne that the scheme was not Government policy: in fact it was unacceptable and would remain unacceptable until the objections of the Hierarchy set out in McQuaid's letter had been cleared.

In reply, Browne had asserted that several members of the Hierarchy had declared themselves to be in favour of the scheme, and he
accused Costello of using the Hierarchy to destroy it. Browne said he
would put the matter to the Archbishop of Armagh for a decision by the
bishops at their spring meeting.

It was to Drumcondra, not Armagh, that Browne chose to go next
day, March 22. Ironically, this was Holy Thursday, a busy liturgical day for
McQuaid who had risen at 4.30am for the Holy Oil ceremonies. 'Learned at
11 a.m. in Pro-Cathedral that Dr B. had phoned,' McQuaid noted. 'Said I
would be free only after 2 p.m., as this was most occupied day of the year.'

When McQuaid phoned Costello just after midday, he was told that
the previous night Browne had been very cold and had demanded to know
why the Taoiseach had countermanded his statement. Costello had said:
'Because I am Taoiseach.' Browne also accused Costello of neglecting his
duty in not answering the Hierarchy's letter. McQuaid told Costello that

he would deal with Browne only on the basis that he would report back to Costello everything said between them.

At the 3.15pm interview McQuaid held the upper hand and used it to advantage over the distraught Browne:

> Dr B. began by 'abject apology' for troubling me on such a day. Described his notes and impression concerning our interview in October. I told him exactly how he had behaved. He was very surprised and apologised, saying he had been very nervous. But he was convinced that all points had been most happily cleared. And T. [Taoiseach] after the interview gave him same impression.
>
> Then letter was delivered to Taoiseach in November. He was amazed to find that the Taoiseach had never sent to Hierarchy his answer. To all this I made no comment.
>
> Dr B. asked me to believe he wanted to be only a good Catholic and to accept fully Church's teaching. I accepted that attitude.
>
> Dr B. asked me if Scheme, in my opinion, was against Catholic teaching. I said that in my view, it was undoubtedly contrary to Cath. teaching, but I added that I was only one Bishop. In my opinion, it was contrary to Catholic teaching in that
>
> a. State arrogated to itself a power in respect of education not properly its own.
>
> b. The rights of parents were not respected.
>
> c. Free-for-all scheme was an unjust tax. For a tax must be reasonably necessary in view of the common good. This tax could not be so regarded. I added that I was only one Bishop, not the Hierarchy.
>
> Dr Browne then said: 'Well, that is the end. It will be very serious for the Government and the people and me. I shall leave the cabinet and political life. It is a rotten life. (I interjected 'it need not be.') He answered: 'But it is. I thought I could make it different. It is a life I was forbidden to take up, for I was given only a few years to live, and I have a wife and two children.'
>
> I remarked: 'You must not ask me for any advice on your political life. That I could not give. I do not understand your politics.'

> Dr B. answered: 'Of course, I would not think of asking such advice.'
>
> Then Dr B. asked me to arrange to have the Scheme considered in Low Week. I said he should see Taoiseach and have Taoiseach forward his representations for the Bishops would consider only a Government letter. He agreed.
>
> I agreed to see Taoiseach same evening and go down to see Dr Staunton, Sec. Dr B. thanked me effusively. Again apologised for all in which he had been faulty.

That Holy Thursday evening Costello called to the Palace by arrangement and McQuaid briefed him on the interview with Browne. While Costello agreed with McQuaid that this was an advance, he warned that Browne was quite capable of changing overnight.

McQuaid captured Costello's steely mood: 'T. reiterated his determination not to pass the Scheme, even if the Hierarchy should find it acceptable, for he was convinced of its impossibility and of the impossibility of fighting the Doctors, who were intensely opposed to the Scheme. We agreed to have Scheme considered at Low Week if possible, and have a covering letter sent to Dr Staunton.'

Costello called to McQuaid, as arranged, at 5.30pm on March 27. He handed the Archbishop Browne's memorandum along with a covering letter from the Government to the bishops.[27] Costello concurred with McQuaid's immediate observation that the Minister's memorandum was inaccurate in stating that the scheme was a Government scheme. 'The covering letter contained no phrase accepting Government responsibility.'

McQuaid's visit to Staunton in Wexford next day almost overlapped with Browne's arrival there on March 29. Browne was desperately looking for a court of appeal against McQuaid, but he had chosen the wrong man.

Reporting to McQuaid, Staunton depicted an apologetic Browne, ready to accept a declaration on grounds of faith and morals from the bishops. Staunton told Browne that he had left their October meeting 'under the clear impression that he [Browne] was unwilling to accept the views of the Bishops and that this was confirmed in our minds by his mention of ecclesiastical dialectics over the radio.'[28]

'Politely we exchanged pleasantries, and parted,' Browne wrote of his meeting with Staunton, unaware that the previous day McQuaid had delivered the documentation on which he would be judged.[29]

Browne's visits to Armagh and Galway were also unproductive. In Armagh on March 31, D'Alton, a pleasant, withdrawn and scholarly-looking man, treated him to fine hock and fish, but Browne failed to elicit a response to his question as to how the bishops could live with the welfare state provisions in the North, and yet oppose his proposals. Browne's

Episcopal namesake in Galway offered him Bond Street cigarettes and champagne, but was also reluctant to talk about the scheme, other than its cost.

'My visits to the bishops were a wanton squandering of valuable time, both mine and theirs,' Browne wrote. 'I was merely a mendicant Government minister uselessly pleading for the underprivileged of the Republic, with the princes of their church ... a final decision dictated by Rome had already been taken in Maynooth'.[30]

Browne was being premature: McQuaid was still putting the finishing touches to the draft.

Maynooth rule

On April 1, McQuaid sent Staunton the Hierarchy's draft reply, which he confined to comments of principle. Two days later he offered a fuller analysis of events, not without some self-drama: 'A slight move on my part could have precipitated a crisis within the Cabinet and caused a General Election, at any moment since January.'

McQuaid strongly urged that the Hierarchy should reject the Minister's proposals:

> On our side we have the Doctors of the country and every member of the Government. If now we reject this particular Scheme, we shall have saved the country from advancing a long way towards socialistic welfare. In particular, we shall have checked the efforts of Leftist Labour elements, which are approaching the point of publicly ordering the Church to stand out of social life and confine herself to what they think is the Church's proper sphere.

Next day, April 4, the Hierarchy came to the unanimous verdict that the scheme was contrary to Catholic social teaching. McQuaid drafted a letter for Staunton as secretary, but was deputised to transmit the Hierarchy's reply to the Government in his own name and by personal delivery.

The Hierarchy, McQuaid wrote, could not approve of any scheme 'which, in its general tendency, must foster undue control by the State in a sphere so delicately and intimately concerned with morals as that which deals with gynaecology or obstetrics and with relations between doctor and patient.' The key passage read:

> The Hierarchy must regard the scheme proposed by the Minister for Health as opposed to Catholic Social Teaching ... In this particular scheme the State arrogates to itself a function and control, on a nationwide basis, in respect of education, more especially in the very intimate matters of

chastity, individual and conjugal.[31]

On his return to Drumcondra, McQuaid telephoned Costello seeking an interview for the following day. He arrived promptly at Government Buildings at the scheduled time of 5pm, and for an hour and twenty minutes explained the bishops' statement to Costello. 'The Taoiseach at once and fully accepted our decision, as one would expect,' McQuaid informed D'Alton next day.[32]

Costello expressed his great relief at a decision which he felt would terminate the enormous worry and waste of time occasioned by Browne's actions. And he told McQuaid that Browne was unpredictable to an extent that was difficult to conceive.

McQuaid described the bishops' letter as a clear-cut, forthright condemnation of socialistic State medicine. It had received more care, word for word, than any document he had seen handled in his ten years as a member of the Hierarchy. Criticism of it by Browne or anybody else would require very careful attention to 'the defining adjectives'. The Minister would not be well served by giving it a hasty reading, let alone making hasty comment.

Costello revealed that Labour Party people had been worked up to a defence of Browne's scheme, and at an Inter-Party meeting he had had to deal very firmly with several of their members' misconceptions. Within the Labour Party there had been a propaganda attempt to secure a confidence vote in the scheme following the TUC's call on its 200,000 members to support it. The chairman, Bill Davin T.D., a member of the Knights of St Columbanus, however, successfully countered this move.

Likewise, there were political tremors within Clann na Poblachta when a meeting at which MacBride was present had censured Browne but passed a vote in favour of his scheme. (This was a reference to a national executive meeting from which Browne stormed out.) When McQuaid expressed surprise that MacBride could do such a thing knowing that the matter was *sub judice* with the bishops, Costello explained that the Clann leader was watching 'his political interest with his party'.

Costello also told McQuaid that James Dillon recalled Browne declaring: 'I am determined to have State medicine.' The Taoiseach promised to keep McQuaid informed of developments.

Next morning, Friday April 6, at 9.15am, McQuaid, eager to hear the latest news, spoke by phone to Costello, who told him that he had given a copy of the bishops' letter to 'the Minister in question'. After reading it, Browne declared to Tánaiste William Norton: 'It is all right. The Bishops have not condemned the Scheme on the grounds of morals.'

Brendan Corish, a parliamentary secretary and a Knight of St Columbanus, who was present when Browne put this spin on the condemnation, commented: 'If I had not heard the remark, I could not believe it to be possible.'

On hearing this news, McQuaid took immediate corrective action. 'Dr Browne's remark proves to you what I have said about him,' he said pointedly to Costello. When Costello explained that Browne took that line because the bishops had spoken of 'Catholic social teaching, not moral teaching', McQuaid asked the Taoiseach to explain to the Cabinet that 'the letter was a definite, clear-cut and forthright condemnation of the scheme on moral grounds. Catholic social teaching meant Catholic moral teaching in regard to things social.'

Costello said he was very pleased to have that statement for the cabinet meeting that day. McQuaid also asked him to bring to the Cabinet's attention the frequency with which the phrase 'this particular scheme' was used: the intention was to show that the bishops had Browne's defective scheme in mind rather than a scheme for mothers and children as such. Again, Costello felt that this background information would be very useful in briefing his Cabinet.

That morning, too, McQuaid informed D'Alton: 'The comment of the minister confirms my report to the Standing Committee. It is not known what the Minister will do next ... I am keeping in close touch with the Taoiseach.'[33]

At 7.30pm that evening Costello asked to see McQuaid. When they met an hour later, Costello told him of a dramatic Cabinet meeting at which each minister had a copy of the bishops' letter on the table as Costello briefed them along the lines of McQuaid's instructions. He asked each minister to give an opinion. All declared their acceptance of the bishops' ruling and rejected the scheme; all, that is, except Browne, who stood up and said, 'Very well, I must consider what is to be done,' and then walked out.

Costello had fresh information for McQuaid: Browne had succeeded in working up the Labour people through his adviser Noel Hartnett and Senator Sheehy Skeffington (both instantly labelled by the Archbishop as Trinity College men), and the women workers through Miss Louie Bennett (a trade unionist whom McQuaid identified as a Protestant!).

The Taoiseach told McQuaid that Browne would now have to resign or be dismissed; he was quite definite that Browne must leave the Cabinet. And he assured McQuaid that the Cabinet understood perfectly clearly that the Hierarchy's condemnation of the scheme had been made on moral grounds.

Browne had by now arranged a public meeting in the Mansion House, and when McQuaid asked Costello who would attend, the Taoiseach said it probably would attract Protestant intelligentsia and the Labour Left. He brooded on the prospect of a Labour Government which included Leftist intellectuals emerging in Ireland; the antidote to their influence, Costello believed, was McQuaid's workers' study circles.

Costello explained that, in the face of Browne's attacks at the

Clann na Poblachta executive meeting, MacBride had protected his 'political prestige' by sanctioning a vote in favour of the scheme, but McQuaid was amazed when Costello showed him a draft text drawn up by MacBride which referred to the imposition of a mother and child plan 'irrespective of ability to pay'. McQuaid and Costello both noted that MacBride's wording was contrary to the bishops' express condemnation. In response to McQuaid's suggestion that Norton was the man to explain the bishops' letter, Costello concurred that the Tánaiste would put things right with Labour.

So close was the McQuaid-Costello collaboration that the Taoiseach called on the Archbishop next day, Saturday April 7, to discuss the draft of the Government's response to the Hierarchy, and together they agreed the reply to be sent by Cabinet.

Browne's media highground

The clock was now ticking away for Browne.

On April 8 Browne defended himself at a 13-hour Clann meeting, where MacBride won the motion by 48 votes to 4.

On April 9 Costello wrote to McQuaid formally setting out the Government's acceptance of the Hierarchy's letter.[34]

On April 10 McQuaid wrote to Costello:

> It will be my duty to convey the decision of the Government to the Standing Committee of the Bishops without delay, and to the General Meeting of the Hierarchy in mid-June. I may, however, be permitted to anticipate the formal reply of the Hierarchy by expressing to you as Head of the Government my deep appreciation of the generous loyalty shown by you and your colleagues in graciously deferring to the judgement of the Hierarchy concerning the moral aspects of the particular Health Scheme advocated by the Minister for Health.
>
> In view of the clear attitude of the Hierarchy I may be allowed to express my conviction that the decision of the Government to proceed to formulate another scheme consonant with Catholic principles will receive the very welcome support of the Bishops. It is our urgent desire, evidenced in our communications with the Government, that due provision should be made by the Government for the health of those mothers and children whose insufficient means would not allow them to avail themselves of the best modern facilities.
>
> The present intention of the Government to prepare such

a Scheme is at once a guarantee of the blessing of God on your deliberations and a presage of practical and peaceful achievement.[35]

On April 10 D'Alton lauded McQuaid. 'It proves that the Minister is not only a very elusive person but quite unreliable. However, we can be thankful that the Taoiseach is so sound on the matter. Your interview with him can have left him in no doubt about our attitude, and about the moral issues involved. I sincerely hope that your Grace's efforts will result in a solution that the Bishops can accept, though one cannot predict what line the Minister will now take. I see that TUC is getting particularly active over the Scheme. I am wondering how far its present activity is inspired.'[36]

'The activity is fully "inspired",' McQuaid replied to D'Alton. 'In view of the confusion, misunderstanding and deliberate misrepresentation of our attitude, a moment may well come, suddenly, when the Taoiseach may ask my leave to publish the correspondence. Already he has spoken of it several days ago. I feel it ought to be. Perhaps you would kindly indicate if you consent. The important thing is to have our attitude clearly grasped by the rank and file of Trade Unionists. The position is very serious.'[37]

On the night of April 10, MacBride instructed Browne to resign. At 7.30pm the following day, Costello phoned McQuaid to tell him that Browne had resigned and had, without permission, sent a long statement to the press. The President had accepted the resignation. The Taoiseach would act as Minister for Health.

On April 12, McQuaid found himself sharing acres of newsprint with Browne. By prior agreement with Bertie Smyllie, *The Irish Times* editor, Browne had handed his correspondence with McQuaid and Costello over to him. In an editorial headed 'Contra Mundum', *The Irish Times* sided with the gallant loser:

> This is a sad day for Ireland. It is not so important that the Mother and Child Scheme has been withdrawn, to be replaced by an alternative project embodying a means test. What matters more is that an honest, far-sighted and energetic man has been driven out of active politics. The most serious revelation, however, is that the Roman Catholic Church would seem to be the effective Government of this country.[38]

That afternoon, Costello phoned McQuaid to tell him that Browne had made 'a most unfortunate and inaccurate statement' in the Dáil and that as Head of Government he must respond in an adjournment debate that evening. Browne had declared: 'While as I have said, I as a Catholic accept unequivocally and unreservedly the views of the Hierarchy on this matter, I have not been able to accept the manner in which this matter has been dealt with by my former colleagues in the Government.' His attack was mainly directed at Costello and MacBride.[39]

McQuaid advised Costello that the only answer was to publish all the correspondence, and he authorised the Taoiseach to publish all his letters in the Dáil statement. He recapitulated several points to refresh Costello's memory, urging him to note especially the Hierarchy's desire for a proper health scheme and his own kindness all through to Browne.

McQuaid wrote to D'Alton: 'The complete surprise of Dr B's publishing the correspondence – without a word of permission of anyone – has made unnecessary my query as to the advisability of your sanctioning publication. The Taoiseach has been obliged to follow up.

'The situation, as regards the Hierarchy, in the opinion of Most Rev Dr Staunton and myself, is sufficiently clear to everyone ... I hope that Your Grace has seen yesterday's *Irish Times* editorial; unjust and typical – even though the writer is, I believe honest.'[40]

The fall-out

On April 13, McQuaid congratulated Costello on putting the truth about the Hierarchy's case so well in his Dáil statement. His satisfaction was shared by other senior bishops.

'It is a very regrettable business. I suppose that many people will now blame the Bishops for not having shown their hand in 1947,' Bishop O'Neill of Limerick wrote to McQuaid from his Palace in Corbally. 'I think, however, that which was done was properly done.'[41] This opinion was shared by D'Alton, who ruminated: 'It is not easy to forecast what line the ex-Minister will now take but I feel that we need not worry.'[42] Writing from Tuam, Archbishop Walsh expressed his gratitude to McQuaid for letting him know how things were moving. 'Everything is now clear: and in spite of mischief-makers I think all will turn out well both for the Church and for the people. In this as in other things all of us owe a deep debt of gratitude to Your Grace.'[43]

McQuaid had ample grounds for feeling satisfied. Not only was he briefed by the Taoiseach about Cabinet discussions during the course of at least seven secret bilateral meetings, in drafting the text of the Government's acceptance of the Episcopal condemnation of the scheme he acted with the kind of advisory authority customarily vested in a Cabinet secretary. More extraordinary still, when Browne made a vigorous defence of his position in his resignation speech to the Dáil, McQuaid came to Costello's assistance, briefing him on the points to be made in his counter-statement against Browne's 'reckless and untrue charges'.

Emotionally volatile and trapped politically, Browne may have compounded his difficulties by not complying fully with the Hierarchy's objections as early as October 1950, and by alienating his Cabinet colleagues, but he was defeated ultimately by the condemnation of the bishops on McQuaid's official dictation. McQuaid's detailed notes confirm that from as early as October he effectively stalked the increasingly beleaguered Browne, until he was fully satisfied that he was isolated in Cabinet and was helpless in the face of the vested interests of the medical profession with whose leaders McQuaid dealt behind the scenes.

Rome Rule is Home Rule

With the praise of senior colleagues ringing in his ears, McQuaid sent his confidential report on the controversy to the Nuncio, Archbishop Felici, in which he wrote that the Hierarchy's judgement against the Mother and Child Scheme was decisive.

> The Government, with admirable loyalty and open courage, has accepted that judgement and rejected Dr Browne's scheme. The whole country has equally accepted.

> The Leftist elements in the Labour groups and Women's Associations, linked with these Groups, have repeated the calumnies of *The Irish Times*. That is to be expected and will continue for some weeks, especially in venomous letters and tendentious resolutions. But *The Irish Times* reaches a small circle of Catholics and the overwhelming majority of Trade Unionists in this country stand with the Church. The attack from Labour is directed from Communist elements in England and in the Irish Workers' League.

> Concerning *The Irish Times*: it has surpassed itself in injustice, first of all in writing a most unfair editorial, at once when only one side, Dr Browne's side, has been published. (And the *Times* forgot or did not know, that Dr Browne in publishing my letters without my permission has gravely violated our civil law.)

> Secondly, *The Irish Times* has opened its columns to very bitter letters and has kept up the disturbance by articles of unfair comment.

McQuaid informed Felici that 'representative' Protestants had sought to condemn wholeheartedly the unjust action of *The Irish Times*, and they had acknowledged that the Archbishop would always deal justly with the Protestant minority. 'And these Protestants and Freemasons mean to deal with the Editor of *The Irish Times* in their own way,' he predicted menacingly.

McQuaid felt that the Browne affair cast an interesting sidelight on life in the Republic, especially in regard to 'the nonsense and dishonest commentary' on Partition.

> This attitude of Protestant and Freemasons is explained by the firm stand I took within the last few months to see that justice was done to the Protestants in the famous case of the Meath Hospital Committee and lawsuit. At the moment, the attitude of the Protestants and the Freemasons, I am quite sure, is such that they will not tolerate any injustice done to the Church. It has not always been thus. But it must be said in fairness that when these people are our friends, they are our friends to a degree that would shame many Catholics. It was a traitorous Catholic, I fear, who helped to produce the most unjust editorial of *The Irish Times*.

McQuaid did not believe that the publicity over the Mother and Child Scheme would set back relations between the Republic and Northern Ireland. Defending Episcopal policy, he told the Nuncio that it might be necessary for the bishops to ignore the suggestions that 'to bring in the Protestant North, we in the Republic ought to permit to Protestants divorce, birth-prevention and removal of censorship of publications.'

McQuaid continued:

> The outcry in the Protestant North, following the unjust presentation of the Bishops' judgement by *The Irish Times*, is indeed typical. But what many fail to see is that the Protestants now see clearly under what conditions of Catholic morality they would have to be governed in the Republic. The political enticements held out to them are now judged by them to be only snares to trap them in a Republic dominated by the Catholic Church. Thus, the arguments of the liberal Catholics, who seem to put national unity before the interests of the Faith, have been discredited in the eyes of Northern Protestants.

The contrary judgement about the impact of these events was sent to London by the British Ambassador, Sir Gilbert Laithwaite:

> In particular it brought out the dominating position and authority claimed by, and conceded to, the Roman Catholic Hierarchy in southern Ireland in matters of public interest which could be presented as having a moral or social aspect. The deference paid by the Government to the views of the Hierarchy has gravely disturbed Protestant, and indeed to some extent Catholic, feeling in the Republic, and the Hierarchy's attitude may well supply

damaging ammunition to opponents of Catholicism in other countries.

Since the core of the hierarchical objection was the absence of a means test, there are signs too of a degree of underground criticism of the attitude of the bishops among the poorer classes in this country, which is far from usual.

Above all, the effect of the incident has been to set back decisively any prospects that there might have been (and these were never more than the slightest) of an understanding between the north and south over Partition.[44]

Laithwaite's observation proved to be the more accurate. The Mother and Child correspondence was published by the Ulster Unionist Council, and the controversy had a profound effect on a rising star of the Unionist Party, Brian Faulkner, who took the view that 'the Roman Catholic Church wields immense power in Southern Ireland. It has brought down Governments.'[45]

The fear which McQuaid instilled in Ulster Protestants living in the Loyalist Tiger's Bay area of Belfast is still recalled by the writer, Sam McAughtry. 'If you can imagine that the essence of our fears was that Catholic politicians were controlled by their priests, John Charles McQuaid embodied those fears. Before then, McQuaid was unknown to us. In destroying Browne, he emerged from the shadows. He was the Catholic leader.'[46]

In Castlebar on the day the newspaper coverage appeared, the young broadcaster, Seán MacRéamoinn,[47] was surprised by how the whole town was in turmoil. Unlikely people expressed the opinion that the bishops had gone too far this time. That critical view persisted.

Of all the media coverage, McQuaid most admired a doughty defence of his action, as setting out important truths against socialist ideas, by Douglas Woodruff in the London-based Catholic journal, *The Tablet*.[48] His stance was commended in continental newspapers such as *La Croix* in France.[49] He revelled in the pleas of loyalty from 'Catholic first' politicians, Costello, MacBride, McGilligan, Norton and for the time being, Browne. Virtually the only voice in the Dáil to defend its independence from Episcopal interference was Peadar Cowan, an Independent. McQuaid ignored publicly – but cursed in private – what McGilligan called 'the Catholics Anonymous who flock to the columns of *The Irish Times*'.

Not for the first time the commentator who angered McQuaid most – because he wrote best – was Seán Ó Faoláin. The Browne case, Ó Faoláin wrote in *The Bell*, showed that the Republic had two parliaments:

[A] parliament at Maynooth and a parliament in Dublin ...
The Dáil proposes; Maynooth disposes. The Dáil had,

when up against the Second Parliament, only one right of decision: the right to surrender.[50]

This verdict was to haunt McQuaid, especially after the collapse of the Costello Government over 'the price of milk, cows' not mothers'.'[51]

The May 1951 election saw de Valera return to Leinster House with the unfinished business from Conor Ward, Jim Ryan and Nöel Browne awaiting his – and McQuaid's – urgent attention. Despite de Valera's silence during Browne's Dáil debacle – 'I think we have heard enough' – he would now have to deal with a McQuaid who had defined the moral and social power of a bishop in absolutist terms.

18

McQuaid's Dreary Eden
1940–73

'John the Bishop promised at the end of our lives unsullied
by the ugliness of human sexuality, he would deliver us
Irish to our heavenly maker.'

Dr Nöel Browne, 'A Virgin Ireland'.

Behind the extravagant external displays of religious fervour, Catholic Ireland in the mid-twentieth century was a grim, inward-looking and deeply
repressive society. Presiding over and controlling that society was the
Archbishop of Dublin and Primate of Ireland, John Charles McQuaid, now
firmly established after his scuttling of Dr Nöel Browne's Mother and
Child Scheme as the arbiter of public morality in all spheres of human
behaviour, particularly sexual conduct.

During the Holy Year of 1950, Browne was the only Government
minister not to attend a religious ceremony at which McQuaid switched
on the lights of a statue to the Virgin Mary at the estuary of the River
Liffey at Ringsend. Browne was intrigued at how hard-bitten dockers had
dug into their pockets to pay for a statue which proclaimed the virtue of
virginity to the world. In a normal society, such absurdity, he believed,
would have made its perpetrator fit for certification.[1]

Similarly, Browne concluded that McQuaid was obsessed with pro-
tecting Catholic Ireland from the evil nature of human sexuality. Under
the country's rigid censorship laws, McQuaid had ensured that the majority of the world's great writers were banned on the grounds of sexual indecency. McQuaid, too, he held responsible for the flight of Irish writers.
Among the less acceptable features of the highly centralised clericalist
system, which McQuaid directed with the assistance of a kitchen cabinet
of young and devoted priest-secretaries, was the confinement by the
courts of thousands of young boys and girls to virtual penal servitude in
orphanages where many of them were physically and sexually abused by
'celibate' priests, Brothers and Sisters. Young men and women who did
not observe the Catholic Church's strict prohibition on sex outside of
wedlock were dealt with harshly and summarily. Unmarried mothers were

sent away or placed in 'Magdalene Penitentiaries', where they were forced by nuns to engage in slave-labour as laundry workers and cleaning women. The chastisement of the body was seen as a means to the salvation of the soul, and the Mother of God was aspired to as the epitome of Irish womanhood. Irish girls flocked to the convents; boys to the priesthood and the Christian Brothers. To direct this popular piety, McQuaid issued a series of publications which laid down a strict, all-encompassing moral code for his flock.

The national catechism, which was launched in 1951, had consumed McQuaid's energies since the early 1940s, and at the height of the Browne controversy he was putting the finishing touches to the 108-page text. It deserves to be known as the McQuaid catechism.[2] 'It was the most important, the most used book in our schoolbags,' Gene Kerrigan writes in his memoir of life in Cabra West in the 1950s.[3]

As was common at the time in the Catholic Church, the catechism taught that the principal dangers to faith were attendance at non-Catholic worship and schools, marriage to non-Catholics, and books or companions hostile to the Church or its teaching. Forbidden by the sixth commandment was not only adultery, but all looks, words and actions which offended against chastity. The chief dangers to chastity were idleness, intemperance, bad companions, improper dances, immodest dress, company-keeping and indecent conversation. Indecent books, indecent plays and indecent pictures were equally a threat. The chief means of preserving chastity were modesty in dress and conduct, the avoidance of occasions of sin, cultivating devotion to the Blessed Virgin Mary and, above all, seeking the help of God through prayer and the sacraments.

Catholics were also bound to observe the six commandments of the Church: to hear Mass on Sundays and holy days of obligation, to fast and abstain on days appointed for penance, to confess their sins at least once a year, to receive worthily the Blessed Eucharist at Easter-time, to contribute to the support of pastors and to observe the marriage laws of the Church.

The catechism required a valid marriage of Catholics to be celebrated in the presence of an authorised priest and two witnesses. A marriage of a Catholic to a non-Catholic in a registry office, or before a non-Catholic minister, was not a true marriage and a Catholic who lived as husband or wife after such a marriage was living in sin.

The Church forbade marriage between a Catholic and a non-Catholic, because mixed marriages were a danger to the faith of the Catholic party, broke the unity of the home and made difficult the Catholic upbringing of the children. Under the *Ne Temere* decree of 1908, the catechism decreed that no mixed marriage could be performed during Mass but must take place in the sacristy, generally before 9am if a dispensation had been granted by the Church authorities.

The best preparation for a happy Catholic marriage was to be chaste, temperate and charitable, to pray to God for guidance in choosing a partner, and to ask the advice of parents and a confessor. When baptised persons had been validly married and had lived together as husband and wife, their marriage bond could not be broken, except by the death of either party. The State had no power to break the bond of a valid marriage: in the Church's view, civil laws authorising divorce were null and void.

Catholic control

At a time when Irish marriage rates were the lowest and the latest in the world, a pamphlet bearing McQuaid's imprimatur, 'The Young Husband,' advised young married Catholics to keep their lives unstained by the crime of birth-prevention. 'The one who desires to limit the number of his children will come under God's anger. There may be very serious reasons for limiting the number of children – illness, great dangers to health, and so on. In such a case, the married pair must use their will-power and prudence and live as brother and sister. Such abstinence is difficult, but possible. And there is no other way.'

Following a decision by the Easter meeting of the bishops in March 1944 to express disapproval of the sale of the new sanitary tampons for women, called Tampax, McQuaid was delegated to communicate the Episcopal censure to the Government. At a meeting with the Parliamentary Secretary for Health, Dr Conor Ward, he explained their fears that tampons could stimulate girls at an impressionable age and lead them into using contraceptives to satisfy their aroused passions. Ward said he shared the bishops' misgivings. For a time the sale of Tampax was prohibited.[4]

A staunch supporter, like the other bishops, of a 'modesty campaign', McQuaid reported regularly to his colleagues the results of his 'continued investigation' into the censorship of films, which he thought was on the whole satisfactory and that the films being shown were morally harmless. On the formation of the National Film Institute McQuaid became its principal patron, personally contributing £250 (about £6,250 today) towards the purchase of films. The institute had ambitious plans 'to direct and encourage the use of the motion picture in the national and cultural interests of the Irish people, in accordance with the teachings of His Holiness, Pope Pius XI in the Encyclical, *Vigilanti Cura*'.[5]

Viewing committees in London and Hollywood were set up to vet the suitability of films for import into Ireland. As part of promoting an indigenous film industry, instructional films were made on the fight against tuberculosis and on the local defence force. Films under the category of civics included *The Great Awakening*, a film on the teachings of Pope Leo XIII on the need for social service, as well as *The Life of Abraham Lincoln* and *The Life of Madame Curie*. Big attractions were the film *Young Farmers* for men and films on homecraft for women.

McQuaid also encouraged the ladies' section of the Legion of Mary to instruct women on dress elegance and deportment. Some reflective women felt themselves caught in the dilemma of either running the risk of ridicule if they became active in 'purity leagueishness' or of ignoring the Archbishop's appeal. One lady Legionary, M.G. Godfrey, expecting her view to be passed on to McQuaid, told Duff that while there was a lot the Legion could do to uphold Christian modesty, she doubted whether the clergy were the best qualified to say how this could be done. The priest, she wrote, 'may be indisputably right about immorality, but wrong in attributing it to bare legs (to put it crudely), stockings, or no stockings – lipstick or not – the length of skirts.'

The Legion debated how they might handle the campaign, a Mrs Donovan pointed that every woman of a certain age knew that ample clothing did not necessarily connote modesty. Sharing this view, Mrs Godfrey remarked: 'There is a type of dress which the priest would probably designate as ugly but at least decent, but which women of my age know to be ugly and quite indecent, though the young girls do not know it. It was designated by the devil.' Mrs Godfrey's not altogether facetious proposal to Duff was that the Legion should hold a meeting on women's work with not a word about modesty in dress – and that the meeting be addressed by a Mrs Partridge who could back up His Grace by speaking in the Franciscan habit of the Third Order![6]

McQuaid and 'dirty' literature

Long remembered by Browne from his visit to the Palace on October 10, 1950, to discuss his Mother and Child Scheme with McQuaid, was the Archbishop's unsolicited remark that 'the little child prostitutes charge sixpence a time'.[7] It struck Browne as an odd comment from a man he regarded as obsessed with the evil of sexuality. What Browne did not know was that McQuaid regularly read specialist manuals on sexology, including works that would have been considered deviant and pornographic. Most of these publications were in Latin and French. McQuaid felt justified in doing so on the grounds that it was necessary for him to be familiar with such publications in his work with Catholic doctors.

In the mid-1930s, when he was active as a priest lobbying against the importation of contraceptives, McQuaid amassed a collection of publicity materials about family planning clinics, mainly in Britain but including one in Belfast, run by the pioneer of birth-control methods, Dr Marie Carmichael Stopes.[8] He sought permission from his confessor, Fr Fennelly, to read Stopes' *A Letter to Working Mothers*, reprinted in 1935 but banned in Ireland. Fennelly advised him to 'Do so if you think that you can find anything in it to perfect your knowledge of that subject. If any priest asked me I would say 'Don't', but your scientific pursuit of that subject changes the situation. No doubt the soiling of the imagination is undesirable but in your case I would think it justifiable.'[9]

Fennelly, who remained McQuaid's confessor after he became Archbishop until his own death in 1972, extended this dispensation to read 'dirty' literature *sine die*. Over the years McQuaid built up a sizable collection of writings on sexology which were not available generally. It was a unique collection in Ireland.

However, he became extremely worried in 1952 at the possible publication in English of such manuals known as the *Cahiers Laennea*. 'I have all these Cahiers and other Laennea publications because of my constant work with Catholic doctors,' he told Bishop Lucey of Cork. 'Quite a high proportion of the publications are meant for the medical profession, for priests and lawyers and so deal with sexology, normal and abnormal. If this material be made available to the general public in an English translation, I should very much fear that it will be a best-seller, and that the results will be quite unfortunate.'[10]

Trapping evil literature

On November 14, 1953, when Éamon de Valera received a request from McQuaid for a meeting on 'a matter of grave social import,' he smelt trouble in the Drumcondra air. Five days later at Government Buildings the Archbishop presented the Taoiseach with two paperbacks 'depicting a frenzied lust, coupled with violence and murder'. Such publications, McQuaid complained, were 'very hurtful to the outlook and morals of the Faithful.'[11]

McQuaid explained that he was calling at the request of the Hierarchy to voice their anxiety at the volume of evil books and booklets which were circulating in the country. Despite the censorship system, young people could get access to this evil literature. To prove his point McQuaid presented the two paperback specimens – *Fires That Destroy* and *Saratoga Mantrap* – which he said were openly obtained in 21 bookshops in Dublin. McQuaid advised de Valera, now virtually blind, that an elderly person should read them cover to cover and give him a clear idea of their contents in their totality.

In an implied criticism of the Irish censors, McQuaid explained that the British authorities were searching for obscene books, fining persons found with them and banning at least twice as many books in the year as the Irish Censorship of Publications Board.

De Valera, who listened 'courteously and sympathetically', explained that because the Department of Industry and Commerce had gone as far as it could in banning English newspapers, this latest problem was a matter for the Department of Justice to tackle. He promised to get the Minister for Justice, Gerald Boland, to read the two paperbacks.

When McQuaid suggested that it might be possible to 'trap' the books at the ports of entry, de Valera dismissed this as unworkable. 'It was a very difficult net to close,' de Valera said. However, he suggested that 'it might be possible, in view of the action of the British, to come to some arrangement concerning the import of books.'

After McQuaid's request, the machinery of Government leapt into action. The Department of Justice instructed customs officers to check all consignments of paperback novels. 'Where a consignment contains novels with titles, jacket designs, or illustrations suggestive of indecent content, it is to be detained and a copy of each book forwarded immediately to the Censorship of Publications Board.'[12]

Gardaí were instructed to warn booksellers that they were liable to prosecution, and if offensive works remained on the shelves they would be brought to court. Shortly before Christmas, de Valera reported to McQuaid on the implementation of the measures.[13] McQuaid undertook to report to the Hierarchy on the improvements.[14]

'Snooper' McQuaid

McQuaid was regarded as a voyeur by Frederick O'Connor, the astronomer who built a telescope for him in the bell-tower at Notre Dames des Bois. O'Connor used to delight in telling friends, including the Clann na Poblachta politician Jack McQuillan, that the telescope was used by the Archbishop to look, not at the stars, but at couples and young males and females on the beach at Killiney, as well as schoolgirls in the nearby convent school.[15] Frequently, McQuaid appeared to sound like a Peeping-Tom character in Brinsley McNamara's novel, *The Valley of the Squinting Windows*. On receiving a tip-off about the dubious marital status of the newly appointed American Ambassador, George Garrett, McQuaid wrote to the Secretary of the Department of External Affairs, Freddie Boland: 'May I ask you a question which you will not think indiscreet? Is it true that Mr Garrett is divorced and has "remarried" a woman who had divorced her husband?'[16]

Brian Moore, another 'Catholic writer' from Belfast, fell foul of McQuaid. Claiming that his first novel, *The Lonely Passion of Judith Hearne*, was banned as a result of McQuaid's displeasure, Moore quoted the Archbishop as telling a relative of his, well known in Dublin: 'I know that boy's connected to your family. It's ridiculous that he would write this sort of book.' Moore decried McQuaid as 'a heavy-duty banner' on whose say-so many books were banned. 'It was a sexual censorship. Also anything that was considered anti-clerical they went out of their way to put down.'[17]

McQuaid's obsession with 'impurity' was consistent throughout his career, whether illustrating to young Vivion de Valera how the drawings of women modelling underwear used in *Irish Press* advertisement actually revealed a mons veneris if one employed a magnifying glass,[18] or scrutinising films in the National Film Institute to ensure they were in accord with the teachings of Pope Pius XI in the Encyclical, *Vigilanti Cura*. Fastidious to a fault – he was known to advise his priests and seminarians to use Cussens soap when washing their genitals,[19] while he himself often wore a *cilicio* or 'hairshirt' under his priestly vestments when saying Mass.[20]

He delegated the Knights of St Columbanus to carry out a clean-up campaign against 'evil literature'[21] and encouraged a zealous laity to report on indecency wherever it might be found in popular art. Reporting to McQuaid on a film, *Behind Closed Shutters*, about an innocent Italian girl duped into prostitution, a leading light in the Knights of St Columbanus, Dermot J. O'Flynn, described the main characters as showing evidence of vice and debauchery and the film as an excursion into the by-ways of sin. Even though the film had a conventional ending, with the girl securing her freedom, McQuaid applauded Flynn's efforts to have the film banned.[22]

When the Bishop of Ossory, Peter Birch, broached the possibility of the Kilkenny Association opening a hostel in Dublin for their county men and women, McQuaid marked his cards: 'If they are thinking of a hostel, they have plenty of trouble coming to them. I do hope that they are not thinking of a mixed hostel.'[23]

On another occasion, McQuaid told journalist Brian Quinn that he had noticed that a play in one of the Dublin theatres carried a title that was suggesting to patrons the height from the ground of a woman's genitals. He sent a doctor friend to see the play and report back to him. The Archbishop did not hide his fury that his fears had turned out to be accurate. He told the startled newspaper editor that the playwright should be 'horse-whipped'.[24]

In his book, *A Thorn in the Side*, Bishop Pat Buckley described how it was McQuaid's practice to meet the seminarians of Clonliffe College twice a year individually. The students had been warned to plead ignorance when he would ask them what they knew about the facts of life. This plea was the cue for the Archbishop to give them a full and frank explanation of the functioning of the sexual organs. It was a bit of a shock, Buckley recalled, to hear graphic words like penis and vagina 'coming from such a holy mouth'.[25]

Bishop James Kavanagh recalled the occasion when, seated for lunch after a Confirmation ceremony, a parish priest opened a conversation with the Archbishop by remarking that he was perished by the cold. 'What kind of underwear have you on, Father?' His Grace enquired. The startled and embarrassed parish priest blurted out that he was wearing the usual winter woollies.

'Tell me, Fathers,' said John Charles, 'do you know what kind of underwear the US forces wear when they are serving in the Arctic?' The priests confessed their ignorance.

'They wear Egyptian cotton mesh,' he said.

Silence.

Then he asked: 'And when they are serving in the desert, Fathers, do you know what kind of underwear they wear then?' For a second time the priests admitted that they were stumped.

'Fathers, they wear Egyptian cotton mesh there too,' the Archbishop said.[26]

Unhealthy interests

Mrs Mercy Simms, who cooperated with McQuaid in opening a school for itinerant children in Ballyfermot, said in an interview shortly before her death that she felt he had an unhealthy attraction towards boys.[27] McQuaid dropped in regularly to see the boys at Our Lady's Hostel in Eccles Street, and he told a Jesuit priest that the boys liked him turning up in 'his gear'.[28]

McQuaid frequently talked to boys about masturbatory fantasies. According to the teaching of the Church, not only was masturbation deemed to be a sin, it also caused blindness. McQuaid was convinced that the Catholic Church had a duty to supply instruction in chastity that was accurate, clear, adequate and supernatural. 'It can be done without hurt to sensitivity and without physical details,' he told a mental health conference at the St John of God hospital in Stillorgan. 'I am equally convinced that very many neuroses have their origin in the defective training in chastity.'[29]

'He took a strong interest in me. I now realise it was an unhealthy interest,' according to 'Y', the son of one of McQuaid's lay staff at Notre Dames des Bois. In 1954, at the age of nine, Y expressed an interest in becoming a priest, and was enrolled first in Willow Park and later at Blackrock College by McQuaid, who paid his fees. Y recalls being summoned to an interview by McQuaid when he was about 12 or 13 years old.

'I was in the garden helping my father when he told me that he wanted to talk to me. We walked up the stairs to his study, which was directly opposite the top stair with a green beige double-door. I tiptoed towards that door; I was considerably nervous. He sat at his desk. I could see Bray Head behind him. He asked me how I was doing at school. As I said I was doing fine and enjoying the school, he fingered his pectoral cross. There was a long silence. I just wanted to get away. He asked if there was anything else that I wanted to tell him. I told him that there was nothing else. There was another long silence. "Are you sure?" he asked again. I insisted that everything was fine. At the time I was too young to know what masturbation was. It was only later that I discovered from my contemporaries that his question was the cue for a discussion on self-abuse.'[30]

A similar experience is recalled by 'X', who was at Belvedere College, run by the Jesuits. Although he was not interested in religion, X, then aged 16, went with his friends on a residential weekend retreat at Clonliffe College at which the priest continually talked about the evils of masturbation and sexual temptation. The highlight of the retreat was the one-to-one meetings which each boy had with McQuaid.

X remembers McQuaid sitting very close to him and talking about masturbation and the facts of life. When McQuaid put his hand on X's knee, the boy felt extremely uncomfortable. He found the encounter a strange and perplexing occasion. He did not tell his parents about what had happened.

After X returned home, his mother received a phone-call from the Palace informing her that the Archbishop wanted to speak to her son. The family was flattered. X travelled out to Drumcondra, and was shown into a room where he found himself alone with McQuaid. The Archbishop tried to encourage him to join his College Volunteers Corps, but X had a sick feeling and showed no interest in joining. He made a quick exit. Even today, years later, X experiences that 'sick feeling' whenever McQuaid's name is mentioned. He considers that McQuaid was 'enormously repressed sexually'.[31]

The school inspector's allegation

An unexpected and previously unpublished sequel to history's linking of McQuaid and Browne occurred nearly 40 years after the Mother and Child controversy and almost 15 years after McQuaid's death, when in January 1988 Browne attended the funeral in Dublin's Pro-Cathedral of his former political colleague and adversary, Seán MacBride.

After the ceremony he was approached by a retired school inspector, who whispered to him that he had highly secret information of the utmost importance about the late Archbishop McQuaid. The man, tall, well dressed and grey-haired, told Browne about an incident in which 'John the Bishop' was alleged to have made sexual advances to a schoolboy.

Wanting to return to his home in Connemara on the next train, Browne told the man to come to Galway and tell him the full story. To Browne's surprise, the man rang next day and they made arrangements to meet in the Great Southern Hotel.

The school inspector, a specialist in the Irish language, wanted to unburden himself of a secret that 'appeared to be burning a hole in his skull'. After a lengthy interrogation of the man, Browne believed in the veracity of 'this truly astonishing story' about the churchman who had contributed so much to the destruction of his political career in the Mother and Child controversy.

Browne wrote an essay entitled 'A Virgin Ireland' based on 'the secret and sordid lifestyle' of the 'revered, respected and above all feared' McQuaid.[32] On 'impeccable authority' the man told of how

McQuaid, dressed in a black polo pullover, black cap and black clerical coat, entered a Dublin public house by a narrow side-door which opened towards a steep set of stairs to a room which led to a large and partially darkened private room. A telephone call in advance secured admission to this special service.

Because the pub was busy that particular evening, the owner asked his son to help in the bar. The boy carried a glass of Jameson's Red Breast whiskey upstairs to the private room. Some ten minutes later the door to the room was thrown violently open; the boy ran out and came clattering down the stairs.

When the father saw his son's flushed face and the astounded look in his eyes – a mixture of shock and revulsion – he brought him into an unoccupied snug where the boy blurted out his story.

After delivering the glass of whiskey, the boy had been waiting to be paid when McQuaid smilingly invited him to sit down beside him for a moment on the settee so that they might talk. McQuaid asked the boy how he was enjoying school.

'Incredulous, trying not to believe it, slowly it became clear to the child that John the Bishop's roving hands and long fingers had intentions other than getting information about school,' Browne wrote. The boy claimed that McQuaid edged closer to him on the settee and he feared that the cleric was intent on sexually assaulting him. Unable to speak and near to tears, at last accepting the unbelievable, the boy stood up abruptly and fled the room, leaving the tray and money behind him.

After hearing the story from his son, the father mounted the stairs to the private parlour where McQuaid was quietly sipping his whiskey. McQuaid welcomed the publican: according to Browne, a trained psychiatrist, McQuaid was acting on the common and valid assumption that a child is too ashamed and fearful to report what has happened to parents. In an exceptional case, such as this, he considered that it would be normal for the child to be afraid to suggest that a distinguished prince of the church could be guilty of such a grave sexual assault.

McQuaid sought to enter into conversation with the publican as if nothing had happened, though the publican was clearly infuriated as he stood over McQuaid. In his rage and disgust, no longer afraid as normally he would have been, the publican confronted the Archbishop. Showing McQuaid the door, the publican accused him of attempting to corrupt his innocent son and of being a disgrace to his cloth, the office of bishop and his Church. Angrily, he ordered McQuaid not to darken the door of the house again.

Browne concluded that in addition to being overcome by a sense of guilt caused by the abandonment of his self-control, McQuaid agonised over the disastrous prospect of his behaviour being discovered. Convinced that the psycho-sexual predictability of the behaviour outlined in the story explained 'the disturbing drives that motivated McQuaid', Browne classified the data as constituting 'a classical story of a paranoid schizophrenic'. He saw McQuaid as a Jekyll and Hyde figure. He felt that the story was shocking but authentic.[33]

However, Browne recoiled from placing the allegation in the public domain because he feared that his claim would be treated as an instance of his *animus* against McQuaid.

19

Ecclesiastical Taoiseach
1951–55

'I suppose you think you are the chief bucko?'
Alfred O'Rahilly to McQuaid.

In the military church of Arbour Hill on Sunday October 7, 1951, Archbishop John Charles McQuaid invited the assembled members of the Army, Navy and Air Corps to take a solemn oath dedicating themselves to Mary, Our Lady, Queen of the Holy Rosary. Led by President Seán T. O'Kelly and Taoiseach Éamon de Valera, the political and military establishment stood to attention and solemnly invoked Mary as the official patroness of the Defence Forces of the Irish Republic. It was a moment in the history of religious fundamentalism that ranks alongside the Ayatollah Khomeini's crusade to transform Iran into a Muslim state.

On the epistle side of the altar stood the famous flag of the 1641 Confederation of Kilkenny with its entrancing picture of Our Lady encircled by Rosary beads that inspired an earlier generation of Irish soldiers to go into battle against the English with the words 'Sancta Maria' on their lips. This flag was donated by the first Papal Legate to Ireland, Archbishop John Baptist Rinnuccini, to the Irish commander and victor of the Battle of Benburb, Owen Roe O'Neill. This flag symbolised the direct connection between the Catholic nation in the seventeenth century and the Catholic State which McQuaid was moulding in the 1950s. For McQuaid, the flag represented the battle lost almost three hundred years earlier to achieve religious freedom from the Protestant English crown but which was now being belatedly won by the Catholics of his generation in the new post-Independence Ireland. The Kilkenny Flag, as the *Irish Press* noted, was an appropriate link with Ireland's Catholic past.[1]

McQuaid's foremost biblical scholar, Monsignor Patrick Boylan, consolidated the historical link in a sermon that traced Ireland's passage from the Penal Days to its status as a Catholic nation. The solemn act of acknowledging Mary as the nation's Queen, he told the political and military leaders, was an act of homage to one who was 'veritably more dear and more real' to the people than even the members of their own homes.

As Boylan descended from the pulpit, McQuaid glided to the centre of the altar and recited a ten-verse dedication prayer which he himself had composed:

> O Immaculate Virgin Mary, Mother of God, Queen of the Most Holy Rosary,
> humbly kneeling at Thy feet today, we choose Thee as Our Heavenly Patroness,
> We salute Thee, Who didst learn from the Archangel that by the power of the Holy Ghost
> Thou shouldst become the Mother of the Word made flesh.
> We salute Thee, ever Virgin Mother Who didst give birth to the Divine Redeemer,
> Who has atoned for all our sins and restored us to the Life of Sanctifying Grace ...[2]

Throughout the ceremony, McQuaid's equation of Catholicism with Irish culture was accepted without question. The beliefs of Protestants serving in the national forces were ignored. Arbour Hill was a classic example of the Archbishop's spectacular success in harnessing the energies of all sectors of society to the goal of a truly Catholic State.

Like an officer reporting to his commander in chief, when the ceremony was over he sent a telegram to the Pope:

> Faithful children of the Holy See, Officers, non-Commissioned Officers and men, in the Defence Forces of Ireland, assembled in the Military Church, Arbour Hill, Dublin in the presence of the President of Ireland, members of the Government, on the occasion of the Solemn Invocation of the Blessed Virgin, Queen of the Most Holy Rosary, as Patroness of the Defence Forces of Ireland, humbly pledge filial homage and enduring loyalty to the Holy Father ...[3]

McQuaid rule

McQuaid's Arbour Hill ceremony captured the mood of heightened popular piety in the aftermath of the Holy Year and Assumption celebrations. The bells of Dublin churches mourned the passing of the elderly Nuncio, Archbishop Ettore Felici, and welcomed his successor, the brash American, Archbishop Gerald Patrick O'Hara. Having already confronted Communists in Romania, the Cold War churchman marked his arrival in Ireland by walking out of a meeting in protest at criticisms of Cardinal Stepinanc made by the Protestant writer Hubert Butler of Kilkenny. Robustly, he kept McQuaid on his toes with his anxieties about the capacity of Radio Moscow to beam into Ireland and his inquiries as to whether there was anything objectionable in the Legion of Mary's methods and undertakings.[4] With his craze for technology, O'Hara pressed McQuaid to microfilm baptism and marriage registers prior to 1870, but was suitably delighted when McQuaid gifted the Nunciature with an Underwood typewriter.

In an age of uncritical journalism, there were no investigative religious affairs correspondents in Dublin to write the story of McQuaid's quarrel with the powerful secretary at the Nunciature, Monsignor Giovanni Benelli, a strongly opinionated Tuscan. The row, over Clause 269 of the code of Canon Law relating to liturgical protocol, was bruising for both men. McQuaid accused Benelli, on the record, of 'indirectness', and off the record of 'worldliness'. The Tuscan was to avenge himself years later when, as the Sostituto-Secretary of State, he held the second most powerful position in the Vatican of Pope Paul VI.[5]

What the Irish public saw abundantly was the majesty of the Catholic Church personified by its chief pastor in Dublin. McQuaid's prestige was so high that he was frequently asked to intervene in industrial disputes. His settling of the barmen's strike in 1955 made him, literally, the toast of the city's pubs. His negotiating skills added to his aura of power and enhanced the clergy's stature. 'It was with a feeling of pride that I read about the settlement through you,' wrote the founder of Muintir na Tíre, Fr John Hayes.[6]

In spring 1952, McQuaid was building 17 churches, extending existing ones and founding many new schools. 'Hiberno-Romanesque' churches such as St Gabriel's in Mount Prospect and Our Lady Queen of Peace in Mount Merrion were built at enormous expense.[7] 'For all these churches, our priests have to find the means among our people,' McQuaid told Archbishop Hurley of Florida. Although the people were expected to pay for the churches, they were given no say in their design. Towards the end of the Emergency period, McQuaid established a hand-picked diocesan committee to purge designs for ultra-modern church architecture and art: 'No statue or picture is erected in any church or public Oratory, no plan of a church is accepted, without my personal censorship,' he told Rome.[8]

He overruled critics who complained that Hiberno-Romanesque was a hocus-pocus patchwork of architectural styles. Opposition from parishioners to his blueprint for Merrion were swept aside, and when the design for the new Bird Avenue Church at Clonskeagh was competitively selected by professional architects, McQuaid overrode the decision and imposed his own selection.[9]

McQuaid entertained no doubts as to the correctness of his decisions. When he opened a vocational school in Crumlin in 1953, he heralded it as a forerunner of 'a system of education which would be among the best in Europe.'[10] Hard-nosed in business matters, he knew how to expand the independent Church-controlled sector while maximising money from the taxpayer. When Carysfort Training College run by the Sisters of Mercy was due to recruit an extra 115 students, the college head, Sister Teresita, was guided on the building programme by the Archbishop of Dublin, not the Minister for Education. 'The best arrangement would be,' McQuaid advised Sister Teresita, 'for the College to undertake its own alterations and to recoup itself by the extra grant of the additional students.'[11]

In accordance with McQuaid's wishes, Drimnagh Castle was sold to the Christian Brothers for £16,000 (£320,000). Although this sum was substantially reduced to the Church authorities as a charitable bequest, McQuaid's auxiliary, Bishop Dunne, reported that the State had to be paid £4,865 (£90,000) at once, and that there were difficulties in balancing the diocesan books on account of other outflows to the Clonliffe College building programme. 'It became evident very early on that I should have to shelter behind Mr A. O'Hagan & Son [the diocesan legal advisers],' Dunne informed McQuaid. 'It seems that there are complications arising out of the administration of the estate of Hugh Hatch, who predeceased his brother Louis by some months. Things are moving very slowly and the distribution of Louis Hatch's money according to his wishes has to be equally slow.' McQuaid nonchalantly assured Dunne: 'Messers O'Hagan will steer you through the maze.'[12]

Although the management of diocesan funds was kept a secret, McQuaid's annual gifts to the Catholic Social Welfare Conference and other charities were widely publicised. Much of his other charitable work was done in private, mostly to the benefit of Irish nationals, but he gave £100 (£2,000) anonymously to the Lord Mayor of London's appeal after the flooding of the River Thames in winter 1953.[13] The following year he sent a 'princely gift' to help in relief work after the floods in New South Wales, Australia.[14]

In the Marian Year of 1954, Irish workers gave a 'munificent offering' of £3,052 (£61,000) as the 'industrial tribute', a sum which was well received in Rome.[15] The nation's piety was recharged that year when the centenary of the dogma of the Immaculate Conception was widely celebrated. 'It was Dublin's Great Day,' the *Irish Press* proclaimed in a report of how tens of thousands of people, many of them trade unionists, walked in procession through the streets in the warm May sunshine to the Pro-Cathedral, where McQuaid administered Solemn Benediction from a temporary altar erected on the outdoor steps.[16]

Marian fervour reached levels which won comparison with the great Eucharistic Congress of 1932. So popular was the granting of Papal Blessings from Rome that when McQuaid heard reports that the scrolls were being sold by non-Catholic firms, an instruction was promptly sent to the Rector of the Irish College in Rome to prevent such traffic.

The work of moulding the piety of a nation started in the schools, where young boys and girls went through mental torture ahead of their Confirmation as they learned by rote the answers to questions which they barely understood. The novelist Maeve Binchy recalls McQuaid asking her: 'What is sanctifying Grace?' When she answered correctly she was hailed as a credit to her school, but any who hesitated or mumbled in such an awesome presence brought disgrace to their school and punishment on themselves.[17]

McQuaid wrote the foreword to the *Guide for Catholic Teachers* which set out the rules governing classrooms under Church control with as pervasive an emphasis on indoctrination as any Marxist publication. The annual publication of his Lenten Regulations bit deep into the popular psyche, decreeing the rules of fast and abstinence and other church obligations, restating the ban on attendance at Trinity College and non-Catholic schools, and of course decrying membership of Communist organisations. McQuaid's Lenten Regulations also alluded to current social issues – in 1952 he expressed grave disapproval of young women competing in cycling and athletic events, deplored 'a certain regrettable laxity in abstaining from servile work [on the Lord's Day] in the building trade', and disapproved of Dubliners relaxing at dog-racing, horse-racing and pony-racing on Sundays.[18]

Typical of the pervasive prudery fostered by the Palace was the reaction of the Archbishop's medical friends at a British Medical Association meeting held in Dublin in July 1952, which planned to discuss a report calling for a more liberal divorce law in Britain. An alliance of the Guilds of Irish and British Catholic doctors not only forced the report to be withdrawn, but chastised the visitors for their audacity in contemplating the presentation on Irish soil of a proposal which was so insulting to the Archbishop of Dublin.[19]

McQuaid's code of conduct forbade any socialising between Catholic and Protestant youth. 'I regard it as invariably dangerous for our young Catholics, boys or girls, to fraternise with Protestant groups, because, no matter what safeguards are provided, the Catholics take on the colour of the Protestant mentality and morals,' McQuaid told the new Bishop of Cork, Dr Cornelius Lucey. 'Explain it as one may, the result is inevitable.'[20]

After Dublin's auxiliary Bishop, Patrick Dunne, twice refused the architect of a new synagogue in Terenure, Wilfred Cantwell, permission to attend its official opening because he was a Catholic, he checked with his boss to see if he had made the right decision: 'May I continue to say no or would Your Grace think my view is too strict?' McQuaid soon confirmed his decision. 'I would not think of admitting such a flimsy plea,' he replied.[21]

On another occasion, Dunne told McQuaid that in the course of 1952–53 a handful of people had come to him for permission to attend marriages in Protestant churches, and when he refused to permit it they seemed to be surprised. He instanced the case of a Miss Bailey, a Methodist who said that she did not care about his veto on Catholics attending her wedding even though she knew that many others had got permission. 'She may have been misinformed, but it is possible that someone is making it easy,' Dunne told McQuaid. 'There have always been priests in this town who wish to be magnanimous in things outside their sphere.'[22]

McQuaid kept his clergy on a tight rein and did not tolerate priests or religious from other dioceses performing services or taking part in public meetings in Dublin without his permission. He expressed his 'grave surprise' that 'three stranger-ecclesiastics' should take part in a public discussion on matters pertaining to faith and morals without consulting him or bearing a recommendation from their own bishops. When Archbishop Miltenburg of Karachi wrote asking permission to have a Pakistani priest show a documentary film on mission work in order to raise funds in Dublin, McQuaid regretted that his diocese was oppressed by such film-shows and fundraising. 'I would ask Your Grace to desist from the project of sending a priest to Dublin for the purpose,' he said firmly.[23]

McQuaid and his fellow bishops also fretted over the growing number of nuns coming over from England on holidays and staying either in the homes of relatives and friends or, worse still, in hotels and guesthouses. They set up a committee which approached the English bishops to secure their cooperation in ensuring that nuns stayed in 'a religious house of women' in future, and parish priests throughout Ireland were instructed to report to their bishops when any nuns were spotted holidaying in their areas.[24]

McQuaid, however, could bend the rules if he took a liking to a visitor. The Spanish priest, Fr Alvaro de Portillo, who visited the Archbishop to engage his interest in opening Opus Dei centres in Dublin, was not only successful in his mission, he was also invited to Killiney for dinner, so well had they got on together.[25]

Dublin's 'holy hooliganism'

A puzzling aspect of McQuaid's civic record is that he did he not denounce the excesses of the Maria Duce-sponsored Catholic Cinema and Theatre Patrons' Association, which kept him informed of the activities it carried out 'in the name of Christ the King'.

On December 18, 1951, the secretary of the association, Mícheál Ó Tuathail, led a group of protesters outside Dublin's Gate Theatre, where Orson Welles was playing alongside Micheál MacLiammóir and Hilton Edwards. Their placards bore the inscriptions 'Dublin rejects Communist front star,' 'Not wanted: Orson Welles, Stalin's Star,' and 'Welles's spiritual home is Moscow.' As the crowd swelled into a mob, the Gardaí had serious difficulties preventing a rush at the theatre amid cries of 'Burn it down!'

The disgraceful scenes were repudiated by Gabriel Fallon in *The Standard*.[26]

When Edwards approached McQuaid to complain about the incident, McQuaid told him that the association was 'an adult group' which was 'responsible for its own activities', a response which was totally at variance with his active vigilance of the Mercier Society's debates. McQuaid also kicked for touch when his Vicar General, Monsignor O'Reilly, brought to his attention the hurt felt by Tomás Roseingrave over Fallon's claim that Maria Duce was inciting hatred and anti-semitism in Dublin.

'I should be unwilling to give them [Maria Duce] any advice concerning an action taken without any consultation of Ecclesiastical Authority,' McQuaid informed O'Reilly. 'And I fail to understand their squeamishness in dealing with Fallon, after they have received from him criticism of their action.'[27]

Whatever about McQuaid's claim that he was not consulted in the Orson Welles case, he received notice from Ó Tuathail on June 7, 1952, of a letter sent to the manager of the Theatre Royal in protest against the scheduled appearance there of Danny Kaye for the week commencing June 22.[28] Ó Tuathail's letter pointed out that Danny Kaye ('real name Daniel Kominski') was cited in the 1948 California Senate Fact-finding Committee on Un-American Activites, and he expected the management to call off Kaye's appearance in view of his Communist-front activities. Maria Duce had copied the methods of Senator Joe McCarthy. 'We recall your ready cooperation with us on the occasion of the proposed visit of Larry Adler to your theatre in August 1950,' Ó Tuathail concluded. 'We trust that in this instance also you will extend to us the same measure of cooperation by taking steps to ensure that the Catholic conscience of your Dublin patrons will not be offered the offence of the presentation to them of Danny Kaye.'[29]

A few months later McQuaid acknowledged receipt of a similar letter from Ó Tuathail to the manager of the Metropole Cinema protesting against the presentation of a film based on Arthur Miller's *Death of a Salesman*. Not only was Miller connected with Communism, so too was the star of the film, Frederick March, whose connections with Communist front groups were well established. The film was not fit material for showing in the Catholic city of Dublin.[30]

Liberalism: the enemy

In his confidential Quinquennial Report to Rome in 1952 on the state of the Dublin archdiocese, McQuaid identified liberalism as the constant enemy. In his own words, liberalism's power was based on the presence of a Protestant minority with its centre of operations in Trinity College; powerful in finance and in the professions, they were organised on a Masonic basis with strong affiliations to London and Belfast. In

McQuaid's mind, such a powerbase demanded unremitting vigilance on the part of the Catholic Church, particularly in education.[31]

When Trinity provost Henry Alton died in 1952, McQuaid refused to allow Catholics on the university staff attend the funeral. He instructed the chaplains at University College, Dublin, not to allow a group which sang Compline on Sundays to put up invitations in the College of Surgeons and Trinity College, and he secured the compliance of the Department of Foreign Affairs in making Trinity ineligible for scholarships from the French Government organisation, *Fondations Catholiques Irlandaises en France*.[32]

In 1954, McQuaid built Marian College in Ballsbridge to counter the effect of the nearby mixed non-denominational Sandymount High. 'The schools were right next to each other, with a barbed-wire fence reminiscent of the Berlin Wall separating them,' recalls a former pupil, Eamon Delaney. 'The Marist Order wanted to call the school Waterside College in view of its closeness to the River Dodder, but McQuaid insisted that it be called Marian College, as it opened in 1954.'[33]

However, McQuaid was encouraged by signs that younger Catholics wanted to assimilate a Catholic philosophy which would give them a distinctive outlook on social and political developments. In October 1952 he presented diplomas in social studies to 90 young workers from the Dublin Catholic Institute of Sociology, which he had established in Gardiner Street, and for the first time the opening of the Dublin Vocational Schools' academic year was marked by Mass, presided over by McQuaid. That month, too, UCD opened evening classes in Commerce and Public Administration. McQuaid had been critical of UCD president Michael Tierney for having allowed a situation to develop where 'most of our future administrators will have been trained in Trinity' – in 1951, he had given 100 students permission to enter the Protestant university.[34]

The UCD breakthrough was welcomed as 'a great service to us all' by Bishop James MacNamee of Ardagh,[35] while Bishop Denis Moynihan of Ross felt deeply indebted to McQuaid for having secured 'favourable facilities' which meant that he was now in a position to insist that there was no longer a valid reason for young Catholics to attend evening lectures in Trinity College.[36] Although Bishop Patrick Collier of Ossory suggested that UCD's popularity could be increased if it stopped making Irish compulsory, he agreed that a wide public would thank McQuaid. 'All of us – both bishops and people – are most grateful to Your Grace for securing such a satisfactory solution of a difficult question. In future no student can plead that he is compelled to go to Trinity College.'[37]

The principle ally in McQuaid's strategy of moulding UCD in his integral brand of Catholicism was the Professor of Metaphysics and Dean of the Faculty of Philosophy, Fr John Horgan, who was rewarded by being made a Domestic Prelate in November 1952, giving him the status of Monsignor and the nickname 'the Mons'. According to Professor Tom Garvin, Horgan radiated power. A large bald man with piercing blue eyes and an intensely inquisitive style of conversation, he had a manipulative manner which reminded Garvin of Squealer, the spokesperson for Napoleon in George Orwell's *Animal Farm*. Another UCD academic, Maurice Manning, referred to Horgan as 'McQuaid's buttonman'. This assessment was accurate: Horgan was McQuaid's chief spy on the campus, sending him regular and detailed reports.[38]

Five university chairs effectively under McQuaid's control were occupied by priests: Ethics and Politics, Logic and Psychology, Education, Sociology and Metaphysics. Little publishing, certainly little of any international repute, emanated from these departments because of 'the terror of error', Garvin recalls.[39]

To promote Catholic interests at university level nationally, since 1950 McQuaid had informally convened meetings between a select group of bishops and the three presidents of the National University of Ireland. On the academic side were Tierney of UCD, Monsignor Pádraig de Brún of UCG and Alfred O'Rahilly of UCC. On the Episcopal side were Cardinal D'Alton, who chaired meetings, Bishop Browne of Galway and Bishop Cornelius Lucey of Cork, who acted as secretary.[40]

McQuaid and the bishops faced a dilemma as to whether they were going to stick to the hated 1908 Act establishing the National University of Ireland, or put themselves in the hands of the politicians by conceding to the Dáil the moral right to pass university acts. McQuaid was wary in case politicians, rather than pass legislation to refashion the National University in a more Catholic fashion, would instead claim further rights for the State on the grounds of nondenominationalism. Legal opinion was sought on the extent to which religious initiatives could be taken in the colleges.

At times McQuaid was like a ring-master between Tierney, who wanted to go beyond the 'agnostic neutrality' of the 1908 Act and transform UCD into an independent Catholic university, and O'Rahilly and de Brún, who wanted to maximise Catholic interests without tampering with the 1908 charter. McQuaid was impressed by the steps which O'Rahilly had taken in Cork, and was receptive to his advice that 'an élite of integral Catholics' could also be formed in Galway and Dublin.[41]

Adoption fixed

The closed nature of Irish society enabled McQuaid to exploit a cloak and dagger atmosphere in which he could influence the legislators. A classic example of McQuaid's political *modus operandi* was his vetting of proposed adoption legislation, the groundwork for which had been prepared by an Episcopal committee under his chairmanship. McQuaid had also deployed two Maynooth theologians to examine the issue with the parliamentary draftsman.[42]

Accordingly, on January 3, 1952, McQuaid handed the Minister for Justice, Gerald Boland, a memorandum which 'excellently solved' the 'very grave spiritual issues' governing the adoption of children.[43] Once Boland nodded his consent, McQuaid announced that 'legal adoption, if it be restricted within certain limits and protected by certain safeguards, is consonant with Catholic teaching.'[44] Boland's Adoption Bill, as presented to the Dáil, mirrored the McQuaid committee's proposals: adoption was open only for illegitimate and orphan children between the ages of six months and seven years; adopting parents were to be 'of the same religion as the child and his parents or, if the child is illegitimate, his mother'; the administering authority had to be satisfied that the applicant was of good moral character, had sufficient means to support the child and was suitable as a parent, and adoption societies were to be registered and regulated.

Each clause of the draft had been vetted by McQuaid and his chief adviser on adoption and social issues, Fr Cecil Barrett. By requiring adopting parents to be of the same religion as the natural parents, the legislation disqualified couples in mixed marriages. To McQuaid's satisfaction, it dealt a heavy blow to proselytism by prohibiting Protestant parents from adopting Catholic children.

McQuaid also negotiated the safeguard that 'it should be made an offence to send or allow to be sent out of the State a child who is a national unless such action is taken directly by the parents or by the natural mother of the child.' This requirement became Section 39 of the Adoption Act. According to the Secretary of the Department of Justice, Tommy Coyne, it was carefully worded to facilitate foreign adoptions which met the McQuaid guidelines, but left the southern Church authorities in a position to restrict Protestant organisations taking children across the Border to live in the Six Counties.[45]

McQuaid's willingness to allow the State establish a legal framework for adoption in 1952 was an advance on his opposition to such a move by Boland in 1944 and by the Inter-Party Minister for Health, General Seán MacEoin, in 1950–51. A major factor in this shift was his desire to avoid a possible public scandal over the sending of illegitimate children to America. In allowing American adoptions, running at 330 in 1953, McQuaid, with the collusion of the departments of State, had been operating in a murky legal zone. With the passage of the 1952 Act, McQuaid not only regularised American adoptions but also had the State endorse his sectarian approach. The technique of engaging the Government in secret negotiations with an Episcopal committee worked 'with excellent smoothness and eliminated even the semblance of opposition', McQuaid informed Bishop D'Alton.[46]

Mother and Infant Scheme

McQuaid was eager to use the same secretive technique to settle the unfinished matter of maternity services, still unresolved from the time of Dr Nöel Browne. He grew extremely annoyed that the new Fianna Fáil Minister for Health, Jim Ryan, a Wexford man who had served in the GPO in 1916 and was close to Éamon de Valera, had not consulted him before publishing a White Paper which had been sent to him in July. Known as the Mother and Infant Scheme, the Bill scaled down Browne's plans and proposed to provide assistance to the mother and child for a maximum of six weeks after birth. It met one of the Hierarchy's previous objections by demanding a nominal contribution from women in the upper income bracket, but it did not specify a figure. The service was to be free only for the poorest.[47]

McQuaid, who found Ryan polite but slow to do his bidding, was frustrated at not being able to deal directly with de Valera, who was in Utrecht, Holland, for treatment for what McQuaid said was 'his blindness'.[48] Despite having undergone six operations for a detached retina, de Valera continued to direct Government policy from his hospital bed.

Determined to act before any 'troubling discussions' about the Bill were held in public, McQuaid persuaded D'Alton to establish an ad hoc Episcopal committee to deal with Ryan. The committee consisted of the same team as formed the adoption group – Archbishop Kinane of Tuam, Bishop Browne of Galway, Bishop Staunton of Ferns, plus a recent newcomer to the Hierarchy, Bishop Cornelius Lucey of Cork. McQuaid was chairman.[49]

McQuaid was in a hurry. From Professor John Cunningham and the surgeon T.C.J. O'Connell of St Vincent's Hospital, he learned that Ryan was pressing for an early response from the Irish Medical Association to his White Paper. The two doctors wanted to know the Hierarchy's views before finalising the IMA's position, but McQuaid told them evasively that he had not had time to study the Government paper. 'It must not be possible for the doctors to quote a Bishop or the Bishops in their tussle with the Government,' McQuaid told D'Alton. Even though his meeting with the doctors had been private, McQuaid assured D'Alton that he 'gave no opinion as a Bishop'.[50]

Fearing that the Catholic position might go by default, McQuaid met the acting head of Government, Seán Lemass, in early September. 'I saw him, because Dr Ryan had never asked to see me (or any Bishop) before issuing the White Paper,' he told D'Alton. Lemass undertook to suggest to Ryan that he should meet the bishops for an informal discussion before presenting the Bill to the Dáil.[51]

McQuaid urged Lemass to remove the 'offensive sections' in the 1947 Act relating to the provision of family planning advice for mothers.

He stressed the need for an income threshold to be set on mothers receiving benefits, and he complained about the 'State powers' which he said were being given to medical officers. McQuaid told D'Alton that Lemass 'fully agreed, and indicated that Ryan would move the amendment. The atmosphere, then, is more propitious than I had believed,' McQuaid wrote. 'In Mr Lemass we have a man of common sense who greatly believes in negotiation with a view to settlement.'[52]

McQuaid's expectations were dented two days later when Ryan presented him with a different version of what Lemass had undertaken. Ryan understood that Lemass had outlined the three-stage procedure of a White Paper, setting out Government intentions, its reception of comments by interested parties and, in the light of representations, proceeding with the implementation of its proposals.

'I gathered from Mr Lemass also that there was some misunderstanding of the provisions of the White Paper and it would be well to have this cleared up,' Ryan added. However, he indicated to McQuaid that the Bill would not be ready for the Dáil before mid-November. He proposed to meet the Archbishop on his return from a short holiday.[53]

McQuaid was not prepared to be fobbed off so lightly. Next day, he requested permission from Lemass to meet the Secretary of the Department of Health, as Ryan would be away on holidays until the end of September. 'The Minister believes that I misunderstood somewhat the provisions of the White Paper,' McQuaid explained to Lemass. 'It would be well to sift the matter before I see the Minister or my colleagues of the Bishops' Committee.'[54] He was quite clear about the function of the meeting: 'In this way, the very tangled issues of a spiritual character involved in the Adoption Act were with complete success smoothed out.'

Simultaneously, McQuaid informed Ryan that in his absence he had asked Lemass for the benefit of 'a conference' with the Secretary so that he would have a clear understanding of the provisions of the Bill when meeting Ryan after his holidays.[55] This letter spurred Ryan into a change of plan: his secretary, Sean Forde, phoned to say that Ryan, though on holiday, would be in his office at the Custom House on September 16 and an appointment could be made to suit His Grace any time that afternoon.[56] McQuaid indicated that he could meet Ryan at any time that was convenient, but thought it would be much more private if the Minister would call to Drumcondra.[57] Not only was an appointment fixed, Lemass phoned to ask if everything had been satisfactorily arranged. 'Excellently arranged,' McQuaid concurred.[58]

When Ryan called on McQuaid at the Palace, the Archbishop found him 'very pleasant'. According to McQuaid's note, Ryan was completely willing to amend the offensive clauses of the 1947 Act but was less clear on the bishops' insistence of a £600 (about £15,000) upper income limit for eligibility to the scheme.[59] In Ryan's account, the minister felt

McQuaid had accepted his arguments against an income level. McQuaid informed him of the Episcopal committee and warned him against 'running into trouble'.[60] Ryan does not appear to have taken on board McQuaid's stricture that his Bill was too close to Dr Browne's 'free for all' plan.

On September 26, McQuaid chaired a meeting with Lucey and Browne at which they drew up a detailed list of demands.[61] Ryan's first meeting with the bishops' committee on October 6 at Drumcondra was described as 'cordial, frank, calm and courteous,' by McQuaid. This glossed over what Ryan regarded as a 'far-fetched and ridiculous' attack by Bishop Browne on the powers enabling health officers use compulsion to detain persons suffering from infectious disease. When the sparring between Ryan and Browne stopped, McQuaid renewed his objections to the 'offensive' sections on motherhood and infant care which he claimed violated the Constitution's acceptance of the natural law and Catholic moral teaching, which favoured the family providing for its own needs. Ryan promised to meet McQuaid's concerns, but did not give him an assurance that he would provide him with an advance copy of the relevant clauses of the Bill.[62]

In his report to the bishops at Maynooth on October 14, McQuaid displayed a fascination for poker-style politics: he raised the intriguing question: what would happen if the Government did not accept the views of the bishops on motherhood. 'Does the Hierarchy wish to issue a public statement to meet the situation?' he asked. 'If so, how is that statement to be made?'

Presenting his own analysis of the likely political responses, McQuaid anticipated that 'a grave situation' might arise before or during the Committee Stage of the Bill, and that any sign of a deviation by the Government from the markers laid down by the committee would best be met by the publication of an Episcopal statement. That comment, McQuaid advised, ought 'to be calm, doctrinal and so simply worded that all the Faithful could understand its import'. It would be 'a test-case for the conscience of Catholic deputies of every party.'[63]

Clearly, McQuaid was preparing for a showdown with the de Valera Government. However, he told his colleagues that he would prefer to avoid public controversy between Church and State and he promised to do his best to prevent a conflict. By this, he envisaged the Government privately suing for peace on the Hierarchy's terms. His colleagues accepted McQuaid's advice, gave him freedom of action to pursue negotiations and the discretion to summon a full meeting of the Hierarchy to make a public statement if one was needed.

McQuaid kept Lemass in the dark about the Maynooth decision, as it would be 'much more useful to retain that weapon for a future use, if the need should arise'.[64] Little progress was made with Lemass, and when he read in the newspaper that the IMA had rejected the Government's proposals, McQuaid lost his patience and demanded that Lemass 'be good enough to accord full weight to the most serious moral objections that I have brought to the notice of the Government.'[65] Lemass assured McQuaid of 'the most correct attention on the Government's part' to the bishops' objections.[66] This show of deference, and Lemass's assurance that he would communicate with McQuaid before publishing the legislation, defused tensions for a time.[67]

At this critical juncture, McQuaid disclosed his views on the political situation in a confidential letter to the Papal Nuncio, Archbishop O'Hara. McQuaid recalled that (with the exception of Browne and MacBride) dealing with Costello's Government had been a very pleasant experience – Costello was not only an excellent Catholic, in immediate sympathy with the Church and its teachings, he was not unduly worried about placating the liberals and Freemasons of North or South. In contrast, McQuaid felt aggrieved that de Valera's Government pursued 'a policy of distance' from the Church. 'That policy is seen in the failure to consult any Bishop on the provisions of a Health Scheme. All the present difficulty results from that failure,' he wrote. De Valera had promised 'to give a Health Scheme based on the Constitution and Social Directives thereof.'

> It would not be in character for him to make any reference to the Hierarchy; such a reference would be felt to be inopportune in view of the Protestant support and the voting-power of the Liberal Independents on whom he has been obliged to lean for a continuance in office. Further, any consultation of the Hierarchy would, if later discovered, bitterly antagonise the North of Ireland Protestants, whom Mr de Valera always considers, in the hope of being able to remove Partition.

And he weighed up the impact of Fianna Fáil's revolutionary past, when the party was on the side opposed to Episcopal direction:

> While, then, the outward courtesies will be accorded, the inner spirit of sympathetic and open collaboration with the Hierarchy will be missing from a Fianna Fáil Government. Not that anti-Catholic measures may be expected from men who faithfully practice now the Faith, but ... a definite liberalism is always present. In my opinion, that liberalism must be incessantly watched. And what I particularly fear is the effect on the rising generation of an attitude which would successfully oppose the Hierarchy on the present Mother and Infant Scheme.[68]

McQuaid did not contemplate losing to the Government.

Meanwhile, from Utrecht, where he was kept informed by Lemass about McQuaid's ultimatum, de Valera instructed his deputy to read Archbishop Kinane's Rockwell speech and the 1947 bishops' letter, two fundamental documents in which the bishops objected to unlimited, unqualified and absolute ministerial powers under the 1947 Health Act. Lemass was also to circulate these two documents to all Government ministers.[69] The Kinane speech was particularly significant. After telling Rockwell students that they were forbidden under grave pain of mortal sin from attending Trinity College, Dublin, he enunciated the principles that 'the prohibition is not a mere arbitrary one, it is based on the natural divine law itself.'

This was a prelude to Kinane's enunciation of the extended principle of the right of bishops:

> **Subject to the supreme magisterial authority of the Holy See, Bishops are the authentic teachers of faith and morals in their own dioceses. And their authority includes the right to determine in case of doubt whether faith and morals are involved, so that one cannot evade their authority by the pretext that they have gone outside their proper sphere.**

Consequently, 'subjects' should not oppose their bishops' teaching: they should carry out what was demanded of them.[70]

De Valera also advised Lemass that the best way to handle McQuaid was to go through each objection and ask him to submit a draft with the qualifications and safeguards that would satisfy him. That draft was to be looked at from 'our point of view' until a text was agreed. Both sides were preparing for battle.

In advance of their meeting with Lemass and Ryan on December 10, McQuaid and his colleagues decided that, because of the approaching Dáil recess, they would not approve amendments offered by the Government. McQuaid calculated that a pre-Christmas approval of the revised legislation could be used by Fianna Fáil for political advantage or propaganda purposes.[71] This deliberate procrastination had an unexpected twist: next day Rome announced the elevation of D'Alton to the College of Cardinals.

'In my lifetime I have sent very few messages which gave me greater pleasure to send,' de Valera wrote from Utrecht. 'I was delighted at the honour done to you personally, at the honour done to the Primatial See of Armagh, and at the manner in which its selection at the present time symbolised the unity of our nation. No wonder your appointment has caused such universal joy. How the Fathers in Blackrock of our day would rejoice if they could see this day.'[72]

From Rome Fr Dan O'Connell S.J., his Clongowes friend, wrote to

McQuaid to offer the consolation that Ambassador Joe Walshe had said the Vatican authorities realised fully that he was the obvious choice as the Irish cardinal. That choice, O'Connell explained, was 'actually made purely for political reasons, as an attempt to conciliate the North and to emphasise the unity of Ireland'.[73]

Against the background of public rejoicing at D'Alton's Red Hat, in January the Government set the income barrier for welfare benefit at £600 in its Mother and Infant Bill. Ryan sent McQuaid drafts of the heads of the more sensitive sections of the Bill without receiving any objections from the Archbishop. In early February, de Valera, now returned from Utrecht, chaired the Government meeting which approved the text of the Bill. He told Ryan to send a copy to McQuaid and consult with him before its circulation to Dáil deputies. McQuaid appears to have been satisfied after a further exchange with Ryan. De Valera felt secure that a Church-State crisis had been averted.

McQuaid 'down under'

While D'Alton was being made a Freeman of Dublin and was fêted at Maynooth, McQuaid was in Sydney, representing Ireland at the Eucharistic Congress. His absence from Ireland from April 3 to June 5, 1953, was his first sustained break from daily administration since his appointment as Archbishop in 1940. Aged 57, he had the opportunity to shine on the world stage.[74]

Chosen by Cardinal Gilroy as the preacher at the Congress's closing session in St Mary's Cathedral, McQuaid spoke of how Catholics in Ireland and Australia had suffered persecution for their faith but were now free to practice their religion in churches, schools and hospitals. He also invoked the presence of 'the host of silent worshippers: the countless numbers of your saintly forebears, the assembly of the priests and prelates who have shepherded your people to the triumph of this hour.'[75]

Lecturing next day at the University of Sydney on 'The Influence of Europe on Australia', McQuaid offered Australia the scholastic philosophy of Aquinas as the antidote to Communism, existentialism and the atomic bomb. He called for 'a return to the Faith that moulded Europe and to the perennial philosophy of St Thomas that links us with our cultural origins'.[76] The origins of contemporary evil he traced to the breakdown of the scholastic world in the late Middle Ages. From the nominalists to Karl Marx had grown a belief in indefinite human progress, but a New Dark Age had emerged instead. Admitting that Picasso could draw old Greek vases with a purity of line, McQuaid remarked scornfully that it was 'surely not necessary to return to the bib-pinafore stage of life to show that we desire to follow a cult of childlike simplicity'. In drama, he dismissed Jean Paul Sartre as a philosopher of nihilism and despair.

Attacking Freud and Jung, he lamented that psychology had been reduced to the study of man as a sexual animal. Ethics and theology had been gradually set aside. Nor could the intellectual soul of man be filled by history, which had become divorced from Thomistic philosophy. His Sydney speech was applauded by church leaders as a *tour de force*, but as John Feeney observed, it 'epitomised the outlook of a churchman who had not yet begun to feel doubts about the relevance of scholastic philosophy.'[77]

Health's 'special position'

During McQuaid's absence, a Church-State crisis flared up suddenly when Cardinal D'Alton sent de Valera an advance copy of a statement which the Hierarchy intended to make public on the Mother and Infant scheme. The statement, while broadly welcoming changes in the 1947 Act, declared that the proposed transfer of a father's responsibility for the welfare of his family to a public authority would lower the people's sense of personal responsibility and seriously weaken their moral fibre.

In panic, de Valera met D'Alton secretly in Drogheda and succeeded in suppressing publication of the bishops' condemnation. A 'summit' meeting of Government ministers and the bishops' committee was held at the President's residence in the Phoenix Park. The bishops squeezed from the Government delegation virtually all the amendments which they sought. It was a remarkable instance of how 'the special position' of the Catholic Church worked in practice, Professor Ronan Fanning has argued.[78]

Writing to McQuaid, Bishop Dunne was scathing of what he and some others, who had wanted their differences with the Government aired in public, felt was a climbdown by D'Alton and other bishops.[79] McQuaid later often remarked that the disarray would not have occurred had he been in Ireland.[80] However, when the Hierarchy met on June 25, McQuaid proposed that the condemnation should be formally withdrawn and the Phoenix Park accord formally approved. Even so, he pressed – and secured as the price of his agreement to the Bill – an amendment permitting the opening of public hospitals to the university medical schools for clinical teaching, even though the medical schools retained control of such appointments. Over tea in Áras an Uachtaráin on July 7, McQuaid clinched this concession from de Valera, extending Catholic control over medical appointments. Next day, Ryan incorporated McQuaid's wishes into the Bill at Report stage without informing deputies of the background to the change.

Subsequently, McQuaid persuaded Drs Cunningham and O'Connell, whom he had encouraged to continue their opposition to the Mother and Infant Bill at the IMA annual meeting in Waterford, to do a U-turn. This they meekly did after McQuaid summoned them and told them that he had changed his mind.[81]

McQuaid's rupture with Dev

McQuaid's latent disenchantment with de Valera's Government surfaced in complaints which he made over aspects of health and education policies. He berated Jim Ryan for not informing him of a planned change in the regulations governing Catholic chaplains in voluntary hospitals and peremptorily requested the Minister to send five copies of these regulations for the attention of the Hierarchy's standing committee. The bishops 'would appreciate the courtesy of being allowed to learn the nature of the change contemplated,' he wrote.[82] Ryan, however, pointed out that these were internal memoranda, assured McQuaid that the independence of the voluntary hospitals would remain untouched and promised that their deficits would be paid from the exchequer's hospital allocation.[83]

Ryan failed to pacify McQuaid, who persisted in using the term 'draft regulations' and complained that the assurance he had given were not binding on his successors. The Minister was puzzled further when McQuaid claimed that de Valera had refused to assist the voluntary secondary schools.

Ryan was particularly disturbed by McQuaid's claim that there was a widespread feeling that the fabric of Irish social life was being subtly and progressively undermined by the very damaging trends in health and education policy. 'I do not need to underline the effect on the educated sections of our society which such a fear of the unitary or Socialistic State continues deeply to disturb,' McQuaid warned.[84]

Ryan discussed McQuaid's complaints with the Minister for Education, Seán Moylan, an ex-IRA man from north Cork. Moylan was dismayed by McQuaid's criticism of Government actions on secondary schools.[85] He told Ryan that it was true that de Valera had discussed school grants at a recent meeting with the Catholic Headmasters' Association, when the association had presented its case for an increase in the capitation grants for secondary schools, which had remained unchanged since 1924. In reply, de Valera had pointed out that an increase to the secondary schools would subsidise the wealthier classes who could afford to pay for their children's education. However, despite these reservations, and subject to budgetary constraints, de Valera had promised that he would take the matter up with the Minister for Finance, Seán MacEntee, and had done so subsequently.

Moylan also told Ryan that the Headmasters' Association was spreading false stories to put pressure on the Government: the Prior of Terenure College had misrepresented de Valera's response 'in a manner lacking in all dignity and restraint', and the President of St Munchin's College, Limerick, had added to the confusion with 'less vehemence but with the same disregard for the facts'.

Moylan knew of no evidence whatsoever to back up McQuaid's claim of 'a deep and widespread apprehension' about Department of Health machinations to undermine the fabric of society. While it was true that, as politicians, neither minister could bind their successors to policy promises, Moylan feared the consequences of an unchecked clericalism. 'We know too that any deviation from truth on the part of the moral leaders of the community will more swiftly ensure an undermining of the social fabric than will the incapacity or dilatoriness on the part of political leadership.'[86]

Moylan advised Ryan that the capitation question should not even be discussed until the situation created by 'the agitatory statements of the clergy was cleared up'. On Moylan's advice, de Valera wrote to McQuaid suggesting that his impressions of the Government's attitude to school grants could only be due to 'some serious misunderstanding' on the Archbishop's part.[87] McQuaid stuck to the evidence from his priests, which he felt obliged to accept as true. 'Your attitude towards the increased capitation,' he replied haughtily to de Valera, 'is now widely known and has gravely disturbed the educated sections of our people. The intimation of a change of attitude on your part would then be a very great pleasure to the Archbishop of Dublin.'[88]

De Valera accused McQuaid of basing his 'wild strictures' on an untrue speech, but McQuaid stuck with his clerical sources rather than accept the word of his long-time friend and mentor. 'It was a painful end to the long-standing friendship,' wrote de Valera's official biographer, the late T.P. O'Neill. 'Relations between the two men were never to be the same again.'[89]

McQuaid's revenge on MacBride?

McQuaid shed no tears for de Valera's defeat in the general election in May 1954, when his party's popularity slumped as a result of Finance Minister Seán MacEntee's austere approach to the economy. A revival in Fine Gael's fortunes seemed to augur the return of John A. Costello as Taoiseach, leading a second Inter-Party Government in alliance once more with Seán MacBride, whose Clann na Poblachta had won three seats.

Immediately on his re-election to Dáil Éireann, MacBride wrote to McQuaid, as in 1947, offering 'to serve Catholicism and Ireland' to the best of his ability and under the Archbishop's guidance.[90] McQuaid thanked MacBride for his assurance that he would 'serve the Faith and our country' and he promised to read MacBride's proposal for a National Government.[91]

From Rome, where he was now preparing for retirement, Ambassador Joe Walshe told McQuaid that he hoped that Jack Costello would under no circumstances make MacBride Minister for External Affairs. Walshe disclosed that during the first Inter-Party Government he had warned Costello, again and again, of the universal distrust surrounding 'this man'. So devious was MacBride that not a single member of the Cabinet, not a single priest, believed in him.

Walshe felt there were solid grounds to believe that 'J.C.' would have a workable majority without MacBride, and he felt there was no reason why the son of W.T. Cosgrave, Liam Cosgrave, should not be appointed Minister for External Affairs. 'He is such a splendid Catholic and will get on well with everybody,' Walshe predicted.[92]

In the event, Costello offered MacBride one post, Post and Tele-graphs, but this offer was turned down. Liam Cosgrave was appointed Minister for External Affairs. MacBride was not in Government.

'I feel certain the credit of bringing Liam Cosgrave out to Rome was entirely yours,' Walshe wrote from Paris. Cosgrave had accompanied McQuaid for the dedication of the chapel to St Columbanus in the crypt of St Peter's. It would appear that McQuaid had used his influence with Costello to stymie MacBride's ambitions.

In his valedictory letter to McQuaid – Walshe was embarking on a tour which would end in Egypt with his death – the Ambassador wrote that he was very glad Monsignor Montini had been appointed as Arch-bishop of Milan. 'If it means – as it almost certainly does – that he becomes *primus papabali*, it is a good thing for us.' No one had built up Montini's interest in Ireland more than the long-serving Ambassador to the Holy See.[93]

From now on, however, McQuaid would have to promote himself in Rome, without either Walshe's or Montini's guiding hand. Compensation for the loss of Walshe's advice was McQuaid's inheritance of his house in Rathgar, a windfall which became a subject of friction between the Arch-bishop and the Department of External Affairs.[94]

McQuaid, the vigilante

While harmony prevailed between the new Costello Government and the Palace, McQuaid's attitude to cultural developments grew more pro-nouncedly Catholic. He told an International Congress of Catholic Doc-tors, debating world population explosion, to close ranks in the face of theories and practices that were 'but a cancellation of human nature'.[95]

On the centenary of the Catholic University of Ireland, he charac-terised it and its successor, UCD, as 'Renaissance agencies of age-old scholarship' which linked 'the early Sophists, the monastic teachers, the medieval philosophers and the scholars of our time'.[96]

Addressing the International Catholic Cinema Congress, McQuaid told its members that they would find in Ireland an outlook that derived from acceptance of the Catholic faith.[97] 'In the judgment of films one must purge one's soul of the decadence caused by the writing of novelists called Catholic, however loud be the world-wide noise of undiscriminating praise,' he said, referring to the placing of Graham Greene's *The Power and the Glory* on the Vatican's Index of Forbidden Books by the head of the Holy Office, Cardinal Pizzardo. Although first published in 1948, Greene's novel about a whiskey priest had come under fire, in the author's own words, from two fronts – Hollywood and the Vatican. A new edition with an introduction by François Mauriac became a success in post-war France, and inspired the Irish-American director, John Ford, to produce a somewhat sanitised film version of the novel as *The Fugitive*.[98]

Fearful that Catholic Ireland could succumb to Communism and liberalism, as in Poland and Hungary, McQuaid had also set up a Vigilance Committee which took as much interest in Teddy Boys as it did in writers. 'Indecency was the order of the night,' a spy reported to McQuaid in 1955 about the Mambo Club, 'a mad house' where teenagers went to dance to the new rock and roll. 'Without any supervision, anything could happen,' the informant wrote.[99]

The Vigilance Committee cast its net wide in search of un-Catholic activity. McQuaid asked the group for information about 104 individuals, a list of suspects which included members of the People's College, the Irish Housewives' Association (he felt not enough Catholic women were joining), Dublin dance-halls, the Unemployed Self Help, the IRA, leading left-wingers and the Irish Workers' League.[100]

Running out of patience with Fr Fahey and Maria Duce, McQuaid rebuked Bishop Staunton for giving an imprimatur to Fahey's book on *The Kingship of Christ and the Conversion of the Jewish Nation* after making it known that he did not want the book sold in Dublin.[101] When Fahey died in January 1954, McQuaid pointedly did not attend the funeral. Maria Duce did not long survive its creator. Having already expressed disapproval of the title Maria Duce, McQuaid directed it to change its name in December 1954.[102]

When the Episcopal-Academic Committee agreed to establish a Chair of Theology at University College, Cork, in 1954, McQuaid's attitude to the appointment gave a telling insight into his outlook on the jurisdiction of an individual bishop. Drafting the statute governing the chair, McQuaid strongly supported giving Bishop Lucey of Cork rather than the Hierarchy the power of appointment and removal. 'The Bishop has to live beside and control such a Professor,' he explained.[103]

Even more remarkably, two days before his sixtieth birthday in July 1955, McQuaid admitted privately to the new Papal Nuncio, Archbishop Alberto Levame, that he was in breach of the law by refusing to sanction the erection in Dun Laoghaire of a major work of religious art by the Irish-American artist, Andrew O'Connor. Responding to enquiries from the Vatican about 'aberrations' in church art and architecture, he told Levame: 'I have succeeded in having quietly set aside a massive bronze statue of Christ the King which in my view and in the opinion of Catholic experts is gravely repugnant to Catholic taste.'[104]

The 5.5 metre bronze sculpture, which was first exhibited at the 1926 Paris Salon, was subscribed to by Protestants and Catholics and in 1932 was chosen as the Christ the King monument for Dun Laoghaire for the Eucharistic Congress celebrations. Cast by Rudier in the 1930s, the 3.5 tonnes of valuable metal were hidden during the Emergency, and in 1949 it was brought to Dun Laoghaire where it would occupy a commanding position for the Holy Year.[105]

However, McQuaid made his opposition to the sculpture clear to the public trustees, Dun Laoghaire Corporation, who felt obliged not to erect it. 'If the question of the erection of the statue were tested in the Civil Courts, I would certainly lose the case,' McQuaid told Levame. 'Therefore I have refrained from any public act which would make an issue of this statue.'[106]

Taken in conjunction with McQuaid's public claim 'to represent the heart of the Catholic people' of Ireland in 'the genuine accents of the Faith,' this private admission of acting above the secular law was his boldest enunciation of his confessional power. But he was about to find out that there were limits to that power as far as a tough-minded section of Dublin soccer supporters were concerned.

20

McQuaid's Drumbeats
1955–59

'Cut off almost completely from the Catholic thought of
our time in Europe, we enjoy the stagnant peace of a
backwater.'

Roland Burke Savage S.J., Studies, *1955.*

A few days before the Republic of Ireland was due to play an international
soccer match against Yugoslavia in October 1955, the secretary of the
Football Association of Ireland, Joe Wickham, received a phone-call from
the Chancellor of the Dublin Diocese, Fr John O'Regan. O'Regan had
three messages for the FAI: Archbishop McQuaid had heard with regret
that the match had been arranged; he further regretted that his views on
the fixture had not been sought, as they had been in 1952; and he suggested that if it were at all possible even at this late stage the game might
be cancelled as a protest against the persecution of Cardinal Aloys
Stepinac by Marshall Tito's Communist regime.[1]

Denying that any discourtesy had been intended towards the Archbishop, Wickham reminded O'Regan that when Yugoslavia had been
scheduled to play in Dublin three years earlier, McQuaid was asked for his
opinion but indicated that he was not interested in soccer. However, His
Grace had suggested that if the association could get out of it discreetly
the match should be called off, which it was.[2]

Arguing that the situation now was different from 1952 when the
Cold War was at its height, Wickham told O'Regan that the Irish Republic
and Yugoslavia belonged to the European Football Federation, which had
no interest in either politics or religion. Anyway, it was too late to call off
the match this time.

O'Regan's phone-call was not the first difficulty which Wickham
had encountered. Two days previously, a Department of Justice official
had phoned to ask him if he was aware that permission was necessary to
allow the Yugoslavs to enter the country. This shook Wickham, who told
the official that for 20 years visiting teams had made their own travel
arrangements and the FAI had never asked for such permission before.

When Wickham, accompanied by the FAI President and former Minister for Defence, Oscar Traynor T.D., went to meet the Secretary of the Department of Justice, Tommy Coyne, Coyne demanded the names of all 22 players and officials in the Yugoslav party and a guarantee that the FAI would pay the expenses of any visiting Iron Curtain player who might seek refugee status in Ireland.

Neither Traynor nor Wickham were aware that Coyne's obstructive approach was the result of a Government decision to oppose the Yugoslav game, which came on foot of a private discussion between the Taoiseach, John A. Costello, and McQuaid. Costello had concurred with the Archbishop's objections and secured Government agreement to advise President Seán T. O'Kelly not to attend the match. This was an embarrassing U-turn for the Government, which had given O'Kelly the go-ahead to welcome the Yugoslav team formally and watch them play at Dalymount Park. When O'Kelly was informed of the decision he asked to speak directly to Costello, but if he had been prepared to dispute the matter his opposition vanished when he was told of the Archbishop's attitude. Two other Government ministers, including Tánaiste William Norton, also cancelled.[3]

Faced with this exceptional turnaround, an emergency meeting of the FAI was convened at which its chairman, S.R. Prole, told members that the match had been arranged in good faith and its cancellation would jeopardise Ireland's standing in international soccer. This stance was supported by the chairman of the Leinster FAI, Leo Carey, who proposed that the fixture should go ahead without further discussion, a move promptly seconded by District Justice E. Ó Riain of Limerick. The only dissenting voice came from the Army Athletic Association representative, Lt. Col. Gunn.

When McQuaid's opposition to the match became news, the No.1 Army Band, which had already begun practising the Yugoslav national anthem, reneged on its engagement. No other band was free to deputise. Transport FC announced that it would not attend a post-match dinner in honour of the Slavs. Soccer commentator Philip Greene said that he would not be available if Radio Éireann went ahead with the broadcast.[4]

Meanwhile, Catholic lay organisations sprang into action, spreading moral indignation throughout the capital in favour of a boycott. The Archbishop's chief associates, the Knights of St Columbanus, made their headquarters the centre for 'a combined protest' from Catholic bodies.[5] The Guilds of Regnum Christi issued a protest statement. The head of the Catholic Boy Scouts, J.B. Whelehan, accused the FAI of entertaining 'the tools of Tito in the capital city of Catholic Ireland'. The Catholic Association for International Relations branded the Yugoslav team as puppets of a Communist state. The League of the Kingship of Christ (*An Ríoghacht*) warned that the Yugoslav team represented 'a tyrannous regime of persecution'. Schoolboys were warned not to go to the match on pain of mortal sin. The Irish team's coach, Dick Hearns, a Garda, made himself unavailable for the game.

The Yugoslav team was oblivious to this unholy rumpus until its aeroplane landed for a stop-over in London, where the players were briefed by Yugoslav diplomats that a churchman had stirred up opposition to the match, though it was going ahead as planned. The Ambassador, Dr Velibit, who had previously worked in Rome, where he saw cardinals attending Italy's matches against Communist countries, expressed his bemusement that the Archbishop of Dublin was not observing the teaching of Pope Pius XII that politics should not interfere with sports. Velibit assigned a Yugoslav journalist to act as press attaché to the team and handle its public relations.

The Yugoslav aeroplane touched down shortly before midnight at Dublin airport, where it was met by FAI chiefs, and the team was taken to the Gresham Hotel in O'Connell St under heavy police escort. At a news conference in the hotel lobby the chairman of the Yugoslav Football Association, Rabo Dugnovic, declared that this was the first time a protest had been made against the team, which had played on all five continents! When a reporter asked for their reaction to Archbishop McQuaid's protest against the imprisonment of Cardinal Stepinac, Dugnovic's interpreter turned away from the Irish journalists and said aloud to his colleagues: 'We completely ignore it.'

That morning *The Irish Times* carried a front-page report that Radio Éireann would not broadcast the match, but that demand for tickets was good. A statement issued in London by Velibit, regretting 'the campaign of intolerance' by the Archbishop of Dublin, was widely quoted, and press coverage aroused a degree of sympathy for the Slavs, who won round one of the propaganda war against the Palace.[6]

On Wednesday evening, the 21,400 supporters who turned out at Dalymount Park had to pass a picket of Legion of Mary members carrying anti-Communist placards. There was a thunderous cheer for Traynor, a former Shelbourne and Belfast Celtic goalkeeper, when he assumed O'Kelly's ceremonial duties and welcomed the Yugoslav team onto the pitch. Liam Tuohy, who was making his debut for the Irish team, recalls the Yugoslav players blessing themselves as they came out of the tunnel. 'There were nearly more Catholics on their side than there were on ours,' he recalled in an interview in 1998.[7]

Although most of the supporters were there to see the match, quite a substantial section of the crowd was composed of non-soccer fans who had decided to register a protest against McQuaid's campaign. In solidarity with Traynor, his colleague in the old IRA, Dan Breen, a Gaelic Athletic Association devotee, attended the match 'to fire his last shot for Ireland'.[8] The Irish could have done with more of his firing power. Yugoslavia beat the Republic of Ireland 4–1.

However, next day, in conversation with one of the Archbishop's secretaries, the secretary at the Papal Nunciature, Monsignor Gaetano Alibrandi, described McQuaid's protest as 'magnificent and splendid'. His assessment concurred with the diocesan office's view that the general impression in Dublin was that the match could not have been allowed to pass in silence. McQuaid received letters from other bishops congratulating him on his 'exceedingly timely intervention'.[9] From Paris, the Croat section of the Confederation of French Christian Workers wrote to express their admiration and gratitude.[10] In response, McQuaid assured the Confederation President, Miro Mrsic, that he was following events closely in Croatia and was praying for a return of peace and justice to their Catholic country.[11]

The emotions stirred up by McQuaid's campaign saw Wickham denounced from the pulpit in his parish church in Larkhill on two consecutive Sundays after the match, when a Fr O'Sullivan called him a Judas who had sold Christ the King for a mere game of football, and worse still, 'a Protestant Catholic'. Angry at being branded as 'a poor class of Catholic' in the eyes of his neighbours, Wickham wrote to the Papal Nuncio, Archbishop Alberto Levame, asking whether the priest was expressing a personal view or was it Church teaching that he was guilty of mortal sin.[12]

Levame passed Wickham's letter on to McQuaid for comment. The Archbishop informed the Nuncio that O'Sullivan was one of his best priests, noted for his visitation of the people, the sick and the dying, but he grudgingly admitted that O'Sullivan had exceeded the bounds of moderation and promised to 'speak to him quietly about the matter'.[13]

McQuaid's stance earned him international notoriety. He was the butt of jokes on BBC television and the organ of the right-wing social movement in Milan, *Il Borghese*, lampooned him as *Un Monsignore D'Altri Tempi* ('a monsignor of olden days').[14] TASS lambasted him as a Cold War churchman. A letter with a Belfast postmark reached him despite bearing the unorthodox address: 'His Grace Archbishop McQuaid, Primate of Ireland and Ruler of Éire, Dublin, The Papal State.' The envelope contained a press report which praised the FAI for showing 'much daring' against the might of the Roman Church, and it claimed the Archbishop's intervention justified Ulster's fear that Dublin rule would mean Rome rule if there were a united Ireland. The anonymous sender added his own jibe: 'THAT SHOOK YOU'.[15]

McQuaid's action had a huge impact on Ulster Protestants, according to the writer Sam McAughtry, who recalls the incident being a topic of heated conversation in the pubs and clubs of East Belfast. 'It was not so much a case of knowing who Archbishop John Charles McQuaid was, though his name did become known,' McAughtry said. 'It was more the fact that a bishop had shown us that it was the Roman Catholic Church that ruled in the South.'[16]

One of the most outspoken critics of the boycott attempt was the Stormont Minister for Education, Harry Midgley. Condemning McQuaid's role as 'one of the most monumental pieces of clerical interference' ever seen in Ireland, Midgley said it vindicated those who believed that the Catholic Hierarchy in Ireland presumed to be not only the controllers of faith and morals but of every other field of human activity.[17]

In a similar vein, a writer in the *Belfast Telegraph* described McQuaid's intervention as grotesque, and said it proved the existence of an 'invisible curtain' of religious division between Northern Ireland and the Republic that was a real as 'the iron one' between East and West. The writer also warned that such misconceived interference in civil affairs could lead tragically to an increase in the already latent anti-clerical feeling in the country.[18]

Perhaps the most damning comment on the Yugoslav episode was a letter to McQuaid from P.J. Kilroy in Manchester, who pointed out that it was only in impoverished, depopulated, whited-sepulchre Ireland that religion was dragged into the sporting scene. 'The Church in Éire, or at least the Hierarchy, have taken a semi-public stand of not wanting to end the evil of Partition,' he wrote. 'They rather appear to envisage a small and semi-Fascist State, dominated by the Hierarchy from whence the people flee, from which the young and the life-blood flows, where old people toil on the land and where whole districts are unnaturally silent, where a Government exists on a false economy of millions of pounds in remittances from emigrants in Britain, America and elsewhere.'[19]

This was a widely shared perception of Ireland in the mid-1950s. In June 1956, provisional census figures put the Republic's population at 2,894,822, the lowest ever recorded and five per cent lower than when the State was founded in 1922. In the decade from 1951 to 1961, some 420,000 Irish people emigrated. Trade and agriculture were depressed, unemployment continued to rise, and marriage rates were dangerously low. A book edited by Irish-American writer John A. O'Brien, *The Vanishing Irish*, asserted that there was powerful evidence that the once populous Ireland was rapidly dying out.

Against such a bleak background, McQuaid's bullying of the FAI has never been forgotten by a section of the Dublin public: it was 'an own goal' that guaranteed him an unenviable place in Dublin folklore. Shortly before his death in 1998, comedian Dermot Morgan was working on a film based on the match, in which he meant to cast McQuaid as a Hitler-like figure.[20] Other writers, like the dramatist Fr Desmond Forristal, have argued that in the Yugoslav episode McQuaid pioneered the sports' boycott as a means of achieving a civil-rights principle, as later practised by the Anti-Apartheid movement against sports' fixtures involving South Africa.[21] Supporters of this viewpoint instance the importance of this principle when another Irish Republic versus Yugoslavia match was opposed in 1999, in protest at the ethnic cleansing being carried out in Kosovo by President Milosevic's forces.

McQuaid was genuinely sincere in his protest, but the records show that his methods, using his chancellor and Catholic lay organisations to spread fear through the city, were secretive and manipulative. His contacts with the Taoiseach, the Department of Justice and the Garda Síochána ensured that the control which he exercised over 'official' Ireland was almost total: no minister of state or municipal representative attended the match.[22]

It was wishful thinking for a member of the Association of Civil Liberties, Christopher Gore-Grimes, to tell a students' meeting that the 21,400 attendance proved that Ireland was no longer a clerical State. Yet he had a point. This was a populist revolt against McQuaid's iron rule; the first of his reign. Coming so soon after the controversy over the Mother and Child Scheme in 1950–51, the long-term loser was McQuaid, who after 1955 never regained the level of respect he had enjoyed among the working class as a result of his social work. Nor was the protest confined to the working class. Quite a number of future public servants, lawyers and schoolteachers defied the McQuaid-inspired vigilantism of Dublin's moral majority. The Archbishop was developing an image of being remote, absolutist, and out of touch.[23]

Soccer padres

Characteristically, the lesson McQuaid drew from the Yugoslav episode was that he needed to gain control over the FAI. This view was shared by Costello, who had told McQuaid privately that the FAI acted in bad faith. McQuaid therefore set up a committee of four priests[24] under the chairmanship of Fr George Finnegan to explore 'the means of apostolate among the Football Association's followers'.[25] Behind the spiritual rhetoric was a hard-headed list of practical objectives drawn up by Finnegan and approved by McQuaid. 'It would prove difficult, especially in the beginning, to influence directly the central committee of the FAI,' Finnegan advised. 'However, it should prove possible to exercise an influence indirectly through club representatives on the Central Committee.'

Finnegan explained that some priests were already presidents or vice-presidents of junior clubs, and that there was room for priests to take up similar honorary positions in senior clubs over time. There was also scope for priests to organise soccer leagues between altar boys from different parishes and streets, and as soccer was played at Clonliffe College, students who were keen on the game could be encouraged to continue their interest after ordination by turning out regularly in a priests' team.[26]

This strategy was implemented, and in due course McQuaid was encouraged by the numbers of 'boy footballers' who were attending retreats. Later, when the question of a special Mass for all FAI members was raised (Protestants had their own service), one of McQuaid's secretaries, Fr J. Ardle MacMahon, advised against it as it would attract publicity.[27] MacMahon also advised Finnegan to have Frank Duff set up a Legion of Mary Praesidium that would encourage boys not to play soccer on Sunday mornings in the Phoenix Park but to go to Mass instead![28] Finnegan had so won McQuaid's trust that he was mandated to approach the FAI to abort a planned B international between the Republic of Ireland and Romania in October 1957. Finnegan was asked to approach some high FAI official to lodge an informal request with FIFA not to embarrass Ireland with these requests.[29]

The workers' faith

Maintaining religious practice among the working class was a basic part of McQuaid's strategy of keeping control in his city. 'Unless Dublin maintains the faith in the working-class families, it will be disastrous for the rest of Ireland,' he told a missionary bishop. 'And that is my aim with the few priests at my disposal.'[30] Always seeking new recruits to the priesthood, McQuaid believed that vocations would come from Catholic homes characterised by simple faith and piety.[31] This 'overwhelming piety' was observed by the German writer, Heinrich Böll, in Westland Row Church after the *Tantum Ergo* at evening Benediction. 'In Germany you would not see that many people coming out of church after Easter Mass or at Christmas,' he wrote in *The Green Island*, a book which romanticised McQuaid's Dublin for several generations of German readers.[32]

As the hectic church and school building programmes went on unabated in areas like Inchicore, Dundrum, Garretstown and Skerries, McQuaid instructed Religious Orders to observe a deal which he had negotiated with the trade unions, giving construction workers a paid day off to attend to their religious duties on feast days.[33] The targeting of the working class was intensified with the setting up of the Dublin Adult Education Committee as an adjunct to the Institute of Catholic Sociology. Lectures were organised in outlying parishes and a Social Study Conference was organised annually. Originally held in Clonliffe College, the attendance grew so large that the venue switched to the National Boxing Stadium on the South Circular Rd.[34]

McQuaid cultivated the traditional promotion of saints to underpin the devotionalism of the working class and enhance the prestige of the diocese. Having failed in his attempt to secure the beatification of his former friend, Brother Gaspard O'Reilly, McQuaid had more success with the process for the reformed alcoholic, Matt Talbot, whose grave in Glasnevin cemetery had become a shrine where the unemployed came to pray for work.[35] A consultative committee selected a list of Irish martyrs

from the post-Reformation period as a representative group, whose cause
for beatification McQuaid believed could be put forward with real hope of
success.[36] As a prelude to opening the cause of his former Clongowes
teacher, Fr John Sullivan S.J., his remains were removed from Clongowes
to Gardiner St Church, where McQuaid blessed them.[37] He also promoted the cause of Père Lamy to baffled Irish audiences, and provided
evidence on his behalf to the French authorities.[38]

The piety of women remained an essential feature of Dublin
Catholic life. McQuaid arranged for each parish to send £2 as 'a collective
gift from the women of Ireland' to help erect a basilica in Rome in honour
of the Queenship of Our Lady.[39] Despite his promotion of Our Lady, he
stamped out any signs of financial or emotional exploitation of her cult –
an attempt by the Oblate Fathers to transform the Inchicore shrine into a
sort of Lourdes was unanimously condemned by his Council as a potential
abuse. When McQuaid heard that pilgrims were coming to Inchicore from
St Peter's parish in Belfast, he asked the Bishop of Down and Connor,
Daniel Mageean, to stop them. 'The parishioners of St Peter's will find
nothing at Inchicore that they cannot find in their own parish of St
Peter's,' he told Mageean.[40]

McQuaid continued to watch over the minutiae of diocesan
administration with a hawk-like eye. The parish priest of Home Farm Rd,
Fr Edward Gallen, received a curt refusal when he asked Fr Mangan for a
letter of introduction for a Mr O'Brien who was to attend a Caritas meeting in Berlin: 'The AB is not a penny-in-the-slot-machine.'[41] In line with
his dislike of modern art, McQuaid disapproved of the cover of *Little Boy
Jesus in a Carpenter's Shop*, which he thought too naturalistic, and forced
the publishers to withdraw the book.[42] He himself enjoyed adulatory
acclaim for his book *Wellsprings of the Faith*, a collection of his Pastoral Letters and addresses which was published in 1957.[43]

McQuaid was especially proud to open Our Lady's Hospital for Sick
Children in Crumlin, the culmination of work which he had begun almost
20 years earlier on behalf of Archbishop Byrne. Addressing 200 members
of the International Hospitals' Federation, he explained that the Crumlin
hospital had received generous grants from the Hospitals' Sweepstake
Fund, but 'without Governmental violation of the free character of its
work' as part of the traditional voluntary sector. McQuaid had reached a
private deal with the Minister for Health which enabled him to reverse
his previous position of shunning Sweepstake monies.[44]

Through his special contacts with Costello, McQuaid also persuaded the Government to accept his proposal for the coordination of
University College Dublin's Medical School with the four hospitals under
his management.[45] So confident had McQuaid become of his control over
the medical sector that he referred to the errors of 'some persons who
have given themselves the vocation to manage us like children and to

control us, soul and body', a clear reference to Dr Nöel Browne and the Labour Party.[46]

The social reality was not as pleasant as McQuaid was wont to portray. In 1955 there were about 4,000 children in foster homes throughout the country, supervised by officers who had no specialised training in child care. Reviewing the problem, the head of the Catholic Social Welfare Bureau, Fr Cecil Barrett, told McQuaid that it was important UCD should provide a child-care course before Trinity College did. 'With proper training, the social workers could be of much assistance to the Church in counteracting the dangers of the Welfare State,' he thought. McQuaid duly took up the matter with the Hierarchy and UCD. [47]

The Minister for External Affairs, Liam Cosgrave, defused a potential crisis in 1956, after a British newspaper breached the news blackout ordered by McQuaid six years earlier about the American adoptions. For the first time, the Irish public learned about what diplomats privately admitted was a 'baby trade' that was not entirely under control. In the Dáil, Cosgrave confirmed that from January 1, 1953, when the Adoption Act came into force, until June 1956, passports had been issued to 543 'illegitimate' children to allow them travel to America. With most Dáil deputies satisfied that the paramount religious needs of the children were being catered for, Cosgrave dampened down a call from Donogh O'Malley of Fianna Fáil for an investigation of the system, warning that he would not attach significance to a yellow British Sunday newspaper which had tried to smear Ireland. The issue was not raised again in the Dáil.

It was raised, however, within Government by the Minister for Health, Tom O'Higgins, who questioned the system in correspondence with Longford County Council, but O'Higgins lost out in the ensuing row between External Affairs and Health. Meanwhile, McQuaid's expert, Fr Barrett, worked with the Department of External Affairs to formulate a new statement of Government policy, though the new line was put on the back burner until disclosures in Washington about the inadequacies of Catholic charities obliged the Department of External Affairs to enforce tighter regulations on child placement in early 1956. However, it was not until July 1957 that McQuaid was able to meet the new practices and have them enforced by nuns in other dioceses.[48]

McQuaid and the bishops enjoyed such a degree of power that they could rely on the Secretary of the Department of Justice, Tommy Coyne, to do battle for them against the the vintners' lobby, which was continuing to press for Sunday opening. 'It must be regarded as a closed issue,' Coyne told the vintners, reminding them of the Episcopal veto on Sunday pints in 1950. 'The Hierarchy cannot be expected to eat their words without losing face; and what is worse, shaking people's faith in their competence to expound the Canon Law.'[49] Costello kept McQuaid informed of

Government policy when the IRA renewed its 'armed struggle', while McQuaid used his influence with the Hierarchy to issue a pastoral condemning 'secret societies' and urged his priests to talk 'quietly' to IRA men to dissuade them from violence.[50]

In response to a suggestion by the Minister for Education, General Richard Mulcahy, that education was in a 'fluid position', the Hierarchy warned him that it would never consent to any reform which would involve any change in the denominational character of the schools at all stages.[51]

McQuaid was crestfallen when he heard that Costello had appointed the writer, Seán Ó Faoláin, as the first director of the Arts Council. Under pressure from McQuaid, Costello tried to withdraw his offer and to persuade the former Director of the National Art Gallery, Thomas Bodkin, to take the post instead. This shocked Bodkin, who had witnessed Costello offering Ó Faoláin the position only a week earlier. McQuaid spent over an hour trying to coax Bodkin to take the job, but Bodkin would not budge even when McQuaid begged him as his Archbishop 'to accept and prevent that man from being appointed'. When Ó Faoláin's appointment was finally confirmed, Costello asked for McQuaid's prayers, if not his blessing. 'I can only hope that the nominee will not let you down,' McQuaid replied.[52]

The Statutes of Maynooth

The Catholic Church's place in Irish history had never been so strong when McQuaid assembled with the other bishops and heads of religious orders at Maynooth on August 6, 1956, for a Plenary Council, the fourth since the Synod of Thurles in 1850. Convened under the presidency of Cardinal D'Alton, its purpose was to update Church law governing the lives of Catholics. In all, the Synod produced 335 decrees, known as the Maynooth Statutes, to which McQuaid and his colleagues signed their names in Latin before solemnly despatching them to Rome for approval.

The Synod was a major triumph for McQuaid, whose ban on attendance at Trinity College was extended to all dioceses. The bishops, declaring it to be a mortal sin to attend Trinity, delegated to McQuaid the supervisory authority over all applications. 'Only the Archbishop of Dublin is competent to decide, in accordance with the norms of the instructions of the Holy See, in what circumstances and with what guarantees against the danger of perversion, attendance at that College may be tolerated.'[53]

It was McQuaid who told the Religious Orders, even those like the Capuchins which enjoyed exemptions granted by Rome, the limits of their jurisdiction when they formed the Conference of Major Religious Superiors to co-ordinate their activities and common interests. 'I felt that it was an occasion for laying down once and for all the principles governing cooperation and thus prevent intrusion into our proper sphere,' he explained to Bishop Collier, who shared his view that coexistence could prosper between the Hierarchy and the conference on the basis of Episcopal supremacy.[54]

The resurgence of anti-Communist feeling following the Soviet Union's brutal suppression of revolution in Hungary in October 1956 reinforced what Professor Tom Garvin has described as the climate of 'clerical absolutism in Ireland. McQuaid submitted an aid scheme to the Government which was read out to the Cabinet by Costello and referred to General Seán MacEoin who, as Minister for Defence, was charged with responsibility for Red Cross intervention.[55] McQuaid collected £31,823 (£576,000) for the victims of Communist tyranny in Hungary which he lodged with Levame for transmission to the Pope.[56]

Older Dubliners recall his spectacular entry to a performance of Handel's *Messiah* by Our Lady's Choral Society in the former Theatre Royal. The place was in darkness; the choir was about to commence its first recital when suddenly a single spotlight picked out the splendid red robes of a thin austere figure who was taking his place in the distinguished visitors' box; at that moment, the choir chanted in Latin – *Ecce Homo* – here is the man. McQuaid bowed slightly in recognition of his due.[57]

Without pastoral experience, McQuaid's managerial style was that of the headmaster of the élite boarding school he once was: he would assign good reports to those priests and laity who pleased him and he would punish or freeze out those who disobeyed his wishes. A superworkaholic, he not only kept duplicated copies of letters in his small but finely chiselled handwriting, he also drafted many of the replies which were sent out in the names of his secretaries.

In a decade during which Irish people emigrated in droves, another important part of McQuaid's power-base was his position as the link between Government and Hierarchy on the issue of looking after the spiritual needs of Ireland's emigrants. He sent two priests to England, one to work at a labour camp, another in the hotels of central London. 'Africa is an easy apostolate in contrast,' he told a missionary bishop.[58] To supplement his diocesan clergy, McQuaid reached agreement with the Columban Fathers to send three of their priests to England also.[59]

McQuaid shared responsibility with the Minister for External Affairs, Liam Cosgrave, for establishing an inter-departmental committee on legislation to licence agencies offering employment for boys and girls in England.[60] McQuaid also urged the Government to request Irish newspapers not to carry advertisement for lodgings in England without consulting the Catholic Social Welfare Bureau, which would advise on their suitability.[61] He also secured the Hierarchy's agreement to help fund a newspaper for emigrants, with each parish subscribing £3 as its contribution to the seed capital. In cooperation with the Archbishop of

Personifying the splendour of the Catholic Church at a ceremony in Meath in 1943, at which McQuaid displays the Borgia ring.

The brash Archbishop of New York, Cardinal Francis Spellman, who was suspected of conspiring to cheat John Charles McQuaid of a Cardinal's Red Hat from Pope Pius XII in 1946.

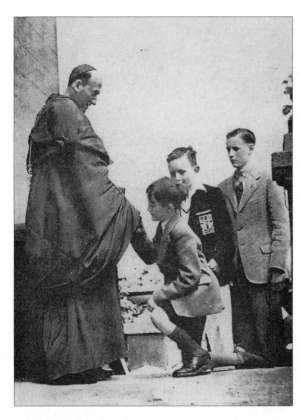

Blackrock boys kiss His Grace's ring on Pentecost Sunday 1949, the year of McQuaid's priestly Silver Jubilee.

Joe Walshe, the devout diplomat who counselled the Archbishop of Dublin to strengthen the influence of Irish Catholicism in the Vatican on the basis of its world-wide diaspora.

Ashurst, the magnificent Victorian Gothic building in Killiney, Co. Dublin, which McQuaid purchased in 1945 and renamed Notre Dame des Bois, Our Lady of the Woodlands.

Taking photographs while relaxing in the grounds of Notre Dame des Bois was one of the Archbishop's hobbies.

In homage of St Columbanus: The Fianna Fáil leader, Éamon de Valera, kisses the ring of the Papal Nuncio to France, Archbishop Angelo Roncalli, later Pope John XXIII, watched by the Minister for External Affairs, Seán MacBride, Archbishop McQuaid and Taoiseach John A. Costello at a jovial luncheon during the Luxeuil Columbanus Congress in 1950.

Greeting Pope Pius XII in Rome during the Holy Year, 1950, escorted by Cardinal Alfredo Ottaviani.

The Old Guard (*from left*): Archbishop Charles Heerey C.S.Sp., Monsignor Alfred O'Rahilly, Cardinal John D'Alton, President Éamon de Valera, McQuaid and the founder of the Legion of Mary, Frank Duff.

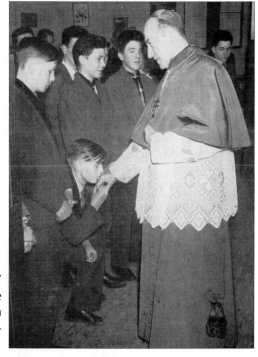

McQuaid in 'his gear' at the boys' club in Eccles Street, which Finance Minister, Charles Haughey, praised in 1963 as an instance of the Archbishop's charitable work.

The Last Hurrah: The Papal Legate to the 1961 Patrician Congress, Cardinal Gregory Peter Agagianian, is met by Taoiseach Seán Lemass and Archbishop McQuaid at Dublin Airport. In the background are the Vatican official and future Bishop of Clonfert, Dr Tom Ryan, and Tánaiste Seán MacEntee.

The Papal Legate, Cardinal Agagianian, and Archbishop McQuaid smile benignly at children brought to meet them at Clonliffe College during the Patrician Congress of 1961.

The 2,500 bishops attending the Second Vatican Council, 1962–65, convened by Pope John XXIII to renew and reform the Roman Catholic Church.

Despite his opposition to ecumenism, Dr McQuaid's admired 'the gentleness' of the Church of Ireland Archbishop of Dublin, George Otto Simms.

Uncertain of his future, Archbishop McQuaid scrutinises Pope Paul VI as the image-conscious Pontiff studiously looks at the Vatican photographer's camera.

Unpublished cartoon by Kilroy (Micheál Ó Nualláin), which was commissioned by *The Irish Tim*
in 1971 at the time of Senator Mary Robinson's Family Planning Bill.

If umbrellas could only shoot! The deposed
McQuaid goes for a walk with his successor
Fr Dermot Ryan.

Westminster, Bernard Griffin, he arranged a system for placing Irish workers under the care of the Irish priests.[62]

In the general election of March 1957, which de Valera won with his biggest ever majority, a former IRA man, Jack Murphy, was elected to the Dáil for the Unemployed Protest Committee. After Finance Minister, Frank Aiken, introduced a severe budget, Murphy implored McQuaid to intercede on behalf of the unemployed, old-age pensioners and lower income groups. Instead of offering public support, McQuaid privately advised Murphy to resign his Dáil seat. Murphy, McQuaid wrote of their meeting, 'was in poor health, unable to work, disillusioned and pursued by Communists. He agreed very honestly. Got him a job on New Church, Gloucester Rd.' Murphy subsequently left Ireland for Canada, another refugee emigré.[63]

Despite the appalling scale of emigration and unemployment, there was a grave shortage of trained women teachers, partly as the result of an explosion in the number of primary-school pupils, but mainly because women teachers were required to give up teaching on getting married. This ban, which dated from the early 1930s, had assumed 'a moral character' that many Catholics thought was an unchangeable feature of their faith. When the Minister for Education, Jack Lynch, indicated that he wanted to repeal the ban, he was advised that the bishops would never agree. 'I cannot say what opposition there was among the members of the Hierarchy, indeed if any, but I know that in Archbishop McQuaid I had a powerful ally in effecting this very necessary reform,' Lynch later recalled.[64] The Hierarchy minute for June 1958 records no dissent. 'A memorandum from the Minister for Education setting out the reasons which induced him to discontinue the marriage ban was duly noted.'

In May 1957, McQuaid's sister, Helen, who had retired from her medical practice in London and returned to Ireland, died suddenly as she was sitting in one of the living rooms at Killiney. She complained of feeling a breeze, and as the curtains were being closed she died, aged 62.[65] McQuaid broke down crying in the sacristy at her funeral Mass. When he regained his composure, he gave a few pounds to the sacristan, Joe Doyle, a future Fine Gael politician and Lord Mayor of Dublin. 'He was at his most human that day,' Senator Doyle recalls.[66] A month later he broke down in front of his secretary. 'Today a month ago I lost Helen,' he explained to Mangan, tears running down his cheeks. This was the first and only experience Mangan had of his real emotions.[67]

Fethard-on-Sea: McQuaid on the fence

At a time when McQuaid was deeply depressed, mourning the loss of his sister, the Taoiseach, Éamon de Valera, turned to him for help in resolving a boycott by Catholics of Protestant businesses in the small Wexford town of Fethard-on-Sea. The boycott had begun to attract widespread and adverse publicity, and was calling Ireland's reputation for tolerance into question internationally. The Archbishop agreed to meet de Valera only on condition that their conversation was 'strictly confidential'.[68] He was well-acquainted with the Hook peninsula in Wexford, where he often stayed on short holidays, and familiar with the background to the boycott, which he regarded fundamentally as a matter of principle relating to implementation of the Catholic Church's law on mixed marriage.

At the centre of the dispute were Sheila Cloney, a member of the Church of Ireland, and her Catholic husband, Seán, a local farmer. Childhood sweethearts, the couple had married in London in the Augustinian church in Hammersmith and had also received a blessing in a nearby Anglican church. As part of the wedding ceremony, Sheila had signed the *Ne Temere* pledge in the presence of an Augustinian priest, promising to bring their children up as Catholics.

The couple returned to Wexford, where they had two daughters. Their eldest girl, Eileen, was approaching her sixth birthday in 1957 and due to start school that Easter. One day when Seán was working on the farm, the local parish priest called and told Sheila that Eileen would be going to the local Catholic school and that there was nothing she could do about it.

The priest's intervention alienated Sheila, who left home in late April with the two children. A few days later Seán was visited by a Northern Ireland lawyer, Desmond Boal, then an associate of the Rev. Ian Paisley, a firebrand preacher who was making a name for himself as the founder of the Free Presbyterian Church in Ireland. Boal offered to facilitate a reunion between Seán and his wife on three conditions: that he would leave Ireland and live in Australia or Canada, the children would be brought up as Anglicans, and he should convert to Protestantism. It emerged that Sheila and the children were living at the City Mission in Edinburgh; later they sought refuge in the northernmost of the Orkney Islands, Westray.[69]

Meanwhile, word spread in Wexford that Protestant friends had encouraged Sheila to defy the priest by leaving Seán and fleeing to Scotland. The local curate ordered his parishioners to boycott Protestant businesses in the area. Among the victims were Sheila's father, who had given her £40 before her departure, and a Cavan farmer who was mistaken for a Northern Ireland man. A Catholic teaching in the Church of Ireland school was advised by Catholic women to stop working there.

The Government discussed the boycott informally on June 3, but it was not until June 21 that de Valera met McQuaid. De Valera left Drumcondra with the impression that the Archbishop shared his anxiety about the adverse effect the controversy was having on the country's reputation for religious tolerance and fair play. De Valera, however, was unsure whether or not McQuaid would help defuse the situation by counselling his Episcopal colleagues to take a conciliatory line on the issue.

In terms of ecclesiastical authority, McQuaid enjoyed the rank of Metropolitan over three other dioceses – Kildare and Leighlin, Ossory, and Ferns. He was also a close friend of Bishop Staunton of Ferns, whose diocese took in Fethard-on-Sea. Staunton had made no public statement on the boycott, but McQuaid would have known that he felt Sheila had been wrong to renege on her marriage pledge to bring up the children as Catholics.

One bishop who had no qualms about publicly supporting the boycott was Bishop Michael Browne of Galway. In an address to the annual conference of the Catholic Truth Society in Wexford at the end of June, Browne said he believed there was a concerted campaign to kidnap Catholic children and deprive them of their faith. Non-Catholics had not protested against this practice – instead, Protestants had tried to make political capital out of 'a peaceful and moderate protest'.[70] Browne delivered his address in the presence of McQuaid, Cardinal D'Alton and other members of the Hierarchy, none of whom dissented from his remarks. By their silence, the bishops were perceived to endorse the boycott.

When Dr Nöel Browne raised the issue in the Dáil on July 4, de Valera, claiming to speak for 90 per cent of the people, denounced the boycott as ill-conceived, unjust and futile. He begged 'all who have regard for the fair name, good repute and well-being of our nation to use their influence to bring this deplorable affair to a speedy end'. But he also appealed to anyone who might have influence with Sheila 'to urge on her to respect her troth and her promise and to return with her children to her husband and her home'.[71]

De Valera had two purposes: firstly, he was courageously denouncing the boycott on behalf of the majority of the Irish people; and secondly, he was indicating to the Hierarchy that Mrs Cloney should fulfil her *Ne Temere* promise. In doing so, de Valera recognised the validity of the Canon Law regulation as the basis for a solution to the dispute.

McQuaid, who was on one of his regular breaks from Dublin, received a copy of the parliamentary reply, which de Valera sent to him ahead of the Dáil exchanges.[72] 'I am grateful for your courtesy in sending me the reply that you feel bound to express on the incident at Fethard-on-Sea,' McQuaid answered. It was a polite but neutral reply. McQuaid had sat silently on the sectarian fence.[73]

Although the controversy was discussed at the Stormont parliament in Belfast and featured prominently in speeches by the Orange Order on the 12th of July, as well as receiving coverage in *Time* magazine, de Valera's speech helped to bring about a calmer atmosphere. A local T.D., who was also a Knight of St Columbanus, issued a joint statement with Sheila's father appealing for her return. A visit by the parish priest to buy cigarettes in a Protestant shop signalled an end to the boycott. Mrs Cloney and the children returned home on December 31. The couple's daughters did not go to the local school and were educated instead by their parents.

Neither Catholics nor Protestants could claim a final victory at Fethard-on-Sea. It is possible that McQuaid was involved latterly through the Knights in the appeal for Sheila's return, but whatever degree of sympathy McQuaid may have had towards de Valera's moral dilemma, he shared Bishop Browne's gung-ho attitude against mixed marriage.

Indeed, a hardening of the Hierarchy's approach to this front-line issue had been taken at the Maynooth Plenary Council, when the bishops agreed to standardise and strengthen the traditional Forms of Promises signed by the partners in a mixed marriage. These were now to be called Forms of Guarantees, involving a legal declaration rather than just a solemn expression of intent, and the signed guarantee was to be addressed to the bishop in each diocese. This change was awaiting Rome's approval and had not yet been announced publicly. McQuaid was hardly going to break ranks on an issue where there was Episcopal unanimity.[74]

Furthermore, McQuaid's lack of cooperation with de Valera in the Fethard-on-Sea boycott contrasted with the willing assistance which he gave a year earlier to John A. Costello in his difficulties with the Coadjutor Bishop of Killaloe, Joseph Rodgers, in 'the Clondara case', another ugly sectarian squabble, this time in Co. Clare. The case arose when two Jehovah Witnesses were assaulted and their bibles destroyed in a fire by a frenzied crowd cheered on by their parish priest in the village of Clondara. Amazingly, at the subsequent trial the local Justice dismissed the charges against the priest and his parishioners under the Probation of Offenders Act, but bound the two Jehovah Witnesses to the peace on bonds of £200 each; their crime was to have committed blasphemy. Rodgers, who had attended the trial, subsequently wrote to the Taoiseach, criticising the Attorney General for treating the priest and loyal Catholics of Clondara like common criminals 'for their defence of the doctrine of the Blessed Trinity, a doctrine so nobly enshrined in our Constitution'. Rodgers warned Costello that the matter would not rest, and he demanded a guarantee of legal protection against vile and pernicious attacks against the Catholic faith.[75]

Turning to the Archbishop for assistance, Costello showed McQuaid his reply to Rodgers, in which he sympathised with 'the just indignation' of the priest and parishioners, but pointed out that once a complaint had been made by the Jehovah Witnesses, the State had no choice but to investigate and, in the event, bring the matter to court.[76] 'Your statement is admirable in clarity and moderation,' McQuaid replied to Costello. 'I saw the Bishop during the Plenary Council and I think that the incident will not be repeated.'[77]

The key to understanding the attitude of McQuaid and the Catholic bishops in these incidents was their fear that their God-given right to determine the Catholic conscience of a Catholic people was being undermined by a rearguard propaganda battle by the minority Protestant community. Even one of the younger bishops, William Philbin, who became Bishop of Clonfert in 1953, was afflicted with this anxiety. 'A concerted effort is being made by the religious minority to secure a dominating position in our public life,' Philbin said in 1957. 'We are opposed by an extremely efficient propaganda machine.'[78]

Four decades further on, the archives show that even though they enjoyed a position of largely undisputed majoritarian rule, McQuaid and the bishops suffered from an inferiority complex in relation to the former Protestant rulers of the country. In particular, they had become paranoid about the activities of the two main organs of Protestantism: *The Irish Times* and Trinity College, Dublin. This formidable 'Protestant propaganda machine', aided and abetted by Catholic liberals and insidious publications from Britain, was they believed undermining the moral monopoly of the Hierarchy.

The minutes of the Hierarchy's meetings for this period show an increasing preoccupation with the need for a public relations bureau which would respond to attacks on the Catholic faith, its bishops and clergy. This was the lesson drawn from the Fethard-on-Sea case by Bishop Staunton, who argued that the defence of Catholic interests through the press was the supremely important challenge facing the Hierarchy.

'The Protestant propaganda, in my opinion successful, was in fact an attack on the Catholic Church, under the guise of an attack on the people of Fethard-on-Sea,' Staunton told McQuaid. 'I felt strongly the want of an organisation, not to defend the people of Fethard-on-Sea, but to put the facts, which I could supply, before the public.'[79]

Neither Staunton nor McQuaid felt disposed to make the kind of apology to the Protestants of Fethard-on-Sea that the Bishop of Ferns, Brendan Comiskey, offered in 1997.

Pius XII's vision

McQuaid's Quinquennial Report to Rome for his *ad limina* visit in September 1957 has not yet been opened by the Dublin diocese, but it probably contains his assessment of the Protestant-liberal propaganda machine's threat to the otherwise solid supremacy of the Hierarchy as the decade entered its last years.

The Rome of Pius XII was also in its final phase. Now aged 81, Pius had become increasingly authoritarian. He had also become more mystical after believing that he was visited by Jesus Christ during an illness in 1953 when it was expected that he would die. The details of what was happening inside the Vatican had been communicated regularly to McQuaid by his Clongowes friend, Daniel O'Connell, now head of the Vatican Observatory at Castel Gandolfo. 'One thing you may take as certain,' O'Connell told McQuaid, 'The Holy Father believes that Our Lord appeared to him at the crisis of his severe illness.'[80]

McQuaid had continued to send the largest sums of money of any Irish prelate to Rome. Prior to his visit, he had given the Pope specially-bound copies of *A Catechism of Catholic Doctrine*, Mary Purcell's biography of Matt Talbot and *Reportorium Novum*, the Dublin diocesan history journal which he had founded. 'The Holy Father is well aware that these volumes owe their publication to Your Grace's pastoral zeal and to your lively interest in all that concerns the historic See of Dublin,' Monsignor Angelo dell'Acqua, Montini's successor in the Secretariat of State, told him. 'He would have me tell you that He was deeply touched by this latest evidence of your unfailing devotion and attachment.'[81]

Yet despite this profession of fealty, the Irish bishops had been at loggerheads with the Curia following a request that the minutes of their meetings be sent to Rome. The bishops took umbrage at this and informed Rome that their meetings were among the first of their kind, and the rules of procedure, which dated from 1882, had long been approved and contained no prescription requiring the sending of minutes to Rome. The bishops wondered if the new demand indicated a want of confidence in them on the part of Pope Pius,[82] but after further discussions they agreed to forward the minutes to the Nunciature for transmission to Rome, though only after they had been approved and authenticated at a further meeting of the Hierarchy.[83]

During his stay in Rome, McQuaid had an audience with the Pope and later met his chief adviser, the German Jesuit Fr Robert Leiber, at a lunch hosted by Dan O'Connell. It was through O'Connell that McQuaid became entangled in the intrigues of the Papal court. After his audience with Pope Pius XII, his housekeeper, Sister Pasqualina, asked O'Connell to give McQuaid a message that the heads of the *Mondo Megliore* (Better World) movement wanted to recruit the Spiritual Director at the Irish College, Monsignor Dominic Conway, but O'Connell replied that such a change would depend on the Irish Hierarchy. According to Pasqualina, the Pope did not mention the matter to McQuaid in case it implied that he was giving an order. There was a hint from Pasqualina that the movement should start in Ireland.[84]

McQuaid was also pleased to learn from O'Connell that the ailing Pontiff had enjoyed a recital by Dublin's Choral Society and had commented on the ladies' dress, which he approved of very highly. 'I mentioned of course that you were responsible for all that,' O'Connell told him.[85]

McQuaid is watching

McQuaid boasted to the Papal Nuncio that Ireland was freer from 'modern aberrations' than any other European country or North America,[86] and indeed it might have been, given the lengths he went to to root out such aberrations at source through his Vigilance Committee and lay societies, principally the Knights of St Columbanus and the Legion of Mary.

The operations of McQuaid's formidable espionage network derived their significance from the reinforcement they afforded to his confidence in his unique understanding of divine providence. Quite how that confidence came to be so complete and could be transmitted so readily to his devoted and uncritical flock is difficult for the contemporary reader to fathom. Psychoanalysts have long held that a person's earliest experiences colour and direct subsequent relationships. The trauma of his early life and consequent need to develop anxiety-reducing strategies would no doubt have led him to simplify, if not indeed to avoid the complexities of day-to-day existence. But this alone cannot fully account for his insistence on the unwavering deference to which he felt his office entitled him. Strongly imbued with a sense of the dignity of that office, McQuaid expected to be deferred to on all matters within his jurisdiction. On hearing that the Bishop of Ardagh and Clonmacnoise, Bishop James McNamee, was in Dublin to have his portrait painted, McQuaid called on the home of the artist, Maurice MacGonigal, to rebuke the visiting prelate for failing to ask his permission 'to enter my diocese'.[87]

The high esteem in which McQuaid held J. Edgar Hoover, the head of the FBI, is one of the most revealing insights into his complex character. McQuaid had little to learn from Hoover in regard to the home-spun intelligence system which he operated. On being told by a New York Monsignor of McQuaid's admiration for the FBI's espionage work against suspected Communist trade unionists, Hoover sent McQuaid a note thanking him for his 'highly valued support'. By separate post, Hoover sent McQuaid a copy of his book, *Masters of Deceit*. Like Hoover, McQuaid was 'a control freak'. He was obsessed with the need to control all aspects of public and private life.[88]

Even Radio Éireann's popular programme, *Hospitals' Requests*, was monitored by McQuaid's spy system. The programme, which was broadcast each Wednesday lunchtime and had a weekly audience of about 1.5 million listeners, kept TB patients in touch with their families and friends through requests for music ranging from Gene Autry to Verdi. The programme's signature tune, ironically, was 'Someone to Watch Over Me'.

One Wednesday, broadcaster Tom Cox included a request for the Cole Porter number *Always True to You*, the lyric of which went:

> **But I'm always true to you, darling, in my fashion;**
> **Yes, I'm always true to you, darling, in my way.**

When Cox finished the programme, he was summoned to the office of the Controller of Programmes, Roibeárd Ó Faracháin, who was also a poet and critic. The office was shrouded in smoke from the Controller's pipe when the nervous young announcer was ushered in. 'The Palace has been on,' Ó Faracháin said. 'You played a record today which contained the words' – he consulted his note-pad in the arms-length way of the courtroom – 'in my fashion and in my way'.

'His Grace is concerned at the somewhat, eh, circumscribed morality of the song,' Ó Faracháin said. 'Indeed, he believes it advocates the proposition that a limited form of fidelity is somehow acceptable.'

Cox, who knew that Ó Faracháin was a distinguished intellectual associated with Austin Clarke and the Abbey Theatre, realised that the Controller was feeling anything but comfortable, faced with his perceived corporate duty to defer to the views of the chief arbiter of faith and morals. Cox decided not to make it any easier for him. 'What do you want me to do?' he asked.

'Well, Tom, let's say that your programmes won't suffer unduly if you left it out.'

On his next *Hospitals' Requests*, Cox's first record was an instrumental version of 'Always True to You', performed by Victor Sylvester and his Ballroom Orchestra – a quickstep, strict tempo.[89]

Radio, films, theatre and books came under the scrutiny of McQuaid's unofficial censorship. A key figure was the economist, Dermot J. O'Flynn, a senior member of the Knights of St Columbanus and a nominee to the Censorship Board. McQuaid praised O'Flynn for his work against obscene films and left it to him to see what the Knights could do 'throughout the country by an ordered and general opposition'.[90]

Unlike books and films, the theatre was exempted from the State's censorship laws, but under an old Act of the Westminster Parliament, an obscene performance could be closed down by the police and the producer charged before the courts. This was exactly what happened in 1957 to Alan Simpson for staging Tennessee Williams' *The Rose Tattoo* in a small theatre club known as the Pike. The general belief at the time was that the proceedings against Simpson for producing a play which referred to a contraceptive were instigated by McQuaid.[91] Certainly, Dr Nöel Browne claimed that the Special Branch acted on 'the direction' of McQuaid. At the very least, the strong suspicion must remain that the clamp-down was organised by the Knights of St Columbanus, with McQuaid's covert approval.[92]

From the start of 1958, a renewed campaign against the importation of 'evil' books and magazines was led by McQuaid and Bishop Michael Browne. A Pastoral Letter, published in the name of the Hierarchy but written mainly by Browne, claimed that such imports were 'flooding' the country. It reminded the Catholic people of Ireland that one of their most important obligations was 'the defence of Catholic morality especially in that sacred sphere where the health and vigour of the race, the purity of domestic life and the sanctity of marriage are involved.'[93]

Browne feared that he had underestimated the scale of the onslaught. On his return to Galway by train after a meeting with McQuaid, he was surprised to see on the bookstall at Westland Row station a number of 'those rather risky publications such as For Men Only,' which he had never seen in Irish bookstalls before. His enquiries confirmed that they were displayed in all railway bookstalls in the front row so as to make them more accessible. 'The bookstalls are run by Messsrs Eason but CIÉ can hardly disclaim all responsibility,' Browne wrote to McQuaid, indicating that a protest must inevitably follow from McQuaid to these two companies.[94]

It was against this background that McQuaid became embroiled in another public controversy when word reached the press that he had withdrawn his permission for Mass to be said at the opening of the annual spring festival, known as An Tóstal, because of its plans to stage *Bloomsday*, an adaptation from James Joyce's *Ulysses*, and Sean O'Casey's *The Drums of Fr Ned*.[95]

A leak to an English newspaper led to O'Casey withdrawing his play, and the situation was made worse for the organisers when Samuel Beckett also withdrew his work. Simultaneously, the Jesuit Provincial, Fr O'Grady, phoned the Palace to leave word that he had directed the Rector of Gardiner St Church to refuse Tóstal's application for permission to stage Beckett's play in the St Francis Xavier Hall. 'It is significant that you are the first to uphold my resistance to the Dublin Tóstal's productions of Joyce and O'Casey,' McQuaid wrote to O'Grady.[96]

While O'Grady may have been the first to help, McQuaid could rely on his loyal followers to follow suit. The mood was summed up by a member of the Guild of St Francis de Sales, a guild of journalists founded by McQuaid through the Knights of St Columbanus, who said that the Archbishop of Dublin's displeasure was a signal to all Catholics in the diocese to boycott the festival. The Lord Mayor phoned to express his disapproval, as did the Christian Brothers. The Supreme Knight, Dr J. O'Mahony, lodged an objection to the choice of plays.

Dublin Corporation threatened to withdraw a £3,000 (£54,000) grant for street decorations if the plays were presented. The Dublin Council of Trade Unions was told by its secretary, John Dunne, a friend of McQuaid's, that he had protested to the festival council against the production of plays of an objectionable nature. On Dunne's advice, the Council of Trade Unions announced its support for the Archbishop's action.[97] In the end, the festival committee announced it was withdrawing the Joyce and O'Casey plays.

'There we go; the streets of Dublin echo with the drumbeats of footsteps running away,' O'Casey wrote in a letter to *The Irish Times*. 'The Archbishop in his Palace and the Customs Officer on the quay viva watch out to guard virtue and Éire; the other Archbishop (Barton) draws the curtains and sits close to his study fire, saying nothing; and so the Hidden Ireland becomes the Bidden Ireland, and all is swell.'

The crusade against the two plays was internationalised when the two secretaries of the Hierarchy's standing committee, Bishop MacNeeley of Raphoe and Bishop Fergus of Achonry, sent a letter to the American bishops explaining why McQuaid 'had felt compelled' to cancel the Mass on account of Tóstal's selection of O'Casey and Joyce. In an extraordinary initiative, they asked their powerful American counterparts to apply pressure on de Valera's Government to ban objectionable plays from the stage. The Irish bishops further confronted the Government by stressing that a recent decision by the Minister for External Affairs, Frank Aiken, to vote for discussion of China's admission to the United Nations 'did not reflect the views of Irish Catholics'.

This letter was dynamite in the hands of Cardinal Spellman. At a lunch in the Cardinal's New York residence with Frank Aiken and Freddie Boland, the Cardinal brought up the subject of the bishops' letter. A flaming row ensued, with Boland pointing out that Aiken's vote had been endorsed by a two-thirds majority in the Dáil, a fact which the two Irishmen regarded as 'the crowning argument' against Spellman and McQuaid.[98] The American bishops, however, remained so angry over the vote on China that they encouraged a boycott of pilgrimages to Ireland, which act constituted a tremendous blow to the tourist industry of an ailing economy.[99]

Pope John XXIII

Pius XII died on October 9, 1958. Two days later his mortal remains were removed from Castelgandolfo to the Vatican, but as the cortége reached St John Lateran, a sound like a Guy Fawkes banger was heard from within Pius's coffin. The heat had caused the body to ferment. Overnight the embalmer and Papal doctor, Dr Riccardo Galeazzi Lisi – he was actually an oculist – re-embalmed the body. Next day, mourners filing past the bier saw Pius with a green and ashen-coloured face, and his body had begun to stink. The Pontiff's remains, now bloated and disgorged, were still on display at the long drawn-out funeral on October 13, at which President O'Kelly represented Ireland.

'It is really horrible – but I told you long ago what kind of man he is,' Dan O'Connell wrote to McQuaid from Castel Gandolfo about Galeazzi-Lisi. 'He gets much money for his betrayal.' Next day the Cardinal caretakers dismissed Galeazzi-Lisi.[100]

O'Connell lamented that 'one hears nothing about the late Pope only talk about who is to succeed'. O'Connell had picked up a shift of mood, away from the highly centralised rule under Pius to something more open. The conclave of 51 cardinals, half of whom were over 77 years of age and including the not-so-sprightly 76-year-old D'Alton, was a closely-contested affair between the Armenian, Cardinal Agagianian, and the portly Patriarch of Venice, Angelo Roncalli, known to McQuaid from his visits to France in 1950. Pius's preferred successor, Cardinal Giuseppe Siri of Genoa, at 52, suffered from youthfulness. Roncalli was elected on the eleventh ballot after a three-day conclave, and took the name of Pope John XXIII.

Regarding Pope John as a conservative, McQuaid continued in his old familiar ways. When he heard in December 1958 that the Institute of Public Administration was organising evening lectures attended by Catholic students at Trinity College, McQuaid asked for an explanation from the Institute's president, John Leydon, recently retired from the Department of Industry and Commerce. Leydon summoned his key advisers – Charlie Murray, Tom Barrington and Richard Roche – to lunch in the St Stephen's Green Club and showed them the letter. A sense of alarm spread around the table. Leydon, who had been honoured by McQuaid as a Papal Knight of St Gregory but was known for his combat-iveness, became quite despondent.

According to Roche, Leydon recovered his fighting spirit, and in a robust reply told McQuaid that 'the Institute at no time considered that arrangements made by them would conflict with the obligations of its members as Catholics.' This did not satisfy McQuaid, who returned to the attack, pointedly regretting that the Institute had not arranged for lectures 'in the University that the Hierarchy has accepted because it suf-ficiently safeguards the rights of conscience of Catholics' – that is, Uni-versity College, Dublin. 'I should like, with respect,' Leydon replied, 'to emphasise that the initiative in arranging such lectures in connection with diplomas in Public Administration rests with the College concerned. The Institute was asked by Trinity College, Dublin .... the Institute was not approached by University College, Dublin.' Without conceding any-thing, Leydon had defused the situation.[101]

This kind of petty warfare had become a tiresome feature of McQuaid's rule as Archbishop by the end of the 1950s. Even when de Valera announced in January 1959 his intention to stand for the Presi-dency, his last months as Taoiseach found him on the defensive as McQuaid made insistent overtures on behalf of UCD's rights in regard to veterinary education, as against Trinity College's. 'We are being dogged by this determination to put Trinity into a position not of equality, but of superiority,' McQuaid complained privately to D'Alton.[102]

On June 9, 1959, McQuaid heard 'the good news' of de Valera's election as President and sent him a short note to congratulate him.[103]

Correspondence between McQuaid and Bishop Browne suggests that they looked to Seán MacEntee, who stood on the right wing of Fianna Fáil, as the man most disposed to upholding the interests of the Catholic Church.[104] However, it was the more pragmatic Seán Lemass who became party leader and Taoiseach. From his past dealings with McQuaid, Lemass knew that coping with McQuaid's superior behaviour would be part of the burden of being Taoiseach.

Elder Church Statesman
1959–62

'The illustrious McQuaid.'

Cardinal D'Alton on McQuaid at the centenary of Clonliffe College.

On June 23, 1959, the day on which a new era in Irish politics opened with the election of Seán Lemass as Taoiseach, Archbishop John Charles McQuaid briefed his fellow bishops behind the closed doors of Maynooth College, explaining how he had escalated the campaign against Trinity College, which now spread from the United States and Canada to England, Scotland and Wales. While Lemass was calling in the Dáil for 'an upsurge in patriotism' from all sectors of Irish society, McQuaid was condemning Trinity as an institution founded to destroy the Irish nation and its Catholic faith. Though less than 20 miles separated Leinster House and Maynooth, the messages of Taoiseach and Primate embodied contradictory views of Irish nationalism – Lemass edging towards a concept of cultural pluralism, McQuaid defending religious exclusiveness.[1]

Ireland's past and future clashed that June day, as Lemass began a premiership that would bring Ireland into the modern mainstream of European life, through the dismantling of trade barriers in preparation for Common Market membership, through détente with Ulster Protestants in the North and the fostering of a more liberal outlook in the South. A reversal of the population decline and the introduction of economic planning under a talented and far-seeing civil servant, T.K. Whitaker, were to save Ireland from becoming a failed political and social entity. But Lemass did not inherit a clean sheet; he had to work within the parameters defined by the dominant clericalist culture which McQuaid personified.

More drink

Alcohol was to be the first battle-ground between the old and the new Irelands. Indeed, the one public pronouncement made by the Hierarchy on June 23 was a statement on the Intoxicating Liquor Laws. Issued in the name of all the bishops, it was written by McQuaid and was intended as a shot across the Lemass Government's bows.[2]

The decision to issue the statement was taken after McQuaid informed the bishops that the Government was about to introduce legislation along the lines suggested by the Commission of Inquiry into the vintners' trade, extending the general opening hours all over the country on weekdays from 9.30am to 11.30pm (with a one-hour break in Dublin and other large centres from 2.30pm to 3.30pm which became known as the 'holy hour'). The commission had also recommended limited Sunday opening hours from 12.30pm to 2pm and from 5.00pm to 9.00pm.[3]

Peeved that the Government had chosen to 'disregard' the bishops' views, McQuaid presented a draft statement which was approved for publication in the press. The statement incorporated the main points of McQuaid's memorandum on the matter which had been submitted to de Valera the previous month.[4] It warned that increased drinking would lead to greater alcoholism which would have most serious moral and social effects, an increase in delinquency and widespread danger to life on the roads. It also feared that more drinking would mean less economic prosperity. Arguing that the people welcomed restriction and Garda enforcement of the existing laws, the statement deplored that the proposals would strike at what was most sacred, the Lord's Day. Its conclusion rang a warning bell for the new Taoiseach: 'The Irish Hierarchy confidently hopes that legislation, when it is introduced, will not weaken the moral fibre of our nation, and will respect the deep-seated convictions of our Catholic people.'

The Intoxicating Liquor Bill fell short of the commission's recommendations and provided for only one hour's opening on Sundays. After it was circulated to the bishops, in October McQuaid informed the Minister for Justice, Oscar Traynor, that he disagreed with its terms. 'The Government,' he complained, 'has not seen fit to accept the representations of the Hierarchy. It cannot then be supposed that any view expressed by the Archbishop of Dublin will have any avail.'[5] Although held at arm's length by Traynor, who may have relished this turn of events since the Yugoslav match nearly four years earlier, McQuaid predicted that the legislation would fail, a hint that the clergy might attempt to frustrate its enactment.

McQuaid pressed for an 11pm closing on weekdays all year round instead of the proposed closing time of 11.30pm. At a meeting with the new Secretary of the Department of Justice, Peter Berry, in late November, McQuaid asked that his disapproval of the Liquor Bill be conveyed to the Government, but Lemass, speaking in the Dáil four days later, countered McQuaid's argument that the civil law should reflect Church law when he declared that 'drunkenness is a sin for which men are responsible to a higher court than ours'.[6]

In retrospect, the Bill's passage can be viewed as a small but significant moment in Church-State relations. The citation of Canon Law no longer automatically held sway in the Dáil. McQuaid's efforts to amend the Bill had not only been dismissed, but Lemass had taken the high moral ground from the Archbishop by invoking the counter-argument that legislators had to take human frailty into account. Although Lemass had gone for a minimalist change in the law, he was pioneering a gradualist approach that would be followed by his successors over the next 35 years, reclaiming areas of public legislation which had been abdicated to the Catholic Church since the foundation of the State. A gambler, Lemass may have taken some personal pleasure in facing down McQuaid, who had recently forced him to abandon a Bórd Fáilte-supported proposal for the building of a casino.[7]

For the first known time since he became Archbishop in 1940, McQuaid came away from the corridors of Government without a success to report. The extent of his rebuff is reflected in the terse note with which the Hierarchy recorded its position on October 13, 1959: 'It was agreed that no further action on the part of the Hierarchy was called for'.[8] As Tommy Coyne had anticipated, the bishops did not want to lose face by highlighting the consequences for their authority of politicians deciding for the first time to reject the import of Canon Law.

'Bishop' de Valera

De Valera's move to the Presidency enhanced the Irish Republic's outward appearance as a solidly unchanging Catholic State. The general perception of de Valera as 'the Father of the Nation' was articulated by Cardinal Francis Spellman of New York.[9] As President, de Valera conceived himself as a lay Catholic statesman, and utilised the facilities of Áras an Uachtaráin as a spiritual guesthouse, especially for visiting church dignitaries. De Valera had once confided to Mary McSwiney, 'every instinct of mine would indicate that I was meant to be a dyed-in-the wool Tory or even a bishop rather than the leader of a revolution.'[10] As President, de Valera was able to combine the lifestyle of a Tory grandee with that of a bishop manqué. Both McQuaid and D'Alton must have felt that the Irish nation had acquired a third prelate, and one who had a more stately residence than either Notre Dame des Bois in Killiney or Ara Coeli in Armagh.

Once again, McQuaid was at the centre of the ecclesiastical and civil pomp that attended de Valera's installation as the third President of Ireland. Knowing Éamon and Sinéad de Valera's attachment to the Mass, McQuaid appointed Fr Joseph Carroll as chaplain to the President and responded attentively to their requirements. Before long, de Valera's overriding interest in matters Irish was being brought to McQuaid's attention. He asked McQuaid to secure the Hierarchy's approval of 'Serving of Mass', with directions in Irish by Fr Ó Floinn, for insertion in a booklet of Irish prayers.[11]

Generally, the McQuaid Papers relating to the de Valera Presidency indicate that their relationship returned to the harmonious level that had existed between them in the 1930s, when McQuaid was President of Blackrock College and de Valera was Taoiseach. McQuaid wrote to de Valera on his eightieth birthday to wish him many happy years in his exalted office, and next day de Valera phoned to thank him. Troubled by religious scruples when he was invited to review the Boys' Brigade at a function at which the Protestant Archbishop, George Otto Simms, would give a blessing, de Valera consulted McQuaid, who advised that it was lawful for him to attend provided he took no active part in the proceedings. Grateful for this advice, de Valera promised not to take his hat off during the function which included the singing of a Vespers hymn.[12]

However, the papers also reveal that McQuaid had aspirations to succeed de Valera as Chancellor of the National University of Ireland when it was thought unlikely that de Valera would retain this job along with the Presidency. Correspondence between McQuaid and Bishop Michael Browne of Galway refer to their plans for securing the chancellorship, with Browne, who was a domineering and flamboyant figure in university politics, acting to smooth the way for McQuaid's elevation to the post. The clue to the intrigue is to be found in Browne's advice to McQuaid that he would not like an application by Archbishop Charles Heerey of Onitsha for academic facilities at UCD 'to be connected with Your Grace's candidature for Chancellor'.[13]

However, McQuaid's temperamental dislike of the rough and tumble of academic politics ensured that he had no stomach for the kind of open and semi-public infighting that Browne relished. 'Nothing would induce me to let my name go forward in such a morass of politics,' McQuaid informed Browne after hearing that Monsignor Boylan was being excluded by the Government as a candidate for the NUI seat in the Senate.[14] However strong his ambitions of succeeding to the chancellorship which had been held by his predecessor, Archbishop William Walsh, before de Valera's accession to the post in 1921, McQuaid congratulated and thanked de Valera for consenting to continue in the office.[15]

Inside Maynooth

The agenda for the October 1959 bishops' meeting at Maynooth shows the extent of the Episcopal hold over the nation's affairs which confronted a reforming Taoiseach like Seán Lemass. The Hierarchy presumed to tell the Minister for Education on which days examinations should be held in the schools; the Society of St Vincent de Paul was rapped on the knuckles for publishing an abridged adaptation of the McQuaid catechism without approval; nuns were told that they could not join the Irish Nurses' Organisation; nuns with Froebel certificates were to be recognised as teachers by the Department of Education as a result of pressure from the Archbishop of Tuam; the chairman of the Electricity Supply Board was resisting pressure to subsidise the heating of churches; youth groups were to be better coordinated under the control of the clergy; the Irish National Teachers' Organisation was to be rebuked for having acted against charity in calling for a national boycott against the Marist Brothers over a management dispute with Bishop O'Boyle of Killala,[16] and Advent Sunday was fixed as Temperance Sunday.[17]

The dominance of the Archbishop of Dublin at the Maynooth meeting figures in three other items on the agenda. Having 'happily averted' the danger that Catholic adoption agencies would be inspected by the local authorities, a National Council of Catholic Adoption Societies was approved and its membership selected by the bishops. Secondly, McQuaid reported on how he had objected to the right of the departments of Education and Agriculture to select lecturers on social ethics at Government-organised winter schools for young farmers, and had persuaded them that it was their 'duty' to assign this function to the local clergy. Thirdly, McQuaid undertook to check the accuracy of a widespread allegation that the Westminster Crusade of Rescue excluded from its charity Irish girls who 'got into trouble' before leaving Ireland.[18]

Most significant of all, the Hierarchy had before it a report from a sub-committee which concluded that a proposed national television service would represent 'one of the most powerful forces which has appeared in Irish life and one of which the Church will have to take cognisance.' While recognising the positive opportunities for bringing the teaching of the Church to a wide audience and even to non-Catholics, the report stressed that the negative aspects were 'the more immediate and urgent'.

Three out of every four programmes on the new station were expected to be imported, the report noted, and a high percentage of those produced in Britain were highly objectionable from a moral point of view; the same was true to a lesser extent of programmes from America. 'The danger of harm being caused to the moral sense of the country through imported programmes is the most urgent aspect of this matter for the Bishops,' the report warned. It recommended a system of censorship analogous to that exercised over the cinema, with a bishop sitting on a panel of religious advisers.[19]

That month, McQuaid stopped J.P. Donleavy's *Ginger Man*, starring Richard Harris, Rosalie Westwater, Godfrey Quigley and Genevieve Lyons, from being staged in the Gaiety Theatre. One of the Archbishop's secretaries arrived at the theatre to convey His Grace's disapproval of the play, which had been described in the newspapers as an insult to religion and decency. 'There goes a battleship,' Richard Harris remarked as the priest left the theatre. However, the clerical mission was successful.

According to Donleavy the play was forced off the Dublin stage by 'the intervention of the awesome power of the Catholic authority wielded by the Archbishop of Dublin'.[20]

McQuaid was also continuing his crusade to keep Catholics and non-Catholics apart. In response to a query from the new Bishop of Limerick, Henry Murphy, about how to treat non-Catholic youth activities, he replied: 'I have no cognisance of non-Catholic activities that are not professedly sectarian, unless the Baden-Powell Boy Scouts be such a category. And these Scouts I actively discourage. All approved Youth Organisations are placed under the direction of the Diocesan Youth Council.'[21]

Meanwhile, in Hamburg, where Catholics counted for about four per cent of the population, Denis O'Kelly and his wife wanted to adopt an Irish boy and were introduced to a home in Dublin through the good offices of a Columban priest, Fr Aedan McGrath. 'It was at that stage the requirements of Archbishop McQuaid before signing permission for a child to be adopted became known to us,' O'Kelly recalled. Sending a copy of a recent bank statement was a problem for O'Kelly, a young academic who was just starting his career, but he got over this hurdle by sending a copy of his bank statement on the last day of the month, when his salary was credited to his account. O'Kelly and his convert wife were disgusted at having to sign a sworn affidavit that they would send the boy to a Catholic school and subsequently to a Catholic university, but very reluctantly consented to it. The O'Kellys succeeded in adopting the baby with the assistance of Ambassador Warnock of the Irish Embassy in Bonn and a German judge, 'in spite of McQuaid's blocking activities'.[22]

Books: Papist and Prod

Having lost to Lemass on pub opening hours, McQuaid regained the upper hand shortly afterwards when he forced the Taoiseach to abandon a proposal for a book-sharing arrangement between the National Library and Trinity College that was designed to cut costs to the taxpayer. The plan, first presented to de Valera in early 1959 by the Director of the National Library of Ireland, Dr Richard Hayes, aimed to avoid duplication in 90 per cent of academic publications.[23]

Advised in his first week as Taoiseach by Government secretary Maurice Moynihan that the proposal would require very careful handling, Lemass was attracted to the scheme's practical merits, especially after talks with the Provost of Trinity, Dr A.J. McConnell. Lemass allowed several months to elapse before he asked McQuaid for his opinion on 'tentative suggestions' for a long-term solution at the National Library and Trinity College libraries, both of which had reached the limits of their storage capacity.[24]

At a meeting on May 4, 1960, McQuaid told Lemass that the

bishops had unanimously agreed that the Government should not proceed with the proposal because they did not want to create the impression that Trinity College was the most important centre of higher education in the State. In McQuaid's own words, the bishops believed that 'the chief University institution in a mainly Catholic community should manifestly be a Catholic institution'. This response sealed the fate of the Hayes project. 'The proposal to conjoin Trinity College's new library and the National Library will not be heard of again,' McQuaid wrote to D'Alton.[25] Five days later Lemass informed McConnell that the scheme was impracticable.

At this juncture, the Minister for Education, Dr Patrick Hillery, made a speech in the Dáil on university education which McQuaid regarded as hugely significant. 'For the first time, after its loss more than 400 years ago, the principle of our right to Catholic education has been publicly and officially accepted by the Government,' McQuaid informed a new Nuncio, Archbishop Antonio Riberi. 'It is my hope that at last we are entering on a period of security in university education for Catholics, but there are many reasons for vigilance still existing.'[26]

McQuaid's confidence in UCD achieving its rightful 'predominant position' soared as a result of its move from Earlsfort Terrace to a new site at Belfield on the south-west of the city. McQuaid had persuaded the President of UCD, Dr Michael Tierney, to make the change, because Earlsfort Terrace was too small to accommodate an expanding campus.[27] Similarly, the country's largest Catholic teaching hospital, St Vincent's, was moving from St Stephen's Green to Elm Park, close to Belfield. The strategy aimed to create a great Catholic suburban axis to neutralise the city-centre dominance of Trinity and the Protestant teaching hospitals.[28] The McQuaid-Tierney partnership was facilitated by Dublin Corporation's chief planning officer, Michael O'Brien, who was a zealous member of the Knights of St Columbanus.[29] Through O'Brien, McQuaid vetoed a Corporation plan to build two-bedroom houses in a new estate in the north Dublin area of Finglas, because couples needed bigger houses to accommodate the large families which they were likely to have as good Catholics.[30]

Yet when a young idealistic doctor, the future parliamentarian and Minister for Health, Dr John O'Connell, asked McQuaid to take a stand on the deprivation which existed in the inner city, the Archbishop was loath to do so. O'Connell was appalled by the level of poverty and unemployment which he saw in the heart of Dublin, and wrote to McQuaid saying that the dispensary system was inadequate to cope with the situation. 'I believed that something could be done if every school, every church and every factory took on an extra worker as a gesture towards the poor,' O'Connell recalled. 'I said it was dreadful that people were left to deteriorate and lose their will to work for ever.' O'Connell asked McQuaid to make a public plea on the matter, but the Archbishop indicated that he did not feel the problems O'Connell outlined were his concern. Undeterred, O'Connell wrote a second letter about the housing problem, because he was concerned about the possibility of incest in such crowded conditions. He received another curt answer: it was not the Archbishop's concern.[31]

McQuaid at 65

McQuaid turned 65 in July 1960, the normal retirement age in the professions. He had surrounded himself with a culture of cronyism, and an inner circle of clerical advisers who had become a group of courtiers offering flattery as well as advice. His clergy were so cowed that they did not even write a letter to a newspaper, let alone pen anything of a literary nature, while the laity competed to ingratiate themselves with him. If anyone offended him, he or she was instantly snubbed, as Dr Louis O'Brien discovered when he composed a hymn to St Andrew which he played without the Archbishop's clearance. So displeased was McQuaid by the composition that he left the ceremony without speaking to the dismayed hymnist.[32]

McQuaid enjoyed his pre-eminence in the world of medicine, and took special pride in Our Lady's Hospital, Crumlin, which had been commended by the World Health Organisation as the finest children's hospital in Europe. As a princely benefactor, he had presented the hospital with equipment for advanced cardiac treatment and for advanced work in pathology. He also had endowed the Mater Hospital with a library and provided the seed capital for its department of encephalography.

As chairman of the National Maternity Hospital at Holles St, the largest general hospital at Jervis St, the children's hospital at Our Lady's, the Mater Misericordiae Hospital and St Michael's, Dun Laoghaire, McQuaid held a tight grip over appointments. He had encouraged Orders of nuns such as the Sisters of Mercy, the Bon Secours Sisters and the Holy Rosary Sisters to play a dominant role in medicine, where they could act as the custodians of Irish motherhood.[33]

Doctors in the hospitals under his management had to make special efforts to acknowledge His Grace's particular expertise in medical matters. Doctors such as Bryan Alton were his collaborators in medical politics. Formal dress was required to be worn even by junior doctors on occasions attended by McQuaid and it was a blot on an ambitious doctor's career prospects if he or she did not kneel to kiss his Borgia ring. One doctor who had not lived up to McQuaid's expectations was summoned to his presence and told: 'Remember, I made you.' That doctor's appointment was not renewed.[34]

A believer in the fiction that the Church took precedence over State at the opening and blessing of new hospitals, McQuaid insisted on arriving last, though on occasions he met with competition from a dogged Tánaiste and Minister for Health, Seán MacEntee, who believed that as the taxpayers' representative he should be last to arrive. This rivalry led to the spectacle of their respective drivers circling the hospital buildings until, invariably, the Minister had to yield to the Archbishop.[35]

McQuaid prided himself on being *au fait* with developments in modern theology. He kept abreast of French spiritual writings and communicated regularly with one of the pioneers of ecumenism, Fr Guy de Broglie S.J., who taught at both the Institut Catholique in Paris and at the Gregorian University in Rome. De Broglie's work, *La Liberté Religieuse*, was one of McQuaid's favourites books, as was *Questions Théologiques* by Fr Charles Boyer S.J. of the Gregorian University.[36]

Several years ahead of an instruction from the Holy See banning the philosophical and theological works of the French Jesuit, Teilhard de Chardin, McQuaid had forbidden his students at Clonliffe College to read them. 'I will see to it that the instruction be observed in my seminary, and will secure, as far as I can, the exclusion of the work from Catholic bookshops,' he informed the Nunciature in Dublin.[37]

A sense of the passing years haunted McQuaid. 'The years left are few. You will pray that I will use them well,' he asked of the West German Ambassador, Dr Felician Prill, a scholar with a particular interest in the problems of nationalism and religion in nineteenth-century Europe. Prill admired McQuaid and recommended him for an honour from the fledgling West German State. 'It is awkward,' McQuaid replied, 'for the one country that ought to decorate the AB is France.'[38]

The years had not diminished McQuaid's love of travel or church architecture, and he enjoyed visits to Chartres, Troyes, Vence, Ronchamp and the churches of Paris and Switzerland with his companions, Fr Dinan and Comte Paul Biver, an acknowledged authority on church design. McQuaid had been made an Honorary Canon of the Cathedral of Tarbes and Lourdes diocese, and was appointed to the international medical committee which met regularly at the headquarters of the Lazarists in the Rue de Sèvres in Paris to investigate claims of miracles at Lourdes.[39] He gave a large donation for the building of the St Pius X Basilica in Lourdes.[40]

The Dublin diocesan pilgrimage to Lourdes had become an important source of annual revenue for Aer Lingus, which had acquired specially fitted DC10s for the needs of the sick and the invalided. On the flights the pilgrims were provided with a menu card on the back of which was a map of Dublin sponsored by Guinness's brewery showing places of interest such as Trinity College, Christ Church Cathedral, St Patrick's Cathedral and St Michan's Church. The highlighting of Protestant buildings offended McQuaid, who wrote to the Aer Lingus Sales Manager, Arthur J. Walls, saying that 'It is extraordinary that the national airline lists only sights of the other denomination.' Walls replied spiritedly: 'You can hardly blame Aer Lingus for the fact that every building of note in Dublin was handed over to the Protestants.'[41]

For all his years in public life, McQuaid still felt the need to prepare speeches. Following the death of Archbishop Kinane, Fr Tom Morris was appointed Archbishop of Cashel and invited McQuaid to propose the toast at his reception. McQuaid asked to be excused. 'I do not even know who will be present and I do not speak with any facility but I have to prepare everything very carefully,' he explained.[42]

His work rate was still impressive. When the Maynooth Statutes came into force in August 1959, he circulated all the bishops with the application forms for permission to attend Trinity College and dealt with this extra work load personally. He completed the building of a lavish chapel, an Aula Maxima with a cloister and a new wing in time for the centenary celebrations of Clonliffe College, at which he was acclaimed as the worthy successor of Cardinal Cullen. Pope John XXIII commended his achievements in a letter published in *L'Osservatore Romano* which was picked up by the Dublin media. De Valera, Lemass, ministers and bishops flocked to the centenary Mass, where the preacher, Archbishop Joseph Walsh, marvelled at how the highly disciplined Clonliffe-trained clergy had made the diocese 'as fine an example of Catholic life and ecclesiastical administration as can be found the world over'.[43]

The centenary fostered a new drive to promote vocations. By 1960 the Catholic population of Dublin had soared to nearly 700,000, served by 537 diocesan priests, almost 100 of whom were engaged in university and college teaching, executive work, and as chaplains to convents and teachers in vocational schools. Religious Houses were bulging with clergy and students. McQuaid had admitted to his diocese, and given university residences, to the Society of St Columban, the Mill Hill Fathers, the Salesian Fathers, the White Fathers, the Society of the Divine Word, the Pallotines and the Rosminians. Women religious included the Holy Rosary Sisters, the Medical Missionaries of Mary, the Congregation of Notre Dame des Missions, the Salesian Sisters and the Sisters of Jesus and Mary.[44]

So attractive was Dublin as a religious base that McQuaid boasted he had the pick of 270 applications for religious foundations in the city, but knew that his Council would not even think of allowing another congregation.[45] He gruffly rejected a plea from Bishop Nguyen Van Thien of Vinh-Long in Vietnam to look after the upkeep and university training of a Fr Vu-Sun. 'I regret I am not in a position to undertake this responsibility,' he replied, 'Nor is there a single Religious House where he can stay. Two Fathers of an Irish Congregation have sought in vain for weeks to obtain a place in a Religious House or Hostel. And my Council will not tolerate any priest living outside such a House or Hostel.' McQuaid took grave exception to Fr Vu-Sun entering the Dublin diocese from Falkirk, unannounced and without any papers from his bishop. 'This is not the first occasion on which I have had reason to complain of the action of Oriental priests. Your Lordship will be good enough to see that Fr

Vu-Sun is removed from my Diocese without delay, if he has not already obeyed my instructions given some time ago to return to Falkirk from whence he came.'[46]

New and old horizons

McQuaid began his third decade as Archbishop with a request from the Papal Nuncio, Archbishop Antonio Riberi, to respond to an appeal by Pope John for the special needs of Latin America, and to set out his ideas for presentation to His Holiness.[47] McQuaid outlined his views in a six-page memorandum which argued that Catholic schools based on the Irish model would be pivotal in developing a pastoral strategy for Latin America. 'The very concept of the priesthood has perished in South America,' McQuaid wrote. 'If vocations from families of good social standing are to be obtained only schools can supply the answer.'

McQuaid suggested that if the faith was to be preserved in Latin America, it must be through a native Hierarchy and clergy on whose virtue and professional training the Holy See could confidently depend. He was also of the opinion that priests must not identify themselves too closely in their standards of living and in their social habits with the upper classes:

> It seems to me that our apostolate, while it embraces all classes, must, if we are to overcome the Communist menace, boldly address itself to the underprivileged and the poor. Our priests can be trusted to endure difficult conditions and sustained hard work.

At a practical level, McQuaid felt that language was a grave barrier but he noted that, in recent years, interest in Spanish had grown and he was confident that the priests who knew Latin would master the language. 'I should like to assure the Holy Father,' he concluded, 'that I will assist in every way that is open to me in providing in our country the apostolate of South America.'[48]

Years earlier, McQuaid had been coached by Ambassador Joe Walshe to forge links with Spain. McQuaid had responded to the overtures of the leadership of the secretive Opus Dei, and attended the opening of its first residence centre in Dublin at Nullamore, Dartry, in 1954 accompanied by the Taoiseach, John A. Costello. He also blessed the organisation's new residence in Hume St.[49]

As part of his response to the Latin American Mission, McQuaid showed a preference towards the Legionaries of Christ, a missionary group of Spanish origins which stressed loyalty to authority with as much gusto as Opus Dei. He persuaded his fellow bishops to allow the Legionaries of Christ's scouts to seek recruits each year, not only in Dublin schools but in almost every diocese in Ireland, enabling it to achieve 25 or 30 postulants in

Dublin and the same number from the rest of the country.[50]

The year 1961 also marked the launching by McQuaid of a renewed offensive against Trinity College. In his booklet, *Higher Education for Catholics*, McQuaid denied that the Hierarchy was being bigoted in making Church legislation against Trinity binding in conscience on Catholic parents: 'It is not in the atmosphere of a non-Catholic University that one trains by choice the picked exponents of Catholic Faith and morals.'

After warning of the dangers of indiscipline and indifference facing youth in non-Catholic institutions, McQuaid reaffirmed the claims of a truly Catholic university. His mood was defiant:

> It must have seemed long to wait some four hundred years to secure only what approximated to parity of opportunity for higher education. But, should the need arise, we should gladly reckon another four hundred years as short to wait until, in our own land, we might achieve the full development of University formation that is our imprescriptible right, as citizens and as Catholics.[51]

The Provost of Trinity, Dr A.J. McConnell, let McQuaid know that his board intended to make a submission to the Commission on Higher Education, then reviewing the options for the future. McConnell, an Ulster Protestant, bluntly informed the Archbishop that the submission would stress that the last vestiges of religious disqualification disappeared from Trinity College under the terms of the Fawcett Act of 1873 – and that at no time since then was the description of the college as a Protestant university appropriate. 'Today there are many Catholics in the College – on the Board, on the staff and among the student body – and members of the College of all denominations work together harmoniously in an atmosphere of mutual confidence and respect,' McConnell told McQuaid.[52]

Alfred O'Rahilly, who had become McQuaid's adviser on university education, was fielded as a robust apologist in a series of articles for *Studies*, though O'Rahilly had detected the new undercurrents of tolerance and openness and felt privately that the Archbishop was losing the public relations battle. 'The insidious propaganda of TCD and of *The Irish Times* has had a devastating effect,' he wrote. 'The students – at least the vocal element – and the good Catholic professional men are for TCD. Even the clergy I feel are so bewitched by ecumenism that they think it is wrong to stand up for their own rights – even if we concede equal rights for Protestants.'[53]

While never lessening his opposition to Trinity, McQuaid did not fully trust UCD either, though he had recognised that its organisation and atmosphere were suitable for Catholics. Consulted by Bishop William Philbin of Clonfert as to whether he should take part in a debate run by the

Literary and Historical Society, McQuaid advised that 'There is only one answer: avoid such a meeting. It is not clear that the dignity of a Bishop's position could be safeguarded in the circumstances of the L&H.'[54]

So closed were UCD's intellectual horizons that when news reached McQuaid that a young political scientist, John Whyte, was working on a book on Church-State relations, word was conveyed to the head of the Department of Ethics and Politics, Rev. Dr Conor Martin, that this was an intrusion into the affairs of the diocese. As a priest of the diocese, Martin felt obliged to instruct Whyte not to write the book. Whyte found another job at Queen's University, Belfast, and produced his classic work.[55]

Last hurrah

McQuaid was at the zenith of his power in 1961, the year which celebrated the 1500th anniversary of the death of St Patrick. For him the Patrician Congress had only one meaning: 'a renewed appreciation of the gift of the One True Faith'.[56] Pope John's decision to send as his Legate Cardinal Gregory Peter Agagianian, the Vatican's Minister for the Missions, delighted McQuaid, who saw this as recognition of Dublin's unique place in world Catholicism. Described by Bishop Dunne as 'somewhat inscrutable, uncommunicative but always charming,' Agagianian was met by McQuaid at a windswept Dublin airport and escorted to Áras an Uachtaráin, where de Valera had invited him to stay.[57]

On June 15, the bells of 300 churches in the diocese pealed in triumph, as Agagianian solemnly inaugurated the Patrician Congress at a service in the Pro-Cathedral presided over by McQuaid. The previous evening, a ten-foot-tall 'congress candle' in Dublin's O'Connell St was lit from a fire at Slane, the hill in Co. Meath associated with St Patrick as a shepherd boy. Throughout the nine days of the congress the candle shone as a symbol of 'the fealty of the Capital and the Nation to the Light of Faith kindled by St Patrick'.[58]

A novel feature of the ceremonies was the presence of an élite corps of Catholic schoolboys, distinguished in uniforms and yellow berets. McQuaid had assigned one of his closest priests, Fr Tom Fehily, the task of creating this body, which became known as the Colleges' Volunteers Forces. It was under the command of Brendan Glennon. Other highlights included a huge garden party hosted by McQuaid; a turnout of over 20,000 people in Ballyfermot, singing *Faith of Our Fathers* to the music of the de La Salle Accordion Band in greeting to the Papal Legate; and the unveiling of a statue of Our Lady at Ringsend. Most spectacular of all was the attendance of 90,000 people at Mass in Croke Park. McQuaid basked in the applause of the crowd (described by one commentator as being like a vast mosaic of living faith), as he was driven around the ground in an open limousine before joining 12,500 robed priests, soldiers and his volunteers on the pitch, where a huge altar had been erected. The laity watched the ceremony in passive awe.

An evening of speeches in the Theatre Royal is recalled by broadcaster Seán MacRéamoinn for the famous TV evangelist Bishop Fulton Sheen's oratorical slip when he praised the 'passionate chastity of the men of Ireland'.[59] Apart from this slip of the tongue, Sheen, a master of broadcasting, held his audience and television viewers fascinated. 'On television I said that if the telecast was good, it was because, like Elisha, I was wearing the mantle of the real Eliah,' Sheen told McQuaid, a compliment that cast the Archbishop in the role of a biblical prophet.[60]

The success of the Patrician celebrations was an immense boost to McQuaid's morale, and there was renewed speculation that he would be honoured with a Red Hat. 'We were all thrilled to the depths of our being by the way Dublin and Diocese rose to the occasion,' wrote Archbishop John Norton from Balthurst. 'It was all a personal triumph for you, especially when Cardinal Döpfner [Archbishop of Munich] paid tribute to the remarkable organisation.'[62]

'All the reports that have come through about your Patrician Congress are unanimous in saying it was an overwhelming success,' Archbishop Finbar Ryan wrote from Cork. 'I am sure it gave Cardinal Agagianian a new perspective on Irish faith and apostolicity.'[63] On his return to the Eternal City, Agagianian reported to Pope John on how impressed he had been with the Congress and of how harmonious were the relations between Church and State in Ireland, a relationship personified by de Valera. McQuaid, however, did not figure on the list of new cardinals in Pope John's next batch.[64]

Four decades later the Congress can be viewed as the last hurrah of a triumphant Church. It was viewed as such at the time by the editor of *The Furrow*, Fr J.G. McGarry, who remarked to Seán MacRéamoinn that it was 'a most impressive occasion for 1961'.[65] More significant for Ireland's future direction was the lodging a few weeks later of the Government's application for membership of the European Economic Community, and the arrival of Irish television.[66]

Television, nude models and lonely girls

The first black-and-white programme from Ireland's new television station, RTÉ, was broadcast from the Gresham Hotel at 7pm on New Year's Eve 1961. A young soldier unfurled the Tricolour as the national anthem was played, and the station broadcast the solemn speeches of President de Valera, Taoiseach Seán Lemass and Cardinal D'Alton, each of whom emphasised the need to maintain proper standards, parental control and national values on the airwaves.

The speeches on screen reflected life in a cultural ghetto, while in a studio in Donnybrook a former BBC producer, Chlöe Gibson, dressed in jeans to meet Archbishop John Charles McQuaid on his arrival at the station. McQuaid had insisted that because Montrose, the new station's headquarters in Donnybrook, was in his diocese, it should have a chapel. He had also insisted that he should conduct the first act of worship there.

McQuaid arrived with his driver, Robert, who was carrying His Grace's vestments for a benediction which was to be televised live. 'Sweetheart,' Gibson said to Robert, 'you can leave the gear down here.' Robert nearly dropped the vestments with embarrassment. To the amazement of colleagues, Gibson kept a finicky John Charles sweet in the RTÉ oratory prior to his television debut, when McQuaid conducted solemn benediction of the Blessed Sacrament with all the pomp and presence of an ecclesiastical Micheál MacLiammóir. The bishop and the producer got on so well together that their friendship endured.[67]

Since the first discussions by the Hierarchy sub-committee on television, McQuaid had broken ranks from his colleagues and selected two priests, Fr Joseph Dunn and Fr Desmond Forristal, to go to New York to learn television techniques. Dunn had drawn up a memorandum, approved by McQuaid, which led to the formation of the religious broadcasting unit *Radharc* (Vision), to which McQuaid gave a £300 gift (£2,500) to purchase equipment from Ulster Television.[68] It was, arguably, the most far-sighted and progressive decision of McQuaid's career.

Informally, McQuaid had mentioned to de Valera that he would like to have a priest appointed as religious adviser to RTÉ. The President referred this wish to Seán Lemass, who passed the message on to Éamonn Andrews. Although the Catholic TV Committee had an agreement in principle with RTÉ that the priest to be appointed would be McQuaid's choice – Fr Dunn – it called for a list of three candidates. The two others were the Dublin diocesan priest, Desmond Forristal, and a Dominican, Romuald Dodd.

Although a devout Catholic, Andrews had not forgiven McQuaid for ordering the Franciscans to remove the first chaplain to the Catholic Stage Guild, Fr Cormac Daly O.F.M., and while he was polite and outwardly friendly towards the Archbishop, Andrews was determined not to allow McQuaid extensive control over television. Knowing that a priest of a Religious Order would be more independent than a priest of a diocese, Andrews ensured that Dodd was selected. Faced with a *fait accompli*, McQuaid registered his displeasure by ordering Dunn to have no dealings with Dodd.[69]

McQuaid found that he could not control television as easily as he had radio. The most dramatic instance of this came when McQuaid, in the company of Archbishop Morris, approached Lemass and requested him to remove senior broadcasters Jack White and Shelagh Richards, two Protestants, and Proinsias MacAonghusa, for what he regarded as their liberal and subversive influence. Lemass refused.[70]

Despite the onset of this new medium, McQuaid stuck to his old tactics of orchestrating letter campaigns against 'indecency', wherever it might be found. Driving down O'Connell St, his car stopped beside Clery's department store, where to his horror he saw nude models in the window. A campaign was launched through the Conference of Convent Secondary Schools against the display of life-sized models in the shop windows of Dublin.[71]

The popularity in 1960 of a novel describing the suppressed sexual desires of young women deeply shocked McQuaid. Although the censors banned *The Country Girls*, its author Edna O'Brien, a former Mercy Convent student from Co. Clare, became a cult figure for young people who were eager to buy and read her book illegally. The publication in 1962 of O'Brien's second book, *The Lonely Girl*, added to her notoriety when it was also banned.

'May I ask your Eminence to be good enough to read the item 'The Ages of Innocence' by Isobel English, page 3, *Catholic Herald* of June 1,' McQuaid requested the Archbishop of Westminster, Cardinal Godfrey. 'The item is a review of *The Lonely Girl* by Edna O'Brien. The review has set flowing a stream of protests from Catholic layfolk to the editor.'

McQuaid told Godfrey that he had been so taken aback that 'such stuff' would be printed that he gave the book to the Minister for Justice, Charles Haughey, who came to him next day to express his disgust and revulsion. 'Like so many decent Catholic men with growing families, he was just beaten by the outlook and descriptions,' McQuaid wrote of Haughey's reaction. 'I was very surprised that the Literary Lounger of the *London Illustrated* let it down so lightly. He is normally sane. Perhaps Your Eminence will have the book read.[72]

'I am in complete agreement with Your Grace that we must try to prevent such things happening again,' Godfrey replied. 'I was startled by what I have seen of the writings of Edna O'Brien and have written to the editor of the *Catholic Herald*, a new one as you may know. I have met him on a number of occasions and he seems quite well-intentioned and I trust will attend to the matter.'[73]

That new editor was an Irishman, Desmond Fisher, formerly of the *Irish Press* and later to become a senior executive in RTÉ. When shown this correspondence decades later, Fisher is adamant that Godfrey did not raise the question of Edna O'Brien with him. 'Godfrey must have been humouring McQuaid, whose attitudes were considered old-fashioned by the English bishops,' Fisher surmises.[74]

Despite McQuaid's efforts to ban her writings in Ireland, O'Brien had other notable successes such as *Girls in their Married Bliss* and *August is a Wicked Month*. When the Dominican priest, Fr Austin Flannery O.P., said publicly that he liked O'Brien's work, the Dominican Provincial received a handwritten letter from McQuaid expressing his opposition to such sentiments being held by a religious. The Provincial passed a copy of the rebuke on to Flannery but took no action against him. Another indication of how out of touch McQuaid had become with liberal opinion in Ireland itself was the story circulating that, in the absence of the Dominican Provincial, Flannery, as his stand-in, received the complaint about Edna O'Brien, to which he replied: 'Your Grace, I acknowledge your complaint about Fr Flannery. Yours in Christ, Austin Flannery.'[75]

Yet despite his hidebound attitudes, McQuaid had a progressive interest in the new science of sociological research. He advised the Maynooth academic, Fr Jeremiah Newman, that sociologists made the mistake of regarding a priest in a teaching post as not being engaged in the pastoral ministry, a suggestion which enabled Newman to include priest-teachers in his pioneering work on the state of religion in Ireland.[76]

In 1962, McQuaid privately engaged an American Jesuit to conduct the first sociological study of public opinion in the Dublin area, in a survey interviewing Catholics about their attitudes toward religion and clerical authority. The findings produced by Fr Biever were mainly but not all to McQuaid's liking.[77] Across all categories of age, class and region of birth, almost nine out of ten of those interviewed regarded the Catholic Church as the greatest force for good in Ireland. The people looked to priests as the natural leaders, not only in religious matters but also in political and economic affairs. Almost nine out of ten Dubliners said they would support the Catholic Church in a conflict with the State. Describing the politicians as helpless against a clerically dominated social climate which cleared in advance the most important legislation, Biever concluded that the political process was heavily tinged by theocracy.

However, even in 1962 there were warnings that the seeds of decline for the Irish Catholic Church had been sown. A staggering statistic showed the huge gulf between this educated group and the masses: 83 per cent of the educated disagreed with the proposition that the Catholic Church was the greatest force for good in Ireland, while 87 per cent of the less well educated supported the proposition. Though cut off from political power by the clergy and by the mass of their compatriots, the intellectual élite formed an important but isolated and alienated group. According to Biever, the intellectuals were disillusioned as to the efficacy of the Church in the performance of its social functions. McQuaid's Church was almost forcing the talented intellectual to seek his or her fortunes in other countries. This was a reservoir of alienation that was to swell in the 1960s, highlighted by memories of McQuaid's roles in the Mother and Child controversy and the Yugsolav soccer boycott.[78]

However, as McQuaid prepared in autumn 1962 to travel to Rome for the Second Vatican Council, neither he nor his Episcopal colleagues detected this undercurrent of anti-clericalism running through the educated stratum of a relatively uneducated nation. So confident were McQuaid and the Irish bishops that the Vatican Council would be of short duration and traditional tone that they petitioned Rome to be excused from making their *ad limina* visits in 1962: they saw no need to go there twice in the one year.[79] However, McQuaid was to see more of Rome in the next three years than at any other time in his life. He was unprepared for the revolutionary changes in Catholicism that would alter the course of both his episcopacy and his country.[80]

PART IV

VATICAN II –
CHANGE & DOWNFALL OF
JOHN CHARLES MCQUAID
1962–73

Roman Winds of Change
1962–65

'I am as well as my enemies allow me to be.'
McQuaid to John A. Costello.

'The bells of Your Grace's diocese are even now ringing out their prayerful peals in union with the sentiments of the absent Chief Pastor of Dublin,' Monsignor John O'Regan wrote to Archbishop McQuaid on October 11, 1962, the day on which Pope John XXIII opened the Second Vatican Council in St Peter's with ceremonial splendour and Latin oratory. 'The Press, Radio and Television coverage of events so far has been most impressive, but nothing to the scenes and events which are now such a part of Your Grace's life. We are all very proud that the diocese has such a very distinguished and worthy representative at this great Council and I know that your work in Rome will shed further lustre on the great achievements of Your Grace for the Church and for this diocese.'[1]

As O'Regan penned this sycophantic note from Dublin, McQuaid was being spotted among the 2,500 prelates by a young Australian priest, Fr Michael Keating, who was assigned to assist Archbishops to their places. 'He was humbly placed, and I told him as the Primate of Ireland he could have a more prominent position. He declined but spoke at some length to me about Australia. His humility struck me as I had heard of his strictures.'[2]

During a five-hour ceremony, Pope John redrew the map of Roman Catholicism. Attacking 'the prophets of doom' who saw in modern times 'nothing but prevarication and ruin', the 80-year-old Pontiff charted a new route for Catholic renewal and ecumenical progress. His remarks laid the basis for what became known as 'the spirit of the Council', a phrase which distinguished between the substance of the ancient doctrine of 'the deposit of the faith' and the way in which it was expressed.[3]

In outlook and conviction, McQuaid ranked among Pope John's 'prophets of doom'. McQuaid had represented Pope John as a traditionalist who anguished over 'insidious errors' endangering Catholic spirituality and had confidently anticipated that the council would invite 'the dissident Christians to seek that unity that so many souls desire'. Dampening expectations of momentous change arising from the council, he warned the faithful against new and startling moves towards the unity of Christians.[4]

Furthermore, in his preparatory submission to Rome, McQuaid envisaged the council updating the Syllabus of Errors, published by Pope Pius IX in 1864, with fresh condemnations of evolution, polygamy, existentialism, situation ethics, moral re-armament, socialism and Communism. He also favoured a strengthening of the powers of diocesan bishops over the religious Orders and advocated a dogmatic proclamation of the Blessed Virgin Mary as the Universal Mediatrix of All Graces.[5]

Aged 67 and in excellent health, McQuaid had no small regard for the role which he was about to play on the world ecclesiastical stage. Just as his predecessor Cardinal Cullen had been prominent at the First Vatican council of 1869–70, so McQuaid expected that he would be a major figure at Vatican II as a beacon of Catholic certitude in the age of Sartre and Beckett. Owing to Cardinal D'Alton's continual illness, McQuaid was the acknowledged leader of the Irish representation. Fluent in Latin and with passable Italian, he knew his way around Rome, and since his arrival on October 7 had visited heads and officials of the various departments of the Curia.

Pope John's 'prophets of doom' in the Curia were led by the head of the Holy Office, Cardinal Alfredo Ottaviani, and Cardinal Michael Browne, the Irish Dominican. This faction was also strong within the Italian Hierarchy, and centred around Cardinal Giuseppe Siri of Genoa and Cardinal Ernesto Ruffini of Palermo. Ottaviani had deluged the council fathers with 2,000 printed pages of preparatory documentation and was pressing for a quick, one-session council that would ratify the prepared texts.

However, at the first working session, Ottaviani faced a mutiny when Cardinal Achille Liénart of Lille and Cardinal Joseph Frings of Cologne took over the microphone and insisted that the council should elect its own members to specialist commissions rather than accept the Curia's picked list. This procedural sparring was overshadowed in the media by the threat to world peace, as US President John F. Kennedy and Soviet leader Nikita Khruschev confronted each other over the siting of Soviet missiles in Fidel Castro's Cuba.

The threat of nuclear war hung over the world as McQuaid delivered his first address to the council on October 24, when, speaking on behalf of the Irish Hierarchy, he argued for the retention of Latin in the Mass. According to the chronicler of the council, Xavier Rynne (a *nom de plume* for the American Redemptorist priest, Francis Xavier Murphy) McQuaid 'announced that he was not at all against the Latin language. He wanted it retained as now in the Mass, but could see the utility of allowing the vernacular in the administration of the sacraments.'[6]

McQuaid's defence of Latin as the language of universal Church worship followed speeches in favour of the use of modern languages – 'the vernacular' – from the head of the Vatican Library, Cardinal Eugene Tisserant, and the head of the Secretariat for Christian Unity, Cardinal Augustin Bea. It signalled that McQuaid was firmly on the far right of the council.

To the relief of the council – and the world – Khruschev agreed on October 26 to withdraw his missiles from Cuba, partly as a result of Pope John's mediation. With the spotlight back on the council's procedural tussle, McQuaid submitted suggestions to the Secretary General, Archbishop Pericle Felici, a nephew of the late Nuncio to Ireland. His second brief intervention against change in the administration of the Eucharist was well received, according to his secretary, Fr Ardle MacMahon, who reported to the Dublin diocesan staff: 'A number of people present spoke of the intervention as being clear, concise and commanding very close attention from the Fathers of the Council.'[7] Bishop John T. Scanlan felt that McQuaid's remarks received many expressions of approval from the American bishops.[8]

The attention of most Fathers was fixed not on McQuaid but on the burly Ottaviani, known as *Il Baluardo*, the Bulwark. When Ottaviani exceeded his ten minutes' speaking time at one debate, the presiding prelate, Cardinal Bernard Alfrink of the Netherlands, cut off his microphone. Ottaviani was doubly mortified when a round of applause signalled support for Alfrink's move. McQuaid, however, was not amused: the council needed order. With the aim of giving direction to the proceedings, McQuaid attended an informal meeting of the Hierarchies of England and Wales, Scotland and Ireland at the English College on Saturday November 3. The joint session was convened after Monsignor Derek Worlock, secretary to the ailing Cardinal William Godfrey, proposed the meeting to McQuaid.[9] The meeting set up a sub-committee under McQuaid's chairmanship which drew up a five-point plan to streamline council debates. Preference was to be given to bishops who spoke on behalf of a group, orations were to be succinct (McQuaid's October 24 script was to be a model), a maximum of five minutes should be allocated to each speaker, a guillotine procedure should be used to speed up voting on texts and the agenda should be drastically reduced to cover only matters of vital interest.[10]

This British-Irish Episcopal gathering was noteworthy for the late arrival of the Archbishop of Liverpool, John Carmel Heenan, who had just come from a meeting with the Secretary of State, Cardinal Amleto Cicognani, to whom he had mentioned the English College caucus. Cicognani had asked for a copy of its recommendations by next day. McQuaid duly sent him the text, but not until after he prevented the British-Irish sub-committee from becoming a permanent forum.

McQuaid won support at a meeting of the Irish Hierarchy for an alternative strategy designed to maintain Ireland's independence from a British Isles' formation. The Irish bishops endorsed a seven-point procedural blueprint worked out by McQuaid and Browne. This blueprint, which was to be submitted to the Pope, reinforced the thrust of the English College document but was more precise and rigorous on technical details, and bore the imprint of McQuaid's experience in expediting Maynooth business, not least in its proposal that the names of speakers should not be given to the media.[11]

Having preserved the right of the Irish Hierarchy to send its own proposals to Cicognani while maintaining a loose contact with the British, McQuaid sent letters to Cardinals Norman Gilroy of Sydney and James Francis McIntyre of Los Angeles, as well as to Bishop Joyce of Auckland, with the aim of forming a lobby among the Irish diaspora. 'We are particularly anxious to have freedom of action in linking with other Hierarchies especially with the American,' McQuaid told McIntyre.[12] However, neither the British-Irish plan nor the McQuaid-Browne blueprint became the formula for a swift and peremptory end to the council as desired by the traditionalist camp.

The way forward was being charted elsewhere – in the house where the triumvirate of Cardinals Frings, Liénart and Paul-Émile Léger of Montreal agreed on a daring scheme to throw out the Curia's agenda and to start afresh. This group cooperated closely with the two prelates who were to produce the master-plan for the council: Cardinal Léon Joseph Suenens of Brussels-Malines and Cardinal Giovanni Battista Montini of Milan. As far back as March 1962, Suenens had been encouraged by Pope John to produce an overall plan in consultation with Montini. Their scheme divided topics into the church *ad intra* and *ad extra*, encompassing domestic and external issues. The Suenens approach was given shape by Montini in a letter to Cicognani stressing that the council would need a second session to deal with the mission of the Church and a third session to deal with the Church's relationship with other groups in society.[13]

As the council moved forward on the lines proposed by the Montini-Suenens partnership, McQuaid and Browne opposed a far-reaching proposal to grant greater powers of decision-making to the National Episcopal Conferences based on the principle that these bodies should work collegially with the Pope. McQuaid and Browne saw this proposal as a move to limit the power exercised by an individual bishop in his own diocese.[14]

From Rome, McQuaid was also preventing attempts to promote new theological thinking in Dublin. The text of a Milltown Park public lecture on 'Adam and Anthropology' by Fr Martin Brennan S.J., a lecturer in biology at UCD, was 'delated', that is, complained of, to McQuaid, who ordered that press releases of future Milltown lectures should be subject to censorship by his office.[15] McQuaid's writ also extended to Palmerstown in Co. Dublin, where a young Mayo man and future Labour Government minister, Emmet Stagg, was informed by the Archbishop's secretary, Fr Liam Martin, that he was 'directed to say that His Grace the Archbishop will oppose your accepting the position offered to you as Trainee Laboratory Technologist in Trinity College.' Stagg ignored the ban.[16]

Meanwhile, on November 14, Ottaviani strode back into St Peter's to introduce the *schema* (council proposal) on the Sources of Revelation, which was based on the traditionalist view that there were 'two sources' of revealed truth, namely the teaching of scripture and tradition as taught by the Church. Dismissing alternative drafts circulated by French, German, and Dutch theologians, Ottaviani haughtily asserted that 'the presentation of a *schema* belongs solely to the Holy Father'. It was a stand-off between Ottaviani and the council reformers that could only be decided by the Pope.

Next evening a telephone message from Bishop Joyce was left at the Irish College for McQuaid, informing him that the anti-Curialist group were very active, especially among the Africans, and was claiming to have the support of the Pope. As Gilroy was worried at this development, Joyce wanted to know if McQuaid planned to speak next day. 'This is only one of the alarms to which we shall be subjected all through the council,' McQuaid noted. 'And it will get worse.'[17]

A shrewd Cavan man, McQuaid was determined on 'a wait and see' approach. He would not be speaking next day: 'The issue is not at all clear yet,' he explained to Joyce. But even at this early stage, McQuaid felt uneasy that the conciliar tide was moving against the integralist view of the Church as unchanged and unchanging that he had been taught in Rome in 1925.

The tide was changing, and Joyce was correct in fearing that the anti-Curialists had the Pope on their side. Round two went against Ottaviani. The opposition, led by Lienart, argued that the Word of God was the unique source of revelation and dismissed 'the cold and scholastic two-sources formula' as inadequate. The decisive speech was delivered by Bishop Émile-Joseph de Smedt of Bruges, who warned that the council would fail if the draft was not modified. It was described by *Le Monde* as 'one of the great moments of the council'.[18]

None of the dramatic change sweeping Rome was conveyed by Cardinal D'Alton to the Irish people when he spoke at Dublin airport as the Irish bishops returned from the Vatican Council's first session. Their most abiding collective memory was their pious enjoyment of the privilege of celebrating Mass each day at the tomb of St Peter with bishops of every race and colour from all corners of the world.[19] Attention centred instead on the chalice which had been presented to Cardinal Lauri during the 1932 Eucharistic Congress which was now being brought back to Dublin like a football trophy by McQuaid. The return of the Eucharistic Congress chalice seemed to symbolise that intellectually the Irish Hierarchy was still stranded in 1932.[20]

1963: Business as usual

In the opening weeks of 1963, McQuaid continued to act as if what was happening in Rome had no relevance to life in Ireland. He was absorbed in Church-State negotiations on education, adoption, company law and a proposed change in the age of consent for marriage. He was the Hierarchy's principal figure in these complex matters, and was now dealing with the ambitious and able ministers of a younger post-Civil War generation.

The Minister for Education, Dr Patrick Hillery, a Clare man who had been educated by the Holy Ghost Fathers at Rockwell College, was causing alarm in Episcopal ranks over his plan to extend nationally an experiment in comprehensive schools begun in the western and border counties. In a briefing note for the Hierarchy, McQuaid described this new type of secondary school as unconstitutional and 'a simulacrum of British-type schools'. Instead of accommodating the preference of Catholic parents for fully Catholic schools, as required by the Catholic Church, McQuaid argued that Hillery was proposing to use taxpayers' money to establish State secondary schools which would be non-denominational and sexually coeducational, whose curriculum would be biased in favour of literary education at the expense of science. He complained that the role of Catholic bishops was so nebulous in law that Protestant Bishops could claim the same position.[21]

McQuaid's analysis confirmed the worst fears of the Bishop of Elphin, Vincent Hanly, who had taught Latin and mathematics at Summerhill College, Sligo. 'We are on the edge of an educational crisis,' Hanly informed McQuaid after he had met Hillery in Dublin. Hanly feared that Hillery was a secularist.[22]

In this panic atmosphere, McQuaid met Hillery and the Secretary of the Department of Education, Tomás Ó Raifeartaigh, and subsequently assured the bishops that there was no threat whatsoever to the schools. 'The definitely denominational, non-coeducational character of the comprehensive schools, with management by the parish clergy, gives us the necessary guarantee in regard to Catholic teachers and curriculum and discipline,' he assured them.[23]

McQuaid's confidence calmed Bishop James Fergus, co-secretary of the Hierarchy. 'The Bishop of Elphin and myself can now feel that the position is safe as long as Your Grace has a grip on it,' he told McQuaid, who had been assured by Hillery that the proposed legislation would not be presented to the Dáil until it had been vetted by the bishops.[24]

At around the same time, the Minister for Industry and Commerce, Jack Lynch, a former Cork hurling star and a lawyer by profession, called a young civil servant into his office. Lynch had met McQuaid, who told him that he was concerned about the Companies Bill. Lynch instructed the official to run out to Drumcondra and settle the matter with the Chancellor of the Archdiocese, Monsignor O'Regan, and to relieve McQuaid's anxieties about the Bill, a massive tome running to several hundred clauses and a ream of schedules. The official was left with an abiding recollection of the efficiency of McQuaid's diocesan system when it came to dealing with material matters affecting its interests. He also marvelled at the promptness of the response McQuaid elicited from the civil authorities.[25]

McQuaid reported to the bishops that the Companies Bill was a matter of concern to dioceses organised as companies without share capital, as they would now be legally required to present annual audited accounts to the Registrar of Companies. To forestall this, McQuaid was seeking an amendment which would exempt dioceses from these provisions. McQuaid had already secured an exemption for the dioceses in an earlier Street Collections Act. Lynch, like Hillery on the comprehensive schools, accommodated McQuaid's stipulations.[26]

McQuaid was also keeping a watchful eye on the progress of the Minister for Justice, Charles J. Haughey, the most colourful and able of the new crop of ministers, who was married to Maureen, the eldest daughter of Taoiseach Seán Lemass. McQuaid had met Haughey, then parliamentary secretary to the ageing Minister for Justice, Oscar Traynor, early in 1961 and had given him the wording of a text to protect the Catholic Church's financial interests in regard to Mass bequests which was incorporated into the Charities Act.[27]

Later that year, Haughey, now Minister for Justice, had dealings with McQuaid, including a midnight meeting, when the Archbishop attempted to settle a dispute with Gardaí that led to the setting up of the Garda Representative Association.[28]

Having co-authored the 1952 Adoption Act, McQuaid instructed Bishop Fergus 'to block' new proposals from Haughey on adoption before they were finalised by Government, 'lest a wrong scheme be advanced'.[29] From McQuaid's comment to Fergus, it is clear that his strategy was to influence legislation before it reached the Dáil. In due course, McQuaid studied Haughey's amending Bill which related to the issue of citizenship, a point that had been raised by the Hierarchy in its original recommendations before the 1952 Act was passed. 'This is merely a technical matter that on careful examination I find of no substantial importance to Catholic adopters,' McQuaid concluded. 'But I insist with Justice on referring every such change to all the Bishops.' Haughey, like Hillery and Lynch, learned that a basic rule of Irish politics was to consult and placate

McQuaid. Knowing that McQuaid occasionally took a glass of wine, Haughey sent him a few vintages fit for the palate of an Archbishop. Thanking him for the gift, McQuaid wrote that when abroad he drank wine but very rarely at home.[30]

McQuaid, however, was unhappy with proposals to change the marriage laws. He had raised his reservations with the departments of Health and Justice but was concerned that the former department had not taken these on board, and had therefore notified the Tánaiste and Minister for Health, Seán MacEntee, of his concerns. 'The Department of Health is blandly proceeding with a legal question, having refused to listen to the points made by Justice, (at my instigation, I may say confidentially),' McQuaid told Bishop Fergus. 'At least, I shall halt Health in its progress.'[31] MacEntee arranged to negotiate with two Dublin priests, appointed by McQuaid, Fathers Gerard Sheehy and Jeremiah Curtin. The outcome was judged to be 'very satisfactory' from the bishops' point of view.[32]

1963: New leaders emerge

To the annoyance of the Westminster authorities, McQuaid did not attend the funeral of Cardinal Godfrey, who died in January 1963.[33] D'Alton, though ill himself, braved the winter bleakness and travelled to London, but fatally damaged his own health. A few weeks later, McQuaid received a telegram from the Auxiliary Bishop of Armagh, William Conway, informing him that D'Alton had died. McQuaid drove through heavy snow to Armagh, where he chanted the Absolutions at D'Alton's funeral Mass along with Cardinal Spellman, Archbishop Walsh of Tuam and Archbishop Murphy of Cardiff. So cold was the weather that the heating system broke down and the Mass was said by candlelight, without organ music. The dimness of the church seemed suited to the passing of an era.

The deaths of D'Alton and Godfrey made the leadership of the Irish and English Hierarchies a burning issue at a sensitive stage in the proceedings of the Vatican Council, and once again speculation mounted as to whether McQuaid would be confirmed as the official leader of the Irish Hierarchy. While Armagh remained vacant, McQuaid handled administrative matters relating to the second session of the council scheduled for September.[34] He declined to take over the position of patron of the Catholic Truth Society from D'Alton, even though he recognised that it 'needed a shot in the arm'. His mind was focused on organising the Irish bishops, and he proposed the holding of special conferences to allow them coordinate their views on the agenda prior to embarking for Rome.[35]

McQuaid, like the other Irish bishops, did not appear to have fully grasped the new *détente* between the Vatican and the Kremlin which shaped Pope John's classic Encyclical, *Pacem in Terris*, published in April.

The Encyclical was addressed to 'all men and women', not just to Catholics, and while the Pope condemned Communism as a philosophy, he recognised 'good and commendable elements' in its programmes. This was a recognition of the liberalising policies of Nikita Khrushchev, especially his decision to release the Ukrainian Metropolitan, Archbishop Josef Slipyi, from a Soviet labour camp.

As well as teaching that Communists could be men and women of good will, John also defined human rights as belonging to individuals of every race and creed, a marked change from the Catholic Church's traditional upholding of its own institutional rights vis-a-vis the State. Rather than condemning the world for its anti-Catholicism, its materialism and its faith in science, Pope John praised the improved conditions of workers, welcomed the increasing role of women in public life, and rejoiced that Western imperialism was on the decline. He also questioned the just war theory by arguing that war no longer made sense in a nuclear age.[36]

This powerful Encyclical was to be John's last testament: the 81-year-old Pontiff was dying from stomach cancer. It was not until Whit Monday evening, June 3, as the Pro-Vicar of Rome, Cardinal Luigi Traglia, said the words *Ite Missa Est* at the conclusion of the Mass for the Sick in a crowded St Peter's Square, that Pope John gave his last shudder in the Papal bedroom of the Apostolic Palace. McQuaid prepared a tribute which he agreed to broadcast on television at the prompting of RTÉ Programme Controller Pádraig Ó Raghailligh.[37] In his broadcast, McQuaid compared the reign of John XXIII with that of Pius X, 'by reason of the flame of charity that visibly burned in the spirit of each Pontiff'.[38] His evaluation of the late Pope told more about John McQuaid than John XXIII. The Union Jack flying at half mast outside City Hall in Belfast, spoke more tellingly of Pope John's work in breaking down barriers between Catholics and Protestants than McQuaid was prepared to admit.

McQuaid presided at Solemn Pontifical Requiem Mass in the Pro-Cathedral before flying to Rome as the senior Irish churchman for the official mourning ceremonies. In Rome he attended the Consecration of Monsignor Tom Ryan as Bishop of Clonfert,[39] but his high profile in the city served to highlight the fact that Ireland was unrepresented at the conclave which on June 21 elected Cardinal Montini, who assumed the Papal throne as Paul VI. Montini's election was welcomed by McQuaid, who could not have forgotten Ambassador Joe Walshe's prediction that Montini would become Pope and that his appointment would be good for Ireland. McQuaid must have felt within himself that Montini's accession to the Papacy would pave the way, at last, for recognition of his credentials for a cardinal's hat.

Five days after Montini's election as Pope, McQuaid stood in the queue of dignitaries awaiting the arrival at Dublin Airport of President John F. Kennedy, the first Catholic President of the United States.

Privately, McQuaid had made representations to the Minister for External Affairs, Frank Aiken, about the protocol for the visit. Dublin Airport was in his diocese, McQuaid maintained, thus he should be the first dignitary to meet the President. A ruffled Aiken rushed to find Lemass, who was in the Dáil canteen with some ministers, including Charles Haughey. When Aiken blurted out the problem raised by McQuaid, Lemass told him that if the Archbishop wished to meet the President at the airport, then all the church leaders, including the Nuncio, should be invited. This solution snookered McQuaid: diplomatic protocol gave the Nuncio precedence over the Archbishop of Dublin. On the day, Lemass, after welcoming Kennedy, had the pleasure of introducing him to the church leaders in a line that was headed by Sensi, with McQuaid second, ahead of Archbishop George Simms of the Church of Ireland.[40]

On foot of the Kennedy visit, McQuaid returned to Rome for the Coronation of Montini as Pope Paul VI, which was also attended by de Valera, Aiken, and the Irish Ambassador to the Holy See, Thomas Commins, who were granted an audience by Paul VI.[41]

A few months later, on September 14, Bishop William Conway was appointed Archbishop of Armagh. Unlike Cardinals MacRory and D'Alton, who had been his seniors in age, Conway was nearly 18 years younger than McQuaid. Indeed, McQuaid was already a member of the Hierarchy in June 1942 when Fr Conway of St Malachy's College, Belfast, applied for the chair of Moral Theology at Maynooth. McQuaid supported the candidature. As well as teaching English and Latin, Conway, known as 'Big Bill' by his friends, had built up an impressive academic record at Maynooth and the Gregorian University. A highly organised man, he had studied not only how the Roman Curia and the Roman Rota worked, but had also gained practical experience there in 1941, when he worked for a short time in the private office of the Under-Secretary of the Congregation of the Sacraments, Monsignor Zerbi.[42]

More adept at public relations than McQuaid, Conway struck the right chord in his first message when he referred to 'a certain sense of spring in the air through the Church as a whole and, if I mistake not, in Ireland also'. On September 25, McQuaid attended Conway's Consecration in Armagh, only four days before they both were present in Rome for the opening ceremony of the second session of the Vatican Council by Pope Paul.

Although McQuaid was given the honour of celebrating Mass in St Peter's on October 1, it was Conway who now led the Irish delegation, especially after his appointment as a member of the Commission on Clergy. With an energy that had not been seen in the higher echelons of the Irish Hierarchy since McQuaid's own appointment in 1940, Conway plunged into the council's three main themes – the nature of the Church, the promotion of Christian unity, and dialogue with the modern world.

As chairman of the Episcopal Conference, Conway liked to hold press conferences and give interviews, two methods of communication which McQuaid continued to shun, preferring to shower Monsignor Felici and the council secretariat with technical amendments in Latin. McQuaid attended an Irish-Belgian luncheon at the Irish Embassy to the Holy See in the Villa Spada at which he was joined by the man whose views he deeply suspected, Cardinal Suenens. More congenially, McQuaid was guest at lunch in the Corso d'Italia hosted by the Superior General of the Holy Ghost Fathers, Marcel Lefebvre, who shared his anxieties that the council was losing coherence in its pandering to neo-Modernist and neo-Protestant tendencies.

McQuaid's only intervention of the second session, and his last of the council, came on the subject of ecumenism. It was a short, terse speech warning of its dangers. His style and approach was contrasted with the speech delivered shortly afterwards by Archbishop Heenan, who had succeeded Godfrey at Westminster. A highly perceptive report sent to the Department of External Affairs by Ambassador Commins noted:

> In the Council Hall the general atmosphere Dr Heenan's statement managed to create was one of oncomingness to the separated brethren, whereas that created by Dr McQuaid's was a rather sober reflection on the reality of the doctrinal differences dividing Catholics from the separated brethren. This impression derived from the shortness (two minutes), conciseness and directness of Dr McQuaid's statement. Dr Heenan, speaking for the Bishops of England and Wales, spoke much longer and knew how to coat the pill, whereas Dr McQuaid (speaking for himself) administered it quite clinically. But it would be a great mistake to conclude that Dr Heenan's approach to ecumenism is, in the last resort, in any way more forthcoming than Dr McQuaid's.

According to Commins, McQuaid was not gifted – or burdened – with the ability to project his views in a manner designed to win sympathy.

> What he has to say he will say if he feels it to be the truth, and without apparent regard for tangential niceties. He seems to be temperamentally incapable of 'padding' a statement in the interest of making its essential import more easily acceptable to those to whom it is addressed. In other words, it is not in his nature 'to coat the pill' and this can often be a costly drawback as it materially must tend to make the average person interpret his crisp style as reflecting an unrelenting and dogmatic attitude

generally towards the entirety of the subject matter on which he is expressing himself. And this could be a quite mistaken interpretation.[43]

Similarly, Commins detected a deeply conservative bent in Conway, based on private discussions at the Villa Spada which the Archbishop of Armagh had with prelates such as Cardinal Julius Dopfner of Munich. This observation was borne out in a speech in which Conway frowned on mixed marriages. However, like Heenan, Conway knew how 'to coat the pill' for Protestants, by comparing the Reformation, for example, to a quarrel among neighbours.

Just as the first session was distracted by Kennedy's confrontation with Khruschev, the second was temporarily knocked off course by the news of Kennedy's assassination in Dallas. McQuaid immediately sent telegrams of condolences to Washington and to Jacqueline Kennedy. Dinner at the Irish College that evening took place in a shocked and hushed dining-room.[44]

Despite the world media focus on Kennedy's death, McQuaid went ahead two days later with the publication from Rome of an announcement that the Cause for the Beatification of Matt Talbot had reached the final stage of the Apostolic Process. It was bad timing. Irish eyes were on the funeral preparations in Washington and the memories of his wonderful visit to Ireland. Poor Matt Talbot was a casualty of the Kennedy assassination: his process still stands where it was in that tragic November of 1963.

By early December the council had regained its momentum and promulgated *Sacrosanctum Concilium*, The Constitution on the Sacred Liturgy, its first achievement and one which was to have dramatic effect on ordinary Catholics: Latin was now to be replaced in the Mass by the national language of each country. As McQuaid indicated in his Pastoral Letter on the Liturgy, he was among the 2,147 who voted in favour of the change rather than among the four who opposed it. There was an element of back-tracking in his memory: 'Forgotten now the words of controversy, the moments of tension, when in our anxiety to be faithful to our sacred trust, each had striven, in his human way, but with earnest Faith, to formulate the teaching that would benefit the Church.' Dubliners, eager for information about the changes, were left baffled by McQuaid's sonorous assurance that the new liturgy was 'an instrument of sanctity for this our time and for succeeding generations of mankind'.[45]

McQuaid's Christmas reading included the collected works of the *Apparitions of Our Lady to Bernadette at Lourdes* by Canon Réné Laurentin, a present which he received from Bishop Théas of Lourdes and Tarbes.[46] He also read an account of the Vatican Council by Antoine Wegner, the correspondent of the French Catholic newspaper, *La Croix*. McQuaid obviously appreciated this version of conciliar events, for he presented a copy of it to Archbishop Simms. Much of what McQuaid was to read in the year of 1964 was not to be so edifying or enjoyable.

1964: McQuaid's annus horribilis

The year 1964 proved to be an *annus horribilis* for McQuaid. In February his stepmother Agnes died.[47] This personal mourning was compounded by a spate of adverse publicity. Much to his dismay, he became the subject of a more critical style of journalism. In the fourth part of a series on 'Censorship in Ireland' in the *Guardian*, Dubliner Peter Lennon profiled McQuaid as the *éminence grise* behind the collapse of Dr Nöel Browne's Mother and Child Scheme in 1951 and the campaign against the Yugoslav match in 1955. McQuaid's record, Lennon concluded, showed that he was generally on the side of the obscurantists. 'His concern with keeping what he considers to be troublesome information from the people, or ideas which he might admit to being intrinsically valid and worthy, but of a rather too subtle nature, reveals less of a concern for the well-being of his flock than a most unchurchmanlike contempt of their intelligence.' [48]

In *The Open Church*, published in the same year, the American writer Michael Novak depicted McQuaid as rigid and scholastic. Disapprovingly, he quoted McQuaid's remark that it was his experience that 'converts want only certain Catholic doctrines as proposed by the Holy See, not nebulous formulations by private theologians'. McQuaid, he said, shared the general tendency of the Irish Hierarchy of placing authority above any other value and avoiding public competition in the teaching of religion.[49]

Both accounts were avidly picked up in Dublin, particularly as they recycled the stories of how in late 1963 McQuaid had banned two major theologians of the Vatican Council, the Canadian Augustinian priest, Gregory Baum, and the American Jesuit, John Courtney Murray, from speaking in his diocese and of how they outflanked him by speaking, respectively, in Maynooth and Milltown. (In the former case, the Professor of Moral Theology, Dr Enda McDonagh, resisted pressure by letter from McQuaid; in the latter case, Martin was wrong: Murray called off his speaking engagement, but came privately to Ireland.)

Baum, an expert on ecumenism, gave an incisive interview on RTÉ to Kevin O'Kelly in which he explained the new thinking about the role of bishops. 'In the past we thought of the influence which the Church had played in the world as being the actions of the Princes of the Church, of the Bishops in touch with the leaders of society and in that way seeking to influence the development of the world. Today we know that this time has passed.' It was a devastating critique of the monarchical style of episcopacy personified by McQuaid. Nothing like this had been said on Irish television before.[50]

McQuaid wrote to the Director General of RTÉ, Kevin McCourt, asking him to explain on whose authority 'the stranger-priest' had spoken in his diocese on matters of faith and morals. McCourt replied that it was a routine interview with an interesting person, defending the editorial freedom of the national broadcasting station against McQuaid's claim that he had an ecclesiastical right to censor theological opinion.[51]

Coming on top of the Baum-Murray episodes, the writings of Lennon and Novak unsettled McQuaid, who was determined to nip an incipient intellectual revolt in the bud. An orchestrated letter campaign swung into action against the Paris-based Lennon and Novak's book was rubbished by McQuaid himself. Journalist Louis McRedmond recalls McQuaid discussing Novak's book with him in Rome, saying, 'Mr McRedmond, it is a pernicious book.'[52]

A third international profile in 1964 consolidated McQuaid's unenviable stature as a *bête noire* of the council. This was the bestselling *The Pilgrim* by Michael Serafian, a pseudonym for an Irish-born priest, Malachy Martin, who was a brother of one of McQuaid's secretaries, Liam Martin. Serafian bracketed McQuaid with Cardinal Santos of the Philippines as a prelate who considered his authority was sacrosanct. In McQuaid's opposition to Murray and Baum, as well as his 'running battle' with Trinity College, Serafian discovered 'the same high-minded attitude, the same substitution of juridical norms for the one irreplaceable quality of a Christian – genuine charity.' Referring to how a Catholic, Freddie Boland, had been elected Chancellor of Trinity College, Serafian noted that 'this fact, plus the new Catholic interest in ecumenism, has left Dr McQuaid's innate hatred of Protestants and his life-long drive against them somewhat at a loss.'[53]

McQuaid shouldered the blame for hierarchical Ireland, even though most of his colleagues shared his immobility in the face of change. As the editor of the *Catholic Herald*, Desmond Fisher, wrote: 'The whole Irish attitude at the Council was cautious, concerned about disturbing the simple faithful, and reluctant to change the existing disciplines too hastily.'[54] More fundamentally, McQuaid was deeply traumatised by what he judged to be a doctrinal crisis for the Catholic Church. Halfway through the third session of the council in autumn 1964, he informed the Secretary of the Congregation of Seminaries and Studies, Archbishop Dino Staffa, one of John's 'prophets of doom', that he disagreed in principle with the draft text on ecumenism. He was particularly troubled by a section dealing with the circumstances in which Catholics could attend services with Protestants to pray 'for unity'. This section was 'a grave worry to me', McQuaid told Staffa. 'It is altogether repugnant to me.'[55]

To McQuaid's dismay not only were the Council Fathers being asked to tolerate inter-denominational prayers, they were about to give them their solemn blessing. The emerging text even suggested that it was 'desirable' for Catholics to join in prayer with their separated brethren, a prescription that ran completely contrary to the ruling which

Cardinal Marchetti-Selvagianni had delivered to McQuaid against the Mercier Society 20 years earlier.

McQuaid baulked, too, at the recommendations that prayers in common were an effective means of petitioning God for the grace of unity and that they were a genuine expression of the ties which still bound Catholics to their separated brethren. Such recommendations were anathema to his Kimmage Manor and Biblical Institute lectures, which had treated Protestants as wayward sects rather than as sincere Christians.[56]

This sea-change in attitudes struck at the root of McQuaid's belief that lack of allegiance to Rome among the Protestant churches was essentially a lack of recognition of his own position as a spiritual Lord Archbishop of Dublin. His belief was simple: authority was the foundation stone on which the Church in Dublin was built. No allegiance, no authority; no authority, no foundation; no foundation, no Church.[57]

Despite McQuaid's opposition, the ecumenism decree was approved overwhelmingly on November 21, 1964, along with the council's most important document, 'The Light of Nations', which placed special emphasis on 'the local church' as part of a communion of churches which shared supreme authority in the Church under the primacy of the Bishop of Rome. Rather than merely being a provincial outpost of a centralised headquarters in Rome, this local church was to be viewed as having an organic life of its own through the cooperation of different dioceses with one another in the National Episcopal Conference. This principle of co-responsibility was further outlined in the council's stress on the concelebrated Mass and in the idea of 'presbyterial collegiality' – the notion that the bishop and the priest cooperate in their common mission through councils or senates of priests. This latter document demolished the idea of the Church as a kind of military command system on which McQuaid had been nurtured.

The hardening of McQuaid

The New Year began as badly as 1964 had for McQuaid. He found himself at the centre of public controversy after he ordered the removal of modernistic, non-representational carved wooden figures from the crib in the church at Dublin Airport. The workers who had contributed to the £40,000 (£380,000) cost of the church on land donated by the State felt aggrieved by what they regarded as his high-handed ecclesiastical intervention. McQuaid's unseemly skirmishing contrasted with the historic visit by Taoiseach Seán Lemass to Stormont for talks with the Unionist Prime Minister of Northern Ireland, Captain Terence O'Neill.

The death of Sir Winston Churchill on January 24 found McQuaid reluctant to hold a service for the English statesman's soul. However, he was forced to do so by diplomatic gamesmanship on the part of the

Nunciature and the British Embassy. The secretary at the embassy, Monsignor Edward Cassidy, now President of the Pontifical Council for the Promotion of Christian Unity under Pope John Paul II, was the go-between in one of the few instances when McQuaid made an unexpected liturgical-ecumenical gesture.[58]

A few days later, Rome announced that Conway was to become a Cardinal. Rome had again passed McQuaid by. A clear reference to McQuaid having put up a struggle for the honour was made later by the Nuncio, Archbishop Sensi, in a private conversation with the Minister for External Affairs, Frank Aiken.[59]

'You have been much in mind since the announcement of the new Cardinals,' Archbishop Finbar Ryan wrote to McQuaid from Port-of-Spain. 'Neither you nor I was named, despite your merits nor the wish of our brave Prime Minister here!' Consolingly, Ryan noted that a long period of uncertainty, talk and attack had ended for McQuaid, and this had, to a certain extent, left him happier. 'Your single-minded integrity remains, thanks be to God and your own courage.'[60]

Conway's elevation was a cause of celebration in the Irish Republic, as D'Alton's had been in 1953.[61] It came as a surprise, therefore, when McQuaid set up a press relations office and put an experienced journalist, Ossie Dowling, in charge. Its purpose, McQuaid told Sensi, was 'to execute more effectively the pastoral aims of the Decree on the Instruments of Social Communications.'[62] This decree, the worst of all council documents, was in itself to limit the effective scope of this pioneering appointment, irrespective of McQuaid's personality.

Far from being prepared to adapt to a more open Church, McQuaid became noticeably more hardened in his attitudes in 1965. Even his closest advisers observed a heightened intolerance on his part. Increasingly, McQuaid ostracised former collaborators and became even more susceptible to sycophants and informers.

Since 1961, McQuaid had encouraged about 50 members of his Youth Volunteer Force to report directly to him on what priests and laity were saying and doing. As these boys matured into manhood and entered professional or student life in the second half of the 1960s, McQuaid could call on a new corps of eager intelligence-gatherers to supplement the work of the vigilance committee system set up in the early 1950s. Still determined to root out signs of indecency or Communism, McQuaid was also becoming increasingly distrustful of his own clergy.[63]

Priests whose sermons received an unfavourable report from McQuaid's moral vigilantes, received two-sentence warnings from chancellery staff. One priest who delivered a sermon on the changing role of the priesthood was severely reprimanded; others faced demotion to outlying parishes in Wicklow and Kildare under elderly, authoritarian parish priests. 'The atmosphere,' John Feeney wrote, 'of a closely-supervised state within a state was built up.'[64]

A graphic instance of McQuaid's siege mentality was when in early 1965 he wrote to the Dominican Prioress General, Mother Jordan Keary, requesting the lecture notes of a recently appointed lecturer to the Department of History at UCD, Sister Benvenuta O.P., who was to become better known by her own name of Margaret MacCurtain, or, more familiarly still, Sister Ben. Recently returned from working in the Vatican archives, Sister Benvenuta was recruited by Professor Desmond Williams to give courses on the historiography of the Reformation and Counter-Reformation in Europe and Ireland. She had also contributed to a book of essays on theology in the universities, edited by the English theologian, Fr Charles Davis, in which she argued that because the NUI was non-denominational, it would be difficult to set up a department of theology there, unlike Trinity College which had such a department. These views had triggered McQuaid's inquisitive interest in this nun-scholar.

Asked whether she would comply with the Archbishop's request, Benvenuta discussed the dilemma with a former prioress, Sister Maria Joseph Malone, who pointed out that the Dominican Order was subject not to diocesan rule but was under Papal jurisdiction, a principle which had been defended in the nineteenth century. Sister Mary Joseph under-took to explain this point of principle to Mother Jordan. ' You are right,' Mother Jordan replied. 'I should not be giving my authority to the Arch-bishop. I shall phone and tell him this is my jurisdiction.' McQuaid lost the argument.[65]

However, McQuaid's moral vigilantes were more successful in orchestrating a letter campaign in protest at reports that a staff member of *Playboy* magazine would take part in the *Late Late Show* to recruit 50 Irish women as Bunny Girls. The letter-bombardment of Montrose forced RTÉ to instruct presenter Gay Byrne to cancel the item.[66]

Persisting in his efforts to prevent imports of evil books, McQuaid made representations to Jack Lynch, who was now Minister for Finance. Lynch later recalled McQuaid talking about books and magazines with 'suggestive covers and unseemly content'. Lynch felt this was an appro-priate representation for a churchman to make under the laws of the time.[67]

Not for the first time McQuaid confused literature with pornogra-phy. In June 1965 the Censorship Board banned *The Dark*, a novel written by a primary-school teacher, John McGahern, which described a young boy masturbating. McGahern took leave of absence during the display of public outrage that followed the book's publication, and his headmaster urged him not to return to the school but instead to go to England. 'It turned out that he was taking direct orders from the Archbishop of Dublin, John Charles McQuaid,' McGahern later said. 'The Archbishop was behind the whole thing, and he had an absolute obsession with what he called impure books.'

Significantly, McGahern disclosed that the parish priest, Canon Patrick Carton, actually said that it was the Archbishop who was behind his dismissal. 'Then I heard privately, but there was no way you could prove this, that John Charles McQuaid said if the Irish National Teachers' Organisation backed me, he wouldn't give them any support in pay negotiations that were coming up for the department, and that he'd back them to the hilt if they would have nothing to do with my case.'[68]

McQuaid's treatment of McGahern came on the eve of the fourth and final session of the Vatican Council. Determined to hold onto a closed Church in a closed society, he announced defiantly that 'No doctrine of the Church can be changed by the Council,' as he made ready to travel to Rome in September. 'No doctrine taught by the Infallible Church can be changed. It is we who must change.'[69]

Like his friend Archbishop Finbar Ryan, McQuaid had a sense of foreboding that Pope Paul would need all his courage to deal with the reformers.[70] Yet though Paul was steering the council to its reformist conclusions, he made several major concessions to the ultra-right led by Archbishop Lefebvre: he banned discussion of clerical celibacy and ruled that birth control could no longer be an open question in the council as it was to be the subject of an investigation by a special commission.

By now McQuaid appears to have become semi-detached from the Irish Hierarchy, which under Conway's chairmanship had set up eight Episcopal commissions. McQuaid caucused with the minority group, *Coetus Internationalis Patrum*, in which Lefebvre figured prominently.[71] He had also become friendly with the founder of the Legionaries of Christ, Fr Marcial Maciel.[72]

As the council *schemas* were put to the vote, McQuaid, according to John Feeney, 'meekly acquiesced in the vote and went with the massive majorities'.[73] Unlike the First Vatican Council in 1870, which portrayed the Papacy as an absolutist monarchy, the Second Vatican Council defined the Church as the People of God, a pilgrim people living in a specific historical situation and geographical location. Vatican One's emphasis on the supremacy of the Pope was modified by Vatican Two's teaching on collegiality, that the Pope acts in concert with his bishops, sharing co-responsibility on pastoral and doctrinal matters.

The council also redefined the Church's relationship with society in the pastoral constitution on 'The Church in the Modern World'. Here the idea of the Church as a perfect society gave way to the more realistic view that the Church is part of the modern world, an institution integrated into human society. A Church which in the nineteenth century had condemned religious liberty now brought that concept to the fore. A Church which had opposed the modern world now committed itself to dialogue with all currents of religious thought and none.

'You may have been worried by much talk of changes to come,' McQuaid said in a sermon in Dublin's Pro-Cathedral when he returned from the Second Vatican Council:

> Allow me to reassure you. No change will worry the tranquillity of your Christian lives ... As the months will pass, gradually the Holy Father will instruct us how to put into effect the enactments of the Council. With complete loyalty as children of the one, true Church, we fully accept each and every decree of the Vatican Council.[74]

Only three days previously, Pope Paul had told the Italian bishops: 'We, and We above all, must make some change – and it will not be a trifling change.' McQuaid was about to find out how unsettling the postconciliar change would be for Ireland, and for himself.

23

Crisis of Obedience
1965–68

'The loss of respect for the divine dignity of the
episcopate is terrifying – very terrifying in view of the
Irish tradition.'

Archbishop Finbar Ryan to McQuaid.

On December 27, 1965, the Nuncio to Ireland, Archbishop Giuseppi Sensi,
and the Dublin clergy gathered at Clonliffe College to pay homage to John
Charles McQuaid on the twenty-fifth anniversary of his Consecration as
Archbishop. The Nuncio read out a tribute from Pope Paul VI, praising
McQuaid for making Dublin a model diocese. As to the future, Paul urged
him to 'carefully seek out and energetically complete the new policies'.

McQuaid also had a major announcement to make. He disclosed
that he had brought with him from Rome a Decree of the Sacred Congregation of Seminaries and Universities affiliating Holy Cross College,
Clonliffe, with the Pontifical University of St Thomas Aquinas in Rome.
'Clonliffe therefore will have the power to confer a degree in Sacred Theology,' he declared. 'Would not the Founder of the College, Cardinal
Cullen, rejoice that our diocese is thus more closely bound, particularly at
this time, to the traditional, sure teaching of the Apostolic See of Rome?'

In an emotional peroration, he said:

> I shall not ever again, I may presume, be given the occa-
> sion of meeting at once all the body of the clergy. I would,
> then, ask your forgiveness for the faults that have certainly
> been mine, in dealing with you personally and in adminis-
> tering the diocese ... A Jubilee is a moment of rejoicing; but
> there ever lurks a sorrow at the heart of human beings. I
> am reminded by the fleeting years that 'it groweth now
> towards evening and the day is far advanced'.[1]

Not only was McQuaid, now 70 years of age, aspiring to stay in
office 'to the end', he was determined to do so with his authoritarian style
of episcopacy unchanged. In effect, he was launching a counter-strategy

to maintain Clonliffe as a traditional-style seminary which would function as a bastion against the new ideas for a changed priesthood. Yet Pope Paul had given him a subtle hint to implement the policies of Vatican II without causing any more controversy in Dublin. It was a clear marker from the Holy See.

The empty chair

In early January, 1966, *The Irish Times* reported that for the first time since the Reformation the Roman Catholic and Protestant Archbishops of Dublin would say the 'Our Father' together in Dublin's Mansion House during the Week of Prayer for Church Unity. This front-page story was accompanied by an agency report that the Archbishop of Canterbury, Dr Michael Ramsey, was to meet Pope Paul VI in Rome. Suddenly, ecumenism was happening in Dublin as well as Rome.[2]

The report, however, had a distinctly unsettling effect on the tranquillity of the Palace. After reading it with growing anger, McQuaid phoned the organiser, Fr Roland Burke Savage S.J., and accused him of misinforming journalists, because there would no question of his praying publicly with Archbishop George Simms. When McQuaid came off the phone, he instructed his staff not to take any return call from the traumatised Jesuit.

Hastily, McQuaid arranged a meeting with the Nuncio at his residence in the Phoenix Park where, according to León Ó Broin, for two hours he 'pranced' about the room threatening repeatedly to lodge a formal complaint against Burke Savage to the Jesuit Provincial, Fr Brendan Barry S.J. McQuaid's sense of outrage, however, was not shared by Sensi, who was in favour of the Mansion House meeting as being entirely in accordance with the council's Decree on Ecumenism.[3]

McQuaid eventually reached a compromise with Sensi: he agreed to sit on one side of President de Valera, while Simms sat on the other, all of them listening to a lecture on ecumenism by the Belfast priest, Monsignor Arthur Ryan. It was also agreed that after Ryan finished speaking, Sensi would lead the prayers from the platform, where he would be accompanied by Ryan and Burke Savage. McQuaid would come forward to the platform to say the Our Father, while Simms would do so from his seat in the front row.

More than 700 people crowded into the Round Room in the Mansion House for the historic event, which was being televised live by RTÉ. In the rush for places, people sat wherever they could, even taking reserved seats in the front two rows. At 8pm President de Valera, as agile as ever despite his blindness; Simms, dressed in his gaiters and overcoat; the Lord Mayor, Alderman Eugene Timmons, in civic gown and chain; the leader of the Opposition, Liam Cosgrave T.D. and the Chief Justice, Cearbhall Ó Dálaigh, walked down the aisle to spontaneous applause, only to find that there were no seats for them! Spotting the predicament for the President, James Dillon T.D. jumped to his feet and gallantly gave de Valera his chair. The President, however, was forgotten as all eyes turned on McQuaid, who entered in his customary Renaissance-prince style, dressed in his cape, robes and skull-cap, with his air of aloof mystery. Avoiding the confusion in the front row, McQuaid moved directly to the platform where he took a chair alongside Sensi, Ryan and Burke Savage. A fifth chair remained untaken.

For an hour Monsignor Ryan proved he was no Cardinal Bea: his emphasis was on the dangers involved in dialogue and the need for the local bishop to direct and, if need be, correct ecumenical activities. He singled out McQuaid's intervention in the council for special praise, for its defence of Catholic doctrine as well as its parsimony of words, the latter a virtue which the Belfast man failed to imitate. To the discomfort of the genteel Protestants in the audience, Ryan paid 'a well-earned tribute' to the Catholic authorities in the Republic for having maintained a record of tolerance since Independence that entitled them to hold their heads up high. McQuaid was more than pleased by the address.

After polite applause, Burke Savage announced that Sensi would lead them in saying the Lord's Prayer. McQuaid, on the platform, and Simms, in the front row, joined in the reciting of the prayer, along with the 700 people in the Round Room including Taoiseach Seán Lemass. It was a worthy but conventional occasion. Public reaction, however, was less polite. The talking point became 'the empty chair', which it was assumed had been placed there for Simms.

The correspondence columns in *The Irish Times* were dominated by 'The Mansion House'. A 'Catholic Televiewer' felt that he had witnessed a *tour-de-force* by McQuaid. Richard Strahan deplored the sight of McQuaid towering over everyone as if he had won a great battle, and he asked 'why wasn't Dr Simms on the platform and why was Dr McQuaid?' The Church of Ireland *Gazette* hoped that ecumenism in Dublin had not suffered too severe a setback. The *Catholic Sentinel* in Portland, Oregon, judged that 'another gesture has been wrung from the unwilling hands of His Grace the Archbishop of Dublin'. In the *St Louis Review*, John Horgan commented that ecumenism was running the risk of becoming Ireland's number one bloodsport.

Simms too came under fire from those within the Church of Ireland who were suspicious of ecumenism. Some were relieved that he had not been seated beside McQuaid, a gesture that might have signified agreement with Ryan's ill-judged polemic. Others felt that McQuaid had treated Simms as a second-class churchman. Despite his obvious embarrassment at McQuaid's uncourtly behaviour, Simms was most gracious when he told an *Irish Press* reporter that it was a joy for him to attend, that he was deeply interested in everything Ryan said, and that he detected a sincere and profound desire for a greater understanding on doctrinal differences.

An editorial in *The Irish Times* summed up the mood of the meeting as one of 'sackcloth and ashes'. On McQuaid's side was the memory of Penal Laws, of Mass Rocks and a faith which was the only thing in life; on Simms's was a sense of isolation which was intensified by the thought that, in the eyes of people whom they regarded as fellow Christians, they were heretics. But whatever its shortcomings, the newspaper concluded that at least the meeting was a beginning.

Afterwards McQuaid wrote to Mrs Mercy Simms, acknowledging that she and her husband must have suffered because of the Mansion House. 'If we had set out to be discourteous and hurtful, a more sure result could not have been secured – and all because of a good man's failure to coordinate and organise,' he wrote, firmly placing the blame for the calamity on Burke Savage. 'I knew nothing of the Press releases: nothing about the empty chair. In fact, I did not know too well which chair I was meant to take! I find it difficult to say what I have been called on to endure in the English-speaking press because of 'my discourtesy and ecumenical obtuseness': but all these things work together unto good for those that love God.'[4]

This previously unpublished letter reveals the anxious state of McQuaid's own mind about an incident which consolidated nationally and internationally his notoriety as an anti-ecumenical die-hard. An event which was meant, in McQuaid's eyes, to be a formal ecumenical gesture towards the Church of Ireland Archbishop of Dublin, had gone badly wrong because an over-zealous Burke Savage had taken licence to promote the event as a major advance towards Church unity.

Had the occasion not been so badly mismanaged, the Mansion House gathering might have passed off as a modest step towards a formal public relationship between the two Archbishops of Dublin. McQuaid had come to like and respect Simms, who had been a member of the Mercier Society and whose Trinity College background McQuaid feared initially. On Simms's appointment as Archbishop in 1957 after a period as Bishop of Cork, McQuaid expected that he 'would attend everything and speak at everything', and vowed to 'take care of him quietly'.[5]

Over the years, McQuaid met Simms privately and enjoyed his and Mrs Simms's company; she had taught French at Trinity College and took an active interest in social issues. On one occasion, McQuaid presented Simms with a book on Abbé Huvelin, the spiritual director of Charles de Foucauld and an adviser to the 'Modernist' writer, Baron Friedrich von Hügel. Simms appreciated this present as he was interested in von Hügel and recalled as a child meeting Maud Petre, a close friend of von Hügel and of the excommunicated Dublin Jesuit, Fr George Tyrrell. In return, Simms asked Waddingtons to frame a reproduction of one of the pages from the *Book of Kells* for McQuaid.[6]

A successful Mansion House meeting would have improved McQuaid's public image, especially as he had been named Irishman of the Year for 1965 by Sean Mitchell in *The Corkman*.[7] A success might have encouraged him to move further along the ecumenical route. About this time, he accepted an invitation from Lt. Col. Joseph Adams to become a patron of the National Association for the Mentally Handicapped of Ireland, a non-denominational body comprising 60 organisations in the Republic; he would not have done so in earlier years.[8] To the surprise of observers, McQuaid warmed to Ramsey when the Archbishop of Canterbury came to Dublin for the centenary of St Bartholomew's Church in 1967. Asked by reporters about his discussions with McQuaid, Ramsey replied: 'We talked as scholars talk when they find that they have things in common.'[9] As a courtesy, McQuaid nominated his Vicar General, Monsignor Charles Hurley, to attend Ramsey's lecture at the Royal Dublin Society, at which he said he detected a new spirit of ecumenism in Ireland. McQuaid went to Dublin Airport next day to bid Ramsey farewell. Thanking McQuaid, Simms wrote: 'He is a most genial person and appreciated the friendliness he met on all sides.'[10] Simms had in fact introduced the two Archbishops in 1956, when Ramsey was Archbishop of York, and McQuaid had presented him with a copy of his *Wellsprings of Faith*.[11]

Clearly, there was a discrepancy between McQuaid's personal reaction to eminent figures like Ramsey and his Pavlovian distrust of Trinity College Protestantism. But whatever his response to individual Protestants, McQuaid withheld his assent to the new ecumenism. In the last analysis, the empty chair highlighted this incorrigible defect in his outlook. The episode inflicted massive damage on McQuaid's image as an ecclesiastical Canute. He glossed over the extent to which his narrow outlook made him the author of his own 'ecumenical obtuseness', and his attribution of blame for the fiasco to Burke Savage revealed a mean and unforgiving streak. The reviled Jesuit priest found himself out of favour with the Archbishop and was hurt emotionally and psychologically by McQuaid's display of venom.[12]

Furthermore, McQuaid had cut a pathetic figure in the eyes of Sensi, a hard-working but fastidious Nuncio. Having previously worked in the Middle East as Apostolic delegate to Jerusalem and Palestine, Sensi placed a high value on dialogue and told Burke Savage that if the Archbishop had carried out his threat to make a formal complaint, he would have told the Jesuit Provincial to throw the letter in the rubbish bin. The Mansion House episode was a black mark in McQuaid's file in Rome.[13]

'Guying' McQuaid

McQuaid's stock was unprecedently deflated as a result of the Mansion

House debacle when on February 16, 1966, the winter 1965 issue of *Studies* appeared belatedly, carrying a 50-page defence of the Archbishop by its editor, the bruised but gallant Fr Roland Burke Savage. 'The Church in Dublin, 1940–1965: A study of the episcopate of Most Reverend John Charles McQuaid D.D.' was given massive coverage in the Dublin media, which was losing its traditional inhibitions – if not quite its fear – of the Hierarchy. Though somewhat sycophantic in tone, the article marked an important stage in the Irish Catholic Church's transition from public unaccountability to critical scrutiny. Designed largely as a reply to media criticism, especially to Peter Lennon's *Guardian* article and *The Irish Times*, Burke Savage set out to portray McQuaid in a positive light. Instead, he unwittingly put McQuaid in the dock in a way no Irish churchman had been put before.

Cast in the role of defence counsel, Burke Savage introduced an iron-willed prelate who was not so much a domineering figure as a man obsessively conscious of the dignity and responsibility of the high office for which he was accountable only at the court of God. Accepting that McQuaid was not a Hollywood-style Archbishop, Burke Savage claimed that 'the slightly sinister figure with the cloak-and-dagger air' was simply the result of McQuaid's inability to relax before a camera. This was a dubious defence. There are many pictures of McQuaid in which he is relaxed – he enjoyed photography. He used shyness as an excuse for shunning journalists and photographers.

On the charge of religious bigotry, Burke Savage was adamant that McQuaid was never anti-Protestant as such, but conceded that he was most definitely and vigorously anti-non-sectarian in his outlook. This is a most ingenious but unconvincing distinction.

On the third charge of delaying progress on the liturgy, Burke Savage argued that McQuaid knew the value of making changes slowly, almost imperceptibly, so that no one was suddenly steam-rolled into a completely new way of life. This defence underrated both the extent of McQuaid's personal distaste for the new practices and the seismic nature of the change in outlook within Catholicism.

Burke Savage defended the Archbishop's design of churches on the grounds of providing the great body of the faithful of his diocese with churches which came up to their image of one. This was a paternalistic defence and ignored the number of Dublin Catholics who wanted more experimentation in church design.

On the allegations of 'meddling in politics', Burke Savage defended McQuaid's roles in the Yugoslav match and in the Mother and Child controversy. 'Not for him the easy task of climbing on band-wagons when victory was assured; he must guide or else fail in his office,' Burke Savage wrote, coming close to the philosophy of 'my leader, right or wrong'.

Burke Savage accused Peter Lennon of trying 'to guy' the

Archbishop, a charge that provoked Lennon to reply that if there were any possibility of civilised dialogue between bishops and the people, such attacks would be unnecessary. Lennon explained that he had picked the Yugoslav match because it was one of the few documented cases which gave a reasonably clear picture of McQuaid's methods.

Lennon chided Burke Savage for failing to acknowledge that in his account of the Mother and Child Scheme he had overlooked the fact that Nöel Browne was put into a position where he had to resign. Lennon also questioned Burke Savage's good faith in claiming that McQuaid did not have even indirect control in the running of UCD. 'Dr McQuaid controls the whole pattern of education in the diocese of Dublin,' Lennon asserted. 'Not a single subject, not a single textbook could survive on any curriculum from kindergarten up to university level if it met with Dr McQuaid's disapproval.'[14]

The Burke Savage portrait provoked the international theology review, *Herder Correspondence*, into publishing a highly critical article on McQuaid. The writer argued that the root cause of McQuaid's difficulties lay in his character. His 'personal one-sidedness' had produced a pastoral situation which called urgently for repair. 'Every public man has unfortunate incidents, and Dr McQuaid's share, by now so ridiculously magnified, would have been forgotten long ago if his language were different and if he came across as an inspiring guide of men,' the review noted. 'Certainly he has his malicious detractors, but they merely exploit a situation – they did not create it.'[15] This was the nub of the case against John Charles.

Even Burke Savage would have found it impossible to defend McQuaid had he been privy to the way in which the Archbishop forced the Taoiseach, Seán Lemass, to abandon a plan to hold an ecumenical service at the opening of a Garden of Remembrance on the fiftieth anniversary of the Easter Rising. McQuaid ruled out taking part in a simultaneous blessing with Protestant and Jewish clergymen; nor was he prepared to be present at successive blessings by non-Catholic and Jewish clergymen.[16] Even when Lemass invited McQuaid to be the sole churchman officiating at the ceremony, it appears that Archbishop Sensi had to coax McQuaid to overcome his revulsion for the armed revolt which the ceremony commemorated. This led to the nationally televised blessing by McQuaid of all the dead, no matter their religion, in the presence of President de Valera, members of the Government, both Houses of the Oireachtas, representatives of the various religious denominations and survivors of the Rising.[17]

Off camera, however, as a consequence of McQuaid's ecumenical objections, separate religious services were held on Easter Monday prior to the opening of the Garden of Remembrance. Unfortunately, Archbishop Simms and several Presbyterian ministers arrived late for the ceremonies, and discovered that some zealous official had already closed the gates. This embarrassment was highlighted by Cyril James in *The People* and became the subject of a Government inquiry.[18]

Although McQuaid attended a State reception in Dublin Castle for the Rising, he declined an invitation from the Minister for Finance, Jack Lynch, to attend the ceremonial unveiling by President de Valera of the Thomas Davis statue at College Green. Nor did he accept an invitation to sit in the Hogan Stand at Croke Park for the opening performance of *Aiseirí*, a dramatic reconstruction of the events of Easter Week. Privately, he was not unamused by the IRA's demolition of Nelson's Pillar in Dublin's O'Connell Street.[19]

Nor was there an ecumenical whiff at the Inauguration of de Valera's second term as President on June 25, 1966. It was a Catholic service for a Catholic President as McQuaid occupied the special prie-dieu at the Mass in the Pro-Cathedral and, on Lemass's request, imparted the blessing of Almighty God on the President.[20] McQuaid's refusal to countenance an ecumenical dimension at worship on State occasions kept alive memories of how on the death 20 years earlier of former President Douglas Hyde, Government ministers had not been allowed to attend the funeral service at St Patrick's Cathedral.

However, times were changing, and even McQuaid could not prevent one of the most tangible and popular social changes of twentieth century Ireland when the Hierarchy announced that 'for considerations of friendship' with Protestants, Catholics in future could take part in services from which they had been banned under pain of mortal sin for most of McQuaid's lifetime. Catholics could now go into Protestant churches to attend the baptisms of the children of their non-Catholic friends and neighbours. They could be bestman or bridesmaid at the marriage of Protestant friends. They could attend the funerals of non-Catholics. Most significantly, mixed marriages would now take place before the high altar during Mass instead of furtively in the early morning at a side altar or in the sacristy. Public representatives and civic officials would be able to attend non-Catholic services on official occasions. English was to be used at funerals.[21]

No surrender

Far from being subdued, McQuaid was preparing to fight a rearguard battle to prevent what he believed was the break-up of the Catholic Church. He found an ally in Belfast in the recently promoted Bishop William Philbin, whose pastoral writings he admired. 'I feel one has to put the brake on this persistent effort to set up a new kind of Catholic Church,' Philbin assured McQuaid.[22] Ironically, McQuaid had become even more adept at slamming the brakes on change just when Pope Paul VI had abolished the Index of Forbidden Books.

In spring 1966, McQuaid objected to an article on mixed marriages by a staunch advocate of church unity, Fr Michael Hurley S.J., in the monthly review for the clergy, *The Furrow*, and he put pressure on Hurley, through the Jesuit Provincial, to withdraw permission to allow *The Irish Times* publish the article. Only the courage of the Provincial, Fr Cecil McGarry, prevented McQuaid from succeeding in his objective of expelling Hurley from the Dublin diocese. On another occasion, Hurley was banned by McQuaid from giving a highly advertised lecture on original sin at Milltown Park.[23]

Nuns, too, came under McQuaid's critical scrutiny. Up until the Second Vatican Council, nuns generally had kept to their convents and were not allowed to take part in radio or television programmes. Worried for some time, however, about a loosening of religious discipline, especially among 'student-sisters' who were living in hostels or hospitals and were prone to wearing skirts, McQuaid summoned the Reverend Mothers of the diocese to a private meeting at the Palace on August 16, 1966, at which he asked them to introduce a code of conduct for nuns under their charge. 'I should like to see a greater uniformity in the permissions that are accorded,' McQuaid said in a transcript kept in the archives of the Irish Sisters of Charity. He wanted rules governing visits by nuns outside of their convents, on times of receiving visitors, on excursions, on the hour of their return at night and even on the personal use of transistors and expensive cameras. 'I should like, particularly, to see a better code of deportment in the streets,' he said.[24]

Reminding the Mother Superiors of their duty to safeguard religious life, McQuaid lamented:

> We are enduring a period of ferment, during which young Religious are reading all manner of articles and books that give personal views, rather than the established tradition of the Church. Under cover of renewal to meet modern circumstances, changes are being advocated that are not a renewal, but a destruction.

The Holy Faith nuns were McQuaid's model organisation. 'They are solidly formed, hard-working, well-governed, academically equipped; no airs and graces. They will do anything to aid a parish priest. They are untouched by the modern craze for *aggiornamento*.'[25] Among the 'crazes' to be stamped out were liturgical innovations that smacked of the Protestant Reformation. McQuaid was advised by Archbishop Finbar Ryan OP, now in retirement in Cork from Trinidad, to direct his architects and clergy not to substitute a table for the altar. Ryan also shared McQuaid's distress over the decline in the traditional devotion of the Rosary, even its rejection by priests and religious.[26]

Ryan encouraged McQuaid to transform Clonliffe College into 'a bastion of sacerdotal dignity and orthodoxy'. The 'first fruits' of the 'new' Clonliffe were celebrated by McQuaid in May 1966 when he ordained eleven students to the priesthood. At prize-giving, McQuaid advised students to fix their minds 'chiefly on the eternal stabilities of Thomist philosophy and on the authentic teaching of the Church's *magisterium* in theology.' There could be no more disappointing waste of their energy and time, he warned, than 'the futility of mastering avidly articles in reviews or ephemeral concepts of private theologians while neglecting the primary sources of ascertained truth.'[27]

Although the Hierarchy planned to develop Maynooth as a centre of higher studies which would admit brothers, nuns and laity (even women!) in Arts, Science, Philosophy and Religion, McQuaid was intent on withdrawing all Dublin diocesan students from the college. He did not trust Maynooth, especially after the shockwaves caused by the resignation at the end of 1966 from both the priesthood and the Catholic Church of Fr Charles Davis, theological adviser to Cardinal Heenan. Davis, the editor of *The Clergy Review*, had lost his faith in the biblical and historical origins of the Catholic Church and now believed that the Church was corrupt.

McQuaid, who had a supervisory role as an Episcopal Visitor to Maynooth, worked closely with Bishop Michael Browne of Galway to prevent theologians and students there from reading reports about the challenges to traditional authority and practice that were taking place elsewhere, especially in the Netherlands, England and the United States.

Both men were gobsmacked by the radical theological journalism that was appearing in periodicals such as *The Tablet* in London, *Commonweal* in New York and the *National Catholic Reporter* in Kansas City. When Browne, to his horror, came across a copy of the *National Catholic Reporter* within the sacred precincts of Maynooth, he informed McQuaid at once that the copy belonged to a member of the staff!

The McQuaid-Browne partnership feared that *The Furrow*, under the editorship of Fr J.G. McGarry, 'was doing harm' and they tried to put pressure on Bishop Patrick Lennon, in whose diocese of Kildare and Leighlin the monthly review was published, to make him realise that 'he should not allow his diocese to be an escape route for heretics'.[28]

Browne boasted of how he had prevented an even more dangerous subversive from speaking in Galway – Fr Herbert McCabe, the Dominican editor of *New Blackfriars*, who had written an editorial agreeing with Davis's critique of the institutional church, but explaining why he was staying in the Catholic Church to try to bring about change. The possibility of a visit to Ireland by the 'radical' English catechist, Fr Peter de Rosa, sounded alarm bells in Dublin and Galway. Nor was the popularity of the appearances on the *Late Late Show* of the Dominican lecturer in Politics at UCD, Fr Fergal O'Connor, appreciated by McQuaid and Browne. [29]

The McQuaid papers relating to Maynooth for the turbulent post-

council period have not yet been opened for inspection, on the grounds
that they contain references to clergy who are still alive. The evidence
suggests that McQuaid and Browne pressed for an official investigation –
or a purge. Brief and cryptic references in the correspondence between
McQuaid and Browne convey an impression of hysteria over any sign of
mutiny in Maynooth. For instance, there is a self-satisfying reference to a
successful interference which stopped the former Archbishop of Bombay,
Thomas Roberts, from giving a talk at Maynooth.

An *Irish Press* report on the visit of Maynooth students to Trinity
College, where they made contacts with Catholic students, drew a sharp
protest from McQuaid, who pointed out that the Trinity prohibition was
still in force. McQuaid was furious that the visit had been made without
any request to him for permission. Nor was he aware that any permission
had been given to the Maynooth students to join the non-denominational
Union of Students of Ireland (USI) or to associate themselves with Trinity College 'in regard to the magazine *Agora* or other activities'.[30]
McQuaid's intervention was applauded by Browne as having a most salu-
tary effect on both the administration and the students. 'Non-
-intervention would have led to more extreme and scandalous activities,'
he wrote to McQuaid from Galway. While fearing the link-up of Maynooth
students with the USI, McQuaid and Browne dismissed *Agora* as 'poor
stuff, very immature', but they were worried that one of its contributors
was the Professor of English at Maynooth, Fr Peter Connolly.[31]

In opposition to the Hierarchy's policy of opening Maynooth up to
Religious Orders, McQuaid put pressure on the Orders in his diocese to
send their personnel instead to the Mater Dei Institute which he opened
in the grounds of Clonliffe College to train teachers of religion for secondary schools. Its first president was Fr Joseph Carroll, who had become his
favourite adviser. Like Clonliffe College, Mater Dei was affiliated by
McQuaid to the Angelicum. It offered a three-year course leading to a
diploma and a four-year course leading to a master's degree.[32]

McQuaid told the Mother Superiors at his private 'summit' meeting that improved educational standards could be achieved by their giving
support to his plan for an Institute of Religious Formation. 'It is my determination that our courses of theology will maintain the firm teaching of
the authority in the Church,' he said. 'Our link with the Angelicum is our
guarantee, for in the Angelicum the Popes have said, the purest doctrine
has its home. I can guarantee to you sound doctrine.'[33]

Proof of McQuaid's continuing hold over the Department of Education was the ease with which he ensured that Mater Dei graduates were
admitted to the register of secondary teachers as teachers of religion.
Although only 'apprentices' in the principles of sane philosophy and in
the authority of the magisterium of the Church, Mater Dei students were
assured by McQuaid that in later life they would have the power to judge

justly what was being called new, because they had grasped and appreciated what was old.[34]

As part of his policy to contain new ideas, McQuaid commissioned a new series of six textbooks written by Mary Purcell and Brother J.C. Moore, which were to replace the old primary-school catechism over three years.[35] Yet McQuaid had no illusions about the low level of religious understanding among the products of the Irish school system. He admitted to Bishop MacFeely:

> **Very few indeed can defend the Faith. If the young people can be firmly grounded in the belief in the Church as infallible by Christ's establishment they will realise that there is an answer, even if they have not the training to formulate it.**[36]

The 'swinging sixties'

In his book, *The Best of Decades: Ireland in the 1960s,* Fergal Tobin detects 'the nice coincidence' that only a week before the Minister for Justice, Brian Lenihan, announced his intention of reforming the censorship laws, an old-fashioned contretemps took place in Co. Kerry between the Catholic clergy and the buxom film star, Jayne Mansfield.[37] The McQuaid archives reveal that this clerical campaign against Miss Mansfield was triggered off by a letter from McQuaid, though he escaped any public identification with this shameful incident.

On April 18, 1967, the tranquillity of the rural life of the elderly Bishop Denis Moynihan at his Episcopal residence of St Brendan's in Killarney was interrupted with the arrival in the morning post of a letter from the Archbishop of Dublin. The letter confirmed that the world's sexiest celluloid figure was booked to perform her risqué cabaret act at the Brandon Hotel in Tralee. Accompanied by press cuttings of the pouting Miss Mansfield, McQuaid's letter indicated that the blonde bombshell's cabaret act would be no blushing Rose of Tralee-style performance.

'We got to know of the approaching visit of Jayne Mansfield to Tralee at the week-end,' Moynihan replied by return post. Pointing out that there was no mention of Miss Mansfield's date even in the ordinary edition of *The Kerryman,* Moynihan told McQuaid that it had been too late to make a protest from the pulpits that weekend. However, he assured him that there would be a protest 'in every parish in the diocese the following Sunday'.[38]

'This woman boasts that her New York critics said of her that she sold sex better than any other performer in the world,' Bishop Moynihan thundered, in a statement co-signed by his dean, Monsignor John Lane. Miss Mansfield's presence in Tralee, he said, would be a slur on the town's good name. The management bowed to this righteous condemnation and cancelled the engagement only a few hours before the star was about to take the stage. In vain, an upset Jayne Mansfield assured journalists that she had been misquoted and that she was a good Catholic – in fact, one of her happiest moments in Ireland had been when she lit a candle for herself and her young son when she visited the church in Castleisland while a flat tyre in her car was being fixed by the local garage mechanic.

On July 11, 1967, the Government decided to remove a ban on books that had been proscribed for more than 12 years – some 5,000 titles in all. However, it decided not to amend laws banning the sale of contraceptives 'until the moral problems are clarified for Catholics'. In a memorandum to the Government, Lenihan based his case on a liberalisation of the law in Britain, where D.H. Lawrence's *Lady Chatterley's Lover* was declared not to be obscene on the grounds that a person might not be convicted if it was proved that publication was for the public good and in the interests of science, art or literature.[39]

Fifteen months earlier, in February 1966, McQuaid had narrowly escaped becoming a figure of public ridicule along with his colleague over the famous incident on the *Late Late Show* that became known as 'the Bishop and the nightie' incident. When Gay Byrne interviewed a couple about their wedding night, he amused the audience by asking the wife if she could recall the colour of her nightie. Even greater amusement was caused by a phone-call from Bishop Tom Ryan of Clonfert, who announced that he would denounce the programme from the pulpit next day in Loughrea. This threat received massive publicity in the newspapers.

McQuaid was no less amused by the programme than Bishop Ryan, but he had the guile to make his protest in private. He wrote to RTÉ's Director General, Kevin McCourt, to complain that the questions and answers in the interview were 'vulgar, even coarse, and suggestive'. In a wider criticism of Byrne, McQuaid considered that the *Late Late Show* was a wilful exception to the norm of good programming at RTÉ. 'You have not been fairly treated,' McQuaid told McCourt, 'for this type of thing is quite unlike what you have been so warmly thanked for.'[40]

Another source of McQuaid's irritation was the publicity which the *Late Late Show* had given to the American owner of *Playboy* magazine, Hugh Heffner, and his famous Bunny Girls. 'I think Gay Byrne need not, for a second week, return to the Bunnies,' McQuaid advised McCourt, referring to an article in the *Irish Independent*. 'I wonder if you saw Weekender's article and pictures describing the strange American who conceived the plan. You would not, I think, let it into the house.'[41]

No one in RTÉ leaked the McQuaid letter, which would have done colossal damage to his standing – respect for authority was diminishing as the more materialistic values of the era of pop culture began to take root in Ireland. Perhaps McQuaid already had an intuition that he had reacted wrongly a few years earlier when, on receiving a report of the mob hysteria that had accompanied the Beatles on their trip to Dublin, he had predicted that the young would return to the old reverences.[42]

Nor had McQuaid's representations been listened to by the Minister for Local Government, Neil Blaney, when the Ballymun housing estate was being built.[43] McQuaid was also taken by surprise when the Minister for Education, Donogh O'Malley, announced in September 1966 that he was introducing free post-primary education. Although O'Malley made media capital out of not having consulted McQuaid, he later met the Hierarchy to explain his proposal. Accompanied by the Secretary of the Department of Education, Tomás Ó Raiffeartaigh, and two assistant secretaries, O'Malley travelled to Maynooth on October 3 to discuss his policies with Cardinal Conway and McQuaid. No statement was issued afterwards, but O'Malley at least professed to be very happy with the meeting.[44]

Although there was some dissent from religious Orders, by the summer of 1967 the O'Malley scheme was supported by the Hierarchy and it was implemented that September. McQuaid and his colleagues saw the financial benefits to the Church authorities in the scheme.

McQuaid had little liking for O'Malley. Addressing secondary-school teachers in the Gresham Hotel after the annual Votive Mass, McQuaid said there was no such thing as free education, as the taxpayer was obliged to bear the burden. According to McQuaid, O'Malley was presenting as his own the aim of enlarging the facilities for instruction and formation long advocated by the Archbishop of Dublin.

He also berated O'Malley for his attempts to question the role of the religious in education:

> How little they know of the history of education or of the
> organisation of a school who, in myopic ignorance, have
> accused the Brothers and the Sisters of reluctance to assist
> the poor. Were it not for the intelligent preparation and
> constant self-sacrifice of the Congregations that, in such
> very great part, have provided secondary education, the
> present system of free education could not have been even
> partially initiated.[45]

It was a deliberate put-down of the Minister for launching an initiative that was to open higher education to generations of young Irish men and women. This new opportunity was a blow to McQuaid's system, which relied for its authority on the existence of a largely uneducated laity.

When O'Malley first mooted his free education scheme, Lemass was still Taoiseach. By the time of its introduction, Jack Lynch had taken over the leadership, a move which appears to have pleased McQuaid, who found Lynch a more congenial figure than the gruff Lemass. Not only did McQuaid and Lynch exchange greetings by letter, McQuaid called on

Lynch at Government Buildings and Lynch paid a return call to Drumcondra.[46] Only days after Lynch assumed power, the former President, Seán T. O'Kelly, died. The old guard, it seemed, was giving way to the new.

However, anyone who thought McQuaid was mellowing was rudely awakened in the opening weeks of 1967 when, in his Christian Unity Week letter, he called for prayers for the return of Protestants to the One True Church. This provoked a sharp reaction, led by the Vicar of St Bartholomew's Church in Dublin, the Rev. Maurice Carey, who claimed that McQuaid was out of step with Cardinal Bea and the Vatican Secretariat for Unity.[47] The general verdict was summed up by a letter in *The Irish Times* which stated that if McQuaid's concept of ecumenism was correct, then 'dialogue' was a euphemism for conversion to Roman Catholicism.[48]

Having made no mention of the Trinity regulations in his 1966 Lenten Regulations, speculation mounted that McQuaid was bowing to the spirit of the age and letting them lapse into history. With a vengeance, in February 1967, however, McQuaid reminded his flock that the Trinity ban had not gone away. He was particularly scathing of the argument that the ban's removal would facilitate the union of Christendom, which he dismissed as 'a form of charity, not the conclusion of a reasoning process'.[49] This provoked *The Irish Times* into making one of its most trenchant attacks on McQuaid. 'To those outside his flock,' its editorial stated, 'he represents the very incarnation of all that it was believed Pope John with his loving heart was trying to rid his Church of – obscurantism, self-righteousness and spiritual apartheid.'[50]

An even more stinging criticism came from the Ulster Unionist M.P., Phelim O'Neill. Speaking in the Stormont parliament, O'Neill, who faced expulsion from the Orange Order for having attended the funeral of a Roman Catholic, implied that McQuaid was the Catholic equivalent of the Rev. Ian Paisley. 'There are people on both sides of the fence who seem to be living in the days of the stake, the rack and the thumbscrew,' O'Neill said. 'There are bigots on both sides. There is the Archbishop of Dublin – or perhaps I should call him the Archbigot of Dublin.'[51]

The *Sunday Independent* hastened to McQuaid's defence. By special arrangement with the Palace, it gave prominent space to an article headlined 'Reason for the ban on Catholics going to Trinity', by 'The Archbishop of Dublin, the Most Rev. Dr McQuaid'. It was a scoop; or at least, that was the impression which the newspaper created: 'In this article, His Grace outlines the teaching of the Church on higher education for Catholics.' John Charles had become a newspaper columnist!

An editorial accompanying the piece dismissed the attacks on the Archbishop as a savage abuse of freedom of speech, and argued that it was imperative that 'fundamental principles of the Church be proclaimed and adhered to'. In its haste to defend the Archbishop, however, the newspaper forgot to tell its readers that the article was a reproduction of

McQuaid's 1961 pamphlet.[52]

'It is magnificent,' wrote the Bishop of Sydney, Thomas Muldoon, likening it to a Michelangelo masterpiece that would inspire generations. 'The power of truth in it must move anyone who is not totally mentally blind ... Your critics who tried to make you appear as the antithesis of everything Pope John stood for should now feel like confused youngsters.'[53]

McQuaid's article, however, provoked a further round of criticism. Trinity's Provost McConnell accused him of doing 'a grave injustice' to the college, and hoped that a less harsh era was dawning in which Trinity would no longer be treated by McQuaid in a manner which had few, if any, parallels in the Western world. The Cork University Philosophical Society petitioned Rome for clarification of 'this unrealistic ruling'. On the *Late Late Show* panellists including David Thornley, Jim Lydon, Fr Paddy Brophy and Vincent Grogan agreed that the ban was outmoded and indefensible, as did the studio audience. The gulf between McQuaid and public opinion over 'the ban' was already wide.

It was at this juncture that the long-awaited report of the Commission on Higher Education was published. It recommended that the NUI be broken up and replaced by three independent universities in Dublin, Cork and Galway, and proposed that Trinity College would remain a separate university. The Minister for Education, Donogh O'Malley, went further when he announced that the Government would establish by law one multi-denominational University of Dublin based on a merger of Trinity College and UCD. O'Malley, who had not consulted the churches in advance, said that he wanted 'to end an insidious form of Partition on our own doorstep'.[54]

This remark was regarded as snide by the Fine Gael spokesman on Education, Pat Lindsay, who defended McQuaid in the Dáil as a man of principle and suggested that the worst people could say about him was that he adhered to fundamentals.[55] In half an hour's work at Cabinet, O'Malley had presumed to render irrelevant the arguments of half a century over Catholic attendance at Trinity College, the *Irish Independent* noted.[56] Within a year the merger negotiations had stalled. O'Malley died suddenly, leaving behind unfinished plans for the future of education, and a reputation which would grow into a legend. At his graveside, Jack Lynch acknowledged that O'Malley had seen horizons that few dared to contemplate.[57] The Apostolic Nuncio, Dr Joseph McGeough, was present at the funeral; the Archbishop of Dublin was not.

1968: Year of student revolt

In 1968, the year which witnessed student rebellion in France led by Daniel Cohn-Bendit, McQuaid faced an unprecedented breakdown in his relations with Catholic students at UCD. Even in the early days of the

Vatican Council the chaplaincy at UCD reported continued docility to traditional devotional practices, but by the mid-1960s a new generation of students regarded their Archbishop as an interloper who raised more laughter than fear as a result of his outdated attitudes.

Television gave the student protest a wider constituency. On RTÉ's current affairs programme, *Seven Days*, student leader John Feeney criticised McQuaid for claiming to speak 'authoritatively for his diocese' when it was now clear that many Catholics disagreed with his views. Feeney's attack was highlighted by the newspapers. Overnight, Feeney, the son of a doctor, became the Cohn-Bendit of UCD Catholic student politics.

Prior to his television appearance Feeney, along with a member of the non-Catholic Student Christian Movement, had written to the newspapers as the representatives of the College's theological societies to apologise to all non-Catholics for the lack of consideration shown to them by McQuaid. This was a rejection of a Pastoral Letter, *Our Faith*, in which McQuaid issued his sternest warning to date against ecumenical experimentation. 'It is not a renewal in the spirit of the Second Vatican Council,' he wrote, 'to exchange the certain teaching of the Church of Christ for the partial vision of a private judgement. One may not tamper with the doctrine of the Church.'[58]

Fearlessly, Feeney revealed on television the details of his difficulties with McQuaid. He explained that when he phoned the Palace to make his complaint known to a secretary, he was told that McQuaid regretted his 'very serious offence' of having written to the press. McQuaid's secretary pointed out that, 'If Mr Feeney's society felt the need for direction, it had available the accredited chaplain at UCD, Fr Paul Boland.'[59] Feeney also disclosed that this was the second time he had been rebuked by the Palace. He had received a letter previously from the Archbishop's secretary rebuking him for convening a study session of seminarians and students at which it was suggested that parish priests should be appointed on merit and for fixed terms. Defiantly, Feeney called on McQuaid to respond to the laity's valid demands to have some part in running the Church.

For the first time on national television ordinary viewers were given a first-hand account of McQuaid's high-handed method of communicating with church members. Feeney's contribution highlighted McQuaid's inaccessibility. It confirmed that students were expected to address the Archbishop, if at all, through the chaplain. Likewise, if McQuaid had a point to make to either the assistant chaplains or students, he would do so in writing to the chaplain or in private consultations. Such a system was seen to be out of step with the Second Vatican Council's concept of the Church as the People of God. It was also out of step, as Michael Sheehy observed in his book, *Is Ireland Dying?* with the radical, if intemperate trend in Irish undergraduate opinion.[60]

The unrest among the UCD students prompted McQuaid to send a spy to report on what was happening, especially in regard to the popularity of the organisation known as Pax Romana, which was attracting more recruits than the mainstream Catholic Student Society on account of its willingness to engage in topical debate, including ecumenism, under the popular assistant chaplain, Fr Brian Power. 'Your Grace, your worst fears have been confirmed,' the informant reportedly wrote to McQuaid.

On foot of this report, McQuaid instructed the head chaplain, Fr Paul Boland, to restore matters to normality, and summoned Fr Power to the Palace. Brought before McQuaid, who was seated on his throne, Power was accused of saying Mass for a clerical students' conference in Newman House without the Archbishop's permission, and berated for allowing speakers to address the conference contrary to His Grace's wishes. Most seriously of all, Power was charged with having said Mass with no altar-stone.

When Power tried to explain the circumstances in which Mass was said without an altar, McQuaid jumped off his throne with the speed of a bullet from a gun and left the room. Power delayed for a while before it dawned on him that McQuaid was standing at the front door, waiting for him to leave. McQuaid held his arms stiffly by his sides, signalling the ultimate insult that Power was not allowed to kiss the Episcopal ring. As he left with as much dignity as he could muster, Power sensed that McQuaid was unbalanced mentally by the sheer depth of his outrage.

The sequel to this bizarre encounter came in a summary notice from the Palace informing Power of his imminent transfer to the working-class parish of Inchicore, a humbling demotion for an intellectual and literary man who was highly popular with students. However, there was a further twist to the story. Just as Power was packing his belongings at the chaplaincy, he received word that the head of the Philosophy Department, Monsignor John Horgan, wanted to see him. 'If you play ball you can remain as chaplain,' Horgan told Power. 'Playing ball' meant undertaking to reform Pax Romana, cut off its funding from the university authorities and pass the grant over to the diocese. Power refused to cooperate on those terms and was duly despatched to a curacy in Inchicore, while Boland was instructed by McQuaid to form a new Pax Romana which would be strictly Catholic in membership, a venture doomed to failure in view of the disaffection felt by the students at the shabby treatment of their assistant chaplain.[62]

Nor were Catholic students at Trinity College enamoured by the way their Archbishop treated them. Further insight into McQuaid's aloofness was provided in the letters page of *The Irish Times* by the president of the Laurentian Society, Donal O'Sullivan, in connection with a controversy that had arisen over a visit to Dublin of the English Jesuit scholar, Fr Martin D'Arcy. It emerged that on hearing of D'Arcy's planned visit, the secretary of the Laurentian Society had arranged for him to add a speaking engagement at Trinity to his programme and had written to McQuaid for permission for the talk. Back came the surprise reply from the Archbishop's secretary: 'I am directed by His Grace to inform you that no application has been received from the Superior of the Rev. Martin D'Arcy S.J. to address a meeting anywhere in the diocese of Dublin. In these circumstances a reply to your question does not arise.' The Trinity meeting did not take place.[63]

A second distinguished English Jesuit who encountered McQuaid's pathological hatred of Trinity College was Archbishop Roberts, known to his friends as 'Tommy'. Roberts wrote to McQuaid informing him that he had been asked by the Trinity College Historical Society to chair a debate on the subject: 'Ecumenism is an excuse for charity'. Seeking McQuaid's permission to enter Trinity, Roberts noted pointedly: 'I am advised by the secretary that I am asked to do no more than chair the meeting.'[64]

This carefully nuanced request came shortly after McQuaid had declined to take part in a debate on Church–State relations at Trinity. McQuaid had informed the organiser, Gully Standford, that he feared he was not competent to speak on the relations between the Anglican Church and the Irish State.[65] The debate had gone ahead with other speakers and had been widely publicised. But it was not to McQuaid's liking, as he made clear to Roberts. 'If the debate resembles the recent paper on Church and State, it will be a mirror of the unchanged Elizabethans in Trinity College, Dublin.'[66]

Now approaching 73 years of age, McQuaid found constant reassurance from his friend Archbishop Finbar Ryan, who explained to him that the reason he continued to be 'the object of scorn' was because his critics saw in him 'an indomitable rock of Catholic defence and their own weakness'.[67]

It is clear from private conversations which McQuaid had with Mrs Simms that he made an attempt to understand the changing attitudes of a younger generation towards organised religion, but that he was incapable of transcending the theological approach which he had been taught as a student at Kimmage. McQuaid was unreceptive to books which Mrs Simms gave him on secularisation by Bishops John Robinson and Lesslie Newbigin and Harvey Cox.[68] On one occasion, McQuaid confessed to Mrs Simms that he found it 'a problem of stating the claims of Christianity to people who have cast aside, not God, but the revelation of God in our Divine Lord – what they call institutional Christianity.' While he was convinced that such people would not hear of a 'Church', he could not understand why 'if they accept the historicity of the Gospels, how can they escape our Divine Lord's own statement that He would build His Church?'[69]

Fearful that 'forces of dissolution' were trying to break the unity of the Catholic Church, McQuaid, by mid-1968, saw all around him signs of apostacy, confusion and hostility. Yet he clung to his belief that the Holy Ghost always guided the Church. In near desperation, McQuaid prayed that Christ's Vicar on earth – Pope Paul VI – would put a halt to the spiralling crisis of obedience.

24

No Change
1968–70

'His sense of commitment is unquestioned. What is in
doubt is his position in a changing church and a
changing Ireland.'

Seán MacRéamoinn on McQuaid, 1969.

Archbishop John Charles McQuaid was like a born-again churchman as he celebrated his seventy-third birthday on July 28, 1968. He had just received a confidential communication from Rome, whose contents were to be made public worldwide the following day. So positive was the news that for the first time in his 28 years as Archbishop he attended a national news conference. For once, the 'Ogre', as he referred to himself, was looking forward to an encounter in his den with the Fourth Estate.[1]

Next morning at the Mater Dei Institute, journalists sat with growing impatience as McQuaid awaited the arrival of a camera crew for RTÉ before introducing the priest who had been chosen to explain Pope Paul's momentous decision on birth control. For months, even years, speculation had grown into a widespread conviction that Pope Paul would reverse the Catholic Church's traditional ban on artificial methods of contraception. It was already known that the majority of the members of the advisory commission set up to examine the issue had recommended change. Now the moment had arrived for Paul's ultimate decision to be announced.

McQuaid handed the platform over to the small, rotund figure of the Professor of Moral Theology at Maynooth College, Monsignor Frank Cremin, who had been his adviser in Rome during the Vatican Council. There was a hush as the Monsignor held up the document to the glare of the television cameras. With dramatic effect, Cremin summed up 34 pages of Latin text in two words: 'No change.'

While Cremin explained, at length, the contents of the Papal statement, *Humanae Vitae* – On Human Life – McQuaid, who had left the press conference, issued his own commentary. 'This is an essential document for it sets forth once again the nature and purpose of marriage, as they are manifested by the natural law and the law of the Gospel,' he said. 'In a sphere of intimate delicacy, and in the circumstances of modern life, *Humanae Vitae*, with great firmness and immense compassion, reasserts the moral law that has been constantly proposed by the teaching authority of the Church.'[2]

McQuaid had also received a covering letter from the Papal Secretary of State, Cardinal Amleto Cicognani, urging the Irish Episcopal Conference to ensure that the Pope's teaching was understood and obeyed.[3] In a telegram to Cicognani, McQuaid welcomed the reaffirmation of 'the constant doctrine of the Church on marriage' and assured Pope Paul of 'our total acceptance of his official teaching'. McQuaid confidently predicted that the doctrine would result in an immediate renewal of the loyalty of his priests to their Church.[4]

McQuaid's wholehearted endorsement of Pope Paul's Encyclical contrasted sharply with the reaction in London of the former Archbishop of Bombay, Thomas Roberts S.J., who forecasted that the Papal pronouncement would raise a storm. Perceptively, the *Irish Press* religious affairs correspondent, T.P. O'Mahony, warned that the Catholic Church might be on the threshold of one of the greatest crises in its history.[5]

Whatever private opinions were held among the clergy in Dublin, not one of them broke ranks. The only dissenter in Ireland was the Professor of Theology at University College, Cork, Rev. Dr James Good, who described the Encyclical as 'a major tragedy'. When Bishop Cornelius Lucey suspended Good from his priestly functions, McQuaid congratulated the Bishop of Cork on his firm action. Describing Good as a man of firm views once his mind was made up, Lucey was relieved that the summer vacation meant that university teachers were not on campus to offer him support.[6]

Armed with *Humanae Vitae*, McQuaid enforced the contraception ban in the hospitals under his control. His first target was Holles St, where in April 1963 the Master, Dr Kieran O'Driscoll, had established the first family planning clinic in Ireland. Based on the safe period, this initiative, O'Driscoll claimed, had McQuaid's 'full knowledge and at least the tacit support'. From 1967, Dr Declan Meagher and Dr Dermot MacDonald, who ran the clinic, offered the pill to couples who felt in conscience able to take it. According to the 'Clinical Report' for 1967, half of those women offered it went on the pill. The service was provided in expectation of the Papal commission authorising a more liberal approach, but on foot of Pope Paul's Encyclical, the experiment came to end. O'Driscoll announced that the pill would no longer be prescribed to women attending Holles St.[7]

An opinion poll conducted by the *Irish Medical Times* showed that 65 per cent of doctors were opposed to the Papal ruling on birth control.[8] Although at least one couple wrote directly to McQuaid announcing their departure from the Catholic Church, the main channels for dissent were the letters' columns of the newspapers. So strong was the opposition that many Catholics stopped practising their religious duties, particularly the confessing of their sins to a priest. As Fergal Tobin noted in *The Best of Decades*, genuine opposition to *Humanae Vitae* within the Catholic Church could neither be wished away nor banned.[9]

Humanae Vitae was criticised at a conference in Bargy Castle, Wexford, attended by theologians, doctors, academics and journalists. The conference report concluded that contraceptive methods often fostered conjugal love and helped towards the attainment of maturity in married relationships. A copy was sent to McQuaid by the coordinator, Vincent Grogan, a former Supreme Knight of St Columbanus. 'Thank you for your manifesto,' McQuaid replied. 'I feel sure that you would prefer to go to your judgement with the knowledge that you had done all in your power to secure full assent to the teaching of the Vicar of Christ.'[10]

In October, Pope Paul sent McQuaid a special message thanking him for his 'token of fidelity' in loyally supporting *Humanae Vitae*. 'Such ready acceptance of the teaching of Christ's Vicar on Earth is a sign of the lively faith which animates the heart of a true Christian,' the Vatican Secretary of State, Cardinal Cicognani, wrote specifically on the Pope's instruction.[11] This commendation lifted McQuaid's spirits.

Although Pope Paul did not claim that *Humanae Vitae* was an infallible document, McQuaid upheld the teaching authority of the Church as infallible when he addressed the diocesan pilgrimage in Lourdes in late August.[12] Loyalty to Paul was foremost in McQuaid's mind at the October meeting of the Hierarchy at Maynooth when the Irish bishops issued a statement that ranked with those of Scotland, Australia, New Zealand and Italy in 'the most loyal to Rome' category. Echoing McQuaid's July response, the bishops declared that they were confident that their people would give it wholehearted assent.[13]

McQuaid was shocked by the uproar in Washington DC, where Cardinal Patrick O'Boyle was confronted by a revolt from 51 of his 300 priests, which he met head-on with suspensions and removals if recantations were not forthcoming at private interviews. In a letter of support, McQuaid assured O'Boyle of his prayers for God to give him the courage to withstand steadfastly the disobedience of his priests. 'Where there is confusion, one must seek the action of the demon,' McQuaid wrote. 'And to counter his deceit Our Blessed Lady is all-powerful under God.'[14]

Fundamentally, McQuaid saw the battle over *Humanae Vitae* in terms of Christ versus Satan. He had no sympathy for the argument that by acting against the majority opinion of the commission on birth control, Pope Paul did more than Martin Luther ever had to undermine the concept of Papal authority. On the contrary, McQuaid was elated that Paul had ignored the principle of collegiality and had published *Humanae Vitae* without the cooperation of the world's bishops. For McQuaid, it was imperative that the Pope should uphold the 1930 Encyclical of Pius XI, *Casti Connubii*, in which he declared that sexual intercourse was immoral if a couple did anything to 'deliberately frustrate that act in its natural power to generate life'. According to Pius XI, contraception was an offence against the law of God and of nature. Only the rhythm method, because it was 'natural', was permissible – all other methods were 'unnatural' and therefore immoral. Pius XII had gone even further in declaring that his predecessor's teaching on this question was valid for all time. Paul VI had now endorsed that view emphatically.

Paul's shift to the right

Paul's upholding of traditional Catholic teaching did not come as a surprise to McQuaid, who had observed a gradual shift by the Pontiff from post-conciliar experimentation towards conservative stability. In early January 1966, McQuaid was delighted to receive a case of 'exquisite confectionery' accompanied by a Christmas card from Pope Paul. McQuaid requested Cardinal Cicognani to tell the Pope that he appreciated this 'charming gesture of paternal benevolence' – 'It is but another stimulus to a filial loyalty in which I trust I shall never, with God's help, be found wanting.' [15]

Late that year Paul helped to subsidise *Renovatio*, a journal edited by the conservative former Archbishop of Sao Paulo, Cardinal Angelo Rossi, as a counterweight to the liberal journal, *Concilium*. Evidence of McQuaid's ongoing links since the council with the right-wing leaders of Catholicism was his receipt in late September 1966 of a note from the Superior General of the Holy Ghost Congregation, Archbishop Marcel Lefebvre, along with a letter from Cardinal Siri, recommending *Renovatio* as a review that aimed to refortify the interior life of the Catholic Church.[16] Paul's shift to the right was confirmed in 1967 when he unilaterally issued the Encyclical *Saceredotalis Coelibatus*, which upheld the law on priestly celibacy.

Unlike Cardinal Conway, who was appointed a president of the newly created International Synod of Bishops, McQuaid took little interest in the preparations for the first Synod, which took place in Rome in October 1967 and discussed the revision of Canon Law, seminaries, mixed marriages, doctrinal dangers and liturgy.[17] When requested by Conway for his comments on the Synod's programme, McQuaid replied: 'Mine will be brief, and they will have no effect on the ultimate decision.'[18]

Although the Synod was a modest success, the more important development in 1967 was Paul's reform of the Curia. He streamlined the Secretariat of State by making the two senior officials, Antonio Samoré and Angelo Dell-Aqua, cardinals, assisted by two dynamic younger men, Agostino Casaroli in foreign policy and Giovanni Benelli as substitute Secretary of State. In this way, Paul became a centralised Pope in a reorganised

Curia, while theoretically adhering to the concept of collegiality.

Paul was now showing a more sympathetic attitude to churchmen who had been discomfited by the Second Vatican Council. As a gesture to the right wing led by Cardinal Siri of Genoa and Archbishop Lefebvre, Paul accepted the resignation, under new rules for bishops on reaching 75 years of age, of the prelate who had overseen liturgical reform, Cardinal Giacomo Lercaro. One day, Lercaro picked up his copy of *L'Osservatore Romano* to read that his resignation had been accepted on the grounds of advanced age and ill health, both of them spurious reasons.[19]

Just as McQuaid feared 'the forces of dissolution', so too did Paul begin to speak out against unorthodoxy. McQuaid's Pastoral Letter, *Our Faith*, which he issued in support of Paul, was warmly received by the Pontiff.[20] When Rome informed McQuaid in early 1968 of its inquiry into the Dutch Catechism on account of its humanistic treatment of Christ, he told the Nuncio, Archbishop Joseph McGeough: 'I have never tolerated it; nor shall I, until the Holy See has declared it free from error.'[21]

Nor did McQuaid hold in esteem the Swiss theologian, Hans Küng, who was under investigation in 1968 by the Doctrinal Congregation, the former Holy Office, for his book *The Church*, which according to his biographer, Robert Nowell, marked a break with tradition in Catholic ecclesiology by focusing on the Church, not as a strictly sacrosanct entity, but as an institution that shared the sinful condition of mankind.[22] McQuaid informed the Nunciature that he was so opposed to Küng that he even disapproved of Sheed and Ward for publishing *The Church*.[23]

When McQuaid learned that there was an overall decrease of 5 per cent in Peter's Pence from Ireland in 1968, he sent a special letter to priests asking them to assist the charities of the Holy Father more effectively. Privately he was not surprised at the decline. 'This city alone is honeycombed with collecting organisations,' he told the Nuncio. 'A very large sum has been sent out of the country to allay distress in India and Vietnam. Soon we are to have a collection in aid of Nigeria. The Irish Red Cross is insistently campaigning for funds. Nonetheless, I will do all I can to see that the Holy Father's fund be generously supported.'[24]

Containment policy

The shift to the right in Rome encouraged McQuaid to keep the lid on debate in Ireland. When he heard that the winter 1968 edition of *Studies* planned to carry an article by a senior member of the Department of Education questioning the traditional relationship between Church and State on schooling, he made enquiries. To his dismay, the Archbishop discovered that the new editor, Fr Peter Troddyn, had not only commissioned the article by the assistant secretary, Sean O'Connor, he was devoting the whole issue of the journal to reactions to it by leading educationalists,

Catholic and Protestant.[25]

Determined to scuttle Troddyn's ambitious project, McQuaid summoned the Provincial of the Jesuits. It was a brief encounter. McQuaid asked Fr Cecil McGarry if *Studies* intended to publish O'Connor's article. McGarry replied, 'Yes', and gave his reasons. 'The Archbishop then courteously sent the Provincial on his way,' the current editor of *Studies*, Fr Nöel Barbour S.J., has written.[26]

This defiance of McQuaid stands out in the history of twentieth-century Ireland as a milestone in the championing of the democratic right of freedom of expression. In a seminal article, O'Connor made an unprecedented call for the Catholic Church authorities to declericalise the education system and share decision-making responsibility with the laity. His article, 'Post Primary Education Now and in the Future', called for dialogue at the highest level between Church and State. McQuaid, however, saw O'Connor's position not as a friendly appeal for partnership, but as a venture which would undermine the Catholic Church's control of education. It earned O'Connor the nickname of 'the Great Seculariser'.

O'Connor spelled out the implications for Church and State of a decline in the numbers of religious at a time of exploding school numbers. These circumstances opened the way for more responsibility to be given to lay secondary teachers, who until then were treated like hired hands whose responsibility ended at the classroom door. 'No one wants to push religious out of education,' he stressed. 'That would be disastrous, in my opinion. But I want them in it as partners, not always as masters.'

Unless agreement was reached by Church and State to match the changing circumstances, educational advance at both primary and post-primary levels would be hindered. 'The dialogue must be frank and must range over a wide area,' O'Connor concluded. 'The prospects for education are good, but only if the major providers are in harmony.'[27]

McQuaid, however, found the Redemptorists more pliable than the Jesuits. The Redemptorist Provincial, Fr Jack Whyte, bowed to severe pressure from Drumcondra to muzzle the order's pioneering monthly magazine, *Reality*, which was founded and edited by Fr Michael O'Connor, a Kerryman from Tralee. O'Connor had already encountered McQuaid's iron fist over an article which he wrote in the *Redemptorist Record* (*Reality*'s predecessor) questioning why young Dublin boys and girls should have to learn to say the Mass in Irish when English was their actual mother tongue. For this criticism O'Connor was caught in what he recalls as 'a pincer movement' between McQuaid, President de Valera and the President of *Cumann na Sagart*, Fr Tomás Ó Fiaich, the future Cardinal Archbishop of Armagh. Under this combined pressure, the Provincial, Fr Whyte, capitulated and published a grovelling letter apologising for the article, even though its writer, O'Connor, remained unrepentant.

As a new product, *Reality* targeted a readership of young school-leavers who were interested in the changes being brought about by the Vatican Council. This proved to be a popular move – the magazine reached a circulation of 55,000, its articles were quoted in the daily newspapers, and it began to have an influence nationally.

Eager to implement the Vatican Council's idea of encouraging the laity to participate in the work of the Church, O'Connor set up an editorial board which included the religious affairs correspondent of *The Irish Times*, John Horgan, Andrew Hamilton, a Protestant, and Maeve Binchy of *The Irish Times*, Louis McRedmond, Miriam Hederman O'Brien and Máire Mullarney.

Reality, however, was constantly censored by the Palace. McQuaid forced the Redemptorists to accept a system of supplying galley proofs of each edition to three censors led by Monsignor Patrick O'Connell, former Mercier spy and now parish priest in Rathmines. The other two censors were not known to O'Connor, who had to meet O'Connell to discuss each edition. Whenever O'Connell ordered an article to be cut or dropped altogether, O'Connor would ask for the basis in Canon Law for the diocesan decision. Invariably, he would not be given a reasoned argument. The bottom line for O'Connell was simply that McQuaid would not like it.

Such a system made it virtually impossible for the editor and his board to commission articles with any degree of certainty that they would be published. The situation became worse when, in conjunction with one of the chaplains at UCD, *Reality* initiated the first sociological study of the attitudes of Catholic undergraduates. The findings exploded the McQuaidian myth that those who went to UCD were confirmed in their faith and those who went to Trinity lost it. Such a reality was too much for McQuaid to stomach any longer. O'Connor was moved by Whyte to the West Indies to renew his faith, and spent the next 30 years teaching in the United States.[28]

McQuaid's world was severely patriarchal and the culture it promoted left little room for 'the other', whether that other be female, dissenter or simply not mainstream Irish. On being asked to endorse the aims of the Irish Council of Women, which was formed in 1967, McQuaid conducted an investigation into its president and issued the instruction to pay no attention to her association.[29]

'Make sure it is not a combined Catholic-Protestant affair,' he told a Columban priest before addressing the Tuairim discussion group, run by young Catholic intellectuals such as Dr David Thornley, Donal Barrington, Patrick Kilroy, Miriam Hederman O'Brien, Con Smith and Frank Winder, whose activities he was infiltrating through a priest-spy.[30]

To his priests, McQuaid was increasingly a remote and pedantic disciplinarian, out of touch with the undercurrents which were so drastically to change the society they served. The clerical joke circulating in the diocese about McQuaid's top of the range Citroen car number, 5270, was that it stood for working 52 weeks in a year, seven days a weeks, and no chance of a lift![31] Those priests who fell foul of him would be banished at short notice to difficult parishes.[32] One day when McQuaid called to a parish house and discovered that the priest was out playing golf, he sat by the phone until the unsuspecting cleric came home. 'Father, I was looking after your sick calls,' he said cuttingly.[33]

For almost all of his long reign, Irish journalism was non-intrusive. Normally he did not send his annual Pastoral Letter to *The Irish Times* which had to send a reporter around to the *Irish Press* to take notes of what was invariably a dense script full of biblical quotations without a contemporary news angle. The precondition of receiving his texts was that the *Irish Independent* and the *Irish Press* would carry them verbatim.[34]

On the rare occasions when reporters dared to approach him, McQuaid would be invariably rude and haughty towards them. The story is told of how Maurice Liston of the *Irish Press* and John Healy of the *Irish Independent* approached him to check their verbatim note of what he had just said. 'Did I say that?' McQuaid asked. 'You did, Your Grace,' Liston assured him. 'Well, I did not mean to say that,' said McQuaid, daintily tearing up the note.[35]

When McQuaid learned that the *Irish Press* photographer, Tom McElroy, had arranged for him to be pictured with a newly ordained priest – who was in a wheelchair – alongside his proud parents, McQuaid scolded his priest-secretary and stormed out of the room, leaving everyone totally embarrassed. On another occasion, McElroy took a picture of the Archbishop at a service after he had discarded his crozier on turning a corner of the church only to be ordered by the Archbishop not to use the photograph.[36]

The one writer who threatened to inform the public of McQuaid's retinue of priest-servants, nun-attendants, a gardener, a valet and a chauffeur was his former pupil, Brian O'Nolan, in his column as Myles na gCopaleen. McQuaid, he claimed, had 'more able-bodied persons of both sexes in personal attendance than anything attempted by the Holy Father.' He also threatened to make a public statement about McQuaid's palaces and private transport, and he requested that any further letter in coarse praise of himself be signed by himself and not by (still another) servant.[37]

By the late 1960s, McQuaid's paranoia was beginning to manifest itself in public. During an address to 300 nuns attending the Conference of Convent Secondary Schools, he suddenly looked up and asked if there were any journalists in the audience. When Peadar Cearr from the *Cork Examiner* made himself known, he was told that the meeting was private and was ordered to walk down to the podium to hand his notes over to the Archbishop. Denis Coghlan of *The Irish Times* quietly left the hall but was spotted by McQuaid in the hallway after the meeting. McQuaid approached him and harshly demanded his notebook. This time Coghlan looked 'the terrifying figure in the eye' and told him 'No.' Explaining that he had been invited officially, Coghlan said that his notes were not his to surrender as they were the property of the newspaper. If His Grace wished, he could take the matter up with the editor. He refused to give his name but showed his invitation from the Dublin Diocesan Press Office. Muttering that there must have been a mistake, McQuaid flounced away in a rage, leaving Coghlan in a state of near nervous collapse.[38]

Later, the press officer, Ossie Dowling, explained that he was requested by the organisers to arrange press coverage of the event, which he did. 'It now seems that this was not what was desired, and I regret any inconvenience or embarrassment caused to my colleagues of the press as a result of the misunderstanding,' he said. Dowling had joined Burke Savage as one of the Archbishop's scapegoats.

So insistent was McQuaid on keeping diocesan affairs out of the news that he denied to an *Irish Press* reporter the existence of a draft plan to introduce a pay scheme for all curates and parish priests which would eliminate the disparity between rich and poor parishes.[39] When the *Evening Herald* rang the Palace to enquire about pending changes in the Mass, a harassed secretary pleaded that he would have to put the question to the Archbishop! When *The Herald* published a report suggesting what the alterations in the Mass were likely to be based on what was happening in England, the editor, Brian Quinn, duly received a letter from the Archbishop accusing him of 'an intrusion into the See of Dublin'.[40]

McQuaid stifled attempts to open up a Christian-Marxist dialogue, and in October put the Provincial of the Irish Dominicans, Fr L.C. Coffey, under pressure to ban two English Dominicans, Herbert McCabe and Laurence Bright, from addressing a conference in Dublin on 'Marxism, Christianity and Ireland'. After being sacked for a period after his editorial on Charles Davis, McCabe had been reinstated as editor of *New Blackfriars*. Bright was the leading light behind *Slant*, a journal promoting debate between Christians and Marxists, which had a following among UCD students.[41]

Nor was McQuaid in tune with the new buzz words about 'social consciousness' and 'social conscience'. His Catholic Social Service Conference had lost much of its original dynamism and there was a marked slackening in demand for its clothes and soup-runs as a result of the economic prosperity of the 1960s. The growing willingness of Government to intervene in social policy, especially after Pope John's 1961 Encyclical, *Mater et Magistra*, made the CSSC's activities seem marginal. In typical fashion, McQuaid rounded on critics who suggested that the Catholic Church was unconcerned about the poor. 'The Catholic Social Service Conference is not a discussion group bandying about theories of social structures and economic measures. While others write and talk, its members silently, for the love of God, devote themselves to the works of charity that are at hand. No measures of social security can eliminate human poverty.'[42]

McQuaid also encouraged one of his favourite younger priests, Fr Michael Cleary, a curate in Marino, to make a public speech attacking the Sinn Féin movement and the Citizens Advice Bureau as organisations which were Communist-led and controlled. While working in London as part of McQuaid's group of emigrant chaplains, Cleary had met a Communist who had spoken of coming to Ireland 'to do a job'. According to Cleary, Sinn Féin was recruiting genuine young Irish lads who were full of nothing but nationalist patriotism, unaware of the Communist agenda of the organisers.[43]

In his Lenten regulations for 1969, McQuaid condemned the growing mood of social protest in Ireland. 'Those who seek to promote social justice have themselves the grave obligation first to observe elementary justice in regard to individual persons and groups and the civil authorities,' he declared. 'Any policy that claims to promote social justice but fails to respect the Natural Law and the Christian Law, as the Church proposes them by her Divine mandate, is of its very nature injustice.'[44]

The growing permissiveness in society was also a target for McQuaid. 'It is to be deplored that following the licentious example of people who have rejected God and Christianity some publications, films and stage plays are lending their aid to the provocation of sensuality in thought and action.'[45]

McQuaid's liturgical directives to his clergy in spring 1969 were presented at a private conference in Drumcondra by Bishop Joseph Carroll. Priests were not obliged to say Mass facing the people. Concelebration of Mass by priests was to be allowed on Holy Thursdays, but only if the parish priest thought it advisable. Plans for the reconstruction of a High Altar and for the re-siting of the tabernacle were to be submitted by parish priests to the Archbishop. Temporary structures set in front of the High Altar were prohibited. The use of any musical instrument other than the organ was strictly forbidden; no profane tunes were to be sung; Holy Communion was to be received kneeling and offertory processions involving lay people were not to be permitted. The laity were not to be allowed to place a host in a ciborium on entering the Church.

The widespread dissatisfaction and distress over the directives among the Dublin clergy, especially in the religious Orders, was reported by Louis McRedmond in the *Irish Independent* on April 1.[46] The changes fell short of public expectations and were unfavourably compared with more sweeping changes in England, Holland and the United States, where readings were taken not from the Bible but from novels and newspapers, while the Gregorian Chant gave way to the songs of Bob Dylan or the folk group Peter, Paul and Mary. In response to criticisms, McQuaid asserted that he was the sole regulator under the Holy See of public worship in the Dublin diocese.[47]

This adverse reaction was followed by the news that a Dominican liturgical scholar, Fr Liam Walsh, had been removed from the Diocesan Liturgical Commission as well as from his teaching posts at Mater Dei and the Dublin Institute of Adult Education. Walsh, who went abroad to teach, spoke out. 'I found it difficult to reconcile being associated with the recent decision of the Archbishop on liturgy with my work as a teacher,' he explained. 'I want to disassociate myself from it so that my teaching can be free and more effective.'[48]

McQuaid's struggle against 'Protestantisation' of the liturgy was applauded by his friend, Archbishop Finbar Ryan. 'What you say in your directive,' he told McQuaid, 'has a very stabilising impact – imperative in this day of youthful effervescence. The news of publication of the definitive dismissal is very welcome. I hope there will be concerted action by all the Bishops to bring about conformity in practice, and that diversity of rites for the Mass will not continue.'[49]

An indicator of just how heated discussions on liturgy had become was the instance in which eight Maynooth theologians argued the pros and cons of giving Communion in both kinds to participants at the annual summer school. Although it was well known that McQuaid was opposed to such innovation in his diocese, it was proposed that this should be done without seeking his permission. After all, it was happening elsewhere in the Catholic world and what McQuaid did not know would not trouble him. At the outset of the meeting it looked as if the experiment would be quickly endorsed: seven of the eight theologians were in favour. The eighth staff member, who was in the chair, opposed it uncompromisingly, so much so that the meeting dragged on. Eventually, the seven capitulated to the Professor of Dogmatic Theology, Fr Kevin McNamara, who was to become Archbishop of Dublin from 1985 to 1988.[50]

McQuaid was watching what was happening at Maynooth closely. When the Archbishop of Westminster, Cardinal John Heenan, wrote to McQuaid informing him that he had been invited to address the Maynooth Summer Union, McQuaid raised no objection, but advised him to scrutinise very carefully the persons who were listed to speak and whose addresses would be published with his. Only the previous Saturday, McQuaid had refused the imprimatur to a chapter on the 1968 Summer School proceedings. 'The Maynooth Summer School is – though it is still unaware – to be made the object of a special inquiry,' McQuaid told Heenan in confidence. Heenan addressed the school, but he surprised the progressive clergy by telling them to get back into the habit of saying their Rosary, a sentiment shared by McQuaid! [51]

Tension between the Hierarchy and Maynooth College staff mounted after three professors criticised a pastoral on Christian marriage. The unprecedented reaction came in a series of comments made by the Professor of Theology, Donal Flanagan, the Professor of Philosophy, P.J. McGrath and the Professor of Classics, Gerard Watson in *The Irish Times*.

'If their publication is unprecedented,' wrote *Hibernia*, 'so too is the current state of controversy within the church. And the fact that they were read with such interest is surely a most healthy sign of the commitment involved. It is to be hoped that the Hierarchy will view it in that light.'[52]

On the contrary, McQuaid took a dim view of the three commentaries and brought them to the attention of Bishop Michael Browne of Galway. 'I had seen the three Maynooth articles,' Browne replied, 'I hope the case of these three will be raised by the Visitors.'[53]

In view of his plans for Mater Dei, McQuaid gave minimum cooperation to the foundation of the Milltown Institute in 1968. This initiative amalgamated the houses of studies of the Augustinians, Carmelites (Calced and Discalced) Camillians, Jesuits, Marists, Oblates, Passionists and Sacred Heart Missionaries. The inspiration behind the move was the Jesuit priest, Fr Jim Healy S.J., who encountered many obstacles from the Palace.[54]

Restlessness among the clergy was not confined to Maynooth or the Religious Orders. The Council of Priests, which McQuaid had handpicked in 1966, was pressing for a more representative composition, which McQuaid accommodated in late 1969 with the election of a new council whose chairman was the Professor of European Languages at UCD, Fr Dermot Ryan, a priest considered to hold progressive views at odds with McQuaid.[55] Ryan was also among the theologians pressing for the inclusion of theology as an academic subject in the universities. 'This group would tell us what to think and do,' McQuaid wrote dismissively to Conway, noting that the question of theology was 'a very troublesome venture where a Hierarchy is concerned, not to mention the Archbishop in whose City the new University-whatever-its-form is to be physically sited.'[56]

McQuaid was presented with another 'sign of the times' when Bishop Patrick Dunne informed him that students at Clonliffe were showing disrespect for the conventional rules of silence. McQuaid wrote in the margin of the note: 'There is nothing I can do about it.'[57] More worrying still was the decrease in numbers coming forward for the priesthood. 'Sorry, am myself straitened for priests,' was his limp response to a request for priests from the Apostolic Administrator of Grenada.[58]

Censoring theology tapes

In March 1969, McQuaid's attention was drawn by Bishop Browne to the popularity of tape recordings of conferences and lectures given by theologians, which Mercier Press of Cork was promoting as classroom texts in all the leading seminaries in the English-speaking world. Three of these were by the Professor of Moral Theology at the Catholic University of Washington, Fr Charles Curran, on penance, natural law and abortion, and two were by the Professor of Moral and Social Theology at the Lateran

University, the Redemptorist, Fr Bernard Häring, on morality and the post-Encyclical Church – a lecture in which he gave his reasons for opposing *Humanae Vitae*. Three others were on marriage, women and the new nun. 'Where are we going?' Browne wanted to know.[59]

McQuaid was particularly disturbed by Curran, who had added considerably to Cardinal O'Boyle's distress by organising a protest statement signed by over 600 theologians pointing out that *Humanae Vitae* was not infallible.[60] His investigations established that a series of 40 tapes had been put on the commercial market by Mercier, covering topics such as the theology of vocation, original sin, and the spirituality of Teilhard de Chardin. Other well-known lecturers included the English Jesuits, Edward Yarnold and Thomas Corbishley, the Irish Redemptorist Seán O'Riordan and the American Redemptorist, F.X. Murphy.

Although prelates in Ireland, England, Scotland, the United States, Australia, New Zealand and the Philippines had welcomed the tapes as a useful teaching aid, McQuaid was perturbed that there was no provision in Canon Law governing the censorship of taped lectures, as there was for books and pamphlets. However, he sent the provincials of Religious Orders a private directive, which stated: 'I want you to note that the conferences on tape, issued by Mercier Communications, Mercier Press Ltd, 4 Bridge Street, Cork, may not be used in any hostel or convent of religious in the diocese unless they have been previously censored, and passed by the censor in charge, Monsignor P. O'Connell, 54 Lower Rathmines Road, Dublin. On application it may be learned which conferences have been allowed. This matter must be regarded as binding gravely for it is a question of safeguarding the Faith in doctrine and in morals. You will therefore take measures to see that this regulation is faithfully observed.' [61]

When the directive was leaked to the media, McQuaid looked daft. When his press officer, Ossie Dowling, asked how he should comment, McQuaid instructed him to say nothing. In contrast, the head of Mercier Press, Captain Seán Feehan, claimed that as there was no provision in Canon Law for the official censorship of tapes, McQuaid's action was 'entirely arbitrary'. Feehan also stated that it was company policy to ensure that all tapes issued were first approved by competent theologians as being in complete conformity with the teachings of the Church. 'It would seem that the views of some of the leading theologians are in conflict with those of the Archbishop of Dublin,' he said. 'The speakers on the tapes are men of absolute orthodoxy; they are in good standing with their religious order or diocese, their teaching institution, and with the Church.'[62]

Inside the Hierarchy

In May 1969, McQuaid attended dinner at the Department of External Affairs to welcome the new Nuncio, Gaetano Alibrandi, a Sicilian prince from Castiglione who later became legendary for playing the theme tune of *The Godfather* on the organ. McQuaid already knew Alibrandi from his period as counsellor at the Nunciature from 1954–56. What McQuaid could not yet know was that Alibrandi would become the most influential Nuncio since Paschal Robinson, and would have as potent an influence on his career as Robinson had had. But adversely.[63]

Alibrandi was an experienced Vatican diplomat, trained in the Pontifical Ecclesiastical Academy and apprenticed in the Secretariat of State. He served in Papal Nunciatures in Turkey and Mexico as well as Ireland before rising to the rank of Nuncio in postings to Indonesia, Chile and the Lebanon. The Ireland to which he returned in 1969 was a more complex place than it had been in 1954, when he had been told that he could be sure that all Dubliners were in God's grace.

In view of the ageing profile of the Irish Hierarchy, one of the important tasks assigned to Alibrandi was the nomination of a new generation of bishops more in line with the thinking of the Second Vatican Council. This process had begun under his predecessor, Archbishop Sensi, who had boasted to the Minister for External Affairs, Frank Aiken, of his interventions in the proceedings of the Hierarchy.[64] Alibrandi's continuation of this policy came at a time when Rome was modifying the criteria for the selection of bishops.[65]

A struggle was already taking place between McQuaid and Conway to influence appointments. Within the Dublin metropolitan area, two of McQuaid's allies in the Hierarchy, Bishop Staunton of Ferns and Bishop Collier of Ossory, had died in 1963 and 1964 respectively. McQuaid had promoted the appointments of the Rector of the Irish College in Rome, Donal Herlihy, and the educationalist at Kieran's College, Kilkenny, Peter Birch. Although Herlihy and Birch had cultivated McQuaid when they were priests, they were increasingly discomfited as bishops by his dog-in-the-manger approach to the agenda of the Episcopal Conference. McQuaid's third suffragan bishop, Thomas Keogh, had retired in September 1967 and was succeeded by the Rockwell-educated Patrick Lennon. Although somewhat in awe of McQuaid, Lennon had taught moral theology at St Patrick's College, Carlow, and was more disposed to the new theological trends than McQuaid deemed advisable. McQuaid came to regard Lennon as a Trojan horse for the liberal faction in the Irish Church. In late 1968, McQuaid had strengthened his voting power within the Hierarchy with the appointment of a second Auxiliary Bishop, Joseph Carroll, the President of Clonliffe College. A conservative who could be relied upon to preach 'the sound doctrine of the Church', Carroll was seen as being groomed to succeed McQuaid.

However, the most significant recruit to the Hierarchy was the Professor of Scholastic Philosophy at Queen's University, Cahal Daly, an Antrim man who had been adviser to Cardinal Conway at the Vatican

Council. A prodigious writer and speaker, Daly took over as Bishop of Ardagh and Clonmacnoise from Bishop James MacNamee. He took a special interest in liturgical change and in drafting Hierarchy documents. Close to Cardinal Conway, Daly also related well to McQuaid, to whom he confided his qualms that 'all the aberrations in the Church today have been committed over and over again in the Church's history'.[66] Other new appointments to the Hierarchy were Michael Harty, a liturgy expert, who replaced Joseph Rodgers as Bishop of Killaloe, and John McCormack, a Canon lawyer, became Bishop of Meath in early 1968 in succession to John Kyne. However, the appointment which captured the public imagination was the announcement in August 1969 that the new Bishop of Kerry was to be Fr Eamonn Casey, the colourful head of the London-based housing organisation known as Shelter. This appointment was interpreted as an achievement of Cardinal Conway's in his efforts to rid the Hierarchy of its stiff and remote image. McQuaid, who had been supporting the candidature of Monsignor Cremin, took the news of Casey's appointment badly.[67]

Nonetheless, McQuaid immediately sent a message congratulating Casey, whom he knew from his work with Irish emigrants. 'The spontaneity and warmth of your greeting helps to allay a little the many fears and apprehensions,' Casey wrote back. 'May I take this opportunity to acknowledge the debt I owe to you, the inspiration, encouragement and unfailing support that Your Grace has given to all of us in the emigrant mission that made whatever we have accomplished possible.' [68]

Another Conway protégé was Patrick Mulligan, who succeeded Eugene O'Callaghan as Bishop of Clogher in early 1970. Mulligan, an expert in church history and education, invited McQuaid to concelebrate the Mass at his Consecration in St Macartan's Cathedral. McQuaid agreed to attend but asked to be excused from concelebrating, a clear indication of withholding his personal assent to an important element in the new liturgy.[69]

Eruptions in the North

On August 14, 1969, the day on which the British Prime Minister, Harold Wilson, authorised the deployment of troops in Northern Ireland to deal with a sudden upsurge of sectarian violence, Archbishop McQuaid called for prayers for peace in 'the disturbed areas of our country'. As well as revealing his support for a united Ireland, McQuaid had identified himself exclusively with the minority Catholic community.[70]

Four days earlier, riots had broken out in Derry after the Orange Apprentice Boys paraded through the Catholic Bogside district. The unrest spread to other parts of the North, particularly Belfast, where hundreds of Catholics were driven from their homes by Protestants. In a special television address, the Taoiseach, Jack Lynch, warned that the Irish Government could not stand by, and announced the setting up of Irish army field hospitals close to the border.

McQuaid responded to Lynch's appeal for support for refugees by signing a cheque for £1,000, worth £9,000 in today's money.[71] The cheque was delivered by hand to Government Buildings on Monday morning after a weekend of rioting in the North. Anxious to receive publicity for this contribution, McQuaid instructed his secretary, Fr Ardle MacMahon, to telephone the private secretary to the Taoiseach, Bertie O'Dowd, informing him that reference to 'the charitable funds at the disposal of the Archbishop would be much appreciated in any announcement'.[72]

Lynch thanked McQuaid for his contribution towards 'the relief of those affected by the tragic occurrences in the Six Counties', and confirmed that he had instructed the Minister for Finance, Charles Haughey, to pass the cheque on to the Irish Red Cross which was administering the government's aid fund. £100,000 (£900,000) had been set aside by the government for relief of distress in the North.[73]

Relations between the Irish and British Governments became extremely tense after Lynch was told by Wilson when they met in Downing St that the border was not an issue and the affairs of Northern Ireland were entirely a domestic matter for the United Kingdom.[74] Lynch's warning that his Government 'would not stand by' had intensified tensions in the North, where it was interpreted as signalling a military intervention, an option which was impracticable as a badly equipped Irish Army did not have the capacity for such a manoeuvre. Fearing attacks from Loyalists, citizen committees were established and barricades were erected in Catholic areas in Belfast.

McQuaid sent a large cheque to the Bishop of Down and Connor, William Philbin, after the situation deteriorated further in August.[75] 'We have been going through dreadful times,' Philbin informed McQuaid. 'There has been more of a pattern to the events than may appear. Fifty Catholic-owned public houses have been burned throughout the whole city, this being ... the only business in which our people preponderate.'

One good thing that had emerged, Philbin continued, was that Belfast Catholics, notably troublesome young ones, had become mature and responsible citizens overnight, taking over maintenance of law and order and eliminating petty crime in the absence of a police presence.[76]

Appraised of the threat to the Catholic community in Belfast, McQuaid sent a second cheque for £500 (£4,500) to Bishop Philbin through the Catholic Social Service Conference. This cheque, which Philbin regarded as 'a source of the greatest comfort', was received on the morning the Bishop had a long discussion in Belfast with the Home Secretary, James Callaghan. Philbin reported to McQuaid: 'I believe he means to do a number of things which will definitely change the situation responsible for so many eruptions of trouble, and I think the changes will come gradually but will very soon begin. His approach is quite revolutionary by comparison with the attitude of previous British politicians.'[77]

At this juncture, McQuaid visited the Secretary of the Department of Justice, Peter Berry, who was receiving urgent treatment in Mount Carmel Hospital, Rathgar. It is highly likely that Berry informed McQuaid of his unease about how Government monies were likely to be used for supplying arms to the besieged Catholics in the North. With his interest in military matters, McQuaid probably followed closely the series of events that led the following May to the Arms Crisis in which Lynch dismissed Charles Haughey and Neil Blaney from his Government on the grounds of having been involved in a conspiracy to import arms for the North.[78]

In early September 1969, the chairman of the Northern Ireland Inter-denominational Distress Organisation, Dermot A. Ryan, a prominent businessman with an address in Dublin's fashionable Ailesbury Road, invited McQuaid to become a patron of the organisation. The group, Ryan explained, had distributed over £8,000 (£72,000) worth of food, clothing and bedding and had raised almost £6,000 (£54,000) in cash for the relief of the distressed people in Northern Ireland. 'I know that you have this cause very deeply at heart and are helping the Bishops in the North in every way possible,' Ryan wrote.[79] Ryan, however, failed to enclose a list of the organisation's other patrons and he did not impress McQuaid by the cheap quality of the paper he used in his circular. McQuaid did not become a patron on the pretext of not wishing to be invidious to the many organisations wishing to relieve distress in the North.[80]

Five days later 'peace lines' were erected by the British Army in parts of Belfast to keep Catholics and Protestants apart. As the situation worsened, Cardinal Conway and Bishop Philbin were perceived to be pro-British in placing a high priority on the maintenance of grants for Catholic schools and hospitals. Philbin, in particular, became alienated from a large section of the Belfast Catholic working class and was humiliated when his orders to pull down barricades were mocked. McQuaid, however, continued to regard Philbin as a sound barometer of Catholic opinion in Belfast.[81]

The ugly nature of sectarianism revealed in the television coverage of murderous events in Northern Ireland did not cause McQuaid to rethink, let alone question, his attitude to Catholics mixing with Protestants in the Republic. When Bishop-elect Eamonn Casey was invited by Geoffrey Corry to address the Irish Christian Youth Assembly, which was affiliated to the Irish Council of Churches but was seeking to recruit Catholics and non-Christians, McQuaid advised Casey to decline courteously. 'The Irish Christian Youth Assembly is not known to us Catholics here and the new venture, which hopes to embrace Catholic youth, has some worrying aspects,' McQuaid told him. 'It is liable to intensify an existing confusion.'[82]

McQuaid's sectarian outlook must have taken a severe knock a few weeks later when the Taoiseach, Jack Lynch, promised to hold a referendum in which the voters would be asked if Article 44 of the Constitution defining the special position of the Catholic Church was regarded as an obstacle to Irish unity. McQuaid made no public comment, unlike Cardinal Conway who said that he would not shed a single tear over its disappearance. 'It confers no legal privilege whatever on the Catholic Church, and if the only way to convince our fellow Christians in the North about this is to remove it, then that might be worth the expense of a referendum,' the Cardinal said.[83]

The likelihood of a referendum increased when Archbishop Simms welcomed a reconsideration of the special position of the Catholic Church in the light of the new thinking of Vatican Two on Church–State relations and ecumenism. Nor was there any opposition from the Fine Gael and Labour parties, whose leaders, Liam Cosgrave and Brendan Corish, both devout Catholics, also supported it. The October meeting of the Hierarchy endorsed Conway's views.

Later that month, Conway reported to McQuaid that the extraordinary Synod of Bishops, convened by Pope Paul to deal with the question of authority in the Church, had gone well. 'No explosive proposals were pushed – I think those who might have been inclined to do so sensed that the general mood of the bishops was not propitious for their ideas,' Conway wrote.[84] This was a reference to the Belgian Primate, Cardinal Suenens, who had revived demands for change in an interview with the Paris-based *Informations Catholiques Internationales*, which captured world headlines for his criticism of Pope Paul's 'obstruction' of the collegiality advocated by the council. Although there were fears that the Curia wanted to suppress debate at the Synod, there was a generally positive discussion on ways of ensuring better communications between Rome and the national Episcopal conferences. The tide had turned against Suenens.[85]

After attending a meeting of European Bishops at Chur in Switzerland, the Irish representative, Bishop Cahal Daly, informed McQuaid of his anger at the fact that Cardinal Suenens had addressed an alternative meeting of dissident priests and gave them the impression that he supported the ending of obligatory celibacy. In his report to McQuaid of Suenens's performance, Daly enclosed critical comments that he had presented to the Belgian Primate. On the margin of Daly's correspondence, McQuaid wrote: 'The simple truth is that Card. Suenens is not a gentleman.'[86]

Shortly before Christmas, the bishops held a special meeting to discuss a document which Conway had written and circulated, 'Ireland in the Seventies', in which he set out the challenges facing the Irish Catholic Church in the decade ahead. This became the basis for a reorganisation and development of Episcopal commissions involving lay experts.[87]

To the surprise of many of his critics, in early 1970 McQuaid introduced liturgical changes which he had resisted previously. He allowed altars to be turned towards the congregation. Laymen were to be allowed to read at Mass and offertory processions were to be permitted. 'You have effectively silenced the critics who accused you of soft-peddling the Church's wishes,' Archbishop Finbar Ryan wrote from Cork.[88]

Lifting of the ban

By 1970 the toll on McQuaid's reputation was considerable. An index of his unenviable status was his portrayal in Donald S. Connery's book, *The Irish*, as the foremost symbol of the Irish Church's outdated character and the single greatest obstacle to its modernisation.[89] Nothing exemplified this more than the ban on Catholics attending Trinity College, Dublin.

In February, *Hibernia* published a position paper written by the Irish Federation of University Teachers (IFUT) in favour of removing the ban. This was presented to the Hierarchy after specific references to McQuaid were deleted.[90] By 1970, 1,400 of the 4,000-strong student body were Catholics, most of whom had received a dispensation from McQuaid, an instance of what the religious affairs commentator, Louis McRedmond, described as McQuaid's 'practical liberality'.[91] It was practical in the sense that McQuaid felt that a Catholic studying at Trinity was less dangerous than one going to Oxford or Cambridge.

The presence of such large numbers of Catholics made the ban seem even more irrelevant. Although McQuaid frequently professed that he merely implemented the ruling on behalf of the Hierarchy, it is clear that after the 1956 Synod gave him an exclusive executive role in applying the ban, Trinity was outlawed to Catholics to a greater extent than it had ever been in its long history.[92] This was certainly so until about 1965, when the pace of change overtook McQuaid. A harbinger of change was the sight of nuns in Trinity's library: in 1968 McQuaid allowed the Sisters of Charity to use it to find books that were unobtainable elsewhere.[93]

McQuaid declined an invitation to attend an address by Senator Edward Kennedy at Trinity College, but the presence there of the President of Maynooth College, Dr Jeremiah Newman, intensified the publicity about the outdatedness of the ban. It seemed absurd to people that a Boston Catholic could lecture at Trinity while Dublin Catholics were still forbidden under pain of mortal sin to enter the portals of an institution which had taught Wolfe Tone, Robert Emmet, Thomas Moore, Thomas Davis, John Blake Dillon, Isaac Butt and Oscar Wilde. An editorial in *Hibernia* described the ban as a unique academic anachronism in the Christian world, and noted that the initiative for a review of the position would have to come from McQuaid.[94]

McQuaid and Browne, however, found the insistence that the ban must and would go 'really disturbing'. They feared the propaganda of the Catholic staff in Trinity, and loathed the demand for abolition of the law from what they called 'the humanist and radical section in UCD who want no denominationalism of any kind'.[95]

The file containing McQuaid's contribution to the repeal of the ban has not yet been made available by the Archdiocese of Dublin. However, the evidence indicates that the initiative in fact came from Cardinal Conway. On June 25, 1970, the Hierarchy issued a statement at the end of its summer meeting at Maynooth, announcing that it was applying to Rome for permission to lift the ban on attendance by Catholics at Trinity College. Significantly, the statement identified Donogh O'Malley's 1967 proposal to merge Trinity and UCD as the development which had cleared the way for a new Episcopal policy. The merger proposal had provided 'some hope of a change that would make this institution acceptable to the Catholic conscience,' the statement added, a distinctive phrase that appears to have been drafted by McQuaid.[96]

Asked at a news conference whether the statement was unanimous, Cardinal Conway said: 'I think yes. We don't normally say, but my recollection is that it was. There were several votes taken on the wording.' The Cardinal also disclosed that discussions about removing the ban had been going on since 1965, when there had been 'a major discussion' about it between the Irish bishops attending the Second Vatican Council. The decision to repeal the ruling represented 'the conclusion of a process of rethinking'. Its rescinding was not contingent on the proposed merger taking place between UCD and Trinity.[97]

Later, in an interview with the academic, Brian Burke, Conway explained that the decision was based on a complex series of causes, including the new attitudes towards Protestantism and religious freedom inaugurated by the Second Vatican Council. Religious, political and social circumstances had conspired, he added, to ensure the removal of a piece of legislation which was no longer tenable in theory and no longer effective in practice.[98] Clearly Conway, as in regard to the special position of the Catholic Church in the 1937 Constitution, was not losing any sleep over the removal of the Trinity ban. Nor had Rome any difficulties about its removal, and granted the Hierarchy's request on September 7, enabling Catholics to enter Trinity for the start of the autumn term without a shadow of mortal sin hanging over them. By the end of October, McQuaid had appointed Fr Brendan Heffernan as the first Catholic chaplain to Trinity.[99]

Prior to this, McQuaid had rejected all invitations to appoint chaplains on campus, though this left him vulnerable to the argument that in refusing to do so he was in breach of the Vatican Council's decree on education, which stipulated that 'at colleges and universities which are not Catholic' bishops should provide 'Catholic residences and centres where priests, religious and laymen ... can serve as on-campus sources of spiritual and intellectual assistance to young college people.'[100]

Shortly before the decision, McQuaid had refused to meet the president of the TCD Students' Representative Council, Paul Tansey, to discuss the ban. There were no negotiations between the Hierarchy and the IFUT, and neither was there any secret deal between the Hierarchy and Trinity, whose Provost, Albert McConnell, believed that as the ban was withering, the less said about it the quicker it would die.[101]

The removal of the Trinity ban was an overdue recognition by the Hierarchy that it was an embarrassing remnant from a past age. However cogent the reasons for the change, as so ably spun by Cardinal Conway, the Hierarchy made no attempt to explain the underlying philosophical question of why an edict which had been presented as absolute moral teaching by prelates like McQuaid and Kinane, was now being discarded as incompatible with ecumenical theology. Although the Hierarchy still maintained that the ban had been amply justified in the past, the 1970 decision was a turnaround of such enormity that it did call into question policies which had for years been pursued with such certitude. Although McQuaid went along with the ban's removal, there was a growing feeling that he belonged to an era that was now passing into history.

25

'Until the End'
1970–73

'Dr McQuaid's service to the Truth was shown in his
pursuit of right doctrines.'
Archbishop Dermot Ryan, April 1973.

On Tuesday July 28, 1970, as John Charles McQuaid celebrated his seventy-fifth birthday, journalists asked the pipe-smoking and congenial press officer, Ossie Dowling, whether the Archbishop would be submitting his resignation to Pope Paul VI under the new retirement rules introduced by the Vatican. 'It is just another working day,' Dowling said chirpily. Over tea and sponge cake in the Palace, however, McQuaid told one of his assistants, Margaret McMahon, that officially he retired that day.[1]

Busy at his desk from early that morning after his drive from Killiney, McQuaid had ample reason to believe that his resignation would not be accepted. Indeed, he was serenely confident that he would be allowed to prolong his episcopacy for as long as his health and vigour held. Furthermore, a most flattering article reciting his 'numberless achievements' appeared in that day's *Irish Independent* by the religious affairs correspondent, Joe Power, who suggested that thousands of Dubliners would be poorer, spiritually and physically, without McQuaid's watchfulness. The suggestion was that McQuaid was an integral part of a benign institution and would be at the helm for many more years.[2]

The Nuncio, Archbishop Alibrandi, called to convey the Holy See's greetings. President de Valera phoned to offer his and Mrs de Valera's good wishes. Messages of good-will were received from the Taoiseach, Jack Lynch, the Minister for External Affairs, Dr Patrick Hillery, and members of the diplomatic corps. At noon, representatives of the newsboys' organisation presented him with 'a spiritual bouquet' and a cheque for £500 (£4,500) which he donated to the chairman of the Dublin Itinerants Settlement Committee, Fr Thomas Fehily.

Meanwhile, the media continued to try to guess when McQuaid would step down and who would replace him. Two days before his birthday the *Sunday Press* reported that the Archbishop planned to travel to Rome in September and would personally present his resignation to Pope Paul.[3] Next day, Joe Power, well briefed, reported that the talk of an impending resignation was without foundation. 'Why?' Power asked, 'was McQuaid being singled out by journalists?' Other bishops were continuing in office, among them Bishop Neil Farren of Derry, aged 77, Bishop O'Boyle of Killala, 82, Bishop Quinn of Kilmore, 77, and Bishop Browne of Galway who would be 75 in December.[4]

Power, who had special access to McQuaid, answered that the Archbishop would stay on for another two years, and his report tipped Bishop Joseph Carroll as the likely successor. 'Whenever Dr McQuaid offers his resignation to the Holy See, his loss to the Archdiocese of Dublin will be incalculable,' Power wrote. 'And one cannot help feeling that when he does the Holy Father will request him to remain to complete the many projects which he has initiated in the diocese.'[5]

Speculation about McQuaid's resignation had begun the previous year when the *Irish Press* religious affairs correspondent, T.P. O'Mahony, highlighted the importance of the succession for the future direction of the Irish Catholic Church and named as possible successors Bishop Donal Herlihy of Ferns and Bishop Michael Harty of Killaloe.[6] Speculation flared up again when journalists learned that McQuaid would be in Rome from October 22 to November 11, 1969, on what Dowling said was his annual visit. While McQuaid was in Rome, however, the *Irish Press* editor, Tim Pat Coogan, had a tip-off that McQuaid had indeed offered his resignation. Coogan instructed a staff reporter, Michael O'Toole, to meet McQuaid at Dublin airport and ask him directly if this was the case. This was an awesome assignment as journalists were not in the habit of 'door-stepping' bishops, certainly not the Archbishop of Dublin. O'Toole's direct question provoked a vintage McQuaid response. 'The subject of my retirement was never mentioned,' he said. 'There was, I believe, some speculation on this matter in Dublin, but it is quite without foundation.'

McQuaid confirmed that he had a private audience with Paul VI, who presented him with a gold and ivory chalice. 'Since my audience with the Holy Father was a private one I naturally cannot tell you what transpired,' he told the reporter. 'The Holy Father did, however, ask me to convey to the people of Ireland his gratitude and admiration for their continuity, fidelity and loyalty to the faith. The Holy Father expressed this message with unusual feeling.'[7]

Lobbying Rome

What McQuaid concealed from the press was that on July 18, ten days before his birthday, he had written to Pope Paul VI tendering his resignation and declaring his willingness to do whatever the Pontiff decided.[8] McQuaid expected that Paul would ask him to stay on. All the evidence available to him was that he stood high in Paul's estimation. His Pastoral Letter marking Paul's fiftieth anniversary as a priest was well received in Rome and had been published in *L'Osservatore Romano*.[9]

Lauding Paul's priesthood, McQuaid declared that his penetrating intelligence and unflinching will had won the deepest gratitude of the Church. 'They who have been allowed to know Paul VI, as his inner life reveals him, of one accord bear witness to the depth of divine Faith that is the mainspring of his thought and word and action,' McQuaid wrote, in a style of Papal adulation more appropriate to the age of Pius XII than to the post-*Humanae Vitae* period. As if writing his own epitaph, McQuaid noted how it had been Paul's lot to be misrepresented, opposed, reviled and even hated.

McQuaid also assured Paul of the staunch loyalty of Dublin. 'Not a single priest of this diocese has, by word or writing, failed fully to respect the teaching of the Pope on Faith and Morals,' he wrote. 'The faithful, too, for all the pressure of evil and all the influences of the mass media, remain, in very greatest proportion, true to the Faith and the practice of the Faith, especially to Holy Mass and Holy Communion.'[10]

McQuaid's letter gave Pope Paul 'much joy and he was greatly comforted and encouraged by this latest manifestation of Your Grace's deep devotion and loyal attachment to His August Person,' the substitute Secretary of State, Archbishop Giovanni Benelli, informed McQuaid.[11] Benelli also thanked McQuaid for his kind remarks about himself – McQuaid had offered his 'deep thanks for the gentle friendship with which Your Excellency has always treated me over a long space of years.'[12]

This correspondence indicates clearly that, ahead of his retirement, McQuaid had launched a charm offensive to prolong his period as Archbishop. It also reveals that McQuaid offered Pope Paul £10,000 (£90,000) for the reconstruction of the Papal Nunciature in the Phoenix Park. 'I shall see to it that the necessary funds will not be wanting,' he wrote to Archbishop Benelli. 'It is just one way of expressing to His Holiness my gratitude for a Fatherly kindness that has never failed me.'[13]

Remarkably, without waiting for a response from Rome, McQuaid sent a cheque for £10,000 to Archbishop Alibrandi next day.[14] In the circumstances, this offer smacks of 'a sweetener' to maintain his position. In one of those twists of fate, however, it was McQuaid's misfortune that he was dealing not just with Pope Paul, but also with Benelli, who had not forgotten his difficulties with McQuaid during his stint at the Dublin Nunciature from 1950 to 1953. Now firmly ensconced as chief of staff to Pope Paul, Benelli had become the most influential official in the Vatican, regularly making decisions without reference to his immediate boss, the ineffectual Frenchman, Cardinal Jean Villot. So significant was Benelli's role during the Pontificate of Pope Paul that George Bull, author of *Inside the Vatican*, described him as an aggressive figure who drew the threads of power into his own very capable and conservative hands.[15] A blunt Tuscan, who was nicknamed the *carabiniere* – the military policeman – Benelli handled all important Church business from his office on the third floor of the Apostolic Palace. 'The reports, complaints, and requests from the world's Roman Catholic Bishops sooner or later came to his desk,' Paul Hofmann wrote in *Anatomy of the Vatican*. The question of McQuaid's retirement, as well as the gift for £10,000, landed on Benelli's desk.[16]

McQuaid must have felt dumbfounded when he was informed by Benelli that, while Pope Paul appreciated his donation of £10,000, it had been decided not to modernise the Nunciature. 'In all propriety, therefore, His Holiness cannot accept for this purpose the gracious offer,' Benelli wrote. 'So, of course, he would wish you be completely free to utilise the money for your beloved archdiocese or in whatever way you would judge fitting.'[17]

Meanwhile, Benelli had responded positively to a request by McQuaid to see him during his visit to Rome in September.[18] Documents in the archives of the Irish Department of Foreign Affairs indicate that this was the occasion when McQuaid formally offered his resignation to Pope Paul. However, the Ambassador to the Holy See, Thomas Commins, only discovered this later on, during a conversation at dinner offered by the new auxiliary Bishop of Elphin, Dr Dominic Conway, in the Columbus Hotel close to St Peter's. The information came from an authoritative source – McQuaid's schooldays' companion, Fr Dan O'Connell, who had recently retired from the Vatican Observatory but was still President of the Pontifical Academy of Sciences at the Pope's request.

O'Connell confided to Commins that McQuaid had offered his resignation to the Pope on the grounds of having reached the age of 75, but his resignation was declined because of McQuaid's 'obviously undiminished vigour, physical capacity and competence to continue the administration of the diocese'. This vital information was sent by Commins to Dublin in a confidential report to the head of External Affairs, Hugh McCann: 'Archbishop McQuaid does not appear to have let anything of this be known to anyone else here'.

> That is in character since as you know he is extremely reserved. In fact, apart from his visit to the Pope, he does not appear to have contacted anyone here except Fr O'Connell. He certainly did not contact either the Embassy or the Irish College; indeed the Irish College did not know where he was staying when I enquired of the rector. I only ascertained, after the Archbishop had gone home, that he stayed with some nuns in Nemi which is in

the Castelli area just outside the city of Rome.[19]

As a result of O'Connell's indiscretion, McQuaid's secret had filtered through to the Irish Government, but it was still confined to a limited circle and was not leaked to the media. McQuaid himself told only a few trusted friends that he would not be stepping down. This news thrilled Archbishop Finbar Ryan, who told McQuaid that there was no one with his grasp of facts and principles to face the coming educational struggle. 'We are strong enough to hold our own but there must be a leader to keep our teaching bodies together,' Ryan wrote. 'By God's Providence, you are the man.'[20]

The duration of McQuaid's staying-on, however, was not as clearcut as O'Connell indicated, nor as McQuaid himself believed. Dr Stafford Johnson, who together with Fr Vincent Dinan accompanied the Archbishop on his journey to Rome, picked up a qualification in Pope Paul's remarks. Stafford became apprehensive when he heard Paul say that he would be consulting his advisers. Intuitively, he read this as a signal that there would be a change.[21]

Foremost among those advisers was the substitute Secretary of State, Giovanni Benelli, whom McQuaid also met on this visit. Benelli found 'valuable' McQuaid's comments on the new Northern Ireland desk set up in the Department of External Affairs under the direction of diplomat, Éamonn Gallagher, and he heartily agreed with the Archbishop on the necessity of keeping constant watch 'to maintain and strengthen the Church's teaching on such vital questions as divorce and birth prevention'.[22]

Before leaving Rome, McQuaid had further urgent business to expedite with Benelli and entrusted Fr Dan O'Connell with a letter to deliver to him. 'I very much hope that the letter arrived in time,' O'Connell wrote to McQuaid. 'I was in fact lucky to reach Mons. Benelli as soon as I did.' Intriguingly, O'Connell added: 'Please God your own problems are not too difficult.'[23]

Curse upon the nation

McQuaid returned to Dublin believing that his mandate as Archbishop had been renewed with the specific task of opposing the encroachment of what became known as 'the liberal agenda'. Both Paul VI and Benelli shared his view that Ireland should adhere to its Catholic ethos and principles irrespective of the pressure building up from liberals who argued that the South should make accommodations with the majoritarian Protestant population in Northern Ireland on issues like contraception and divorce.

This matter had first arisen after Seán Lemass embarked on his policy of détente with the North. In 1965, while McQuaid was attending the final session of the Vatican Council, Lemass instructed his Minister for Justice, Brian Lenihan, to make discreet enquiries as to what the

Church's reaction would be to an alteration or removal of the Constitutional ban on divorce. After consulting with the Chancellor of the diocese, Monsignor Gerard Sheehy, Lenihan informed Lemass that there would be 'violent opposition from the Hierarchy to any proposal to allow divorce in the State'. Both Lemass and Lenihan understood that Sheehy was speaking on behalf of McQuaid, and dropped the matter.[24]

However, Lemass later set up a Committee on the Constitution chaired by George Colley T.D. which he sat on after he stepped down as Taoiseach. Shortly before Christmas 1967, the committee proposed that civil divorce should be made available to Protestants who wished to have recourse to it. It also called for the deletion of the name of religions from the Constitution, and for the modification of Article 3, which established the legal right of the Oireachtas to legislate for Northern Ireland.[25]

McQuaid's Lenten Regulations for February 1968 noted that 'an informal committee' had put forward a proposal on divorce that was 'contrary to the law of God'. The experience of other countries had provided that civil divorce produced 'the gravest ills in society,' he warned. 'The effort, even well-intentioned, to solve hardship within marriage by civil divorce, has invariably resulted for society in a series of greater sufferings and deeper evils.' [26]

As McQuaid had detected, the committee's terms of reference did not commit the political parties to implementing its recommendations. The Republic's politicians, or at least a progressive minority, were defining two main strands in national debate: the first viewpoint advocated changes in the Constitution to reduce fears of undue Catholic influence and thus, hopefully, pave the way for the reunification of Ireland; the second maintained that the Constitution was outdated, that it bore the marks of a pre-Vatican Council Catholicism and it therefore should be updated to reflect the values of a pluralist society in the Republic.[27]

Neither McQuaid nor Rome liked the thrust of this new thinking. A battle for public opinion was underway for what McQuaid regarded as the soul of Ireland. By coincidence, while McQuaid was in Rockwell College finalising a major statement against contraception, he received news of the death of General De Gaulle on November 11, 1970. In a letter to the French Ambassador, Emmanuel d'Harcourt, McQuaid joined with 'the whole of Ireland in saluting the memory of a great Frenchman of old Catholic stock, who was the incarnation in his so worthy life of the spirit of the true France, his native land.'[28] It was as if the death of de Gaulle galvanised McQuaid, the Cavan man of old Catholic stock, into a defence of the spirit of what he believed was the true Ireland. Over the next few months he issued three statements on contraception that became increasingly vehement in their language and tone.

In his first statement, issued in late November, McQuaid warned that any writer who wished to venture into the area of moral law was gravely obliged to understand correctly and to state accurately the objective moral law as the teaching authority in the Church explained it. 'In a diocese there is only one teaching authority, who, under the Pope and in union with him, is competent, by virtue of his sacred office, to declare the authentic and objective moral law, that is binding on all the faithful of his diocese, both priests and lay people,' he declared. 'That authority is the bishop.' To correct the 'confusion' that had been caused in the minds of Dublin Catholics, he formally declared that the doctrine of the objective moral law concerning the regulation of birth taught that 'any contraceptive act is wrong in itself'.[29]

McQuaid's second anti-contraception salvo came in his Lenten Regulations in February 1971. He regretted that 'our faithful people continue to be assailed by public pleas for civil divorce and contraception'. Civil divorce, he noted, was proposed as the right of minorities, while contraception was proposed as the right of married persons to birth control. The words 'right' and 'control' were lending a false appearance of reason and morality to the debate, McQuaid complained, and added magisterially: 'But civil divorce is evil and contraception is evil. There cannot be, on the part of any person, a right to what is evil.'[30]

At their spring meeting at Maynooth, the bishops expressed their disquiet at pressures being exerted on public opinion on questions concerning the civil law and divorce, contraception and abortion. 'These questions involve issues of grave import for society as a whole, which go far beyond purely private morality or religious belief,' they declared. 'Civil law on these matters should respect the wishes of the people who elected the legislators, and the bishops confidently hope that the legislators themselves will respect this important principle.'[31]

McQuaid, however, was disappointed by the moderate tone of the statement, which bore more the imprint of Cardinal Conway, Bishop Cahal Daly and Bishop Peter Birch than himself. It was too polite a statement in view of the gathering forces for change led by a young Catholic lawyer from the West of Ireland, Senator Mary Robinson, née Bourke. The beneficiary of a McQuaid-granted dispensation to study at Trinity, Robinson was the first Catholic to become a Trinity Senator.

On February 26, Robinson had notified the Senate that she had drafted a Bill to legalise contraceptives. She had also appeared on the *Late Late Show* as the legal advisor to the newly formed Women's Liberation Movement. Privately, she had met Cardinal Conway in Dundalk but found him to be 'a bully' who did not accept her intellectual integrity.[32]

On March 30, Robinson placed on the Senate order book her Criminal Law Amendment Bill 1971, which aimed to repeal section 17 of the 1935 Act along with the Censorship of Publications Acts 1929 and 1946. The Bill was co-sponsored by John Horgan, who in addition to his job as religion and education correspondent of *The Irish Times* was a Senator representing the National University, and Trevor West of Trinity College. They were a lethal triumvirate in McQuaid's eyes. Robinson posed a direct challenge to the Constitutional status quo; Horgan was a liberal Catholic who was self-taught in theology,[33] and an outspoken West had told an exclusive Protestant audience at the King's Hospital, Palmerstown, that McQuaid's remarks 'sometimes send shivers down Protestant spines'.[34] However, the Bill failed to secure the support of the six Senators required to allow it to be published and discussed in the Senate.

On March 28, McQuaid issued a theological Exocet that launched what was to be a 25-year 'moral civil war' between the Hierarchy and the legislature on matters of public and private morality. If legislation were passed which 'offended the objective moral law,' he warned, 'it would be, and would remain a curse upon our country.' To speak of 'a right to contraception on the part of the individual, be he Christian, non-Christian or atheist, is to speak of a right that cannot even exist.'[35]

McQuaid spelt out in highly emotive language why such legislation would be 'disastrous' for Ireland:

> Given the proneness of our human nature to evil, given the enticement of bodily satisfaction, given the widespread modern incitement to unchastity, it must be evident that an access, hitherto unlawful, to contraceptive devices will prove a most certain occasion of sin, especially to immature persons. The public consequences of immorality that must follow for our whole society are only too clear to see in other countries.

McQuaid was also scathing in his contempt for the argument that a uniformity of sexual outlook and practise could, in some obscure way, assist the reunification of Ireland. 'One must know little of the Northern people,' he wrote, 'if one can fail to realise the indignant ridicule with which good Northern people would treat such an argument.'

Reaction in the North to McQuaid's Pastoral confirmed, however, that Protestants considered contraception a major test of relations between the Republic and Northern Ireland. While agreeing with McQuaid that the liberalisation of the law on contraceptives would not entice Northern Protestants into a united Ireland, the right-wing Unionist leader, Bill Craig, feared that there would be difficulties and tensions if the Roman Catholic community did not have family planning in keeping with modern times. A leading member of the Young Unionist Association, Jim Rodgers, predicted that contraception would be one of the big issues in any attempt to unite the country because Protestants felt it was their right to decide for themselves whether or not to use contraceptives. The Presbyterian press officer, the Rev. Donald Frazer, who revealed that church committees were examining the issue of contraception, said that many Northern Protestants were concerned by the fact that Government policies in the South seemed to be influenced by one church. The chairman of the New Ulster Movement, Brian Walker, regretted that the interference in the Republic on issues like contraception confirmed Northern Protestants in their conviction that the Church of Rome was able to manipulate the Government of the day, however much this was denied by the politicians and the civil service.[36]

The following Sunday, when McQuaid's Pastoral was being read in all the churches of the diocese, the Irish Women's Liberation Movement formed a 40-foot chain across the entrance to Archbishop's House at Drumcondra and waved placards denouncing him as a dictator. At evening Mass in the Church of the Three Patrons, Rathgar, a man who interrupted the reading of the Archbishop's letter was shouted down by the congregation.

McQuaid's 'stern words' were interpreted by the *Irish Independent* as a shot across the Lynch Government's bows.[37] The Church of Ireland Archbishop of Dublin, Alan Buchanan, came out strongly in favour of relaxing the laws, provided there was adequate control over the sale of contraceptives. The *Belfast Telegraph* predicted that the birth-control issue looked like developing into the biggest clash between the Catholic Church and the Southern State since the Mother and Child row. But it also noted the unsettling effect McQuaid's intervention had had on Lynch and Fianna Fáil: 'After the uncompromising restatement of traditional opposition to birth control from the Archbishop of Dublin, Dr McQuaid, the ruling party is waiting and watching to see which way the wind of public opinion seems to be blowing.'[38]

From the reaction in their constituencies, the politicians deduced that the wind was blowing in McQuaid's favour. A second attempt by Senator Robinson to introduce her Bill was easily defeated. Lynch and Hillery engaged in what columnist John Healy described as 'verbal politics' – they talked about changing sections of the Republic's laws and the Constitution which gave offence to liberty of conscience, but they did nothing that would merit a belt of McQuaid's crozier.

McQuaid was not the only bishop to speak out against the Robinson Bill. The Bishop of Killala, Dr Thomas McDonnell, preached a sermon against her in St Muredach's Cathedral directly across from the Robinson homestead on the River Moy. His words were sent by a local reporter to the national newspapers, which gave it prominent display. It was read by McQuaid, who wrote to McDonnell congratulating him on his statement. The publicity-shy McDonnell replied that he had not intended his remarks to receive national attention. 'Senator Robinson is, I regret to say, a Ballina girl and of excellent Catholic parents.'[39]

Support for McQuaid came privately from Bishop Dominic Conway of Elphin, who described his intervention as timely and welcome, courageous and forthright. 'Thank God you have spoken out,'

Conway wrote from Sligo. 'The whole of our solid Catholic population welcomes this statement. It is deplorable that only the few individual crackpots in the pressure groups get publicity. Long may you continue in the See of Dublin.'[40]

Conway's good wishes were badly needed. Only four days earlier, John Horgan had revealed in *The Irish Times* that Archbishop Alibrandi was conducting a poll among a select number of priests on their choice of a possible successor as Archbishop of Dublin. Without naming individuals, Horgan identified three front-runners: a priest in an academic post in Dublin, at least one member of the Hierarchy, and a Dublin priest attached to the Secretariat of State in Rome. These referred to Professor Dermot Ryan, Bishop Donal Herlihy of Ferns and Monsignor John Gordon, who had been assigned by McQuaid to the Secretariat of State and was now an Apostolic Delegate to several African countries.

Horgan's report, though brief, was significant. It highlighted that this was the first consultation of its kind in Dublin. 'The fact that the consultation is actually taking place also suggests,' Horgan wrote, 'that Dr McQuaid's retirement may take place in the reasonably near future' – otherwise the uncertainty created by the soundings would have deleterious effect on the morale of the Dublin priests.[41] Further light on the process was shed in the *Evening Herald* by Joe Power, who confirmed that the soundings had been going on since October. However, Power claimed that the procedure was not unusual, having been adopted in other dioceses where bishops had reached the retiring age of 75, and he further claimed that it was accepted throughout the diocese that McQuaid would stay in office for at least another year.[42]

North on the brink

On August 20, 1971, following the news that the Stormont Government had used emergency powers to intern suspect republicans without trial, McQuaid called for a day of prayer in all Dublin churches to make reparation for sins of injustice, hatred and revenge committed against God. Through the intercession of Mary, he hoped that God might mercifully grant a peace that would be the fruit of justice in Northern Ireland. His appeal, couched in religious language, was given little publicity by the media, especially RTÉ, which was grappling with the more immediate problems of reporting horrendous cases of injustice arising from a major miscalculation by the Unionist Government headed by Brian Faulkner. Dissatisfied with the lack of coverage, McQuaid instructed his officials to send his statement by post to parish priests and rectors. He also gave a £1,000 (£9,000) gift to the Red Cross.[43]

Behind the scenes, Dublin Corporation and the Government were seeking more than financial aid from McQuaid. The Dublin City

Manager, Matthew Macken, asked McQuaid for help in providing sufficient accommodation for refugees from the North,[44] while the Minister
for Defence, Jerry Cronin, consulted McQuaid about how church buildings could be used as temporary settlements because the numbers of refugees had risen beyond the army's capacity to handle the crisis.[45] Within a
few hours, McQuaid arranged accommodation with Religious Orders and
lay groups for 1,635 mothers and children in 39 houses. 'I feel I simply
must offer my warmest congratulations on the magnificent day's work
Your Grace did for the refugees today,' Fr Cecil Barrett told McQuaid.
'You were marvellous.'[46]

McQuaid held a church collection at the end of August to assist 'our
suffering brethren in the North', and he called attention to the fact that
'the greatest strain will be put on the Bishops of the afflicted areas, as
they strive to meet the overwhelming calls upon their charity by refugees
returning to the North in coming weeks.'[47] McQuaid was himself receiving reports on the effects of internment on the Catholic community. In
early September, Hugh Bredin of the Department of Scholastic Philosophy, Queen's University, sent McQuaid a protest petition against internment with the plea: 'We hope that you will exert whatever influence you
can to have this policy reversed.'[48]

Not only was McQuaid being pressed to help bring about a change
in Stormont's anti-terrorist legislation, he was under pressure within the
Hierarchy from Cardinal Conway to contribute to an unprecedented
statement in the name of all the bishops that would have enormous implications for the relationship of the Catholic Church in Ireland towards
both the Irish Republic and Northern Ireland.

'I think it will be necessary to issue a major statement from our
forthcoming meeting on the situation in Northern Ireland which, of
course, can have profound repercussions in the Republic,' Conway wrote
to McQuaid on September 7. He requested McQuaid, along with the
other bishops, to send him a list of the points which ought to be emphasised in such a statement.[49]

From Rome, where he received the letter, McQuaid administered a
masterly exposition on the *realpolitik* of Church-State relations in regard
to the status of Northern Ireland. McQuaid told Conway that all the bishops could properly concentrate on were the normal human rights that a
citizen ought to be allowed to enjoy:

> Are we to consider civil disobedience which Northern
> Catholics are advocating and practising?' he asked. 'Such
> civil disobedience was advocated by the Bishops in the
> matter of general conscription during the First World War
> and had very far-reaching political effects.
>
> Are we to support the campaign for fuller participation by

Catholics in the Government of Northern Ireland? If we enter that area we must be very clear about the consequences of recognition of Northern Ireland. It is in this area that repercussions in the Republic must be very seriously considered.'

In effect, McQuaid was warning Conway that the kind of statement which he envisaged would be tantamount to a *de jure* recognition by the Hierarchy of the independent status of Northern Ireland, and, as such, would be a blow to the moral claim of Northern Catholics to belong by right to the ancient Irish nation.

Furthermore, McQuaid warned that if any statement were to be made by the bishops, account would have to be taken of the tripartite talks already arranged for the end of the month at Chequers between the British Prime Minister, Ted Heath, the Taoiseach, Jack Lynch, and the Stormont Prime Minister, Brian Faulkner. The bishops, too, would have to consider the effect of their statement on the future negotiations of the political leaders. 'It may well be,' he concluded, 'that developments within the next three weeks, as a result of the tripartite talks, may render inopportune any major statement from all the Bishops.'[50] Nothing of significance emerged from the Chequers talks. No major joint Pastoral Letter on the North was issued by the Hierarchy.

Meanwhile, the *Irish Independent* reported from Rome that Pope Paul received McQuaid in private audience. No details of the meeting were released, but Vatican sources assumed that one topic was the situation in Northern Ireland. Three weeks previously, the Pope had criticised the Stormont Government by stating that the situation there was 'further aggravated following the adoption of the exceptional security measures which were strongly resented by at least a part of the citizens.' McQuaid's public relations unit was also at work in Dublin assuring journalists that the Archbishop's visit had no special significance.[51]

On his return to Dublin, McQuaid signed a cheque for £25,000 (£220,000) which he handed personally to Bishop Philbin for 'the needs of the Belfast Catholics in their sufferings'. Describing this as an extraordinarily generous contribution, Philbin assured him that the money would 'be put to good account in attempting to restore the position here, in many respects'.[52]

Philbin was unsure how to make a public acknowledgement of the assistance. 'Last time I referred to the matter in a Lenten Pastoral, which the *Irish Independent* quoted. More than this ought to be done, and I shall be more than agreeable to carry out any suggestion that seems good to your Grace.' McQuaid left it to Philbin to 'use some public occasion that press and TV could report to our people'.[53]

McQuaid's office continued to monitor developments in the North closely. Put on file was a cutting from *The Irish Times* of a speech in October by the student leader Éamonn McCann advocating the building up of an open Marxist revolutionary party.[54] McQuaid also received an anonymous letter about the torture of nationalists in North, which was critical of Conway's perceived pro-British stance but praised the outspokenness of the Dungannon priest, Fr Denis Faul, who merited a 'high place in heaven'.[55]

McQuaid and the IRA truce

As Christmas 1971 approached, McQuaid concentrated his attention on bringing about 'a God's Truce', based on the old Papal practice of the *Tregua Dei* under which hostilities should cease on the days of religious festival, especially Christmas day, the birth of Christ. Since September the Provisional IRA, the militant republicans who had broken away from the more Marxist and socialist tendency which regrouped as the Official IRA, had mounted a bombing campaign of a ferocity never witnessed before in Northern Ireland. In retaliation, Loyalist groups formed the Ulster Defence Association and stepped up their killings of Catholics.

On Thursday December 16, McQuaid asked Ossie Dowling to contact the Provisional IRA leaders, Seán MacStíofáin and Ruairí Ó Brádaigh, as well as Tomás MacGiolla, President of Sinn Féin, and Cathal Goulding chief of staff of the Official IRA. Dowling's purpose was to invite the republican leaders to meet Archbishop McQuaid. Four days later, Dowling brought Ó Bradaigh and MacStiofáin by car to meet the Archbishop at 2.45pm, Goulding at 3.30pm and MacGiolla at 8.15pm. McQuaid asked each of them to support a Christmas truce. He also informed them that he would be issuing a public appeal that evening.[56]

In his statement, McQuaid appealed, in the name of Our Divine Lord, to all the parties concerned to consider observing a truce, if only from Christmas Eve until Tuesday, December 28:

> This plea is not a judgement on the situation, North or South. Least of all is it a political initiative. It is only an appeal, in the name of the Prince of Peace, for the conditions that could allow all Christians, free from the fear of hostilities or searches or arrests, to commemorate, in peace, the coming of God made man on earth. May His gentle Mother, who bore him to be the Saviour of the world, intercede with Him for us, one and all, without exception, at this feast of Christmas.[57]

MacStíofáin, the English-born chief-of-staff of the Provisional IRA, later recalled that:

> [W]ith the success of the bombing campaign at the end of November 1971 the Republican leadership took a general decision to observe a Christmas truce if one could be

arranged. Ruairí Ó Brádaigh and I received an invitation
to meet the Catholic Archbishop of Dublin, the late Dr
McQuaid, to discuss the possibility of such a truce. It was
with great pleasure that I was able to tell him that this had
already been decided upon. We had a brief and friendly
conversation with him, and left him some literature outlining the Republican social and economic programme.

What I particularly appreciated was that he had gone privately about proposing the truce instead of exploiting the
situation by calling for it in the media first, the usual tactic
of certain other churchmen who won more publicity than
concrete results.[58]

A three-day truce was to be observed from December 24, but Mac-
Stíofáin described as spiteful Brian Faulkner's Christmas message to the
people in which he gave a guarantee that there would be 'no let-up whatsoever in the drive to combat the IRA'. The ceasefire broke down.
McQuaid received a message signed by 'an IRA Sufferor [sic]'. 'My Lord,
we the above respected your plea of a two day truce but we are forced out
again to the streets by the British Soldiers attack on our homes yesterday
morning. Pray for us as we are suffering to free our land from the English.
Please pray for us. May God bless you and keep you.' [59]

End of an era

That same day, December 27, 1971, the thirty-first anniversary of his
Episcopal Consecration, McQuaid received a request from the Papal
Nuncio, Archbishop Gaetano Alibrandi, to call at his residence in Killiney.
McQuaid readily agreed, expecting that the Nuncio was coming to pay his
respects. However, it proved not to be a joyous occasion. Wringing his
hands, Alibrandi broke the news that Pope Paul had accepted McQuaid's
resignation.[60] Worst still, his successor was not his preferred choice,
Bishop Joseph Carroll. Instead, it was one of his sternest critics, the 47-
year-old Professor of Eastern Languages at UCD, the Rev. Dermot Ryan.
Ryan, a biblical scholar, was a protégé of Monsignor Patrick Boylan, the
man who was beaten for the job in 1940.[61]

McQuaid contacted Boylan to arrange a meeting of the diocesan
administrative council at Drumcondra. After McQuaid announced the
name of his successor to his Vicars General, Ryan, somewhat gauchely in
view of his lanky six-foot-four frame, walked in from an adjoining room.
Arrangements were made for the announcing of Ryan's appointment on
Tuesday January 4. Contact between McQuaid and Ryan was formal,
frosty and brief. A product of the exclusive Jesuit-run Belvedere College,
Ryan was popular at UCD, though his record of publication was derisory.

He had posed as a liberal in the Priests' Council to attract the support of the middle ground and the younger clergy, and a campaign to promote him as McQuaid's successor had been led by priests such as Peter Lemass and Joe Dunn, who were well versed in communications.

Ahead of the public announcement, on Monday January 3 McQuaid was received at Áras an Uachtaráin where he informed President de Valera of his pending departure from office. De Valera was shocked. 'Not half as shocked as I am,' McQuaid is reported to have replied.[62]

The transfer of power was stage-managed with the issue of a press release in which Ryan said that he was greatly honoured to have been asked to become Archbishop by Pope Paul but was anxious at the task ahead of him. 'My anxiety is to some extent eased by my appreciation of what Dr McQuaid has done for the diocese during 31 years of unselfish ministry,' he added, referring to 'the excellent preparedness' in which his predecessor had left the diocesan administration.

Unlike McQuaid, who made no public appearance or comment, Ryan made himself available to the press for photographs. His appointment was welcomed by Cardinal Conway, who said Ryan's great gifts would redound to the benefit of the whole Irish Church. Conway, who was a member of the Congregation of Bishops, had had a decisive say in the UCD professor's appointment.[63]

McQuaid's resignation was described as a watershed, not only in the life of the Irish Church, but also for politics and society. The Taoiseach, Jack Lynch, called him 'a distinguished scholar and educationalist who has given outstanding service to the Church', while his old opponent, Dr Nöel Browne, told television viewers that McQuaid's appointment had been disastrous for Irish Catholicism and for the unification of Ireland.

The hallmark of McQuaid's career, both as President of Blackrock College and as Archbishop, was summed up by John Horgan in *The Irish Times* as 'a mixture of institutional severity and personal kindness'. His policy was based on the principle that error has no rights, and on his desire to protect his flock from what he considered were harmful influences. Such a policy was framed for a static and conservative society. 'Given its premises, it was a consistent and accurate policy,' Horgan wrote. 'But it was one which was made increasingly redundant by the emergence, or re-emergence, of pluralism in Irish society, by the spread of the media of communication, by urbanisation, and by inevitable sociological change.'[64]

Although McQuaid appeared to be at odds with the liberalising trend in Irish society, he remained popular with many Dublin Catholics, whose traditional outlook he shielded. As a typical instance of popular reaction, an elderly Dublin man was quoted as saying John Charles was 'a great man' who would be missed by 'a hell of a lot of people who were in favour of him anyway.' One old lady said: 'He's magnificent. He's done his time and he's done it very well. He couldn't have done it any better. We are all proud of him.' The most frequently-used adjectives to describe him were gentle, kind, shy and simple. One woman said he was 'beautiful in his robes'. People and commentators alike were puzzled as to why the Cardinal's Red Hat had never come to McQuaid's Dublin.[65]

Admirers and critics praised his administration of a diocese which had expanded enormously in his 31 years as Archbishop. The number of Catholics grew from 630,000 to over 800,000; the diocesan clergy from 370 to 600; the religious from 500 to 800. He constituted over 60 new parishes, bringing the total to 131. In addition, some 80 new churches were built, and over 250 primary schools. It was a record of phenomenal expansion.

The Dublin Diocesan Press Office announced that McQuaid would continue to govern the diocese until Archbishop-elect Ryan's Consecration. In his final letter for Unity Week on January 16, 1972, McQuaid showed no change of heart towards ecumenism: as he had done in past years, he warned Dublin Catholics not to put ecumenical meetings before prayer when it came to unity with other denominations. 'The Catholic Church has been founded on Peter and the Apostles,' he declared. 'Alone it guarantees to us the full and genuine teaching of Jesus Christ until the end of time, for to it alone is promised the unfailing guidance of the Holy Spirit that preserves his Church from error in doctrine of faith and morals.'[66]

Poignantly, the last letter in the McQuaid Northern Ireland file was issued in response to Bloody Sunday in Derry on January 30, 1972, when 14 persons were killed and 13 wounded by the British Army. It is a message to 'Most Rev. Doctor Farren, Bishop's House, Derry. I offer your Lordship and bereaved families my profound sympathy.'[67]

On his last working day, McQuaid told a member of his staff, Fr John Patrick Batelle: 'I am no longer wanted here, Father.'[68] On another occasion, he told Fr Aidan Lehane C.S.Sp.: 'I have great peace of mind because I have done absolutely no juggling. I will enthrone the Archbishop and then I will disappear completely. The next few years will be tough and perhaps I would not have been able for them. Perhaps I would let the Church down.' [69]

'Today for the last time I speak to you as Archbishop of Dublin,' McQuaid declared in his valedictory letter read out at Masses in the Dublin diocese. 'The Second Vatican Council earnestly requested the bishops to put themselves at the disposal of the Pope, on the completion of their 75th birthday. In obedience to that direction, I declared my willingness to do whatsoever His Holiness should decide. Eighteen months later the Holy Father appointed my successor in the See of Dublin. That decision is at once for me a declaration of the will of God which I have accepted in complete obedience. It is a very great grace to be allowed to know with certainty what God wishes us to do in this life.'[70]

Privately, McQuaid was devastated by his enforced contemplative leisure. 'The last few weeks have been torrential,' he wrote to his nephew,

Dr Paul McQuaid.[71] Once the most powerful ecclesiastic in the Irish Republic, he found himself overnight powerless, unoccupied and unwanted for public engagements. The pro-McQuaid clergy did not dare visit him, as a call would be construed by the Ryan insiders as a snub to the new régime.[72] Nor could McQuaid do favours, as of old. 'There was a time when I could have helped you,' he told Fr Aidan Lehane, 'But remember I am in the vaults, in the vaults entirely.'[73]

'The good heart of all who have written to me amazes me and humiliates me,' McQuaid wrote to Mrs Mercy Simms in Armagh. 'If I am here in Ballybrack it is due to the kindness of the Holy See, which unasked arranged this for me. I had never expected it.'[74]

McQuaid had made his last will and testament on March 14, 1967, and appointed Monsignor Patrick O'Connell, Fr Gerard Sheehy and Fr Desmond Williams as his executors and trustees. He directed that all property and funds over which he had sole power of selection and appointment should be used for the relief of the poor in the diocese. In foremost place was to be expenditure on Clonliffe College; his other priorities were the Catholic Social Service Conference and the Catholic Social Welfare Bureau. As to the remainder of his property, that was to be bequeathed to his successor, who would have absolute and sole discretion over its use, though McQuaid expressed the wish that such residue should be spent on Clonliffe College. The will was based on the assumption that a successor would only be appointed after McQuaid's death – he had not expected to become the first Archbishop of Dublin to retire.[75]

'The Holy See has made all the arrangements for my support,' he told Aidan Lehane. 'They have left me my house, my car and a chaplain. I am grateful to them.'

'So well they might, after all your years of service,' Lehane said. 'So well they mightn't,' McQuaid replied.[76]

McQuaid professed not to follow current affairs, such as the overwhelming vote for membership of the EEC in May 1972. Each day he said Mass in Latin in his chapel, and greeted Sister Denis of his household with the blessing, '*Benedicamo Dei*.'[77] He broke his wrist when he tripped over his Irish terrier, Rex, in the garden that summer and spent four days in St Colmcille's hospital at Loughlinstown. Previously endowed with a strong constitution, he appeared frail and vulnerable. Lonely, he was pleased to accept an invitation from the former chaplain at UCD, Fr Paddy Tuohy, to come to dinner. [78] When Mary Purcell visited McQuaid in the summer of 1972 at his Killiney residence, he said he had many callers and was reading de Gaulle and Malraux in French and General Weygand in English. 'I am watching a hawk to get a chance of shooting him ... and I have to pray and do penance, I may not have much time left,' he told her.[79]

The one time McQuaid came out of his voluntary exile was to visit the Provisional IRA chief-of-staff, Seán MacStíofáin, who was on a hunger and thirst strike in the Mater Hospital. MacStíofáin had mentioned to the chaplain of Mountjoy Prison, Fr Billy Farrell, that he had met McQuaid previously and had taken a great liking to him. 'Would you like to see him?' Fr Billy asked me,' MacStíofáin later wrote in a memoir. 'It had not occurred to me that this was likely, but when I said I would he went off and arranged it. Dr McQuaid subsequently visited me and gave me Absolution. Dr Ryan, who was Archbishop now, came into the hospital the following day and told me that he had said Mass for me and my family that morning. Their visit in no way indicated strong support for my action in going on this strike, or for the Republican movement. They were two church dignitaries who understood what Christian charity is all about in visiting a very sick man and giving him spiritual consolation. I was very upset later when I heard of all the fuss their visit caused, and how it was misrepresented by British and Irish politicians alike.'[80]

McQuaid's visit created a storm of protest in the House of Commons, where it was condemned by three outraged British Conservative M.P.s led by a Catholic, Sir John Biggs Davison. That row was just settling down when in early December a majority of more than five to one voted in favour of deleting the two sub-sections of Article 44 of the Constitution relating to the special position of the Catholic Church and the list of other denominations. A Limerick man, Ger Cleary, who visited McQuaid, asked him what he thought of the poll. McQuaid said Article 44 had merely stated a fact – that the majority of the Irish people professed the Catholic faith – and predicted that 'its removal wouldn't satisfy anybody.'[81]

In February 1973, McQuaid was driven by his chauffeur, Robert, to Maudabawn, close to his native Cootehill in Co. Cavan, for the funeral of his uncle, Patrick McQuaid. He told his life-long friend, Jim Fitzsimons, that he would return to Cootehill before Easter for a whole day and that he would call to see another boyhood friend, Pat Smith of Bridge St, and others he had known. 'It was his desire to drive slowly through all the streets, especially Bridge St and Church St, the areas in which his father did such wonderful work,' the *Anglo-Celt* reported.[82]

McQuaid was never to make that journey home. On April 1, he was alarmed by an article in the *Sunday Press* headlined: 'The Church and its Money – How Archbishop Ryan is facing the colossal task of balancing the books.' Without mentioning McQuaid by name, the full-page investigation into the chaotic affairs of the Dublin diocese was a damning indictment of his administration. He read the article with mounting anger and incredulity.

The report claimed that Archbishop Ryan had discovered 'what a financial mess the diocese was in'. He had inherited limited resources and spiralling debt, amounting to millions of pounds. Stunned, Ryan had phoned Louis Heelan, a prominent industrialist who had been a classmate at Belevedere College, requesting him to call to Drumcondra. T.K. Whitaker of the Central Bank was also invited to the meeting. 'Ryan was clearly worried and just as clearly he was preoccupied with financial problems,' the report continued. 'Heelan was concerned with what he saw as 'waste within the church community' and that 'some of these big, empty churches' seemed to be monuments to the priest who built them and not to God.'

The report explained how Ryan set up a financial committee composed of the best money experts he could find, both clerical and lay, who were to review the entire financial structure of the diocese. While Ryan would not disclose the exact amount of debt, he indicated that 'it would take at least five years to even begin to sort out the financial problems'. In future, they would make public the amounts raised from fund-raising. Any cost over £5,000 (£45,000) would have to be referred to the diocesan committee for consideration. Committee members were sculptor John Behan, the director of the National Gallery, James White, hotelier P.V. Doyle, trade unionist Donal Nevin, Monsignor Cecil Barrett, Fr Peter Lemass and Fr Denis Coogan.

Ryan also asked the Arts Council to come up with plans for new prototype churches. The aim was to provide new buildings that would be viewed as amenities for the city. More involvement by lay members in Church activities was to be encouraged. The report also referred to the aim of cultivating 'a quiet revolution in Irish religious activity' that would help bring about 'the establishment of a clerical system that can move with the times, rather than remaining rigidly in the past'.[83]

So distressed was McQuaid by the report that he visited his old friend, Cecil Barrett, then parish priest in Booterstown. 'What will I do?' he asked. 'It is putting my whole period in office in question.' Barrett counselled him to do nothing, because any statement would be seized upon by the media. McQuaid was also sufficiently distressed by the report to mention it to Sister Denis.[84] In his anxiety, he had completely lost the composure which had once prompted him to claim years earlier, as Rector of the Catholic University of Ireland, a special affinity to Cardinal Paul Cullen. 'Of Cardinal Cullen,' he had said in 1955, 'no writer has done adequate justice to his character or stature. Silent, magnanimous, far-seeing, Cardinal Cullen would seem to be as heedless of justification after death, as he was intrepid in administration during life.'[85] McQuaid now felt both besieged and in need of vindication. Anxiety ate in to him.

On Saturday morning, April 7, McQuaid was too ill to get up at his usual time of 6.30am to say Mass. He rang his bell to alert his chaplain, Fr John FitzPatrick, who phoned Dr Bill Roach in nearby Newcastle. Sister Denis brought Dr Roach to him. After examining McQuaid, Roach recommended that he should be admitted to hospital immediately. 'Whatever you decide, Doctor,' McQuaid said resignedly. He insisted that his sister,

Mrs Deenie Murtagh, who was staying in the house, should not be disturbed. When the ambulance arrived, McQuaid was carried out on a stretcher. Fr Fitzpatrick accompanied him, while his chauffeur, Robert, drove behind as the ambulance headed to Loughlinstown Hospital.

Matt McQuaid, who lived at Woodlands Park in Blackrock, was told of the attack and came at once to the hospital. He reassured Charley, as he called the former Archbishop, that he would get better, but McQuaid had a second attack in the hospital and was dead within an hour of his admission. The Last Rites of the Church were administered to him by Fr Fitzpatrick.

Prompted by Matt McQuaid, staff nurse Margaret O'Dowd told reporter Jimmy Walsh of the *Irish Press* that the Archbishop had been given pain-killing injections, but never complained. Rising up from his pillow, he asked Nurse O'Dowd if he had any chance of reaching heaven. She told him that if he as Archbishop could not get to heaven, few would. This answer appeared to satisfy him and he lay back on the pillow to await death. He died at about 11am.

The announcement was made by Archbishop Ryan, who said that priests and people would long remember his unfailing fidelity during his 31 years of dedicated service to the diocese. The news was carried on the front-page of Dublin's *Evening Herald*, which noted that on account of his shyness the advent of an age of communication had intensified the burden of his office in his last difficult decade. McQuaid may have been in sympathy with an age prior to the age of Pope John, but 'it was never yet established that to be out of vogue is to be any less a man of God'.[86]

President de Valera was 'deeply grieved' to hear the news of McQuaid's death. Taoiseach Liam Cosgrave sent a message of sympathy to Ryan, expressing his 'deep regret at the death of your illustrious predecessor'. Cardinal Conway praised McQuaid's 'utter steadfastness and dedication to duty as well as his unrecorded acts of charity'. Archbishop Simms recalled 'his wonderful care for the poor and his concern for individuals during his time as Archbishop'. The Chief Rabbi of Ireland, Dr Isaac Cohen, praised him as 'a church leader of profoundly strong religious convictions'. The *Anglo-Celt* said that he 'forever stood four-square against the erosion of permissiveness which threatened modern society'.[87]

Even in death, McQuaid aroused controversy. Chris Ryder referred to him in the *Sunday Times* as a powerful and conservative figure, wielding considerable influence behind the political scene, and largely responsible for the banning of many books, plays and films that offended against decency and morality. [88]

Dr Nöel Browne claimed that the most important development in political life during his episcopacy was the relationship established between himself and de Valera under the 1937 Constitution, when each of them worked together. 'The Church used the State; the State used the Church. This in my view led to the setting up of the sectarian society of the North because of their fear of becoming part of a society which was essentially as this society had become, a theocratic state in which Catholic law and moral teaching became State law.'[89]

Dr Stafford Johnson was convinced that it was the *Sunday Press* report which contributed to the strain that precipitated the double heart-attack. 'It was the trigger that brought about his death and no doubt God had his own designs on this. I have his own annotated copy.'[90]

He had often told the sisters of the Poor Servants of the Mother of God that he wished to die in their hospital. However, according to his nephew, Dr Paul McQuaid, he might have lived for a number of years more had a right diagnosis been made of his condition and had he been taken to a different hospital. Recalling events from the perspective of 1995, Dr McQuaid noted that Loughlinstown Hospital would have been a very much less adequately established hospital than it is today. 'By all accounts, he was not diagnosed as having a Dissecting Abdominal Aneurysm. This is, nowadays, an eminently operable condition given the availability of resources and facilities. Had he been transferred, perhaps, directly to St Vincent's Hospital, Elm Park, perhaps the outcome might have been quite different. By the time it became clear what was wrong with him it was already too late to effect transfer, although that, again, might be open to question.' [91]

President de Valera and Taoiseach Cosgrave attended the Requiem Mass at which Cardinal Conway presided. Cardinal Heenan represented the Hierarchy of England and Wales, and the Auxiliary Bishop of Glasgow, James Ward, represented the Scots. The Mass was concelebrated by Archbishop Ryan with the Provincial of the Holy Ghost Fathers, Fr Christopher O'Brien, and Fr Joseph Coyne, the last priest to have been ordained for Dublin by McQuaid.

The chief mourners who walked behind the coffin were Deenie, Tom and Matt, with their children, and his niece Mary Meade. Among the mourners was his school friend, Jim Fitzsimons. John Charles McQuaid lies buried in the vaults under the High Altar of Dublin's Pro-Cathedral.

Notes

Principal Sources

DDA	Dublin Diocesan Archives
DVA	De Valera Archives
HGA	Holy Ghost Archives
ICD	Irish Catholic Directory
ISC	Irish Sisters of Charity Archives
IJA	Irish Jesuit Archives
NAI	National Archives of Ireland
NLI	National Library of Ireland
OLD	Oireachtas Library, Dublin
RAI	Redemptorist Archives, Ireland
RCB	Representative Church Body Library
HRA	Holy Rosary Archives

INTRODUCTION: THE MCQUAID SHADOW

1   Russell Braddon in his introduction to *Roy Thomson of Fleet Street*.
2   Purcell Manuscript in the McQuaid Papers, DDA.
3   Memoir on Life of Brother Gaspard O'Reilly, in the McQuaid Papers, DDA.
4   Conspectus Vitae of Hugo Kerr C.SS.R., Redemptorist Archives.
5   Nöel Browne, *Against the Tide*, p. 151.
6   John Cooney, 'McQuaid's Shadow', *The Irish Times Weekend*, April 4, 1998.
7   'McQuaid told of priest's indecent pictures' was a headline in *The Irish Times*, July 4, 1997, in regard to Fr Magennis, who was convicted for indecently assaulting a 13-year-old girl in a hospital bed while chaplain to Our Lady's Hospital for Sick Children in Crumlin in 1960. That same day, McQuaid's photograph appeared on the front page of the *Evening Herald* under the headline: 'Victim tells of how ordeal was hushed up by Archbishop – My Abuse Hell.'
8   An indicator of the changing times in Ireland is that the first edition in 1986 of *Moral Monopoly* by Tom Inglis carried a cover photograph of personnel attending the New Ireland Forum, while the second edition in

1998 highlights a picture of de Valera kissing McQuaid's ring: This
reflects a reassessment of McQuaid's influence.

9   The programme disclosed that in 1962 McQuaid was deeply unhappy
about the management of Artane Industrial School by the Christian
Brothers. The Archbishop's dissatisfaction was reported by the chaplain
to Artane, Fr Henry Moore, when interviewed by an Inter-Departmental
Government Committee on the Prevention of Crime and Treatment of
Offenders. I am grateful to the RTÉ producer, Mary Raftery, for this reference. The section of the Dublin Diocesan Archives relating to Artane
and Goldenbridge has not yet been made available to researchers.

10 The Commission's terms of reference are to give victims an opportunity
to tell of the abuse that they suffered; to establish a complete picture of
the causes and nature of abuse in state-funded institutions since the
1940s; to employ specialists, and to publish its findings and recommendations. For a critique of the Commission's terms of reference, see
Padraig Ó Móráin, 'Plan to help abused children falls short', *The Irish
Times*, May 12, 1999.

11 In the *Irish Independent* on September 4, 1999, Bruce Arnold called for an
investigation into the role of the Catholic Church as an institution within
the Irish State.

PART I: MAKING OF A MILITANT – EDUCATION TO PRIESTHOOD:
1895–1925

Chapter 1: Faith of his Fathers, 1895–1910

1   John McQuaid's baptismal record in the genealogical centre in Cavan
pours cold water on the pious story that 'during his Christening ceremony his mother's coffin rested on the catafalque in front of the altar' as
told by M. Clare Crowe in *Sisters of Mercy, Kilmore*. The exact cause of
Jennie's death on August 5, 1895, cannot be ascertained as her death
certificate has not been traced.

2   John McQuaid is listed in *Slater's Directory* for 1856 as one of five Cootehill residents in the leather trade. One of John's brothers, William, studied medicine, but there is no record of his having practised: the family's
medical dynasty effectively began with Drs Matt and Eugene.

3   Quoted in Purcell Manuscript, DDA. This is a history of McQuaid's early
life which the writer, Mary Purcell, was compiling before his death.

4   According to the *Anglo-Celt*, August 10, 1895, Jennie was highly cultivated and endowed with the social graces, but she was also meek,
gentle and retiring, 'finding her greatest happiness with her own by
whom she was idolised.'

5   Ibid.

6   Quoted in Michael McCarthy, *Priests and People*, p. 92.

7   The Bishop of Kilmore, Edward Magennis, told Rome that Cavan was 'practically solid' against Parnell. 'An eloquent preacher and an able administrator,' Magennis 'disliked publicity in any form and lived to work unostentatiously for faith and fatherland,' according to Bernard Canning, *Bishops of Ireland, 1870–1987*, p. 138.

8   According to Cavan folklore, Dr Eugene was not known for his piety.

9   Information from Aidan Boyle and Terry Molloy, Cootehill.

10   Record from registry of St Joseph's Church, Terenure. I am grateful to the parish priest, Mgr John Greehy, for this reference. Parochial records of marriage dispensations have not been kept in the DDA. Agnes's father, Thomas, attended the Catholic University, Dublin.

11   Obituary of Agnes McQuaid, *Irish Press*, February 24, 1964; *Catholic Standard*, February 28, 1964.

12   Purcell Manuscript, p. 4.

13   Fr Brady's obituarist in the *Anglo-Celt*, March 27, 1897, wrote: 'Great was his love for the island of saints and scholars, the land of Saint Patrick and Saint Brigid, the country of missionary priests and holy nuns.' The Cootehill area abounded in Catholic folklore: the site of a house in Drumgill in the neighbouring parish of Kill was reputed to have been one of the hiding places of the seventeenth-century martyred Archbishop of Armagh, Oliver Plunkett, who was canonised in 1975.

14   Jane Corry, death certificate, Lombard Street, Dublin. Her death on November 17, 1897, was witnessed by the official in charge of the Workhouse, Thomas Connolly, and was signed by Dr Eugene. Her treatment included 'amputation eight days, delirium six days.'

15   *Anglo-Celt*, November 12, 1897. This Protestant background in his family genealogy was not acknowledged by John McQuaid. However, Purcell was adamant that Jane Corry was 'a convert from Protestantism' (p. 7).

16   Purcell Manuscript, DDA, p. 5.

17   Agnes also had a child which died in infancy (Purcell, p. 5). She employed a governess, Jennie McMahon.

18   Pat Smith is quoted in Purcell Manuscript, p. 7. Veronica Blessing, whose mother, Mary Jane McCudden, went to school with Jennie Corry, remembered John as a distant, aloof figure. John Rice, who was friendly with young Matt McQuaid, spoke of John as detached. A cousin, Orla O'Brien, was reputed to have been the only girl given a kiss by John. Author's interviews with Veronica Blessing, John Rice and Diarmuid Teevan took place in 1995.

19   From Co. Armagh and educated at Knox College, in Toronto, Canada, Henry was respected not only in his own congregation but by the entire community, according to his obituary in *The Missionary Herald*, April, 1929. I am grateful to the Assistant Secretary of the Presbyterian Historical Society of Ireland, Robert H. Bonar, for a copy.

20   Lavinia Greacen, *Chink*, p. 10.

21 Ibid, p. 14.

22 Francis J. MacKiernan, 'The O'Reillys and MacQuaids of Lisdoagh,' *Breifne*, 1991, Vol. VIII, No. 2.

23 For this reconstruction of life in Cootehill I am indebted to Hugh O'Brien, author of *The Celtics of the GAA Cootehill* and *St Michael's Cootehill*.

24 Confidential medical source to author.

25 In the 1960s seminarian Seán Brady, from Drumcalpin in the parish of Laragh, met Archbishop McQuaid at the Irish College in Rome, and suggested to His Grace that he would have forgotten the names of the Cavan townlands. 'I have forgotten nothing,' McQuaid replied to the future Archbishop of Armagh. Quoted by Patsy McGarry in *The Irish Times*, April 27, 1998.

26 For a description of the dispensary system, see Ruth Barrington, *Health, Medicine and Politics in Ireland, 1900–1970,* p. 134.

27 Purcell Manuscript, p. 6.

28 Ibid, p. 7. Dr Eugene dealt severely with 'land-grabbing, murder and horn-blowing.'

29 M. Clare Crowe in *Sisters of Mercy, Kilmore*, pp. 126–46.

30 Mrs Eileen Maloney, née Finlay, recalls how Fr O'Connell 'went so far as to pass Agnes McQuaid at the altar when she went to receive Holy Communion – this showed the bitterness that existed in Cootehill in those years.' Maloney to author, February 23, 1998. The conflict with Fr O'Connell was confirmed by John Rice's recollection of Matt McQuaid being taken out of national school by Dr Eugene.

31 For profiles of Fr Patrick O'Connell, see Hugh O'Brien, *St Michael's Cootehill,* pp. 32–55 and Bishop Francis J. MacKiernan, *Diocese of Kilmore, Bishops and Priests,* 1136–1988, Breifne Historical Society, p. 724.

32 Purcell Manuscript, DDA, p. 8. Apart from the Church of Ireland, Cootehill numbered places of worship for Presbyterians, Methodists, Moravians and Quakers.

33 T.K. Whitaker interview with author.

34 The diary extract was quoted widely in newspapers at the time of McQuaid's appointment to Dublin in 1940. Purcell writes that Fitzsimons inserted in the school register 'a boy of remarkable promise' after McQuaid's name.

35 Purcell Manuscript, DDA, p. 8.

36 Margaret Cusack, *The Life of the Most Rev. Joseph Dixon*, pp. 253–360. The Drogheda Synod, which shaped the Catholic environment in which John McQuaid grew up, recommended that sound moral and religious education was the best way to combat Protestant proselytism. See also article by James Kelly, 'The Formation of the Modern Catholic Church in the Diocese of Kilmore 1580–1880,' in *Cavan*, edited by Raymond Gillespie. John would have revered Fr Eugene as a martyr for the priesthood, and he would have heard the stories of how Fr Matt denounced an eviction in Kill.

'It is not enough to drive out the mother and children like a parcel of swine on a stormy night,' he bewailed, 'Nor enough to tumble their cabin, wound their feelings and see their tears; but some of these monsters grinned at their victims' decrepitude.'

37 Purcell Manuscript, p. 8. He was enrolled as Charles McQuaid. According to Dr Paul McQuaid, he went to Cavan on a McQuaid bursary. A fellow boarder, James Galligan, often cut his hair.

38 Daniel Gallogly, *St Patrick's College, Cavan.*

39 Purcell Manuscript, p. 8.

40 An intellectual reign of terror was established by Pius X through the secret 'thought police' run by Monsignor Humberto Benigni, which Christopher Hollis compared to Dostoevski's Grand Inquisitor and Lenin's dreaded Cheka, or secret police, in Bolshevist Russia. For vivid reconstructions of the new climate of fear brought about in Irish provincial Catholicism by the campaigns against Modernism and mixed marriages, read Gerald O'Donovan's novels, *Father Ralph* and *Waiting.*

41 'The yarn that he was expelled for smoking has no basis whatsoever,' Purcell wrote, p. 8.

42 Interview with Miss Dempsey, April, 1995.

43 Purcell Manuscript, p. 8.

44 Coldrey, *Studies*, Vol. 85, No. 340.

45 St Patrick's College Registers state that John McQuaid was a student there from September 1905 until June 1910. Letter from Bishop Francis MacKiernan to author.

Chapter 2: Chosen by God, 1910–1913

1   McQuaid memoir, in McQuaid's hand, of Brother Gaspard, 3 pp, DDA, AB8/A/1/5.

2   Obituary of Gaspard O'Reilly, HGA, Dublin.

3   Ibid.

4   McQuaid memoir of Brother Gaspard.

5   Ibid.

6   Libermann's original Congregation of the Holy Heart of Mary (1839) merged in 1848 with the Society of the Holy Ghost, founded in 1703 by Breton, Claude Poullart des Places. Libermann was an epileptic. See Michael O'Carroll, *Francis Libermann, Apostle of Africa.*

7   Fr Seán Farragher, *Blackrock College.*

8   McQuaid memoir of Brother Gaspard, DDA.

9   Author's interview with Fr Farragher.

10 McQuaid memoir of Brother Gaspard.

11 Fergal McGrath S.J., *Fr John L. Sullivan S.J.*

12 I am grateful to Fr Stephen Redmond S.J., Jesuit Archives, Dublin, for

biographical details of Dan O'Connell. Dan claimed to be a kinsman of Daniel O'Connell, the Liberator.

13 Fergal McGrath S.J. in *The Clongownian*, 1941.

14 McQuaid memoir of Brother Gaspard.

15 Hugo Kerr, Conspectus Vitae, and 'Necrology' or Life of Hugo Kerr, 1895–1986. Redemptorist Provincial Archives, Marianella.

16 Kerr, Conspectus Vitae. Also, Purcell Manuscript recounts this episode.

17 This is the version given innocently by Purcell.

18 This is the oral evidence from a reliable medical source.

19 From the scrapbook of Andy Smith, Cootehill. Dr Eugene found himself in the thick of the growing sectarian polarisation in Cootehill, where the Orangemen of Dawson's Hall had become militant.

20 Kerr, Conspectus Vitae.

21 The piety of the period is captured well in Alfred O'Rahilly's *Fr William Doyle S.J.*

22 Kerr is quoted in Purcell Manuscript, p.10.

23 Burke Savage, *Studies*, Winter, 1965.

24 Purcell Manuscript, p. 10.

Chapter 3: Sanctity and Terror, 1913–1924.

1   In the McQuaid Papers in the DDA (AB8/A/I.1–11) there are numerous notebooks in John McQuaid's handwriting, mainly lecture notes on theology, philosophy, scripture and history, with the occasional personal insight. There are few observations on politics. The purpose of life on Earth, he wrote, was 'to seek God's glory and eternal bliss hereafter'.

2   'Our Novitiate, Kimmage Manor,' by a Novice, *Missionary Annals*, July-August 1925. Retreats were based on the exercises laid down by the founder of the Society of Jesus, St. Ignatius Loyola, consisting of meditations on church teachings, silent examinations of conscience and reflections on the duties of life.

3   'God is all; man is nothing' was the essence of Libermann's teaching. Michael O'Carroll, *Libermann* (p.18). According to Edmund M. Hogan, the author of *The Irish Missionary Movement*, the end result of this training was 'a rigid, uncompromising, ascetical spirituality which placed a premium on obedience, expiation, self-sacrifice, detachment and supremacy of will over other faculties' (p.164).

4   H. Daniel-Rops, *The Church in the Seventeenth Century*, pp. 51–131.

5   Exhibits in DDA, McQuaid Papers, AB8/A/I.4.

6   Finín O'Driscoll, 'In search of a Christian Social Order: the impact of Social Catholicism in Ireland' in *Celebrating Columba, Irish-Scottish Connections*, 597–1997, edited by T.M. Devine and J.F. McMillan, pp. 102–136.

7   McQuaid Papers, DDA, Box AB8/A/I.

8   From 1934 to1947 Dan Murphy was Provincial and in the 1950s he was Procurator General in Rome. His circumspection was legendary and he left no memoirs. McQuaid did not get on well with Murphy, according to Holy Ghost sources.

9   John Feeney, *The Man and the Mask*, p. 4.

10   Meenan, *Centenary History of the Literary and Historical Society*, p. 110.

11   John Touhill, Murphy obituary, HGA.

12   Michael O'Carroll, *Leen C.S.Sp.*, p. 38.

13   Farragher, *Dev and his Alma Mater*, pp. 107–119.

14   A typescript copy of the 188-page thesis is to be found in AB8/A/I.8 in the McQuaid Papers, DDA. On religion, he wrote that Seneca 'fingered, if he could not make to fit the lock, the Christian key to suffering, when he realised it to be God's hand on the chosen soul. That he saw in the world a commonwealth of God and man, and in death, the birthday of eternity, and in eternity, the life with God for ever. All this did Seneca teach his fellow-Romans, not so much because he was a Stoic, but because he was Seneca.'

15   Walsh obituary, HGA. Aged 38, he was 'a wise and spiritual priest'. He refused Gaspard admission to Kimmage to see McQuaid.

16   McQuaid, 1932, Cavan sermon, p. 12, DDA, AB8/A/VIII.74.

17   Corcoran obituary, *Irish Press*, March 24, 1943. An appreciation by Dermot F. Gleeson appeared in *Studies*, Vol. XXXII, 1943.

18   In McQuaid's possession were the papers of Robert O'Benkett, the French delegate at the Irish Race Convention in Paris in 1920, an indication of McQuaid's interest in contemporary issues.

19   Logbook of *Studies* in possession of author.

20   Patrick Maume, *D.P. Moran*, p. 23.

21   *Missionary Annals*, 'Father James Laval, Apostle of Mauritius,' September 1920. The previous April the *Annals* proudly carried a letter from Cardinal Gasparri conveying the Apostolic Blessing of Pope Benedict XV.

22   Farragher interview.

23   *Missionary Annals*, November 1920.

24   *Missionary Annals*, July 1921.

25   Daly, Gabriel, *Transcendence and Immanence*, pp. 187–89.

26   Fahey was a convoluted lecturer. His obituarist in the *General Bulletin* of the Holy Ghost Province of Ireland, March 1954, described his Philosophy lectures as solid and profound but 'at times they may have lacked simplicity.'

27   For a profile of Billot, see Daly, *Transcendence and Immanence*.

28   Denis Fahey, 'The Mission of St Thomas Aquinas', the *Catholic Bulletin*, May 1925. McQuaid was impressed by how Pope Benedict encouraged study of St Thomas as a mystic. In McQuaid's opinion, Benedict 'perfectly outlined the mysticism of St Thomas' in a letter to the editor of *La Vie Spirituelle*, Father Bernadot, on September 15, 1921.

29 McQuaid, Cavan sermon, DDA. AB8/A/VIII.74.

30 McQuaid's Kimmage papers, DDA.

31 Seán Cronin, *Wolfe Tone and the United Irishmen*, Repsol, 1991, p. 10.

32 Integralism was given juridical expression in the new Code of Canon law which gave sweeping powers to the Roman civil service in the name of the Pope.

33 Peter Donnelly, 'Bishops and violence', *Studies*, Autumn 1994.

34 Pope Benedict, of Genoese nobility, was dubbed *Il Picoletto* – the Midget – by the Romans on account of his small and frail physique.

35 Ger Cleary to John Cooney, April 13, 1998.

36 Personal note in McQuaid's handwriting, July 26, 1922, DDA.

37 Interview with Mrs Eileen Maloney, Cavan, February 1998.

38 The *Freeman's Journal*, February 24, 1923; February 27, 1923.

39 Typescript copy of letter, Army of the Irish Free State, Togher to McQuaid, March 10, 1923, DDA, AB8/A/I.10.

40 *Reality*, 1989.

41 According to the *General Bulletins* of the Holy Ghost Congregation, the main steps on McQuaid's way to the priesthood were: on September 23, 1922, he took first minor orders covering the functions traditionally ascribed to door-keepers, lectors, exorcists and acolytes; on October 18, 1922, he took his perpetual vows of poverty, chastity and obedience; on March 19, 1923, he took second stage of minor orders; on March 16, 1924, the sub-diaconate was conferred on him; on June 14, 1924, in Dublin's Pro-Cathedral, Archbishop Byrne conferred the diaconate on him.

42 Obituary of Bishop Wilson, ICD 1939, Events for 1938, p. 65. Wilson was mentioned in despatches for bravery in World War One.

43 For the text of the anti-Modernist oath, see appendix 2, pp. 235–36 of Daly, *Transcendence and Immanence*.

44 The letter, April 26, 1924, was published by Fr Fahey in the *Catholic Bulletin*, May 1925.

45 Boylan acknowledged McQuaid's help in the preface. 'To the Rev. J. McQuaid C.S.Sp., M.A., who undertook and patiently carried through the task of verifying the Biblical references in the Commentary, and read the entire work in proof, the author is very specially indebted.' Also helping Boylan was Fr Patrick J. Walsh who wrote the biography of Archbishop William J. Walsh.

Chapter 4: Biblical Scholar, 1924–25

1 Fr Michael O'Carroll C.S.Sp., in *The Blackrock College Annual*, 1943.

2 The Scottish priest, Fr Thomas Taylor, describes the canonisation in his biography of Thérèse, *A Little White Flower*. The ceremony was attended

by the Governor General of the Irish Free State, Tim Healy, whom McQuaid may have met at a reception.

3   Fr Michael O'Carroll C.S.Sp., in *The Blackrock College Annual*, 1943.

4   A vivid description of Rome at this time is provided by Sir Alec Randall, in his *Vatican Assignment*.

5   Fr Michael O'Carroll C.S.Sp., in *The Blackrock College Annual*, 1943.

6   J.F. McMillan, France, in *Political Catholicism in Europe, 1918–65*, p. 41, edited by Tom Buchanan and Martin Conway.

7   Cavan sermon, 1932, DDA, AB8/A/VIII.74.

8   S.W. Halperin, *Mussolini and Italian Fascism*, p. 20.

9   A.J.C. Jemolo, *Church and State in Italy*, 1850–1950.

10   I am grateful to Malcolm Sinclair for a photocopy of Fonck's biographical details in the *New Catholic Encyclopaedia*, Vol. V, pp. 994–95, 1967.

11   McQuaid studied the works of three leading authorities on St Thomas Aquinas: James M. Vosté O.P., Édouard Hugon O.P. and Joseph le Rohellec C.S.Sp.

12   *Missionary Annals*, Roman Notes, 'In the home of St Thomas Aquinas', August 1925. This was probably Fr Michael Browne O.P.

13   Typescript article on St Catherine of Siena, based on a sermon to the Missionary Sisters of Our Lady of the Holy Rosary in Killeshandra, Co. Cavan, published in the *Apostolate*, January 1929, DDA, AB8/A/73.

14   Farragher, *Blackrock College*, p. 260.

15   'I never forgot his word and I can see the spot on the road where he suddenly made this remark as we were walking him home,' McQuaid recalled years later to Mrs Mercy Simms. Mrs Simms cited this as an instance of 'a father complex' on McQuaid's part.

16   *Anglo-Celt*, December 19, 1925, reported a message of sympathy passed by the Cavan Health Board. Agnes was the sole beneficiary of Dr Eugene's will. He had shares in *The Irish Times*, and held ordinary stock in the Great Northern Railway as well as Imperial Japanese Government Bonds. His debts included two years' rent for an office owing to Major Eric Dorman-Smith.

PART II: BUILDING A POWERBASE, 1925–1940

Chapter 5: Man of Mystery, 1925–32

1   *Studies*, Winter, 1998.

2   Anthony Cronin, *No Laughing Matter*, p. 34.

3   Ciarán Ó Nualláin, *The Early Years of Brian O'Nolan*, p. 70

4   The McQuaid Papers in the DDA contain a wide range of materials relating to his Blackrock period from 1925–1940 as Dean of Studies and as

President: AB8/A/II.

5   Interview with Robert Geldof.

6   McQuaid to Howell, October 24, 1930, DDA, AB8/A/II.

7   McQuaid Papers, DDA, AB8/A/II.

8   Burke Savage, *Studies*, Winter, 1965.

9   Máirín Egan to author.

10   Quoted by Desmond Forristal, *Edel Quinn, 1907–1944*, p. 29.

11   Michael O'Carroll, C.S.Sp.

12   McQuaid Papers, DDA, Blackrock College section.

13   Belloc lectured at Blackrock in March 1928 on 'The Conspiracy against Christendom.'

14   Anthony Cronin, *No Laughing Matter*, p. 34.

15   Clerical source.

16   In *Studies*, 1998, Aidan Lehane C.S.Sp. writes that McQuaid had a fine feeling for words. For example, after leaving his glasses in Rockwell College, he enquired: 'I have mislaid a pair of glasses in a dark blue case with a tiny fringe of gold decoration. Could I have left them also in your unconscious keeping?'

17   Farragher interview.

18   John Cooney, *The Crozier and the Dáil, 1922–1986*.

19   McQuaid, The Hague text, August 1, 1933, DDA, AB8/A/VII.70.

20   Educated at Clongowes, Newman's Catholic University and Heidelberg University, O'Sullivan was described by Mary Macken as devoutly child-like : 'This intellectual giant had the faith of a child.' Quoted by E. Brian Titley, *Church, State and the Control of Schooling in Ireland, 1900–1944*, p. 105.

21   Michael O'Carroll, 'Defunctus adhuc loquitur', obituary article in HGA.

22   Finín O'Driscoll, 'In search of a Christian Social Order: the impact of Social Catholicism in Ireland', pp. 102–136.

23   Notes on the Projected National Programme, drawn up by Edward Cahill S.J.

24   His card, or Tessera, number 323, is in the DDA.

25   Comte de Biver, *Père Lamy*. It was perhaps through the philosopher, Jacques Maritain, that McQuaid had been introduced to Lamy and Biver.

26   Fennelly to McQuaid, July 2, 1928, DDA, AB8/A/II.

27   Recalled in 'A Golden Page in Ireland's History', in *Irish Independent Eucharistic Congress*, Number, June 1932.

28   Farragher interview.

29   Despite his lugubrious public persona, Paschal Robinson, a Franciscan, had a colourful career already behind him. Born in Dublin in 1870, he moved to New York, aged five. After college he became a journalist and joined the *North American Review* where he became friendly with the writer, Mark Twain. He swopped the editorial chair for the Franciscan

habit and was ordained a priest in 1901 in Rome. He was Professor of History at the Catholic University of America in Washington D.C. from 1914 to 1925 when he was appointed the Vatican's Apostolic Visitor to Palestine. Promoted to the rank of Archbishop in 1927, Robinson had been the special mediator of Pius XI in a church-state controversy in Malta. He was renowned for being secretive and discreet, but disarmed visitors by personal charm and warmth. He lived in the former Chief Secretary's lodge in the Phoenix Park, which was specially made available to him by the Government.

30 Farragher, *Dev and His Alma Mater,* p. 160. The *College Journalist* called for a more balanced guest list.

31 Ibid. The de Valera family moved from Sandymount to Blackrock in April 1930.

32 The Foundation inspired by Bishop Shanahan and Fr Leen was the Missionary Sisters of Our Lady of the Holy Rosary, who purchased Dromullac House, outside Killeshandra, in McQuaid's native Cavan. Invited in January 1929 to preach there, McQuaid marvelled at the rugged beauty of the location and detected the seal of divine providence in the initiative. It was 'a fair setting for such an ambitious religious foundation: it has the good odour of Christ about it,' he said. McQuaid's gift of prophecy, however, proved fallible: the convent and adjoining farm were sold for £½ million in 1980 to a COOP, and the lavishly ornate building and church have since fallen into ruin.

33 In a foreword to Leen's *Voice of a priest*, Fr Bernard J. Kelly C.S.Sp alludes to the breakdown. 'Trials and failures in all the different spheres in which he was engaged appeared in a synchronised array. He felt unequal to the burden of administering Blackrock College' (p. 21).

34 It is intriguing that this letter of appointment was taken by McQuaid from Blackrock College when he moved as Archbishop to Drumcondra, where it is to be found in the Blackrock section of his archives, AB8/A/II.15.

35 Farragher, *Dev and his Alma Mater,* p. 161.

36 *Blackrock College Annual,* 1930, p. 193.

37 *Blackrock College Annual,* 1932, pp. 39–44.

38 McQuaid's address to the Society of St Vincent de Paul, January 24, 1932, DDA.

Chapter 6: War against Satan, 1932–34

1 The manuscript (24 pages) of 'Our Divine Lord Jesus Christ or Satan? The real struggle in the modern world,' is located in box AB8/ VIII. 74, DDA.

2 The *Anglo-Celt,* March 16, 1932, reported how Bishop Finegan pointed out the distinguished contribution to Kilmore Catholicism made by the McQuaids: 'The large audience followed the distinguished lecturer's

address with the closest attention, and at its close they gave expression by loud and prolonged cheer.'

3   Published in Tony Farmar, *Ordinary Lives*, p. 125.

4   In his laudatory foreword, McQuaid recommended Fahey's latest work as presenting 'a synthesis of dogmatic truths and historical facts.'

5   Finín O'Driscoll, 'In search of a Christian Social Order: the impact of Social Catholicism in Ireland.' p. 116.

6   Farragher, *Dev and his Alma Mater*, p. 163.

7   McQuaid to de Valera, March 10, 1932, DVP, 1440/7.

8   Farragher, *Dev and his Alma Mater*, pp. 163–65. When the showdown with the Governor General duly took place, McNeill was replaced by the accommodating republican veteran, Dónal Ó Buachalla. One of the first to congratulate him was McQuaid.

9   Boylan, *The Eucharistic Congress Record*, 1932.

10 Burke Savage, *Studies*, Winter, 1965.

11 The *College Journal* for April 9, 1932, noted: 'Fr Superior is confined to his room. He is suffering from an attack of flu.' I am grateful to Fr Farragher for this reference.

12 Thomas Arnold Harvey, a graduate of Trinity College, had tutored Robert Gregory, the son of Lady Gregory, at Coole, where he met and became friendly with the painter, Jack B. Yeats. (See Hilary Pyle, *Jack B. Yeats*, p. 56.) As rector of Portrush in Co. Antrim, Harvey won the admiration of the Presbyterian liberal, J.B. Armour for refusing to allow Orangemen in 1912 to put the Union Jack on his church tower (J.R.B. McMinn, *Against the Tide*, p. 117).

13 Press cuttings in DDA, AB8/A/II.21. The typescript of the sermon preached in aid of the Society of St Vincent de Paul is located in AB8/A/VIII.74.

14 Tony Cronin interview.

15 *Wellsprings of the Faith*, pp. 122–28.

16 Byrne personally thanked McQuaid for his 'courteous and tactful assistance.' Box AB8/A/II.24, DDA.

17 *The Irish Independent*, August 2, 1933. The paper, 'Some aspects of the present condition of Catholic Secondary Education in Ireland', is in the DDA. AB8/A/VII.70.

18 Ibid.

19 Bishop John Dignan, *Catholics and Trinity College*, 1933.

20 McQuaid, who had contributed £5 towards the total cost of just over £75, was reimbursed £4 for the advance, which he paid to the illuminating artist.

Chapter 7: Catholic campaigner, 1934–36

1 The cutting from *The Irish Times*, February 7, 1934, is to be found in the McQuaid Papers in the DDA as part of a file which he kept during his campaign. Box AB8/A/II.26.

2 *Irish Press*, February 9, 1934.

3 Ibid.

4 The *East Galway Democrat*, February 10, 1934.

5 McGilton to McQuaid, February 9, 1934, DDA, Box AB8/A/II.26.

6 The *Sunday Chronicle*, February 11, 1934.

7 Fr Peter O.P. to McQuaid, February 8, 1934, DDA, Box AB8/A/II.26.

8 Noonan to McQuaid, February 9, 1934, DDA, Box AB8/A/II.26.

9 Roe to McQuaid, February 12, 1934, DDA, Box AB8/A/II.26.

10 McGilton to McQuaid, February 20, 1934, DDA, Box AB8/A/II.26.

11 McQuaid to McGilton, February 23, 1934. Arguing that the controversy should be resolved by the principles of Christian modesty and medical science, McQuaid wrote: 'Mixed athletics and all cognate immodesties, are abuses that right-minded people reprobate, wherever and whenever they exist.' In his draft text, McQuaid cited mixed swimming and mixed sunbathing as instances of abuse.

12 McQuaid press cuttings.

13 McQuaid to McGilton, March 23, 1934, DDA, Box AB8/A/II.26.

14 Walshe to McQuaid, February 12, 1934, DDA, Box AB8/A/II.26.

15 Invitations were sent to the Association of Secondary School Teachers of Ireland (ASTI), the Irish Technical Education Association, the Vocational Officers' Association, the Managers' Associations, the Headmasters' and Schoolmasters' Associations, Trinity College, University Colleges, Dublin, Cork and Galway, the Irish Christian Brothers, the Training Colleges, the Association of Assistant Mistresses in Secondary Schools and the Conference of Convent Secondary Schools.

16 O'Connell's letter of October 3, 1933, is in the section of the McQuaid Papers on the Catholic Headmasters' Association, 1933–40, DDA, AB8/A/VI/63.

17 *Irish Press*, November 9, 1933.

18 McQuaid memorandum on first meeting, DDA, AB8/A/VI/63.

19 McQuaid statement, November 11, 1933, marked private and confidential, DDA, AB8/A/VI/63. A standing committee meeting of the CHA on November 9 deputed McQuaid and Staunton to attend as a courtesy. McQuaid and Staunton were not to accept any decision unless it had first been referred back to their standing committee.

20 McQuaid account of second meeting, DDA, AB8/A/VI/63.

21 O'Donnell to McQuaid, November 15, 1933, DDA, AB8/A/VI/63.

22 McQuaid memorandum, DDA, AB8/A/VI/63.

23 Education Conference minutes of November 11, 1933, DDA, AB8/A/VI/63.

24 Memorandum on proposed (Advisory) Council of Education, as supplied to His Grace of Dublin, DDA, AB8/A/VI/63.

25 Ibid.

26 Second Memorandum, Education Council, third meeting, May 26, 1934, DDA, AB8/A/VI/63.

27 Memorandum on an annual Education day in CTS week, DDA, AB8/A/VI/63.

28 MacRory to McQuaid, DDA, AB8/A/VI/63.

29 Confidential memorandum, titled, 'The proposed non-denominational Council or Federation of all educational bodies,' DDA, AB8/A/VI/63.

30 McQuaid to Byrne, October 1, 1934, DDA, AB8/A/VI/63. McQuaid also informed de Valera that O'Connell and Burke had agreed not to support the proposed Federation of Educational Bodies, DVA, 1440/4, three pages typescript, marked in MS, 'Dr McQuaid, private.'

31 O'Donnell to McQuaid, October 3, 1934, DDA, AB8/A/VI/63.

32 MacRory to McQuaid, October 6, 1934, DDA, AB8/A/VI/63.

33 McQuaid to MacRory, October 7, 1934, DDA, AB8/A/VI/63.

34 Minutes of Half Yearly Meeting of CHA, April 11, 1935, DDA, AB8/A/VI/63.

35 In 'Catholic education: its function and scope,' published in August 1935, McQuaid argued that 'instruction and discipline are essential portions of Catholic training, and of the two activities, discipline is, in the Catholic tradition, the more important.'

36 McQuaid sermon to Guilds of Regnum Christi. For background see Finín O'Driscoll, 'In search of a Christian Social Order: the impact of Social Catholicism in Ireland.'

37 'The Guild Movement in Ireland', a personal recollection of the earlier days, by Dr J. Stafford Johnson, DDA, AB8/A/III.34. It was McQuaid who suggested to Johnson to write a memoir of the origins and development of the Guilds. All of this was in accord with McQuaid's aim of creating Catholic professional élites.

38 McQuaid and his Catholic doctor friends saw the Presbyterian sortie into the Free State as proof of proselytism. Letter to McQuaid, February 16, 1936, DDA, AB8/A/IV.44.

39 DDA, Box AB8/A/VIII/82.

40 AB8/A/II.27/28. On April 6, 1936, McQuaid received a paper from Waters on 'Saorstat and National Finance'. Other papers from B.B. Waters included, 'Economics and Catholic Morality', 'The Education of Girls' and 'Child Guidance Clinics.'

41 Finín O'Driscoll, 'In search of a Christian Social Order: the impact of Social Catholicism in Ireland.'

42 McQuaid to de Valera, November 19, 1934, DVA, 1440/1.

43 DVA, mainly 1440/7.

44 McQuaid to de Valera, March 23, 1934, DVA, 1440/1.

45 McQuaid to de Valera, DVA, 1440/2.

46 McQuaid to de Valera, DVA, 1440/2.

47 McQuaid to de Valera, May 11, 1935, DVA, 1440/2.

48 McQuaid to de Valera, December 1, 1934, DVA, 1440/4.

49 DVA, 1440/4. McQuaid gave de Valera a copy of his Catholic Education Day proposal.

50 McQuaid to de Valera, November 19, 1934, DVA, 1440/3.

51 McQuaid to de Valera, enclosing letter 'just received from His Grace of Cashel' (Harty), May 22, 1934, DVA, 1440/3.

52 DVA, 1440/3.

53 Farragher, *Blackrock College*, p. 172.

54 Fahey to McQuaid, March 1936, DDA, Blackrock Papers.

55 DVA, 1440/7.

56 Farragher, *Dev and his Alma Mater*, p. 178. McQuaid had assumed 'a role that one does not readily associate with the austere image he projected in later years as Archbishop.'

57 De Valera to McQuaid, May 22, 1936, DVA, 1440/7.

58 McQuaid wrote to the editor of the *Irish Press*, Frank Gallagher, to have the sports editor, Joe Sherwood, an Australian, removed because of a paragraph that did not do justice to the Blackrock College rugby team, according to Bill Sweetman, in 'Devotion to duty and survival,' *Irish Press*, Fiftieth anniversary edition, September 5, 1981.

59 Piondar to McQuaid, June 2, 1936, DDA, Blackrock Papers.

60 Allen to McQuaid, August 27, 1936, DDA, Blackrock Papers.

61 Fleming, Lionel, *Head or Harp*.

62 *Irish Independent*, August 16, 1936.

63 McQuaid illuminated his attitude to the Spanish Civil War when referring, during the Italian crisis in 1948, to his anti-Communist perspective.

64 Allen to McQuaid, August 27, 1936, DDA, Blackrock Papers.

65 Allen to McQuaid, September 5, 1936, DDA, McQuaid's letter of September 3 is not on file.

66 Jack White, *Minority Report*, p. 108. Paul Blanshard, in *The Irish and Catholic Power*, cited this campaign as an instance of how the Catholic Church bred 'fanaticism and moral childhood.' Writing in 1954, Blanshard did not know that McQuaid was the martinet behind the drive against the newspaper.

67 Kevin Collins to McQuaid, August 13, 1935, DDA, Blackrock Papers.

68 William Robert Fitzgerald Collis (1900–1975), wrote two plays on the underprivileged, *Marrowbone Lane* and *The Barrel Organ*. The author of a standard textbook on diseases of children, he was Director of the Department of Paediatrics at Rotunda Hospital, Dublin, and in 1932 became Physician to the National Children's Hospital, Harcourt St.

69 Observer, *Irish Independent*, October 17, 1936, DDA.

70   Marcus Bourke to author, June 25, 1998.

Chapter 8: Co-maker of the Constitution, 1937–38

1   'John Charles McQuaid, the persistent adviser' by Joe Carroll and Fergus
Pyle, *The Irish Times*, July 2, 1987, captured McQuaid's role neatly. Dr
Dermot Keogh, in his article, 'The Irish Constitutional Revolution: An
Analysis of the Making of the Constitution, *Administration*, January 1988,
pinpointed McQuaid's central role but highlighted how more liberal De
Valera was in philosophy and ecclesiology than his Blackrock neighbour.
In a subsequent Thomas Davis lecture, Dr Keogh argued that McQuaid
was much more centrally involved than either Fr Edward Cahill S.J. or the
Jesuits. In his Submission to the Forum for Peace and Reconciliation,
published as *Building Trust in Ireland*, Keogh suggested that McQuaid was
perhaps the most central figure in the writing of the Constitution. Dr
Keogh's changing perspective reflects a growing awareness of McQuaid's
pivotal role and was based on a research thesis on the Constitution by
Cathal Condon (who argues that McQuaid was the main architect of a
number of Articles.) In turn, Dr Keogh has come under fire from Dr
Finola Kennedy, in the Winter 1998 issue of *Studies,* for downplaying the
role of Fr Cahill S.J. Less polemically, Seán Faughnan, in 'The Jesuits and
the drafting of the Irish Constitution of 1937', *Irish Historical Studies*,
helps unravel the drafting process and shows how McQuaid quarried
from – and developed – the Jesuit text.

I have drawn on these publications, while anchoring the material in the
McQuaid Papers (AB8/A/V)and the de Valera Archives (1091, mainly relat-
ing to Articles 40–45). I am also grateful for guidance from Mr Breandán
Mac Giolla Choille, who prepared the de Valera Papers for access to
researchers at the Franciscan Institute of Celtic Studies and Historical
Research, Killiney, Co Dublin. Some of the letters are undated.

2   Box AB8/A/V, DDA, includes typescripts of work done by Jesuit Fathers,
sent by de Valera to McQuaid, and notes by McQuaid on Roman Catholic
dogma and doctrine. According to Fr Farragher, in 1960 de Valera paid
tribute to the valuable assistance he received from McQuaid in drafting
the Constitution. There are two hundred items in this Box alone, covering The Preamble, The Nation (Articles 1–3), The State (4–11), Constitutional Guarantees (40), Rights (40), Natural Law, The Family (41), Religion
(44), Directive Principles of Social Policy (45), Education (42) and Property (43). The period covered is 1936–37.

3   Information from David Sheehy.

4   Viv (Vivion de Valera) to his father, no date, DVA, 1091.

5   A perusal of box DDA, AB8/A/V, confirms the gusto with which McQuaid
approached the drafting process. There are typescript and manuscript
drafts of constitutional Articles by McQuaid, some annotated.

6   McQuaid to de Valera, February 16, 1937, DDA, AB8/A/V.

7   McQuaid to de Valera, February 17, 1937, DVA, 1091. This section laid
     the foundation for the State's right to prevent competition from result-
     ing in the concentration of the ownership or control of essential com-
     modities in a few individuals to the common detriment. McQuaid was
     disappointed by an earlier draft written by Dr Alfred O'Rahilly, then Reg-
     istrar of UCC.

8   This is reflected in Article 45.4.1: 'The State pledges itself to safeguard
     with especial care the economic interests of the weaker sections of the
     community, and, where necessary, to contribute to the support of the
     infirm, the widow, the orphan and the aged.'

9   McQuaid to de Valera, March 8, 1937, DVA, 1091. A study of Bishop
     Cohalan of Cork is long overdue.

10   McQuaid to de Valera, March 10, 1937, DVA, 1091. McQuaid made com-
     ments on Articles 11, 12, 13, 14, 16, 18 and 21.

11   McQuaid to de Valera, March 16, DVA, 1091.

12   Farragher, *De Valera and his Alma Mater,* p. 173.

13   DDA, AB8/A/V.48, McQuaid referred to how 'our fathers have endured so
     many centuries of pain' for the right to worship. Its drafting was com-
     pleted on April 10 in the light of comments from the Nuncio and other
     church leaders consulted by de Valera.

14   Articles 1–3, DDA, AB8/A/V.

15   McQuaid to de Valera, March 25, 1937, DVA, 1091.

16   McQuaid to de Valera, March 25, 1937, DVA, 1091.

17   McQuaid to de Valera, March 26, 1937, DVA, 1091.

18   McQuaid to de Valera, March 27, 1937, DVA, 1091.

19   Material on the Family, DDA, AB8/A/V.48.

20   Ibid.

21   Keogh, *Building Trust in Ireland*, p. 123.

22   Ibid, pp. 123–24.

23   McQuaid's input on the family is much closer, if not identical to that of
     Fr Edward Cahill than generally acknowledged. See Dr Finola Kennedy,
     'Two priests, the Family and the Irish Constitution', in *Studies,* Winter,
     1998.

24   As well as heavily influencing the section on the Directive Social Princi-
     ples, McQuaid 'practically wrote the Article on Education,' Dermot
     Keogh writes, *Building Trust in Ireland*, p. 124.

25   Seán Faughan argues that McQuaid drafted a new Article on religion,
     based on Pope Leo XIII's Encyclical, *Immortale Dei*. This text asserted that
     'the Church of Christ is the Catholic Church.'

26   Keogh, 'The Constitutional Revolution,' IPA, p. 30. According to de
     Valera, MacRory, at a meeting on April 3 at the Nunciature, indicated
     that there would be difficulties over the proposed religion wording,
     though 'he himself would not attack.' Archbishop Byrne of Dublin, how-
     ever, took a more positive approach. MacRory was still obdurate when

he received the revised text on April 11.

27 This may be a reference to Michael Browne O.P.

28 Article 44.1.2 declared: 'The State recognises the special position of the Holy Catholic Apostolic and Roman Church as the guardian of the Faith professed by the great majority of the citizens.' Article 44.1.3 read: 'The State also recognises the Church of Ireland, the Presbyterian Church in Ireland, the Methodist Church in Ireland, the Jewish Congregations, and the other religious denominations existing in Ireland at the date of the coming into operation of the Constitution.' The formula was suggested to de Valera by Archbishop Gregg.

29 McQuaid to de Valera, April 15, 1937, DVA, 1091.

30 McQuaid to de Valera, April 15, 1937, DVA, 1091.

31 Revised *Pro Memoria*, April 16, 1937, DVA, 1995/2G.

32 Walshe report, April 22, 1937, DVA, 1995/1D.

33 McQuaid to de Valera, DVA, 1091.

34 Dáil debates, LXVII, 1890, June 4, 1937. Dr Rowlette, deputy for Dublin University, objected to the 'special position' clause as unnecessary.

35 McQuaid to de Valera, undated letter, DVA. McQuaid 'stung the feminists' in 1937 but his ideal of 'women in the home', which lay at the heart of Catholic social thought, has come under heavy fire. In 1996 a Constitutional Review Group recommended a revised gender neutral clause. See Dr Yvonne Scannell, 'The Constitution and the role of women,' in *De Valera's Constitution and Ours* (ed. Brian Farrell); Rosemarie Rowley, 'Women and the Constitution,' *Administration*, Vol. 37, No. 1, 1989; Katie Donovan, 'When Éamon de Valera tried to ignore the women of Ireland,' *The Irish Times*, April 24, 1991.

36 T.P. Coogan, *De Valera*, pp. 495–97

37 McQuaid to de Valera, May 10, DVA, 1091.

38 Working under the direction of John J. Hearne, the legal expert in the Department of External Affairs, was a team of civil servants who included Maurice Moynihan, Stephen Roche, Michael McDunphy and Philip P. O'Donoghue. Others worked on the Irish version. See Brian Kennedy, 'The special position of John Hearne,' *The Irish Times*, April 8, 1987.

39 *Irish Press*, August 7, 1937. McQuaid's involvement in the international Catholic peace movement was his response, he wrote in the *College Journal*, to 'a project which the Holy Father had orally blessed.' Among the speakers were the English Dominican scholar, Gerald Vann, and the Rev. J. Delos O.P. of Lille University.

40 De Valera wrote on November 10. McQuaid replied next day from Hughenden, DVA, 1091.

41 Quoted in *The New Ireland* by J.B. Morton, p. 97.

42 McQuaid to de Valera, December 29, 1937. McQuaid would have taken pleasure from the review by Fr John F. O'Doherty, 'The Catholic Church in 1937', in the *Irish Ecclesiastical Record*, where he referred to 'the

unanimous chorus of admiration' which greeted the Constitution throughout Europe, in contrast to those at home who opposed its enactment 'on the grounds of a false and un-Catholic feminism, or as if it were a party-political measure.'

43 McQuaid to de Valera, January 3, 1938, DVA, 1091.

44 Installation of the President, the *Catholic Bulletin*, July 1938, pp. 547–49. McQuaid, no doubt, attended the reception given by de Valera in St Patrick's Hall, Dublin Castle, where guests 'represented every department of life on an occasion which has already done much to soften old acerbities and remove prejudices that have long militated against national harmony.'

45 De Valera's speech quoted in the *Catholic Bulletin*, July 1938, p. 548.

46 Newspaper cuttings on the court cases from October-November 1938 are in the McQuaid Papers, AB8/A/II.33.

47 McQuaid to Kinane, October 7, 1938, DDA, AB8/A/II.33. Memorandum on the new Domestic and Household Workers' Union of Ireland. Despite his lofty stance, McQuaid's handling of the strike is not the only instance of personnel-managerial difficulties. In December 1933 he had issued one week's notice to the Reverend Mother of the Bon Secours Sisters that their services in the College would not be needed after Christmas, only to be embarrassed when word spread of his negotiations for a replacement with an English order of nuns. See DDA AB8/A/VIII/83 for McQuaid's correspondence with the Superior General of the Sisters of Charity of St Paul the Apostle, Selly Oak, Birmingham, 1933–34.

48 McQuaid memorandum to bishops, AB8/A/II.33.

49 Patrick Daly to McQuaid, November 11, 1938, DDA, AB8/A/VIII/83.

50 The letter was signed by a disciple of Canon Kelleher, one of the Maynooth social priests.

Chapter 9: Dev's Man, 1939–40

1 Quoted in Farragher, *Blackrock College*, p. 242. Fr Timothy Corcoran S.J. was among those urging McQuaid to lobby the Holy Ghost authorities in Paris.

2 Robinson to Le Hunsec, July 1,1939, quoted in Farragher, *De Valera and his Alma Mater*, p. 187.

3 Le Hunsec to Robinson, July 5, 1939, quoted in Farragher, *De Valera and his Alma Mater*, p. 188.

4 McQuaid to de Valera, July 7, 1939, DVA, 1440/7.

5 McQuaid to Le Hunsec, July 8, 1939, quoted in Farragher, *De Valera and his Alma Mater*, pp. 188–89.

6 Farragher, *Blackrock College*, p. 240.

7 Farragher, *Blackrock College*, p. 241.

8   O'Reilly to McQuaid, May 5, 1939, DDA, AB8/A/III.36

9   Corcoran to McQuaid, December 21, 1938, DDA, AB8/A/VI.

10 Author's interview with Tony Cronin.

11 Author's interview with Fr Michael O'Carroll C.S.Sp.

12 Joscelyne Finberg to McQuaid, September 17, 1939, DDA, AB8/A.

13 Cardinal Hinsley's pastoral is in a collection of his wartime addresses, *The Bond of Peace*. For a valuable study of Hinsley, see Thomas Moloney, *Westminster, Whitehall and the Vatican*, p. 134.

14 Joe Lee, *Ireland 1912–85*, p. 238. Professor Lee was unaware of how de Valera's preoccupation with accommodating McQuaid influenced the mechanics of this cabinet reshuffle.

15 O'Kelly was in touch with McQuaid, who had congratulated him on his new duties. O'Kelly to McQuaid, September 13, 1939, DDA, AB8/A/1.

16 Since March 1935 McQuaid had been in the thick of negotiations with the Association of Secondary Teachers of Ireland (ASTI) on conditions governing employment and dismissal of lay teachers in Catholic secondary schools. DDA, AB8/A/VI.

17 Minute by Very Rev. James Ryan, St Kieran's College, Kilkenny, of the Catholic Headmasters' Association half-yearly meeting, October 19, 1939, DDA, AB8/A/VI.

18 Ibid.

19 McQuaid to de Valera, October 20, 1939, DDA, AB8/A/VI.

20 De Valera's private secretary to McQuaid, October 26, 1939, DDA, AB8/A/VI.

Chapter 10: Father 'X', 1940

1   English to de Valera, March 4, 1940, DVA, 1440/7.

2   Information from Dr Denis Carroll.

3   Author's interview with Fr Farragher.

4   Dublin clerical sources.

5   The memorandum stated that the next Archbishop 'must be in general sympathy with the Government.' According to Fr Farragher, de Valera in later years said that he opted for McQuaid rather than John D'Alton because of the former's 'competence in the social question.'

6   This and subsequent exchanges between Dublin and the Vatican (Walshe-Macaulay-Donovan) are to be found in Secretary files, DFA, p.15(i), NAI, which provides the central narrative of this chapter's account of the 'X' campaign.

7   John Cornwell, *Hitler's Pope, The Secret History of Pius XII*. This book takes a critical look at the role of this autocratic Pope, whose outlook and temperament resembles that of McQuaid.

8   Dermot Keogh, *Ireland and the Vatican*, p. 145.

9   Kinane to McQuaid, June 28, 1940, DDA, AB8/A/VI. McQuaid had also distinguished himself in negotiations on behalf of Archbishop Byrne with Dublin Corporation for the purchase of ground on what became Our Lady's Hospital for Sick Children in Crumlin. In a memorandum, February 16, 1938, McQuaid showed a mastery of hospital administration and finances as well as (Catholic and Protestant) population trends in an expanding city. He also threw chunks of Canon Law at unsuspecting councillors by upholding the right of Catholic parents to Catholic hospital beds for their sick children.

10 Fr Michael O'Carroll C.S.Sp, on *John Charles McQuaid: What the Papers Say.*

11 Information from Fr. Farragher.

12 Farragher, *De Valera and his Alma Mater*, p. 191.

13 McQuaid writings on catechetical instruction in Ireland, December 17, 1939, DDA, AB8/ A/IX.84.

14 Ibid.

15 Ibid.

16 Biographical note on Colman Donovan, supplied by Joe Hayes of the Department of Foreign Affairs.

17 Walshe to de Valera, September 2, 1946, NAI, DFA, S, P15(i), NAI.

18 Matt McQuaid, Radio Éireann interview.

19 Blackrock College Year Book, 1974, pp. 269–70.

20 *Irish Press*, November 12, 1940.

21 John A. Costello, *Mission Outlook*, 1973.

22 PRO DO 130/45 Political Affairs, 1944. I am grateful to John Horgan for this reference.

23 Author's interview with Fr Brian Power.

24 PRO DO 130/45 Political Affairs, 1944.

25 Information from Dr Denis Carroll.

26 *Irish Press*, November 12, 1940.

27 Farragher interview.

28 *Irish Independent*, November 12, 1940.

29 *Irish Press*, November 12, 1940.

30 *Irish Independent*, November 12, 1940.

31 *The Irish Times*, November 12, 1940.

32 'The Holy Ghost Father,' by Fr Michael O'Carroll C.S.Sp., in *Mission Outlook*, 1973. O'Carroll also recalls that McQuaid had a Gaspard-like friendship with another Holy Ghost Brother in the Blackrock Community, Declan Paschal Mansfield, 'up to the last moment when he came to his deathbed.' p. 13.

33 The *Glasgow Observer*, December 6, 1940.

34 Burke Savage, *Studies*, Winter, 1965.

35 McQuaid to Walshe, DEA, December 1940.

36 I am grateful to Dean Brian Harvey for a copy of his father's letter,

November 18, 1940.

37 J.J. Mooney sales offer. Undated. Copy in author's possession.

38 Farragher, *De Valera and his Alma Mater*, p. 193.

39 Interview with Miss Dempsey, Cootehill, April 1995.

40 I am indebted to Dr Paul McQuaid for a collection of press cuttings on the Consecration.

41 Collier to McQuaid, December 31, 1940, DDA, AB8/B/XV. He thanked McQuaid for 'the delicate attention to our comforts and convenience, while at Archbishop's House.' Collier was a legendary 'Prince-Bishop.' A Co Laois man, educated at Maynooth, he had worked as a curate in England and had been President of St Kieran's College, Kilkenny. His correspondence to McQuaid is lively: he comes across as the new Archbishop's Episcopal mentor, willing to defer to Bishop Wall in the pecking order at the Consecration, and advising McQuaid to dispense with fast and abstinence rules on his Consecration day, a Friday.

42 Farragher, *De Valera and his Alma Mater*, pp. 193–94.

PART III USING POWER – RULER OF CATHOLIC IRELAND: 1940–62

Chapter 11: Pillar of the Emergency, 1940–44

1 ICD 1942, for January 13, 1941, pp. 632–35.

2 ICD 1942, for January 13, 1941, pp. 635–37.

3 ICD 1942, for January 13, 1941, pp. 636–37. McQuaid's social concern was signalled in a letter which he publicly addressed to Bishop Wall on January 2, 1941, when he wrote: 'only the thronging multitude of the poor could adequately satisfy a Bishop that the full rites of his Consecration Day had been suitably witnessed and fulfilled.' He also assured Wall: 'I am given a See at peace within itself.' Forgetful of the political machinations behind his appointment, he claimed he had been chosen 'by a Providence of God.' See ICD 1942, for January 2, 1941, pp. 630–32.

4 McQuaid also petitioned Robinson for a dispensation for the Pallium, a band of white wool worn on the shoulders which was sent by the Pope to new prelates as a token that they possessed the fullness of Episcopal office, DDA, AB8/B/XVII/1.

5 Collier to McQuaid, January 16, 1941, DDA, AB8/B/XV.

6 McQuaid to Robinson, January 12, 1941, DDA, AB8/B/XVII/1.

7 McQuaid to de Valera, January 25, 1941, DVA, 1280. McQuaid also displayed cynicism when he added: 'The Seanad comments on Secondary Education remind me of a number of Irishmen debating the centre of Asia.'

8 Feeney, *The Man and the Mask*, p. 15.

9 Information from Dr Denis Carroll. McQuaid had first met Walsh in 1925 when assisting Boylan in his biblical publication, and he admired Cronin

as a fine Thomist. A study of the Dublin clergy under McQuaid is much needed. However, personnel files of priests have not been released by Archbishop Desmond Connell.

10 McQuaid sent a signed copy of his Pastoral Letter to de Valera on February 20, 1941.

11 The Church of Ireland Archbishop of Dublin, Arthur Barton, also drew up contingency plans for Protestant children to find Protestant homes. These plans were publicised in issues of the *Church of Ireland Gazette* which heatedly debated whether its members in the forces should have their own chaplains.

12 McQuaid, in full Episcopal wear, excelled in inspecting guards of honour in Army barracks and at church functions, as a photograph of him in dashing form at St Bricin's Military Hospital, Dublin, on March 19, 1941, illustrates.

13 Kinane to McQuaid, March 21, 1941, DDA, AB8/B/XV/a.

14 Roche to McQuaid, March 22, 1941, DDA, AB8/B/XV/a.

15 MacNeely to McQuaid, March 22, 1941, DDA, AB8/B/XV/a.

16 McQuaid's relationship with Joe Walshe was pivotal to his access. He was also courted by the leading diplomats such as John Maffey, Edward Gray and Eduard Hempel. When his correspondence was opened by the British authorities, McQuaid asked Walshe to look into the matter. 'May I send you three envelopes addressed fully to me, yet opened by the British censorship. Twelve letters received were opened.' (McQuaid to Walshe, February 12, 1942.)

17 Norton to McQuaid, May 3, 1941, DDA, AB8/B/XVIII. The name Cullen suggested to Norton that the lady was a Catholic but her reference to 'Roman Catholic' baffled him!

18 The material on the Catholic Social Service Conference (DDA, AB8/B/XXI) deserves a detailed monograph.

19 This episode is recounted in Mary Purcell's Golden Jubilee history, *The Catholic Social Service Conference, 1941–91*.

20 Bolster, *Knights of Saint Columbanus*, p. 86.

21 'A most loyal' message to McQuaid was proposed by Dr Hugh Daly, a founder member of the Guilds of Regnum Christi, and was seconded by Fr Edward Coyne S.J., who urged the members 'to view the work we are doing as His Grace would visualise it.' The motion, adopted unanimously, read: 'The members of this Conference, in session assembled, wish to convey to Your Grace their filial devotion and loyalty, and with feelings of the utmost respect, beg Your Grace to accept this assurance of their desires at all times, to render to Your Grace their devoted and loyal service. They humbly beg Your Grace's blessing and the work of the Conference.'

22 Cronin to McQuaid, April 19, 1941, DDA, AB8/B/XXI.

23 For a vivid account of Dublin firemen travelling to Belfast see Robert

Fisk, *In Time of War*, pp. 421–33.

24 The Belfast statement issued by the Hierarchy's standing committee was published in ICD 1942, for April 22, 1941, pp. 652–53.

25 McQuaid to Walshe, May 16, 1941, DDA, AB8/B/XVIII.

26 ICD 1942, for June 4, 1941, pp. 661. An amusing account is provided by Ben Kiely, 'A bomb to begin with', in *The Waves Behind Us*, pp. 1–11.

27 ICD 1942, for June 16, 1941, pp. 663–64.

28 Carew to McQuaid, April 22, 1941, and undated memorandum, Sisters of Charity, Crumlin, DDA, AB8/B/XVIII/26, Education box, 1940–71.

29 O'Carroll to McQuaid, June 20, 1941, DDA, AB8/B/XVIII/26.

30 Sr J. Patricia to Dunne, July 1, 1941, DDA, AB8/B/XVIII/26.

31 McQuaid to Derrig, July 3, 1941, DDA, AB8/B/XVIII/26.

32 McQuaid note, July 24, 1941, DDA, AB8/B/XVIII/26.

33 O'Carroll to O' Muircheartaigh, September 22, 1941, DDA, AB8/B/XVIII/26.

34 Derrig to McQuaid, September 29, 1941, DDA, AB8/B/XVIII/26.

35 Born in Westport, Co. Mayo in 1897 and educated at UCG, Thomas Derrig was a headmaster in Ballina Technical School before becoming Commandant of the West Mayo Brigade in 1920 and was opposed to the Treaty. He took an H. Dip. in Education in 1926, the year before he became T.D. for Carlow-Kilkenny. He was Minister for Education from 1932 to 1948, except for the short period, 1939–40, when he was Minister for Lands.

36 McQuaid to Derrig, September 30, 1941, DDA, AB8/B/XVIII/26.

37 Financial transfers from the public purse in May 1941 alone included the payable order for £3,392 (about £85,000 in today's money), which McQuaid received directly from the Department of Education as the third instalment of an annual grant for the training of students at Our Lady of Mercy Training College at Carysfort in the academic year of 1940–41, and the payable order for £1,890, (worth about £47,000 today) as the third instalment for St Patrick's Training College, Drumcondra. See Department of Education Accountant to McQuaid, May 7 and May 15, DDA, Education box.

38 ICD 1942, for June 27, 1941, p. 665.

39 St Mary's Cabra Centenary Brochure.

40 ICD 1944, May 7, 1943, p. 682. Miss Cruice said that in her 35 years there was no religious discrimination as to patients who needed treatment.

41 ICD 1945, for February 8, 1944, p. 672.

42 ICD 1944, for September 17, 1943, p. 698.

43 ICD 1945, for April 21, 1944, p. 685.

44 ICD 1943, for May 5, 1942, Boland Dáil statement. Quoted in Feeney, pp. 18–19.

45 Derrig to McQuaid, May 10, 1942, DDA, AB8/B/XVIII/26.

46 McQuaid note, January 16, 1943, DDA, CSSC box.

47 McQuaid to Derrig, May 5, 1941, DDA, AB8/B/XVIII/26.

48 Indenture between W.&L. Crowe and Most Rev. John Charles McQuaid. Approved subject to map by A. O'Hagan & Son, September 9, 1941. I am grateful to the bookseller, Sheila Smith, for this document which gives a rare insight into McQuaid's property dealings.

49 The *Irish Catholic Directory* is a basic source for identifying church and school developments.

50 Purcell, CSSC booklet.

51 Huntingfield to McQuaid, August 20, 1941, DDA, AB8/B/XVIII/41. McQuaid courted the company of British royalty, including Lord Louis Mountbatten, whose residence at Classiebawn, Mullaghmore in Co Sligo, he often visited. Although he was uncompromising in his stand against the Reformed religions, he mixed with Protestant Ascendancy families whose social lifestyles matched the dignity of his office.

52 Green Cross Fund and cabinet minutes, September 3, 1941, NAI S 12557. In 1942, when a former republican prisoner, Thomas Mullaly, complained to McQuaid about intimidation by Gardaí in Limerick, McQuaid took up his case with Boland at the Department of Justice but also counselled Mullaly to keep quiet, while persuading him to leave the IRA. See correspondence on Mullaly in McQuaid Papers, DDA, AB8/B/VXIII/11 for September 1941.

53 The correspondence reveals a maudlin streak in Kavanagh. 'Your money is the least part ... I would like to hear from Your Grace and know that I am not quite alone in the world.' As an after-thought he asked McQuaid to 'please ignore any self-pity.' When the 'Poet Laureate of Drumcondra,' was down on his luck, McQuaid fixed him up as film critic with the *Standard* and gave him a regular allowance. According to Brian Behan, Kavanagh, in a public house, accidentally dropped a note from McQuaid which his brother, the rabble-rousing Brendan Behan, picked up and mockingly read. To annoy Kavanagh, Behan and a fellow-drinker, Sean Daly, would play ritual scenes of kissing 'Plug' McQuaid's ring. (Aubrey Malone, *The Brothers Behan*, p. 71.) Joe Mulholland, a Scottish student at UCD in the 1950s, recalls that whatever his reservations about being dependent on McQuaid for patronage, Kavanagh could be heard saying in the Carmelite Church in Clarendon Street that 'the Archbishop was not such an ould bastard.'

54 O'Donovan to author, August 6, 1995.

55 ICD 1942, for September 21, 1941, pp. 674–76.

56 ICD 1942, for October 14, 1941, pp. 679–82. Anonymously, McQuaid sent a 'princely gift' to the Bishop of Kilmore, Patrick Lyons, to help the Poor Clares build a new orphanage after the gruesome death in a fire of children who had been locked in their dormitories. 'It will hearten the poor sisters to face their task,' Lyons told McQuaid. 'They have been

very calm and brave. Every day since, the convent is full of civic guards taking statements! They have put some sisters at least three times through their interrogation. *Cui bono?*' Lyons to McQuaid, March 2, 1943, DDA, AB8/B/XV/a.

57 Joseph Carroll, *Ireland in the War Years*, p. 93. 'Perhaps the censorship was an inhibiting factor, but one suspects that there was never much interest by the bishops in the fate of what the Good Friday liturgy termed the perfidious Jews,' Carroll writes. McQuaid complained about Balinski to London.

58 NAI, D/T, memo on censorship debate, March 1941.

59 Hinsley to McQuaid, September 9, 1941, DDA. Hinsley sent McQuaid a copy of the best known Papal criticism of 'the blood and soil' ideology of Nazism, Pius XI's encyclical, *Mit Brennender Sorge* (With Burning Anxiety), published March 14, 1937. Cardinal Michael Faulhaber of Munich-Freising and Bishop Konrad von Preysing of Berlin were among the German prelates who persuaded Pius XI to condemn Nazism.

60 Collier to McQuaid, October 1941, DDA, AB8/B/XV/a, Irish bishops.

61 Information from Denis Murnaghan.

62 Richard Sherry, Clonliffe College History and Centenary Record, p. 161.

63 Information from David Sheehy, Dublin Diocesan Archivist.

64 ICD listing of the Dublin Diocese for 1941.

65 Mangan, *Doctrine and Life*, 1990, p. 198.

66 M. J. Curran, DDA, *Reportorium Novum*, Vol. 11. No. 1, 1957–58, 1–5.

67 Robinson to McQuaid, February 4, 1943, DDA, AB8/B/XVII/1.

68 'I fear that unless God in His mercy intervenes, a terrible time awaits this world,' Bishop Kinane wrote the day after Pearl Harbor to McQuaid, DDA, AB8/B/XV/a.

69 McQuaid to Derrig, December 21, 1942, DDA, AB8/B/XVIII/26.

70 McQuaid to Maffey, DDA, AB8/B/XVIII/41.

71 McQuaid to Mathew, February 9, 1942, DDA, AB8/B/XV/d.

72 ICD 1943, events for 1942, April 5, p. 619.

73 Purcell, CSSC.

74 Corish, *The Irish Catholic Experience*, p. 248.

75 Minutes of Hierarchy meeting, June 23, 1942, DDA. Initially, 32 priests were engaged in teaching.

76 Collier to McQuaid, October 17, 1941, DDA, AB8/B/XV/a.

77 The bishops agreed to ask priests not to use candles at the close of missions during the Emergency. When there was a shortage of altar wine in the North, McQuaid pleaded with Joe Walshe to allow a month's supply to be imported. Nor did prescriptions against worldly comfort preclude him from sharing his well-stocked cellar with the less fortunate Papal Nuncio during the Emergency. At the height of wartime scarcities, which extended to the most basic commodities, McQuaid was able to offer

those closest to him luxuries imported from far-away places which had mysteriously eluded the otherwise diligent customs service. His nephew, Paul, recalls the thrill of receiving an orange from him at the height of the Emergency scarcities. Reputed to be frugal personally, he cryptically told an honoured guest, 'Though it be Lent, we must eat.'

78 Memorandum, DDA, AB8/B/XV/b. Bishop Staunton read out a letter from the Taoiseach, Éamon de Valera, on the advisability of 'holding a general election or a local government election on a Sunday or church holiday, in view of a probable decision to make the polling areas correspond with parishes or parts of parishes, and having a full and representative poll.' The matter was discussed and it was not considered desirable.

79 Kinane to McQuaid, March 17, 1942, AB8/B/XV/a.

80 McQuaid's note of standing committee meeting of bishops, April 14, 1942, DDA, AB8/B/XV/b. The bishops also recommended the faithful through the annual Peter's Pence collection to 'be more than usually generous in view of the Pope's needs.'

81 In a Pastoral Letter, McQuaid hailed Pius XII as 'the Father of Christendom, the infallible Guardian of Christian revelation and the supreme Judge of Christian morality.' See ICD 1943, Letter, May 10, 1942, pp. 625–26. Earlier, McQuaid coordinated the despatch of congratulatory cables to Rome from the bishops, Maynooth College, the Catholic School Managers, headmasters and teachers, St Vincent de Paul Society and the Catholic Young Men's Society. He also arranged for the publication of edifying profiles of the Pope in the daily newspapers, the provincial press and monthly journals such as *Studies, Irish Ecclesiastical Record* and the *Irish Rosary*. He was rewarded with a Commemorative Medal from Cardinal Maglione.

82 Walshe to McQuaid, June 25, 1941, DDA, AB8/B/XVIII/6.

83 *Mission Outlook*, June 1973.

84 January 7, 1942 and McQuaid's approval, January 17, 1942, DDA, AB8/B/XVIII.

85 ICD 1943, events for June 17, 1942, pp. 269–70.

86 Ibid.

87 Bolster, *The Knights of Saint Columbanus*, p. 85. On June 25, 1942, McQuaid told a meeting of the Knights of St Columbanus that he had often heard them criticised as being too fixed on their personal, social and business advancement as the Catholic counterpart of the Masonic Order. He assured them that he would never accept such vague criticisms. 'I know of your practice of religion. I know too of your devotion to the Hierarchy.'

88 Williams to McQuaid, September 6, 1942, DDA, AB8/B/XV/d.

89 Williams to McQuaid, September 16, 1942, DDA, AB8/B/XV/d.

90 Griffin to McQuaid, September 5, 1942, DDA, AB8/B/XV/d.

91 Griffin to McQuaid, January 10, 1943, DDA, AB8/B/XV/d. One of the early

pioneer missionaries was Fr McDowell, who was directed to serve in the diocese of Northampton as chaplain to emigrants working with the British Sugar Corporation. (McQuaid to Parker, October 16, 1943, DDA, AB8/B/XV/d.)

92 ICD 1943, for September 8, 1942, pp. 636–37.

93 ICD 1944, for June 2, 1943, pp. 686–88.

94 Walshe to McQuaid, January 20, 1943.

95 MacRory to McQuaid, January 24, 1943, DDA, AB8/B/XV/a. This file also contains MacRory's list of objections sent to Gray on October 7, 1942.

96 Mathew to McQuaid, February 12, 1942, DDA, AB8/B/XV/d.

97 Collier to McQuaid, January 28, 1943, DDA, AB/8/B/XV/a.

98 Mooney noted this observation in a return letter of April 24, 1943, DDA, AB/8/B/XV/d/22, American bishops.

99 Quoted in John Cooney (no relation!), *The American Pope*. For a more ecclesiastical version of events, see ICD 1944, for March 31 to April 2, 1943,
pp. 676–78.

100 ibid.

101 Collier to McQuaid, August 18, 1943, DDA, AB/8/B/XV/a.

102 McQuaid to Collier, August 18, 1943, DDA, AB/8/B/XV/a. McQuaid informed Collier that the permission came very appositely, as he had just consecrated his diocese to the Immaculate Heart of Mary, 'a fact which augurs very happily to the new foundation.'

103 Document in author's possession.

104 ICD 1945, for May 21, 1944, pp. 687–92. McQuaid may have had his own career in mind when he said of Rice: 'It is this character of initial failure and mighty renascence which strikes one in considering the life and work of Edmund Ignatius Rice. He himself, in the plan of God, was obliged to grope obscurely towards his definitive vocation.'

105 Interview source with author.

106 Martha's experience was told in 'The sisters of no mercy,' *Irish Independent*, March 21, 1998, based on Channel 4 television documentary, *Sex in a Cold Climate*.

107 ICD 1944, for July 20, 1943, pp. 690–91.

108 Robinson to McQuaid, July 26, 1943, DDA, AB8/B/XVII/a.

109 McQuaid to Boland, August 27, 1943, DEA.

110 Walshe to McQuaid, October 14, 1943, DDA, AB8/B/XVIII/6.

111 ICD 1944, for November 7, 1943, p. 705.

112 Keogh, *Ireland and the Vatican*, pp. 178–84.

113 Correspondence from London Metropolitan Archives, April 12, 1999.

114 The centenary history of the Mater Misericordiae poured lavish praise on how McQuaid endowed the hospital with the latest transistorised E.E.G. machine, and his encouragement for a new Child Guidance Clinic.

115 According to Dr Ruth Barrington, in *Health, Medicine and Politics*, 'a venereal disease clinic was set up on McQuaid's initiative in the Mater Hospital after the Mercy Nuns refused his request to set up a clinic.'

116 Stanley to McQuaid, May 24, 1944, DDA. For obituary of Stanley, 1895–1996, *The Irish Times*, November 15, 1996.

117 McQuaid to Stanley, May 27, 1944, DDA.

118 John Feeney, *The Man and the Mask*, emphasises the 'solely Catholic concern' of McQuaid against the background of deeply felt fear of Protestant proselytism, pp. 14–19.

Chapter 12: Hammering Dissent, 1940–44

1 I am grateful to diplomats, John Dew and Ted Hallett, for locating this document in the files of the former Commonwealth and Dominions Office.

2 McQuaid had spied on Judge Wylie, who had formed his Guild of Goodwill to enlist support for job-creation schemes. McQuaid circulated, from the c/o address of the Knight of St Columbanus activist, Dr Stafford Johnson, at 15 Fitzwilliam Square, a confidential report of a speech delivered by the philanthropic judge in Dublin's Mansion House. The Catholic architect, John J. Robinson, praised McQuaid for his 'very comprehensive' manuscript and made four typed copies of it. The Catholic Social Service Conference challenged a Medical Mission to Roman Catholics in Dublin whose purpose was to proselytise the Catholic poor, who were only given medical attention and food after attending a Protestant religious service in the clinic hall. Even before McQuaid's installation as Archbishop, it was picketed three nights a week by the Legion of Mary.

3 Dobrzynski to Dunne, July 23, 1942, DDA, AB8/B/XVIII/41.

4 July 7, 1941, archives of Sisters of Charity.

5 Kinane to McQuaid, March 14, 1942, DDA, AB/8/B/XV/a.

6 This section is based on the of the SHR archives, Dublin. The paternalism shown by McQuaid to this order of nuns was replicated throughout the diocese. I am indebted to Sister Cori for her assistance. It would be timely for Women's Studies to undertake a major study of McQuaid's relations with orders of nuns.

7 Secretary to Hayes, November 5, 1941, DDA, AB8/B/XXII/b/3.

8 McQuaid to MacMahon, November 5, 1941, DDA, AB8/B/XXII/b/3.

9 Rynne, p. 170.

10 Hayes to McQuaid, May 28, 1942, DDA, AB8/B/XXII/b/3.

11 Information from Tom Fitzpatrick and Jim Quigley.

12 McQuaid to Derrig, May 5, 1941, DDA, AB8/B/XVIII/26.

13 León Ó Broin, *Frank Duff*, p. 57.

14 According to Ó Broin, in *Just Like Yesterday*, the coldness of the rebuff

from McQuaid deeply wounded Duff. Ó Broin concluded that 'Dr McQuaid did no service to faith, morals or anything else' in banning the series.

15 McQuaid to Mathew, December 3, 1942, DDA, AB/8/B/XV/d.

16 Ibid.

17 Duff to McQuaid, December 5, 1942, DDA, AB8/B/XXII/b/3.

18 McKeon, *Frank O'Connor: A Life*, pp. 136–37.

19 The article, but not McQuaid's rebuke, is recounted by Heenan in *Not the Whole Truth*. The article in the McQuaid file, AB8/B/XV/d, is undated.

20 McQuaid to Godfrey, December 19, 1941, DDA, AB/8/B/XV/d.

21 Godfrey to McQuaid, December 26, 1941, DDA, AB/8/B/XV/d.

22 McQuaid to Godfrey, December 31, 1941, DDA. McQuaid also sent a copy, 'for information sake', of Godfrey's letter and his reply to Robinson.

23 McQuaid to MacRory, March 26, 1942, DDA, AB8/B/XV/a.

24 McQuaid's draft reply for his secretary to Alton. Years later, the elderly Alton took his revenge on McQuaid by walking past him at a public function – information from Dean Robert MacCarthy, St Patrick's Cathedral, Dublin.

25 McQuaid's advice was described as excellent by Cardinal MacRory, who praised his 'frankness and courage'. 'I believe that we shall hear no more about this honour on Bishop Mathew, which was more meant to benefit Trinity College than to honour the Catholic Church.' MacRory to McQuaid, July 6, 1942, DDA, AB8/B/XVa.

26 McQuaid to Mathew, August 14, 1942, DDA, AB/8/B/XV/d.

27 *Studies*, Winter, 1998.

28 ICD for 1944, for February 15, 1943, p. 668.

29 Quoted in *Skeff, A Life of Owen Sheehy Skeffington*, pp. 119–20. Some doctors believed that McQuaid nearly managed to stop all preventive work against TB.

30 Mitchell, *A Peculiar Place*, pp. 170–71.

31 Author's interview with Noel Coghlan.

32 Walsh to McQuaid, February 26, 1942, DDA, AB8/B/XV/a.

33 Brendan Ó Cathaoir, *The Irish Times*, February 2, 1990.

34 Ó Broin, *Just Like Yesterday*, p.154.

35 Duff to McQuaid, January 8, 1943, DDA, AB8/B/XXII/a/3.

36 Staunton to McQuaid, February 12, 1943, DDA, AB8/B/XV/a.

37 Hierarchy minutes, June 22, 1943, DDA, AB8/B/XV/b.

38 *Waterford Star*, cutting in McQuaid Papers, AB8/B/XV/a, Bishop Cohalan of Waterford box.

39 Cohalan was a nephew of his namesake, Daniel Cohalan, the Bishop of Cork.

40 McQuaid to Cohalan, December 18, 1943, DDA, AB8/B/XV/a.

41 Cohalan was prominent in the Pioneer Movement, Ferriter, p. 131.

42 McQuaid to Cohalan, December 28, 1943, DDA, AB8/B/XV/a, Irish bishops.

43 The *Church of Ireland Gazette*, February 25, 1944, p. 72.

44 'The Ban on TCD', *The Bell*, Vol. VIII, No.1, April 1944. This article is not cited by Maurice Harmon in his biography of O'Faoláin, nor in Neill Kirwan's analysis, 'The Social Policy of *The Bell*,' in *Administration*, 1989.

45 McQuaid's letter to parish priests containing the anti-Trinity Decree was dated February 12, 1944. Author's copy was sent to Very Rev. Thomas O'Riordan, Kilquade, Delgany, Co. Wicklow.

46 Gay Byrne, *The Time of My Life*, pp. 24–26.

47 McQuaid to Lemass, December 17, 1943, DVA, 1440/5. McQuaid had stated his objections to de Valera as far back as May 8.

48 Lemass to McQuaid, December 18, 1943, DVA, 1440/5.

49 McQuaid to de Valera, February 9, 1944, DVA, 1440/5.

50 De Valera to McQuaid, February 19, 1944, DVA, 1440/5.

51 McQuaid to de Valera, February 20, 1944, DVA, 1440/5.

52 McQuaid to de Valera, February 23, DVA, 1440/5.

53 De Valera to McQuaid, February 25, 1944, DVA, 1440/5.

54 De Valera note re. O'Hanlon, 11.30pm, Monday, February 28, 1944, DVA, 1440/5. Expecting trouble, de Valera instructed his civil servants: 'Get file re. AB prepared.'

55 McQuaid to de Valera, March 4, 1944, DVA, 1440/5. On June 15 the Commission unanimously decided that 'the school leaving age should ultimately be raised to 16 years of age.'

56 Roche to McQuaid, quoted in *The Irish Times*, March 3, 1996, based on S. Files, Department of Justice, NAI.

57 Ibid.

58 Confidential Report of Deans of Residence, 1944–45, submitted to Hierarchy, DDA, AB8/B/XV/b.

59 ICD 1944, for January 7, 1943, p. 66.

60 *Irish Press,* June 5, 1944.

61 Maguire to McQuaid, July 6, 1944, DDA, AB8/B/XVIII.

62 McQuaid to Maguire, July 14, 1944, DDA, AB8/B/XVIII.

63 McQuaid to Mother Paul, July 14, 1944, DDA, AB8/B/XVIII.

64 Burke Savage, *Studies*, Winter, 1965.

Chapter 13: Defending the One True Church, 1942–44

1 O'Connell memorandum of conversation with Rev. Dr Leen, C.S.Sp., September 28, 1942, DDA, AB8/XXII/a/3. The Mercier Society and Pillar of Fire Society are included in the Legion of Mary box.

2   O'Connell's report of Mercier Society committee meeting, October 2, 1942.

3   O'Connell's memorandum of conversation with Leen, October 7, 1942.

4   O'Connell's report of meeting of the Catholic Committee of the Mercier Society, October 15, 1942.

5   O'Connell's memorandum of conversation with Leen, October 7, 1942.

6   O'Connell's report to McQuaid, October 15, 1942.

7   Dempsey to McQuaid, November 3, 1942, and memorandum.

8   McQuaid to Duff, November 6, 1942.

9   Duff to McQuaid, November 10, 1942.

10 McQuaid to Duff, November 12, 1942.

11 McQuaid to Duff, November 16, 1942.

12 Ibid.

13 Ibid.

14 Ibid.

15 Ibid.

16 Mercier Society meeting, November 10, 1942.

17 McQuaid to Duff, November 16, 1942.

18 McQuaid to Ó Broin, November 16, 1942.

19 Duff to McQuaid, November 18, 1942.

20 Adrian Hastings, *A History of English Christianity, 1920–1985*. Hinsley had also been introduced to the exclusive Aetheneum Club by the Archbishop of Canterbury, Cosmo Lang.

21 Duff to McQuaid, November 18, 1942.

22 McQuaid to Duff, November 18, 1942.

23 Duff to McQuaid, November 19, 1942.

24 Duff to McQuaid, November 10, 1942.

25 Duff to McQuaid, January 8, 1943.

26 Ibid.

27 Duff to Mangan, April 16, 1943.

28 McQuaid to Marchetti-Selvaggiani, undated.

29 Ó Broin to McQuaid, December 4, 1942.

30 This is McQuaid's most self-revealing condemnation of Jews. It is a clearly anti-Semitic viewpoint.

31 Ó Broin to McQuaid, January 4, 1943.

32 Mangan to Ó Broin, January 5, 1943.

33 Ó Broin to Mangan, January 7, 1943.

34 Mangan to Ó Broin, February 15, 1943.

35 Leen to McQuaid, March 11, 1943. Leen met McQuaid on Monday, March 15.

36 McQuaid to Leen, November 13, 1943.

37 McQuaid to Kissane, November 29, 1943. McQuaid had also consulted

senior Jesuit priests including the Irish Provincial, Fr John MacMahon, and Fr John Hannon. MacMahon suggested that the Vicar General of the Jesuits at its Curia headquarters in Rome, Fr Magni, might indicate the Society's attitude towards the Legion which McQuaid could show to Duff. McQuaid leaned on MacMahon to get a statement that would be critical of the infant movement. This ploy backfired, however, when Magni told MacMahon that he could not understand why such a declaration was sought about the standing of the Legion of Mary, as 'not even Catholic Action in Italy had asked for such a declaration.' It was the normal Jesuit practice, Magni added, to regard Catholic organisations with great respect and kindly collaboration. (See JAI, Letters of the Generalate in Rome to Ireland, 1806–1959 (ADMN-1) and Provincial's correspondence, 1905–1959 (ADMN 3).

38 McQuaid to Leen, January 21, 1944.

39 McQuaid to Duff, January 26, 1944.

40 O'Connell's report to McQuaid of Mercier Committee meeting, February 5, 1942. O'Connell listed the Catholic members of the Mercier Committee as: Frs Leen, Heuston and Carroll (sic), F. Duff, J. Nagle, J. Cummins, L. Ó Broin, D. Fitzgerald, J. Walsh (sic), B. Sheppard and Mr McAuley.

41 Duff to McQuaid, February 20, 1944.

42 Ibid.

43 McQuaid to Duff, February 21, 1944.

44 McQuaid to Duff, April 6, 1944.

45 Revised proposed constitution of 'The Mercier Society.'

46 Duff to McQuaid, April 20, 1944.

47 McQuaid to Duff, April 22, 1944.

Chapter 14: The Hidden Ruler, 1944–48

1 ICD 1931, for July 13, 1930, pp. 615–17.

2 McQuaid to de Valera, November 12, 1944, DDA, AB8/XVIII.

3 McQuaid's note, November 13, 1944, DDA, AB8/XVIII.

4 McQuaid's note, November 14, 1944, DDA, AB8/XVIII.

5 Mangan interview, *Doctrine and Life*, July-August 1990.

6 Jesuit Provincial Archives, Dublin, Administration File, November 11, 1944.

7 Biographical note, John Dignan, 1880–1953, in Canning, *Bishops of Ireland*, p. 335.

8 Dr John Dignan, *Social Security: Outlines of a Scheme of National Health Insurance*, Sligo, 1945.

9 Dignan to McQuaid, October 21, 1944, DDA, AB8/XV/a.

10 Dignan to McQuaid, March 24, 1945, DDA, AB8/XV/a.

11 McQuaid to Dignan, March 22, 1945, DDA, AB8/XV/a.

12 Whyte, *Church and State in Modern Ireland 1923–1979*, p. 119.

13 At six-foot-four Maffey was taller than de Valera, according to Coogan, *De Valera, Long Fellow, Long Shadow*, p. 537.

14 ICD 1946, for April 18, 1945, p. 684. McQuaid called for special May devotions for the intentions of Pope Pius XII.

15 Note by O'Connell for McQuaid, May 30, 1945, DDA AB8/B/XV/a. Walshe received his confidential information from a girl employed in the Irish Assurance Co., Dorset Street. 'Mr Walshe has reason to believe that this comes from a certain Norah Arkle, whose name is indicative of her Dutch origin. He does not know if she is a Catholic,' O'Connell wrote. 'All this activity could easily be the work of British or American agents-prov.'

16 Churchill victory speech, May 13, 1945. Referring to Britain's crisis after the fall of France in 1940, Churchill said that this was a deadly moment, and if it had not been for the loyalty and friendship of Northern Ireland, 'we should have been forced to come to close quarters with Mr de Valera, or perish for ever from the Earth.'

17 De Valera reply, May 16, 1945, Moynihan, *Speeches and Statements*, pp. 470–71.

18 McQuaid to de Valera, May 17, 1945, DVA, 1440.

19 McQuaid's made his announcement about Magennis and Sir Joseph Glynn (a Knight of St Gregory), on January 25,1944. McQuaid had been assured that there would be no objection to Papal Honours by the Government. This Papal Honours system was used by McQuaid over the years to reward 'obedient servants' in the civil and public service.

20 Magennis to McQuaid, May 18, 1945, DDA, AB8/XVIII.

21 McQuaid to Magennis, May 19, 1945, DDA, AB8/XVIII.

22 Magennis to McQuaid, May 30, 1945, DDA, AB8/XVIII.

23 McQuaid to Magennis, May 31, 1945, DDA, AB8/XVIII.

24 Dáil and Senate reports, November 1945.

25 MacArdle to McQuaid, August 14, 1945, DDA, AB8/B/XVIII/1.

26 Walshe to McQuaid, July 1945, NAI, DEA, S. Correspondence.

27 Hierarchy Standing Committee, McQuaid notes, DDA, AB8/XV/b/5.

28 ICD 1946, for July 12, 1945, pp. 700–701.

29 ICD 1946, for July 29, 1945, p. 704.

30 Patrick O'Donoghue, 'Our Lady's Choral Society', *Link-up*, April 1995.

31 Review of the work of Emigrants' Section, 1946, DDA, AB8/B/XV/b.

32 Feeney, *The Man and the Mask*, p. 35.

33 McQuaid to Carew, July 27, 1945, Archives of the Irish Sisters of Charity.

34 Mellon to McQuaid, October 24, 1945, DDA, AB8/B/XV/d/18, Scottish bishops.

35 ICD 1946, for November 12, 1945, pp. 718–19. McQuaid told the young people that they were saved from the obscurity and confusion of their own research by Catholic education.

36 ICD 1947, for December 2, 1946, pp. 682–83.

37 Youth Clubs, DDA, Keogh to McQuaid, November 20, 1945; and McQuaid to Keogh, November 21, 1945, DDA, AB8/B/XV/a.

38 McQuaid to Robinson, October 3, 1946, DDA, AB8/B/XVII/a. McQuaid reported that the only European contact that had come under his notice was an invitation to the Congress of the Union des Organisations de la Jeunesse Chrétienne, but he had ignored that as suspicious.

39 McQuaid to de Jong, August 14, 1945, DDA, AB8/B/XV/d. 'I am well aware of the danger to the young and the unformed in such times of stress: the elderly will have faith to overcome their difficulties.'

40 McQuaid to Staunton, August 11, 1945, DDA, AB8/B/XV/a.

41 Walshe to McQuaid, August 13, 1945, DDA, AB8/B/XVIII/6.

42 Conveyance document signed January 13, 1945, between Mildred Elinor Dobbs and Henry B. O'Hanlon. Conveyance and endorsement document between O'Hanlon and Archbishop McQuaid, Monsignor Patrick Boylan and Rev. Michael Patrick O'Connell, dated November 30. McQuaid was already in possession by mid-October when Joe Walshe informed him he was looking forward 'to visiting Your Grace in your new home on Thursday.'

43 McQuaid had discussed with the Nuncio a Hierarchy decision to raise Mass offerings from five shillings to ten shillings. Spring 1945, DDA, AB8/B/XV/b.

44 McQuaid to Stafford Johnson, DDA, AB8/B/XVII/2.

48 Walshe to Kiernan, December 18, 1945, DEA, S. Correspondence.

46 Lyons to McQuaid, December 13, 1945, DDA, AB8/B/XV/a.

47 Knights of Malta parchment conferred the most ancient religious Order of Chivalry in Christendom. It was traditionally a nobiliary body, which through appointments of Knights of Magistral Grace extended its membership to well-deserving Catholics of a respectable position, especially in those countries where nobility no longer exists as an institution. The uniform consisted of a red cloth jacket, with gold embroidered cuffs, lapels and collar, and closed in front by twelve buttons embossed with the Cross of the Order. The trousers were dark blue, with a golden braid and red stripes applied on the sides. The belt was embroidered with gold lace. The shoulders were fringed. A cocked hat and spurs completed the uniform.

48 Walshe to Kiernan, December 18, 1945, DEA, S. Correspondence.

49 Keogh, *Ireland and the Vatican*, p. 196.

50 McQuaid to Glennon, December 24, 1945, DDA, AB8/B/XVIII/d/22, American bishops.

51 Walshe to de Valera, June 12, 1946, DVA, 1529.

52 Walshe to de Valera, August 28, 1946, DVA, 1529.

53 De Valera to Walshe, December 6, 1946, DVA, 1529.

54 Ryan to McQuaid, August 5, 1946, DDA, AB8/B/XV/d/26.

55 Ryan to McQuaid, August 9, 1946, DDA, AB8/B/XV/d/26.
56 Walshe to Kathleen O'Connell, July 26, 1946, DVA, 1529. McQuaid sought de Valera's support in his championing of Soeur Olive, who erected a chapel dedicated to Christ the King, and was removed from the Benedictine monastery of the Holy Sacrament in Paris, DVA,1440.
57 Walshe to de Valera, August 21, 1946, DVA, 1529.
58 Walshe to Boland, DFA, October 25, 1946, DDA, AB8/B/XVIII/6.
59 In his foreword to Count Anthony H. O'Brien of Thomond's book, *Archbishop Stepinac: The Man and his Case*, McQuaid acknowledged that the situation in Yugoslavia necessarily required Stepinac 'to enter into relations with every movement and manner of persons.' But, he added, 'the Archbishop was always the spiritual Ruler and Teacher of his flock.'
60 McQuaid's letter in support of Stepinac, October 26, 1946. Brian Fallon, *An Age of Innocence: Irish Culture 1930–1960,* judges Stepinac as 'a highly dubious figure politically, as Hubert Butler and other had shown' (p. 212).
61 Walshe to Boland, November 25, 1946, DDA, AB8/B/XVIII/6.
62 McQuaid to Robinson, July 9, 1946, DDA, AB8/B/XVII/a.
63 By now Robinson was a sick man and his writing had deteriorated badly.
64 Walshe to McQuaid, December 2, 1946, DDA, AB8/XVIII/6.
65 Quoted in T.J. O'Connell, *100 Years of Progress: The Story of the Irish National Teachers' Organisation.*
66 Faulkner, *Studies*, Winter, 1998.
67 McQuaid to Derrig, April 13, 1946, DDA, AB8/B/XV/III/26. McQuaid felt that the Government did not play fair with him.
68 Quoted in O'Connell.
69 Ibid.
70 Gabriel Fallon, letter to *The Irish Times*, April 12, 1973. A vivid account of McQuaid's role preparing Larkin for death is provided by Burke Savage, *Studies*, Winter, 1965.
71 McQuaid to Walsh, DDA, AB8/B/XVIII/6.
72 In his foreword to Mary Purcell's biography of Talbot, McQuaid made no reference to Talbot's extreme bodily mortifications, such as the wearing of chains and self-flagellation. Instead, he compared Talbot to St Joseph in possessing 'a very remarkable spirit, or, rather, gift of prayer, the practice of self-denial in poverty and hard work, the habit of re-collection in the presence of God, a very tender graciousness towards children, and a deep love of the most holy Mother of God.'
73 *Irish Press*, May 16, 1947, 'Honour is paid to memory of Liberator.' McQuaid said that 'it is chiefly to the honour of the County of Kerry that Derrynane should be saved from ruin.'
74 McQuaid had a preference for hand-made buckled shoes and well-tailored clothing. A dilettante, he loved art, architecture, literature and he corresponded with writers such as John Betjeman. For relaxation, he

read detective novels, John Carter-style science fiction pulp and ghost stories He was a fine pianist who loved to play Beethoven and Johann Strauss. Among his hobbies were photography and shooting wild fowl. He loved to drive fast cars, often doing so in the Wicklow Mountains with the latest model from his half-brother, Matt McQuaid, who was in the motor business.

75 Ostorog to McQuaid, March 27, 1947, DDA, AB8/B/XVIII/41.

76 Griffin to McQuaid, October 12, 1946, AB8/B/XV/d.

77 Collier to McQuaid, March 24, 1947, DDA, AB8/B/XV/a.

78 Collier to McQuaid, August 6, 1947, DDA, AB8/B/XV/a.

79 'We will make Dublin jealous!' Collier told McQuaid in a clear reference to the failure of Dublin Corporation to make McQuaid a Freeman of Dublin.

80 Briscoe to McQuaid, August 19, 1947, DDA, AB8/B/XVIII/38.

81 Ryan to McQuaid, 1947, DDA, AB8/B/XV/d/26.

82 Collier to McQuaid, August 25, 1947, DDA, AB8/B/XV/a.

83 Walshe Correspondence in DVA, 1529.

84 MacBride to McQuaid, October 30, 1947, DDA, AB8/B/XVIII/40. 'It is my most earnest desire to discharge my duties to the best of my ability for the good of the people who have placed their trust in me. I would ask Your Grace to pray that I may be guided in this onerous task.'

85 McQuaid to MacBride, November 2, 1947, DDA, AB8/B/XVIII/40.

86 MacBride to McQuaid, November 3, 1947, DDA, AB8/B/XVIII/40.

87 Toolen to McQuaid, September 12, 1947, DDA, AB8/B/XVII/d/22.

88 McQuaid to Boland, January 17, 1947, DDA, AB8/B/XVIII/5. McQuaid suggested the creation of a Pontifical International Aid Society to Pizzardo. Such a body would be 'an instrument of the most serious benefit, not only to the distressed but, from the point of view which now engages my attention, to those who are in a position to assist.'

89 McQuaid to Robinson, January 12, 1948, DDA, AB8/B/XVII/a. Lemass had to wait until 1950 for his Cross of St Gregory, John Horgan, *Lemass*, p. 125.

90 Maffey to Commonwealth and Dominions Office, August 17, 1948. Copy registered 290/22/48 (External Relations Act). I am indebted to John Dew and Ted Hallett for this important report.

Chapter 15: Cold War Churchman, 1948–51

1 *Irish Press*, April 12, 1948.

2 Collier to McQuaid, April 14, 1948, DDA, AB8/B/XV.

3 Garrett to Secretary of State, April 12, 1948, Confidential Files, 865.000/4–1248, RG 59, National Archives, Washington DC.

4 McQuaid told MacBride that his script 'was incapable of misconstruction

except by the persons who wish to misunderstand the religious character of the crisis.'

5   Pius sent 'Our beloved Son' Costello an autographed letter as a mark of particular honour, which was published in *L'Osservatore Romano*. For background, see Dermot Keogh, *Ireland and the Vatican*.

6   McQuaid to Stafford Johnson, March 25, 1948, DDA, AB8/B/XXII.

7   McQuaid to Montini, March 27, 1948, DDA, AB8/B/XVI.

8   McQuaid to de Valera, April 15, 1948, DVA. McQuaid to MacBride, April 5, 1948, DDA, AB8/B/XVIII.

9   LVAA, minutes, Vol. 30, April 17 and 22, 1948.

10   *The Irish Press*, April 12, 1948.

11   Quoted Bolster, *Knights of St Columbanus*, p. 106.

12   ICD 1949, for April 23, 1949, p. 715. Gedda described the outcome as 'this most consoling victory for the Christian forces.'

13   Walshe to McQuaid, May 19, 1948, DDA, AB8/B/XVIII/6.

14   Walshe to McQuaid, May 22, 1948, DDA, AB8/B/XVIII/6. Walshe underestimated – or ignored – the vast sums of US dollars which Cardinal Spellman gave to the Vatican.

15   Walshe to McQuaid, June 23, 1948, DDA, AB8/B/XVIII/6.

16   Hierarchy minutes, June 1948, DDA, AB8/B/XV/b5.

17   Confidential report of the Dean of Residence, UCD, 1947–48, DDA, AB8/B/XV/B5.

18   O'Reilly to McQuaid, August 11, 1948, DDA, AB8/XXII, Lay organisations.

19   MacBride to McQuaid, August 25, 1948, DDA, AB8/B/XVIII.

20   Maffey to Commonwealth and Dominion Office, August 17, 1948. Copy registered 290/22/48 (External Relations Act).

21   MacBride to McQuaid, August 31, 1948, DDA, AB8/B/XVIII. McQuaid told the Auditor at the Nunciature, Monsignor Paro, that he doubted it would be possible to find 'a greater gentleman' than Robinson. September 3, 1948, DDA, AB8/B/XVII.

22   McQuaid to MacBride, November 23, 1949, DDA, AB8/B/XVIII.

23   Memorandum on Emigration, September 1948, DDA. It expressed alarm that many young girls who emigrated to Britain became pregnant. In his memoir, Conor Cruise O'Brien interprets this as an anti-abortion move by MacBride which was designed to appease the bishops. In the event, McQuaid did not take up the proposal.

24   Maffey report, August 1948.

25   Seán Cronin, *Washington's Irish Policy*, pp. 228–30. McQuaid also expected that war would break out in 1950 in which Ireland would become involved. 'Ireland cannot be said to be not neutral,' McQuaid told Garrett. McQuaid assured Garrett that 'the humble people of this land were prepared to resist and fight any manifestations or encroachments of an alien ideology.' In August 1948, McQuaid also asked Fr

Denis Fahey if he agreed that 'further crisis (or doom) is close at hand.' McQuaid to Fahey, August 26, 1948, HGA, Dublin.

26   Cronin, pp. 228–30.

27   Information from Dr Dermot Keogh.

28   Frings to McQuaid, December 13, 1948, DDA, AB8/B/XV/d. McQuaid had purchased a piano for two German girls staying in a Legion hostel. Frings gave a Miss Fiertel permission to found the Legion of Mary in Cologne and to find out the addresses of girls planning to emigrate to Ireland, mostly coming from the south of Germany, the American and French zones.

29   Fliesser to McQuaid, April 10, 1948, DDA, AB8/B/XV/d.

30   McQuaid to McNicholas, January 1, 1949, DDA, AB8/B/XV/d.

31   Maffey report, August 1948.

32   Costello to McQuaid, February 27, 1968, DDA, AB8/B/XVIII/38. 'I did not, as has been alleged, make a declaration of the Republic on my own initiative and without the consent of my colleagues in the then Government.' Costello told McQuaid twenty years later, supplying him with a confidential memoir.

33   McQuaid to Masterson, January 19, 1949, DDA, AB8/B/XV/d.

34   Hierarchy minutes, October 1948, DDA, AB8/XV/b. The holding of public inter-college games on Sundays was condemned by the Hierarchy in October 1948 by a majority of one.

35   Masterson to McQuaid, January 22, 1949, DDA, AB8/XV/b.

36   McQuaid to Masterson, January 24, 1949, DDA, AB8/XV/b.

37   ICD 1949, for December 28, 1948, pp. 705–706. Mindszenty had written to McQuaid on January 31, 1945, asking him to direct the Irish Catholic newspapers to use the semi-official Hungarian Catholic agency, *Magyar Kurir*, for news from and for South Eastern Europe. McQuaid appears to have ignored the request.

38   McQuaid to Boland, January 5, 1949, quoted by Keogh, *Ireland and the Vatican*, p. 263.

39   McQuaid to Boland, February 11, 1949, DDA.

40   Walshe to McQuaid, March 3, 1949, DDA, AB8/XVIII/6.

41   *Irish Press*, February 19, 1949. Tierney also described McQuaid as 'a man who was above all praise, and at the same time demanded the veneration of all good men, because of his princely office in the Church.'

42   Walshe to McQuaid, March 3, 1949, DDA, AB8/B/XVIII/6.

43   McQuaid to Montini, May 2, 1949, DDA, AB8/B/XVI.

44   McQuaid to McCarron, May 29, 1949, quoted in Ferriter, *A Nation of Extremes*.

45   Catholic Information Bureau Report, 1949, DDA, Hierarchy box, AB8/B/XV/I/b.

46   Dublin Lenten Regulations.

47   McQuaid to D'Alton, March 5, 1948, DDA, AB8/B/XV/a.

48   D'Alton to McQuaid, March 11, 1948, DDA, AB8/B/XV/a.

49   Kavanagh, Social Activist, *Studies*, Winter, 1998.

50   ICD 1949, for December 20, 1948, p. 704.

51   Durnin to Dublin Archdiocese, January 2, 1950, DDA, AB8/B/XVIII.

52   Mangan to Roseingrave, October 30, 1949, DDA, AB8/B/XXII.

53   Ryan to McQuaid, November 13, 1949, DDA, AB8/B/XXII.

54   Confidential report of the Dean of Residence, UCD, 1948–49, DDA, AB8/B/XV/b.

55   Mangan to McCarthy, May 7, 1949, DDA, AB8/B/XXII.

56   Montini to McQuaid, July 16, 1949, DDA, AB8/B/XVI.

57   McQuaid to Montini, August 4, 1949, DDA, AB8/B/XVI.

58   McQuaid to Montini, (second letter) August 4, 1949, DDA, AB8/B/XVI. MacBride noted that McQuaid had looked worried at their meeting but did not tell him that he had received a letter from Montini.

59   NAI, DFA Secretary's Files, P 126/1.

60   Dermot Keogh, in *Ireland and the Vatican* devotes a chapter to 'Seán MacBride and the Nuncio crisis,' pp. 265–311.

61   Quoted by Keogh, *Ireland and the Vatican*, p. 310.

62   Conor Cruise O'Brien, *Memoir*, pp. 99–103.

63   Anonymous to McQuaid, 1951, DDA, AB8/B/XVIII/18.

Chapter 16: 'The Arch-Druid of Drumcondra', 1950–51

1   ICD 1951, for events for 1950. Even the expenses of illuminating St Peter's (oil-lamps lighted by hand) were borne by Ireland, with McQuaid's lead. For the adulation of Pius XII in the Holy Year, see *Angelic Shepherd* by Fr Senan O.F.M., C.A.P., with an imprimatur from Joannes Carolus.

2   ICD 1951, for August 15, 1950, p. 752. In *Just Like Yesterday,* León Ó Broin disclosed that the introduction of a Sunday Mass broadcast on radio for the sick and housebound was proposed by him and accepted by McQuaid.

3   McQuaid to Lucas, January 8, 1950, DDA, AB8/B/XV/d. Lucas asked McQuaid for a ten-year loan of up to £50,000 (£1 million), free of interest, to build a major seminary in Pretoria.

4   Not once in the nine years of his reign had McQuaid trusted in the charity of the faithful, without immediately benefitting from 'the touching loyalty of their full cooperation.'

5   Subscribers to the fund were enrolled among the benefactors of the College and shared in the Masses and prayers for their souls. McQuaid thanked Mother Mary Carew for a generous cheque of £250 towards the Maynooth appeal.

6   Towey, *Irish De la Salle Brothers in Christian Education*. I am grateful to

Loreto Byrne for this reference.

7   McQuaid to Lucas, January 8, 1950, DDA, AB8/B/XV/d.

8   McQuaid to Treacy, April 1, 1948, quoted in 'Celebrating a Jubilee: Mari-anella 1910–1994', by Brendan McConvery C.SS.R.

9   McQuaid to Treacy, June 10, 1948, 'Celebrating a Jubilee.'

10 Ibid.

11 McQuaid to the Chief Rabbi Jakobovits, May 26, 1949, DDA, AB8/B/XV.

12 McQuaid to Paro, June 13, 1949, DDA, AB8/B/XVII. 'I have kept my Gov-ernment informed of these interviews in view of the interest that the Government is taking in the Holy Places,' McQuaid wrote. 'I shall have pleasure in letting you know any further developments which could interest the Secretariate of State.'

13 Ryan to McQuaid, June 11, 1949, DDA, AB8/B/XXII/a/7, Maria Duce. The previous August, McQuaid had decided not to interfere in the policy of Maria Duce.

14 Denis Fahey, *Apologia Pro Vita Sua*, DDA, AB8/B/XXII/a/7.

15 Mangan to Agar, December 12, 1948, DDA, AB8/B/XXII/a/7.

16 Agar to Mangan, November 5, 1948, DDA, AB8/B/XXIIa/7. The names and addresses of the original executive committee of Maria Duce, with an address at 5 Cavendish Row, Dublin, were: John Cullen, 90 Haddington Rd; A. O'Connor, 269 Harold's Cross Rd; A.J. Sheerin, 9 Palmerston Park; Capt. G. O'Gorman-Quinn, 26 Garville Ave, Rathgar; F. Murtagh, St Declan's Terrace, Marino; J. Smith, Garda Depot, Phoenix Rd; V. Collins, 99 Seafield Rd, Clontarf; John Ryan, 34 Terenure Park, Terenure; T. Roseingrave, 26 Highfield Rd; J.M. Desbonnet, 5 Cavendish Rd; P.B. Cos-tello, 11 Lower Abbey St; and T.J. Agar, 56 Shandon Park.

17 Agar to Mangan, January 3, 1949, DDA, AB8/B/XXII/a/7.

18 Agar to Mangan, January 19, 1949, DDA, AB8/B/XXII/a/7. Generally, McQuaid remained sympathetic towards Fahey, a review of whose work in the Roman journal *Civilita Cattolica* he had admired. McQuaid also thanked Fahey for his critique of the Irish dramatist and Socialist, George Bernard Shaw. He expressed his regret at Fahey's difficulties in obtaining an imprimatur from Bishop Staunton of Ferns for his booklet on *The Tragedy of James Connolly*. Fahey sent, and McQuaid read, intelli-gence reports on American Jewish spies, the most successful being Newman Levy, who operated under the name Wilson Warren Colby. Pri-vately, McQuaid told Fahey that he was 'nauseated' by a particularly savage attack on him in the *Irish Catholic*.

19 Agar to Mangan, April 21, 1949, DDA, AB8/B/XXII/a/7.

20 In the late 1950s the focus of vexation was the pamphlet, 'The Church, the State and the Constitution,' by Donald Barrington, the future Supreme Court Judge, published by the Catholic Truth Society of Ireland.

21 Curley to McQuaid, October 4, 1949, DDA, AB8/B/XXII/a/7.

22 Secretary to Curley, October 10, 1949, DDA, AB8/B/XXII/a/7.

23 'Censorship and worse,' *Standard*, October 21, 1950.

24 McQuaid note, November 23, 1949, DDA, AB8/B/XXII/a/7.

25 Roseingrave became the first Irish chairman of the EEC's Economic and Social Committee.

26 ICD 1951, for June 1950, pp. 744–45.

27 Kavanagh to McQuaid, April 24, 1951, DDA, AB8/B/XXII/a/2.

28 Hierarchy minutes, October 1949, DDA, AB8/B/XV/b.

29 Minutes of Hierarchy meeting, June 1949, DDA, AB8/B/XV/b.

30 Blanshard, *The Irish and Catholic Power*, p. 103.

31 McKenzie to McQuaid, January 13, 1950, DDA, AB8/B/XXII/a/2.

32 Devane to McQuaid, September 26, 1950, DDA, AB8/B/VXIII/14.

33 Quoted in Blanshard, p. 116. Devane also warned that 'the alien pen will accomplish in a few decades what the alien sword failed to achieve in centuries.'

34 Blanshard, p. 119.

35 Ryan to McQuaid, July 19, 1949, DDA, AB8/B/XXII/a/7.

36 Ó Tuathail to McQuaid, August 18, 1950, DDA, AB8/B/XXII/a/7.

37 Michael Gorman to author.

38 Ibid.

39 Peter Gatenby, *Dublin's Meath Hospital*.

40 Bowen, *Protestants in a Catholic State*; White, *Minority Report*.

41 McQuaid to Cohalan, July 19, 1949, DDA, AB8/B/XV/a.

42 Bolster, *Knights of St Columbanus*, p. 112.

43 McQuaid note, June 1950, DDA, AB8/B/XV/b.

44 Walshe to McQuaid, August 24, 1950, DDA, AB8/B/XV111/6.

45 Tilson Infants, Court Judgements, *Irish Ecclesiastical Record*, June 1951.

46 Ibid.

47 I obtained a copy from an anonymous 'source' after an introduction by journalist Susan McKay.

48 For a more detailed account, see Mike Milotte, *Banished Babies*.

49 McQuaid to McKenzie, DDA, AB8/XXII/a/2.

50 *Irish Press*, September 22, 1950.

51 Walshe to McQuaid, March 13, 1950, DDA, AB8/B/XVIII/6. 'You will be glad to hear,' Walshe wrote in May,' that the President (O'Kelly) gave your affectionate good wishes to the Holy Father.' Pius was at the height of his autocracy as 'Emperor of Rome' (John Cornwell's phrase) – Vatican officials took phone calls from him on their knees.

52 Walshe to McQuaid, April 17, 1950, DDA, AB8/B/XVIII/6. Montini realised the Columbanus Chapel's full import as 'a unifying and Romanising symbol for our Catholic people all over the world.' A key figure in the expediting of the project was Monsignor Ludwig Kaas, the former chair-man of the German Centre Party. 'As you know he is an intimate adviser

of the Holy Father with whom he constantly confers,' Walshe told McQuaid. Pope Pius XII's lay adviser was Count Enrico Galeazzi. Walshe counselled McQuaid to thank Montini, Kaas and Galeazzi for their support of the Chapel project. Kaas wanted an immediate financial instalment for the project; McQuaid obliged diligently.

53 In his address to Pius, Stephen McKenzie said, 'Dr McQuaid ... has the love and esteem of the people of Ireland.' It was not until 1954 that McQuaid said the inaugural Mass in the Chapel of St Columbanus.

54 *Irish Press*, July 22, 1950: 'Tricolours display at Luxeuil.'

55 Before reaching Luxeuil de Valera and his son Vivion honoured Père Lamy at his birthplace.

56 ICD 1951, for events 1950, pp. 750-51.

57 Walshe to McQuaid, August 24, 1950, DDA, AB8/B/XVIII/6. Walshe wanted McQuaid to look after Commendatore Menini, the Manager of the Roman Opere di Religione, the Vatican Bank, who was planning to visit Ireland. In 1951 McQuaid met Archbishop Montini while he was in Ireland on holiday.

58 Collier to McQuaid, August 2, 1950, DDA, AB8/B/XV/a.

59 MacNamee to McQuaid, November 11,1948, DDA, AB8/B/XV/a.

60 McQuaid to Costello, May 1950, DDA, AB8/B/XVIII. 'Cardinal has now varied purpose of centre 'for all denominations.' No one had ever mentioned this aspect.'

61 *Irish Independent*, October 16, 1950.

62 Peter Hebblethwaite, *John XXIII.*

63 ICD 1951, for October 8, 1950.

64 Bolster, *Knights of St Columbanus*, p. 106.

65 *Irish Press*, November 2, 1950.

66 Conroy's Presidential address, July 18, 1951.

Chapter 17: Mother and Child, 1950–51

1 The documents written in McQuaid's own hand in the Dublin Diocesan Archives, AB8/B/XVIII/20, listed as Mother and Child Scheme (MCS), provide a wealth of new material about the inside story of the Mother and Child controversy. Principally, these are: report to Standing Commitee of Hierarchy, January 16, 1951; notes on events in March, 1951; report to Standing Committee of Hierarchy, April 3, 1951; summary report to the General Meeting of Hierarchy, April 4, 1951; notes on events since Hierarchy's Meeting; draft of answer presented to Standing Committee of Hierarchy, April 3, 1951, and accepted at the General Meeting on April 4, 1951; secret report to Apostolic Nuncio, April 15, 1951; and notes and events since Hierarchy's Meeting.

2 For the background, see Ruth Barrington's excellent *Health, Medicine and*

Politics in Ireland 1900–70.

3   McQuaid to de Valera, January 23, 1946, NAI, Cabinet Files, S 13444C.

4   Barrington, Ruth, *Health, Medicine and Politics*, p. 172.

5   Barrington, p. 172

6   Statement of the Hierarchy on the Health Act, 1947, DVA, 1440/6. Appendix A.

7   De Valera to Staunton, February 16, 1948, DVA, 1440/6. Appendix B.

8   Michael McInerney, 'Nöel Browne: Church and State', *University Review*, Vol. V, No. 2, 1968.

9   Richard Whyte to Dr O'Connell, February 1, 1950, DDA, MCS.

10 Patrick Dargan to McQuaid, February 20, 1950, DDA, MCS.

11 Bolster, Evelyn, *The Knights of Columbanus*, p. 97.

12 These examples are cited by Browne in *Against the Tide*, pp. 143–47. Browne was aghast when McQuaid dismissed a proposal for nuns to visit in their homes children who had temporarily lost their mothers who were in sanatoria with tuberculosis – the Archbishop claimed that the sight of nuns going into a a home where the wife was known to be absent 'would give scandal.'

13 Ibid. P. 157.

14 Staunton to Costello, October 10, 1950, DDA, MCS.

15 *Against the Tide*, pp. 159–161.

16 Dail Debates, CXXV, pp. 739–40.

17 *Against the Tide*, pp. 161–62.

18 Irish Medical Association, Report of the Conference held at the Department of Health on November 24, 1950, between the Minister for Health and a deputation appointed by the Association to discuss Proposals in connection with a Mother and Child Health Scheme under Part III of the Health Act, 1947.

19 Roantree to McQuaid, November 7, DDA, MCS.

20 McQuaid to Bishop Browne, December 9, 1950, DDA, MCS.

21 Dr Browne to McQuaid, March 6, 1951, DDA, MCS.

22 As to the origins of the phrase, former Army Officer J.P. Duggan recalls a discussion at McKee Barracks about the Mother and Child Scheme in which he remarked that a belt of the crozier would quickly bring Browne into line. The phrase went into circulation. Duggan to author, June 14, 1995.

23 McQuaid to Costello, March 8, 1951, DDA, MCS.

24 McQuaid to Browne, March 8, 1951, DDA, MCS.

25 Costello to McQuaid, March 9, 1951, DDA, MCS.

26 Costello to Browne, March 15, 1951, DDA, MCS.

27 Memorandum of observations of the Minister for Health on various matters relating to the Mother and Child Scheme.

28 Staunton to McQuaid, March 31, DDA, MCS.

29 *Against the tide*, p. 169

30 Ibid p. 170.

31 McQuaid to Costello, April 4, 1951, DDA, MCS

32 McQuaid to D'Alton, April 5, 1951, DDA, MCS.

33 McQuaid to D'Alton, April 6, 1951, DDA, MCS.

34 Costello to McQuaid, April 9, 1951, DDA, MCS.

35 McQuaid to Costello, April 10,1951, DDA, M.C.S.

36 D'Alton to McQuaid, April 10,1951, DDA, MCS.

37 McQuaid to D'Alton, April 11,1951, DDA, MCS.

38 *The Irish Times*, April 12, 1951.

39 Dail Debates, Browne's Personal Statement, April 12, 1951, pp 667–75.

40 McQuaid to D'Alton, April 12, DDA, MCS.

41 O'Neill to McQuaid, April 13, DDA, MCS.

42 D'Alton to McQuaid, April 13, DDA, MCS.

43 Walsh to McQuaid, April 14, DDA, MCS.

44 Foreign and Commonwealth Papers. Quoted in *The Irish Times*, January 1–2, 1982.

45 Quoted in *Faulkner* by Andrew Boyd, p. 35.

46 Author's interview with Sam McAughtry.

47 *John Charles McQuaid: What the Papers Say.* To explain his stance McQuaid commissioned Fr James Kavanagh to write a popular exposition of the Catholic Church's case.

48 McQuaid mistakenly thanked Michael Derrick for writing the article.

49 *La Croix*, April 24, 1951.

50 Quoted in Cooney, *The Crozier and the Dáil*, p. 23.

51 Lee, J.J., *Ireland, 1912–85*. p. 319. For a more pro-McQuaid view, see 'Medics, Mitres and Ministers' by Joe Dunn in *No Vipers in the Vatican,* pp. 177–95.

Chapter 18: McQuaid's Dreary Eden, 1940–73

1 Nöel Browne, 'A Virgin Ireland.' The manuscript in Trinity College, Dublin, is dated, October 1989. He described McQuaid as 'a cardboard figure of fear.'

2 D'Alton congratulated McQuaid on the completion of 'a very efficient task,' though it would probably not satisfy all the critics, April 19, 1951, DDA, AB8/B/XVIII/20.

3 Gene Kerrigan, *Another Country, Growing Up in '50s Ireland.*

4 Ruth Barrington, *Health, Medicine and Politics*, p.149, based on notes of an interview conducted by John Whyte with Dr F.C. Ward, June 18, 1966.

5 Memorandum on The National Film Institute of Ireland from the Hon. Secretary, Brigid Redmond to McQuaid, October 3, 1943, DDA, AB8/B/XXII.

6   Godfrey to McQuaid, December 16, no year given, c.1943–44, DDA, AB8/B/XXII.

7   Browne, *Against the Tide*, p. 157. Browne described the remark as 'this strange interlude.'

8   Stopes literature, DDA, AB8/A, Blackrock College Years section.

9   Fennelly to McQuaid, October 8, 1935, DDA, AB8/A/II.

10   McQuaid to Lucey, December 31, 1952, DDA, AB8/B/XV/a.

11   McQuaid Note on Evil Literature, November 19, 1953, DDA, AB8/B/XV/III. Writing on this episode in the *Sunday Independent*, April 12, 1998, Professor Ronan Fanning also noted that McQuaid declined to attend a Pageant of St Patrick at Croke Park because a Protestant was playing the part of the national saint and, to add injury to insult, it was being directed by Dublin's most celebrated gay couple, Hilton Edwards and Micheál MacLiammóir.

12   NAI, D/T, S2321A.

13   Unsigned Dept. of Justice Minute, December 14, 1953, NAI, D/T, S2321A.

14   McQuaid to de Valera, December 29, 1953, NAI, D/Taoiseach, S2321A.

15   Interview by author with the late Jack McQuillan.

16   McQuaid to Boland, DDA, AB8/B/XVIII/5.

17   Moore quoted in Carlson, *Banned in Ireland*, p. 113.

18   T.P. Coogan, *De Valera*, p. 652.

19   Confidential source.

20   Michael McCann to author.

21   McQuaid to McKenzie, DDA, AB8/B/XXII/a/2.

22   Flynn to McQuaid, DDA, AB8/B/XXII/a/2.

23   McQuaid to Birch, April 19, 1970, DDA, AB8/B/XV/a.

24   Information from Brian Quinn.

25   Buckley, *A Thorn in the Side*, p. 20.

26   'A thoroughly laid-back prelate', *Evening Herald*, June 90, 1986.

27   Author's interview with Mrs Simms, 1995.

28   Burke Savage, *Studies*, Winter, 1965. McQuaid persuaded the Gárdaí to run a Catholic boys club in Finglas headed by Chief Superintendant O'Meara, supported by Dublin Vocational Education Committee and the Department of Education.

29   *Irish Independent*, December 11, 1961.

30   Interview with author.

31   Interview with author.

32   Nöel Browne, 'A Virgin Ireland.'

33   Browne was interviewed by the then Fr Pat Buckley, now a Bishop of the Tridentine ritual, for an academic thesis for Queen's University Belfast, during which the inspector's allegation against McQuaid was discussed. Specifically, Browne was asked to define the nature of McQuaid's sexual drive. 'He was a pederast really,' Browne replied.

Chapter 19: Ecclesiastical Taoiseach, 1951–55

1 *Irish Press*, October 8, 1951.
2 Ibid for the full text of the prayer composed in the genre of the seventeenth-century French school of devotional writing.
3 McQuaid addressed the message to Monsignor Montini.
4 O'Hara to McQuaid, September 12, 1952, DDA, AB8/B/XVII/5.
5 Benelli correspondence, DDA, AB8/B/XVII/4, Senior Vatican church sources still speak of the Benelli-McQuaid stand-off.
6 Hayes to McQuaid, 1955, DDA, AB8/B/XXII/ b/3.
7 McQuaid to Hurley, April 2, 1952, DDA, AB8/B/XV/d. McQuaid could spare no priests for the American mission.
8 McQuaid to Levame, July 26, 1955, DDA, AB8/B/XVII/6.
9 Colin Conroy, *Historic Merrion*, p. 17.
10 Feeney, *The Man and the Mask*, p. 38. The McQuaid Papers reveal that even though the Catholic Church on continental Europe was modernising liturgy, in 1953 he refused the German Ambassador permission to hold a Christmas midnight Mass for select guests in a small church at which the celebrant would preach in German. 'Your Excellency is scarcely aware that the fixed tradition of this diocese is opposed to the project,' he wrote.
11 McQuaid to Sr Teresita, February 18, 1954, DDA, AB8/B/XVIII/26.
12 McQuaid annotation on letter from Dunne, March 13, 1954, DDA, AB8/B/XV/a.
13 Lord Mayor of London to McQuaid, February 24, 1953, DDA, AB8/B/XVIII/41. McQuaid also sent telegrams to the British Royalty on occasions of bereavement.
14 Farrelly to McQuaid, March 24, 1954, DDA, AB8/B/XVII/d.
15 Dell'Acqua to McQuaid, January 28, 1955, DDA, AB8/B/XVI/3.
16 *Irish Press*, May 16, 1954; ICD 1955, events for 1954, p. 633.
17 'Old girls remember old times,' *The Irish Times*, May 11, 1997.
18 Dublin Lenten Regulations: 'Fast to be kept', *Irish Press*, February 25, 1952.
19 Paul Blanshard, *The Irish and Catholic Power*, pp. 165–66.
20 McQuaid to Lucey, November 11, 1953, DDA, AB8/B/XV/a.
21 McQuaid to Dunne, August 25, 1953, DDA, AB/8/B/XV/a.
22 Dunne to McQuaid, July 1, 1953, DDA, AB8/B/XV/a.
23 McQuaid to Miltenburg, May 19, 1954, DDA, AB8/B/XV/d.
24 Minutes of Hierarchy meeting, October 13, 1953, DDA, AB8/B/XV/b/7.
25 Obituary appreciation by R.M. (Richard Mulcahy) of Bishop Alvarro de Portillo, *The Irish Times*, May 4, 1994.
26 Gabriel Fallon, 'Dublin's holy hooliganism', *Standard*, January 4, 1952.
27 McQuaid to O'Reilly, January 21, 1952, DDA, AB8/B/XXII.

28 Ó Tuathail to McQuaid, June 7, 1952, DDA, AB8/B/XXII.

29 Ó Tuathail to Manager, Theatre Royal, June 7, 1952, DDA, AB8/B/XXII.

30 Ó Tuathail to Manager, Metropole Cinema, September 24, 1952, DDA, AB8/B/XXII.

31 On account of his attendance in 1950 at the proclamation of the dogma of the Assumption, McQuaid was dispensed by Cardinal Aeodato Piazza of making an *Ad Limina* visit to Rome in 1952.

32 When the Vatican Library received microfilms of 67 manuscript volumes removed by Napoleon Bonaparte, but subsequently obtained by Trinity College, McQuaid noted, cynically, 'interesting that Trinity did not restore the loot.'

33 Éamon Delaney to author, September 23, 1998.

34 McQuaid to D'Alton, December 29, 1951, DDA, AB8/B/XV/a.

35 MacNamee to McQuaid, DDA, AB8/B/XV/a.

36 Moynihan to McQuaid, November 6, 1952, DDA, AB8/B/XV/a.

37 Collier to McQuaid, October 24, 1952, DDA, AB8/B/XV/a.

38 Tom Garvin, 'The strange death of clerical politics in University College, Dublin,' in *Irish University Review*, Vol. 28, No. 2, Autumn-Winter, 1998, pp. 308–14. Horgan was noted for being friendly with students with Grecian features, according to university sources.

39 Ibid.

40 J. Anthony Gaughan. On a suggestion from O'Rahilly that a booklet should be published on the minimum Catholic requirements in university education, McQuaid opted for an update of the 1933 brochure by the late Bishop of Clonfert, John Dignan, *Catholics and Trinity College*.

41 O'Rahilly regarded McQuaid as holy, but difficult and peculiar. McQuaid found O'Rahilly completely docile. Lucey and UCC staff members were against O'Rahilly's ordination.

42 McQuaid to Rev. Professors Lucey and McCarthy, DDA, AB8/B/XV/b.

43 Statement issued by McQuaid, January 10, 1952.

44 Coyne to Mangan, November 4, 1952, DDA, AB8/B/XVIII/11.

45 Ibid.

46 McQuaid to D'Alton, Personal, September 8, 1952, DDA, AB8/B/XV/a.

47 Proposals for Improved and Extended Health Services, July 1952.

48 McQuaid, DDA, AB8/B/XVIII/21.

49 McQuaid to D'Alton, September 8, 1952, DDA, AB8/B/XVIII/21.

50 Ibid.

51 Ibid.

52 Ibid.

53 Ryan to McQuaid, September 10, 1952, DDA, AB8/B/XVIII/21.

54 McQuaid to Lemass, September 11, 1952, DDA, AB8/B/XVIII/21.

55 McQuaid to Ryan, September 11, 1952, DDA, AB8/BXVIII/21.

56 Secretary's note, September 13, 1952, DDA, AB8/B/XVIII/21.

57 McQuaid note, September 13, 1952, DDA, AB8/B/XVIII/21.

58 Ibid.

59 McQuaid note of Ryan interview, September 16, 1952, DDA.

60 Barrington, *Health, Medicine and Politics*, p. 230.

61 McQuaid note, September 26, 1952, DDA, AB8/B/XVIII/21.

62 McQuaid note, October 6, 1952, DDA, AB8/B/XVIII/21. 'Points for the meeting with the Minister of Health.'

63 Report to the General Meeting of the Hierarchy, October 14, 1952, DDA, AB8/B/XVIII/21.

64 McQuaid to D'Alton, October 22, 1952, DDA, AB8/B/XVIII/21.

65 McQuaid to Lemass, October 6, 1952, DDA, AB8/B/XVIII/21.

66 Lemass to McQuaid, October 8, 1952, DDA, AB8/B/XVIII/21.

67 McQuaid to Lemass, October 8, 1952, DDA, AB8/B/XVIII/21.

68 McQuaid to O'Hara, November 7, 1952, DDA, AB8/B/XVIII/21.

69 De Valera to Lemass, November 19, 1952, Lemass Papers. I am grateful to Michael O'Sullivan for this reference.

70 Kinane address, DVA, 1281. This speech is a key source expressing the prerogatives of the Irish Hierarchy at the height of their power in the mid-twentieth century.

71 McQuaid note, DDA, AB8/B/XVIII/21.

72 De Valera to D'Alton, DVA, 1281.

73 O'Connell to McQuaid, October 14, 1953, DDA, AB8/B/XVI/20.

74 Accompanied by Monsignor Glennon, McQuaid travelled to Shannon Airport on Good Friday for a flight to New York. The next leg of the journey brought him to Sydney via San Francisco, Honolulu and Fiji. During stopovers McQuaid and Glennon had meetings with Cardinal Spellman, Archbishop John Mitty and Bishop James J. Sweeney at which they reviewed Irish adoptions and the application of McQuaid's guidelines.

75 McQuaid, *Wellsprings of the Faith*, pp. 228–33.

76 Ibid, pp. 213–22.

77 Feeney, *The Man and the Mask*, p. 30.

78 Ronan Fanning, 'Fianna Fáil and the bishops', *The Irish Times*, February 13 and 14, 1985.

79 Dunne to McQuaid, May 1, 1953, DDA, AB8/B/XV/a.

80 Author's interview with Aidan Lehane C.S.Sp.

81 McQuaid note, DDA, AB8/B/XVIII/21.

82 McQuaid to Ryan, January 24, 1954, DVA, 1440/6.

83 Ryan to McQuaid, DVA, 1440/6.

84 McQuaid to Ryan, DVA, 1440/6.

85 Moylan to Ryan, DVA, 1440/6.

86 Ibid.

87 De Valera to McQuaid, DVA, 1440/6.

88 McQuaid to de Valera, DVA, 1440/6.

89 Typescript article by the late T.P. O'Neill.

90 MacBride to McQuaid, May 25, 1954, DDA, AB8/B/XVIII/40.

91 McQuaid to MacBride, May 26, 1954, DDA, AB8/B/XVIII/40.

92 Walshe to McQuaid, May 26, 1954, DDA, AB8/B/XVIII/6.

93 A detailed study of Walshe would help further illuminate his relationship with McQuaid in promoting their shared vision of Irish Catholicism.

94 Cited by former General Secretary of the Department of Foreign Affairs, Seán Donlon, in an address to the Humbert Summer School, Co. Mayo, August 1999.

95 Transactions, Sixth International Congress of Catholic Doctors, Dublin, 1954.

96 As McQuaid delivered his address he was puzzled by the absence of the Archbishop of Tuam. Next day Walsh explained that he missed the celebration because his ring got damaged and he had to take it to a jeweller. Walsh to McQuaid, July 20, 1954, DDA, AB8/B/XV/a.

97 *Wellsprings of the Faith*, July 4, 1954.

98 *Graham Greene: The Man Within*, Michael Shelden. Greene called Pizzardo 'Pissardo'.

99 *John Charles McQuaid: What the Papers Say*.

100 Ibid.

101 McQuaid note, November 11, 1954, DDA.

102 In a note on the history of Maria Duce (AB8/B/XXII/7), McQuaid accepted its change of name to Fírinne (Truth). He ordered this because of 'the disedification and resentment' which 'Ducists' caused among Catholics by views and methods that were linked to Our Blessed Lady's name. McQuaid informed Archbishop Levame that since the death of Fr Fahey, Maria Duce was almost isolated from the clergy. McQuaid had ordered two priests to investigate its activities and when opposition to it emerged, the Holy Ghost Superior had ordered six of his priests to withdraw. While accepting that Article 44 of the Constitution was defective, McQuaid felt that Maria Duce's methods to repeal this section 'have given grave cause for anxiety.'

103 McQuaid to Lucey, June 16, 1954, DDA, AB8/B/XV/a.

104 McQuaid to Levame, July 26, 1954, DDA, AB8/B/XVII/6. McQuaid had also informed Archbishop O'Hara in July 1952 of this breach of civil law.

105 Dáithi Hanly, *The Irish Times*, January 22, 1999. McQuaid's role was unknown to Peter Pearson in his reference to the sculpture in his marvellous book, *Between the Mountains and the Sea*.

106 McQuaid to Levame, July 26, 1954, DDA.

Chapter 20: McQuaid's Drumbeats, 1955–59

1   *The Irish Times*, October 17, 1955. The McQuaid Papers cast new light on the Archbishop's role in an incident that remains fixed in the popular mind as ill-judged pantomime, DDA, AB8/B/XXII/b/1.

2   In his letter to McQuaid, dated January 17, 1952, Wickham indicated that the FAI had already turned down an invitation to play Yugoslavia in 1951 and therefore needed 'a reasonable excuse' to say no a second time. McQuaid, though he regarded the proposed match as very inadvisable, did not meet a delegation from the Association as requested, confirming in Wickham's mind that he had little time for soccer.

3   'O'Kelly told not to attend soccer match,' by Stephen O'Brien, *Irish Independent*, January 1–2, 1991. Report based on release of State papers.

4   *The Irish Times*, October 17, 1955.

5   Evelyn Bolster, *Knights of St Columbanus*, p. 107. Bolster claims that McQuaid took umbrage because of the failure of the FAI to consult him.

6   *The Irish Times*, October 18, 1955.

7   'Red card that failed to see Communists off,' by Denis Walsh, *The Sunday Times*, September 15, 1998.

8   Quoted by Michael McInerney in 'Nöel Browne: Church and State', *University Review*, Vol. V, No. 2, 1968.

9   Secretary to McQuaid, October 20, 1955, DDA, AB8/B/XXII/b/1 Alibrandi complained about the timid attitude of the *Irish Independent* and termed the *Irish Press* anti-clerical. The incident, he concluded, showed the need for a daily Catholic paper. McQuaid later unsuccessfully tried to establish an Irish publication modelled on *The Tablet*, the London-based Catholic weekly.

10 Mrsic to McQuaid, October 21, 1955, DDA, AB8/B/XXII/b/1.

11 McQuaid to Mrsic, November 5, 1955, DDA, AB8/B/XXII/b/1.

12 Wickham to Levame, November 4, 1955, DDA, AB8/B/XXII/b/1.

13 McQuaid to Levame, November 9, 1955, DDA, AB8/B/XXII/b/1.

14 Ryan to Mangan, December 7, 1955, DDA, AB8/B/XXII/b/1. This was sent by Fr Tom Ryan of the Vatican Secretariat of State.

15 Anonymous, DDA, AB8/B/XXII/b/1.

16 Author's interview with Sam McAughtry.

17 Quoted in *Irish Independent* report of Cabinet archives, January 1/2, 1991.

18 *Belfast Telegraph,* no date on cutting in McQuaid Papers.

19 P.J. Kilroy, October 26, 1955, DDA, AB8/B/XXII/b/1.

20 John Cooney broadcast on Today FM, April 5, 1998.

21 *John Charles McQuaid: What the Papers Say*.

22 Secretary's Note, October 20, 1955, DDA, AB8/B/XXII/b/1.

23 *Sunday Times*, September 15, 1998. The Yugoslav match sowed the seeds of McQuaid's image as a bogeyman.

24 The four priests were W. Byrne, John McCarthy, Thomas Menton and Martin Byrne.

25 McQuaid to Finnegan, February 26, 1957, DDA, AB8/B/XXII/b/1.

26 Meeting of the committee of priests to consider the means of apostolate among the Association Football, February 1956, DDA, AB8/B/XXII/b/1.

27 MacMahon to McQuaid, note of Finnegan interview, October 10, 1957, DDA, AB8/B/XXII/b/1.

28 Ibid.

29 Interview with Finnegan, October 13, 1955, DDA, AB8/B/XXII/b/1.

30 McQuaid to Moynagh, October 15, 1957, DDA, AB8/B/XV/d.

31 McQuaid's annotation on letter of Cowderoy, November 7, 1955, DDA, AB8/B/XV.

32 McQuaid himself never romanticised Germany, regarding it as the land of Luther. He did not attend the festival of St Kilian in Würzburg.

33 Mangan to Mother Heskin, archives of the Irish Sisters of Charity. McQuaid ensured that nuns observed the Regulations for Holy Week including provisions limiting the number of candles on the Altar of Repose to twenty, a maximum of four vases of flowers, and public adoration was to end at midnight. As regards the law of Eucharistic Fast, the following rules were to be observed by convents in the Dublin Diocese – solid food could be taken only up to three hours before a ceremony; no alcoholic spirits were to be taken later than the previous midnight; alcoholic table-drinks such as wine and beer might be taken during a meal, but only in suitable moderation and to the exclusion of spirits; and non-alcoholic drinks such as tea and coffee might be taken up to one hour beforehand. Water might be taken at any time beforehand.

34 James Kavanagh, 'Social Activist,' Studies, Winter, 1998.

35 Purcell, Remembering Matt Talbot, p.123.

36 Hierarchy meeting, DDA, AB8/B/XV/b.

37 Burke Savage, Studies, Winter, 1965.

38 Rupp to McQuaid, November 29, 1957, DDA, AB8/B/XV/d. The Auxiliary Bishop of Paris also enlisted McQuaid onto the Committee of Honour of the Friends of Joan of Arc.

39 Hierarchy minutes, DDA, AB8/B/XV/b.

40 McQuaid to Mageean, July 24, 1958, DDA, AB8/B/XV/a. More than 1,400 workers marched in procession to the Church of Mary Immaculate, Inchicore, in honour of their forefathers, who a century earlier had built in five days the first Oblate Church in Ireland.

41 McQuaid annotation on letter from Gallen, July 16, 1956, DDA, AB8/B/XXII.

42 McQuaid's instruction to Lord Wicklow backfired as his publishing company did not engage in the sale of books of other publishers. Wicklow exonerated himself.

43 Archbishop Finbar Ryan told McQuaid that the book would be 'a

monument of your consuming zeal for the souls of young people.' In *Studies,* Fr Fergal McGrath described McQuaid's letters as 'models of pastoral instruction.' Cardinal Gilroy of Sydney wrote that 'every address and article written by his Grace is a gem.'

44 ICD 1957, p. 649. McQuaid took a special pride in his mastery of medical matters, but his sense of intellectual superiority was unable to distinguish the boundaries between informed and professional knowledge. For instance, as President of the Catholic Institute for the Deaf, he opted for the oral system of education rather than the more successful bilingual system, but after being frustrated in getting the management of St Joseph's School for Boys in Cabra to adopt it, he built a new school for deaf boys in Stillorgan which failed to win the confidence of parents and is now closed. I am grateful to Ned Crean for this information.

45 McQuaid to Costello, DDA, AB8/B/XVIII. Securing State grants without relinquishing control over Catholic hospitals was a major priority for McQuaid, as illustrated in a letter to him from Dr A.B. Clery, September 3, 1956, suggesting that representation on the Cancer Association could be achieved for grant-purposes without in any way being put 'under' that body. Clery signed himself as 'Your Grace's obedient child.'

46 ICD 1957, p. 649.

47 Barrett to Mangan, June 3, 1955, DDA, AB8/B/XV/b.

48 This section follows the narrative revealed in Mike Milotte's investigative, *Banished Babies*.

49 Coyne, November 15, 1955, quoted in Ferriter.

50 DDA, AB8/B/XV/b, Hierarchy box.

51 Hierarchy minutes, DDA, AB8/B/XV/b.

52 Costello to McQuaid, December 20, 1956, DDA, AB8/B/XVIII.

53 Statute No. 287, ICD 1961, p. 694. It came into force on November 15, 1960. The tender of Messrs. Gill & Son, for £93.11. 0d being the lowest, it was accepted by the Hierarchy for the right of publication of the *Acta et Decreta.* Only to be read by clerics, it was sold behind Catholic bookshop counters and was not on public display. It can now be bought as a collector's item.

54 McQuaid to Collier, September 1, 1958; Collier to McQuaid, August 29, 1958, DDA, AB8/B/XV/a.

55 Costello's note about Cabinet response, DDA, AB8/B/XVIII.

56 McQuaid to Levame, December 18, 1956, DDA. In November, McQuaid sent Pius £10,000, raised as Peter's Pence, for his personal use. Dell'Acqua to McQuaid, December 14, 1956, DDA.

57 I am indebted to Dermot Flynn for this recollection. Flynn believes that part of McQuaid's power was based on the impact which he made on the public through restrained exposure.

58 McQuaid to Moynagh, DDA, AB8/B/XV/d.

59 Connolly to Mangan, DDA, AB8/B/XV.

60 Hierarchy minutes, 1956, DDA, AB8/B/XV/b.

61 Hierarchy minutes, 1958, DDA, AB8/B/XV/b.

62 Hierarchy minutes, June 1958, DDA, AB8/B/XV/b. Maynooth students were prohibited from taking vacation employment in England. The first Sunday of October was fixed as Emigrants' Day, but a collection was not considered feasible.

63 Murphy's correspondence with McQuaid is poignant. It is clear that McQuaid broke his spirit by weaning him from the error of Communism before offering him material assistance. McQuaid's treatment of Murphy contrasts with his denunciation of the unrepentant Michael O'Riordan. Not afraid to show the Catholic Church's electoral muscle, McQuaid used the pulpits of the diocese to order his flock, under the pain of mortal sin, not to vote for O'Riordan, a public transport worker and veteran of the Spanish Civil War, who was standing in the 1951 General Election as a Communist. I am grateful to Fr Austin Flannery O.P. for introducing me to Michael O'Riordan.

64 Jack Lynch, *Mission Outlook*, June 1973.

65 *British Medical Journal,* June 8, 1957, described Dr Helen McQuaid as a very fine physician with a marvellous clinical instinct. Excellent company, 'her many English friends loved to listen to her charming Irish voice, with its infectious chuckle, telling stories grave and gay in her own inimitable fashion.' On hearing of her death a former patient said: 'All Putney is in mourning.' She left John Charles £500 in her will for charitable purposes.

66 Author's interview with Senator Joe Doyle.

67 Mangan interview, *Doctrine and Life*, 1990.

68 Moynihan note, NAI, Department of the Taoiseach (D/T), S16247.

69 Carol Coulter, *The Irish Times*, May 10, 1997.

70 *Irish Press*, July 1, 1957.

71 Quoted in Keogh, *Twentieth-Century Ireland*, p. 240.

72 De Valera to McQuaid, July 4, 1957, NAI, D/T. S 16247.

73 McQuaid to de Valera, July 5, DDA, AB8/B/XVIII. McQuaid was in Rockwell College.

74 Forms of Guarantees in mixed marriages, pp. 34–35 in *Acta et Decreta*, 1956.

75 Rodgers to Costello, July 27, 1955, NAI, D/T, S. 16073A.

76 Costello to Rodgers, August 14, 1956, NAI, D/T S. 16073A. Costello to McQuaid, December 20, 1956, DDA, AB8/B/XVIII; Costello to McQuaid, November 13, 1956, DDA, AB8/XVIII.

77 McQuaid to Costello, August 16, 1955, NAI, D/T. S.2321B.

78 The Philbin-McQuaid rapport is worth further study. For example, Philbin warned McQuaid that he had heard severe criticisms of how the Franciscan missionaries of Mary managed a Hospital and Nursing School at Portiuncula, Ballinasloe, Co. Galway.

79 Staunton to McQuaid, January 21, 1958, DDA, AB8/B/XV/a.

80 O'Connell to McQuaid, December 1954, DDA, AB8/B/XVI/20.

81 Dell'Acqua to McQuaid, June 8, 1956, DDA, AB8/B/XVI/4.

82 Hierarchy minutes, June 1956, DDA, AB8/B/XV/b. The bishops were unanimous that the Statutes, approved by the Holy See and tested by long experience, had proved fully adequate for their guidance in all circumstances and needed no revision.

83 Hierarchy minutes, 1958, DDA, AB8/B/XV/b.

84 O'Connell to McQuaid, September 21, 1957, DDA, AB8/B/XVI/20. O'Connell indicated to Pasqualina that the movement might not be suitable in Ireland. He cautioned McQuaid, 'I have not discussed this matter with you.' O'Connell to McQuaid, October 23, 1957.

85 O'Connell to McQuaid, October 10, 1957, DDA, AB8/B/XVI/20.

86 McQuaid to Levame, July 26, 1956, DDA, AB8/B/XVII/6.

87 Information from Ciarán MacGonigal.

88 Hoover to McQuaid, September 17, 1958, DDA, AB8/B/XVIII. It was addressed to Most Reverend John G. McQuaid, D.D. – a classic instance of FBI efficiency!

89 Tom Cox to author. Prof. T.B.H. McMurray also recalls how McQuaid withdrew from a conference under the auspices of the British Association for the Advancement of Science when he discovered that world population problems would be discussed.

90 McQuaid to O'Flynn, July 16, 1954, DDA, AB8/B/XXII/a/2.

91 Swift, *Stage by Stage*, p. 247.

92 Nöel Browne, 'A Virgin Ireland'.

93 ICD 1959, for January 31, 1958, pp. 656–57.

94 Browne to McQuaid, January 29, 1958, DDA, AB/8/B/XV/a. CIÉ has a correspondence file from Archbishop McQuaid in its archives.

95 Gabriel Fallon, 'The Tóstal Affair', *Hibernia*, March 1958.

96 *John Charles McQuaid: What the Papers Say*.

97 Tony Gray, *The Irish Answer*, pp. 244–46.

98 'Bishops pressurised Aiken through US', *Irish Independent*, January 2, 1995.

99 Éamonn Gallagher interview with author.

100 O'Connell to McQuaid, 1958, DDA, AB8/B/XVI/20.

101 Richard Roche's obituary of John Leydon, *Administration*, Vol. 27, No. 3. Crossing McQuaid took its toll – Leydon stepped down from the IPA Presidency.

102 McQuaid to D'Alton, January 9, 1959, DDA, AB/8/B/XV/a.

103 McQuaid to de Valera, July 5.

104 Browne to McQuaid, DDA, AB/8/B/XV/a.

Chapter 21: Elder Church Statesman, 1959–62

1   Hierarchy minutes, June 23, 1959, DDA, AB8/B/XV/b/8.
2   Hierarchy statement on Intoxicating Liquor Laws, June 23, 1959, DDA, AB8/B/XV/b/8.
3   Hierarchy minutes, June 23, 1959, AB8/B/XV/b/8.
4   McQuaid sent the memorandum to D'Alton on May 9, 1959.
5   McQuaid to Traynor, October 28, 1959, AB8/B/XVIII.
6   Dáil debates, Vol. 178, November 25, 1959. Lemass to McQuaid, NAI, DT, S16524D, November 3, 1955.
7   Diarmaid Ferriter has drawn attention to the significance of the passage of this Bill in *A Nation of Extremes*, p. 190. The extent of the disagreement should not be exaggerated as McQuaid needed the support of Lemass to recover money from General Franco for dues owed to the Irish College in Salamanca.
8   Hierarchy minutes, October 13, 1959, AB8/B/ XV/b/8.
9   Spellman to de Valera, June 22, 1959, DVA, 1280.
10 De Valera to MacSwiney, DVA, 1444.
11 De Valera to McQuaid, September 2, 1959, DDA, AB8/B/XVIII/1.
12 De Valera to McQuaid, July 14, 1962, DDA, AB8/B/XVIII/1.
13 Browne to McQuaid, March 31, 1959, DDA, AB/8/B/XV/a.
14 McQuaid to Browne, October 27, 1959, DDA, AB/8/B/XV/a.
15 McQuaid to de Valera, DDA, AB8/B/XVIII/1.
16 As chairman of the Hierarchy's education committee, McQuaid became embroiled in this long-running controversy between O'Boyle and INTO. A row erupted after O'Boyle appointed a Marist Brother as principal of the local school in succession to a layman, Mr Courell. On April 19, O'Connell led an INTO delegation to Drumcondra to brief McQuaid, who seemed very perturbed that a strike should have been called and strongly urged the executive not to proceed with it. McQuaid felt also that the executive should not have gone to the Papal Nuncio without first calling on him or other members of the Irish Hierarchy. The McQuaid Papers show that the bishops told the Holy See that the INTO executive committee did not reflect the views of the vast majority of the Catholic lay teachers of Ireland.
17 Hierarchy minutes, October 13, 1959, DDA, AB8/B/XV/b.
18 The Westminster Diocese's Catholic Women's League had reported to Taoiseach John A. Costello and Archbishop McQuaid in 1953 that there was 'an abnormal flight' of Irish girls to England who were pregnant. In 1959 McQuaid helped to finance a £25,000 (more than £300,000) extension to the Irish Centre in London. Cardinal Godfrey arranged for Irish priests to be assigned to parishes and districts with sizable numbers of Irish parishioners. Frs Aedan McGrath of the Maynooth Mission to China, Paul Boland and Éamonn Gaynor of Killaloe were working in Britain.

McGrath's specific instructions were to foster the Legion of Mary among immigrants, to counteract the influence of the Connolly Clubs and 'to try to get the immigrants to be more apostolic.'

19   Hierarchy minutes, October 1959, Minute 14. 'The Proposed Television Service,' DDA, AB8/B/XV/b/8.

20   J.P. Donleavy, *Ireland – In All Her Sins and In Some of Her Graces*, pp. 209–210. Geraldine Hone, however, recalls McQuaid saying to her that he was being blamed for something for which he was not responsible. On one occasion McQuaid commented wryly to a member of the medical profession about how the saying – 'the Archbishop would not approve' – was readily ascribed to situations without his being in any way consulted. (Quoted by Thomas J. Morrissey in his biography of William Delany S.J.)

21   McQuaid to Murphy, July 1, 1959, DDA, AB8/B/XV/a.

22   Letter of Denis O'Kelly to author, June 29, 1998.

23   De Valera to McQuaid, September 2, 1959, DDA, AB8/B/XVIII/1. Dr John Bowman dissects 'The Wolf in Sheep's Clothing: Richard Hayes's proposal for a new National Library of Ireland, 1959–60', in *Modern Irish Democracy: Essays in honour of Basil Chubb*, edited by Ronald J. Hill and Michael Marsh.

24   Moynihan, note of May 5, 1960, quoted in Bowman.

25   McQuaid to D'Alton, May 4, 1960, Armagh Diocesan Archives.

26   McQuaid to Riberi, March 25, 1960, DDA, AB8/B/XVII/8. Two days earlier Hillery told the Dáil: 'I would not be a party to the creation of a position in which the parents of any religious denomination ... who seek university education for their children, should find themselves with no alternative to the placing of their children, in violation of conscience, in a particular educational institution.'

27   'It was that advice from the Archbishop that made me make up my mind to get well outside the centre of the city,' Tierney said on a radio programme after McQuaid's death.

28   Frank McDonald, *The Destruction of Dublin*. O'Brien had been a Blackrock College student. In conversation with the author former Senator, Jim Dooge, said that copies of all major planning applications were sent to McQuaid as a matter of course in the 1950s.

29   Ibid.

30   Ibid.

31   O'Connell, *Doctor John*. Also see O'Connell's correspondence with McQuaid after he became a T.D., DDA, AB8/B/XVVIII/38.

32   Information from Dr Tony Peacock.

33   Burke Savage, *Studies*, Winter, 1965, p. 304. Further research should confirm that McQuaid supported the practise at the National Maternity Hospital of symphysiotomy as an alternative to Caeserian sections. This operation, which was based on religious grounds, was described by

British obstetricians as 'the midwifery of darker times.' The operation which 'opened the pelvis like a hinge' was common from the mid-1940s until 1960. See Jacqueline Morrisey, *The Irish Times,* September 6, 1999.

34 Medical source.

35 Joseph Robins, *Custom House People*, p. 132. I am grateful to Jim O'Donnell for this reference.

36 Burke Savage, *Studies*, Winter, 1965, p. 324.

37 McQuaid to Riberi, January 30, 1960, DDA, AB8/B/XVII/8.

38 Prill to McQuaid, DDA, AB8/B/XVIII/41. Two years after McQuaid's death, Prill published *Ireland, Britain and Germany, 1870–1914: Problems of Nationalism and Religion in Nineteenth-Century Europe.*

39 Théas to McQuaid, September 8, 1960, DDA, AB/8/B/XV/d. McQuaid stayed in the best establishment, the Metropole Hotel.

40 Théas to McQuaid, April 4, 1959, DDA, AB/8/B/XV/d. In 1959 McQuaid was appointed to the International Lourdes Medical Committee which investigated the authenticity of reported miracles.

41 Arthur J. Walls to author.

42 McQuaid to Morris, February 27, 1960, DDA, AB/8/B/XV/a.

43 Monsignor Boylan, however, appealed to priests to improve the stock of theological works available in the library. Clonliffe library was never renowned for its store of knowledge.

44 Burke Savage, *Studies*, p. 316.

45 McQuaid to Ackerman, September 26, 1962, DDA, AB8/B/XV/d.

46 McQuaid to Van Thien, October 22, 1960, DDA, AB8/B/XV/d.

47 Riberi to McQuaid, January 3, 1961, DDA, AB8/B/XVII/8.

48 McQuaid to Riberi, January 1961, DDA, AB8/B/XVII/8.

49 By the mid-1960s, McQuaid had become distrustful of Opus Dei. 'I had better wait to see you,' he told Bishop William Philbin when the latter enquired about Opus Dei activities in Dublin. 'I never know who these people are or how many they are or what they are doing or what they will next want to do.' (McQuaid to Philbin, February 18, 1965.)

50 Michael McCann to author, June 25, 1998.

51 This was the thundering last paragraph of *Higher Education for Catholics*, issued during Lent, 1961.

52 McConnell to McQuaid, April 18, 1961, DDA, AB8/B/XV/b. McConnell was an Antrim Protestant who was committed to bringing Trinity College into the mainstream of Irish life.

53 J. Anthony Gaughan, *Alfred O'Rahilly*, Vol. III, Part 2, pp. 174–191. McQuaid's secretary, Fr Liam Martin, appealed to O'Rahilly's vanity by describing his case as 'unanswerable', but Brian Fallon, in *An Age of Innocence, Irish Culture, 1930–1960*, p. 266, observes that the scale had fallen from many readers' eyes and they increasingly saw O'Rahilly as 'a pontificating old ass.'

54 McQuaid to Philbin, January 2, 1961, DDA, AB/8/B/XV/a. The Very Rev. Dr J.C. McQuaid C.S.Sp. had addressed the L&H in 1933/4 when Vivion de Valera was Auditor – the subject was 'Pride: The Vice of Modern Times.' Other speakers were Prof. R. Donovan, Prof. William Magennis and Dr J.C. Flood.

55 Tom Garvin, 'The strange death of clerical politics in UCD,' in *Irish University Review*, Vol. 28, No. 2, Autumn-Winter, 1998, pp. 308–314. Ironically, Whyte's book, which underestimates the extent of McQuaidian clericalist control over Irish politics and society, is quoted as Holy Grail by Irish Catholic Church apologists today! Whyte was told by McQuaid that ministers always accorded him courtesy and cordial cooperation, and that he was most struck by the absence of contention (p. 366).

56 Pastoral Letter, 1961.

57 Dunne to McQuaid February 28, 1961, DDA, AB8/B/XV/a. McQuaid replied that he had never sought the honour. 'Honour it is, but a great worry'. The possibility of a public monument to St Patrick, which would replace the Nelson Pillar in O'Connell Street, was raised by McQuaid with Lemass, but it was not feasible.

58 *Irish Independent*, June 17, 1961. Four Army Vampire jets, flying at 11,000 feet over Wicklow Head, escorted Agagianian in the jetliner, *Pádraig*, from the coastline to Dublin Airport.

59 Dunne to McQuaid, DDA, AB8/B/XV/a.

60 Sheen to McQuaid, DDA, AB8/B/XV/d.

61 McQuaid had asked Lemass to speak on 'The Church in the Modern World.'

62 Norton to McQuaid, DDA, AB8/B/XV/d. Nostalgically, Norton recalled reading poetry with McQuaid during his 1953 Australia trip.

63 Ryan to McQuaid, August 7, 1961, DDA, AB8/B/XV/d/26.

64 Agagianian to de Valera, July 9, 1961, DVA.

65 Seán MacRéamoinn recollection.

66 Hederman O'Brien, *The Road to Europe*. McQuaid was offered, but did not accept, the Presidency of the European Movement in Ireland.

67 Obituary of Chlöe Gibson by Tony Barry, *Sunday Tribune*. The opening night was like a Blackrock Old Boys' reunion: de Valera, D'Alton, Jimmy O'Dea and Kevin McCourt, the first Director General, as well as McQuaid were all old 'Rock boys.

68 Information from Brum Henderson.

69 Joe Dunn, *No Vipers in the Vatican*, pp. 263–74.

70 Feeney, *The Man and the Mask*, p. 43.

71 Annual Report Catholic Convent Secretary Schools, 1962, p. 42.

72 McQuaid to Godfrey, June 5, 1962, DDA, AB8/B/XV/d.

73 Godfrey to McQuaid, August 27, 1962, DDA, AB8/B/XV/d.

74 Author's interview with Desmond Fisher.

75 Author's interview with Austin Flannery O.P.

76 *Irish Ecclesiastical Record*, 'The Priests of Ireland: A socio-religious survey', by Jeremiah Newman, August 1962: 'Catholic education is properly the formation to Catholic life. Whoever then in the priesthood is appointed to a post of education, is, by the fact, appointed to assist the bishop in the most fundamental task of the pastoral ministry,' McQuaid wrote to Newman.

77 B.F. Biever, *Religion, Culture and Values: A Cross-Cultural Analysis of Motivational Factors in Native Irish and American Irish Catholicism*, New York, Arno Press, 1976.

78 Tom Garvin, 'Change and the Political System', *Unequal Achievement* (ed. Frank Litton, pp. 30–31).

79 Hierarchy minutes, 1961, DDA, AB8/B/XV/b/8.

80 The artist, Derek Hill, whose haunting portrait of a frightened McQuaid is to be seen in the foyer of St Vincent's Hospital, Dublin, believes that had McQuaid died in 1962 he would be regarded in history as a truly great churchman.

Chapter 22: Roman Winds of Change, 1962–65

1   The McQuaid Papers relating to Vatican Two have not been officially opened, though a preview was allowed to journalists in 1998. O'Regan already missed McQuaid's 'unerring judgment' in administering the Dublin diocese. O'Regan to McQuaid, October 11, 1962, DDA.

2   Keating to author, June 1, 1998. 'I was only 23 years old and it was not common for prominent prelates to be as friendly and courteous' towards a Locus Assignator,' he writes.

3   Hebblethwaite, *Pope John XXIII*, is the best biography of this truly great Pope.

4   John Charles McQuaid, *What is a General Council?* p. 17.

5   John Feeney, *The Man and the Mask*, p. 45. McQuaid had sought the views of senior clergy and religious.

6   Rynne, *Letters from Vatican City*, p. 108.

7   MacMahon was reporting to Fr, later Bishop, Desmond Williams.

8   Scanlan to McQuaid, DDA.

9   For details see John Cooney, *McQuaid at Vatican II, Doctrine and Life*, April 1998. McQuaid reported to D'Alton that there was no evidence whatever about the purposes of meeting. 'We could scarcely refuse the courtesy of the invitation. The same link-up was made in the First Vatican Council.' The French Hierarchy through its expert, Père Gy O.P., invited McQuaid to liaise between French and Irish Hierarchies.

10 Ibid.

11 Ibid.

12 Ibid.

13 For insider analysis of the first session see Peter Hebblethwaite's *John XXIII* and Cardinal Suenens' *Memories and Hopes*.

14 Report of Ambassador Tommy Commins to the Department of External Affairs, NAI, S. 24/184, marked Secret. A former Rockwell College student, Commins displayed an incisive knowledge of Council developments.

15 Hurley, *Christian Unity*, pp. 244–5. De Valera attended and enjoyed the lecture.

16 I am grateful to Emmet Stagg T.D. for a copy, dated November 15, 1962.

17 The American bishop, Joseph Fenton, who kept a diary, was even more unsettled than McQuaid. 'I always thought this Council was dangerous... Now I am afraid real trouble is on the way.' Fenton later blamed Pope John. 'The Pope is definitely a lefty.' Quoted by Guiseppe Alberigo and Joseph A. Komanchak, in *History of Vatican II: Volume 2*, Peeters, Leuven.

18 Henri Fesquet, *Le Bilan du Concile*, the most detailed daily account of the Council proceedings by a great Religious Affairs Correspondent.

19 ICD, 1964, for Events of 1963, p. 686.

20 As McQuaid recorded, this was gifted by the gravely ill Pope John, who at a private audience told the Irish Bishops, smilingly, 'I am not afraid to die for I shall go to the embrace of Our Lord.' Cicognani informed McQuaid that the Chalice should be disposed of at his pleasure. McQuaid sent a copy of Cicognani's letter to President de Valera.

21 McQuaid to Hanly January 5, 1963, DDA, AB/8/B/XV/b.

22 Hanly to Fergus, February 18, 1963, DDA, AB/8/B/XV/b.

23 McQuaid to Hanly , March, 1963, DDA, AB/8/B/XV/b.

24 Fergus to McQuaid, March 5, 1963, DDA, AB/8/B/XV/b.

25 'The Bishops have no right to be silent', by Fergus Pyle, *The Irish Times*, March 12, 1987.

26 Hierarchy minutes, June 1963, DDA, AB8/B/XV/b/9.

27 Note of McQuaid's meeting with Haughey, March 22, 1961.

28 *Irish Independent*, November 14, 1961. A Gárda source claims that the deal was struck between a Gárda officer and Haughey, not between Haughey and McQuaid's intermediary. 'You seem to have done a good day's work with regard to the Gárda,' Cardinal D'Alton wrote to McQuaid from Rome.

29 McQuaid to Fergus, January 18, 1963, DDA, AB/8/B/XV/b.

30 This cordial exchange is to be found in DDA, AB8/B/XVIII.38.

31 McQuaid to Fergus, August 30, 1963, DDA, AB/8/B/XV/b.

32 O'Doherty to McQuaid, September 4, 1965, DDA.

33 Irish diplomats in London reported the disappointment in Westminster at McQuaid's non-appearance. An absence such as this would explain McQuaid's ineffectual role in ecclesiastical diplomacy, especially when

the Taoiseach Seán Lemass asked him at the start of the Council to use his influence to prevent the Apostolic Delegate to Britain being raised to the full Ambassadorial rank of Nuncio. Lemass appears to have turned more to Armagh under William Conway than to McQuaid.

34 Sensi to McQuaid, DDA, AB8/B/XVII/9. A memorandum from the Secretariat of State urged the bishops to bring medical certificates with them. The Vatican officials also told the bishops that the travelling expenses and cost of the stay in Rome of their private secretaries and experts would not be met by the Holy See.

35 Bishop Eugene O'Doherty thought conferences suggested by McQuaid would be 'most useful'.

36 Hebblethwaite, *Pope John XXIII*, pp. 484–88.

37 McQuaid, however, refused to give an *Irish Times* reporter an advance copy of his script which would have been under embargo until Pope John's death. McQuaid was apparently anxious for the soul of columnist, John Healy, on account of his innovative and irreverent style of reportage – information from Douglas Gageby.

38 RTÉ broadcast script, June 4, 1963. McQuaid explained John's Pontificate to 'charity, informed by deep Faith and unending confidence.'

39 For biography of Ryan, ICD 1964, pp. 719–20.

40 Recollection of Charles Haughey to author. In contrast to his friendly relationship with Haughey, McQuaid was suspicious of another rising star of Fianna Fáil, George Colley, who was the first Minister of Education to stand up to the Hierarchy. 'This new Minister for Education, a cold, forceful lawyer, is examining how privato (sic) are our schools, if we take a State subsidy,' McQuaid wrote referring to proposed comprehensive schools.

41 McQuaid's written submissions included amendments on 'The Church in the World' (to Monsignor Morcillo), to Mgr Pericle Felici, the general secretary of the Council, on the 'Sacrament of Marriage', and a written submission to the Theological Commission on 'The call to sanctity in the Church.'

42 Rev. William Conway, qualifications and testimonials, June 1942, DDA, AB8/B/XV/b.

43 Commins described the contribution of the Irish bishops as 'sadly feeble' reflecting the degree to which thy were 'outside the climate of the Council'. Commins' Council reports are lodged in the NAI under S. Correspondence of the Department of External Affairs.

44 Cahal Daly, *Steps On My Pilgrim Journey*, p. 141.

45 Pastoral Letter on Liturgy, February 20, 1964.

46 Theas to McQuaid, December 17, 1963, DDA, AB8/B/XVd.

47 'Death of Mrs Agnes McQuaid,' aged 93, *Irish Press*, February 24, 1964. In her will, dated May 1959, and in a codicil of December 1961, Agnes bequeathed John Charles £100, the same amount as she left her maid,

Bridget Lawlor. Her remaining estate was divided between Matthew, Thomas and her daughter Deenie.This compared with tax-free legacies of £1,000 each to her sons Matthew and Thomas, and to her grand-daughter Mary Meade.

48 Peter Lennon landmark series including 'Dublin's Grey Eminence' appeared in *The Guardian*, January 8–11, 1964.

49 Novak, *The Open Church*. Neither McQuaid nor any Irish Bishop figured in a book profiling the leaders of the Council, edited by Novak. The leaders were named as Cardinals Bea, Suenens, Lercaro, Ritter, Tisserant, Patri-arch Maximos 1V Saygh, Archbishop Josef Beran, Cardinal Paul Émile Léger, Alfredo Ottaviani, Frings, Albert Gregory Meyer, and Franz König of Vienna.

50 Baum was interviewed by the late Kevin O'Kelly. Baum later reminisced about how he evaded McQuaid's ban by lecturing at Maynooth. See 'The-ologian in the Age of Crisis,' by John Cooney, *The Irish Times*, May 10, 1974.

51 Kevin McCourt was interviewed on *John Charles McQuaid: What the Papers say*.

52 Author's interview with Louis McRedmond.

53 Michael Serafian, *The Pilgrim*, p. 38.

54 Desmond Fisher, 'The Church and Change,' Thomas Davis Lecture, broadcast February 2, 1986.

55 McQuaid to Dino Staffa, October 6, 1964, DDA.

56 The Decree was giving Finbar Ryan 'a great headache,' the Dominican Archbishop of Trinidad confided to McQuaid, November 1964, DDA, AB8/B/XV/D/26.

57 Michael McCann to author, June 25, 1998.

58 McQuaid, felt snookered – he wrote: 'the (British) Ambassador puts pres-sure on the Nuncio, who in turn, puts all the onus on me and himself escapes, by saying it is not to be an official function. So there is some 'function' then to be envisaged: and the specific suggestion of my decid-ing on a Sat. service is made. Therefore I am to have a Sat. service.' McQuaid proved himself to be more cooperative with Lemass in attend-ing a Mass on the return of the body of Sir Roger Casement. 'I appreci-ated greatly Your Grace's personal cooperation in the making of the funeral arrangements and in particular in your decision to preside at the Solemn Requiem Mass,' Lemass wrote. McQuaid did not go to Glasnevin cemetery.

59 Sensi, when leaving Ireland in 1967, surprised Aiken and the Secretary of the Department of External Affairs, Con Cremin, by claiming credit for Conway's selection as Archbishop of Armagh but that his nomination as Cardinal was 'a separate and more difficult question'. NAI, DFA/98/2/6. The McQuaid papers show that he knew how to look after Sensi's mate-rial welfare by doing him the odd favour, such as arranging for his half-brother Matt to help out when the Nuncio needed a new car.

60 Ryan to McQuaid, February 2, 1965, AB8/B/XV/d/26.

61 Lemass attended the ceremony in Rome and held a reception for the Cardinal at Iveagh House, which McQuaid attended. Conway's more modern style appealed to Lemass, who was taking an interest in the theological issues reshaping the Catholic Church. After an audience with Pope Paul, Lemass discussed with Conway the Pontiff's ideas for a Catholic Radio Station in Ireland, a College in Ireland for seminarians from developing countries and periodic international conferences in Ireland under Catholic auspices.

62 McQuaid to Sensi, March 10, 1965, AB8/B/XVII/9.

63 Feeney, *The Man and the Mask*, p. 50. McQuaid ignored members of his Drumcondra staff for weeks and sent most of them to Coventry. He even banished the loyal Fr Chris Mangan.

64 Ibid, p. 51. McQuaid was 'in reaction'.

65 Author's interview with Margaret McCurtain.

66 *John Charles McQuaid: What the Papers Say*. McQuaid watched the *Late Late Show* and had admired the performance of one of his favourites priests, Father Michael Cleary who 'was just great.'

67 Jack Lynch, *Mission Outlook*, June 1973.

68 Author's conversation with John McGahern. See Julia Carlson, *Banned in Ireland*, pp. 99–121.

69 Feeney writes that McQuaid in Rome travelled by car while the other Bishops went to and from the Irish College by bus – his aloofness was reflected in passive voting with the majority.

70 Ryan to McQuaid, April 20, 1965, and April 30, 1965, DDA, AB8/B/XV/d/26.

71 Author's interview with Fr. Michael O'Carroll C.S.Sp.

72 Michael McCann to author, June 25, 1998.

73 John Feeney, *The Man and the Mask*, p. 54. Feeney also points out how the Dublin diocese continued to grow. In 1964 McQuaid announced a school building programme. The previous year the first Irish Missionary Summer School took place in Dublin.

74 These much-quoted remarks came to haunt McQuaid.

Chapter 23: Crisis of Obedience, 1965–68

1 The McQuaid episcopal silver jubilee address appeared in *Studies*, Winter, 1965. McQuaid was determined that Clonliffe College should resist the tendency to disregard the learning and use of Latin. He believed that the study of Greek and Latin had been maintained in Ireland when even Oxford had relinquished its tradition of classical learning. 'I very deeply regret to say that the progressive elimination of Latin from the Liturgy has inevitably induced the mentality everywhere that Latin is not necessary,' he complained to Archbishop Sensi on August 25,

1965. 'We are approaching the position in which the clergy can no longer be regarded as a learned body in the old sense. And nothing can halt the process. There will soon be no more desire to cultivate Latin than to observe, as Pope Piux XII recommended, the old laws of the Eucharistic fast.

2   *The Irish Times*, January 14, 1966.

3   *All in a Life*, pp 185–6. It was agreed the previous month that Sensi would chair the meeting.

4   McQuaid to Mercy Simms, April 15, 1966. One of the most powerful articles had been 'Dublin tip-toes into Ecumenism' by Gary MacEoin, syndicated throughout the United States and published in Ireland by the Redemptorist magazine, *Reality*.

5   McQuaid to Philbin, January 9, 1957, DDA, AB8/B/XV/a.

6   George Simms to McQuaid, March 7, 1957, DDA, AB8/B/XV.

7   *Corkman*, January 8, 1966.

8   Adams to McQuaid, May 31, 1966, DDA, AB8/B/XXII/b.

9   Obituary of Archbishop George Otto Simms, *The Irish Times*, November 16, 1991.

10   Simms to McQuaid, DDA, February 25, 1961, AB8/B/XV/a.

11   Ramsey to McQuaid, February 27, 1956, DDA, AB8/B/XV. 'It was such a pleasure to meet you and to talk of many matters,' Ramsey wrote. 'And now, I have also to thank you for your book, which I am very delighted to have both for its contents and as your gift. I pray that God will give you great blessing and your flock.' Simms was thrilled by the rapport between McQuaid and Ramsey. 'I know that this gift will be greatly appreciated by him,' Simms wrote to McQuaid. 'He is able to fit in quite a lot of reading and writing in his busy life – and he is particularly interested in doctrines and in the elements of the spiritual life.'

12   Author's interview with Mrs Mercy Simms, 1995.

13   In correspondence with the author, the late Fr Burke Savage S.J. admitted that his 1965 *Studies* article was 'incomplete' and 'for the most part one-sided' though he was adamant that it was 'factually accurate.' He expressed a desire 'to help to redress the balance of my own hastily written script.' Illness, however, prevented him from meeting the author for an interview. (Burke Savage to author, February 8, 1995, April 27, 1995 and May 25, 1995.)

14   Peter Lennon to *Irish Independent*, March 14, 1966.

15   *Herder Correspondence*, July, 1965, republished in Desmond Fennell, *The Changing Face of Catholic Ireland*, pp. 119–20. This comment was much more critical than an earlier defence of McQuaid against Serafian – see Fennell, pp. 109–119.

16   Blessing of Garden of Remembrance, DAA, AB8/B/XVIII. This message was conveyed by Fr Ardle MacMahon to Dan O'Sullivan on January 13,1966.

17   Con Cremin report of confidential remarks made by Archbishop Sensi to

the Minister for External Affairs, Frank Aiken, in 1967, NAI, DFA, 98/2/6.

18 'Lemass orders big parade probe,' *People*, April 17, 1966.

19 *John Charles McQuaid: What the Papers Say*.

20 Sinéad de Valera praised McQuaid for publishing the Catechism in Irish. 'All who are interested in the restoration of the language should be grateful to those who have given such a book to the country,' adding, 'It is a joy to see the Sacred words in Irish. I hope St Colmcille, St Brigid and our other friends in heaven will remember the country and its needs.' (March 6, 1966, DDA). The Gaelic League paid tribute to McQuaid for the help and encouragement which he gave to the Irish language movement. McQuaid ordered that Mass be said in Irish on Sundays in parishes where the number of clergy and the number of Masses made it practicable to do so, Tomás Ó Cofaigh, former Secretary of the Department of Finance, remembers in the Archbishop's favour. (Letter to author, August 7, 1995.)

21 'Irish Hierarchy permits mixed marriages,' *The Irish Times*, June 23, 1966. McQuaid had been unhappy that his half-brother, Thomas, had entered a mixed marriage with Thelma Greer. They lived in Sheffield.

22 Philbin to McQuaid, February 23, 1966, DDA, AB8/B/XV/a.

23 Michael Hurley S.J., *Christian Unity*, pp. 246–47.

24 McQuaid transcript, August 16, 1966, Archives of Irish Sisters of Charity

25 McQuaid claimed that he could pick out the children taught by the Holy Faith nuns for excellence at Catechism and for deportment in Church.

26 Ryan to McQuaid, January 6, 1966, DDA, AB8/B/XV/d/26.

27 *Irish Independent*, May 23, 1966, report on the Clonliffe ordinations. The prize-giving ceremony was in early June when McQuaid offered his advice against 'private theologians.'

28 Browne to McQuaid, DDA, AB8/B/XV/a.

29 McQuaid's sternest critic on the *Late Late Show* was John Feeney, who accused the Archbishop of having shares in a condom company. Another student, Brian Travaskis, condemned McQuaid, the Christian Brothers and the Irish language – and described Bishop Browne as 'a moron.' The television station's Director General, Kevin McCourt, apologised for 'disparaging remarks' against Browne and for 'an unkind reference' to the Archbishop of Dublin (*Irish Press*, March 30, 1966). A participant on the Show confirms that he was approached to stay off the programme by one of McQuaid's media-watchers.

30 Seminarians at Maynooth were under particular scrutiny by McQuaid and Browne.

31 Browne to McQuaid, March 17, 1966, DDA, AB8/B/XV/a. Fr Connolly was one of the most outspoken clerical critics of censorship.

32 On December 15, 1967, McQuaid blessed the Mater Dei Institute.

33 August 16, 1966, Archives of Irish Sisters of Charity.

34 ICD 1968, for June 13, 1967.

35 Hierarchy minutes, DDA, AB8/B/XV/b.

36 McQuaid to McFeeley, December 31, 1966, DDA, AB8/B/XV/a.

37 Tobin, *The Best of Decades*, p. 162.

38 Moynihan to McQuaid, April 18, 1967, DDA, AB8/B/XV/a.

39 In 1964 Lenihan had indicated reformist tendencies to McQuaid in regard to changes in the personnel of the Censorship of Films Appeal Board. 'I hope to appoint a Board whose decisions will command general respect,' he informed the Archbishop, signing himself 'Yours sincerely, Brian Lenihan.' (Lenihan to McQuaid, December 14, 1964, DDA, AB8/B/XVIII).

40 McQuaid to McCourt, February 14, 1966, quoted in *John Charles McQuaid: What the Papers Say*.

41 Ibid.

42 Ibid.

43 Neil Blaney was adamant in an interview with the author that no such representation was made to him by the Archbishop. McQuaid came to the defence of the people of Ballyfermot when a priest of the diocese of Waterford, Fr Ryan, addressing the Federation of Catholic Boy Scouts, made what Bishop Russell, admitted was an 'intemperate' statement' (McQuaid to Russell, November 12, 1966, DDA, AB8/B/XVa).

44 ICD 1967, for October 1966, p. 790. 'All the indications are that it took place in the most cordial and cooperative spirit.' See 'How O'Malley launched free schooling,' *The Irish Times*, September 10, 1986. The civil servant, Seán O'Connor, was told by a nun that McQuaid issued what was tantamount to a directive to the convents to join the scheme. 'One would surmise that he (McQuaid) wanted the convent schools to attract to themselves the newcomers to secondary education', O'Connor is quoted as saying in James Downey, *Lenihan*, p. 60.

45 ICD 1968, for October 13, 1967, pp. 840–41.

46 Lynch to McQuaid, November 17, 1966, DDA, AB8/B/XVIII. 'Please accept my humble thanks for your message of congratulation on my appointment as Taoiseach,' Lynch wrote. 'With God's help I shall endeavour to live up to the trust now placed in me.'

47 *Church of Ireland Gazette*, January 14, 1968.

48 Letter, *The Irish Times*, January 15, 1968.

49 Pastoral Regulations, 1967.

50 *The Irish Times*, February 6, 1967.

51 Being called an 'Archbigot' so hurt McQuaid that, for once, he contemplated suing *The Irish Times* for endorsing O'Neill's statement made originally under parliamentary privilege, according to a clerical source.

52 *Sunday Independent*, February 12, 1967.

53 Muldoon to McQuaid, February 28, 1967, DDA, AB8/B/XV/d.

54 *Irish Independent*, February 28, 1967.

55 O'Malley statement, April 18, 1967. O'Malley at times knew how to bend

the knee to McQuaid, as when he joined with the Archbishop in criticising 'variety TV' debates on education. *Irish Independent*, October 10, 1967.

56 Lindsay, *Memories*, pp. 188–89. 'In view of the recent barrage of criticism,' McQuaid told his Fine Gael apologist, 'I only hope I have the grace to stress the fundamentals until the end.'

57 Bishop Browne also watched O'Malley closely. On one occasion he complained to McQuaid that O'Malley was 'talking some strange lines which should be immediately opposed that boarding schools should be made available as tourist centres and that 100 teachers be trained in psychiatry – but all lay, not one priest or nun.'

58 In *Our Faith* McQuaid defended the perpetual virginity of Our Blessed Lady and the Roman Missal as the chief fount of Sacred Liturgy, p. 11.

59 Tragically, John Feeney was killed in an air crash at the height of a remarkably talented career in journalism.

60 Sheehy, p. 195. The same hierarchical procedure applied in other spheres of Catholic life. It was McQuaid's practice to write to a parish priest, a Provincial Religious Superior or a Mother Superior rather than to a curate, a religious priest or a nun.

61 Feeney, *The Man and the Mask*, p. 62.

62 Author's interview with Fr Brian Power.

63 *The Irish Times*, February 9, 1967, O'Sullivan claimed that afterwards McQuaid attempted to discredit the students by stating falsely that they give themselves the title of intellectuals. Rounding on McQuaid, O'Sullivan wrote: 'He achieved his rank without any of the parochial experience which fits a man for the episcopate and to say more would be superfluous.'

64 Roberts to McQuaid, November 13, 1967, DDA, AB8/B/XV/d.

65 W.A.C. (Gully) Standford, *The Hist and Edmund Burke Club: An Anthology of the College Historical Society, the Student Debating Society of TCD from its Origins in Edmund Burke's Club, 1747–1997.* Edited by Declan Budd and Ross Hinds. Standford had proposed to address the relations of the 'majority, Catholic Church with the state.' On July 4, 1967 McQuaid wrote: With respect to your scholarship, I venture to believe that you have not, and cannot have, the evidence that would allow a full and just estimate of a thesis so vast and so complex.' p. 229.

66 McQuaid to Roberts, November 16, 1967, DDA, AB8/B/XV/d.

67 Ryan to McQuaid, February 21, 1968, DDA, AB8/B/XV/d/26.

68 Author's interview with Mrs Simms.

69 McQuaid to Mercy Simms, February 1, 1967.

Chapter 24: No Change, 1968–70

1 McQuaid described himself as 'the ogre in his den' at a reception to

open his press office.

2   ICD 1969, for July 28, 1968, pp. 751–53. Cremin's press conference in *The Irish Times, Irish Press and Irish Independent* reports, July 29, 1968.

3   Cicognani to McQuaid, September 6, 1968, DDA, AB8/B/XVI/4.

4   ICD 1969, for July 28, 1968, pp. 751–53.

5   *Irish Press*, July 29, 1968.

6   Lucey to McQuaid, DDA, AB/8/B/XV/a.

7   Farmar, *Holles St*, p. 154.

8   ICD 1969, for August 21, 1968, p. 757.

9   Fergal Tobin, *The Best of Decades*, p. 195.

10 Quoted by Garret FitzGerald, *All in a Life*, p. 84. Grogan became a major public critic of McQuaid, especially after he left the Knights of St Columbanus.

11 Cicognani to McQuaid, October 4, 1968, DDA, AB8/B/XVI/4.

12 *The Irish Times*, August 25, 1968.

13 Hierarchy statement, issued on October 9, 1968. For text see Horgan and Flannery (eds) *Humanae Vitae and the Bishops*, pp. 138–39.

14 McQuaid to O'Boyle, October 2, 1968, DDA, AB8/B/XV/d/22.

15 McQuaid to Cicognani, January 4, 1966, DDA, AB8/B/XVI/4.

16 Lefebvre to McQuaid, September 25, 1966, DDA, AB8/B/XV/d.

17 Peter Hebblethwaite, *Understanding the Synod*.

18 McQuaid to Conway, September 20, 1967, DDA, AB/8/B/XV/a.

19 Hebblethwaite, *Paul VI*, p. 508.

20 *Our Faith*. This Pastoral letter captures McQuaid's entrenched outlook and his loathing of Martin Luther's legacy.

21 McQuaid to McGeough, January 31, 1968, DDA, AB8/B/XVII/10.

22 *A Passion for Truth*, pp. 237–40.

23 McQuaid to McGeough, April 29, 1968, DDA, AB8/B/XVII/10.

24 McQuaid to McGeough, July 1, 1968, DDA, AB8/B/XVII/10. As the Dublin Diocese's contribution towards defraying the expenses of the Second Vatican Council, McQuaid sent Rome a cheque for £17,400 (£150,000).

25 Brian Kennedy, 'Seventy-five Years of *Studies*', *Studies,* Winter, 1986. Burke Savage had resigned in March 1968.

26 *Studies*, Winter, 1998, 'His Grace is not pleased,' pp. 400–401.

27 *Studies*, Autumn 1968.

28 Fr Michael O'Connor interview. O'Connor was given only ten days to leave Ireland, not enough to comply with medical requirements abroad, and he nearly died in the West Indies. O'Connor's request for an interview with McQuaid was turned down. 'You are obviously a young man who does not fully appreciate the impact of his own words,' McQuaid replied. 'No purpose would be fulfilled by the requested interview. Your Major Religious Superior has adequately dealt with the matter.'

29 Irish Council of Women, DDA, AB8/B/XXII. McQuaid instructed the parish

clergy to report on the President, Mrs E. Cahill, who had sought Church of Ireland support through Mrs Mercy Simms. He also sent a priest-spy to the Council's inaugural press conference in the Gresham Hotel. In its report, *The Irish Times* pictured Mrs Cahill with Mrs Catherine McGuinness and Mrs Monica McEnroy.

30 The Tuairim spy was Fr Bertram Crowe, lecturer in Ethics and Politics at UCD.

31 Information from Fr Tom Stack.

32 Fr Dermod McCarthy in conversation with Fr Bernard Cotter, *Intercom*, June 1999. He was shifted to Athy on the fringe of the diocese after being involved in a Radharc programme on the slow implementation of Vatican Two in regard to nuns.

33 Ciarán MacGonigal recalls this episode.

34 Information from Gerry Mulvey and the late Nigel Brown of *The Irish Times*. Brown recalled the rare occasion when McQuaid's script was in Irish and he went to the Church of Ireland Dean of St Patrick's Cathedral (John Armstrong, later Archbishop of Armagh) for an English translation – readers unwittingly enjoyed an Irish Protestant version of McQuaid!

35 Michael O'Toole, *More Kicks than Pence*.

36 Information from Tom McElroy, now with the *Sunday World*. Another instance of McQuaid's prickliness when he felt that his dignity as a churchman was being questioned was when a trade unionist, Patrick Lyons, wrote urging him to rectify a scandalous situation in St Joseph's Asylum for the Blind. McQuaid took this request as a threat which fell far short of treating him with the respect which his office as a church dignatory demanded.

37 Quoted in John Feeney, *The Man and the Mask*, p. 56.

38 Denis Coghlan interview.

39 Feeney, *The Man and the Mask*, p. 68.

40 Brian Quinn interview.

41 ICD 1969, for October 18, 1968, p. 766. McCabe had been dismissed by Apostolic Delegate, Gerald Patrick O'Hara, who had only read news reports of the finely nuanced editorial. Another victim of McQuaid's exalted sense of his prerogatives was the veteran Fianna Fáil politician, P.J. Little, who was assisting the Benedictines in promoting literature on the Moral Re-armament Movement. 'I must ask you to desist from all attempts to promote MRA in my diocese,' McQuaid directed him. DDA, AB8/B/XV/a.

42 Letter, September 15, 1968.

43 ICD 1969, for November 23, 1968, p. 771.

44 Pastoral regulations, February 1969.

45 Ibid.

46 Louis McRedmond, *Irish Independent* April 1, 1969.

47 McQuaid had issued his regulations after consulting the members of his

own hand-picked Commissions on Sacred Liturgy and Sacred Music.

48 Liam Walsh O.P. statement.

49 Ryan to McQuaid, April 26, 1969, DDA, AB8/B/XV/d/26.

50 Profile of Archbishop Kevin McNamara by John Cooney, *The Irish Times*, January 17, 1985.

51 McQuaid to Heenan, DDA, AB8/B/XV/d.

52 *Hibernia*, March 28, 1969.

53 Browne to McQuaid, March 29, 1969, AB8/B/XV/a.

54 Author's interview in 1976 with the late Fr Jim Healy S.J.

55 Feeney, *The Man and the Mask*, p. 68.

56 McQuaid to Conway, February 17, 1970, DDA, AB/8/B/XV/a.

57 John Charles McQuaid: *What the Papers Say*.

58 McQuaid to Webster, September 9, 1969, DDA, AB8/B/XV/d/25.

59 Browne to McQuaid, March 10, 1969. Browne indicated his intention to follow McQuaid's example about Mercier Recordings.

60 James Mackey, an Irish theologian who signed the Curran statement, was later overlooked for a teaching post at Maynooth.

61 *The Irish Times*, March 10, 1969.

62 Ibid.

63 The tune was 'Speak Softly, Love' – Archbishop Alibrandi played this theme song from *The Godfather* when I interviewed him in Sicily for the *Irish Press* in Autumn 1994.

64 External Affairs memorandum, marked most secret, July 19, 1967, NAI.

65 Conway to McQuaid, December 8, 1969, DDA, AB8/B/XV/a.

66 Cahal Daly to McQuaid, December 7, 1967, DDA, AB/8/B/XV/a. Cahal Daly, as a new bishop, sought McQuaid's help on his first Pastoral.

67 *Studies*, Winter, 1998.

58 Casey to McQuaid, July 30, 1969, DDA, AB/8/B/XV/a. McQuaid did not attend Casey's Consecration on November 9 as he was abroad. When shown 'the nice letter' from Casey, Fr Cecil Barrett wrote 'what he says is only the truth and all of them know that the chaplaincy scheme and much else would have ceased to exist long ago, but for Your Grace's strong sustaining hand.' (August 2, 1969.)

69 McQuaid to Mulligan, DDA, AB8/B/XV/a. McQuaid refused to concelebrate Mass at other Episcopal ordinations, a blatant breach of Vatican Two.

70 McQuaid statement, August 4, 1970. There is a special file in the DDA on McQuaid's reaction to the Troubles in the North, AB8/B/XVIII/4.

71 McQuaid to Lynch, August 16, 1969, DDA, AB8/B/XVIII/4. He said that the monies were from 'charitable funds' at his disposal.

72 Ardle MacMahon note to McQuaid, August 18, 1969, DDA, AB8/B/XVIII/4.

73 Lynch to McQuaid, August 18, 1969, DDA, AB8/B/XVIII/4.

74 Religious tolerance file in the National Archives, released in January

1999. This event marked what historians now see as the opening of a new Thirty Years' War between nationalists and unionists in the North. The file, mainly of newspaper cuttings, reveals the absence of an Irish Government policy hitherto on the issue.

75 McQuaid to Philbin, August 25, 1969, DDA, AB8/B/XVIII/4.

76 Philbin to McQuaid, August 28, 1969, DDA, AB8/B/XVIII/4.

77 Philbin to McQuaid, August 29, 1969, DDA, AB8/B/XVIII/4.

78 Michael Mills, 'Cabinet dilemma over "doomsday,"' *The Irish Times*, April 29, 1998.

79 Ryan to McQuaid, September 4, 1969, DDA, AB8/B/ AB8/B/XVIII/4.

80 Secretary to Ryan, September 5, 1969, DDA, AB8/B/ AB8/B/XVIII/4.

81 McQuaid deferred to Philbin for advice about J. Christopher Napier of the Bombay Street Housing Association, room 37, 16 Donegall Square South, Belfast, which aimed to rebuild the area devastated in the August 1969 riots. An entirely non-political and non-sectarian body, it wanted McQuaid's permission to announce a collection at the gates of all churches in Dublin and have it mentioned from the pulpits – Napier to McQuaid, March 19, 1970. Philbin was negative. McQuaid refused to support the collection.

82 McQuaid to Casey, September 6, 1969, DDA, AB8/B/XV/a. Fr Aidan Lehane C.S.Sp. recalls that on hearing of Casey's appointment while on a visit to Rockwell, McQuaid said nothing 'but ice formed on the upper slopes.' (*Studies,* Winter, 1998.)

83 Conway's statement was given massive media coverage.

84 Conway to McQuaid, October 31, 1969, DDA, AB8/B/XV/a.

85 St John Stevas, *The Agonising Choice*, p. 208.

86 Daly to McQuaid, August 3, 1969, AB/8/B/XV/a.

87 McQuaid to Conway, October 1, 1969, DDA, AB8/B/XV/a. 'Thank you. The schema seems at first glance to be relevant and comprehensive. Shall study it.'

88 Ryan to McQuaid, DDA, AB8/B/XV/d/26.

89 Donald S. Connery, *The Irish*, p. 139.

90 *Hibernia*, February 20, 1970.

91 Louis McRedmond, 'The bishops lift the ban,' *The Tablet*, July 4, 1970.

92 Andrew Burke, 'Trinity College and the religious problem in Irish education,' p. 119, in Kelly and MacGearailt (eds) *Dublin and Dubliners*, Dublin, 1990.

93 McQuaid to Mother Heskin, November 14, 1968.

94 The editor, John Mulcahy, was an early – and courageous – critic of McQuaid. I am grateful to the current editor of *Phoenix*, Paddy Prendeville, for allowing me access to the *Hibernia* files.

95 Browne to McQuaid, February 8, 1969, DDA, AB/8/B/XV/a.

96 John Horgan, 'Bishops end Trinity ban,' *The Irish Times*, June 26, 1970.

97 Ibid.

98 Andrew Burke interviewed Conway on December 4, 1973, as part of his research for a Boston College thesis.

99 Brendan Heffernan, 25 years of Roman Catholic chaplaincy at Trinity College, *Link-up*. When Heffernan demurred that he might not have the qualifications for the job, McQuaid said: 'Father, I have chosen you, all will be well.' The first Mass said by Heffernan in Trinity was in the Examination Hall on May 14, 1971.

100 Author's interview and correspondence with George Dawson.

101 *Gravissimum Educationis*, p. 10, in Austin Flannery O.P., Vatican Council II, *The Conciliar and Post-Conciliar Documents*. Scholarly Resources Incorporated, Wilmington, Delaware, 1975.

Chapter 25: Until the End, 1970–73

1 *John Charles McQuaid: What the Papers Say*.

2 'Archbishop's concerns with many fields,' *Irish Independent*, July 28, 1970.

3 *Sunday Press*, July 26, 1970.

4 'Prelate not to retire', *Irish Independent*, July 27, 1970.

5 Ibid.

6 *Irish Press*, 'Who will succeed Dr McQuaid?' Date blurred on fading cutting.

7 Michael O'Toole tells the story in *More Kicks than Pence*.

8 McQuaid to Paul VI, July 18, 1970, DDA, AB8/B/XVI/3.

9 *L'Osservatore Romano* , June 11, 1971.

10 McQuaid to Paul VI, May 23, 1970, DDA, AB8/B/XVI/3.

11 Benelli to McQuaid, July 9, 1970, DDA, AB8/B/XVI/4. A young student in Rome, Diarmuid Martin, now Bishop of Glendalough and secretary of the Pontifical Council for Justice and Peace, sometimes acted as courier between Benelli and Drumcondra.

12 McQuaid to Benelli, May 23, 1970, DDA, AB8/B/XVI/4. McQuaid may have been aware of the remark in 1962 of Cardinal Richard Cushing of Boston to an Irish diplomat – 'The Vatican doesn't give a damn for Ireland because Ireland hasn't any money to hand them.'

13 Ibid.

14 McQuaid to Alibrandi, May 24, 1970, DDA, AB8/B/XVII/11.

15 George Bull, *Inside the Vatican*, pp. 122–23.

16 Paul Hofman, *Anatomy of the Vatican*, pp. 116–120.

17 Benelli to McQuaid, August 24, 1970, DDA, AB8/B/XVI/4

18 Benelli to McQuaid, August 8, 1970, DDA, AB8/B/XVII/4. Benelli advised him to have his secretary phone his *Assesore* in the Secretariat of State, Monsignor Sabastiani, to arrange the appointment.

19 Commins to Hugh McCann, November 11, 1970, NAI, DFA, S. 14/105.

20 Ryan to McQuaid, December 19, 1970, DDA, AB8/B/XV/26.

21 I am indebted to Fr Lehane for an extract from Dr Stafford Johnson's letter.

22 Benelli to McQuaid, August, 8, 1970, DDA, AB8/B/XVII/11.

23 O'Connell to McQuaid, October 25, 1970, DDA, AB8/B/XVI/20.

24 Lemass-Lenihan correspondence is lodged in NAI, DFA, 96/2/14.

25 'Report of the Committee on the Constitution', December 1967. I am indebted to the late John Kelly T.D. for a copy.

26 Lenten Regulations, 1968.

27 John Cooney, *The Crozier and the Dáil*, p. 28.

28 From Rockwell McQuaid phoned his office to arrange for Bishop Carroll to call at the French Embassy in Ailesbury Road to sign the book of condolence. On his return to Dublin McQuaid presided at a special Mass in the Pro-Cathedral which struck Ambassador d'Harcourt as corresponding exactly to General de Gaulle's taste in beautiful church music and scriptural texts. McQuaid to D'Harcourt, November 11, 1970, DDA, AB8/B/XVIII/41. D'Harcourt to McQuaid, November 19, 1970, DDA.

29 November 11, 1970.

30 Lenten Regulations, February 1971.

31 Bishops' Statement, March 1971.

32 Olivia O'Leary and Helen Burke, *Mary Robinson*, pp. 55–6.

33 John Horgan speaking on *John Charles McQuaid: What the Papers Say*.

34 McQuaid remained particularly sensitive to criticism from Trinity College Protestants. He was even reputed to bristle if they spoke Irish.

35 Archbishop's Pastoral Letter, published March 29, 1971, in *The Irish Times*.

36 *Irish Independent*, March 29, 1971.

37 *Irish Independent*, March 29, 1971.

38 *Belfast Telegraph*, April 5, 1971.

39 Quoted by John Cooney, *Magill*, 1998.

40 Conway to McQuaid, March 30, 1971, DDA, AB/8/B/XV/a.

41 *The Irish Times*, March 26, 1971, 'Views on Dr McQuaid's sucessor sought.'

42 *Evening Herald*, March 26, 1991, 'Dublin prelate not yet to retire.'

43 Miss Mary B. Murphy , a Red Cross official, requested McQuaid to release the news to papers of his donation as 'headlines would help a lot.'

44 Macken to McQuaid, August 16, 1971, DDA, AB8/B/XVIII/4. 'Without Your Grace's help and the generous personal interest which you took in this problem as a whole we would not have been able to solve it as successfully as we have and I have pleasure in acknowledging our great debt of gratitude to you.'

45 Cronin to McQuaid, August 27, 1971, DDA, AB8/B/XVIII/4. 'I personally

and the Government, as well as the refugees concerned, have special
cause to be appreciative of your Grace's benevolence during this very
critical time,' the Minister for Defence, Jerry Cronin, wrote to McQuaid.

46 Barrett to McQuaid, August 12, 1971, DDA, AB8/B/XVIII/4.

47 McQuaid's statement, 1971, AB8/B/XVIII/4.

48 Bredin to McQuaid, September 3, 1971, DDA, AB8/B/XVIII/4.

49 Conway to McQuaid, September 7, 1971, DDA, AB8/B/XVIII/4.

50 McQuaid to Conway, September 14, 1971, DDA, AB8/B/XVIII/4.

51 *Irish Independent*, September 21, 1971.

52 Philbin to McQuaid, October 1, 1971, DDA, AB8/B/XVIII/4.

53 McQuaid to Philbin, September 22, 1971, DDA, AB8/B/XVIII/4

54 *The Irish Times*, October 6, 1971.

55 Anonymous to McQuaid, October 12, 1971, DDA, AB8/B/XVIII/4.

56 McQuaid notes, DDA.

57 McQuaid peace appeal, December, 20, 1971.

58 Author's interview with Seán MacStíofáin.

59 IRA message to McQuaid,

60 Author's interview with Fr Michael O'Carroll C.S.S.p

61 Biographical sketch of Dermot Ryan in Canning, *Bishops of Ireland*, pp.
    185–6.

62 Information from Michael O'Toole.

63 'Dublin's new Archbishop', by Pat Holmes, *Irish Press,* January 5, 1972.

64 'Resignation a watershed in Irish church life,' by John Horgan, *The Irish
    Times*, January 5, 1972.

65 *The Irish Times*, January 5, 1972.

66 Church Unity letter, January 1972.

67 McQuaid to Farren, January 30, 1972, DDA, AB8/B/XVIII/4.

68 *John Charles McQuaid: What the Papers Say*.

69 Aidan Lehane C.S.Sp, *Studies*, Winter, 394.

70 *The Irish Times*, February 14, 1972. 'To close the files of the most Rever-
    end John C. McQuaid D.D.' is written with stark finality on a single sheet
    of paper for February 16, 1972, DDA.

71 Archbishop McQuaid to Paul McQuaid, February 25, 1972. ' It will, I
    hope, now be more possible to see you all.' It was signed 'your affection-
    ate and Uncle John.' In other correspondence he signed himself as 'Uncle
    Charlie.'

72 Author's interview with the late Fr. Joe Dunn.

73 Aidan Lehane C.S.Sp, *Studies*, Winter, 1998. Johnson exonerated Arch-
    bishop Dermot Ryan from any complicity in the leaking of data harmful
    to McQuaid. However, the information about the chronic state of dioce-
    san finances was conveyed to journalists by Ryan's spin-doctor, the late
    Fr Peter Lemass, no doubt with his boss's sanction. Ryan must have felt a
    twinge of conscience when he heard of McQuaid's death.

74   McQuaid to Mercy Simms, March 2, 1972. McQuaid indicated to Mrs Simms that it would be some time before he would see France again and he deplored the fact that the horrifying tragedy of the North continued undiminished. 'His Grace must suffer from it acutely. I wonder if we are praying and doing penance sufficiently for God to hear us. What I find so frightening is the legacy of hate that is being accumulated, apart from the offence against God, which so few persons mention.'

75   Will of Archbishop John Charles McQuaid, D.D., Probate Office, the High Court.

76   Aidan Lehane C.S.Sp., *Studies*, Winter, 1998.

77   Sr Denis interview with author.

78   Author's interview with Fr Aidan Lehane C.S.Sp.

79   Purcell, *Irish Catholic*, May 5, 1988.

80   MacStíofáin, *Memoirs of a Revolutionary*, pp. 348–49. Fr Bernard Canning in *Bishops of Ireland*, p. 184, sees parallels in McQuaid's visit with the intervention of Cardinal Paul Cullen to save the Fenian General Thomas F. Burke from the gallows and Archbishop William Walsh's signing of a petition to reprieve Roger Casement.

81   Letter to author from Ger Cleary, April 14, 1998.

82   *Anglo-Celt*, April 13, 1973. McQuaid was also in mourning following the deaths of his close friends Archbishop Finbar Ryan O.P. and Fr Bernard Fennelly C.S.Sp.

83   *Sunday Press*, April 1, 1973.

84   Interview with Fr Michael O'Carroll C.S.Sp.

85   *Wellsprings of the Faith*, p. 209. In his eulogy of Cullen, the nine-teenth-century 'Romaniser' of the Irish Catholic Church, McQuaid also said : 'Not his the multitude of letters and scrupulous autobiography that help a later age to reconstruct the picture of the unspeakable dead.' In McQuaid's case he kept so much of his correspondence that, like President Richard Nixon with the tape recorder, he may have left more than he intended. (McQuaid and Nixon met during his visit to Ireland in October 1970.) However, some of McQuaid's correspondence was destroyed or lost, according to John O'Hara, the flamboyant business-man, who bought Notre Dame des Bois and found the house full of let-ters, many of which dealt with Latin America.

86   *Evening Herald*, April 7, 1973.

87   *Anglo-Celt*, April 13, 1973.

88   Quoted in Canning, *Bishops of Ireland*, p. 183.

89   Quoted in *The Irish Times*, April 9, 1973.

90   Extract of letter from Dr Stafford Johnson to Fr Aidan Lehane C.S.Sp. I am indebted to Fr Lehane for the extract. An abiding memory for Fr Lehane is of McQuaid sitting on his bed in Rockwell College dangling his feet and looking at the coal fire and saying 'This is Heaven!'

91   Dr Paul McQuaid to author, July 14, 1995.

SOURCES

ARCHIVES

DUBLIN DIOCESAN ARCHIVES (DDA)

In 1997 Archbishop Desmond Connell decided to open the archives covering McQuaid's episcopate from 1940 to 1972 with annual releases to follow over an extended period. The McQuaid Papers run to seven hundred archival boxes making it the largest collection held by the Dublin Diocesan Archives. The first tranche, released in early 1998, covered the Irish Government, the Holy See, the Apostolic Nunciature and Bishops.

A second tranche, released in January 1999, included files relating to the Catholic Social Service Conference, the Department of Education and correspondence with Ambassador Joe Walshe. Its section on Lay Organisations included: Football Association of Ireland, Ireland-America Society, Irish Council of Women, Irish Farmers' Association, Irish German Society, Irish Nurses' Organisation, Irish Save the Children Fund, Legion of Mary including the Mercier Society, the Pillar of Fire Society, Mount Street Club, Moral Re-armament (MRA), Muintir na Tíre, National Council for the Blind, Royal National Life Boat Institution, Rotary Club and Tuairim.

Of major interest is the file on Maria Duce (later called Fírinne), including correspondence between McQuaid and Fr Denis Fahey C.S.Sp. There is also a key document written by Fahey explaining his background and ideas.

Significantly, diocesan papers relating to personnel, church finances and McQuaid's relations with Religious Orders are not open for inspection. To bridge this deficit, I have been facilitated by several Religious Orders who gave me access to their archives relating to the Archbishop.

An exceptionally important new source is McQuaid's collection of minutes, notes and observations of Hierarchy meetings from 1940 to 1965. (Closed are his Hierarchy files for the turbulent period from 1966 to 1971; to be reviewed in 2007.) This is a major goldmine for historians of the modern Irish Catholic Church, especially when taken in conjunction with McQuaid's correspondence with other Irish bishops.

Also of great importance are the files of McQuaid's correspondence with the Holy See and the Papal Nuncios in Dublin (though Archbishop Alibrandi's file from 1969 to 1972 is closed; to be reviewed in 2007). McQuaid's sense of his own position as the ecclesiastical head of the Irish diaspora can be gauged from his wide-ranging correspondence with church leaders worldwide. Particularly instructive, too, are two sets of personal correspondence with his close friends, the Archbishop of Trinidad, Finbar Ryan O.P., and Daniel O'Connell S.J.

In addition, it should be stressed that since 1994 a substantial volume of material has been open for inspection in the Dublin Diocesan Archives relating to McQuaid's life prior to his appointment as Archbishop of Dublin in 1940. Foremost among this material was a draft biography of his boyhood and adolescence, which had been begun by the Catholic writer, Mary Purcell. There is also a manuscript memoir, in McQuaid's own hand, of Brother Gaspard O'Reilly of Blackrock College. There is also a wide range of material which McQuaid kept in his possession from his days as a member of the Holy Ghost Congregation. This material has been cataolgued by the archivist, Mr David Sheehy, under the following headings: Seminarian and priest, 1913–26; Dean of Studies and President of Blackrock College, 1925–40; Catholic affairs, 1934–40; Medical affairs, 1933–38; Drafting of the Irish Constitution, 1922–39; Catholic Headmasters' Association, 1933–40; Education, 1933–37; Addresses and homilies, 1929–40; Miscellaneous.

The Archives holds an extensive run of the annual *Irish Catholic Directory* (ICD), an annual record of church personnel and events. An invaluable guide through the McQuaid Papers is Archivist David Sheehy, a master of his craft, who is compiling a detailed catalogue of sources.

DE VALERA ARCHIVES (DVA)

The release of the second tranche of the Éamon de Valera Archives, by the Franciscans in Killiney, County Dublin, in 1994, produced valuable material relating to McQuaid's attitude to de Valera both personally and politically. The first tranche of de Valera Papers relating to the Constitution was released in 1987. This highly important collection is now being re-catalogued at University College, Dublin.

NATIONAL ARCHIVES OF IRELAND (NAI)

Fuelling the renewed interest in McQuaid's career is the annual January release of papers from Government Departments by the National Archives of Ireland. Particularly important was the 1994 release which chronicled the efforts of the de Valera Government to persuade the Vatican to appoint McQuaid Archbishop of Dublin in 1940. Thanks go to Dr David Craig, Caitríona Crowe and staff.

HOLY GHOST ARCHIVES (HGA)

Fr Leo Laydan C.S.Sp., Provincial Archivist, briefed me on the Congregation's scholasticate system and the relations between the Irish Province and the Mother House in Paris. He also kindly made available the Bulletin of the Province of Ireland and the personnel files containing obituaries of: Bishops John Heffernan (1883–1966), John G. Neville (1858–1943), Bartholomew Wilson (1885–1938); Frs Jeremiah Vincent Dinan (1907–1975), John English (1884–1959), Denis Fahey (1883–1954), Richard Harnett (1879–1959), James Murphy (1878–1952); Brother Gaspard O'Reilly (John) (1846–1923).

REDEMPTORIST PROVINCIAL ARCHIVES (RPA)

Fr Brendan McConvery C.SS.R. kindly made available the curriculum vitae written in 1914 by Hugo Kerr as a novice before his profession; also a conspectus vitae, written in 1984, which refers to John McQuaid; and *The Life of Father Hugo Kerr C.SS.R. (1895–1986)* by Patrick O'Donnell C.SS.R

Hugo Kerr contributed the introductory article to *Two Hundred Years with the Redemptorists*, published by the Four Candles, 1933.

IRISH JESUIT ARCHIVES (IJA)

Fr Stephen Redmond S.J. kindly provided a photocopy of the handwritten curriculum vitae of Daniel O'Connell which he wrote on November 16, 1914, during his novitiate with the Society of Jesus, aged eighteen. This should be supplemented by a profile ('Astronomer and Seismologist') which appeared in *The Clongownian* in 1953, after O'Connell moved from the post of Director of Riverview Observatory, New South Wales, Australia, to the Vatican Observatory at Castel Gandolfo, which he directed until 1970. From 1968 until 1972, he was, by the appointment of Pope Paul VI, President of the Pontifical Academy of Sciences. He died in Rome on October 14, 1982. His obituary appeared in *L'Osservatore Romano*, October 16, 1982.

Archivist, Orna Somerville, made available Letters of the Generalate in Rome to Ireland, 1806–1959 (ADMN–1) and Provincial's correspondence, 1905–1959 (ADMN 3).

In the course of 1999 the papers of Fr Edward Cahill, S.J. (1870; 1913–1947; reference J55), and Fr Timothy Corcoran S.J. (1869 to 1943, reference J 49), were released.

IRISH SISTERS OF CHARITY ARCHIVES (ISC)

I wish to thank Sr Marie Bernadette for allowing me to read the correspondence between the Superioress-Generals in Mount St Anne's Milltown (Mother Mary Bernard Carew; Mother Teresa Anthony Heskin and Mother Frances Rose O'Flynn) and Archbishop McQuaid.

HOLY ROSARY SISTERS ARCHIVES (HRS)

I am indebted to Sr Cori of the Missionary Sisters of Our Lady of the Holy Rosary, Cross Avenue, Blackrock, for allowing me to read the correspondence between the Superioress-Generals and the Dublin diocese.

BLACKROCK COLLEGE (BC)

Important contributors to the McQuaid revival are the veteran Blackrock College priests, Frs Seán Farragher C.S.Sp. and Michael O'Carroll C.S.Sp., both of whom generously recalled their memories of the Archbishop and Éamon de Valera in interviews. I am indebted to Fr Farragher for giving me an advance copy of the proofs of his book, *Blackrock College, 1860–1995*, which contained an important digest of the correspondence between Paris and Dublin relating to the attempt to prolong McQuaid's Presidency of Blackrock College in 1939. Another major quarry was Fr Farragher's earlier book, *Dev and his Alma Mater: Éamon de Valera's Lifelong Association with Blackrock College, 1898–1975*. The *Blackrock College Annuals* capture the glory days of the McQuaid era in the College's history.

NATIONAL LIBRARY OF IRELAND (NLI)

Despite McQuaid's legendary aloofness from the Fourth Estate, he was a regular fixture in newspapers both as President of Blackrock College and as Archbishop of Dublin. Photocopies provided by the library of reports from the *Irish Press, Irish Independent, The Irish Times*, the *Catholic Standard* and the *Irish Catholic* are an important source for gauging McQuaid's image.

REPRESENTATIVE CHURCH BODY LIBRARY (RCB)

The occcasional reference to Archbishop McQuaid in the Church of Ireland *Gazette* from 1940 underlines the religious apartheid that so deeply marked Ireland until the early 1960s. The Librarian and Archivist, Dr Raymond Refaussé, and the Church of Ireland House of Bishops, are likely to come under pressure to open the Archives of Archbishop George Otto Simms, following the opening by Archbishop Connell of correspondence between McQuaid and Simms. I am also indebted to the late Mrs Mercy Simms for allowing me to read her correspondence with McQuaid.

OIREACHTAS LIBRARY DUBLIN (OLD)

Patrick Melvin and Séamus Haughey were superb finders of forgotten Dáil debates.

THE JOHN GILBERT LIBRARY

Librarian Máire Kennedy provided important newspaper references.

DUBLIN CITY ARCHIVES (DCA)

Mary Clark and her staff were helpful in supplying biographies of City Fathers.

JOURNALS

Administration, Blackrock College Annual, Capuchin Annual, Catholic Bulletin, Catholic Truth Quarterly, Capuchin Annual, Christus Rex, Church Record, The Clongownian, Crane Bag, Doctrine and Life, Fiat, The Furrow, Hibernia, Irish Ecclesiastical Record, Irish Medical Association, Irish Messenger, Medical Press and Circular, Missionary Annals, Irish Rosary, Irish Monthly, The Month, New Blackfriars, Reality, Reportorium Novum, Rockwell College Annual, Studies, University Review.

NEWSPAPERS

Anglo-Celt, Catholic Herald, Standard (later *Catholic Standard*), *Catholic Times, Church of Ireland Gazette, Evening Herald, East Coast Gazette, Freeman's Journal, Kilkenny People, Glasgow Observer, Irish Independent, Irish Press, The Irish Times, Mayo Post, Sunday Graphic* and *Sunday News, The Tablet, The Sunday Times, Western People.*

BROCHURES

Catholic University School, 1949–50; Clonliffe College, 1859–1959; Mater Misericordiae Hospital, 1861–1961; Medical Missionaries of Mary, 1937–1962; Our Lady of Mercy College, 1877–1977; Sisters of Mercy, Cootehill, 1880–1980; St Mary's School for the Deaf, Cabra, 1846–1946; St Patrick's College, Drumcondra, 1875–1975; The Catholic Institute for the Deaf, Official Opening of St Vincent's Centre for the Deaf, 1991.

CUTTINGS BOOK

Councillor Andy Smith, Cootehill, Co. Cavan, from *Anglo-Celt*, November 12, 1910–12.

ACKNOWLEDGEMENTS

In search of John Charles McQuaid I interviewed or received help from numerous individuals including: Archbishop Gaetano Alibrandi; Dawne Bailey; Robert Ballagh; Mr Justice Donal Barrington; Tom Barrington; the late Neil Blaney T.D.; Veronica Blessing; Marcus Bourke; John Bowman; Seán Boyd; Andrew Boylan T.D.; Aidan Boyle; Leonard Boyle O.P.; Seán Boyne; Martin Brady T.D.; Mrs Phyllis Browne; the late Nigel Brown; Tony Brown; Bishop Pat Buckley; the late Rev. Roland Burke Savage S.J.; Mike Burns; Archbishop Donald Caird; Helen Callanan; Peter Canning; Michael Carroll C.S.Sp.; Denis Carroll; Ger Cleary; Denis Coghlan; Noel Coghlan; Colin Conroy; Tim Pat Coogan; James Craig; Ned Crean; Anthony Cronin; Prof. George Dawson; John de Courcy Ireland; Éamon Delaney; Elizabeth Dempsey; Sr Denis; John Dew; Elizabeth Douglas; Senator Joe Doyle; Peter Doyle; the late Fr Joe Dunn; J.P. Duggan; Máirín Egan; Brendan Ellis; Rev. Seán Fagan; Bernadette Fahy; Enzo Farinella; Frank Feely; Alex Findlater; Seán Farragher C.S.Sp.; Sally Ann Flanagan; Austin Flannery O.P.; Chris Finnegan; Tom and Carmel Fitzpatrick; Seán Flynn; Fr Des Forristal; Joseph Foyle; Michael Fry; Douglas Gageby; John Garvey; Prof. Tom Garvin; John Gilmartin; Michael Gorman; Dean Brian Harvey; Charles Haughey; Joe Hayes; Bill Heaney; John F. Hickey; Pat Hickey; Michael D. Higgins T.D.; Derek Hill; John Horgan; John Hume M.P., M.E.P.; Michael Hurley S.J.; Max Keane; Hugh Kennedy; Fr Michael Keating; John Kelly; Ben Kiely; Peadar Kirby; Mr Justice Vivion Lavan; Michael Leddy; Aidan Lehane C.S.Sp.; the late Brian Lenihan T.D.; Eddie Linden; Máirín Lindsay; Charles Lysaght; Prof. George McDonald; Count Randal McDonnell of the Glens; Paul McQuaid; Prof. Alan MacInnes; Seán MacRéamoinn; Michael McCann; Rev. Robert MacCarthy; Sinéad McCarthy; Margaret McCurtain O.P.; Tony McGarry; Bishop Francis McKiernan; Prof. Jim McMillan; Jim McNeive; Deirdre McQuillan; the late Jack McQuillan; Louis McRedmond; Geraldine McSweeney; Fidelma Magee and the O'Brien family; Eileen Maloney; Terry Molloy; John Moran; Gerry Mulvey; Denis Murnaghan; Paul Murphy; Jim Murray; Martin Naughton; Donal Nevin; Dick O'Brien; Hugh O'Brien;

Tomás O'Cofaigh; Michael O'Connor C.SS.R; Ulick O'Connor; Canon Desmond O'Dowd; Mary O'Doherty; Donal O'Donovan; John O'Hara; Johnny O'Hanlon; Deirdre O'Keeffe; Denis O'Kelly; Tommy O'Leary; Andy O'Mahony; T.P. O'Mahony; Daragh O'Malley; the late Prof. T.P. O'Neill; Mícheál Ó Nualláin; Martin O'Rourke; Michael O'Sullivan; Tommy Owens; Dr Tony Peacock; Noel Pearson; Fr Brian Power; Joseph Power; Fr Sean Quigley; Brian Quinn; David Quinn; Eoin Ryan; Tim Ryan; Tom Ryan; Léan Scully; Henry Sheridan; the late Mrs Mercy Simms; Malcolm Sinclair; Finbarr Slattery; Michael Smith; Patricia and George Smith; Tommy Smith; Fr Tom Stack; Emmet Stagg T.D.; Bernard Treacy O.P.; Ronan Tynan; Paddy Walley; Arthur J. Walls; Niall Walsh; Dr Tony Ward; Prof. George Watson; T.K. Whitaker; John Wilkins; Fr Desmond Wilson; John Wilson.

PRINCIPAL WRITINGS OF JOHN CHARLES McQUAID

Retreat Notes at Holy Ghost Novitiate, Kimmage, 1913–18, circa 300 items (DDA).

Seminary lecture notes, 1913–21 (DDA).

'A Roman of the Early Empire: Lucius Annaeus Seneca', M.A. Thesis, University College, Dublin, 1918 (DDA).

'Memoir on the Life of Brother Gaspard'. Undated. (DDA). Written prior to McQuaid's appointment as Archbishop of Dublin in 1940. (HGA).

'Fr James Laval, Apostle of Mauritius', *Missionary Annals*, September 1920 (HGA).

'Fr D. O'Sullivan', *Missionary Annals*, August 1921 (HGA).

Roman Notes – 'In the Home of St Thomas Aquinas', *Missionary Annals*, August 1925 (HGA).

Article on 'St Catherine of Siena', based on sermon to Missionary Sisters in Killeshandra, Co. Cavan, in *Apostolate*, January 1929 (DDA).

Article on 'Our New Film' (a Life of the 'Little Flower'), *Blackrock College Annual*, September 1930 (HGA).

Preface to *The Kingship of Christ*, by Rev. Denis Fahey, Dublin, Browne and Nolan, 1931.

Address on *The Schools and the St Vincent de Paul Society*, January 24, 1932 (DDA).

Sermon in the Chapel of Blackrock College at the first meeting of the Guilds of Regnum Christi, October 28, 1934. Published in *Irish Nursing News*, December 1934 (DDA).

Catholic Education – its Function and Scope, CTSI, 1935.

Pastoral Letters and Lenten Regulations, 1941–71.

Foreword to *Archbishop Stepinac, the Man and his case*, by Count Anthony H. O'Brien, Dublin, the *Standard*, 1947.

A Catechism of Catholic Doctrine, Approved by the Archbishops and Bishops of Ireland, Dublin, M.H. Gill, 1951.

Foreword to *Matt Talbot and His Times*, Mary Purcell, November 14, 1954.

Address of welcome in *Transactions of Sixth International Congress of Catholic Doctors, 1954*, Dublin, Irish Overseas Publications Company, 1955.

Foreword to first issue of *Reportorium Novum*, Dublin Diocesan Historical Record, December 1, 1955.

Wellsprings of the Faith, Clonmel and Reynolds, 1956.

'St Vincent de Paul', in *Irish Ecclesiastical Record*, November 1960.

Higher Education for Catholics, Dublin, MH Gill, 1961.

Centenary Address to the Mater Hospital, Dublin, October 8, 1961.

'What is a General Council?', *Irish Messenger*, 1962.

'Our Faith', *Irish Messenger*, 1968.

'Prayer', *Irish Messenger*, 1970.

'Contraception and Conscience', Three statements, 1971.

WILLS
John Charles McQuaid – extracted from the Probate Office, the High Court, Republic of Ireland, March 14, 1967; oath for Executors, June 28, 1976.
Dr Eugene McQuaid; Mrs Agnes McQuaid; Dr Helen McQuaid.

ARTICLES ON JOHN CHARLES McQUAID

Anglo-Celt, 'Illustrious Co. Cavan man', April 13, 1973.

Boland, John, 'Ecclesiastical Taoiseach in a clericalist state', *Irish Independent*, April 11, 1998.

Bowman, John, 'McQuaid's huge archive reveals deal that helped defeat Browne', *Irish Independent*, April 4, 1998.

Bowman, John, 'The Wolf in Sheep's Clothing: Richard Hayes's Proposal for a New National Library of Ireland, 1959–60,' in *Modern Irish Democracy: Essays in honour of Basil Chubb*, edited by Ronald J. Hill and Michael Marsh, Dublin, Irish Academic Press., 1993.

Burns, John, 'McQuaid's gifts to poet revealed', *Sunday Times*, April 5, 1998.

Burke Savage, Roland, 'The Church in Dublin: 1940–1965, a study of the episcopate of the Most Rev. John Charles McQuaid, D.D.', in *Studies*, Vol. LIV, No. 216, Winter, 1965.

Byrne, Frank, 'The enigmatic archbishop', *Irish Independent*, September 19, 1971.

Carroll, Michael, 'Most Rev. John Charles McQuaid, D.D.', in *Blackrock College Annual*, 1942.

Cooney, John, 'Mother's death at birth shaped archbishop's destiny', in *The Irish Times*, July 28, 1995.

Cooney, John, 'Adopted child's religion McQuaid's main concern', in *The Irish Times*, March 18, 1996.

Cooney, John, 'Battles of will with the "alternative Taoiseach"', in *Irish Independent*, April 14, 1994.

Cooney, John, 'Dev's pressure on the Vatican', in the *Irish Press*, January 2/3, 1995.

Cooney, John, 'McQuaid's shadow', *The Irish Times Weekend*, April 4, 1998.

518   John Charles McQuaid

Cooney, John, 'McQuaid had role of aide to Taoiseach (against Nöel Browne)', *The Irish Times*, April 6, 1998.

Cooney, John, 'McQuaid used Dev to advance conservative Catholicism', *The Irish Times*, April 7, 1998.

Cooney, John, 'McQuaid at Vatican II', *Doctrine and Life*, April 1998.

Doyle, Diarmuid, 'Putting the spotlight on J.C. McQuaid', *Sunday Tribune*, April 12, 1998.

Fanning, Ronan, 'McQuaid's country's on bended knee', *Sunday Independent*, April 12, 1998.

Fennell, Desmond, 'Dublin's Archbishop', in *The Changing Face of Catholic Ireland*, London, Geoffrey Chapman, 1968.

Feeney, John, *The Man and the Mask*, Cork, Mercier Press, 1974.

Horgan, John, Appreciation on McQuaid's retirement, January 5, 1972.

The Irish Times, April 9, 1973, carried a full-page obituary.

Lennon, Peter, 'Dublin's Grey Eminence', in *The Guardian*, February 1964.

Kirby, Peadar, 'Memories of John Charles, an Archbishop at home, based on interview with Rev. Chris Mangan', in *Doctrine and Life*, July-August 1990.

Mitchel, Seán, 'Our Irishman of the year is a leading churchman', *The Corkman*, January 8, 1966.

McGrath, Fergal, 'Most Rev. J.C. McQuaid', in *The Clongownian*, 1941.

McGrath, Fergal, Review of *Wellsprings of Faith*, in *Studies*, Vol. XIVI, 1957.

McRedmond, Louis, 'John Charles McQuaid', in *Modern Irish Lives*, Dublin, Gill and Macmillan, 1996.

O'Brien, Breda, 'Paen to one of the great churchmen of the century', *Sunday Business Post*, April 12, 1998.

O'Kelly, Emer, 'McQuaid is exposed as a bully and a bigot', *Sunday Independent*, January 10, 1999.

O'Neill, Thomas P., Dr J.C. McQuaid and Éamon de Valera, off-print.

Power, Joseph, 'Archbishop's concerns with many fields', *Irish Independent*, July 28, 1970.

Power, Louis, 'The Last Overlord', three articles in *Catholic Standard*, January 11, 18 and 25, 1996.

Purcell, Mary, 'The Dr McQuaid I knew', *Irish Catholic*, May 5, 1988.

Studies, Winter 1998, contained articles on McQuaid by Dermot Keogh, Deirdre McMahon, Finola Kennedy, Fr Michael O'Carroll C.S.Sp., Fr Aidan Lehane, C.S.Sp., Fr Ardle MacMahon, Pádraig Faulkner and Dr Paul McQuaid.

DOCUMENTARIES: TV AND RADIO
John Charles McQuaid: What the Papers Say, presented by John Bowman, produced by Peter Kelly, Esras Films.
Man of God, by Nollaig McCarthy.
Bowman Saturday 8.30, *Twenty-fifth Anniversary Retrospective on John Charles McQuaid*, April 1998.

BIBLIOGRAPHY

Adams, Michael, *Censorship, the Irish Experience*, USA, University of Alabama Press, 1968.

Andrews, C.S., *Dublin Made Me*, Cork, Mercier Press, 1979.

Anonymous, *The Life and Work of Mother Mary Aikenhead*, With a Preface by Rev. John Sullivan S.J., London, Longmans, 1924.

Aretin, Karl Otmar von, *The Papacy and the Modern World*, London, Weidenfield and Nicholson, 1970.

Arnold, Mavis and Heather Lasky, Children of the Poor Clares, 1985.

Barrett, Cecil, *Adoption, the Parents, the Child, the Home*, Dublin, 1952.

Barrington, Ruth, *Health, Medicine and Politics in Ireland 1900–1970*, Dublin, Institute of Public Administration, 1987.

Battersby, W.J., *De La Salle*, London, Longmans, 1950.

Beevers John, *Shining as Stars*, Dublin, Browne and Nolan, 1955.

Bestic, Alan, *The Importance of Being Irish*, London, Cassell, 1969.

Birch, Peter, *Saint Kieran's Kilkenny*, Dublin, Gill, 1951.

Biver, Comte Paul, *Père Lamy*, translated by Jacques Maritain, Dublin, Browne and Nolan, 1951.

Blanchard, Jean, *The Church in Contemporary Ireland*, Dublin, Burns and Oates, 1963.

Blanshard, Paul, *The Catholic and Irish Power*, London, Vershoyle, 1954.

Bolster, Evelyn, *The Knights of Saint Columbanus*, Dublin, Gill and Macmillan, 1979.

Bowen, Kurt, *Protestants in a Catholic State*, Dublin, Gill and Macmillan, 1983.

Bowers, Fergal, *The Work: an Investigation into Opus Dei and how it operates in Ireland today*, Dublin, Poolbeg Press, 1989.

Boylan, H., *Dictionary of Irish Biography*, Dublin, Gill and Macmillan, 1998.

Brown, Terence, *Ireland, a Social and Cultural History: 1922–79*, London, Fontana, 1981.

Browne, Alan (ed.), *Masters, Midwives and Ladies-in-waiting: The Rotunda Hospital, 1745–1995*, Dublin, A.A. Farmar, 1995.

Browne, Nöel, *Against the Tide*, Dublin, Gill and Macmillan, 1986.

Browne, Phyllis, *Thanks for the Tea, Mrs Browne*, Dublin, New Island Books, 1998.

Buchanan, Tom and Conway, Martin (eds), *Political Catholicism in Europe 1918–65*, Oxford, Clarendon Press, 1996.

Buckley, Pat *A Thorn in the Side*, Dublin, The O'Brien Press, 1994.

Bull, George, *Inside the Vatican*, London, Hutchinson, 1982.

Byrne, Gay, *The Time of My Life*, Dublin, Gill and Macmillan, 1989.

Byrne, Peter, *Football Association of Ireland 75 Years*, Dublin, 1996.

Cahill, Edward, *The Framework of a Christian State, An Introduction to Social Science*, Dublin, M.H. Gill, 1932.

Callanan, Frank, *T.M. Healy*, Cork, Cork University Press, 1996.

Canning, Bernard, *Bishops of Ireland 1870–1987*, Ballyshannon, Donegal Democrat, 1987.

Cannon, Seán, *Irish Episcopal Meetings 1788–1882*, Rome, 1979.

Carlson, Julia, *Banned in Ireland*, London, Routledge, 1990.

Carroll, Denis, *They Have Fooled You Again, Michael O'Flanagan, 1876–1942*, Dublin, Columba Press, 1993.

Carroll, Joseph T., *Ireland in the War Years 1939–45*, London, David Charles, 1975.

Chadwick, Owen, *A History of the Popes, 1830–1914*, Oxford, Oxford University Press, 1998.

Chesterton, G.K., *Christendom in Dublin*, London, Sheed and Ward, 1932.

Chubb, Basil (ed.), *Federation of Irish Employers 1942–1992*, Dublin, Gill and Macmillan, 1992.

Coldrey, Barry M., *Faith and Fatherland: The Christian Brothers and the Development of Irish Nationalism 1838–1921*, Dublin, Gill and Macmillan, 1993.

Collins, Stephen, *The Cosgrave Legacy*, Dublin, Blackwater Press, 1996.

Connery, Donald S., *The Irish*, London, Eyre and Spottiswoode, 1969.

Coogan, Tim Pat, *De Valera, Long Fellow, Long Shadow*, London, Hutchinson, 1993.

Cooney, John, *No News is Bad News*, Dublin, Veritas, 1974.

Cooney, John, *The Crozier and the Dáil: Church and State 1922–86*, Cork, Mercier Press, 1986.

Cornwell, John, *Hitler's Pope: The Secret History of Pius XII*, London, Viking, 1999.

Crean, Edward J., *Breaking the Silence: The Education of the Deaf in Ireland*, Dublin, Irish Deaf Society Publications, 1997.

Cronin, Anthony, *No Laughing Matter: The Life and Times of Flann O'Brien*, London, Grafton Books, 1989.

Cronin, Mike, *The Blueshirts and Irish Politics*, Dublin, Four Courts Press, 1997.

Cronin, Seán, *Washington's Irish policy*, Dublin, Anvil Press, 1987.

Cross, Eric, *The Taylor and Ansty*, Cork, Mercier Press, 1992.

Crowe, Sr M. Clare, *Sisters of Mercy, Kilmore, Ireland, 1868–1994*, Congregation of Sisters of Mercy, 1994.

Cunningham, Terence and Gallogly, Daniel, *St Patrick's College Cavan, a Centenary History*, Cavan, 1974.

Daly, Gabriel, *Transcendence and Immanence*, Oxford, Clarendon Press, 1980.

Devine, T.M. and McMillan J.F., *Celebrating Columba, Irish-Scottish Connections, 597–1997*, Edinburgh, John Donald.

Donleavy, J.P., *Ireland in All Her Sins and Some of Her Graces*, London, Michael Joseph, 1986.

Downey, James, *Lenihan*, Dublin, New Island Books, 1998.

Dudley Edwards, Owen, *The Sins of the Fathers*, Dublin, Gill and Macmillan, 1970.

Dudley Edwards, Owen (ed.), *Conor Cruise O'Brien Introduces Ireland*, London, André Deutsch, 1969.

Dunn, Joseph, *No Vipers in the Vatican*, Dublin, Columba Press, 1996.

Dunn, Joseph, *No Lions in the Hierarchy*, Dublin, Columba Press, 1994.

Dunn, Joseph, *No Tigers in Africa*, Dublin, Columba Press, 1989.

Fallon, Brian, *An Age of Innocence: Irish Culture 1930–1960*, Dublin, Gill and Macmillan, 1998.

Fanning, Ronan, *Independent Ireland*, Dublin, Helicon Press, 1983.

Farmar, Tony, *Holles Street, 1894–1994*, Dublin, A.A. Farmar, 1994.

Farmar, Tony, *Ordinary Lives*, Dublin, A.A. Farmar, 1995.

Farragher, Seán, *Dev and his Alma Mater: Éamon de Valera's Lifelong Association with Blackrock College 1898–1975*, Dublin, Paraclete Press, 1984.

Farragher Seán and Annaroi, Wyer, *Blackrock College, 1860–1995*, Dublin, Paraclete Press, 1995.

Farren, Seán, *The Politics of Irish Education, 1920–65*, Belfast, Institute of Irish Studies, 1996.

Ferriter, Diarmaid, *A Nation of Extremes*, Irish Academic Press, 1999.

Fesquet, Henri, *Le Journal du Concile*, Paris, Robert Morel, 1966.

Fisk, Robert, *In Time of War*, London, Andre Deutsch, 1983.

FitzGerald, Garret, *All in a Life*, Dublin, Gill and Macmillan, 1991.

Flannery, Tony C.SS.R, *The Death of Religious Life*, Dublin, Columba Press, 1997.

Fonck, Leopoldus, S.J., *Primium Quinsquenium Pontificii*, Rome, Scripta Pontifici Instituti Biblica, 1915.

Fonck, Leopold, S.J., *The Light of the World*, Edinburgh, Sands, 1926.

Gallogly, Daniel, *Diocese of Kilmore, 1800–1950*, Breifne Historical Society, 1999.

Gailey, Andrew, *Ireland and the Death of Kindness: The Experience of Constructive Unionism, 1890–1905*, Cork, Cork University Press, 1987.

Gannon, Robert, *The Cardinal Spellman Story*, London, 1963.

Gatenby, Peter, *Dublin's Meath Hospital*, Dublin, Town House, 1996.

Gaughan, J. Anthony, *Alfred O'Rahilly, Controversialist and social reformer*, Dublin, Kingdom Press, 1992.

Gaughan, J. Anthony, *Olivia Maria Taaffe*, Dublin, Kingdom Books, 1995.

Gillespie, Raymond (ed.), *Cavan: Essays on the History of an Irish County*, Dublin, Irish Academic Press, 1995.

Glynn, Sir Joseph A., *A Life of Matt Talbot*, Dublin, CTSI, 1928.

Greacen, Lavinia, *Chink, Biography of Eric Dorman-Smith*, London, Macmillan, 1989.

Halperin, S.W., *Mussolini and Italian Fascism*, USA, Princeton University Press, 1964.

Hamilton, Phyllis, with Paul Williams, *Secret Love, My Life with Michael Cleary*, Edinburgh, Mainstream Press, 1995.

Harmon, Maurice, *Seán Ó Faoláin*, Dublin, Wolfhound Press, 1984.

Hastings, Adrian, *A History of English Christianity, 1920–1985*, London, Collins, 1986.

Hebblethwaite, Peter, *Pope John XXIII*, London, Geoffrey Chapman, 1984.

Hebblethwaite, Peter, *Paul VI*, London, Harper Collins, 1993.

Hederman, Miriam, *The Road to Europe: Irish Attitudes, 1948–61*, Dublin, Institute of Public Administration, 1983.

Heenan, John C., *Cardinal Hinsley, a Memoir*, London, Burns and Oates, 1944.

Heenan, John C., *Not the Whole Truth*, London, Hodder and Stoughton, 1971.

Hickey, Des and Smith, Gus, *A Paler Shade of Green*, London, Leslie Frewin, 1972.

Hinsley, Arthur, Cardinal, *The Bond of Peace*, London, Burns and Oates, 1941.

Holland, C.H. (ed.), *Trinity College Dublin & the Idea of a University*, Dublin, University College Dublin Press, 1992.

Hoppen, K. Theodore, *Ireland since 1830, Conflict and Conformity*, London, Longman, 1989.

Hogan, Edmund M., *The Irish Missionary Movement, A Historical Survey, 1830–1980*, Dublin, Gill and Macmillan, 1990.

Horgan, John, *Humanae Vitae and the Bishops*, Dublin, Irish University Press, 1972.

Horgan, John, *Seán Lemass: the Enigmatic Patriot*, Dublin, Gill and Macmillan, 1997.

Horgan, John, *Mary Robinson*, Dublin, The O'Brien Press, 1997.

Hug, Chrystel, *The Politics of Sexual Morality in Ireland*, London, Macmillan, 1999.

Hunt, Hugh, *Seán O'Casey*, Dublin, Gill and Macmillan, 1980.

Hurley, Michael, S.J., *Christian Unity: An Ecumenical Second Spring?* Dublin, Veritas, 1998.

Jemolo, A.J.C., *Church and State in Italy, 1850–1950*, Oxford, 1960.

Jordan, Anthony J., *Seán MacBride*, Dublin, Blackwater Press, 1993.

Jung-Inglesias, E.M., *Augustin Bea*, Paris, Éditions St. Paul, 1963.

The Irish Times, The Liberal Ethic, June 1950.

Keatinge, Patrick, *The Formulation of Irish Foreign Policy*, Dublin, Institute of Public Administration, 1973.

Kearney, John, C.S.Sp., *My Yoke is Sweet*, London, Burns, Oates & Washbourne, 1937.

Kearney, John, C.S.Sp., *You Shall Find Rest*, London, Burns, Oates & Washbourne, 1938.

Keenan, Desmond, *The Catholic Church in Nineteenth-Century Ireland*, Dublin, Gill and Macmillan, 1983.

Kenny, Mary, *Goodbye to Catholic Ireland*, London, Sinclair-Stevenson, 1997.

Keogh, Dermot, *The Vatican, the Bishops and Irish Politics*, Cambridge, Cambridge University Press, 1986.

Keogh, Dermot, *Ireland and Europe 1919–1989*, Cork, Hibernian University Press, 1989.

Keogh, Dermot, *Jews in Twentieth-Century Ireland*, Cork, Cork University Press, 1998.

Keogh, Dermot, *Twentieth-Century Ireland*, Dublin, Gill and Macmillan, 1994.

Kerrigan, Gene, *Another Country: Growing Up in '50s Ireland*, Dublin, Gill and Macmillan, 1998.

Kiernan, Colm, *Daniel Mannix and Ireland*, Dublin, Gill and Macmillan, 1984.

Lee, J.J., *Ireland 1912–85*, Cambridge, Cambridge University Press, 1990.

Lindsay, Patrick, *Memories*, Dublin, Blackwater Press, 1992.

MacEoin, Gary, *Northern Ireland : Captive of History*, Holt, Reinhart Winston, 1974.

MacDermott, Eithne, *Clann na Poblachta*, Cork, Cork University Press, 1998.

Mac Giolla, Pádraig, *History of Terenure*, Dublin, Veritas, 1954.

MacStíofáin, Seán, *Memoirs of a Revolutionary*, Cremonesi, 1975.

Mansergh, Martin (ed.), *The Spirit of the Nation, Speeches of Charles J. Haughey*, Cork, Mercier Press, 1986.

Martindale, C.C., S.J., D.P., *Robert Hugh Benson*, 2 Vols, London, Longmans, 1916.

Maule, Patrick, *D.P. Moran*, Dublin, Historical Association of Ireland, 1995.

Maye, Brian, *Arthur Griffith*, Dublin, Griffith College Publications, 1997.

McCarthy, Michael, *Five Years in Ireland*, Dublin, Hodges Figgis, 1901.

McCarthy, Michael, *Priests and People in Ireland*, London, Hodder and Stoughton, 1902.

McCartney, Donal, *The National University of Ireland and Éamon de Valera*, Dublin, The University Press of Ireland, 1983.

McDonald, Frank, *The Destruction of Dublin*, Dublin, Gill and Macmillan, 1986.

McDonald, Walter, *Reminiscences of a Maynooth Professor*, Cork, Mercier Press, 1967.

McKiernan, Francis, *Diocese of Kilmore, Bishops and Priests, Breifne Historical Society, 1989.*

McMinn, J.R.B., *Against the Tide: J.B. Armour, Irish Presbyterian Minister and Home Ruler*, Belfast Public Records Office of Northern Ireland, 1985.

McNiffe, Liam, *A History of the Gárda Síochána*, Dublin, Wolfhound Press, 1997.

Meagher, William, *Most Rev. Daniel Murray*, Dublin, Gerald Bellow, 1853.

Meenan, F.O.C., *St Vincent's Hospital 1834–1994*, Dublin, Gill and Macmillan, 1995.

Milotte, Mike, *Banished Babies, The Secret History of Ireland's Baby Export Business*, Dublin, New Island Books, 1997.

Milotte, Mike, *Communism in Modern Ireland: the Pursuit of the Workers' Republic Since 1916*, Dublin, Gill and Macmillan, 1984.

Moloney, John, *Westminster, Whitehall and the Vatican, The Role of Cardinal Hinsley, 1935–43*, London, Burns and Oates, 1985.

Morris, Charles R., *American Catholic*, New York, Vintage Books, 1997.

Morrissey, Thomas, S.J., *Towards a National University, William Delany S.J.*, Dublin, Wolfhound Press, 1983.

Morton, J.B., *The New Ireland*, London, Sands, 1938.

Murphy, John A., *Ireland in the Twentieth Century*, Dublin, Gill and Macmillan, 1975.

Neeson, Eoin, *The Civil War, 1922–3*, Dublin, Poolbeg Press, 1989.

Nevin, Donal (ed.), *James Larkin, Lion of the Fold*, Dublin, Gill and Macmillan, 1998.

Ó Broin, León, *Frank Duff, a Biography*, Dublin, Gill and Macmillan, 1982.

Ó Broin, León, *Protestant Nationalists in Revolutionary Ireland, the Stopford Connection*, Dublin, Gill and Macmillan, 1985.

Ó Buachalla, Séamus, *Education Policy in Twentieth-Century Ireland*, Dublin, Wolfhound Press, 1988.

O'Carroll, Michael, *Edward Leen C.S.Sp.*, Dublin, Laetare Press, 1952.

O'Connell, John, *Doctor John, Crusading Doctor and Politician*, Dublin, Poolbeg Press, 1989.

O'Connell, T.J., *100 Years of Progress, the Story of the Irish National Teachers' Organisation*, INTO, Dublin, 1969.

O'Connor, John, *The Workhouses of Ireland*, Dublin, Anvil Press, 1995.

Ó Faoláin, Sean, *Vive Moi!*, Dublin, Sinclair-Stevenson, 1993.

O'Farrell, Patrick, *The Catholic Church in Australia, 1788–1967*, Chapman, 1969.

O'Leary, Olivia and Burke, Helen, *Mary Robinson*, London, Hodder and Stoughton, 1998.

Oram, Hugh, *A History of Newspapers in Ireland 1649–83*, Dublin, MO Books, 1983.

O'Riordan, John Jo, *Irish Catholics*, Dublin, Veritas, 1980.

O'Sullivan, Michael, *Mary Robinson*, Dublin, Blackwater Press, 1993.

O'Sullivan, Michael, *Seán Lemass*, Dublin, Blackwater Press, 1994.

O'Toole, Michael, *More Kicks Than Pence*, Dublin, Poolbeg Press, 1992.

Peters, Walter H., *The Life of Benedict XV*, Milwaukee, The Bruce Publishing Company, 1959.

Phoenix, Éamon, *Northern Ireland – Nationalist Politics, Partition and the Catholic Minority, 1890–1940*, Belfast, Ulster Historical Foundation, 1994.

Purcell, Mary, *Matt Talbot and His Times*, Dublin, M.H. Gill, 1954.

Roberts, Thomas (ed.), Contraception and Holiness – The Catholic Predicament, London, Fontana Press, 1964.

Robins, Joseph, *Custom House People*, Dublin, Institute of Public Administration, 1993.

Ryan, Dermot, *Archbishop of Dublin 1972–84, Selected Writings and Addresses* (ed. Desmond Forristal), Dublin, Veritas, 1984.

Rynne, Stephen, *Father John Hayes*, Dublin, Clonmore and Reynolds, 1960.

Rynne, Xavier, *Letters from the Vatican City*, London, Faber, 1962.

Rynne, Xavier, *The Second Session*, London, Faber, 1963.

Rynne, Xavier, *The Third Session*, London, Faber, 1964.

Rynne Xavier, *The Fourth Session*, London, Faber, 1966.

Santamaria, B.A., *Daniel Mannix*, Melbourne, Melbourne University Press, 1984.

Sherry, Richard, *Holy Cross College, Clonliffe, 1859–1959*, Dublin, 1959.

Sheehy Skeffington, Andrée, *Skeff, A Life of Owen Sheehy Skeffington, 1909–1970*, Dublin, Lilliput Press, 1991.

Skinner, Liam C., *Politicians by Accident*, Dublin, Metropolitan Press, 1946.

St John Stevas, Norman, *The Agonising Choice*, London, Eyre and Spottiswoode, 1971.

Taylor, T.N.A., *Little White Flower*, London, Burns, Oates & Washbourne, 1925

Titley, E. Brian, *Church, State and the Control of Schooling in Ireland 1900–1944*, Montreal, McGill-Queen's University Press, 1983.

Tobin, Fergal, *The Best of Decades – Ireland in the 1960s*, Dublin, Gill and Macmillan, 1984.

Touher, Patrick, *Fear of the Collar*, Dublin, The O'Brien Press, 1991.

Tynan, Michael, *Catholic Instruction in Ireland, 1720–1950*, Dublin, Four Courts Press, 1985.

Walker, Reginald F., *The Holy Ghost Fathers in Africa, A Century of Missionary Effort*, Dublin, Senior House of Studies, Blackrock College, 1933.

Walsh, Michael, *The Popes*, London, Marshall Cavendish, 1980.

White, Jack, *Minority Report – The Anatomy of the Southern Irish Protestant*, Dublin, Gill and Macmillan, 1975.

Whiteside, Lesley, *George Otto Simms*, Gerrards Cross, Bucks, Colin Smythe, 1990.

Whyte, John, *Church and State in Modern Ireland 1922–1979*, Dublin, Gill and Macmillan, 2nd edition, 1980.

ARTICLES AND PAMPHLETS

Agnew, Una, S.S.L., 'The bishop and the poet' (Patrick Kavanagh), *Intercom*, September 1994.

Andrews, C.S., 'A personal recollection of Éamon de Valera', Lille, *Études Irlandaises*, University, 1982.

Approaches, 'The Scandal of Maynooth', October 1973, No. 35.

Barkley, John, 'Presbyterian-Roman Catholic relations in Ireland 1780–1975', *The Month*, July 1981.

Boylan, Patrick, 'Catholicism and citizenship in self-governed Ireland', *Irish Messenger*, Pamphlet No. 14.

Browne, Rev. M.J., 'The Synod of Maynooth, 1927, Decrees which affect the Catholic laity', CTS of Ireland, 1930.

Browne, Vincent, 'The Arms Crisis', 1970, *Magill*, May 1980.

Buckley, Pat, 'Archbishop McQuaid's ideas on education', *The Irish Times*, 1991.

De Bháldraithe, Eoin, O.Cist., 'Mixed marriages and Irish politics: the effect of *Ne Temere*', *Studies*, Autumn, 1988.

Coldrey, Barry, 'The sexual abuse of children', in *Studies*, Vol. 85, No. 340.

Crowe, Michael Bertram, 'A Great Irish Scholar: Monsignor Patrick Boylan, 1879–1974', *Studies*, Autumn, 1978.

Curran, C.P., 'Evie Hone: Stained-glass Worker', *Studies*, Summer 1955.

Fanning, Ronan, 'The United States and Irish participation in NATO: the debate of 1950', *Irish Studies in International Affairs*, Vol. I, No. 1, 1979.

Faughnan, Seán, 'The Jesuits and the drafting of the Irish Constitution of 1937', *Irish Historical Studies*, Vol. XXVI, No. 101, May 1988.

Heffernan, Brendan, '25 Years of Roman Catholic Chaplaincy at Trinity College', *Link-Up*, 1996.

Kavanagh, James, 'Social policy in Modern Ireland', the Seán Lemass Memorial Lecture of Exeter University, *Administration*, Vol. 26, No. 3.

Keogh, Dermot, 'Church, State and Society', in *De Valera's Constitution and Ours*, edited by Brian Farrell, 1988.

Keogh, Dermot, 'The Irish Constitutional Revolution: An Analysis of the Making of the Constitution', *Administration*, January 1988, 4–84.

Keogh, Dermot, 'Church, State and Pressure Groups', in a *Doctrine and Life* Special, January 1995.

Kirwan, Bill, 'The Social Policy of the Bell', *Administration*, 1989.

Leslie, Shane, 'Archbishop Walsh', in *The Shaping of Modern Ireland*, edited by Conor Cruise O'Brien, Routledge & Kegan Paul, 1970.

Lyons, Very Rev. Canon, 'A Catholic Nation: its governing authority and functions', CTS of Ireland, 1929.

McInerney, Michael, 'Church and State', *University Review*, Vol. V, No. 2, 1968.

Mellett, James, C.S.Sp., 'Rockwell at the turn of the century', *Rockwell College Annual*, 1961/2, Vols. XXXIII and XXXIV.

Moran, Gerard, 'Church and State in Modern Ireland: the Mayo County Librarian Case, 1930–2' in *Cathair na Mart*, Journal of the Westport Historical Society, Vol. 7, No. 1, 1987.

Newman, Jeremiah, 'The Priests of Ireland: A religious survey', *Irish Ecclesiastical Record*, August 1962.

O'Donoghue, Patrick, 'Our Lady's Choral Society', in *Link-Up*, April 1995.

Ó Fiaich, Tómás, 'The Catholic clergy and the Independence movement', in *The Capuchin Annual*, 1970.

O'Neill, Joseph, 'Departments of Education: church and state', *Studies*, Vol. 38, December 1949.

Roche, Richard, Obituary of John Leydon, in *Administration*, Vol. 27, No. 3, 1979.

Wall, Mervyn, 'O'Faoláin at 90: The censor's implacable foe', *The Irish Times*, February 22, 1990.

Index